The Guru's Guide to Transact-SQL

Ken Henderson

ADDISON–WESLEY

Boston • San Francisco • New York • Toronto • Montreal
London • Munich • Paris • Madrid
Capetown • Sydney • Tokyo • Singapore • Mexico City

Many of the designations used by manufacturers and sellers to distinguish their products are claimed as trademarks. Where those designations appear in this book and we were aware of a trademark claim, the designations have been printed in initial caps or all caps.

The author and publisher have taken care in the preparation of this book but make no expressed or implied warranty of any kind and assume no responsibility for errors or omissions. No liability is assumed for incidental or consequential damages in connection with or arising out of the use of the information or programs contained herein.

The publisher offers discounts on this book when ordered in quantity for special sales. For more information, please contact:

Pearson Education Corporate Sales Division
201 W. 103rd Street
Indianapolis, IN 46290
(800) 428-5331
corpsales@pearsoned.com

Visit AW on the Web: www.awl.com/cseng/

Library of Congress Cataloging-in-Publication Data
Henderson, Kenneth W.
    The guru's guide to Transact-SQL / Kenneth W. Henderson.
      p. cm.
    Includes bibliographical references and index.
    ISBN 0-201-61576-2
    1. SQL (Computer program language) I. Title.
    QA76.73.S67 H47 2000
    005.75'6 — dc21   99-057209

Text printed on recycled and acid-free paper.

ISBN 0201615762

8 9 10111213 MA   06 05 04 03

8th Printing   August 2003

For H

Contents

Foreword

What Ken Henderson wanted to do is to write the best possible book on real, practical programming in Transact-SQL available, bar none. He succeeded. Ken had most of these tricks in his head when he started this book. When you work for a living, you tend to pick things up. If you are smart, you save them, study them, and figure out why they worked and something else did not work. If you are a nice person, you write a book so someone else can benefit from your knowledge. It is very hard for a person new to a language to walk into a project knowing only the syntax and a few rules and write a complex program. Ever try to get along in a foreign country with only a dictionary and a pocket grammar book?

Okay, we now have a goal for this book. The next step is how to write so that someone can use it. Writing in the age of the Internet is really different from the days when Victor Hugo would stand by a writing desk and write great novels on one continuous strip of paper with a quill pen. Today, within the week that a book hits hardcopy, the author can expect some compulsive geek with an email connection to read it and find everything that the author left out or got wrong and every punctuation mark that the proofreader or typesetter missed. In short, you can be humiliated at the speed of light.

But this can work both ways. When you are writing your book, you can exploit this vast horde of people who have nothing better to do with their time than be your unpaid research staff!

Since I have a reputation for expertise in SQL standards and programming, I was one of the people he emailed and asked to look over the manuscript. Neat stuff and some tricks I had not seen before! Suddenly, we are swapping ideas and I am stealing—er, researching—my next book, too. Well, communication is a two way street, you know.

I think you will find this book to be an easy read with a lot of good ideas and code samples. While this is specifically a Transact-SQL book, you will find that many of the approaches and techniques will work with any SQL product. Enjoy!

—Joe Celko

Preface

This is a coder's book. It's intended to help developers build applications that make use of Transact-SQL. It's not about database administration or design. It's not about end-user or GUI application development. It's not even about server or database performance tuning. It's about developing the best Transact-SQL code possible, regardless of the application.

When I began writing this book, I had these design goals in mind:

- Be very generous with code samples—don't just tell readers how to do something, show them.

- Include complete code samples within the chapter texts so that the book can be read through without requiring a computer or CD-ROM.

- Use modern coding techniques, with specific emphases on ANSI compliance and current version features and enhancements.

- Construct chapters so that they're self-contained—so that they rely as little as possible on objects created in other chapters.

- Provide real-world code samples that have intrinsic value apart from the book.

- Avoid rehashing what's already covered extensively in the SQL Server Books Online.

- Highlight aspects of Transact-SQL that differentiate it from other SQL dialects; don't just write another ANSI SQL book.

- Avoid excessive screenshots and other types of filler mechanisms often seen in computer books.

- Proceed from the simple to the complex within each chapter and throughout the book.

- Provide an easygoing, relaxed commentary with a de-emphasis on formality. Be the reader's indulgent, amiable tutor. Attempt to communicate in writing the way that people speak.

You'll have to judge for yourself whether these goals have been met, but my hope is that, regardless of the degree of success, the effort will at least be evident.

About the Sample Databases

This book uses SQL Server's Northwind and pubs sample databases extensively. You'll nearly always be able to determine which database a particular example uses from the surrounding commentary or from the code itself. The pubs database is used more often than Northwind, so, when it's not otherwise specified or when in doubt, use pubs.

Usually, modifications to these databases are made within transactions so that they can be reversed; however, for safety's sake, you should probably drop and recreate them after each chapter in which they're modified. The scripts to rebuild them (instnwnd.sql and instpubs.sql) can be found in the \Install subdirectory under the root SQL Server folder.

Results Abridged

If I have a pet peeve about computer books, it's the shameless use of space-filling devices to lengthen them—the dirty little secret of the computer publishing industry. Many technical books these days overflow with gratuitous helpings of screenshots, charts, diagrams, outlines, sidebars, icons, line art, etc. There are people who assign more value to a book that's heavy, and many authors and publishers have been all too happy to accommodate them. They seem to take the old saying that "a picture is worth a thousand words" literally—in some cases turning out books that are little more than picture books.

I think there's a point at which comprehensiveness gives way to corpulence, a time when exhaustiveness becomes exhausting. In this book, I've tried to strike a balance between being thorough and being space-efficient. To that end, I've often truncated or clipped query result sets, especially those too wide to fit on a page and those of excessive length (I always point this out). On occasion I also list them using reduced font sizes. I don't include screenshots unless doing so benefits the discussion at hand materially (only one chapter contains *any* screenshots). This is in keeping with my design goal of being complete without being overwrought. Nearly 600 SQL scripts are used in this book, and they are all included in the chapters that reference them. Hopefully none of the abridgements will detract from the book's overall usefulness or value.

On Formality

Another of my pet peeves is formality for the sake of formality. An artist once observed that "it's harder to draw a good curved line than a straight one." What he meant was that it's in some ways more difficult to do something well for which there is no exact or stringent standard than to do something that's governed by explicit rules and stuffy precedents. All you have to do to draw a straight line is pick up a straightedge. The rules that govern formal writing, particularly that of the academic variety, make writing certain kinds of books easier because they convert much of the subjective nature of writing into something more objective. They're like training wheels on the would-be author's bicycle. Writing goes from being a creative process to a mechanical one. Cross all the T's, dot all the I's, and you're halfway there. Obviously, this relieves the author of many of the decisions that shape creative writing. It also turns otherwise good pieces of work into dreary, textbook-like dissertations that are about as interesting as the telephone book White Pages.

So, I reject the notion that formal writing is better writing, that it is a higher standard and is the ideal for which all technical writers should strive. Instead, I come from the Mark Twain school of thought—I "eschew surplusage"—and I believe that, so long as common methods of speech do not become overly banal (a subjective distinction, I freely admit), the ultimate goal of the technical writer should be to write the way that readers speak. It is the way people—even technical people—are most accustomed to communicating and the way they are the most able to learn and share ideas. I did not invent this way of thinking; it's simply the way most of my favorite authors—Mark Twain, Dean Koontz, Joe Celko, Ernest Hemingway, Robert Heinlein, Andrew Miller, Oscar Wilde, P. J. O'Rourke, Patricia O'Connor—write. Though it is far more difficult to structure and write a narrative that flows naturally and reads easily, it's worth the effort if the ideas the writer seeks to convey are understood as they were intended.

So, throughout this book, you'll see a number of the rules and pseudo rules of formal writing stretched, skirted, bent, and sometimes outright broken. This is intentional. Sometimes I split infinitives, begin sentences with conjunctions, and end them with prepositions.[1] Sometimes *record* is used interchangeably with *row;* sometimes *field* takes the place of *column;* and I never, ever treat *data* as a plural word. I saw some software recently that displayed a message to the effect "the data are being loaded," and I literally laughed out loud. The distinction between the plural *data* and its obscure singular form *datum* is not maintained in spoken language and hasn't really ever been (except, perhaps, in ancient Rome). It has also been deprecated by numerous writing guides[2] and many authors.[3] The tendency for technical communication to become self-important or ostentatious has always baffled me: why stoop to pretension? Why trade the fluid conveyance of ideas between people for nonsense that confuses some and reads like petty one-upmanship to others?

Acknowledgments

I'd like to thank my wife, who not only makes it possible for me to write books but also makes it worthwhile. The book you see before you is as much hers as it is mine. I'd like to thank Neil Coy, who made a real programmer of me many years ago. Under Neil's tutelage, I learned software craftsmanship from a master. Joe Celko, the dean of the SQL language, has been a good friend and a valuable source of information throughout this project. Kudos to John Sarapata and

---

[1] According to Patricia T. O'Connor's excellent book, *Words Fail Me* (Harcourt Brace & Company, 1999), a number of these rules are not really rules at all. The commonly cited prohibitions against split infinitives, beginning sentences with conjunctions, using contractions, and ending sentences with prepositions are all pseudo rules—they are not, nor have ever been, true English grammatical rules. They originate from dubious attempts to force Latin grammar on the English language and have been broken and regularly ignored by writers since the 1300s.

[2] See, for example, *The Microsoft Manual of Style for Technical Publications* (Microsoft Press, 1995), p. 48.

[3] See, for example, *Joe Celko's Data and Databases: Concepts in Practice* (Morgan-Kaufmann Publishers, 1999), p. 3, where Joe refers to *data* in the singular as he does throughout the book.

Thomas Holaday for helping me come up with a title for the book (I'll keep *Sybase for Dummies* in mind for future use, John). Thanks to the book's technical reviewers, particularly Wayne Snyder, Gianluca Hotz, Paul Olivieri, and Ron Talmage. Heartfelt thanks to John Gmuender, Joe Gallagher, Mike Massing, and Danny Thorpe for their equanimity and for keeping me sane through the recent storm. Congratulations and genuine appreciation to the superb team at Addison-Wesley—Michael Slaughter, Marisa Meltzer, J. Carter Shanklin, and others too numerous to list. Special thanks to Nancy Cara-Sager, a friend, technical reviewer, and copyeditor who's been with me through several books and a couple of publishers now. Her tireless attention to detail has saved me from embarrassing myself more times than I can count.

About the Author

Ken Henderson is a database programmer who lives in Dallas with his wife, four children, and a dog. When he's not writing software or books, he likes to spend time watching his kids grow up. Henderson may be reached via email at khen@khen.com.

Introductory Transact-SQL

The single biggest challenge to learning SQL programming is unlearning procedural programming.—Joe Celko

SQL is the *lingua franca* of the database world. Most modern DBMSs use some type of SQL dialect as their primary query language, including SQL Server. You can use SQL to create or destroy objects on the database server such as tables and to do things with those objects, such as put data into them or query them for that data. No single vendor owns SQL, and each is free to tailor the language to better satisfy its own customer base. Despite this latitude, there *is* a multilateral agreement against which each implementation is measured. It's commonly referred to as the ANSI/ISO SQL standard and is governed by the National Committee on Information Technology Standards (NCITS H2). This standard is actually several standards—each named after the year in which it was adopted. Each standard builds on the ones before it, introducing new features, refining language syntax, and so on. The 1992 version of the standard—commonly referred to as SQL-92—is probably the most popular of these and is definitely the most widely adopted by DBMS vendors. As with other languages, vendor implementations of SQL are rated according to their level of compliance with the ANSI/ISO standard. Most vendors are compliant with at least the entry-level SQL-92 specification, though some go further.

Transact-SQL is Microsoft SQL Server's implementation of the language. It is largely SQL-92 compliant, so if you're familiar with another vendor's flavor of SQL, you'll probably feel right at home with Transact-SQL. Since helping you to become fluent in Transact-SQL is the primary focus of this book and an important step in becoming a skilled SQL Server practitioner, it's instructive to begin with a brief tour of language fundamentals.

Much of the difficulty typically associated with learning SQL is due to the way it's presented in books and courseware. Frequently, the would-be SQL practitioner is forced to run a gauntlet of syntax sinkholes and query quicksand while lugging a ten-volume set on database design and performance and tuning on her back. It's easy to get disoriented in such a situation, to become inundated with nonessential information—to get bogged down in the details. Add to this the obligatory dose of relational database theory, and the SQL neophyte is ready to leave summer camp early.

As with the rest of this book, this chapter attempts to keep things simple. It takes you through the process of creating tables, adding data to them, and querying those tables, one step at a time. This chapter focuses exclusively on the practical details of getting real work done with SQL—it illuminates the bare necessities of Transact-SQL as quickly and as concisely as possible.

Note
In this chapter, I assume you have little or no prior knowledge of Transact-SQL. If you already have a basic working knowledge of the language, you can safely skip to the next chapter.

Like most computer languages, Transact-SQL is best learned by experience. The view from the trenches is usually better than the one from the tower.

Choosing a SQL Editor

The first step on the road to Transact-SQL fluency is to pick a SQL entry and editing tool. You'll use this facility to enter SQL commands, execute them, and view their results. The tool you pick will be your constant companion throughout the rest of this book, so choose wisely.

The Query Analyzer tool that's included with SQL Server is a respectable SQL entry facility. It's certainly capable of allowing you to work through the examples in this book. Those familiar with previous versions of SQL Server will remember this tool as ISQL/W. The new version resembles its predecessor in many ways but sports a slightly more modern interface. The name change reflects the fact that the new version is more than a mere SQL entry facility. In addition to basic query entry and execution facilities, it provides a wealth of analysis and tuning info (see Chapter 16, "Transact-SQL Performance Tuning," for more information).

The first order of business when you start Query Analyzer is to connect to the server, so make sure your server is running. Enter your username and password when prompted (if your server is newly installed, username **sa** defaults to an empty password) and select your server name. If Query Analyzer and SQL Server are running on the same machine, you can use "**.**" (a period—with no quotes) or **(local)** (don't forget the parentheses) for the server name. The user interface of the tool is self-explanatory: You key T-SQL queries into the top pane of the window and view results in the bottom one.

The databases currently defined on your server are displayed in a combo-box on each window's toolbar. You can select one from the list to make it the active database for the queries you run in that window. Pressing Ctrl-E, F5, or Alt-X runs your query, while Ctrl-F5 checks it for syntax errors.

Hot Tip
If you execute a query while a selection is active in the edit window, Query Analyzer will execute the selection rather than the entire query. This is handy for executing queries in steps and for quickly executing another command without opening a new window.

If you're a command-line devotee, you may prefer the OSQL utility to Query Analyzer. OSQL is an ODBC-based command-line utility that ships with SQL Server. Like Query Analyzer, OSQL can be used to enter Transact-SQL statements and stored procedures to execute. Once you've entered a query, hit return to drop to a new line, then type **GO** and hit return again to run it (**GO** must be leftmost on the line). To exit OSQL, type **EXIT** and hit return.

OSQL has a wealth of command-line and runtime options that are too lengthy to go into here. See the SQL Books Online for more info.

A third option is to use the Sequin SQL editor included on the CD with this book. Sequin sports many of Query Analyzer's facilities without abandoning the worthwhile features of its predecessors.

Creating a Database

You might already have a database in which you can create some temporary tables for the purpose of working through the examples in this book. If you don't, creating one is easy enough. In Transact-SQL, you create databases using the CREATE DATABASE command. The complete syntax can be quite complex, but here's the simplest form:

```
CREATE DATABASE GG_TS
```

Run this command in Query Analyzer to create a scratch database for working through the examples in this book. Behind the scenes, SQL Server creates two operating system files to house the new database: GG_TS.MDF and GG_TS_Log.LDF. Data resides in the first file; transaction log information lives in the second. A database's transaction log is the area where the server first carries out changes made to the data. Once those changes succeed, they're applied atomically—in one piece—to the actual data. It's advantageous for both recoverability and performance to separate user data from transaction log data, so SQL Server defaults to working this way. If you don't specifically indicate a transaction log location (as in the example above), SQL Server selects one for you (the default location is the **data** directory that was selected during installation).

Notice that we didn't specify a size for the database or for either of the files. Our new database is set up so that it automatically expands as data is inserted into it. Again, this is SQL Server's default mode of operation. This one feature alone—database files that automatically expand as needed—greatly reduces the database administrator's (DBA's) workload by alleviating the need to monitor databases constantly to ensure that they don't run out of space. A full transaction log prevents additional changes to the database, and a full data segment prevents additional data from being inserted.

Creating Tables

Once the database is created, you're ready to begin adding objects to it. Let's begin by creating some tables using SQL's CREATE TABLE statement. To ensure that those tables are created in the new database, be sure to change the current database focus to GG_TS before issuing any of these commands. You can do this two ways: You can execute a USE command—**USE GG_TS** —in the query edit window prior to executing any other commands, or (assuming you're using

Query Analyzer) you can select the new database from the **DB:** combo-box on the edit window's toolbar (select <Refresh> from this list if your new database is not visible at first). The **DB:** combo-box reflects the currently selected database, so be sure it points to GG_TS before proceeding.

Execute the following command to create the **customers** table:

```
USE GG_TS     — Change the current database context to GG_TS
GO
CREATE TABLE customers
(
CustomerNumber int       NOT NULL,
LastName       char(30) NOT NULL,
FirstName      char(30) NOT NULL,
StreetAddress  char(30) NOT NULL,
City           char(20) NOT NULL,
State          char(2)  NOT NULL,
Zip            char(10) NOT NULL
)
```

Once the **customers** table is built, create the **orders** table using similar syntax:

```
CREATE TABLE orders
(
OrderNumber    int          NOT NULL,
OrderDate      datetime     NOT NULL,
CustomerNumber int          NOT NULL,
ItemNumber     int          NOT NULL,
Amount         numeric(9,2) NOT NULL
)
```

Most SQL concepts can be demonstrated using three or fewer tables, so we'll create a third table. Create the **items** table using this command:

```
CREATE TABLE items
(
ItemNumber   int          NOT NULL,
Description  char(30)     NOT NULL,
Price        numeric(9,2) NOT NULL
)
```

These commands are fairly self-explanatory. The only element that might look a little strange if you're new to SQL Server is the NOT NULL specification. The SQL NULL keyword is a special syntax token that's used to represent unknown or nonexistent values. It is not the same as zero for integers or blanks for character string columns. NULL indicates that a value is not known or completely missing from the column—that it's not there at all. The difference between NULL and zero is the difference between having a zero account balance and not having an account at all. (See Chapter 3, "Missing Values," for more information on NULLs.) The NULL/NOT NULL specification is used to control whether a column can store SQL's NULL token. This is formally referred to as column *nullability*. It dictates whether the column can be truly empty. So, you could read NULL/NOT NULL as NOT REQUIRED/REQUIRED, respectively. If a field can't contain NULL, it can't be truly empty and is therefore required to have some other value.

Note that you don't have to specify column nullability when you create a table—SQL Server will supply a default setting if it's omitted. The rules governing default column nullability go like this:

- If you explicitly specify either NULL or NOT NULL, it will be used (if valid—see below).

- If a column is based on a user-defined data type, that data type's nullability specification is used.

- If a column has only one nullability option, that option is used. Timestamp columns always require values, and bit columns can require them as well, depending on the server compatibility setting (specified via the sp_dbcmptlevel system stored procedure).

- If the session setting ANSI_NULL_DFLT_ON is set to **true** (it defaults to the setting specified in the database), column nullability defaults to **true**. ANSI SQL specifies that columns are nullable by default. Connecting to SQL Server via ODBC or OLEDB (which is the normal way applications connect) sets ANSI_NULL_DFLT_ON to **true** by default, though this can be changed in ODBC data sources or by the calling application.

- If the database setting **ANSI null default** is set to **true** (it defaults to **false**), column nullability is set to **true**.

- If none of these conditions specifies an ANSI NULL setting, column nullability defaults to **false** so that columns don't allow NULL values.

Inserting Data

Use the Transact-SQL INSERT statement to add data to a table, one row at a time. Let's explore this by adding some test data to the **customers** table. Enter the following SQL commands to add three rows to **customers**:

```
INSERT INTO customers
VALUES(1,'Doe','John','123 Joshua Tree','Plano','TX','75025')
INSERT INTO customers
VALUES(2,'Doe','Jane','123 Joshua Tree','Plano','TX','75025')
INSERT INTO customers
VALUES(3,'Citizen','John','57 Riverside','Reo','CA','90120')
```

Now, add four rows to the **orders** table using the same syntax:

```
INSERT INTO orders
VALUES(101,'10/18/90',1,1001,123.45)

INSERT INTO orders
VALUES(102,'02/27/92',2,1002,678.90)
```

```
INSERT INTO orders
VALUES(103,'05/20/95',3,1003,86753.09)

INSERT INTO orders
VALUES(104,'11/21/97',1,1002,678.90)
```

Finally, insert three rows into the **items** table like so:

```
INSERT INTO items
VALUES(1001,'WIDGET A',123.45)

INSERT INTO items
VALUES(1002,'WIDGET B',678.90)

INSERT INTO items
VALUES(1003,'WIDGET C',86753.09)
```

Notice that none of these INSERTs specifies a list of fields, only a list of values. The INSERT command defaults to inserting a value for all columns in order, though you could have specified a column list for each INSERT using syntax like this:

```
INSERT INTO items (ItemNumber, Price)
VALUES(1001,123.45)
```

Also note that it's unnecessary to follow the table's column order in a column list; however, the order of values you supply must match the order of the column list. Here's an example:

```
INSERT INTO items (Price, ItemNumber)
VALUES(123.45, 1001)
```

One final note: The INTO keyword is optional in Transact-SQL. This deviates from the ANSI SQL standard and from most other SQL dialects. The syntax below is equivalent to the previous query:

```
INSERT items (Price, ItemNumber)
VALUES(123.45, 1001)
```

Updating Data

Most people eventually want to change the data they've loaded into a database. The SQL UP-DATE command is the means by which this happens. Here's an example:

```
UPDATE customers
SET Zip='86753-0900'
WHERE City='Reo'
```

Depending on the data, the WHERE clause in this query might limit the UPDATE to a single row or to many rows. You can update all the rows in a table by omitting the WHERE clause:

```
UPDATE customers
SET State='CA'
```

You can also update a column using columns in the same table, including the column itself, like so:

```
UPDATE orders
SET Amount=Amount+(Amount*.07)
```

Transact-SQL provides a nice extension to the SQL UPDATE command that allows you to update the values in one table with those from another. Here's an example:

```
UPDATE o
SET Amount=Price
FROM orders o JOIN items i ON (o.ItemNumber=i.ItemNumber)
```

Deleting Data

The SQL DELETE command is used to remove data from tables. To delete all the rows in a table at once, use this syntax:

```
DELETE FROM customers
```

Similarly to INSERT, the FROM keyword is optional. Like UPDATE, DELETE can optionally include a WHERE clause to qualify the rows it removes. Here's an example:

```
DELETE FROM customers
WHERE LastName<>'Doe'
```

SQL Server provides a quicker, more brute-force command for quickly emptying a table. It's similar to the dBASE ZAP command and looks like this:

```
TRUNCATE TABLE customers
```

TRUNCATE TABLE empties a table without logging row deletions in the transaction log. It can't be used with tables referenced by FOREIGN KEY constraints, and it invalidates the transaction log for the entire database. Once the transaction log has been invalidated, it can't be backed up until the next full database backup. TRUNCATE TABLE also circumvents the triggers defined on a table, so DELETE triggers don't fire, even though, technically speaking, rows are being deleted from the table. (See Chapter 4, "DDL Insights," for more information.)

Querying Data

The SELECT command is used to query tables and views for data. You specify what you want via a SELECT statement, and the server "serves" it to you via a result set—a collection of rows containing the data you requested. SELECT is the Swiss Army knife of basic SQL. It can join tables, retrieve data you request, assign local variables, and even create other tables. It's a fair guess that you'll use the SELECT statement more than any other single command in Transact-SQL.

We'll begin exploring SELECT by listing the contents of the tables you just built. Execute

```
SELECT * FROM tablename
```

in Query Analyzer, replacing *tablename* with the name of each of the three tables. You should find that the customer and items tables have three rows each, while orders has four.

```
SELECT * FROM customers
```

(Results abridged)

```
CustomerNumber LastName FirstName StreetAddress
-------------- -------- --------- -------------
1              Doe      John      123 Joshua Tree
2              Doe      Jane      123 Joshua Tree
3              Citizen  John      57 Riverside
```

```
SELECT * FROM orders
```

```
OrderNumber OrderDate                 CustomerNumber ItemNumber Amount
----------- ------------------------  -------------- ---------- --------
101         1990-10-18 00:00:00.000 1                1001       123.45
102         1992-02-27 00:00:00.000 2                1002       678.90
103         1995-05-20 00:00:00.000 3                1003       86753.09
104         1997-11-21 00:00:00.000 1                1002       678.90
```

```
SELECT * FROM items
```

```
ItemNumber Description Price
---------- ----------- --------
1001       WIDGET A    123.45
1002       WIDGET B    678.90
1003       WIDGET C    86753.09
```

Column Lists

SELECT * returns all the columns in a table. To return a subset of a table's columns, use a comma-delimited field list, like so:

```
SELECT CustomerNumber, LastName, State FROM customers
```

```
CustomerNumber LastName State
-------------- -------- -----
1              Doe      TX
2              Doe      TX
3              Citizen  CA
```

A SELECT's column can include column references, local variables, absolute values, functions, and expressions involving any combinations of these elements.

SELECTing Variables and Expressions

Unlike most SQL dialects, the FROM clause is optional in Transact-SQL when not querying database objects. You can issue SELECT statements that return variables (automatic or local), functions, constants, and computations without using a FROM clause. For example,

```
SELECT GETDATE()
```

returns the system date on the computer hosting SQL Server, and

```
SELECT CAST(10+1 AS CHAR(2))+'/'+CAST(POWER(2,5)-5 AS CHAR(2))+'/19'+CAST(30+31
AS CHAR(2))
```

returns a simple string. Unlike Oracle and many other DBMSs, SQL Server doesn't force the inclusion of a FROM clause if it makes no sense to do so. Here's an example that returns an automatic variable:

```
SELECT @@VERSION
```

And here's one that returns the current user name:

```
SELECT SUSER_SNAME()
```

@@VERSION is an automatic variable that's predefined by SQL Server and read-only. The SQL Server Books Online now refers to these variables as functions, but they aren't functions in the true sense of the word—they're predefined constants or automatic variables (e.g., they can be used as parameters to stored procedures, but true functions cannot). I like *variable* better than *constant* because the values they return can change throughout a session—they aren't really constant, they're just read-only as far as the user is concerned. You'll see the term *automatic variable* used throughout this book.

Functions

Functions can be used to modify a column value in transit. Transact-SQL provides a bevy of functions that can be roughly divided into six major groups: string functions, numeric functions, date functions, aggregate functions, system functions, and meta-data functions. Here's a Transact-SQL function in action:

```
SELECT UPPER(LastName), FirstName
FROM customers

                FirstName
--------------  ---------
DOE             John
DOE             Jane
CITIZEN         John
```

Here, the UPPER() function is used to uppercase the LastName column as it's returned in the result set. This affects only the result set—the underlying data is unchanged.

Converting Data Types

Converting data between types is equally simple. You can use either the CAST() or CONVERT() function to convert one data type to another, but CAST() is the SQL-92–compliant method. Here's a SELECT that converts the Amount column in the orders table to a character string:

```
SELECT CAST(Amount AS varchar) FROM orders

--------
123.45
678.90
86753.09
678.90
```

Here's an example that illustrates how to convert a datetime value to a character string using a specific format:

```
SELECT CONVERT(char(8), GETDATE(),112)
--------
19690720
```

This example highlights one situation in which CONVERT() offers superior functionality to CAST(). CONVERT() supports a style parameter (the third argument above) that specifies the exact format to use when converting a datetime value to a character string. You can find the table of supported styles in the Books Online, but styles 102 and 112 are probably the most common.

CASE

In the examples throughout this book, you'll find copious use of the CASE function. CASE has two basic forms. In the simpler form, you specify result values for each member of a series of expressions that are compared to a determinant or key expression, like so:

```
SELECT CASE sex
WHEN 0 THEN 'Unknown'
WHEN 1 THEN 'Male'
WHEN 2 THEN 'Female'
ELSE 'Not applicable'
END
```

In the more complex form, known as a "searched" CASE, you specify individual result values for multiple, possibly distinct, logical expressions, like this:

```
SELECT CASE
WHEN DATEDIFF(dd,RentDueDate,GETDATE())>15 THEN Desposit
WHEN DATEDIFF(dd,RentDueDate,GETDATE())>5 THEN DailyPenalty*
DATEDIFF(dd,RentDueDate,GETDATE())
ELSE 0
END
```

A searched CASE is similar to an embedded IF...ELSE, with each WHEN performing the function of a new ELSE clause.

Personally, I've never liked the CASE syntax. I like the idea of a CASE function, but I find the syntax unwieldy. It behaves like a function in that it can be nested within other expressions, but syntactically, it looks more like a flow-control statement. In some languages, "CASE" *is* a flow-control keyword that's analogous to the C/C++ **switch** statement. In Transact-SQL, CASE is used similarly to an inline or "immediate" IF—it returns a value based on if-then-else logic. Frankly, I think it would make a lot more sense for the syntax to read something like this:

```
CASE(sex, 0, 'Unknown', 1, 'Male', 2, 'Female', 'Unknown')
```

or

```
CASE(DATEDIFF(dd,RentDueDate,GETDATE())>15, Deposit,
DATEDIFF(dd,RentDueDate,GETDATE())>5, DailyPenalty*
DATEDIFF(dd,RentDueDate,GETDATE()),0)
```

This is the way that the Oracle DECODE() function works. It's more compact and much easier to look at than the cumbersome ANSI CASE syntax.

Aggregate Columns

Aggregate columns consist of special functions that perform some calculation on a set of data. Examples of aggregates include the COUNT(), SUM(), AVG(), MIN(), STDDEV(), VAR(), and MAX() functions. They're best understood by example. Here's a command that returns the total number of customer records on file:

```
SELECT COUNT(*) FROM customers
```

Here's one that returns the dollar amount of the largest order on file:

```
SELECT MAX(Amount) FROM orders
```

And here's one that returns the total dollar amount of *all* orders:

```
SELECT SUM(Amount) FROM orders
```

Aggregate functions are often used in tandem with SELECT's GROUP BY clause (covered below) to produce grouped or partitioned aggregates. They can be employed in other uses as well (e.g., to "hide" normally invalid syntax), as the chapters on statistical computations illustrate.

Filtering Data

You use the SQL WHERE clause to qualify the data a SELECT statement returns. It can also be used to limit the rows affected by an UPDATE or DELETE statement. Here are some queries that use WHERE to filter the data they return:

```
SELECT UPPER(LastName), FirstName
FROM customers
WHERE State='TX'

      FirstName
--- ---------
DOE John
DOE Jane
```

The following code restricts the customers returned to those whose address contains the word "Joshua."

```
SELECT LastName, FirstName, StreetAddress FROM customers
WHERE StreetAddress LIKE '%Joshua%'

LastName FirstName StreetAddress
-------- --------- ---------------
Doe      John      123 Joshua Tree
Doe      Jane      123 Joshua Tree
```

Note the use of "%" as a wildcard. The SQL wildcard % (percent sign) matches zero or more instances of any character, while _ (underscore) matches exactly one.

Here's a query that returns the orders exceeding $500:

```
SELECT OrderNumber, OrderDate, Amount
FROM orders
WHERE Amount > 500

OrderNumber OrderDate                Amount
----------- ----------------------- --------
102         1992-02-27 00:00:00.000 678.90
103         1995-05-20 00:00:00.000 86753.09
104         1997-11-21 00:00:00.000 678.90
```

The following example uses the BETWEEN operator to return orders occurring between October 1990 and May 1995, inclusively. I've included the time with the second of the two dates because, without it, the time would default to midnight (SQL Server datetime columns always store both the date *and* time; an omitted time defaults to midnight), making the query noninclusive. Without specification of the time portion, the query would return only orders placed up through the first millisecond of May 31.

```
SELECT OrderNumber, OrderDate, Amount FROM orders
WHERE OrderDate BETWEEN '10/01/90' AND '05/31/95 23:59:59.999'

OrderNumber OrderDate                Amount
----------- ----------------------- --------
101         1990-10-18 00:00:00.000 123.45
102         1992-02-27 00:00:00.000 678.90
103         1995-05-20 00:00:00.000 86753.09
```

Joins

A query that can access all the data it needs in a single table is a pretty rare one. John Donne said "no man is an island," and, in relational databases, no table is, either. Usually, a query will have to go to two or more tables to find all the information it requires. This is the way of things with relational databases. Data is intentionally spread out to keep it as modular as possible. There are lots of good reasons for this modularization (formally known as *normalization*) that I won't go into here, but one of its downsides is that what might be a single *conceptual* entity (an invoice, for example) is often split into multiple *physical* entities when stored in a relational database.

Dealing with this fragmentation is where joins come in. A join consolidates the data in two tables into a single result set. The tables aren't actually merged; they just appear to be in the rows returned by the query. Multiple joins can consolidate multiple tables—it's quite common to see joins that are multiple levels deep involving scads of tables.

A join between two tables is established by linking a column or columns in one table with those in another (CROSS JOINs are an exception, but more on them later). The expression used to join the two tables constitutes the *join condition* or *join criterion*. When the join is successful, data in the second table is combined with the first to form a composite result set—a set of rows containing data from both tables. In short, the two tables have a baby, albeit an evanescent one.

There are two basic types of joins, *inner* joins and *outer* joins. The key difference between them is that outer joins include rows in the result set even when the join condition isn't met, while an inner join doesn't. How is this? What data ends up in the result set when the join condition fails? When the join criteria in an outer join aren't met, columns in the first table are returned normally, but columns from the second table are returned with no value—as NULLs. This is handy for finding missing values and broken links between tables.

There are two families of syntax for constructing joins—legacy and ANSI/ISO SQL-92 compliant. The legacy syntax dates back to SQL Server's days as a joint venture between Sybase and Microsoft. It's more succinct than the ANSI syntax and looks like this:

```
SELECT customers.CustomerNumber, orders.Amount
FROM customers, orders
WHERE customers.CustomerNumber=orders.CustomerNumber
```

```
CustomerNumber Amount
-------------- --------
1              123.45
2              678.90
3              86753.09
1              678.90
```

Note the use of the WHERE clause to join the customers and orders tables together. This is an inner join. If an order doesn't exist for a given customer, that customer is omitted completely from the list. Here's the ANSI version of the same query:

```
SELECT customers.CustomerNumber, orders.Amount
FROM customers JOIN orders ON (customers.CustomerNumber=orders.CustomerNumber)
```

This one's a bit loquacious, but the end result is the same: customers and orders are merged using their respective CustomerNumber columns.

As I mentioned earlier, it's common for queries to construct multilevel joins. Here's an example of a multilevel join that uses the legacy syntax:

```
SELECT customers.CustomerNumber, orders.Amount, items.Description
FROM customers, orders, items
WHERE customers.CustomerNumber=orders.CustomerNumber
AND orders.ItemNumber=items.ItemNumber
```

```
CustomerNumber Amount    Description
-------------- --------  -----------
1              123.45    WIDGET A
2              678.90    WIDGET B
3              86753.09  WIDGET C
1              678.90    WIDGET B
```

This query joins the composite of the customers table and the orders table with the items table. Note that the exact ordering of the WHERE clause is unimportant. In order to allow servers to fully optimize queries, SQL requires that the ordering of the predicates in a WHERE clause must not affect the result set. They must be associative—the query must return the same result regardless of the order in which they're processed.

As with the two-table join, the ANSI syntax for multitable inner joins is similar to the legacy syntax. Here's the ANSI syntax for the multitable join above:

```
SELECT customers.CustomerNumber, orders.Amount, items.Description
FROM customers JOIN orders ON (customers.CustomerNumber=orders.CustomerNumber)
JOIN items ON (orders.ItemNumber=items.ItemNumber)
```

Again, it's a bit wordier, but it performs the same function.

Outer Joins

Thus far, there hasn't been a stark contrast between the ANSI and legacy join syntaxes. Though not syntactically identical, they seem to be functionally equivalent.

This all changes with outer joins. The ANSI outer join syntax addresses ambiguities inherent in using the WHERE clause—whose terms are by definition associative—to perform table joins. Here's an example of the legacy syntax that contains such ambiguities:

```
-- Bad SQL - Don't run
SELECT customers.CustomerNumber, orders.Amount, items.Description
FROM customers, orders, items
WHERE customers.CustomerNumber*=orders.CustomerNumber
AND orders.ItemNumber*=items.ItemNumber
```

Don't bother trying to run this—SQL Server won't allow it. Why? Because WHERE clause terms are required to be associative, but these aren't. If customers and orders are joined first, those rows where a customer exists but has no orders will be impossible to join with the items table since their ItemNumber column will be NULL. On the other hand, if orders and items are joined first, the result set will include ITEM records it likely would have otherwise missed. So the order of the terms in the WHERE clause is significant when constructing multi-level joins using the legacy syntax.

It's precisely because of this ambiguity—whether the ordering of WHERE clause predicates is significant—that the SQL-92 standard moved join construction to the FROM clause. Here's the above query rewritten using valid ANSI join syntax:

```
SELECT customers.CustomerNumber, orders.Amount, items.Description
FROM customers LEFT OUTER JOIN orders ON
(customers.CustomerNumber=orders.CustomerNumber)
LEFT OUTER JOIN items ON (orders.ItemNumber=items.ItemNumber)

CustomerNumber Amount   Description
-------------- -------- -----------
1              123.45   WIDGET A
1              678.90   WIDGET B
2              678.90   WIDGET B
3              86753.09 WIDGET C
```

Here, the ambiguities are gone, and it's clear that the query is first supposed to join the customers and orders tables, then join the result with the items table. (Note that the OUTER keyword is optional.)

To understand how this shortcoming in the legacy syntax can affect query results, consider the following query. We'll set it up initially so that the outer join works as expected:

```
SELECT customers.CustomerNumber, orders.Amount
FROM customers, orders
WHERE customers.CustomerNumber*=orders.CustomerNumber
AND orders.Amount>600

CustomerNumber Amount
-------------- --------
1              678.90
2              678.90
3              86753.09
```

Since every row in customers finds a match in orders, the problem isn't obvious. Now let's change the query so that there are a few mismatches between the tables, like so:

```
SELECT customers.CustomerNumber+2, orders.Amount
FROM customers, orders
WHERE customers.CustomerNumber+2*=orders.CustomerNumber
AND orders.Amount>600
```

This version simply adds 2 to CustomerNumber to ensure that at least a few of the joins will fail and the columns in orders will be returned as NULLs. Here's the result set:

```
CustomerNumber Amount
-------------- --------
3              86753.09
4              NULL
5              NULL
```

See the problem? Those last two rows shouldn't be there. Amount is NULL in those rows (because there are no orders for customers 4 and 5), and whether it exceeds $600 is unknown. The query is supposed to return only those rows whose Amount column is known to exceed $600, but that's not the case. Here's the ANSI version of the same query:

```
SELECT customers.CustomerNumber+2, orders.Amount
FROM customers LEFT OUTER JOIN orders ON
(customers.CustomerNumber+2=orders.CustomerNumber)
WHERE orders.Amount>600
```

```
CustomerNumber Amount
-------------- --------
3                86753.09
```

The SQL-92 syntax correctly omits the rows with a NULL Amount. The reason the legacy query fails here is that the predicates in its WHERE clause are evaluated together. When Amount is checked against the **>600** predicate, it has not yet been returned as NULL, so it's erroneously included in the result set. By the time it's set to NULL, it's already in the result set, effectively negating the **>600** predicate.

Though the *inner join* syntax you choose is largely a matter a preference, you should still use the SQL-92 syntax whenever possible. It's hard enough keeping up with a single way of joining tables, let alone two different ways. And, as we've seen, there are some real problems with the legacy outer join syntax. Moreover, Microsoft strongly recommends the use of the ANSI syntax and has publicly stated that the legacy outer join syntax will be dropped in a future release of the product. Jumping on the ANSI/ISO bandwagon also makes sense from another perspective: interoperability. Given the way in which the DBMS world—like the real world—is shrinking, it's not unusual for an application to communicate with or rely upon more than one vendor's DBMS. Heterogeneous joins, passthrough queries, and vendor-to-vendor replication are now commonplace. Knowing this, it makes sense to abandon proprietary syntax elements in favor of those that play well with others.

Other Types of Joins

Thus far, we've explored only left joins—both inner and outer. There are a few others that are worth mentioning as well. Transact-SQL also supports RIGHT OUTER JOINs, CROSS JOINs, and FULL OUTER JOINs.

A RIGHT OUTER JOIN isn't really that different from a LEFT OUTER JOIN. In fact, it's really just a LEFT OUTER JOIN with the tables reversed. It's very easy to restate a LEFT OUTER JOIN as a RIGHT OUTER JOIN. Here's the earlier LEFT OUTER JOIN query restated:

```
SELECT customers.CustomerNumber+2, orders.Amount
FROM orders RIGHT OUTER JOIN customers ON
(customers.CustomerNumber+2=orders.CustomerNumber)
```

```
Amount
------ --------
3      86753.09
4      NULL
5      NULL
```

A RIGHT JOIN returns the columns in the first table as NULLs when the join condition fails. Since you decide which table is the first table and which one's the second, whether you use a LEFT JOIN or a RIGHT JOIN is largely a matter a preference.

A CROSS JOIN, by contrast, is an intentional Cartesian product. The size of a Cartesian product is the number of rows in one table multiplied by those in the other. So for two tables with three rows each, their CROSS JOIN or Cartesian product would consist of nine rows. By definition, CROSS JOINs don't need or support the use of the ON clause that other joins require. Here's a CROSS JOIN of the customers and orders tables:

```
SELECT customers.CustomerNumber, orders.Amount
FROM orders CROSS JOIN customers

CustomerNumber Amount
-------------- --------
1              123.45
1              678.90
1              86753.09
1              678.90
2              123.45
2              678.90
2              86753.09
2              678.90
3              123.45
3              678.90
3              86753.09
3              678.90

(12 row(s) affected)
```

A FULL OUTER JOIN returns rows from both tables regardless of whether the join condition succeeds. When a join column in the first table fails to find a match in the second, the values from the second table are returned as NULL, just as they are with a LEFT OUTER JOIN. When the join column in the second table fails to find a matching value in the first table, columns in the first table are returned as NULL, as they are in a RIGHT OUTER JOIN. You can think of a FULL OUTER JOIN as the combination of a LEFT JOIN and a RIGHT JOIN. Here's the earlier LEFT OUTER JOIN restated as a FULL OUTER JOIN:

```
SELECT customers.CustomerNumber+2, orders.Amount
FROM customers FULL OUTER JOIN orders ON
(customers.CustomerNumber+2=orders.CustomerNumber)

       Amount
------ --------
3      86753.09
4      NULL
5      NULL
NULL   123.45
NULL   678.90
NULL   678.90
```

Subqueries

A SELECT statement that's enclosed in parentheses and embedded within another query (usually in its WHERE clause) is called a subquery. A subquery is normally used to return a list of items that is then compared against a column in the main query. Here's an example:

```
SELECT * FROM customers
WHERE CustomerNumber IN (SELECT CustomerNumber FROM orders)
```

Of course, you could accomplish the same thing with an inner join. In fact, the SQL Server optimizer turns this query into an inner join internally. However, you get the idea—a subquery returns an item or set of items that you may then use to filter a query or return a column value.

Grouping Data

Since SQL is a set-oriented query language, statements that group or summarize data are its bread and butter. In conjunction with aggregate functions, they are the means by which the real work of SQL queries is performed. Developers familiar with DBMS products that lean more toward single-record handling find this peculiar because they are accustomed to working with data one row at a time. Generating summary information by looping through a table is a common technique in older database products—but not in SQL Server. A single SQL statement can perform tasks that used to require an entire COBOL program to complete. This magic is performed using SELECT's GROUP BY clause and Transact-SQL aggregate functions. Here's an example:

```
SELECT customers.CustomerNumber, SUM(orders.Amount) AS TotalOrders
FROM customers JOIN orders ON customers.CustomerNumber=orders.CustomerNumber
GROUP BY customers.CustomerNumber
```

This query returns a list of all customers and the total amount of each customer's orders.

How do you know which fields to include in the GROUP BY clause? You must include all the items in the SELECT statement's column list that are not aggregate functions or absolute values. Take the following SELECT statement:

```
-- Bad SQL - don't do this
SELECT customers.CustomerNumber, customers.LastName, SUM(orders.Amount) AS TotalOrders
FROM customers JOIN orders ON customers.CustomerNumber=orders.CustomerNumber
GROUP BY customers.CustomerNumber
```

This query won't execute because it's missing a column in the GROUP BY clause. Instead, it should read:

```
GROUP BY customers.CustomerNumber, customers.LastName
```

Note that the addition of the LastName column doesn't really affect the results since CustomerNumber is a unique key. That is, including LastName as a GROUP BY column won't cause any additional grouping levels to be produced since there is only one LastName for each CustomerNumber.

HAVING

The HAVING clause is used to limit the rows returned by a SELECT with GROUP BY. Its relationship to GROUP BY is similar to the relationship between the WHERE clause and the SELECT itself. Like the WHERE clause, it restricts the rows returned by a SELECT statement. Unlike WHERE, it operates on the rows in the result set rather than the rows in the query's tables. Here's the previous query modified to include a HAVING clause:

```
SELECT customers.CustomerNumber, customers.LastName, SUM(orders.Amount) AS TotalOrders
FROM customers JOIN orders ON customers.CustomerNumber=orders.CustomerNumber
GROUP BY customers.CustomerNumber, customers.LastName
HAVING SUM(orders.Amount) > 700


CustomerNumber LastName TotalOrders
-------------- -------- -----------
3              Citizen  86753.09
1              Doe      802.35
```

There is often a better way of qualifying a query than by using a HAVING clause. In general, HAVING is less efficient than WHERE because it qualifies the result set *after* it's been organized into groups; WHERE does so *beforehand*. Here's an example that improperly uses the HAVING clause:

```
-- Bad SQL - don't do this
SELECT customers.LastName, COUNT(*) AS NumberWithName
FROM customers
GROUP BY customers.LastName
HAVING customers.LastName<>'Citizen'
```

Properly written, this query's filter criteria should be in its WHERE clause, like so:

```
SELECT customers.LastName, COUNT(*) AS NumberWithName
FROM customers
WHERE customers.LastName<> 'Citizen'
GROUP BY customers.LastName
```

In fact, SQL Server recognizes this type of HAVING misuse and translates HAVING into WHERE during query execution. Regardless of whether SQL Server catches errors like these, it's always better to write optimal code in the first place.

Ordering Data

The ORDER BY clause is used to order the rows returned by a query. It follows the WHERE and GROUP BY clauses (if they exist) and sorts the result set just prior to returning it. Here's an example:

```
SELECT LastName, State
FROM customers
ORDER BY State
```

Here's another example:

```
SELECT FirstName, LastName
FROM customers
ORDER BY LastName DESC
```

Note the use of the DESC keyword to sort the rows in descending order. If not directed otherwise, ORDER BY always sorts in ascending order.

Column Aliases

You might have noticed that some of the earlier queries in this chapter use logical column names for aggregate functions such as COUNT() and SUM(). Labels such as these are known as *column aliases* and make the query and its result set more readable. As with joins, Transact-SQL provides two separate syntaxes for establishing column aliases: legacy or classical and ANSI standard. In the classical syntax, the column alias immediately precedes the column and the two are separated with an equal sign, like so:

```
SELECT TodaysDate=GETDATE()
```

ANSI syntax, by contrast, places a column alias immediately to the *right* of its corresponding column and optionally separates the two with the **AS** keyword, like so:

```
SELECT GETDATE() AS TodaysDate
```

or

```
SELECT GETDATE() TodaysDate
```

Unlike joins, the column alias syntax you choose won't affect query result sets. This is largely a matter of preference, though it's always advisable to use the ANSI syntax when you can if for no other reason than compatibility with other products.

You can use column aliases for any item in a result set, not just aggregate functions. For example, the following example substitutes the column alias LName for the LastName column in the result set:

```
SELECT customers.LastName AS LName, COUNT(*) AS NumberWithName
FROM customers
GROUP BY customers.LastName
```

Note, however, that you cannot use column aliases in other parts of the query except in the ORDER BY clause. In the WHERE, GROUP BY, and HAVING clauses, you must use the actual column name or value. In addition to supporting column aliases, ORDER BY supports a variation on this in which you can specify a sort column by its ordinal position in the SELECT list, like so:

```
SELECT FirstName, LastName
FROM customers
ORDER BY 2
```

This syntax has been deprecated and is less clear than simply using a column name or alias.

Table Aliases

Similar to column aliases, you can use *table aliases* to avoid having to refer to a table's full name. You specify table aliases in the FROM clause of queries. Place the alias to the right of the actual table name (optionally separated with the AS keyword), as illustrated here:

```
SELECT c.LastName, COUNT(*) AS NumberWithName
FROM customers AS c
GROUP BY c.LastName
```

Notice that the alias can be used in the field list of the SELECT list before it is even syntactically defined. This is possible because a query's references to database objects are resolved before the query is executed.

Managing Transactions

Transaction management is really outside the scope of introductory T-SQL. Nevertheless, transactions are at the heart of database applications development and a basic understanding of them is key to writing good SQL (see Chapter 14, "Transactions," for in-depth coverage of transactions).

The term *transaction* refers to a group of changes to a database. Transactions provide for change *atomicity*—which means that either all the changes within the group occur or none of them do. SQL Server applications use transactions to ensure data integrity and to avoid leaving the database in an interim state if an operation fails.

The COMMIT command writes a transaction permanently to disk (technically speaking, if nested transactions are present, this is true only of the outermost COMMIT, but that's an advanced topic). Think of it as a database save command. ROLLBACK, by contrast, throws away the changes a transaction would have made to the database; it functions like a database undo command. Both of these commands affect only the changes made since the last COMMIT; you cannot roll back changes that have already been committed.

Unless the IMPLICIT_TRANSACTIONS session variable has been enabled, you must explicitly start a transaction in order to commit or roll it back. Transactions can be nested, and you can check the current nesting level by querying the @@TRANCOUNT automatic variable, like so:

SELECT @@TRANCOUNT AS TranNestingLevel

Here's an example of some Transact-SQL code that uses transactions to undo changes to the database:

```
BEGIN TRAN
DELETE customers
GO
ROLLBACK
SELECT * FROM customers
```

CustomerNumber	LastName	FirstName	StreetAddress	City	State	Zip
1	Doe	John	123 Joshua Tree	Plano	TX	75025
2	Doe	Jane	123 Joshua Tree	Plano	TX	75025
3	Citizen	John	57 Riverside	Reo	CA	90120

As you can see, ROLLBACK reverses the row removals carried out by the DELETE statement.

Caution
Be sure to match BEGIN TRAN with either COMMIT or ROLLBACK. Orphaned transactions can cause serious performance and management problems on the server.

Summary

This concludes Introductory Transact-SQL. You should now be able to create a database, build tables, and populate those tables with data. You should also be familiar with the basic syntax required for querying tables and for making rudimentary changes to them. Be sure you have a good grasp of basic Transact-SQL before proceeding with the rest of the book.

Transact-SQL Data Type Nuances

"Don't fix it if it ain't broke" presupposes that you can't improve something that works reasonably well already. If the world's inventors had believed this, we'd still be driving Model A Fords and using outhouses.
—H. W. Kenton

SQL Server includes a wide variety of built-in data types—more, in fact, than most other major DBMSs. It supports a wealth of character, numeric, datetime, BLOB, and miscellaneous data types. It offers narrow types for small data and open-ended ones for large data. SQL Server character strings can range up to 8000 bytes, while its BLOB types can store up to 2GB. Numeric values range from single-byte unsigned integers up to signed floating point values with a precision of 53 places. All except one of these data types (the cursor data type) are scalar types—they represent exactly one value at a time. There is an abundance of nuances, caveats, and pitfalls to watch out for as you use many of these types. This chapter will delve into a few of them.

Dates

SQL Server dates come in two varieties: *datetime* types and *smalldatetime* types. There is no separate time data type—dates and times are always stored together in SQL Server data. Datetime columns require eight bytes of storage and can store dates ranging from January 1, 1753, to December 31, 9999. Smalldatetime columns require four bytes and can handle dates from January 1, 1900, through June 6, 2079. Datetime columns store dates and times to the nearest three-hundredths of a second (3.33 milliseconds), while smalldatetime columns are limited to storing times to the nearest minute—they don't store seconds or milliseconds at all.

   If you wish to store a date without a time, simply omit the time portion of the column or variable—it will default to 00:00:00.000 (midnight). If you need a time without a date, omit the date portion—it will default to January 1, 1900. Dates default to January 1, 1900 because it's SQL Server's *reference date*—all SQL Server dates are stored as the number of days before or since January 1, 1900.

The date portion of a datetime variable occupies its first four bytes, and the time portion occupies the last four. The time portion of a datetime or smalldatetime column represents the number of milliseconds since midnight. That's why it defaults to midnight if omitted.

One oddity regarding datetime columns of which you should be aware is the way in which milliseconds are stored. Since accuracy is limited to 3.33 milliseconds, milliseconds are always rounded to the nearest three-hundredths of a second. This means that the millisecond portion of a datetime column will always end in 0, 3, or 7. So, "19000101 12:00:00.564" is rounded to "19000101 12:00:00.563" and "19000101 12:00:00.565" is rounded to "19000101 12:00:00.567."

Y2K and Other Date Problems

With the arrival of year 2000, it's appropriate to discuss the impact the Y2K problem on SQL Server apps and some ways of handling it. A lot of hysteria seems to surround the whole Year 2000 issue—on the part of technical and nontechnical people alike—so it seems worthwhile to take a moment and address the way in which the Y2K problem affects SQL Server and applications based on it.

First, due to the fact that SQL Server sports a datetime data type, many of the problems plaguing older applications and DBMSs simply don't apply here. Dates are stored as numeric quantities rather than character strings, so no assumptions need be made regarding the century, a given datetime variable, or column references.

Second, given that even a lowly smalldatetime can store dates up to 2079, there's no capacity issue, either. Since four bytes are reserved for the date portion of a datetime column, a quantity of up to 2,147,483,647 days (including a sign bit) can be stored, even though there are only 3,012,153 days between January 1, 1753 and December 31, 9999.

Despite all this, there are still a number of subtle ways the Y2K and other date problems can affect SQL Server applications. Most of them have to do with assumptions about date formatting in T-SQL code. Consider the following:

```
SELECT CAST('01-01-39' AS datetime) AS DadsBirthDate
```

What date will be returned? Though it's not obvious from the code, the date January 1, 2039 is the answer. Why? Because SQL Server has an internal century "window" that controls how two-digit years are interpreted. You can configure this with Enterprise Manager (right click your server, select Properties, then click Server Settings) or with sp_configure (via the **two digit year cutoff** setting). By default, two-digit years are interpreted by SQL Server as falling between 1950 and 2049. So, T-SQL code that uses the SELECT above and assumes it references 1939 may not work correctly. (Assuming 2039 for Dad's birth year would mean that he hasn't been born yet!)

The simplest answer, of course, is to use four-digit years. This disambiguates dates and removes the possibility that changing the two-digit year cutoff setting might break existing code. Note that I'm not recommending that you require four-digit dates in the user interfaces you build—I refer only to the T-SQL code you write. What you require of users is another matter.

Another subtle way that Y2K can affect SQL Server apps is through date-based identifiers. It's not uncommon for older systems (and some newer ones) to use a year-in-century approach to number sequential items. For example, a purchase order system I rewrote in the eighties used the format YY-SequenceNumber to identify POs uniquely. These numbers were used as unique identifiers in a relational database system. Each time a new PO was added, a routine in the front-end application would search a table for the largest SequenceNumber and increment it by one. About five years before I became associated with the project, the company had merged with another company that had the same numbering scheme. In order to avoid duplicate keys, the programmer merging the two companies' data simply added 10 to the year prefixes of the second company's purchase orders. This, of course, amounted to installing a time bomb that would explode in ten years when the new keys generated for the first company's data began to conflict with the second company's original keys. Fortunately, we foresaw this situation and remedied it before it occurred. We remerged the two databases, this time adding to the SequenceNumber portion of the PO number, rather than its year prefix. We added a number to the second company's sequence numbers that was sufficient to place them after all those of the first company, thus eliminating the possibility of future key conflicts.

This situation was not so much Y2K related as it was an imprudent use of date-based keys; however, consider the situation where the keys start with the year 1999. A two-digit scheme could not handle the rollover to 2000 because it could no longer retrieve the maximum sequence value from the database and increment it.

A common thread runs through all these scenarios: omitting the century portion of dates is problematic. Don't do it unless you like problems.

Date Functions

SQL Server includes a number of functions to manipulate and work with datetime columns. These functions permit you to extract portions of dates, to add a quantity of date parts to an existing date, to retrieve the current date and time, and so on. Let's explore a few of these by way of some interesting date problems.

Consider the classic problem of determining for company employees the hire date anniversaries that fall within the next thirty days. The problem is more subtle than it appears—there are a number of false solutions. For example, you might be tempted to do something like this:

```
SELECT fname, lname, hire_date
FROM EMPLOYEE
WHERE MONTH(hire_date)=MONTH(GETDATE())
```

But this fails to account for the possibility that a thirty-day time period may span two or even three months. Another false solution can be found in attempting to synthesize a date using the current year and the hire date month and day, like this:

```
SELECT fname, lname, hire_date
FROM EMPLOYEE
WHERE CAST(CAST(YEAR(GETDATE()) AS varchar(4))+
SUBSTRING(CONVERT(char(8), hire_date,112),5,4) AS datetime) BETWEEN GETDATE()
AND GETDATE()+30
```

This solution fails to allow for the possibility that the synthesized date might not be valid. How? If the employee was hired in a leap year and the current year isn't also a leap year, you'll have a problem if her hire date was February 29. A rare possibility, yes, but one a good solution should take into account.

The best solution doesn't know or care about the exact date of the anniversary. It makes use of the SQL Server DATEDIFF() function to make the actual anniversary date itself irrelevant. DATEDIFF() returns the difference in time between two dates using the date or time unit you specify. The function takes three parameters: the date part or unit of time in which you want the difference returned (e.g., days, months, minutes, hours) and the two dates between which you wish to calculate the amount of elapsed time. You can supply any date part you want, including q or qq for calendar quarters, as well as h, mi, ss, and ms for time parts. Here's the code:

```
SELECT fname, lname, hire_date
FROM EMPLOYEE
WHERE DATEDIFF(yy, hire_date,GETDATE()+30) > DATEDIFF(yy, hire_date,GETDATE())
```

This code basically says, "If the number of years between the hire date and today's date plus thirty days exceeds the number of years between the hire date and today's date, a hire date anniversary must have occurred within those thirty days, regardless of the actual date."

Note the use of simple arithmetic to add days to a datetime variable (in this case, the return value of the GETDATE() function). You can add or subtract days from datetime and smalldatetime variables and fields via simple arithmetic. Also note the use of the GETDATE() function. This does what its name suggests—it returns the current date and time.

Similar to DATEDIFF(), DATEADD() adds a given number of units of time to a datetime variable or column. You can add (and subtract, using negative numbers) all the normal date components, as well as quarters and time portions. In the case of whole days, it's syntactically more compact to use simple date arithmetic than to call DATEDIFF(), but the results are the same.

DATEPART() and the YEAR(), MONTH(), and DAY() functions extract portions of a given date. In addition to the date parts already mentioned, DATEPART() can return the day of the week, the week of the year, and the day of the year as integers.

Dates and Simple Arithmetic

Beyond being able to add or subtract a given number of days from date via simple arithmetic, you can also subtract one date from another to determine the number of days between them, but you must be careful. SQL Server will return the number of days between the two dates, but if either of them contains a time portion, the server will also be forced to include fractional days in its computation. Since we are converting the result to an integer (without the cast, subtracting one SQL Server date from another yields a third date—not terribly useful), a time portion of twelve hours or more will be considered a full day. This is somewhat counterintuitive. For example, consider this code:

```
SELECT CAST(GETDATE()-'19940101' AS int)
```

If GETDATE() equals 1999-01-17 20:47:40, SQL Server returns:

```
1843
```

However, DATEDIFF(dd, GETDATE(),'19940101') returns:

1842

Why the discrepancy? Because DATEDIFF() looks at whole days only, whereas SQL Server's simple date arithmetic considers fractional days as well. The problem is more evident if we cast to a floating point value instead of an integer, like so:

```
SELECT CAST(GETDATE()-'19940101' AS float)
```

1842.8664351851851

So, there are 1842.87 days between January 1, 1994 and January 17, 1999 20:47:40, or, rounded to the nearest integer, 1843.

To get the two methods to return the same result, we could adjust the first date's time to something before noon, like so:

```
SELECT CAST(CAST('1999-01-17 11:47:40' AS datetime)- '19940101' AS int)
```

Although this would work, your users may not appreciate having their data changed to accommodate schlocky code. It would be kind of like performing heart surgery to fix a broken stethoscope. Far better simply to remove the time from the computation since we don't care about it:

```
SELECT CAST(CAST(CONVERT(char(8),GETDATE(),112) AS datetime)-'19940101' AS int)
```

This technique converts the date to an eight-byte character string and then back to a date again in order to remove its time portion. The time then defaults to '00:00:00.000' for both dates, alleviating the possibility of a partial day skewing the results.

Determining Time Gaps

A common problem with dates is determining the gaps between them, especially when a table of dates or times is involved. Consider the following scenario: Per company policy, employees at a given factory must clock in and out each time they enter or leave the assembly line. The line supervisor wants to know how much time each of her employees spends away from the factory floor. Here's a script that sets up their timecard records:

```
CREATE TABLE timeclock
(Employee varchar(30),
TimeIn smalldatetime,
TimeOut smalldatetime
)
INSERT timeclock VALUES('Pythia','07:31:34','12:04:01')
INSERT timeclock VALUES('Pythia','12:45:10','17:32:49')
INSERT timeclock VALUES('Dionysus','9:31:29','10:46:55')
INSERT timeclock VALUES('Dionysus','10:59:32','11:39:12')
INSERT timeclock VALUES('Dionysus','13:05:16','14:07:41')
INSERT timeclock VALUES('Dionysus','14:11:49','14:57:02')
INSERT timeclock VALUES('Dionysus','15:04:12','15:08:38')
INSERT timeclock VALUES('Dionysus','15:10:31','16:13:58')
INSERT timeclock VALUES('Dionysus','16:18:24','16:58:01')
```

Pythia seems to be a dutiful employee, while Dionysus appears to be playing hooky quite a bit. A query to determine the number of minutes each employee spends away on break might look something like this:

```
SELECT t1.Employee,
   DATEADD(mi,1,t1.TimeOut) AS StartOfLoafing,
   DATEADD(mi,-1,t2.TimeIn) AS EndOfLoafing,
   DATEDIFF(mi,t1.TimeOut,t2.TimeIn) AS LengthOfLoafing
FROM timeclock t1 JOIN timeclock t2 ON (t1.Employee=t2.Employee)
WHERE (DATEADD(mi,1,t1.TimeOut) <= DATEADD(mi,-1,t2.TimeIn))
```

```
Employee     StartOfLoafing         EndOfLoafing           LengthOfLoafing
-----------  ---------------------  ---------------------  ---------------
Pythia       1900-01-01 12:05:00    1900-01-01 12:44:00    41
Dionysus     1900-01-01 10:48:00    1900-01-01 10:59:00    13
Dionysus     1900-01-01 10:48:00    1900-01-01 13:04:00    138
Dionysus     1900-01-01 11:40:00    1900-01-01 13:04:00    86
Dionysus     1900-01-01 10:48:00    1900-01-01 14:11:00    205
Dionysus     1900-01-01 11:40:00    1900-01-01 14:11:00    153
Dionysus     1900-01-01 14:09:00    1900-01-01 14:11:00    4
Dionysus     1900-01-01 10:48:00    1900-01-01 15:03:00    257
Dionysus     1900-01-01 11:40:00    1900-01-01 15:03:00    205
Dionysus     1900-01-01 14:09:00    1900-01-01 15:03:00    56
Dionysus     1900-01-01 14:58:00    1900-01-01 15:03:00    7
Dionysus     1900-01-01 10:48:00    1900-01-01 15:10:00    264
Dionysus     1900-01-01 11:40:00    1900-01-01 15:10:00    212
Dionysus     1900-01-01 14:09:00    1900-01-01 15:10:00    63
Dionysus     1900-01-01 14:58:00    1900-01-01 15:10:00    14
Dionysus     1900-01-01 15:10:00    1900-01-01 15:10:00    2
Dionysus     1900-01-01 10:48:00    1900-01-01 16:17:00    331
Dionysus     1900-01-01 11:40:00    1900-01-01 16:17:00    279
Dionysus     1900-01-01 14:09:00    1900-01-01 16:17:00    130
Dionysus     1900-01-01 14:58:00    1900-01-01 16:17:00    81
Dionysus     1900-01-01 15:10:00    1900-01-01 16:17:00    69
Dionysus     1900-01-01 16:15:00    1900-01-01 16:17:00    4
```

Obviously, there are too many breaks—even Dionysus couldn't have had more breaks than work periods. The deceptive thing about this is that the first row looks correct—Pythia appears to have taken a forty-one minute lunch. But problems begin to arise as soon as there are more than two TimeIn/TimeOut pairs for a given employee. In addition to correctly computing the time between Dionysus' work periods, the query computes the difference in minutes between clock-outs and clock-ins that don't correspond to one another. What we should be doing instead is computing each break based on the most recent clock-out, like so:

```
SELECT t1.Employee,
   DATEADD(mi,1,t1.TimeOut) AS StartOfLoafing,
   DATEADD(mi,-1,t2.TimeIn) AS EndOfLoafing,
   DATEDIFF(mi,t1.TimeOut,t2.TimeIn) AS LengthOfLoafing
FROM timeclock T1 JOIN timeclock T2 ON (t1.Employee=t2.Employee)
WHERE (DATEADD(mi,1,t1.TimeOut)=
   (SELECT MAX(DATEADD(mi,1,t3.TimeOut))
   FROM timeclock T3
   WHERE (t3.Employee=t1.Employee)
   AND (DATEADD(mi,1,t3.TimeOut) <= DATEADD(mi,-1,t2.TimeIn))))
```

Employee	StartOfLoafing	EndOfLoafing	LengthOfLoafing
Pythia	1900-01-01 12:05:00	1900-01-01 12:44:00	41
Dionysus	1900-01-01 10:48:00	1900-01-01 10:59:00	13
Dionysus	1900-01-01 11:40:00	1900-01-01 13:04:00	86
Dionysus	1900-01-01 14:09:00	1900-01-01 14:11:00	4
Dionysus	1900-01-01 14:58:00	1900-01-01 15:03:00	7
Dionysus	1900-01-01 15:10:00	1900-01-01 15:10:00	2
Dionysus	1900-01-01 16:15:00	1900-01-01 16:17:00	4

Notice the use of a *correlated subquery* to determine the most recent clock-out. It's correlated in that it both restricts and is restricted by data in the outer query. As each row in T1 is iterated through, the value in its Employee column is supplied to the subquery as a parameter and the subquery is reexecuted. The row itself is then included or excluded from the result set based on whether its TimeOut value is greater than the one returned by the subquery. In this way, correlated subqueries and their hosts have a mutual dependence upon one another—a correlation between them.

The result set is about a third of the size of the one returned by the first query. Now Dionysus' breaks seem a bit more believable, if not more reasonable.

You could easily extend this query to generate subtotals for each employee through Transact-SQL's COMPUTE extension, like so:

```
SELECT t1.Employee,
   DATEADD(mi,1,t1.TimeOut) AS StartOfLoafing,
   DATEADD(mi,-1,t2.TimeIn) AS EndOfLoafing,
   DATEDIFF(mi,t1.TimeOut,t2.TimeIn) AS LengthOfLoafing
FROM timeclock T1 JOIN timeclock T2 ON (t1.Employee=t2.Employee)
WHERE (DATEADD(mi,1,t1.TimeOut)=
   (SELECT MAX(DATEADD(mi,1,t3.TimeOut))
   FROM timeclock T3
   WHERE (t3.Employee=t1.Employee)
   AND (DATEADD(mi,1,t3.TimeOut) <= DATEADD(mi,-1,t2.TimeIn))))
ORDER BY t1.Employee
COMPUTE SUM(DATEDIFF(mi,t1.TimeOut,t2.TimeIn)) BY t1.Employee
```

Employee	StartOfLoafing	EndOfLoafing	LengthOfLoafing
Dionysus	1900-01-01 10:48:00	1900-01-01 11:01:00	13
Dionysus	1900-01-01 11:40:00	1900-01-01 13:06:00	86
Dionysus	1900-01-01 14:09:00	1900-01-01 14:13:00	4
Dionysus	1900-01-01 14:58:00	1900-01-01 15:05:00	7
Dionysus	1900-01-01 15:10:00	1900-01-01 15:12:00	2
Dionysus	1900-01-01 16:15:00	1900-01-01 16:19:00	4

```
                                                    sum
                                                    ==========
                                                    116
```

Employee	StartOfLoafing	EndOfLoafing	LengthOfLoafing
Pythia	1900-01-01 12:05:00	1900-01-01 12:46:00	41

```
                                                    sum
                                                    ==========
                                                    41
```

Note the addition of an ORDER BY clause—a requirement of COMPUTE BY. COMPUTE allows us to generate rudimentary totals for a result set. COMPUTE BY is a COMPUTE variation that allows grouping columns to be specified. It's quite flexible in that it can generate aggregates that are absent from the SELECT list and group on columns not present in the GROUP BY clause. Its one downside—and it's a big one—is the generation of multiple results for a single query—one for each group and one for each set of group totals. Most front-end applications don't know how to deal with COMPUTE totals. That's why Microsoft has deprecated its use in recent years and recommends that you use the ROLLUP extension of the GROUP BY clause instead. Here's the COMPUTE query rewritten to use ROLLUP:

```
SELECT ISNULL(t1.Employee,'Total') AS Employee,
   DATEADD(mi,1,t1.TimeOut) AS StartOfLoafing,
   DATEADD(mi,-1,t2.TimeIn) AS EndOfLoafing,
   SUM(DATEDIFF(mi,t1.TimeOut,t2.TimeIn)) AS LengthOfLoafing
FROM timeclock T1 JOIN timeclock T2 ON (t1.Employee=t2.Employee)
WHERE (DATEADD(mi,1,t1.TimeOut)=
   (SELECT MAX(DATEADD(mi,1,t3.TimeOut))
   FROM timeclock T3
   WHERE (t3.Employee=t1.Employee)
   AND (DATEADD(mi,1,t3.TimeOut) <= DATEADD(mi,-1,t2.TimeIn))))
GROUP BY t1.Employee,
   DATEADD(mi,1,t1.TimeOut),
   DATEADD(mi,-1,t2.TimeIn),
   DATEDIFF(mi,t1.TimeOut,t2.TimeIn) WITH ROLLUP
HAVING ((GROUPING(DATEADD(mi,-1,t2.TimeIn))=0)
OR (GROUPING(DATEADD(mi,1,t1.TimeOut))+GROUPING(DATEADD(mi,-1,t2.TimeIn))=2))
```

Employee	StartOfLoafing	EndOfLoafing	LengthOfLoafing
Dionysus	1900-01-01 10:48:00	1900-01-01 10:59:00	13
Dionysus	1900-01-01 10:48:00	1900-01-01 10:59:00	13
Dionysus	1900-01-01 11:40:00	1900-01-01 13:04:00	86
Dionysus	1900-01-01 11:40:00	1900-01-01 13:04:00	86
Dionysus	1900-01-01 14:09:00	1900-01-01 14:11:00	4
Dionysus	1900-01-01 14:09:00	1900-01-01 14:11:00	4
Dionysus	1900-01-01 14:58:00	1900-01-01 15:03:00	7
Dionysus	1900-01-01 14:58:00	1900-01-01 15:03:00	7
Dionysus	1900-01-01 15:10:00	1900-01-01 15:10:00	2
Dionysus	1900-01-01 15:10:00	1900-01-01 15:10:00	2
Dionysus	1900-01-01 16:15:00	1900-01-01 16:17:00	4
Dionysus	1900-01-01 16:15:00	1900-01-01 16:17:00	4
Dionysus	NULL	NULL	116
Pythia	1900-01-01 12:05:00	1900-01-01 12:44:00	41
Pythia	1900-01-01 12:05:00	1900-01-01 12:44:00	41
Pythia	NULL	NULL	41
Total	NULL	NULL	157

As you can see, the query is much longer. Improved runtime efficiency sometimes comes at the cost of syntactical compactness.

WITH ROLLUP causes extra rows to be added to the result set containing subtotals for each of the columns specified in the GROUP BY clause. Unlike COMPUTE, it returns only one result set. We're not interested in all the totals generated, so we use a HAVING clause to eliminate all total rows except employee subtotals and the report grand total. The first set of NULL values in the result set corresponds to the employee subtotal for Dionysus. The second set marks Pythia's subtotals. The third set denotes grand totals for the result set.

Note the use of the GROUPING() function to generate a custom string for the report totals line and to restrict the rows that appear in the result set. GROUPING() returns 1 when the specified column is being grouped within a particular result set row and 0 when it isn't. Grouped columns are returned as NULL in the result set. If your data itself is free of NULLs, you can use ISNULL() in much the same way as GROUPING() since only grouped columns will be NULL.

Building Calendars

Another common use of datetime fields is to build calendars and schedules. Consider the following problem: A library needs to compute the exact day a borrower must return a book in order to avoid a fine. Normally, this would be fourteen calendar days from the time the book was checked out, but since the library is closed on weekends and holidays, the problem is more complex than that. Let's start by building a simple table listing the library's holidays. A table with two columns, HolidayName and HolidayDate, would be sufficient. We'll fill it with the name and date of each holiday the library is closed. Here's some code to build the table:

```
USE tempdb
GO
DROP TABLE HOLIDAYS
GO
CREATE TABLE HOLIDAYS (HolidayName varchar(30), HolidayDate smalldatetime)
INSERT HOLIDAYS VALUES("New Year's Day","19990101")
INSERT HOLIDAYS VALUES("Valentine's Day","19990214")
INSERT HOLIDAYS VALUES("St. Patrick's Day","19990317")
INSERT HOLIDAYS VALUES("Memorial Day","19990530")
INSERT HOLIDAYS VALUES("Independence Day","19990704")
INSERT HOLIDAYS VALUES("Labor Day","19990906")
INSERT HOLIDAYS VALUES("Indigenous Peoples Day","19991011")
INSERT HOLIDAYS VALUES("Halloween","19991031")
INSERT HOLIDAYS VALUES("Thanksgiving Day","19991125")
INSERT HOLIDAYS VALUES("Day After Thanksgiving","19991126")
INSERT HOLIDAYS VALUES("Christmas Day","19991225")
INSERT HOLIDAYS VALUES("New Year's Eve","19991231")

SELECT * FROM HOLIDAYS
```

```
HolidayName             HolidayDate
----------------------  -------------------
New Year's Day          1999-01-01 00:00:00
Valentine's Day         1999-02-14 00:00:00
St. Patrick's Day       1999-03-17 00:00:00
Memorial Day            1999-05-30 00:00:00
Independence Day        1999-07-04 00:00:00
Labor Day               1999-09-06 00:00:00
Indigenous Peoples Day  1999-10-11 00:00:00
Halloween               1999-10-31 00:00:00
Thanksgiving Day        1999-11-25 00:00:00
Day After Thanksgiving  1999-11-26 00:00:00
Christmas Day           1999-12-25 00:00:00
New Year's Eve          1999-12-31 00:00:00
```

Next, we'll build a table of check-out/check-in dates for the entire year. It will consist of two columns as well, CheckOutDate and DueDate. To build the table, we'll start by populating CheckOutDate with every date in the year and DueDate with each date plus fourteen calendar days. Stored procedures—compiled SQL programs that resemble 3GL procedures or subroutines—work nicely for this because local variables and flow-control statements (e.g., looping constructs) are right at home in them. You can use local variables and control-flow statements outside stored procedures, but they can be a bit unwieldy and you lose much of the power of the language in doing so. Here's a procedure that builds and populates the DUEDATES table:

```
USE tempdb
GO
DROP TABLE DUEDATES
GO
CREATE TABLE DUEDATES (CheckOutDate smalldatetime, DueDate smalldatetime)
GO
DROP PROC popduedates
GO
CREATE PROCEDURE popduedates AS
   SET NOCOUNT ON
   DECLARE @year integer, @insertday datetime

   SELECT @year=YEAR(GETDATE()), @insertday=CAST(@year AS char(4))+'0101'
   TRUNCATE TABLE DUEDATES -- In case ran more than once (run only from tempdb)
   WHILE YEAR(@insertday)=@year BEGIN
      -- Don't insert weekend or holiday CheckOut dates -- library is closed
      IF ((SELECT DATEPART(dw,@insertday)) NOT IN (1,7))
      AND NOT EXISTS (SELECT * FROM HOLIDAYS WHERE HolidayDate=@insertday)
         INSERT DUEDATES VALUES (@insertday, @insertday+14)
      SET @insertday=@insertday+1
   END
GO
EXEC popduedates
```

Now that we've constructed the table, we need to adjust each due date that falls on a holiday or weekend to the next valid date. The problem is greatly simplified by the fact that the table starts off with no weekend or holiday check-out dates. Since check-ins and check-outs are normally separated by fourteen calendar days, the only way to have a weekend due date occur once the table is set up initially is by changing a holiday due date to a weekend due date—that is, by introducing it ourselves.

One approach to solving the problem would be to execute three UPDATE statements: one to move due dates that fall on holidays to the next day, one to move Saturdays to Mondays, and one to move Sundays to Mondays. We would need to keep executing these three statements until they ceased to affect any rows. Here's an example:

```
CREATE PROCEDURE fixduedates AS
SET NOCOUNT ON
DECLARE @keepgoing integer
SET @keepgoing=1
WHILE (@keepgoing<>0) BEGIN
   UPDATE #DUEDATES SET DateDue=DateDue+1
   WHERE DateDue IN (SELECT HolidayDate FROM HOLIDAYS)
```

```
SET @keepgoing=@@ROWCOUNT

UPDATE #DUEDATES SET DateDue=DateDue+2
WHERE DATEPART(dw,DateDue)=7
SET @keepgoing=@keepgoing+@@ROWCOUNT

UPDATE #DUEDATES SET DateDue=DateDue+1
WHERE DATEPART(dw,DateDue)=1

SET @keepgoing=@keepgoing+@@ROWCOUNT
END
```

This technique uses a join to HOLIDAYS to adjust holiday due dates and the DATEPART() function to adjust weekend due dates. Once the procedure executes, you're left with a table of check-out dates and corresponding due dates. Notice the use of @@ROWCOUNT in the stored procedure to determine the number of rows affected by each UPDATE statement. This allows us to determine when to end the loop—when none of the three UPDATEs registers a hit against the table. The necessity of the @keepgoing variable illustrates the need in Transact-SQL for a DO...UNTIL or REPEAT...UNTIL looping construct. If the language supported a looping syntax that checked its control condition at the end of the loop rather than at the beginning, we might be able to eliminate @keepgoing.

Given enough thought, we can usually come up with a better solution to an iterative problem like this than the first one that comes to mind, and this one is no exception. Here's a solution to the problem that uses just one UPDATE statement.

```
CREATE PROCEDURE fixduedates2 AS
SET NOCOUNT ON
SELECT 'Fixing DUEDATES' -- Seed @@ROWCOUNT
WHILE (@@ROWCOUNT<>0) BEGIN
   UPDATE DUEDATES
      SET DueDate=DueDate+CASE WHEN DATEPART(dw,DueDate)=6 THEN 3 ELSE 1 END
   WHERE DueDate IN (SELECT HolidayDate FROM HOLIDAYS)
END
```

This technique takes advantage of the fact that the table starts off with no weekend due dates and simply avoids creating any when it adjusts due dates that fall on holidays. It pulls this off via the CASE function. If the holiday due date we're about to adjust is already on a Friday, we don't simply add a single day to it and expect later UPDATE statements to adjust it further— we add enough days to move it to the following Monday. Of course, this doesn't account for two holidays that occur back to back on a Thursday and Friday, so we're forced to repeat the process.

The procedure uses an interesting technique of returning a message string to "seed" the @@ROWCOUNT automatic variable. In addition to notifying the user of what the procedure is up to, returning the string sets the initial value of @@ROWCOUNT to 1 (because it returns one "row"), permitting entrance into the loop. Once inside, the success or failure of the UPDATE statement sets @@ROWCOUNT. Taking this approach eliminates the need for a second counter variable like @@keepgoing. Again, an end-condition looping construct would be really handy here.

Just when we think we have the best solution possible, further reflection on a problem often reveals an even better way of doing things. Tuning SQL queries is an iterative process that requires lots of patience. You have to learn to balance the gains you achieve with the pain they cost. Trimming a couple of seconds from a query that runs once a day is probably not worth your time, but trimming a few from one that runs thousands of times may well be. Deciding what to tune, what not to, and how far to go is a skill that's gradually honed over many years.

Here's a refinement of the earlier techniques that eliminates the need for a loop altogether. It makes a couple of reasonable assumptions in order to pull this off. It assumes that no more than two holidays will occur on consecutive days (or that a single holiday will never span more than two days) and that no two holidays will be separated by less than three days. Here's the code:

```
CREATE PROCEDURE fixduedates3 AS
SET NOCOUNT ON
UPDATE DUEDATES SET DueDate=DueDate+
   CASE WHEN (DATEPART(dw,DueDate)=6) THEN 3
   WHEN (DATEPART(dw,DueDate)=5) AND
   EXISTS
   (SELECT HolidayDate FROM HOLIDAYS WHERE HolidayDate=DueDate+1) THEN 4
   ELSE 1
   END
FROM HOLIDAYS WHERE DueDate = HolidayDate
```

This solution takes Thursday-Friday holidays into account via its CASE statement. If it encounters a due date that falls on a Thursday holiday, it checks to see whether the following Friday is also a holiday. If so, it adjusts the due date by enough days to move it to the following Monday. If not, it adjusts the due date by a single day just as it would a holiday falling on any other day of the week.

The procedure also eliminates the subquery used by the earlier techniques. Transact-SQL supports the FROM extension to the ANSI/ISO UPDATE statement, which allows one table to be updated based on data in another. Here, we establish a simple inner join between DUE-DATES and HOLIDAYS in order to limit the rows updated to those with due dates found in HOLIDAYS.

Strings

SQL Server string variables and fields are of the basic garden-variety type. Variable-length and fixed-length types are supported, with each limited to a maximum of 8000 bytes. Like other types of variables, string variables are established via the DECLARE command:

```
DECLARE @Vocalist char(20)
DECLARE @Song varchar(30)
```

String variables are initialized to NULL when declared and can be assigned a value using either SET or SELECT, like so:

```
SET @Vocalist='Paul Rodgers'
SELECT @Song='All Right Now'
```

Concatenation

You can concatenate string fields and variables using the + operator, like this:

```
SELECT @Vocalist+' sang the classic '+@Song+' for the band Free'
```

Char vs. Varchar

Whether you should choose to create character or variable character fields depends on your needs. If the data you're storing is of a relatively fixed length and varies very little from row to row, fixed character fields make more sense. Each variable character field carries with it the overhead associated with storing a field's length in addition to its data. If the length of the data it stores doesn't vary much, a fixed-length character field will not only be more efficiently stored, it will also be faster to access. On the other hand, if the data length varies considerably from row to row, a variable-length field is more appropriate. Variable character fields can also be more efficient in terms of SQL syntax. Consider the previous example:

```
SELECT @Vocalist+' sang the classic '+@Song+' for the band Free'
```

Because @Vocalist is a fixed character variable, the concatenation doesn't work as we might expect. Unlike variable-length @Song, @Vocalist is right-padded with spaces to its maximum length, which produces this output:

```
Paul Rodgers         sang the classic All Right Now for the band Free
```

Of course, we could use the RTRIM() function to remove those extra spaces, but it would be more efficient just to declare @Vocalist as a varchar in the first place.

One thing to watch out for with varchar concatenation is character movement. Concatenating two varchar strings can yield a third string where a key character (e.g., the last character or the first character of the second string) shifts within the new string due to blanks being trimmed. Here's an example:

```
SELECT au_fname+' '+au_lname
FROM authors
(Results abridged)
-------------------------------------------------
Abraham Bennet
Reginald Blotchet-Halls
Cheryl Carson
Michel DeFrance
Innes del Castillo
Ann Dull
Marjorie Green
Morningstar Greene
Burt Gringlesby
```

Due to character movement and because at least one of the names contains multiple spaces, there's no easy way to extract the authors' first and last names once they've been combined in this way. Since au_fname is a 20-character field, the first character of au_lname is logical character 21 in the concatenated name. However, that character has moved due to au_lname's concatenation with a varchar (nonpadded) string. It is now in a different position for each author, making extricating the original names next to impossible. This may not be an issue—it may be what you intend—but it's something of which you should be aware.

SET ANSI_PADDING

By default, SQL Server doesn't trim trailing blanks and zeros from varchar or varbinary values when they're inserted into a table. This is in accordance with the ANSI SQL-92 standard. If you want to change this, use SET ANSI_PADDING (or SET ANSI_DEFAULTS). When ANSI_PADDING is OFF, field values are trimmed as they're inserted. This can introduce some subtle problems. Here's an example:

```
SET NOCOUNT ON
CREATE TABLE #testpad (c1 char(30))

SET ANSI_PADDING OFF

DECLARE @robertplant    char(20),
        @jimmypage      char(20),
        @johnbonham     char(20),
        @johnpauljones char(20)

SET @robertplant=    'ROBERT PLANT    '
SET @jimmypage=      'JIMMY PAGE      '
SET @johnbonham=     'JOHN BONHAM     '
SET @johnpauljones= 'JOHN PAUL JONES'

INSERT #testpad VALUES (@robertplant)
INSERT #testpad VALUES (@jimmypage)
INSERT #testpad VALUES (@johnbonham)
INSERT #testpad VALUES (@johnpauljones)

SELECT DATALENGTH(c1) as LENGTH
FROM #testpad

SELECT *
FROM #testpad
WHERE c1 LIKE @johnbonham

GO
DROP TABLE #testpad

LENGTH
-----------
12
10
11
15

c1
------------------------------
```

```
Object: sp_soundex_alpha
Description: Returns the soundex of a string
Usage: sp_soundex_alpha @instring=string to translate, @soundex OUTPUT=string in
which to return soundex

Returns: (None)

Created by: Ken Henderson. Email: khen@khen.com

Version: 7.0

Example: sp_soundex_alpha "Rodgers"

Created: 1998-05-15. Last changed: 1998-05-16.

Notes: Original source unknown.

Translation to Transact-SQL by Ken Henderson.

*/

AS
IF (@instring='/?') GOTO Help
DECLARE @workstr varchar(10)

SET @instring=UPPER(@instring)
SET @soundex=RIGHT(@instring,LEN(@instring)-1) -- Put all but the first char in
a work buffer (we always return the first char)

SET @workstr='EIOUY' -- Replace vowels with A
WHILE (@workstr<>'') BEGIN
   SET @soundex=REPLACE(@soundex,LEFT(@workstr,1),'A')
   SET @workstr=RIGHT(@workstr,LEN(@workstr)-1)
END

/*

Translate word prefixes using this table

From To
MAC  MCC
KN   NN
K    C
PF   FF
SCH  SSS
PH   FF

*/

-- Re-affix first char
SET @soundex=LEFT(@instring,1)+@soundex

IF (LEFT(@soundex,3)='MAC') SET @soundex='MCC'+RIGHT(@soundex,LEN(@soundex)-3)
IF (LEFT(@soundex,2)='KN') SET @soundex='NN'+RIGHT(@soundex,LEN(@soundex)-2)
```

```
IF (LEFT(@soundex,1)='K') SET @soundex='C'+RIGHT(@soundex,LEN(@soundex)-1)
IF (LEFT(@soundex,2)='PF') SET @soundex='FF'+RIGHT(@soundex,LEN(@soundex)-2)
IF (LEFT(@soundex,3)='SCH') SET @soundex='SSS'+RIGHT(@soundex,LEN(@soundex)-3)
IF (LEFT(@soundex,2)='PH') SET @soundex='FF'+RIGHT(@soundex,LEN(@soundex)-2)


-- Remove first char
SET @instring=@soundex
SET @soundex=RIGHT(@soundex,LEN(@soundex)-1)


/*

Translate phonetic prefixes (those following the first char) using this table:

From To
DG   GG
CAAN TAAN
D    T
NST  NSS
AV   AF
Q    G
Z    S
M    N
KN   NN
K    C
H    A (unless part of AHA)
AW   A
PH   FF
SCH  SSS

*/

SET @soundex=REPLACE(@soundex,'DG','GG')
SET @soundex=REPLACE(@soundex,'CAAN','TAAN')
SET @soundex=REPLACE(@soundex,'D','T')
SET @soundex=REPLACE(@soundex,'NST','NSS')
SET @soundex=REPLACE(@soundex,'AV','AF')
SET @soundex=REPLACE(@soundex,'Q','G')
SET @soundex=REPLACE(@soundex,'Z','S')
SET @soundex=REPLACE(@soundex,'M','N')
SET @soundex=REPLACE(@soundex,'KN','NN')
SET @soundex=REPLACE(@soundex,'K','C')

-- Translate H to A unless it's part of "AHA"
SET @soundex=REPLACE(@soundex,'AHA','~~~')
SET @soundex=REPLACE(@soundex,'H','A')
SET @soundex=REPLACE(@soundex,'~~~','AHA')

SET @soundex=REPLACE(@soundex,'AW','A')
SET @soundex=REPLACE(@soundex,'PH','FF')
SET @soundex=REPLACE(@soundex,'SCH','SSS')

-- Truncate ending A or S
IF (RIGHT(@soundex,1)='A' or RIGHT(@soundex,1)='S') SET
@soundex=LEFT(@soundex,LEN(@soundex)-1)
```

```
-- Translate ending "NT" to "TT"
IF (RIGHT(@soundex,2)='NT') SET @soundex=LEFT(@soundex,LEN(@soundex)-2)+'TT'

-- Remove all As
SET @soundex=REPLACE(@soundex,'A','')

-- Re-affix first char
SET @soundex=LEFT(@instring,1)+@soundex

-- Remove repeating characters
DECLARE @c int
SET @c=65
WHILE (@c<91) BEGIN
   WHILE (CHARINDEX(char(@c)+CHAR(@c),@soundex)<>0)
     SET @soundex=REPLACE(@soundex,CHAR(@c)+CHAR(@c),CHAR(@c))
   SET @c=@c+1
end

SET @soundex=LEFT(@soundex,4)
IF (LEN(@soundex)<4) SET @soundex=@soundex+SPACE(4-LEN(@soundex)) -- Pad with spaces

RETURN 0

Help:
EXEC sp_usage @objectname='sp_soundex_alpha', @desc='Returns the soundex of a string',
@parameters='@instring=string to translate, @soundex OUTPUT=string in which to
return soundex',
@author='Ken Henderson', @email='khen@khen.com',
@datecreated='19980515', @datelastchanged='19980516',
@version='7', @revision='0',
@example='sp_soundex_alpha "Rodgers"'
RETURN -1
```

To see the advantages of this procedure over the more primitive implementation, try the following query:

```
DECLARE @mysx1 varchar(4), @mysx2 varchar(4)
EXEC sp_soundex_alpha 'Schuller',@mysx1 OUTPUT
EXEC sp_soundex_alpha 'Shuller',@mysx2 OUTPUT
SELECT @mysx1,@mysx2,SOUNDEX('Schuller'),SOUNDEX('Shuller')
```

Thanks to its superior handling of common phonetic equivalents such as "SCH" and "SH," sp_soundex_alpha correctly returns the same soundex code for Schuller and Shuller, while SOUNDEX() returns different codes for each spelling. Beyond the obvious use of identifying alternate spellings for the same name, the real reason we need a more complex routine like sp_soundex_alpha is to render more codes, not less of them. Consider the following test script:

```
DECLARE @mysx1 varchar(4), @mysx2 varchar(4)
EXEC sp_soundex_alpha 'Poknime', @mysx1 OUTPUT
EXEC sp_soundex_alpha 'Poknimeister',@mysx2 OUTPUT
SELECT @mysx1,@mysx2,soundex('Poknime'),soundex('Poknimeister')
```

```
DECLARE @s1 varchar(20),@s2 varchar(20),@s3 varchar(20),@s4 varchar(20),
  @s5 varchar(20),@s6 varchar(20),@s7 varchar(20),@s8 varchar(20),
  @s9 varchar(20),@s10 varchar(20),@s11 varchar(20),@s12 varchar(20)
EXEC master..xp_sscanf
'He Meditated for a Moment, Then Kneeling Over and Across the Ogre , King Arthur
Looked Up and Proclaimed His Wish : Now, Miserable Beasts That Hack The Secret
of the Ancient Code And Run the Gauntlet, Today I Bid You Farewell', 'He %stated
for a Moment, Then Kneeling %cver and A%cross the Og%s , King Arthur Looked %cp
and Proclaimed His %s : Now, %s Beasts That %s The Secret %s the %cncient %s And
%cun the Gauntlet, Today I Bid Your Farewell', @s1 OUT, @s2 OUT,
@s3 OUT, @s4 OUT, @s5 OUT, @s6 OUT, @s7 OUT, @s8 OUT, @s9 OUT, @s10 OUT, @s11
OUT, @s12 OUT

SELECT @s1+@s2+@s3+@s4+'? '+@s5+' '+@s6+', '+@s5+' '+@s7+' '+@s8+' '+@s9+
' '+@s10+' '+@s11+@s12
```

Using the %s and %c sscanf() format specifiers laid out in the second string, this example parses the first string argument for the specified character strings arguments. The %s specifier extracts a string, while %c maps to a single character. As each string or character is extracted, it's placed in the output variable corresponding to it sequentially. A maximum of 50 output variables may be passed into xp_sscanf. You can run the query above (like the other queries in this chapter, it's also on the accompanying CD) to see how xp_sscanf works.

If you've used C's sscanf() function before, you'll be disappointed by the lack of functionality in the Transact-SQL version. Many of the format parameters normally supported by sscanf()—including width specifiers—aren't supported, nor are data types other than strings. Nevertheless, for certain types of parsing, xp_sscanf can be very handy.

Masks

Using the PATINDEX() function, you can search string fields and variables using wildcards. Here's an example:

```
DECLARE @Song varchar(80)
SET @Song='Being For The Benefit Of Mr. Kite!'
SELECT PATINDEX('%Kit%',@Song)
```

As used below, PATINDEX() works very similarly to the LIKE predicate of the WHERE clause. The primary difference is that PATINDEX() is more than a simple predicate—it returns the offset of the located pattern as well—LIKE doesn't. To see how similar PATINDEX() and LIKE are, check out these examples:

```
SELECT * FROM authors WHERE PATINDEX('Green%',au_lname)<>0
```

could be rewritten as

```
SELECT * FROM authors WHERE au_lname LIKE 'Green%'
```

Similarly,

```
SELECT title FROM titles WHERE PATINDEX('%database%',notes)<>0
```

can be reworked to use LIKE instead:

```
SELECT title FROM titles WHERE notes LIKE '%database%'
```

PATINDEX() really comes in handy when you need to filter rows not only by the presence of a mask but also by its position. Here's an example:

```
SET NOCOUNT ON
CREATE TABLE #testblob (c1 text DEFAULT ' ')
INSERT #testblob VALUES ('Golf is a good walk spoiled')
INSERT #testblob VALUES ('Now is the time for all good men')
INSERT #testblob VALUES ('Good Golly, Miss Molly!')

SELECT *
FROM #testblob
WHERE c1 LIKE '%good%'

SELECT *
FROM #testblob
WHERE PATINDEX('%good%',c1)>15
GO
DROP TABLE #testblob
```

(Results)

```
c1
-------------------------------------------------------------------------------
Golf is a good walk spoiled
Now is the time for all good men
Good Golly, Miss Molly!

c1
-------------------------------------------------------------------------------
Now is the time for all good men
```

Here, the first query returns all the rows in the table because LIKE can't distinguish one occurrence of the pattern from another (of course, you could work around this by enclosing the column reference within SUBSTRING() to prevent hits within its first fifteen characters). PATINDEX(), by contrast, allows us to filter the result set based on the position of the pattern, not just its presence.

Executing Strings

The Transact-SQL EXEC() function and the sp_executesql stored procedure allow you to execute a string variable as a SQL command. This powerful ability allows you to build and execute a query based on runtime conditions within a stored procedure or Transact-SQL batch. Here's an example of a cross-tab query that's constructed at runtime based on the rows in the pubs..authors table:

```
USE pubs
GO
IF OBJECT_ID('author_crosstab') IS NOT NULL
   DROP PROC author_crosstab
GO
CREATE PROCEDURE author_crosstab
AS
SET NOCOUNT ON
DECLARE @execsql nvarchar(4000), @AuthorName varchar(80)

-- Initialize the create script string
SET @execsql='CREATE TABLE ##FIautxtab (Title varchar(80)'
```

```
SELECT @execsql=@execsql##+',['+au_fname+' '+au_lname+'] char(1) NULL DEFAULT ""'
FROM authors

EXEC(@execsql+')')
DECLARE InsertScript CURSOR FOR
SELECT execsql='INSERT ##autxtab (Title,'+'['+a.au_fname+' '+a.au_lname+'])
VALUES ("'+t.title+'", "X")'
FROM titles t JOIN titleauthor ta ON (t.title_id=ta.title_id)
JOIN authors a ON (ta.au_id=a.au_id)
ORDER BY t.title

OPEN InsertScript
FETCH InsertScript INTO @execsql
WHILE (@@FETCH_STATUS=0) BEGIN
   EXEC sp_executesql @execsql
   FETCH InsertScript INTO @execsql
END
CLOSE InsertScript
DEALLOCATE InsertScript

SELECT * FROM ##autxtab
DROP TABLE ##autxtab

GO

EXEC author_crosstab
GO
```

(Result set abridged)

Title	Abraham Bennet	Reginald Blotchet
But Is It User Friendly?		
Computer Phobic AND Non-Phobic Individuals: Behavior Variations		
Computer Phobic AND Non-Phobic Individuals: Behavior Variations		
Cooking with Computers: Surreptitious Balance Sheets		
Cooking with Computers: Surreptitious Balance Sheets		
Emotional Security: A New Algorithm		
Fifty Years in Buckingham Palace Kitchens		X
Is Anger the Enemy?		
Is Anger the Enemy?		
Life Without Fear		
Net Etiquette		
Onions, Leeks, and Garlic: Cooking Secrets of the Mediterranean		
Prolonged Data Deprivation: Four Case Studies		
Secrets of Silicon Valley		
Secrets of Silicon Valley		
Silicon Valley Gastronomic Treats		
Straight Talk About Computers		
Sushi, Anyone?		
Sushi, Anyone?		
Sushi, Anyone?		
The Busy Executive's Database Guide	X	
The Busy Executive's Database Guide	X	
The Gourmet Microwave		
The Gourmet Microwave		
You Can Combat Computer Stress!		

The cross-tab that this query builds consists of one column for the book title and one for each author. An "X" denotes each title-author intersection. Since the author list could change from time to time, there's no way to know in advance what columns the table will have. That's why we have to use dynamic SQL to build it.

This code illustrates several interesting techniques. First, note the shortcut the code uses to build the first rendition of the @execsql string variable:

```
SET @execsql='CREATE TABLE ##autxtab (Title varchar(80)'
SELECT @execsql=@execsql+',['+au_fname+' '+au_lname+'] char(1) NULL DEFAULT ""'
FROM authors
```

The cross-tab that's returned by the query is first constructed in a temporary table. @execsql is used to build and populate that table. The code builds @execsql by initializing it to a stub CREATE TABLE command, then appending a new column definition to it for each row in **authors.** Building @execsql in this manner is quick and avoids the use of a cursor—a mechanism for processing tables a row at a time. Compared with set-oriented commands, cursors are relatively inefficient, and you should avoid them when possible (see Chapter 13, "Cursors," for more information). When the SELECT completes its iteration through the **authors** table, @execsql looks like this:

```
CREATE TABLE ##autxtab (Title varchar(80),
[Abraham Bennet] char(1) NULL DEFAULT "",
[Reginald Blotchet-Halls] char(1) NULL DEFAULT "",
[Cheryl Carson] char(1) NULL DEFAULT "",
[Michel DeFrance] char(1) NULL DEFAULT "",
...
[Akiko Yokomoto] char(1) NULL DEFAULT ""
```

All that's missing is a closing parenthesis, which is supplied when EXEC() is called to create the table:

```
EXEC(@execsql+')')
```

Either EXEC() or sp_executesql could have been called here to execute @execsql. Generally speaking, sp_executesql is faster and more feature laden than EXEC(). When you need to execute a dynamically generated SQL string multiple times in succession (with only query parameters changing between executions), sp_executesql should be your tool of choice. This is because it easily facilitates the reuse of the execution plan generated by the query optimizer the first time the query executes. It's more efficient than EXEC() because the query string is built only once, and each parameter is specified in its native data format, not first converted to a string, as EXEC() requires.

Sp_executesql allows you to embed parameters within its query string using standard variable names as placeholders, like so:

```
sp_executesql N'SELECT * FROM authors WHERE au_lname LIKE @au_lname',
N'@au_lname varchar(40)',@au_lname='Green%'
```

Here, @au_lname is a placeholder. Though the query may be executed several times in succession, the only thing that varies between executions is the value of @au_lname. This makes it highly likely that the query optimizer will be able to avoid recreating the execution plan with each query run.

Note the use of the "N" prefix to define the literal strings passed to the procedure as Unicode strings. Unicode is covered in more detail later in this chapter, but it's important to note that sp_executesql requires Unicode strings to be passed into it. That's why @execsql was defined using **nvarchar.**

In this particular case, EXEC() is a better choice than sp_executesql for two reasons: It's not called within a loop or numerous times in succession, and it allows simple string concatenation within its parameter list; sp_executesql, like all stored procedures, doesn't.

The second half of the procedure illustrates a more complex use of dynamic SQL. In order to mark each title-author intersection with an "X," the query must dynamically build an INSERT statement for each title-author pair. The title becomes an inserted value, and the author becomes a column name, with "X" as its value.

Unlike the earlier example, sp_executesql is used to execute the dynamically generated INSERT statement because it's called several times in succession and, thanks to the concatenation within the cursor definition, doesn't need to concatenate any of its parameters.

Since sp_executesql allows parameters to be embedded in its query string, you may be wondering why we don't use this facility to pass it the columns from **authors.** After all, they would seem to be fine examples of query parameters that vary between executions—why perform all the concatenation in the cursor? The reason for this is that sp_executesql limits the types of replaceable parameters it supports to true query parameters—you can't replace portions of the query string indiscriminately. You can position replaceable parameters anywhere a regular variable could be placed if the query were run normally (outside sp_executesql), but you can't replace keywords, object names, or column names with placeholders—sp_executesql won't make the substitution when it executes the query.

One final point worth mentioning is the reason for the use of the global temporary table. A global temporary table is a transient table that's prefixed with "##" instead of "#" and is visible to all connections, not just the one that created it. As with local temporary tables, it is dropped when no longer in use (when the last connection referencing it ends).

It's necessary here because we use dynamic Transact-SQL to create the cross-tab table, and local temporary tables created dynamically are visible only to the EXEC() or sp_executesql that created them. In fact, they're deleted as soon as the dynamic SQL that created them ends. So, we use a global temporary table instead, and it remains visible until explicitly dropped by the query or the connection closes.

The biggest disadvantage to using global temporary tables over local ones is the possibility of name collisions. Unlike their local brethren, global temporary table names aren't unique across connections—that's what makes them globally accessible. Regardless of how many connections reference it, ##autxtab refers to exactly the same object in tempdb. If a connection attempts to create a global temporary table that another connection has already built, the create will fail.

We accepted this limitation in order to be able to create the table dynamically, but there are a couple of other options. First, the body of the procedure could have been written and executed as one big dynamic query, making local tables created early in the query visible to the rest of it. Second, we could create the table itself in the main query, then use dynamic T-SQL to execute ALTER TABLE statements to add the columns for each author in piecemeal fashion. Here's a variation on the earlier procedure that does just that:

```
CREATE PROCEDURE author_crosstab2
AS
SET NOCOUNT ON
DECLARE @execsql nvarchar(4000), @AuthorName varchar(80)

CREATE TABLE #autxtab (Title varchar(80))

DECLARE AlterScript CURSOR FOR
SELECT 'ALTER TABLE #autxtab ADD ['+au_fname+' '+au_lname+'] char(1) NULL DEFAULT ""'
FROM authors
FOR READ ONLY

OPEN AlterScript
FETCH AlterScript INTO @execsql
WHILE (@@FETCH_STATUS=0) BEGIN
   EXEC sp_executesql @execsql
   FETCH AlterScript INTO @execsql
END
CLOSE AlterScript
DEALLOCATE AlterScript

DECLARE InsertScript CURSOR FOR
SELECT execsql='INSERT #autxtab (Title,'+'['+a.au_fname+' '+a.au_lname+']) VALUES
("'+t.title+'", "X")'
FROM titles t JOIN titleauthor ta ON (t.title_id=ta.title_id)
JOIN authors a ON (ta.au_id=a.au_id)
ORDER BY t.title

OPEN InsertScript
FETCH InsertScript INTO @execsql
WHILE (@@FETCH_STATUS=0) BEGIN
   EXEC sp_executesql @execsql
   FETCH InsertScript INTO @execsql
END
CLOSE InsertScript
DEALLOCATE InsertScript

SELECT * FROM #autxtab
DROP TABLE #autxtab
```

Note the use of the AlterScript cursor to supply sp_executesql with ALTER TABLE queries. Since the table itself is created in the main query and since the temporary objects created in a query are visible to its dynamic queries, we're able to get by with a local temporary table and eliminate the possibility of name collisions. Though this solution requires more code than the initial one, it's also much safer.

Note that this object visibility doesn't carry over to local variables. Variables defined by the calling routine are not visible to EXEC() or sp_executesql. Also, variables defined within an EXEC() or call to sp_executesql go out of scope when they return to the caller. Basically, the only way to pass variables between them is via sp_executesql's parameter list or via concatenation within the EXEC call.

Unicode

In the past, character string data was limited to characters from sets of 256 characters. Each character was composed of a single byte and a byte can store just 256 (2^8) different characters. Prior to the adoption of the Unicode standard, all character sets were composed of single-byte characters.

Unicode expands the number of possible characters to 2^{16}, or 65,536, by using two bytes instead of one. This increased capacity facilitates the inclusion of the alphabets and symbols found in most of the world's languages, including all of those from the single-byte character sets used previously.

Transact-SQL's regular string types (char, varchar, and text) are constructed of characters from a particular single-byte character set. This character set is selected during installation and can't be changed afterward without recreating databases and reloading data. Unicode strings, by contrast, can store any character defined by the Unicode standard. Since Unicode strings take twice as much storage space as regular strings, they can be only half as long (4000 characters).

SQL Server defines special Unicode-specific data types for storing Unicode strings: nchar, nvarchar, and ntext. You can use these data types for columns that need to store characters from multiple character sets. As with regular character string fields, you should use nvarchar when a column's data varies in length from row to row and nchar when it doesn't. Use ntext when you need to store more than 4000 characters.

SQL Server's Unicode string types are based on SQL-92's National Character data types. As with SQL-92, Transact-SQL uses the prefix character **N** to distinguish Unicode data types and values, like so:

```
SELECT DATALENGTH(N'The Firm')

-----------
16
```

This query returns "16" because the uppercase N makes 'The Firm' a Unicode string.

Numerics

Transact-SQL supports four general classes of numeric data types: float and real, numeric and decimal, money and smallmoney, and the integer types (int, smallint, and tinyint). Float and real are floating point types—as such, they're approximate, not exact types—and some values within their ranges ($-1.79E + 308$ to $1.79E + 308$ and $-3.40E + 38$ to $3.40E + 38$, respectively) can't be represented precisely. Numeric and decimal are fixed-point numeric types with a user-specified, fixed precision and scale and a range of $-10^{38} - 1$ to $+10^{38} - 1$. Money and smallmoney represent monetary quantities and can range from -2^{63} to $+2^{63} - 1$ and -2^{31} to $+2^{31} - 1$ with a scale of four ($-214,748.3648$ to $+214,748.3647$), respectively.

Integer types represent whole numbers. The int data type requires four bytes of storage and can represent integers between -2^{31} and $+22^{31} - 1$. Smallint requires two bytes and can represent integers between -2^{15} and $+2^{15} - 1$. Tinyint uses just one byte and stores integers between 0 and 255.

Floating Point Fun

The first thing you discover when doing any real floating point work with SQL Server is that Transact-SQL does not correct for floating point rounding errors. This allows the same numeric problem, stated in different ways, to return different results—heresy in the world of mathematics. Languages that don't properly handle floating point rounding errors are particularly susceptible to errors due to differences in the ordering of terms. Here's an example that generates a random list of floating point numbers, then arranges them in various orders and totals them:

```
SET NOCOUNT ON
CREATE TABLE #rand
(k1 int identity,
c1 float DEFAULT (
(CASE (CAST(RAND()+.5 AS int)*-1) WHEN 0 THEN 1 ELSE -1 END)*(CONVERT(int,
RAND() * 100000) % 10000)*RAND()
)
)

INSERT #rand DEFAULT VALUES
INSERT #rand DEFAULT VALUES
INSERT #rand DEFAULT VALUES
INSERT #rand DEFAULT VALUES
INSERT #rand DEFAULT VALUES
INSERT #rand DEFAULT VALUES
INSERT #rand DEFAULT VALUES
INSERT #rand DEFAULT VALUES
INSERT #rand DEFAULT VALUES
INSERT #rand DEFAULT VALUES

SELECT * FROM #rand

SELECT SUM(c1) FROM #rand

SELECT * INTO #rand2 FROM #rand ORDER BY c1

SELECT SUM(c1) FROM #rand2

SELECT * INTO #rand3 FROM #rand2 ORDER BY ABS(c1)

SELECT SUM(c1) FROM #rand3

GO
DROP TABLE #rand, #rand2, #rand3

k1          c1
----------- ------------------------------------
1           2337.1234806786265
2           6133.8947556398543
3           4661.8483968063565
4           -487.1674384075381
5           -5402.6488177346673
6           8548.8042443202648
7           1151.1290584163344
8           1983.5178142724058
9           -48.855436548423761
10          865.11748910633833
```

```
--------------------------------------------------
19742.763546549555


--------------------------------------------------
19742.763546549551


--------------------------------------------------
19742.763546549551
```

Since the numbers being totaled are the same in all three cases, the results should be the same, but they aren't. Increasing SQL Server's floating point precision (via the /p server command line option) helps but doesn't solve the problem—floating point rounding errors aren't handled properly, regardless of the precision of the float. This causes grave problems for applications that depend on floating point accuracy and is the main reason you'll often see the complex floating point computations in SQL Server applications residing in 3GL routines.

The one foolproof answer here is to use fixed-point rather than floating point types. The **decimal** and **numeric** data types do not suffer from floating point rounding errors because they aren't floating point types. As such, they also can't use the processor's FPU, so computations will probably be slower than with real floating point types. This slowness may be compensated for in other areas, so this is not as bad as it may seem. The moral of the story is this: SQL Server doesn't correct floating point errors, so be careful if you decide to use the float or real data types.

Here's the query rewritten to use a fixed-point data type with a precision of 10 and a scale of 4:

```
SET NOCOUNT ON
CREATE TABLE #rand
(k1 int identity,
c1 decimal(10,4) DEFAULT (
(CASE (CAST(RAND()+.5 AS int)*-1) WHEN 0 THEN 1 ELSE -1 END)*(CONVERT(int,
RAND() * 100000) % 10000)*RAND()
)
)

INSERT #rand DEFAULT VALUES
INSERT #rand DEFAULT VALUES
INSERT #rand DEFAULT VALUES
INSERT #rand DEFAULT VALUES
INSERT #rand DEFAULT VALUES
INSERT #rand DEFAULT VALUES
INSERT #rand DEFAULT VALUES
INSERT #rand DEFAULT VALUES
INSERT #rand DEFAULT VALUES
INSERT #rand DEFAULT VALUES

SELECT * FROM #rand

SELECT SUM(c1) FROM #rand

SELECT * INTO #rand2 FROM #rand ORDER BY c1

SELECT SUM(c1) FROM #rand2
```

```
DECLARE @textptr binary(16)

BEGIN TRAN
SELECT @textptr=TEXTPTR(pr_info)
FROM pub_info (HOLDLOCK)
WHERE pub_id='1389'

READTEXT pub_info.pr_info @textptr 29 20
COMMIT TRAN

pr_info
--------------------------------------------------------------------------------
Algodata Infosystems
```

Notice the use of a transaction and the HOLDLOCK keyword to ensure the validity of the text pointer from the time it's first retrieved through its use by READTEXT. Since other users could modify the BLOB column while we're accessing it, the pointer returned by TEXTPTR() could become invalid between its initial read and the call to READTEXT. We use a transaction to ensure that this doesn't happen. People tend to think of transactions as being limited to data modification management, but, as you can see, they're also useful for ensuring read repeatability. (See Chapter 14, "Transactions" for more information.)

Rather than specifying a fixed offset and read length, it's more common to use PATINDEX() to locate a substring within a BLOB field and extricate it, like so:

```
DECLARE @textptr binary(16), @patindex int, @patlength int

BEGIN TRAN
SELECT @textptr=TEXTPTR(pr_info), @patindex=PATINDEX('%Algodata
Infosystems%',pr_info)-1,
@patlength=DATALENGTH('Algodata Infosystems')
FROM pub_info (HOLDLOCK)
WHERE PATINDEX('%Algodata Infosystems%',pr_info)<>0

READTEXT pub_info.pr_info @textptr @patindex @patlength
COMMIT TRAN

pr_info
--------------------------------------------------------------------------------
Algodata Infosystems
```

Note the use of PATINDEX() to both qualify the query and set the @patindex variable. The query must subtract one from the return value of PATINDEX() because PATINDEX() is one-based, while READTEXT is zero-based. As mentioned earlier, PATINDEX() works similarly to LIKE except that it can also return the offset of the located pattern or string.

Handling larger segments requires looping through the BLOB with READTEXT, reading it a chunk at a time. Here's an example:

```
DECLARE @textptr binary(16), @blobsize int, @chunkindex int, @chunksize int
SET TEXTSIZE 64 -- Set extremely small for illustration purposes only
```

```
BEGIN TRAN
SELECT @textptr=TEXTPTR(pr_info), @blobsize=DATALENGTH(pr_info), @chunkindex=0,
@chunksize=CASE WHEN @@TEXTSIZE < @blobsize THEN @@TEXTSIZE ELSE @blobsize END
FROM pub_info (HOLDLOCK)
WHERE PATINDEX('%Algodata Infosystems%',pr_info)<>0

IF (@textptr IS NOT NULL) AND (@chunksize > 0)
WHILE (@chunkindex < @blobsize) AND (@@ERROR=0) BEGIN
   READTEXT pub_info.pr_info @textptr @chunkindex @chunksize
   SELECT @chunkindex=@chunkindex+@chunksize,
     @chunksize=CASE WHEN (@chunkindex+@chunksize) > @blobsize THEN @blobsize-
     @chunkindex ELSE @chunksize END
END
COMMIT TRAN
SET TEXTSIZE 0 -- Return to its default value (4096)
```

(Results abridged)

```
pr_info
-------------------------------------------------------------------------------
This is sample text data for Algodata Infosystems, publisher 138

pr_info
-------------------------------------------------------------------------------
9 in the pubs database. Algodata Infosystems is located in Berke

pr_info
-------------------------------------------------------------------------------
ley, California.
```

The trickiest part of this query is the fact that READTEXT doesn't allow reading past the end of the BLOB. That is, if the BLOB is 100 characters long, you can't specify a starting point of 90 and a chunk size of 30 and expect to get the last 10 characters of the BLOB—READ-TEXT will return an error instead. So, the query is forced to do READTEXT's work for it—it computes the exact size of the remainder of the BLOB and is careful not to exceed it.

This query uses the fact that SQL Server evaluates expressions left to right to keep the code as small as possible. In the initial SELECT, the @blobsize variable is used later in the SELECT list immediately after being set by the same statement. Because SQL Server evaluates the list left to right, this works. The SELECT statement within the loop employs the same technique. @chunkindex is used elsewhere within the SELECT statement that also sets its value. This behavior isn't guaranteed to remain the same in future releases of the product, so you should use it with caution.

In the examples thus far, we've used HOLDLOCK to ensure that a text pointer we retrieve early in the query is still valid later—to ensure read repeatability. HOLDLOCK causes the read lock initiated by the SELECT to remain in effect until the end of the transaction. Depending on the current transaction isolation level, HOLDLOCK may not even be necessary because we're reading the entirety of the segment we're after and have no intention of rereading it (see Chapter 14, "Transactions," for more information). An alternative would be to use SET TRANSACTION ISOLATION LEVEL to force the server itself to ensure repeatable reads, like so:

```
DECLARE @textptr binary(16), @blobsize int, @chunkindex int, @chunksize int
SET TEXTSIZE 64      -- Set extremely small for illustration purposes only

SET TRANSACTION ISOLATION LEVEL REPEATABLE READ
BEGIN TRAN
SELECT @textptr=TEXTPTR(pr_info), @blobsize=DATALENGTH(pr_info), @chunkindex=0,
@chunksize=CASE WHEN @@TEXTSIZE < @blobsize THEN @@TEXTSIZE ELSE @blobsize END
FROM pub_info
WHERE PATINDEX('%Algodata Infosystems%',pr_info)<>0

IF (@textptr IS NOT NULL) AND (@chunksize > 0)
WHILE (@chunkindex < @blobsize) AND (@@ERROR=0) BEGIN
   READTEXT pub_info.pr_info @textptr @chunkindex @chunksize
    SELECT @chunkindex=@chunkindex+@chunksize,
      @chunksize=CASE WHEN (@chunkindex+@chunksize) > @blobsize THEN
@blobsize-@chunkindex ELSE @chunksize END
END
COMMIT TRAN
SET TEXTSIZE 0 -- Return to its default value (4096)
GO
SET TRANSACTION ISOLATION LEVEL READ COMMITTED -- Back to its default (in a
separate batch)
```

By telling the server to ensure the reads we perform are repeatable within the same transaction, we block other users from making changes to pr_info while we're perusing it, which is exactly what HOLDLOCK does.

Updating BLOB Data

Supplying BLOB columns with text or image data that's less than or equal to 8000 bytes in size is as straightforward as updating any other type of column. You can use INSERT, UPDATE, and DEFAULT constraints to supply these values, just as you can other types of data. Here's an example:

```
CREATE TABLE #testnotes (k1 int identity, notes text DEFAULT SPACE(10))

INSERT #testnotes DEFAULT VALUES

INSERT #testnotes (notes) VALUES (REPLICATE('X',20))

UPDATE #testnotes SET notes=REPLICATE('Y',10) WHERE k1=1

SELECT * FROM #testnotes
DROP TABLE #testnotes

k1         notes
---------- ------------------------------------------------------------------
1          YYYYYYYYYY
2          XXXXXXXXXXXXXXXXXXXX
```

Writing values larger than 8000 bytes via Transact-SQL requires the use of the UPDATE-TEXT or WRITETEXT command. UPDATETEXT can modify a portion of a BLOB field, while WRITETEXT rewrites its entire contents. Generally speaking, UPDATETEXT is more flexible than WRITETEXT and should be your tool of choice for writing large amounts of text or image data to a BLOB field. Here's an example:

```
CREATE TABLE #testnotes (k1 int identity, notes text DEFAULT REPLICATE('X',20))

BEGIN TRAN
INSERT #testnotes DEFAULT VALUES

DECLARE @textptr binary(16)

SELECT @textptr=TEXTPTR(notes)
FROM #testnotes (UPDLOCK)

UPDATETEXT #testnotes.notes @textptr 0 0 'ZZZ '

SELECT * FROM #testnotes
COMMIT TRAN

GO
DROP TABLE #testnotes

k1         notes
---------- ----------------------------------------------------------------------
1          ZZZ XXXXXXXXXXXXXXXXXXXX
```

UPDATETEXT takes five parameters: the column to be updated, a valid text pointer to it, the offset at which the update is to occur, the number of characters to delete from the offset location, and the update text. Despite its name, UPDATETEXT deletes, then inserts the updated text. It works similarly to the Transact-SQL STUFF() function, whose purpose is to remove a segment of a string and replace it with another. Since we specified an offset and delete length of zero, the string we specified is simply inserted at the front of the text field.

As with READTEXT, valid text pointers can be acquired via the TEXTPTR() function. Transactions help ensure that a text pointer acquired via a SELECT is valid when UPDATETEXT is called. We use UPDLOCK rather than HOLDLOCK because we're updating the data rather than merely reading it.

The real power of UPDATETEXT shows when you need to update a segment of a BLOB rather than prefix it with a new string or replace it altogether. Here's an example:

```
CREATE TABLE #testnotes (k1 int identity, notes text DEFAULT ' ')

BEGIN TRAN
INSERT #testnotes DEFAULT VALUES

UPDATE #testnotes SET notes='Women and Babies First'

DECLARE @textptr binary(16), @patindex int, @patlength int

SELECT @textptr=TEXTPTR(notes), @patindex=PATINDEX('%Babies%',notes)-1,
@patlength=DATALENGTH('Babies')
FROM #testnotes (UPDLOCK)
WHERE PATINDEX('%Babies%',notes)<>0
```

```
UPDATETEXT #testnotes.notes @textptr @patindex @patlength 'Children'

SELECT * FROM #testnotes

COMMIT TRAN

GO
DROP TABLE #testnotes

k1         notes
---------- -----------------------------------------------------------------
1          Women and Children First
```

Here, we use PATINDEX() to locate an offset within a text field, then we use UPDATE-
TEXT to change the string at that location.

WRITETEXT works similarly to UPDATETEXT. Since it writes the entire field, it doesn't
require an offset or length parameter. Here's an example:

```
CREATE TABLE #testnotes (k1 int identity, notes text DEFAULT ' ')

BEGIN TRAN
INSERT #testnotes DEFAULT VALUES

DECLARE @textptr binary(16)

SELECT @textptr=TEXTPTR(notes)
FROM #testnotes (UPDLOCK)

WRITETEXT #testnotes.notes @textptr 'ZZZ '

SELECT * FROM #testnotes

COMMIT TRAN

GO
DROP TABLE #testnotes

k1         notes
---------- -----------------------------------------------------------------
1          ZZZ
```

Note the use of a constraint to supply a default value to the BLOB column. Since both
UPDATETEXT and WRITETEXT require a valid text pointer, you can't use them to write data
to a BLOB field that's NULL. This makes adding text to a newly inserted row more difficult
than it should be. The best way to deal with this is to set up a DEFAULT constraint for the BLOB
column; then, when a row is added to the table, the column will receive a valid value which you
can then access via a separate TEXTPTR() query. Once you have a valid text pointer in hand,
you can call UPDATETEXT or WRITETEXT to place real data into the BLOB column.

BLOB Updates and the Transaction Log
Both UPDATETEXT and WRITETEXT support a WITH LOG option that determines whether
the changes they make are recorded in the transaction log. The default is for BLOB updates not
to be logged. Unfortunately, this invalidates the transaction log (forcing full database backups)
and requires that **select into/bulk copy** be enabled for the database (via sp_dboption). It's

always preferable to log operations when you can. This preserves your ability to use the transaction log as it was intended and protects the integrity of your databases. Of course, there are exceptions to this rule—you may be adding a large amount of BLOB data at once and wish to disable logging temporarily. If so, leave off the WITH LOG option, and only the database's extent allocations will be recorded in the transaction log.

Bits

Bit columns and variables can have one of three values: 0, 1, or NULL. Bits are stored in groups of eight as bytes, so if there are fewer than eight of them, they require just one byte of storage.

Bits are not allowed to serve as index keys, and for good reason. A column that's limited to three possible values would make a very poor index key because it couldn't possibly be very *selective*. That is, it wouldn't be of much help identifying individual rows in a large group of them (an index's *selectivity* indicates the number of rows that are typically identified by one of its key values). In a 9000 row table with a bit column and an even distribution of bit's possible values, the best selectivity a bit index could hope for would be one third of the total rows, or 3000 rows per key value. This means a query that used the index would have to wade through 3000 rows to find a particular record—not an optimal situation.

SQL Server provides a number of operators for working with bits, bit masks, and bitmaps. A bitmap is a column or variable of a type other than bit—usually an integer or image—that stores an array of bit switches—a *map* of them. A bit mask is a collection of bits—usually in the form of an integer—that's used to extract or manipulate the bit switches in a bitmap. Here's an example:

```
SELECT LEFT(name,30) AS DB,
    SUBSTRING(CASE status & 1 WHEN 0 THEN '' ELSE ',autoclose' END+
    CASE status & 4 WHEN 0 THEN '' ELSE ',select into/bulk copy' END+
    CASE status & 8 WHEN 0 THEN '' ELSE ',trunc. log on chkpt' END+
    CASE status & 16 WHEN 0 THEN '' ELSE ',torn page detection' END+
    CASE status & 32 WHEN 0 THEN '' ELSE ',loading' END+
    CASE status & 64 WHEN 0 THEN '' ELSE ',pre-recovery' END+
    CASE status & 128 WHEN 0 THEN '' ELSE ',recovering' END+
    CASE status & 256 WHEN 0 THEN '' ELSE ',not recovered' END+
    CASE status & 512 WHEN 0 THEN '' ELSE ',offline' END+
    CASE status & 1024 WHEN 0 THEN '' ELSE ',read only' END+
    CASE status & 2048 WHEN 0 THEN '' ELSE ',dbo use only' END+
    CASE status & 4096 WHEN 0 THEN '' ELSE ',single user' END+
    CASE status & 32768 WHEN 0 THEN '' ELSE ',emergency mode' END+
    CASE status & 4194304 WHEN 0 THEN '' ELSE ',autoshrink' END+
    CASE status & 1073741824 WHEN 0 THEN '' ELSE ',cleanly shutdown' END+
    CASE status2 & 16384 WHEN 0 THEN '' ELSE ',ANSI NULL default' END+
    CASE status2 & 65536 WHEN 0 THEN '' ELSE ',concat NULL yields NULL' END+
    CASE status2 & 131072 WHEN 0 THEN '' ELSE ',recursive triggers' END+
    CASE status2 & 1048576 WHEN 0 THEN '' ELSE ',default to local cursor' END+
    CASE status2 & 8388608 WHEN 0 THEN '' ELSE ',quoted identifier' END+
    CASE status2 & 33554432 WHEN 0 THEN '' ELSE ',cursor close on commit' END+
    CASE status2 & 67108864 WHEN 0 THEN '' ELSE ',ANSI NULLs' END+
    CASE status2 & 268435456 WHEN 0 THEN '' ELSE ',ANSI warnings' END+
    CASE status2 & 536870912 WHEN 0 THEN '' ELSE ',full text enabled' END,
2,8000) AS Description
FROM master..sysdatabases
```

```
DB          Description
----------  --------------------------------------------------------------------------------
CM          select into/bulk copy,torn page detection,autoshrink
master      trunc. log on chkpt
model       select into/bulk copy,trunc. log on chkpt,torn page detection,autoshrink
msdb        select into/bulk copy,trunc. log on chkpt,autoshrink,cleanly shutdown
Northwind   select into/bulk copy,trunc. log on chkpt,autoshrink,cleanly shutdown
Northwind2  autoclose,select into/bulk copy,trunc. log on chkpt,torn page detection,autoshrink,cleanl
PM          autoclose,select into/bulk copy,trunc. log on chkpt,autoshrink,cleanly shutdown
PO          autoclose,select into/bulk copy,trunc. log on chkpt,autoshrink,cleanly shutdown
pubs        select into/bulk copy,trunc. log on chkpt,autoshrink
SCW_TS      autoclose,select into/bulk copy,trunc. log on chkpt,torn page detection,autoshrink
tempdb      select into/bulk copy,trunc. log on chkpt,ANSI NULL default
```

Here, we query the sysdatabases table in the master database to decode the two status columns (**status** and **status2**) for each database. The literal numbers specified in each CASE expression are bit masks; the status columns are bitmaps. Each of the possible status flags that a database can have is represented by a bit or bits in one of these two columns. We use the bitwise and operator **&** to match the status columns with the switch values corresponding to each flag.

> **Note**
> As mentioned throughout this book, querying the system tables directly is now discouraged. When possible, you should query the INFORMATION_SCHEMA views or call the catalog stored procedures to access system-level information.

Internally, SQL Server makes extensive use of bitmaps and bit masks because they're an efficient way to store and track status flags. For example, the sysindexes table contains a column named **statblob** that's used to track index statistics. It's an **image** column that doesn't actually store an image—it stores a bitmap representing index key distribution information.

UNIQUEIDENTIFIER

The uniqueidentifer data type stores GUIDs (global unique identifiers). A GUID is a 16 -byte binary number that is guaranteed to be unique across all networked computers in the world. Windows COM interfaces use GUIDs to identify themselves. Since these are unique across all networked computers in the world, this provides a universal numbering scheme for COM interfaces.

The T-SQL NEWID() function generates new GUIDs on demand. It can be used as a column default, like so:

```
SET NOCOUNT ON
CREATE TABLE #guids (c1 uniqueidentifier DEFAULT NEWID())
INSERT #guids DEFAULT VALUES
INSERT #guids DEFAULT VALUES
INSERT #guids DEFAULT VALUES
INSERT #guids DEFAULT VALUES

SELECT * FROM #guids
GO
DROP TABLE #guids
```

```
c1
------------------------------------
07A7DEFF-367F-11D3-92AC-005004044A19
07A7DF00-367F-11D3-92AC-005004044A19
07A7DF01-367F-11D3-92AC-005004044A19
07A7DF02-367F-11D3-92AC-005004044A19
```

Each table can have as many uniqueidentifier columns as you wish and can identify a single uniqueidentifier column as its ROWGUIDCOL column. The ROWGUIDCOL can be used to reference its corresponding uniqueidentifier column indirectly without actually naming it (analogously to IDENTITYCOL). Here's an example:

```
SET NOCOUNT ON
CREATE TABLE #guids (c1 uniqueidentifier DEFAULT NEWID() ROWGUIDCOL)

INSERT #guids DEFAULT VALUES
INSERT #guids DEFAULT VALUES
INSERT #guids DEFAULT VALUES
INSERT #guids DEFAULT VALUES

SELECT ROWGUIDCOL FROM #guids
GO
DROP TABLE #guids
```

```
c1
------------------------------------
07A7DF1D-367F-11D3-92AC-005004044A19
07A7DF1E-367F-11D3-92AC-005004044A19
07A7DF1F-367F-11D3-92AC-005004044A19
07A7DF20-367F-11D3-92AC-005004044A19
```

Uniqueidentifiers have a number of disadvantages. Among them:

- Their values are unwieldy and cryptic. They're random and don't fit or match any sort of mnemonic pattern.

- The uniqueidentifier data type is four times as large as the four-byte int type that's typically used for row identifiers. This makes accessing them slower in general, including building and accessing indexes over them.

- The sequence in which a set of uniqueidentifier values were generated is not discernable from the values themselves—you can't tell which values came first and which ones came later by looking only at the data. Among other things, this means that they make poor ORDER BY columns.

Cursor Variables

A cursor variable stores a reference to a cursor definition. Cursors defined via variables are by definition local cursors (since you can't declare global variables) and can be used in place of direct cursor references in commands such as OPEN, FETCH, CLOSE, and DEALLOCATE.

They support the full Transact-SQL cursor syntax and can be used to define read-only as well as updatable cursors. Cursor variables and the cursor data type can be used most places ordinary variables and data types can with three exceptions:

- You can't define a table column of type cursor.

- You can't define stored procedure *input* parameters as cursors (but you can define cursor *output* parameters).

- You can't assign a cursor variable with a SELECT statement. (They must be assigned using the SET command.)

Here's an example of a simple cursor variable definition:

```
DECLARE @cursor CURSOR

SET @cursor=CURSOR FOR SELECT * FROM authors

OPEN @cursor
FETCH @cursor

WHILE (@@FETCH_STATUS=0) BEGIN
   FETCH @cursor
END

CLOSE @cursor
DEALLOCATE @cursor
```

In this example, we define the cursor using the SET assignment statement. Cursor variables can also be assigned from existing cursors, like so:

```
DECLARE @cursor CURSOR
DECLARE c CURSOR FOR SELECT * FROM authors
SET @cursor=c

OPEN @cursor
FETCH @cursor

WHILE (@@FETCH_STATUS=0) BEGIN
   FETCH @cursor
END

CLOSE @cursor
DEALLOCATE @cursor
DEALLOCATE c
```

Here, we first define the cursor using the traditional DECLARE CURSOR syntax; then we assign it by name to the cursor variable. Note the separate deallocation of the cursor variable and the cursor. Deallocating the cursor alone isn't enough; it remains in memory until it's explicitly deallocated or the last variable referencing it goes out of scope, whichever comes last. For example, consider this variation on the code:

```
DECLARE @cursor CURSOR
DECLARE c CURSOR FOR SELECT * FROM authors

SET @cursor=c

DEALLOCATE c

OPEN @cursor
FETCH @cursor

WHILE (@@FETCH_STATUS=0) BEGIN
   FETCH @cursor
END

CLOSE @cursor
DEALLOCATE @cursor
```

Once you've assigned a regular cursor to a cursor variable, you can reference the cursor using either the original name or the variable—they're almost synonymous. So, for example, once you've opened the cursor via the cursor variable, as in the last example, you can't reopen it using the original cursor name without closing it first—it's already open. Likewise, closing the cursor variable closes the original cursor, too—they refer to the same internal structure. As a rule, they're interchangeable. The lone exception is the DEALLOCATE command.

As you can see from the example code, deallocating the original cursor doesn't prevent you from continuing to access it via the cursor variable. Even though the code deallocates it immediately after assigning it to the cursor variable, it doesn't actually go away. Deallocating a cursor reference other than the final one merely removes your ability to access the cursor via that reference—the cursor itself hangs around until the last variable referencing it is deallocated or goes out of scope.

You can define more than one cursor variable that references a particular cursor, and you can assign cursor variables to one another. Here's an example:

```
DECLARE @cursor1 CURSOR, @cursor2 CURSOR
DECLARE c CURSOR FOR SELECT * FROM authors
SET @cursor1=c
SET @cursor2=@cursor1

OPEN @cursor2
FETCH @cursor2

WHILE (@@FETCH_STATUS=0) BEGIN
   FETCH @cursor1
END

CLOSE @cursor1
DEALLOCATE @cursor1
DEALLOCATE @cursor2
DEALLOCATE c
```

One handy feature of Transact-SQL cursor variables is support for cursor output parameters. In the past, returning a cursor from a stored procedure meant either displaying it immediately or trapping it in a table via INSERT...EXEC. Cursor variables give you more control over when and whether to display a procedure's result set. You can call FETCH to return the result set a row at a time or place it into a variable, or you can simply close and deallocate the cursor—it's up to you.

Several of the system procedures that relate to cursors return cursor output parameters. Sp_describe_cursor, for example, returns a cursor that points to a single-row result set containing a report on the cursor you specify. This necessitates setting up a cursor variable and passing it into the procedure as an OUTPUT parameter, like so:

```
DECLARE @cursor CURSOR
DECLARE c CURSOR GLOBAL FOR SELECT * FROM authors
OPEN c

EXEC sp_describe_cursor @cursor_return=@cursor OUTPUT,
@cursor_source=N'global',
@cursor_identity=N'c'

FETCH @cursor

FETCH c
WHILE (@@FETCH_STATUS=0) BEGIN
   FETCH c
END

CLOSE @cursor
CLOSE c
DEALLOCATE @cursor
DEALLOCATE c
```

(Result set abridged)

reference_name	cursor_name	cursor_scope	status	model	concurrency	scrollable	open_status	cursor_rows
c	c	2	1	3	3	0	1	-1

Once it processes the cursor, the code closes and deallocates the cursor along with its own global cursor. In this case, it can get away with making a single call to FETCH to return sp_describe_cursor's one row. If the cursor returned by the stored procedure referenced a multi-row result set, the code would need to loop through it, fetching each row separately. This call to sp_cursor_list illustrates:

```
DECLARE @authorcursor CURSOR, @authorcursor2 CURSOR, @cursorlist CURSOR
DECLARE AuthorsList CURSOR GLOBAL FOR SELECT * FROM authors

SET @authorcursor=AuthorsList
SET @authorcursor2=AuthorsList

OPEN AuthorsList

EXEC sp_cursor_list @cursor_return=@cursorlist OUTPUT,
@cursor_scope=3
```

```
FETCH @cursorlist
WHILE (@@FETCH_STATUS=0) BEGIN
   FETCH @cursorlist
END

CLOSE @cursorlist
CLOSE AuthorsList

DEALLOCATE @cursorlist
DEALLOCATE AuthorsList
DEALLOCATE @authorcursor
DEALLOCATE @authorcursor2
```

(Results abridged)

reference_name	cursor_name	cursor_scope	status	model	concurrency	scrollable
@cursorlist	_MICROSOFT_SS_0532422748	1	-1	3	1	1
reference_name	cursor_name	cursor_scope	status	model	concurrency	scrollable
@authorcursor2	AuthorsList	1	1	3	3	0
reference_name	cursor_name	cursor_scope	status	model	concurrency	scrollable
@authorcursor	AuthorsList	1	1	3	3	0
reference_name	cursor_name	cursor_scope	status	model	concurrency	scrollable
AuthorsList	AuthorsList	2	1	3	3	0

Sp_cursor_list provides the same basic info as sp_describe_cursor but lists info for more than one cursor (all global cursors, all local cursors, or all cursors of either type). The cursor it returns via @cursorlist is fetched a row at a time until it's fully retrieved; then the cursor is closed and deallocated as before.

Note that the prohibition against cursor input parameters means that a cursor output parameter may not have a cursor allocated to it prior to passing it to a procedure. If SQL Server permitted this, it would allow the input parameter restriction to be circumvented since an output parameter can be inspected and used just like any other stored procedure parameter. Here's an example:

```
-- DON'T DO THIS -- BAD T-SQL
USE pubs
GO
IF (OBJECT_ID('inputcursorparm') IS NOT NULL)
   DROP PROC inputcursorparm
GO
CREATE PROC inputcursorparm @cursor_input cursor VARYING OUT
AS
FETCH @cursor_input

WHILE (@@FETCH_STATUS=0) BEGIN
   FETCH @cursor_input
END
```

```
CLOSE @cursor_input
DEALLOCATE @cursor_input
GO

DECLARE @c CURSOR
SET @c=CURSOR FOR SELECT * FROM authors

-- An error is generated when the procedure is called
-- because @c references an existing cursor
EXEC inputcursorparm @c OUT

Server: Msg 16951, Level 16, State 1, Line 7
The variable '@c' cannot be used as a parameter because a CURSOR OUTPUT parameter
must not have a cursor allocated to it before execution of the procedure.
```

Timestamps

Despite the name, timestamp columns have nothing to do with the time or date. A timestamp is a special binary(8) value that's guaranteed to be unique across a database. A timestamp column is updated each time the data in a row changes. In SQL Server's infancy, timestamp columns were used to effect a simplistic optimistic locking strategy that's best explained by an example. If Juliet updates a row after Romeo reads it but before he posts his own changes, Romeo's update attempt will fail because it will use the original timestamp value to try to locate the row. Romeo's UPDATE statement will include the timestamp column in its WHERE clause but won't be able to locate the original record because the timestamp value has changed due to Juliet's update. This prevents Romeo from overwriting Juliet's changes and provides a means for his application to detect that another user modified the row he was editing.

The TSEQUAL() function can be used to compare timestamp values. If the timestamps aren't equal, TSEQUAL() raises an error and aborts the current command batch.

A table is limited to a single timestamp column. A common convention is to name the column **timestamp,** but that's not required by the server. Here's a code sample that shows how to use the timestamp data type:

```
SET NOCOUNT ON
CREATE TABLE #testts (c1 int identity, c2 int DEFAULT 0, changelog timestamp)

INSERT #testts DEFAULT VALUES
INSERT #testts DEFAULT VALUES
INSERT #testts DEFAULT VALUES
INSERT #testts DEFAULT VALUES
INSERT #testts DEFAULT VALUES

SELECT * FROM #testts

UPDATE #testts SET c2=c1

SELECT * FROM #testts

GO
DROP TABLE #testts
```

```
c1            c2             changelog
-----------   -----------    ------------------
1             0              0x0000000000000085
2             0              0x0000000000000086
3             0              0x0000000000000087
4             0              0x0000000000000088
5             0              0x0000000000000089


c1            c2             changelog
-----------   -----------    ------------------
1             1              0x000000000000008A
2             2              0x000000000000008B
3             3              0x000000000000008C
4             4              0x000000000000008D
5             5              0x000000000000008E
```

Note the different values for each row's timestamp column before and after the UPDATE.

You can access the last generated timestamp value for a database via the @@DBTS automatic variable. Each database maintains its own counter, so be sure you're in the correct database before querying @@DBTS. Here's an example:

```
USE tempdb
GO
SET NOCOUNT ON
CREATE TABLE #testts (c1 int identity, c2 int DEFAULT 0, changelog timestamp)

INSERT #testts DEFAULT VALUES
INSERT #testts DEFAULT VALUES
INSERT #testts DEFAULT VALUES
INSERT #testts DEFAULT VALUES
INSERT #testts DEFAULT VALUES

SELECT * FROM #testts
SELECT @@DBTS AS 'Last timestamp'

UPDATE #testts SET c2=c1

SELECT * FROM #testts
SELECT @@DBTS AS 'Last timestamp'
GO
DROP TABLE #testts
```

```
c1            c2             changelog
-----------   -----------    ------------------
1             0              0x00000000000000B7
2             0              0x00000000000000B8
3             0              0x00000000000000B9
4             0              0x00000000000000BA
5             0              0x00000000000000BB


Last timestamp
------------------
0x00000000000000BB
```

c1	c2	changelog
1	1	0x00000000000000BC
2	2	0x00000000000000BD
3	3	0x00000000000000BE
4	4	0x00000000000000BF
5	5	0x00000000000000C0

```
Last timestamp
------------------
0x00000000000000C0
```

Note the USE tempdb at the first of the script. Since temporary tables reside in tempdb, we have to change the current database focus to tempdb in order for @@DBTS to work properly. @@DBTS always returns the last timestamp value generated for a database, so you can use it to acquire the timestamp of an update you've just performed, similar to the @@IDENTITY automatic variable. One big difference between @@DBTS and @@IDENTITY is that @@IDENTITY is connection specific whereas @@DBTS is database specific. The value returned by @@IDENTITY will rarely be the same for multiple users, but @@DBTS will often be identical for all users connected to a given database.

Summary

In this chapter you've explored SQL Server's wealth of data types. You've learned about date, numeric, string, bit, and BLOB data types, as well as fringe types such as timestamps and uniqueidentifiers. Designing sound databases and writing robust Transact-SQL code require intimate familiarity with the wide variety of data types SQL Server provides. Knowing them well is the first step in writing optimal code to access them.

3

Missing Values

Of the thirty-six alternatives, running away is best.
—Chinese Proverb

Missing values and the proper handling of them is a very delicate subject within the database community. The debate centers on how (or whether) missing values should be stored in relational databases and how many and what types of tokens should be used to represent them in SQL.

There are at least three different schools of thought regarding how to handle missing values. The inventor of the relational database, Dr. E. F. Codd, advocates two separate missing value tokens: one for values that should be there but aren't (e.g., the gender of a person) and one for values that shouldn't be there at all because they are inapplicable (e.g., the gender of a corporation). Chris Date, noted database author and lecturer, takes the minimalist position. He believes that SQL is better off without a missing value token of any kind. ANSI/ISO SQL-92 splits the difference and provides one general-purpose missing value token: NULL.

At the risk of stating the obvious, missing values and empty values are two different things. An integer whose value is missing is not the same as an integer whose value is zero. A null string is not the same as a zero-length string or one containing only blanks. This distinction is important because comparisons between empty values and missing values always fail. In fact, NULL values aren't even equal to one another in such comparisons.

The possibility of missing values in relational data indicates that there are three possible outcomes for any comparison: True, False, and Unknown. Of course, this necessitates the use of three-valued logic. The truth tables in Figure 3.1 illustrate.

Note that I use NULL and Unknown interchangeably, even though, technically speaking, they aren't. NULL is a data value, while Unknown represents a logical value. The distinction is a bit abstruse—especially for veteran software developers—and is the reason you must use **...WHERE column IS NULL** rather than **...WHERE column = NULL** if you want your SQL to behave sensibly. (Transact-SQL doesn't forbid the latter syntax, but since one NULL never equals another—or even itself—it never returns True. See the section below on Transact-SQL's ANSI NULL compliance.) As much fun as it would be, I have no desire to enter the philosophical debate over NULLs and their proper use. So, for simplicity's sake, since our purpose is to view the world of data and databases through the eyes of Transact-SQL, I'll stick with treating NULL and Unknown identically throughout the book.

AND	True	False	Unknown
True	True	False	Unknown
False	False	False	False
Unknown	Unknown	False	Unknown
OR	True	False	Unknown
True	True	True	True
False	True	False	Unknown
Unknown	True	Unknown	Unknown
NOT	True	False	Unknown
	False	True	Unknown

Figure 3.1. Three-valued logic truth tables.

NULL and Expressions

Typically, involving a NULL value in an expression yields a NULL result. For example, SELECT 5+NULL returns NULL, not 5, as does SELECT SUBSTRING('Groucho',3,2+NULL). The notable exceptions to this rule are aggregate functions.

Similarly, NULL values are never equal to one another; in fact, a NULL value is not even equal to itself, as illustrated by the following query:

```
CREATE TABLE #nulltest
(c1 int NULL)
GO
INSERT #nulltest VALUES (1)
INSERT #nulltest VALUES (NULL)
INSERT #nulltest VALUES (3)
GO
DECLARE @nv int
SELECT @nv=c1 FROM #nulltest WHERE c1 IS NULL -- Gets the NULL from row 2
SELECT MyNV=c1 FROM #nulltest WHERE c1=@nv -- Returns no rows
```

NULL and Functions

As with simple expressions, most functions involving NULL values return NULL, so SELECT SIGN(NULL) returns NULL, as do SELECT ABS(NULL) and SELECT LTRIM(NULL). The exceptions to this are functions designed to work with NULL in the first place. In addition to aggregates, functions intended to be used with NULLs include ISNULL() and COALESCE().

ISNULL() translates a NULL value into a non-NULL value. For example,

```
SELECT ISNULL(c1,0) FROM #nulltest
```

translates all NULL values found in c1 to 0. Caution should be exercised when doing this, though, since translating NULLs to other values can have unexpected side effects. For example, the AVG query from the example above can't ignore translated NULLs:

```
SELECT AVG(ISNULL(c1,0)) FROM #nulltest
```

The value zero is figured into the average, significantly lowering it.

Note that ISNULL()'s parameters aren't limited to constants. Consider this example:

```
DECLARE @x int,@y int
SET @x=5
SET @y=2
SELECT ISNULL(CASE WHEN @x>=1 THEN NULL ELSE @x END,
   CASE WHEN @y<5 THEN @x*@y ELSE 10 END)
```

Here, both arguments consist of expressions, including the one returned by the function. ISNULL() can even handle SELECT statements as parameters, as in this example:

```
DECLARE @x int,@y int
SET @x=5
SET @y=2
SELECT ISNULL(CASE WHEN @x>=1 THEN NULL ELSE @x END,
   (SELECT COUNT(*) FROM authors))
```

The NULLIF() function is a rough inverse of ISNULL(). Though it doesn't handle NULL values being passed *into* it any better than any other function, it was designed to *return* a NULL value in the right circumstances. It takes two parameters and returns NULL if they're equal; otherwise it returns the first parameter. For example,

```
DECLARE @x int,@y int
SET @x=5
SET @y=2
SELECT NULLIF(@x,@y+3)
```

returns NULL, while

```
SELECT NULLIF(@x, @y)
```

returns 5.

COALESCE() returns the first non-NULL value from a horizontal list. For example,

```
SELECT COALESCE(@x / NULL, @x * NULL, @x+NULL, NULL, @y*2, @x,
   (SELECT COUNT(*) FROM authors))
```

returns @y*2, or 4. As with ISNULL(), parameters passed to COALESCE() can be expressions and subqueries as well as constants, as the code sample illustrates.

NULL and ANSI SQL

With each successive version, SQL Server's ANSI/ISO compliance has steadily improved. Using a variety of configuration switches and modern command syntax, you can write Transact-SQL code that's portable to other ANSI-compliant DBMSs.

NULLs represent one area in which ANSI compliance improved substantially in version 7.0. A number of new configuration settings and syntax options were added to enhance SQL Server's ANSI compliance in terms of NULL values. Many of these are discussed below.

Regarding the handling of NULL values in expressions, the ANSI/ISO SQL specification correctly separates aggregation from basic expression evaluation (this is contrary to what a couple of otherwise fine SQL books have said). This means, as far as the standard is concerned, that adding a NULL value to a number is not the same as aggregating a column that contains both NULL and non-NULL values. In the former case, the end result is always a NULL value. In the latter, the NULL values are ignored and the aggregation is performed. Per the ANSI spec, the only way to return a NULL result from an aggregate function is to start with an empty table or have nothing but NULL values in the aggregated column (COUNT() is an exception—see below). Since Transact-SQL follows the standard in this regard, these statements apply to it as well. For example, consider the following table from earlier:

```
CREATE TABLE #nulltest
(c1 int NULL)
```

and the following data:

```
INSERT #nulltest VALUES (1)
INSERT #nulltest VALUES (NULL)
INSERT #nulltest VALUES (3)
```

The query:

```
SELECT AVG(c1) FROM #nulltest
```

doesn't return NULL, even though one of the values it considers is indeed NULL. Instead, it ignores NULL when it computes the average, which is exactly what you'd want. This is also true for the SUM(), MIN(), and MAX() functions but *not* for COUNT(*). For example,

```
SELECT COUNT(*) FROM #nulltest
```

returns "3," so SELECT SUM(c1)/COUNT(*) is *not* the same as SELECT AVG(c1). COUNT(*) counts rows, regardless of missing values. It includes the table's second row, even though the table has just one column and the value of that one column in row 2 is NULL. If you want COUNT() behavior that's consistent with SQL Server's other aggregate functions, specify a column in the underlying table rather than using "*" (e.g., **COUNT(c1)**). This syntax properly ignores NULL values, so that SELECT SUM(c1)/COUNT(c1) returns the same value as SELECT AVG(c1).

This subtle distinction between COUNT(*) and COUNT(c1) is an important one since they return different results when NULLs enter the picture. Generally, it's preferable to use COUNT(*) and let the optimizer choose the best method of returning a row count rather than forcing it to count a specific column. If you need the "special" behavior of COUNT(c1), it's probably wise to note what you're doing via comments in your code.

By default, SQL Server's ANSI_WARNINGS switch is set if you connect to the server via ODBC or OLEDB. This means that the server generates a warning message for any query where a missing value is ignored by an aggregate. This is nothing to worry about if you know about your missing values and intend them to be ignored but could possibly alert you to data problems otherwise.

ANSI_WARNINGS can be set globally for a given database via sp_dboption or per session using the SET ANSI_WARNINGS command. As with all database options, session-level settings override database option settings.

Other important ANSI NULL-related settings include SET ANSI_NULL_DFLT_ON/ _OFF, SET ANSI_NULLS, and SET CONCAT_NULL_YIELDS_NULL.

SET ANSI_NULL_DFLT_ON/_OFF determines whether columns in newly created tables can contain NULL values by default. You can query this setting via the GETANSINULL() system function.

SET ANSI_NULLS controls how equality comparisons with NULL work. The ANSI SQL standard stipulates that any expression involving comparison operators ("=," "<>," ">=," and so forth—"theta" operators in Codd parlance) and NULL returns NULL. Turning this setting off (it's on by default when you connect via ODBC or OLEDB) enables equality comparisons with NULL to succeed if the column or variable in question contains a NULL value.

SET CONCAT_NULL_YIELDS_NULL determines whether string concatenation involving NULL values returns a NULL value. Normally, SELECT "Rush Limbaugh's IQ=" +NULL yields NULL, but you can disable this by way of Transact-SQL's SET CONCAT_NULL_YIELDS_NULL command. Note that this setting has no effect on other types of values. Adding a NULL to a numeric value always returns NULL, regardless of CONCAT_NULL_YIELDS_NULL.

I should pause for a moment and mention a peculiarity in the SQL standard that has always seemed contradictory to me. I find the fact that the standard allows you to assign column values using "= NULL" but does not allow you to search for them using the same syntax a bit incongruous. For example,

```
UPDATE authors SET state=NULL WHERE state='CA'
```

followed by:

```
SELECT * FROM authors WHERE state=NULL
```

doesn't work as you might expect. The SELECT statement returns no rows, even when a number of them were just set to NULL. Having NULLs not equal one another is not as difficult to swallow as the obvious syntactical inconsistency. In my opinion, the standard would be more symmetrical if it required something like this instead:

```
UPDATE authors SET state TO NULL WHERE state='CA'
```

If this were allowed, the prohibition against "=NULL" would make more sense, but, alas, that's not the case.

NULL and Stored Procedures

Stored procedures are one area where it's particularly handy to be able to control Transact-SQL's ANSI-compliant behavior. Consider the following stored procedure:

```
CREATE PROCEDURE ListIdsByValue @val int
AS
CREATE TABLE #values (k1 int identity, c1 int NULL)
INSERT #values (c1) VALUES (1)
INSERT #values (c1) VALUES (1)
INSERT #values (c1) VALUES (NULL)
INSERT #values (c1) VALUES (9)
SELECT * FROM #values WHERE c1=@val
DROP TABLE #values
```

Despite the fact that the temporary table includes a row whose c1 column is set to NULL, passing NULL as the procedure's lone parameter will not return any rows since one NULL never equals another. Of course, the stored procedure could provide special handling for NULL values, but this approach becomes untenable very quickly as procedures with large numbers of parameters are considered. For example, a procedure with just two nullable parameters would require a nested IF that's four levels deep and would multiply the amount of code necessary to perform the query. However, thanks to SET ANSI_NULLS, this behavior can be overridden like so:

```
SET ANSI_NULLS OFF
GO
CREATE PROCEDURE ListIdsByValue @val int
AS
CREATE TABLE #values (k1 int identity, c1 int NULL)
INSERT #values (c1) VALUES (1)
INSERT #values (c1) VALUES (1)
INSERT #values (c1) VALUES (NULL)
INSERT #values (c1) VALUES (9)
SELECT * FROM #values WHERE c1=@val
DROP TABLE #values
GO
SET ANSI_NULLS ON
GO
```

This changes the viability of Transact-SQL's "=NULL" extension *for the duration of the procedure.* By "viability" I mean that, beyond not generating an error, the syntax actually works as you expect. Though the syntax is technically valid regardless of SET ANSI_NULLS, it never returns True when ANSI compatibility is enabled. As you might guess from the example code, this extension greatly simplifies the handling of nullable stored procedure parameters, which is the main reason it was added to the language.

This technique works because the status of ANSI_NULLS is recorded at the time each stored procedure is compiled. This provides a virtual snapshot of the environment in which the procedure was built, allowing you to manage the setting so that it doesn't affect anything else. The corollary to this is that regardless of the current state of ANSI_NULLS when a procedure is executed, it will behave as though ANSI_NULLS matched its setting at the time the procedure was compiled, so be careful. For example:

```
SET ANSI_NULLS OFF
GO
EXEC ListIdsByValue @val=NULL
GO
SET ANSI_NULLS ON
GO
```

won't produce any rows if ANSI_NULLS wasn't set OFF when the procedure was compiled.

Note that SET ANSI_NULLS also affects the viability of the IN (value, value, NULL) syntax. This means that a query like:

```
SELECT * from #values where (c1 in (1, NULL))
```

won't return rows with NULL values unless ANSI_NULLS is disabled. If you think of the IN predicate as shorthand for a series of equality comparisons joined by ORs, this makes perfect sense.

> **Note**
> I should point out here that I don't encourage needless departure from the ANSI/ISO SQL specification. It's always better to write code that complies with the standard, regardless of the syntactical offerings of your particular SQL dialect. ANSI/ISO-compliant code is more portable and, generally speaking, more readable by more people. As with using NULL values themselves, you should carefully consider the wisdom of writing deviant code in the first place, especially when working in multi-DBMS environments.

NULL If You Must

As I mentioned earlier, I don't intend to get drawn into the debate on the proper use of NULLs. However, it's worth mentioning that, as a practical matter, NULL values in relational databases can be a royal pain. This is best illustrated by a couple of examples. Assuming we start with the following table and data:

```
CREATE TABLE #values (k1 int identity, c1 int NULL)
INSERT #values (c1) VALUES (1)
INSERT #values (c1) VALUES (1)
INSERT #values (c1) VALUES (NULL)
INSERT #values (c1) VALUES (9)
```

one might think that this query:

```
SELECT * FROM #values WHERE c1=1
```

followed by this one:

```
SELECT * FROM #values WHERE c1<>1
```

would return all the rows in the #values table, but that's not the case. Remember that SQL is based on three-value logic. To return all rows, we have to allow for NULL values, so something like this is necessary:

```
SELECT * FROM #values WHERE c1=1 OR c1 IS NULL
```

This makes perfect sense if you consider that the NULL in row 2 is really just a placeholder. Actually, the value of the c1 column in row 2 is not known, so we can't positively say whether it does or does not equal 1, hence the exclusion from both queries. Unfortunately, this sort of reasoning is very foreign to many developers. To most coders, either something is or it isn't—there is no middle ground. For this reason alone, NULLs are the bane of many a new SQL developer. They continually perplex and frustrate the unwary.

Another problem with NULLs is the inability of most host languages to represent them properly. The increasing use of OLE data types is changing this, but it's not unusual for host languages to use some predefined constant to simulate NULL values if they support them at all. An unassigned variable is not the same thing as one containing NULL, and assuming it is will lead to spurious results. Also, few database servers, let alone traditional programming languages, implement ANSI SQL NULL behavior completely or uniformly, and differences in the way that NULLs are handled between an application's various components can introduce layered obfuscation.

Behind the scenes, SQL Server tracks which columns in a table are NULLable via a bitmap column in the sysobjects system table. Obviously, this carries with it a certain amount of overhead. Every aggregate function must take into account the fact that a column allows NULLs and take special precautions so that NULL values in the column don't skew results. Basically, NULLs are nasty little beasties that require special handling by anything that works with them.

To be fair, NULLs are a necessary evil in many cases. Accurate calculations involving quantities quickly become overly complex when there is no direct support for missing values. The difference between zero and an unknown value is the same as that between any other known value and an unknown one—it's a conceptual chasm. It's the difference between a zero checking account balance and not having a checking account at all. Datetime columns often require NULL values as well because dates are frequently expressed in relative rather than absolute terms.

One accepted method for avoiding the use of NULL is to use dummy values to signify missing data. For example, the string 'N/A' or 'NV' can be used to supplant NULLs in character string columns. -1 can be used to indicate a missing value in many integer columns, '1900-01-01' can be used for dates, and so forth. In these instances, the NULLIF() function comes in handy, especially when working with aggregate functions. For example, to get SUM() to ignore numeric columns containing -1, you could use something like SELECT SUM(NULLIF(c1, -1)) because SUM() ignores NULLs. You could code similar expressions to handle other types of dummy NULL values.

The moral of the story is this: NULL is the kryptonite of the database world—it sucks the life out of anything that gets near it. Use it if you must, but avoid it when you can.

4

DDL Insights

If the auto industry had done what the computer industry has done in the last thirty years, a Rolls Royce would cost $2.50 and get two million miles per gallon.—Herb Grosch

But it would be the size of a Dinky toy and crash every three days. Beware of false analogy.—Joe Celko

The chapter is not intended to cover Transact-SQL DDL (Data Definition Language) comprehensively—the Books Online (BOL) do that well enough already. It is not a syntax guide and makes no attempt to cover every T-SQL DDL command thoroughly, or even to cover every command.

Instead, it's a loose collection of tips, pointers, and advice regarding a variety of DDL-related topics. It's intended to supplement the Books Online, not replace them. The goal of this chapter is to fill in some of the gaps left by the BOL and to highlight DDL topics that could use further emphasis.

One of the challenges of writing a book like this is in trying to avoid replicating what's already covered in the vendor documentation while remaining thorough enough to be truly useful to readers and to assure them that their money was well spent. SQL Server's online documentation has long been one of its strong points. I prefer it hands-down to the online documentation of the other DBMS vendors I regularly work with. That said, the exhaustiveness of its coverage makes writing about relatively mundane topics such as DDL challenging for the author who would aspire to fresh, original work. In short, many subjects are already covered quite well by the Books Online, and rather than rehash what comes in the box with the product, I'd rather spend the limited number of pages in this book covering those that aren't.

As opposed to querying database objects, DDL commands are concerned with creating and managing them. They include Transact-SQL commands such as CREATE TABLE, CREATE INDEX, ALTER TABLE, and CREATE PROCEDURE. These commands have a number of nuances and idiosyncrasies that one has to explore to appreciate fully.

CREATE TABLE

Aside from the obvious function of constructing tables, CREATE TABLE is used to establish declarative referential integrity between tables. It's also used to set up default column values and to establish primary and unique key constraints.

Some Thoughts on Referential Integrity

Generally speaking, declarative RI (referential integrity) is preferable to triggers, and triggers are preferable to stored procedures, but there's a place for each. Declarative RI usually gets the nod over triggers and stored procedures because it's easy to use and because it alleviates the possibility of a bug in a trigger or stored procedure compromising data integrity. Declarative RI is also typically faster than a comparable trigger because it is enforced before the pending change is made. Triggers, by contrast, execute just after a change has been recorded in the transaction log but before it's been written to the database. This is what permits them to work with the before and after images of the changed data. This notwithstanding, sometimes triggers are a better choice due to their increased power and flexibility.

And there's nothing wrong with stored procedures that pull double duty and carry out DML (Data Management Language) requests as well as ensure data integrity. In fact, some shops work exclusively in this mode, creating INSERT, UPDATE, and DELETE procedures for every table in a database. This isn't taboo and has its place in the complex world that is database application development.

One way in which stored procedures are better than triggers for ensuring RI is in their ability to enforce data integrity even when constraints are present. If you use a stored procedure, say, to perform deletes on a given table, that stored procedure can ensure that no foreign key references will be broken prior to the delete and display the appropriate error message if necessary. All the while, a declarative foreign key constraint on the table can serve as a safety net by providing airtight protection against inappropriate deletions. That's not possible with a delete trigger. Since declarative constraints have precedence over triggers, a deletion that would violate referential integrity will be nabbed first by the constraint, and your app may have no control over what message, if any, is displayed for the user. In the case of deletes that violate foreign key references, the delete trigger will never even get to process the delete because it will be rolled back by the constraint before the trigger ever sees it.

It's not as though you can use only one of these methods to ensure referential integrity in the database apps you build—most shops have a mix. It's not unusual to see declarative RI make up the lion's share of an RI scheme, with triggers and stored procedures supplementing where necessary.

Foreign Keys

A foreign key constraint establishes a relationship between two tables. It ensures that a key value inserted or updated in the referencing table exists in the referenced table and that a key value in the referenced table cannot be deleted as long as rows in the referencing table depend on it.

ANSI Referential Actions

The ANSI SQL-92 specification defines four possible actions that can occur when a data modification is attempted: NO ACTION, SET NULL, SET DEFAULT, and CASCADE. Of these, only the first one, NO ACTION, is supported directly by SQL Server. For example, if you attempt an update or deletion that would break a foreign key reference, SQL Server rejects the change and aborts the command—the end result of your modification is NO ACTION.

Though SQL Server doesn't directly support the other three referential actions, you can still implement them in stored procedures and triggers. Triggers, for example, are quite handy for implementing cascading deletes and updates. Stored procedures are the tool of choice for implementing the SET NULL and SET DEFAULT actions since a trigger cannot directly modify a row about to be modified.

The NULL Exception

SQL Server strictly enforces foreign key relationships with one notable exception. If the column in the referencing table allows NULL values, NULLs are allowed regardless of whether the referenced table contains a NULL entry. In this sense, NULLs circumvent SQL Server's declarative RI mechanism. This makes more sense if you think of NULL as a value that's missing rather than an actual column value.

Unique Index Requirement

The target of the foreign key reference must have a unique index on the columns referenced by the dependent table. This index can exist in the form of a primary or unique key constraint or a garden-variety unique key index. Regardless of how it's constructed, SQL Server's declarative RI mechanism requires the presence of a unique index on the appropriate columns in the referenced table.

No TRUNCATE TABLE

The presence of foreign key constraints on a table precludes the use of TRUNCATE TABLE. This is true regardless of whether deleting the rows would break a foreign key relationship. Rows deleted by TRUNCATE TABLE aren't recorded in the transaction log, so no row-oriented operations (such as checking foreign key constraints) are possible. It's precisely because TRUNCATE TABLE deals with whole pages rather than individual rows that it's so much faster than DELETE.

Default Constraints

Default constraints establish default column values. These can be more than mere constant values—they can consist of CASE expressions, functions, and other types of scalar expressions (but not subqueries). Here's an example:

```
CREATE TABLE #testdc (c1 int DEFAULT CASE WHEN SUSER_SNAME()='JOE' THEN 1 ELSE 0 END)

INSERT #testdc DEFAULT VALUES

SELECT * FROM #testdc
```

```
c1
-----------
0
```

Even though they can't contain subqueries, default constraints can be quite complex. Here's an example that defines a default constraint that supplies a random number default value:

```
CREATE TABLE #rand
(k1 int identity,
c1 float DEFAULT (
(CASE (CAST(RAND()+.5 AS int)*-1) WHEN 0 THEN 1 ELSE -1 END)*(CAST(RAND() *
100000 AS int) % 10000)*RAND()
)
)
INSERT #rand DEFAULT VALUES
INSERT #rand DEFAULT VALUES
INSERT #rand DEFAULT VALUES
INSERT #rand DEFAULT VALUES
INSERT #rand DEFAULT VALUES
INSERT #rand DEFAULT VALUES
INSERT #rand DEFAULT VALUES
INSERT #rand DEFAULT VALUES
INSERT #rand DEFAULT VALUES
INSERT #rand DEFAULT VALUES

SELECT * FROM #rand
```

(Results)

```
k1            c1
-----------   ----------------------------------------
1             -121.89758452446999
2             -425.61113508053933
3             3918.1554683876675
4             9335.2668286173412
5             54.463890640027664
6             -5.0169085346410522
7             -5430.63417246276
8             915.9835973796487
9             28.109161998753301
10            741.79452047043048
```

The **(CASE (CAST(RAND()+.5 AS int)*-1) WHEN 0 THEN 1 ELSE -1 END)** expression randomizes the sign of the generated number, allowing for both positive and negative numbers, while the **(CAST(RAND() * 100000 AS int) % 10000)*RAND()** expression generates an integer between 0 and 9999.

These exotic expressions aren't limited to numeric columns. You can specify intricate default expressions for other types of columns as well. Here's an example that supplies a random number for a numeric column and a random character string for a varchar column:

```
CREATE TABLE #rand
(k1 int identity,
c1 float DEFAULT (
(CASE (CAST(RAND()+.5 AS int)*-1) WHEN 0 THEN 1 ELSE -1 END)*(CAST(RAND() *
100000 AS int) % 10000)*RAND()
),
```

```
c2 varchar(30) DEFAULT REPLICATE(
   CHAR((CAST(RAND() * 1000 AS int) % 26) + 97)
   +CHAR((CAST(RAND() * 1000 AS int) % 26) + 97)
   +CHAR((CAST(RAND() * 1000 AS int) % 26) + 97)
   +CHAR((CAST(RAND() * 1000 AS int) % 26) + 97)
   +CHAR((CAST(RAND() * 1000 AS int) % 26) + 97),
   (CAST(RAND() * 100 AS int) % 6)+1)
)
```

(Results)

k1	c1	c2
1	643.18693338310379	mhbxmmhbxm
2	4836.4599252204198	yagrfyagrf
3	5720.9159041469775	hxqnphxqnphxqnphxqnp
4	370.00067169272609	fldbmfldbm
5	3952.0816961988294	gpmcn
6	5106.5869548550918	iekyhiekyhiekyhiekyh
7	-3909.4806439394761	asgdw
8	1416.8140454855652	pweudpweudpweudpweud
9	-3440.4833748335254	xtojg
10	44.783535689721887	yiymb

The technique used to build the **varchar** default is worth discussing. It begins by creating a string of five random lowercase characters (the %26 operation returns a number between 0 and 25; since 97 is the ASCII value of **a,** incrementing the number by 97 and converting it to a character value produces a character between **a** and **z**). It then replicates that five-character string between 1 and 6 times (the %6 operation returns a number between 0 and 5, which we then increment by 1) to create a string with a maximum length of 30 characters—the defined width of the column.

Dropping Objects

Though it's not documented, you can drop multiple objects of a given type simultaneously using the appropriate DROP command. For example, to drop multiple tables, you can issue a single DROP TABLE followed by a comma-separated list of the tables to drop. This also applies to stored procedures, views, and other types of objects. Here's an example:

```
USE tempdb
GO
CREATE PROC #test1 as
SELECT 1
GO
CREATE PROC #test2 as
SELECT 2
GO
CREATE PROC #test3 as
SELECT 3
GO

DROP PROC #test1, #test2, #test3
GO
```

```
CREATE VIEW test1 as
SELECT 1 '1'
GO
CREATE VIEW test2 as
SELECT 2 '2'
GO
CREATE VIEW test3 as
SELECT 3 '3'
GO

DROP VIEW test1, test2, test3
GO
```

CREATE INDEX

There are a number of restrictions related to SQL Server indexes that bear mentioning. These are sensible limitations, but they're ones of which you should be aware as you design databases.

No Bit or BLOB Indexes

First, you can't create indexes on **bit, text, ntext,** or **image** columns. With the exception of **bit,** these are all BLOB data types, so it's logical that you can't create standard indexes on them. (For information on creating BLOB indexes, see Chapter 18, "Full-Text Search.") The reasoning behind not allowing **bit** indexes is also pretty sound. The purpose of an index is to locate a row within a table. SQL Server builds balanced trees (B-trees) using the distinct values in the index's underlying data. If a column has only two distinct values, it's virtually useless as an aid in locating a row. A tree representing it would have exactly two branches, though there could be millions of rows in the table. SQL Server would always choose to read the data sequentially rather than deal with an index branch with only two distinct values, so creating such an index would be a waste of time. That's why the server doesn't allow it—there would be no point in building a **bit** index—it would never be used.

To grasp why a column with just two distinct values is so useless as an index key, imagine being a private investigator with the task of locating a missing person and having no information to go on other than the person's sex. Half the world's population would match your description. That's a lot of missing people!

No Computed Column Indexes

Another limitation of SQL Server indexing is the inability to create indexes on computed columns. SQL Server doesn't allow indexes on computed columns because computed columns do not actually exist in the database—they don't store any real data. A computed column in a table is just like one in a view—they're both rendered when queried, but they do not otherwise exist. Since there's no permanent data to index, indexes on computed columns simply aren't allowed.

PAD_INDEX

When used in conjunction with FILLFACTOR, CREATE INDEX's PAD_INDEX option causes the intermediate pages in an index to assume the same fill percentage as that specified by FILLFACTOR for the leaf nodes. Here's an example:

```
IF INDEXPROPERTY(OBJECT_ID('titles'),'typeind','IsClustered') IS NOT NULL
   DROP INDEX titles.typeind
GO
CREATE INDEX typeind ON titles (type) WITH PAD_INDEX, FILLFACTOR = 10
```

PAD_INDEX is useful when you know in advance that you're about to load a sizable portion of new data that will cause page splits and row relocation in an index's intermediate pages if sufficient space isn't set aside up front for the new data.

DROP_EXISTING

As of SQL Server 7.0, CREATE INDEX's SORTED_DATA and SORTED_DATA_REORG options are no longer supported. In their place is the new DROP_EXISTING option. DROP_EXISTING allows you to drop and recreate an index in one step. DROP_EXISTING offers special performance enhancements for clustered indexes in that it rebuilds dependent nonclustered indexes only once and only when the clustered key values change. If the data is already sorted in the correct order, DROP_EXISTING doesn't resort the data but does compact it using the current FILLFACTOR value (providing the same basic functionality as the old SORTED_DATA_REORG option).

Because the recreation of a clustered index and its dependent nonclustered indexes using DROP_EXISTING is carried out in one step, it's inherently atomic—either all the indexes will be created, or none of them will be. For a comparable set of DROP INDEX/CREATE INDEX statements to have this same atomicity, the whole operation would have to be encapsulated in a transaction.

TEMPORARY OBJECTS

SQL Server supports two types of temporary objects—local temporary objects and global temporary objects. Locals are prefixed with one pound sign (#); globals are prefixed with two (##).

No More Unusable Temporary Objects

As of SQL Server 7.0, the CREATE VIEW, CREATE DEFAULT, and CREATE RULE commands no longer support creating temporary objects. Prior to version 7.0, you could create these objects, but you couldn't do anything with them—not terribly useful. That behavior has now been rectified, so in order to create a view, default, or rule that resides in **tempdb,** you must first change the current database context to **tempdb,** then issue the appropriate CREATE command.

Can't Create Objects in Other Databases

On a related note, these three CREATE statements don't permit you to use qualified object names—the name you specify must be an unqualified, one-part object identifier. If you want to create an object in **tempdb,** you must first switch the database context. Of course, changing to **tempdb** to create an object means that you must fully qualify objects it references that reside elsewhere. This limitation does not apply to CREATE TABLE, which directly supports creating objects in other databases.

Temporary Stored Procedures

As with tables, you can create temporary stored procedures by prefixing the procedure name with a pound sign (#). You can create global temporary procedures by prefixing the name with a double pound sign (##). These stored procedures can then be executed just like any other stored procedure. In the case of global temporary procedures, they can even be executed by other connections.

Increased Temporary Table Name Length

Prior to 7.0, SQL Server reported an error if you attempted to specify a local temporary table name that was longer than 20 characters. This has been fixed, and local temporary table names may now be up to 116 characters long.

Global Temporary Status Tables

Global temporary tables (those prefixed with ##) are visible to all users and, as such, are not uniquely named for each connection. That's what distinguishes them from local temporary tables. This global visibility makes them ideal for status tables for long running reports and jobs. Since the table is globally accessible, the report or job can place in it status messages that can be viewed from other connections. Here's an example:

```
SET NOCOUNT ON
DECLARE @statusid int

CREATE TABLE ##jobstatus
(statusid int identity,
start datetime,
finish datetime NULL,
description varchar(50),
complete bit DEFAULT 0)

INSERT ##jobstatus VALUES (GETDATE(),NULL,'Updating index stats for pubs',0)
SET @statusid=@@IDENTITY
PRINT ''
SELECT description AS 'JOB CURRENTLY EXECUTING' FROM ##jobstatus WHERE
statusid=@statusid
EXEC pubs..sp_updatestats
UPDATE ##jobstatus SET finish=GETDATE(), complete=1
WHERE statusid=@statusid

INSERT ##jobstatus VALUES (GETDATE(),NULL,'Updating index stats for northwind',0)
SET @statusid=@@IDENTITY
PRINT ''
SELECT description AS 'JOB CURRENTLY EXECUTING' FROM ##jobstatus WHERE
statusid=@statusid
EXEC northwind..sp_updatestats
UPDATE ##jobstatus SET finish=GETDATE(), complete=1
WHERE statusid=@statusid

SELECT * FROM ##jobstatus
GO
DROP TABLE ##jobstatus
```

(Results abridged)

```
JOB CURRENTLY EXECUTING
-------------------------------------------
Updating index stats for pubs

Updating dbo.authors
Updating dbo.publishers
Updating dbo.titles
Updating dbo.employee

Statistics for all tables have been updated.

JOB CURRENTLY EXECUTING
-------------------------------------------
Updating index stats for northwind

Updating dbo.employees
Updating dbo.categories
Updating dbo.customers

Statistics for all tables have been updated.
sid start               finish              description                       complete
--- ------------------- ------------------- --------------------------------- --------
1   1999-07-24 16:26:40 1999-07-24 16:26:49 Updating index stats for pubs          1
2   1999-07-24 16:26:41 1999-07-24 16:26:49 Updating index stats for northwind 1
```

Object Naming and Dependencies

Unqualified object names are resolved using the following process:

1. SQL Server checks to see whether you own an object with the specified name in the current database.

2. It then checks to see whether the DBO owns a table with the specified name in the current database.

3. If the object name you specified is prefixed with a pound sign (#), the server checks to see whether you own a local temporary table or procedure with that name.

4. If the object name you specified is prefixed with two pound signs (##), the server checks to see whether a global temporary table or procedure with that name exists.

5. If the object name is prefixed with "sp_" and you are using it in a valid context for a stored procedure, the server first checks the current database and then the **master** database to see whether you or the DBO owns an object with the specified name.

6. If not one of these conditions is met, the object is not found, and an error condition results.

Changing the Database Context Temporarily

You can temporarily change the database context in which a system stored procedure will run by prefixing it with the name of the database in which you want it to execute. That is, even though the procedure resides in the **master** database, you can treat it as though it resides in a different database, like so:

```
EXEC pubs..sp_spaceused
```

Regardless of your current database at the time of execution, the stored procedure will run as though you were in the specified database when you ran it.

Temporary Table Indexes

Thanks to SQL Server 7.0's deferred name resolution, you can now refer to a temporary table's indexes by name within the stored procedure that creates it. In version 6.5 and earlier, you were forced to reference them by number. Since object names aren't translated into their underlying identifiers in SQL Server 7.0 until the procedure runs, you're now able to reference temporary table indexes by name in the same manner as indexes on permanent tables.

Be Wary of Unusable Views

There's a bit of a quirk in SQL Server's CREATE VIEW command that allows you to create views on tables to which you have no access. No message is generated and the CREATE VIEW operation appears to work fine. However, an error is returned if you attempt to access the view, making it basically useless. Since no compile-time message is generated, it pays to verify that proper rights have been granted on the objects referenced by a view before putting it into production.

Object Dependencies

SQL Server's object dependency mechanism (which uses the sp_depends stored procedure) is inherently deficient and you shouldn't rely on it to provide accurate dependency information. The original idea behind sp_depends was for object dependency relationships to be stored in the **sysdepends** table in every database to ensure that dependency info was complete and readily accessible. Unfortunately, it didn't quite work out that way. The mechanism has a bevy of fundamental flaws. Among them:

1. Objects outside the current database are not reported.

2. If an object with dependents is dropped, its dependency information is dropped with it.

3. Recreating an object that has dependents doesn't restore or recreate its dependency information.

4. Thanks to SQL Server's deferred name resolution, you will see dependency information only for those objects that actually exist when an object is created.

5. By design, the only way the information contained in sysdepends can be kept up to date is to drop and recreate all the objects in the database periodically in order of dependence.

Personally, the facility has always felt rather perfunctory—like it was an afterthought that someone squeezed into production right before shipping without thinking it through very well. The best thing you can do with sp_depends is to avoid using it. That goes for the object dependency report in Enterprise Manager, as well. It's just as unreliable as sp_depends.

Summary

This chapter provides a number of DDL-related tips, tricks, and pointers. Some of the information and techniques presented here are more common; some of them are more obscure. You should see the Books Online for exhaustive coverage of Transact-SQL DDL.

5

DML Insights

At some point you have to decide whether you're going to be a politician or an engineer. You cannot be both. To be a politician is to champion perception over reality. To be an engineer is to make perception subservient to reality. They are opposites. You can't do both simultaneously.—H. W. Kenton

As I said in the previous chapter, the goal of this book is not to rehash SQL Server's online documentation. Instead, I assume you'll refer frequently to the Books Online (BOL), as do most people who work regularly with the product.

With this in mind, this chapter doesn't attempt to cover Transact-SQL DML (Data Manipulation Language) commands exhaustively. Instead, the goal here is to get beyond the obvious and provide DML tips, tricks, and techniques that go beyond the BOL. I would rather spend the limited pages in this book covering material with at least a modicum of originality—and hopefully even transcendence occasionally—than merely paraphrase what is only a couple of mouse clicks away for you anyway.

DML statements manipulate data—they delete it, update it, add to it, and list it. Transact-SQL DML syntax includes the INSERT, UPDATE, and DELETE commands. Technically, SELECT is also a DML command, but it's so all-encompassing and so ubiquitous in mainstream Transact-SQL development that it's been allotted its own chapter (see Chapter 6, "The Mighty SELECT Statement").

INSERT

There are four basic forms of the Transact-SQL INSERT statement; each has its own nuances. Here's the first and simplest form:

```
INSERT [INTO] targettable [(targetcolumn1[,targetcolumn2])]
VALUES (value1[,value2...])
```

As with the other forms of the command, the INTO keyword is optional. Unless you're only supplying values for specific columns, the target column list is also optional. Items in the VALUES clause can range from constant values to subqueries. Here's a simple INSERT example:

```
CREATE TABLE #famousjaycees
(jc varchar(15),
 occupation varchar(25),
 becamefamous int DEFAULT 0,
 notes text NULL)

INSERT #famousjaycees VALUES ('Julius Caesar','Military leader/dictator',
-0045,'Took the Roman early retirement program')
INSERT #famousjaycees VALUES ('Jesus Christ','Founded Christianity',
0001,'Birth featured tellurian, ruminative, and tutelary visitors')
INSERT #famousjaycees VALUES ('John Calhoun','Congressman',
1825,'Served as VP under two U.S. presidents')
INSERT #famousjaycees VALUES ('Joan Crawford','Actress',
1923,'Appeared in everything from Grand Hotel to Trog')
INSERT #famousjaycees VALUES ('James Cagney','Actor',
1931,'This prototypical gangster made a dandy Yankee')
INSERT #famousjaycees VALUES ('Jim Croce','Singer/songwriter',
1972,'Would that time were in a bottle because you left us way too soon')
INSERT #famousjaycees VALUES ('Joe Celko','Author/lecturer',
1987,'Counts eating and living indoors among his favorite hobbies')

SELECT * FROM #famousjaycees
```

jc	occupation	becamefamous	notes
Julius Caesar	Military leader/dictator	-45	Took the Roman early retirement program
Jesus Christ	Founded Christianity	1	Birth featured tellurian, ruminative, and tutelary visitors
John Calhoun	Congressman	1825	Served as VP under two U.S. presidents
Joan Crawford	Actress	1923	Appeared in everything from Grand Hotel to Trog
James Cagney	Actor	1931	This prototypical gangster made a dandy Yankee
Jim Croce	Singer/songwriter	1972	Would that time were in a bottle because you left us way too soon
Joe Celko	Author/lecturer	1987	Counts eating and living indoors among his favorite hobbies

DEFAULT and NULL

To insert a default value for columns with default constraints, attached default objects, those that allow NULL values, or timestamp columns, use the DEFAULT keyword in place of an actual value. DEFAULT causes columns with associated default constraints to receive their default values during the INSERT. When DEFAULT is specified with a NULLable column that doesn't otherwise have a default value, the column is set to NULL. Timestamp columns get the database's next timestamp value.

To specify explicitly a NULL value for a column that allows NULLs, use the NULL keyword. If you specify NULL for a column that doesn't allow NULLs (or DEFAULT for a NOT NULL column without a default), your INSERT will fail. Here's an example that illustrates DEFAULT and NULL:

```
INSERT #famousjaycees
VALUES ('Julius Caesar','Military leader/dictator',DEFAULT,NULL)
SELECT * FROM #famousjaycees
```

(Results abridged)

```
jc            occupation               becamefamous notes
------------- ------------------------ ------------ --------------------------
Julius Caesar Military leader/dictator 0            NULL
```

SET IDENTITY_INSERT

Note that, contrary to the Books Online, you're not always required to supply a value for every column in the target column list (or every column in the table if the INSERT doesn't have a column list). Identity columns may be safely omitted from any INSERT statement—even those with target column lists. This is true regardless of where the identity column appears in the table. Here's an example:

```
CREATE TABLE #famousjaycees
(jcid int identity,    -- Here, we've added an identity column
jc varchar(15),
occupation varchar(25),
becamefamous int DEFAULT 0,
notes text NULL
)
-- Notice that we omit it from list of values
INSERT #famousjaycees VALUES ('Julius Caesar','Military
leader/dictator',DEFAULT,NULL)
SELECT * FROM #famousjaycees
```

(Results abridged)

```
jcid        jc            occupation               becamefamous notes
----------- ------------- ------------------------ ------------ ----------------
1           Julius Caesar Military leader/dictator 0            NULL
```

Not only are identity columns optional, but *you are not allowed* to specify them unless the SET IDENTITY_INSERT option has been enabled for the table. SET IDENTITY_INSERT allows values to be specified for identity columns. It's handiest when loading data into a table that has dependent foreign keys referencing its identity column.

Unlike timestamp columns and columns with defaults, you *may not* specify a default value for an identity column using the DEFAULT keyword. You can't include a value of any type for an identity column unless SET IDENTITY_INSERT has been enabled. Here's an example that features SET IDENTITY_INSERT:

```
SET IDENTITY_INSERT #famousjaycees ON
INSERT #famousjaycees (jcid,jc,occupation,becamefamous,notes)
VALUES (1,'Julius Caesar','Military leader/dictator',DEFAULT,NULL)
SET IDENTITY_INSERT #famousjaycees OFF

SELECT * FROM #famousjaycees
```

jcid	jc	occupation	becamefamous	notes
1	Julius Caesar	Military leader/dictator	0	NULL

Note the inclusion of a target column list—it's required when you specify a value for an identity column.

INSERT...DEFAULT VALUES

The second form of the command allows default values to be specified for all columns at once. It looks like this:

```
INSERT [INTO] targettable DEFAULT VALUES
```

Here's a simple example:

```
CREATE TABLE #famousjaycees
(jc varchar(15) DEFAULT '',
 occupation varchar(25) DEFAULT 'Rock star',
 becamefamous int DEFAULT 0,
 notes text NULL
 )

INSERT #famousjaycees DEFAULT VALUES
SELECT * FROM #famousjaycees
```

jc	occupation	becamefamous	notes
	Rock star	0	NULL

Here, default values are specified for all the table's columns at once. As with the first form, if you use DEFAULT VALUES with columns that do not have defaults of some type defined, your INSERT will fail. Note that a target column list is illegal with DEFAULT VALUES. If you supply one (even if it includes all the columns in the table), your INSERT will fail.

As with the DEFAULT value keyword, DEFAULT VALUES supplies NULLs for NULLable fields without defaults. And no special handling is required to use it with identity columns—it works as you would expect.

INSERT...SELECT

The third form of the INSERT command retrieves values for the table from a SELECT statement. Here's the syntax:

```
INSERT [INTO] targettable [((targetcolumn1[,targetcolumn2))]
SELECT sourcecolumn1[, sourcecolumn2]
[FROM sourcetable...]
```

Since Transact-SQL's SELECT statement doesn't require that you include a FROM clause, the data may or may not come from another table. Here's an example:

```
CREATE TABLE #famousjaycees2
(jc varchar(15),
 occupation varchar(25),
 becamefamous int DEFAULT 0,
 notes text NULL)

INSERT #famousjaycees2
SELECT * FROM #famousjaycees
UNION ALL
SELECT 'Johnny Carson','Talk show host',1962,'Began career as The Great Carsoni'

SELECT * FROM #famousjaycees2
```

```
jc              occupation               becamefamous notes
-------------   -----------------------  ------------ -------------------------------
Julius Caesar   Military leader/dictator -45          Took the Roman early retirement
                                                      program
Jesus Christ    Founded Christianity     1            Birth featured tellurian,
                                                      ruminative, and tutelary visitors
John Calhoun    Congressman              1825         Served as VP under two U.S.
                                                      presidents
Joan Crawford   Actress                  1923         Appeared in everything from Grand
                                                      Hotel to Trog
James Cagney    Actor                    1931         This prototypical gangster made a
                                                      dandy Yankee
Jim Croce       Singer/songwriter        1972         Would that time were in a bottle
                                                      because you left us way too soon
Joe Celko       Author/lecturer          1987         Counts eating and living indoors
                                                      among his favorite hobbies
Johnny Carson   Talk show host           1962         Began career as The Great Carsoni
```

This example uses a UNION to add a row to those already in the source table.

INSERT...EXEC

The fourth form of the INSERT command allows the result set returned by a stored procedure or a SQL statement to be "trapped" in a table. Here's its syntax:

```
INSERT [INTO] targettable [(targetcolumn1[,targetcolumn2])]
EXEC sourceprocedurename
--or--
EXEC('SQL statement')
```

And here's an example of how to use it:

```
CREATE TABLE #sp_who
(spid       int,
 status     varchar(30),
 loginame   sysname,
 hostname   sysname,
 blk        int,
 dbname     sysname,
 cmd        varchar(16))
```

```
INSERT #sp_who
EXEC sp_who

SELECT * FROM #sp_who
```

(Results abridged)

```
spid        status      loginame hostname blk dbname cmd
----------- ----------  -------- -------- --- ------ ----------------
1           sleeping    sa                0   master SIGNAL HANDLER
2           background  sa                0   master LOCK MONITOR
3           background  sa                0   master LAZY WRITER
4           sleeping    sa                0   master LOG WRITER
5           sleeping    sa                0   master CHECKPOINT SLEEP
6           background  sa                0   master AWAITING COMMAND
```

The ability to load the results of a SQL command into a table affords a tremendous amount of power and flexibility in terms of formatting the result set, scanning it for a particular row, or performing other tasks based on it.

Extended Procedures

This facility also supports loading the results of extended procedures into tables, though only output from the main thread of the extended procedure is inserted. Here's an example using an extended procedure:

```
USE master
IF OBJECT_ID('sp_listfile') IS NOT NULL
   DROP PROC sp_listfile
GO
CREATE PROCEDURE sp_listfile @filename sysname
AS
IF (@filename IS NULL) RETURN(-1)

DECLARE @execstr varchar(8000)

SET @execstr='TYPE '+@filename

CREATE TABLE #filecontents

(output              varchar(8000))

INSERT #filecontents
EXEC master..xp_cmdshell @execstr

SELECT * FROM #filecontents
DROP TABLE #filecontents
GO
```

(Results abridged)

```
EXEC sp_listfile 'D:\MSSQL7\INSTALL\README.TXT'
output
--------------------------------------------------------------------------------
```

```
****************************************************************
                    SQL SERVER 7.0 README.TXT
****************************************************************
This file contains important information that you should read
prior to installing Microsoft(R) SQL Server(TM) version 7.0.
It also contains information about the following SQL Server
topics that does not appear in SQL Server Books Online:
```

INSERT and Errors

One interesting characteristic of the INSERT command is its imperviousness to fatal command batch errors. An INSERT that fails due to a constraint or invalid duplicate value will not cause the command batch to fail. If a group of INSERTs are executed within a command batch and one of them fails, the other INSERTs will not be affected. This is as it should be; otherwise, loading large amounts of data using INSERT statements would be greatly complicated.

    If you want the whole command batch to fail when an INSERT fails, check the @@ER-ROR automatic variable after each INSERT and respond accordingly. Here's an example:

```
CREATE TABLE #famousjaycees
(jc varchar(15) UNIQUE,    -- Define a UNIQUE constraint
 occupation varchar(25),
 becamefamous int DEFAULT 0,
 notes text NULL)

INSERT #famousjaycees VALUES ('Julius Caesar','Military leader/dictator',
-0045,'Took the Roman early retirement program')
IF (@@ERROR <>0) GOTO LIST
-- Now attempt to insert a duplicate value
INSERT #famousjaycees VALUES ('Julius Caesar','Military leader/dictator',
-0045,'Took the Roman early retirement program')
IF (@@ERROR <>0) GOTO LIST
INSERT #famousjaycees VALUES ('Jesus Christ','Founded Christianity',
0001,'Birth featured tellurian, ruminative, and tutelary visitors')
IF (@@ERROR <>0) GOTO LIST
INSERT #famousjaycees VALUES ('John Calhoun','Congressman',
1825,'Served as VP under two U.S. presidents')
IF (@@ERROR <>0) GOTO LIST
INSERT #famousjaycees VALUES ('Joan Crawford','Actress',
1923,'Appeared in everything from Grand Hotel to Trog')
IF (@@ERROR <>0) GOTO LIST
INSERT #famousjaycees VALUES ('James Cagney','Actor',
1931,'This prototypical gangster made a dandy Yankee')
IF (@@ERROR <>0) GOTO LIST
INSERT #famousjaycees VALUES ('Jim Croce','Singer/songwriter',
1972,'Would that time were in a bottle because you left us way too soon')
IF (@@ERROR <>0) GOTO LIST
INSERT #famousjaycees VALUES ('Joe Celko','Author/lecturer',
1987,'Counts eating and living indoors among his favorite hobbies')

LIST:
SELECT * FROM #famousjaycees
```

```
Server: Msg 2627, Level 14, State 2, Line 0
Violation of UNIQUE KEY constraint 'UQ__#famousjaycees__160F4887'. Cannot insert
duplicate key in object
'#famousjaycees_____
_____00000000002E'.
The statement has been terminated.
```

```
jc              occupation              becamefamous notes
------------- ----------------------- ------------ --------------------
Julius Caesar Military leader/dictator -45          Took the Roman early
                                                    retirement program
```

Using INSERT to Remove Duplicate Rows

On a related note, another interesting aspect of the INSERT command is its ability to remove duplicate rows by way of a unique index with the IGNORE_DUP_KEY option set. That is, if you insert a set of rows into a table with an IGNORE_DUP_KEY index, rows that violate the index's unique constraint will be rejected without causing the other inserts to fail. So, in order to remove duplicate rows from a table, you can create a work table that's identical in structure to it, then build an IGNORE_DUP_KEY index over the second table that includes all the first table's candidate keys and insert the table's rows into it. Here's an example:

```
CREATE TABLE #famousjaycees
(jc varchar(15),
 occupation varchar(25),
 becamefamous int DEFAULT 0,
 notes text NULL)

INSERT #famousjaycees VALUES ('Julius Caesar','Military leader/dictator',
-0045,'Took the Roman early retirement program')
-- Include a duplicate value for the sake of illustration
INSERT #famousjaycees VALUES ('Julius Caesar','Military leader/dictator',
-0045,'Took the Roman early retirement program')
INSERT #famousjaycees VALUES ('Jesus Christ','Founded Christianity',
0001,'Birth featured tellurian, ruminative, and tutelary visitors')
INSERT #famousjaycees VALUES ('John Calhoun','Congressman',
1825,'Served as VP under two U.S. presidents')
INSERT #famousjaycees VALUES ('Joan Crawford','Actress',
1923,'Appeared in everything from Grand Hotel to Trog')
INSERT #famousjaycees VALUES ('James Cagney','Actor',
1931,'This prototypical gangster made a dandy Yankee')
INSERT #famousjaycees VALUES ('Jim Croce','Singer/songwriter',
1972,'Would that time were in a bottle because you left us way too soon')
INSERT #famousjaycees VALUES ('Joe Celko','Author/lecturer',
1987,'Counts eating and living indoors among his favorite hobbies')

CREATE TABLE #famousjaycees2
(jc varchar(15),
 occupation varchar(25),
 becamefamous int DEFAULT 0,
 notes text NULL)

CREATE UNIQUE INDEX removedups ON #famousjaycees2 (jc,occupation,becamefamous)
WITH IGNORE_DUP_KEY
```

```
INSERT #famousjaycees2
SELECT * FROM #famousjaycees
SELECT * FROM #famousjaycees2


Server: Msg 3604, Level 16, State 1, Line 0
Duplicate key was ignored.
```

jc	occupation	becamefamous	notes
Julius Caesar	Military leader/dictator	-45	Took the Roman early retirement program
Jesus Christ	Founded Christianity	1	Birth featured tellurian, ruminative, and tutelary visitors
John Calhoun	Congressman	1825	Served as VP under two U.S. presidents
Joan Crawford	Actress	1923	Appeared in everything from Grand Hotel to Trog
James Cagney	Actor	1931	This prototypical gangster made a dandy Yankee
Jim Croce	Singer/songwriter	1972	Would that time were in a bottle because you left us way too soon
Joe Celko	Author/lecturer	1987	Counts eating and living indoors among his favorite hobbies

Notice that we can't include the **notes** column in the index because, as a **text** column, it's not a valid index key candidate. This notwithstanding, the inclusion of the other columns still provides a reasonable assurance against duplicates.

INSERT and Clustered Indexes

A table without a clustered index is known as a heap table. Rows inserted into a heap table are inserted wherever there's room in the table. If there's no room on any of the table's existing pages, a new page is created and the rows are inserted onto it. This can create a hotspot at the end of the table (meaning that users attempting simultaneous INSERTs on the table will vie for the same resources). To alleviate the possibility of this happening, you should always establish clustered indexes for the tables you build. Consider using a unique key that distributes new rows evenly across the table. Avoid automatic, sequential, clustered index keys as they can cause hotspots, too. Going from a heap table to a clustered index with a monotonically increasing key is not much of an improvement. Also avoid nonunique clustered index keys. Prior to SQL Server 7.0, they caused the creation of overflow pages as new rows with duplicate keys were inserted, slowing the operation and fragmenting the table. Beginning with version 7.0, a "uniqueifier" (a four-byte sequence number) is appended to each duplicate clustered index key in order to force it to be unique. Naturally, this takes some processing time and is unnecessary if you use unique keys in the first place. As with all indexing, try to use keys that balance your need to access the data with your need to modify it.

BULK INSERT

In addition to standard INSERTs, Transact-SQL supports bulk data loading via the BULK INSERT command. BULK INSERT uses the BCP (Bulk Copy Program) facility that's been available in SQL Server for many years. Prior to its addition to Transact-SQL, developers called the external **bcp** utility using xp_cmdshell or accessed the Distributed Management Objects (DMO) API in order to bulk load data from within Transact-SQL. With the addition of the BULK INSERT command to the language itself, this is now largely unnecessary. Here's an example:

```
CREATE TABLE famousjaycees
(jc varchar(15),
 occupation varchar(25),
 becamefamous int DEFAULT 0,
 notes text NULL)

-- Assume the file was previously created
BULK INSERT famousjaycees FROM 'D:\GG_TS\famousjaycees.bcp'

SELECT * FROM famousjaycees
```

jc	occupation	becamefamous	notes
Julius Caesar	Military leader/dictator	-45	Took the Roman early retirement program
Jesus Christ	Founded Christianity	1	Birth featured tellurian, ruminative, and tutelary visitors
John Calhoun	Congressman	1825	Served as VP under two U.S. presidents
Joan Crawford	Actress	1923	Appeared in everything from Grand Hotel to Trog
James Cagney	Actor	1931	This prototypical gangster made a dandy Yankee
Jim Croce	Singer/songwriter	1972	Would that time were in a bottle because you left us way too soon
Joe Celko	Author/lecturer	1987	Counts eating and living indoors among his favorite hobbies

BULK INSERT and Triggers

BULK INSERT circumvents SQL Server's trigger mechanism. When you insert rows via BULK INSERT, INSERT triggers do not fire. This is because SQL Server's BCP facility avoids logging inserted rows in the transaction log if possible. This means that there's simply no opportunity for triggers to fire. There is, however, a workaround that involves using a faux update to force them to fire. See the section "Using UPDATE to Check Constraints" later in the chapter for more information.

BULK INSERT and Constraints

Declarative constraints, by contrast, can be enforced via the inclusion of BULK INSERT's CHECK_CONSTRAINTS option. By default, except for UNIQUE constraints, the target table's declarative constraints are ignored, so include this option if you want them enforced during the bulk load operation. Note that this can slow down the operation considerably.

BULK INSERT and Identity Columns

Another salient point regarding BULK INSERT is the fact that, by default, it causes identity column values to be regenerated as data is loaded. Obviously, if you're loading data into a table with dependent foreign key references, this could be catastrophic. To override this behavior, include BULK INSERT's KEEPIDENTITY keyword.

UPDATE

UPDATE has two basic forms. One is used to update a table using static values, the other to update it using values from another table. Here's an example of the first form:

```
UPDATE #famousjaycees
SET jc='Johnny Cash',
    occupation='Singer/songwriter',
    becamefamous=1955,
    notes='Began career selling applicances door-to-door'
WHERE jc='John Calhoun'

SELECT * FROM #famousjaycees
```

jc	occupation	becamefamous	notes
Julius Caesar	Military leader/dictator	-45	Took the Roman early retirement program
Jesus Christ	Founded Christianity	1	Birth featured tellurian, ruminative, and tutelary visitors
Johnny Cash	Singer/songwriter	1955	Began career selling appliances door-to-door
Joan Crawford	Actress	1923	Appeared in everything from Grand Hotel to Trog
James Cagney	Actor	1931	This prototypical gangster made a dandy Yankee
Jim Croce	Singer/songwriter	1972	Would that time were in a bottle because you left us way too soon
Joe Celko	Author/lecturer	1987	Counts eating and living indoors among his favorite hobbies

And here's one of the second:

```
CREATE TABLE #semifamousjaycees
(jc varchar(15),
 occupation varchar(25),
 becamefamous int DEFAULT 0,
 notes text NULL)

INSERT #semifamousjaycees VALUES ('John Candy','Actor',
1981,'Your melliferous life was all-too brief')
INSERT #semifamousjaycees VALUES ('John Cusack','Actor',
1984,'Uttered, "Go that way, very fast"')
INSERT #semifamousjaycees VALUES ('Joan Cusack','Actress',
1987,'Uncle Fester"s avaricious femme fatale')

UPDATE f
SET jc=s.jc,
    occupation=s.occupation,
    becamefamous=s.becamefamous,
    notes=s.notes
FROM #famousjaycees f
JOIN #semifamousjaycees s ON (f.becamefamous=s.becamefamous)
SELECT * FROM #famousjaycees
```

jc	occupation	becamefamous	notes
Julius Caesar	Military leader/dictator	-45	Took the Roman early retirement program
Jesus Christ	Founded Christianity	1	Birth featured tellurian, ruminative, and tutelary visitors
John Calhoun	Congressman	1825	Served as VP under two U.S. presidents
Joan Crawford	Actress	1923	Appeared in everything from Grand Hotel to Trog
James Cagney	Actor	1931	This prototypical gangster made a dandy Yankee
Jim Croce	Singer/songwriter	1972	Would that time were in a bottle because you left us way too soon
Joan Cusack	Actress	1987	Uncle Fester's avaricious femme fatale

Notice the use of an alias to reference the target of the UPDATE. The actual table is named in the FROM clause. Also note the join between the two tables. It's constructed using normal ANSI SQL-92 join syntax and allows values to be easily located in the UPDATE's source table.

The Halloween Problem

The situation where an updated row moves within the list of rows being updated during the update, and is therefore changed erroneously multiple times, is known as the Halloween Problem. In the early days of DBMSs, this was a common occurrence because vendors usually performed a group of updates one row at a time. If the update changed the key column on which the rows were sorted, it was likely that a row would move elsewhere in the group of rows, perhaps to a location further down in the group, where it would be changed yet again. For example, consider this code:

```
UPDATE sales
SET qty=qty*1.5
```

Provided that the server didn't otherwise handle it and provided that the result set was sorted in descending order on the **qty** column, each update could cause the row to move further down in the result set, resulting in it being updated repeatedly as the UPDATE traversed the table—a classic case of the Halloween Problem. Fortunately, SQL Server recognizes situations where the Halloween Problem can occur and automatically handles them. The Row Operations Manager ascertains when encountering row movement problems and other types of transient errors such as the Halloween Problem is likely (updates to primary keys and foreign keys are examples) and takes steps to avoid them.

Note
Note that deferred updates, the approach SQL Server took to deal with row movement problems prior to version 7.0, are no longer used. In many cases, these were more trouble than they were worth, and many SQL Server practitioners are glad to see them go.

It might seem likely that the combination of a primary key update and an update trigger would increase the likelihood of the Halloween Problem occurring. After all, the trigger would see the data as it's being changed, right? Wrong. SQL Server triggers fire once *per statement,* not per row, and have access only to the before and after picture of the data, not to any of the interim stages it might have gone through during the update.

This may seem counterintuitive since triggers appear to execute in conjunction with the DML statement that fires them, but that's not the case. A trigger's code is not compiled into the execution plan for the INSERT, UPDATE, or DELETE that fires it. Rather, it's compiled and cached separately so that it's available for reuse regardless of what causes it to fire. The execution plan for a DML statement branches to any triggers it fires just before it terminates, after its work is otherwise complete.

Note that this isn't true of constraints. Steps are added directly to the DML execution plan for each of a table's constraints.

UPDATE and CASE

You can use a CASE expression to code some fairly sophisticated changes to a table via UPDATE. Using CASE allows you to embed program logic in the UPDATE statement that would otherwise require arcane function expressions or separate UPDATEs and flow-control syntax. Here's an example:

```
SELECT title_id, type, price FROM titles

title_id type          price
-------- ------------  ---------------------
BU1032   business       19.9900
BU1111   business       11.9500
BU2075   business        2.9900
BU7832   business       19.9900
MC2222   mod_cook       19.9900
MC3021   mod_cook        2.9900
MC3026   UNDECIDED      NULL
PC1035   popular_comp   22.9500
PC8888   popular_comp   20.0000
PC9999   popular_comp   NULL
PS1372   psychology     21.5900
PS2091   psychology     10.9500
PS2106   psychology      7.0000
PS3333   psychology     19.9900
PS7777   psychology      7.9900
TC3218   trad_cook      20.9500
TC4203   trad_cook      11.9500
TC7777   trad_cook      14.9900

UPDATE titles
SET price=price*CASE title WHEN 'business' THEN 1.5
                      WHEN 'mod_cook' THEN .8
                      WHEN 'trad_cook' THEN .6
                      WHEN 'psychology' THEN .5
                      WHEN 'popular_comp' THEN 1.75
                      ELSE .75
    END
```

```
SELECT title_id, type, price FROM titles
```

   (Results)

```
title_id type            price
-------- ------------    --------------------
BU1032   business        14.9925
BU1111   business        8.9625
BU2075   business        2.2425
BU7832   business        14.9925
MC2222   mod_cook        14.9925
MC3021   mod_cook        2.2425
MC3026   UNDECIDED       NULL
PC1035   popular_comp 17.2125
PC8888   popular_comp 15.0000
PC9999   popular_comp NULL
PS1372   psychology      16.1925
PS2091   psychology      8.2125
PS2106   psychology      5.2500
PS3333   psychology      14.9925
PS7777   psychology      5.9925
TC3218   trad_cook       15.7125
TC4203   trad_cook       8.9625
TC7777   trad_cook       11.2425
```

Using UPDATE to Check Constraints

If you use BULK INSERT or any of the other bulk load facilities that SQL Server provides to append data to a table that has an associated INSERT trigger, you'll notice that the trigger does not fire. Also, even though BULK INSERT can be made to respect declarative constraints, you may find that this slows the operation down to a relative crawl. It will probably be significantly faster to ignore the table's constraints during the load. One option here is to check constraints and triggers manually after the operation. This requires separate code for each constraint and trigger and a lot of effort not to make any mistakes. Another, and perhaps better, way is to issue a bogus update against the table in question once the operation completes. This fake update simply sets each column's value to itself. This causes triggers to fire and constraints to be checked. If any of the rows contain bad data, the UPDATE will fail. Here's an example:

```
CREATE TABLE famousjaycees
(jc varchar(15) CHECK (LEFT(jc,3)<>'Joe'),      -- Establish a check constraint
 occupation varchar(25),
 becamefamous int DEFAULT 0,
 notes text NULL)

-- Assume the file was previously created
BULK INSERT famousjaycees FROM 'D:\GG_TS\famousjaycees.bcp'

-- Check that the miscreant is in place
SELECT * FROM famousjaycees

-- Now do the faux update
UPDATE famousjaycees
```

```
SET jc=jc, occupation=occupation, becamefamous=becamefamous, notes=notes
```

(Results)

```
jc occupationbecamefamous      notes
------------- ----------------------- ------------ ------------------------------------
Julius Caesar Military leader/dictator -45          Took the Roman early retirement
                                                    program
Jesus Christ  Founded Christianity    1            Birth featured tellurian,
                                                    ruminative, and tutelary visitors
John Calhoun  Congressman             1825         Served as VP under two U.S.
                                                    presidents
Joan Crawford Actress                 1923         Appeared in everything from Grand
                                                    Hotel to Trog
James Cagney  Actor                   1931         This prototypical gangster made a
                                                    dandy Yankee
Jim Croce     Singer/songwriter       1972         Would that time were in a bottle
                                                    because you left us way too soon
Joe Celko     Author/lecturer         1987         Counts eating and living indoors
                                                    among his favorite hobbies
Server: Msg 547, Level 16, State 1, Line 1
UPDATE statement conflicted with COLUMN CHECK constraint 'CK__famousjaycee__
jc__5E8A0973'. The conflict occurred in database 'tempdb', table 'famousjaycees',
column 'jc'.
The statement has been terminated.
```

As you can see, the error message indicates the database, table, and column in which the bad data resides, so you have some basic information to begin locating the invalid data.

Limiting the Number of Rows Affected by an UPDATE

You can use the TOP *n* option of the SELECT command to limit the number of rows affected by an UPDATE. This SELECT is embedded as a derived table in the UPDATE's FROM clause and joined with the target table, like so:

```
-- Establish what the table looks like before the update (limit to 10 for brevity)
SELECT TOP 10 au_lname, au_fname, contract FROM authors ORDER BY au_id

UPDATE a
SET a.contract=0
FROM authors a JOIN (SELECT TOP 5 au_id FROM authors ORDER BY au_id) u ON
(a.au_id=u.au_id)

-- Now show the table afterward (limit to 10 for brevity)
SELECT TOP 10 au_lname, au_fname, contract FROM authors ORDER BY au_id
```

(Results)

au_lname	au_fname	contract
White	Johnson	1
Green	Marjorie	1
Carson	Cheryl	1
O'Leary	Michael	1
Straight	Dean	1
Smith	Meander	0
Bennet	Abraham	1

```
Dull                                    Ann              1
Gringlesby                              Burt             1
Locksley                                Charlene         1
```

au_lname	au_fname	contract
White	Johnson	0
Green	Marjorie	0
Carson	Cheryl	0
O'Leary	Michael	0
Straight	Dean	0
Smith	Meander	0
Bennet	Abraham	1
Dull	Ann	1
Gringlesby	Burt	1
Locksley	Charlene	1

Swapping Column Values with UPDATE

A nifty side effect of the fact that UPDATE can set local variables at the same time it sets column values is that you can use this variable in the update itself. Since Transact-SQL is processed left to right, you can set the variable early in the SET list, then reuse it later in the same update to supply a column value. For example, you could use it to swap the values of two columns, like so:

```
CREATE TABLE #samples
(k1    int identity,
 samp1 float DEFAULT (rand()*1000),
 samp2 float DEFAULT (rand()*1000)
)

INSERT #samples DEFAULT VALUES
INSERT #samples DEFAULT VALUES
INSERT #samples DEFAULT VALUES
INSERT #samples DEFAULT VALUES
INSERT #samples DEFAULT VALUES
INSERT #samples DEFAULT VALUES
INSERT #samples DEFAULT VALUES

SELECT * FROM #samples

DECLARE @swap float

UPDATE #samples
SET @swap=samp1,
    samp1=samp2,
    samp2=@swap

SELECT * FROM #samples
```

(Results)

k1	samp1	samp2
1	696.54331299037415	985.40886709404242
2	632.62866718204532	312.32844166524393
3	85.737145980088201	997.17767926283261

k1	samp1	samp2
4	198.09202551602621	398.36384650194992
5	117.03223448722392	240.39329824544191
6	853.0948352692468	373.61420498632617
7	597.28655124120712	606.33492026963836

k1	samp1	samp2
1	985.40886709404242	696.54331299037415
2	312.32844166524393	632.62866718204532
3	997.17767926283261	85.737145980088201
4	398.36384650194992	198.09202551602621
5	240.39329824544191	117.03223448722392
6	373.61420498632617	853.0948352692468
7	606.33492026963836	597.28655124120712

This trick is cool enough, but because column values referenced by an UPDATE statement always reflect their values *before* the operation, you don't need an intermediate variable in order to swap them. You can just simply assign the columns to one another, like this:

```
UPDATE #samples
SET samp1=samp2,
   samp2=samp1
```

   (Results)

k1	samp1	samp2
1	696.54331299037415	985.40886709404242
2	632.62866718204532	312.32844166524393
3	85.737145980088201	997.17767926283261
4	198.09202551602621	398.36384650194992
5	117.03223448722392	240.39329824544191
6	853.0948352692468	373.61420498632617
7	597.28655124120712	606.33492026963836

k1	samp1	samp2
1	985.40886709404242	696.54331299037415
2	312.32844166524393	632.62866718204532
3	997.17767926283261	85.737145980088201
4	398.36384650194992	198.09202551602621
5	240.39329824544191	117.03223448722392
6	373.61420498632617	853.0948352692468
7	606.33492026963836	597.28655124120712

UPDATE and Cursors

You can use the UPDATE command to modify rows returned by updatable cursors. This is facilitated via UPDATE's WHERE CURRENT OF clause. Here's an example:

```
CREATE TABLE #famousjaycees
(jc varchar(15),
 occupation varchar(25),
 becamefamous int DEFAULT 0,
 notes text NULL)
```

```
INSERT #famousjaycees VALUES ('Julius Caesar','Military leader/dictator',
-0045,'Took the Roman early retirement program')
INSERT #famousjaycees VALUES ('Jesus Christ','Founded Christianity',0001,'Birth
featured tellurian, ruminative, and tutelary visitors')
INSERT #famousjaycees VALUES ('John Calhoun','Congressman',1825,'Served as VP
under two U.S. presidents')
INSERT #famousjaycees VALUES ('Joan Crawford','Actress',1923,'Appeared in
everything from Grand Hotel to Trog')
INSERT #famousjaycees VALUES ('James Cagney','Actor',1931,'This prototypical
gangster made a dandy Yankee')
INSERT #famousjaycees VALUES ('Jim Croce','Singer/songwriter',1972,'Would that
time were in a bottle because you left us way too soon')
INSERT #famousjaycees VALUES ('Joe Celko','Author/lecturer',1987,'Counts eating
and living indoors among his favorite hobbies')

DECLARE jcs CURSOR DYNAMIC FOR SELECT * FROM #famousjaycees FOR UPDATE
OPEN jcs

FETCH RELATIVE 3 FROM jcs

UPDATE #famousjaycees
SET jc='Johnny Cash',
   occupation='Singer/songwriter',
   becamefamous=1955,
   notes='Began career selling appliances door-to-door'
WHERE CURRENT OF jcs

CLOSE jcs
DEALLOCATE jcs

SELECT * FROM #famousjaycees
```

(Results)

jc	occupation	becamefamous	notes
John Calhoun	Congressman	1825	Served as VP under two U.S. presidents

jc	occupation	becamefamous	notes
Julius Caesar	Military leader/dictator	-45	Took the Roman early retirement program
Jesus Christ	Founded Christianity	1	Birth featured tellurian, ruminative, and tutelary visitors
Johnny Cash	Singer/songwriter	1955	Began career selling appliances door-to-door
Joan Crawford	Actress	1923	Appeared in everything from Grand Hotel to Trog
James Cagney	Actor	1931	This prototypical gangster made a dandy Yankee
Jim Croce	Singer/songwriter	1972	Would that time were in a bottle because you left us way too soon
Joe Celko	Author/lecturer	1987	Counts eating and living indoors among his favorite hobbies

DELETE

Like its INSERT counterpart, the DELETE command has a number of forms. I won't go into all of them here—they correspond closely enough with their INSERT and UPDATE siblings that their use should be obvious.

There are, however, a couple of aspects of the command that bear discussion. First, in addition to limiting the rows removed by a DELETE through the use of constants and variables in its WHERE clause, you can reference other tables. Below is a DELETE that's based on a join to another table. It deletes customers in the Northwind Customers table that have no orders in the Orders table:

```
SET NOCOUNT ON
USE Northwind
GO
BEGIN TRAN

SELECT COUNT(*) AS TotalCustomersBefore FROM Customers

DELETE c
FROM Customers c LEFT OUTER JOIN Orders o ON (c.CustomerID=o.CustomerID)
WHERE o.OrderID IS NULL

SELECT COUNT(*) AS TotalCustomersAfter FROM Customers

GO
ROLLBACK TRAN

TotalCustomersBefore
--------------------
91

TotalCustomersAfter
--------------------
89
```

As with the UPDATE command, the number of rows affected by DELETE can be restricted via the SELECT TOP *n* extension. Here's an example:

```
SELECT TOP 10 ord_num AS Before FROM sales ORDER BY ord_num

DELETE s
FROM sales s JOIN (SELECT TOP 5 ord_num FROM sales ORDER BY ord_num) a
ON (s.ord_num=a.ord_num)

SELECT TOP 10 ord_num AS After FROM sales ORDER BY ord_num

Before
--------------------
423LL922
423LL930
```

```
6871
722a
A2976
D4482
D4482
D4492
N914008
N914014

After
--------------------
D4482
D4482
D4492
N914008
N914014
P2121
P2121
P2121
P3087a
P3087a
```

DELETE and Cursors

You can use the DELETE command to delete rows returned by updatable cursors. Similarly to UPDATE, this is facilitated via the command's WHERE CURRENT OF clause. Here's an example:

```
CREATE TABLE #famousjaycees
(jc varchar(15),
 occupation varchar(25),
 becamefamous int DEFAULT 0,
 notes text NULL)
INSERT #famousjaycees VALUES ('Julius Caesar','Military leader/dictator',-0045,'Took the
Roman early retirement program')
INSERT #famousjaycees VALUES ('Jesus Christ','Founded Christianity',0001,'Birth featured
tellurian, ruminative, and tutelary visitors')
INSERT #famousjaycees VALUES ('John Calhoun','Congressman',1825,'Served as VP under two
U.S. presidents')
INSERT #famousjaycees VALUES ('Joan Crawford','Actress',1923,'Appeared in everything
from Grand Hotel to Trog')
INSERT #famousjaycees VALUES ('James Cagney','Actor',1931,'This prototypical gangster
made a dandy Yankee')
INSERT #famousjaycees VALUES ('Jim Croce','Singer/songwriter',1972,'Would that time were
in a bottle because you left us way too soon')
INSERT #famousjaycees VALUES ('Joe Celko','Author/lecturer',1987,'Counts eating and
living indoors among his favorite hobbies')

DECLARE jcs CURSOR DYNAMIC FOR SELECT * FROM #famousjaycees FOR UPDATE
OPEN jcs

FETCH RELATIVE 3 FROM jcs

DELETE #famousjaycees
WHERE CURRENT OF jcs

CLOSE jcs
DEALLOCATE jcs
```

```
SELECT * FROM #famousjaycees
```

jc	occupation	becamefamous	notes
John Calhoun	Congressman	1825	Served as VP under two U.S. presidents

jc	occupation	becamefamous	notes
Julius Caesar	Military leader/dictator	-45	Took the Roman early retirement program
Jesus Christ	Founded Christianity	1	Birth featured tellurian, ruminative, and tutelary visitors
Joan Crawford	Actress	1923	Appeared in everything from Grand Hotel to Trog
James Cagney	Actor	1931	This prototypical gangster made a dandy Yankee
Jim Croce	Singer/songwriter	1972	Would that time were in a bottle because you left us way too soon
Joe Celko	Author/lecturer	1987	Counts eating and living indoors among his favorite hobbies

TRUNCATE TABLE

Analogous to BULK INSERT, the TRUNCATE TABLE command provides a way of deleting the rows in a table with a minimum of logging. That no logging occurs at all is a common misconception. The page deallocations *are* logged—they have to be. If they weren't, you couldn't execute the command from within a transaction and couldn't reverse its effects on the database. Here's an example:

```
USE pubs
BEGIN TRAN

SELECT COUNT(*) AS CountBefore FROM sales

TRUNCATE TABLE sales

SELECT COUNT(*) AS CountAfter FROM sales

GO
ROLLBACK TRAN

SELECT COUNT(*) AS CountAfterRollback FROM sales

CountBefore
-----------
25

CountAfter
-----------------
0

CountAfterRollback
-----------------
25
```

What's not logged with TRUNCATE TABLE is the process of deleting individual rows. That's because no row deletions actually occur—all that really happens is the deallocation of the pages that make up the table. Since row deletions don't occur, they aren't logged and can't fire DELETE triggers.

You'll find that TRUNCATE TABLE is many times faster than an unqualified DELETE *tablename* statement; in fact, it's often instantaneous with small to medium-sized tables. There are a couple of limitations, though. You can't use TRUNCATE TABLE on a table that's referenced by a foreign key constraint, even if the truncation would not break any foreign key relationships (e.g., when the dependent table is empty). You also can't use TRUNCATE TABLE on a table that's been published for replication. This is because replication relies on the transaction log to synchronize publishers and subscribers, and TRUNCATE TABLE, as I've said, does not generate row deletion log records.

Detecting DML Errors

Normally, you can detect DML runtime errors by inspecting the @@ERROR automatic variable. However, if a DML statement doesn't affect any rows, @@ERROR won't be set because that's technically not an error condition. You'll have to check @@ROWCOUNT instead. In other words, if your code needs to consider the fact that a DML statement fails to affect (or find) any rows as an error, check @@ROWCOUNT after the statement and respond accordingly.

Summary

In this chapter, you became acquainted with some of the more prominent aspects of Transact-SQL DML. You learned about the INSERT, UPDATE, and DELETE commands and how they're used in real queries. You also learned about speedy variations of them and the limitations that accompany them.

6

The Mighty SELECT Statement

The fantasy element that explains the appeal of dungeon-clearing games to many programmers is neither the fire-breathing monsters nor the milky-skinned, semi-clad sirens; it is the experience of carrying out a task from start to finish without user requirements changing.—Thomas L. Holaday

As I said in Chapter 1, the SELECT statement is the workhorse of the Transact-SQL language. It does everything from assign variables to return result sets to create tables. Across all versions of the language, SELECT is the most powerful and the most frequently used SQL command. There was even a time when it was used to clear certain server error conditions in Sybase's version of SQL Server (using a function called LCT_ADMIN()).

While it's handy to be able to perform 75% of your work using a single tool, that tool has to be complex in order to offer so much functionality. A tool with so many features can be a bit unwieldy—you have to be careful lest you take off a finger.

Simple SELECTs

As was also pointed out in Chapter 1, SELECT statements need not be complex. Here are a few simple ones to prime the discussion:

```
USE pubs
SELECT * FROM authors
```

(Results abridged)

au_id	au_lname	au_fname	phone
172-32-1176	White	Johnson	408 496-7223
213-46-8915	Green	Marjorie	415 986-7020

```
SELECT title_id, title FROM titles
```

(Results abridged)

```
title_id title
-------- ----------------------------------------------------------------------
PC1035   But Is It User Friendly?
PS1372   Computer Phobic AND Non-Phobic Individuals: Behavior Variations


SELECT 'One'
----

One
```

Computational and Derived Fields

In addition to garden-variety fields, you can specify functions, computations, and derived fields in the column list of a SELECT statement (commonly referred to as its "SELECT list"). Here are some examples:

```
SELECT PI() AS SSPi, CAST(21.99115 / 7 AS decimal(7,6)) AS RoughPi

SSPi                                                RoughPi
--------------------------------------------------- ---------
3.1415926535897931                                  3.141593
```

You can use parameter-less functions like PI() and functions that require parameters like CAST(). You can use expressions that reference fields and expressions that don't. You can perform basic computations in the SELECT list and can include subqueries that return single values. Here's an example:

```
SELECT pub_name, (SELECT COUNT(*) FROM titles t WHERE t.pub_id=p.pub_id) AS
NumPublished
FROM publishers p

pub_name                                NumPublished
--------------------------------------- ------------
New Moon Books                          5
Binnet & Hardley                        7
Algodata Infosystems                    6
Five Lakes Publishing                   0
Ramona Publishers                       0
GGG&G                                   0
Scootney Books                          0
Lucerne Publishing                      0
```

A derived column consists of a subquery that returns a single value. This subquery can be related to the outer query (correlated) or unrelated, but it must return a result set that is exactly one column by one row in size. We'll cover correlated subqueries in more detail in a moment.

I've built the query using a derived field for illustration purposes only. It would be better written using a join, like so:

```
SELECT pub_name, COUNT(t.title_id) AS NumPublished
FROM publishers p LEFT JOIN titles t ON (p.pub_id = t.pub_id)
GROUP BY pub_name
```

This is frequently the case with subqueries—very often they can be restated as joins. These joins are sometimes more efficient because they avoid executing the secondary query for every row in the main table.

SELECT TOP

Prior to SQL Server 7.0, restricting the number of rows returned by a query required the use of the SET ROWCOUNT command. SET ROWCOUNT is still available, but there's now a better way. SELECT TOP n [PERCENT] [WITH TIES] where n is the number or percentage of rows you wish to return is an efficient way to truncate query results. Here's an example:

```
SELECT TOP 10 t.title, SUM(s.qty) AS TotalSales
FROM sales s JOIN titles t ON (s.title_id=t.title_id)
GROUP BY t.title
ORDER BY TotalSales DESC
```

title	TotalSales
Is Anger the Enemy?	191
Secrets of Silicon Valley	50
The Busy Executive's Database Guide	45
Onions, Leeks, and Garlic: Cooking Secrets of the Mediterranean	40
The Gourmet Microwave	40
You Can Combat Computer Stress!	35
But Is It User Friendly?	30
The Psychology of Computer Cooking	30
Cooking with Computers: Surreptitious Balance Sheets	25
Emotional Security: A New Algorithm	25

As you would expect, including the optional PERCENT keyword limits the rows returned to a percentage of the total number of rows.

Add the WITH TIES clause if you want to include ties—duplicate values—in the result set. Unless you're merely trimming the result set to a particular size, TOP n logically implies ORDER BY. Although ORDER BY is optional with basic TOP n, the WITH TIES option requires it so that ties can be logically resolved. Here's an example:

```
SELECT TOP 4 WITH TIES t.title, SUM(s.qty) AS TotalSales
FROM sales s JOIN titles t ON (s.title_id=t.title_id)
GROUP BY t.title
ORDER BY TotalSale
```

title	TotalSales
Is Anger the Enemy?	191
Secrets of Silicon Valley	50
The Busy Executive's Database Guide	45
Onions, Leeks, and Garlic: Cooking Secrets of the Mediterranean	40
The Gourmet Microwave	40

Even though TOP 4 is specified, five rows are returned because there's a tie at position four. Note that this special tie handling works only for ties that occur at the end of the result set. That is, using the TOP 4 example, a tie at positions two and three will not cause more than four rows to be returned—only a tie at position four has this effect. This is counterintuitive and means that the following queries return the same result set as the TOP 4 query:

```
SELECT TOP 5 t.title, SUM(s.qty) AS TotalSales
FROM sales s JOIN titles t ON (s.title_id=t.title_id)
GROUP BY t.title
ORDER BY TotalSales DESC
```

and

```
SELECT TOP 5 WITH TIES t.title, SUM(s.qty) AS TotalSales
FROM sales s JOIN titles t ON (s.title_id=t.title_id)
GROUP BY t.title
ORDER BY TotalSales DESC
```

Another deficiency in TOP n is the fact that it can't return grouped top segments in conjunction with a query's GROUP BY clause. This means that a query like the one below can't be modified to return the top store *in each state* using TOP n:

```
SELECT t.state, t.stor_name, SUM(s.qty) AS TotalSales
FROM sales s JOIN stores t ON (s.stor_id=t.stor_id)
GROUP BY t.state, t.stor_name
ORDER BY TotalSales DESC, t.state, t.stor_name
```

```
state stor_name                                 TotalSales
----- ------------------------------------      -----------
OR    Bookbeat                                  140
WA    Doc-U-Mat: Quality Laundry and Books      130
CA    Barnum's                                  125
WA    Eric the Read Books                       91
CA    News & Brews                              90
CA    Fricative Bookshop                        60
```

Though the syntax is supported, it doesn't do what we might like:

```
-- BAD SQL -- doesn't work as we'd like
SELECT TOP 1 t.state, t.stor_name, SUM(s.qty) AS TotalSales
FROM sales s JOIN stores t ON (s.stor_id=t.stor_id)
GROUP BY t.state, t.stor_name
ORDER BY TotalSales DESC, t.state, t.stor_name
```

```
state stor_name                                 TotalSales
----- ------------------------------------      -----------
OR    Bookbeat                                  140
```

As you can see, this query returns just one row. "TOP n" refers to the result set, not the rows in the original table or the groups into which they've been categorized. See the "Derived Tables" section below for an alternative to TOP n that returns grouped top subsets.

Derived Tables

Besides direct references to tables and views, you can also construct logical tables on the fly in the FROM clause of a SELECT statement. These are called *derived tables.* A derived table is a subquery that's used in place of a table or view. It can be queried and joined just like any other table or view. Here's a very basic example:

```
SELECT au_lname, au_fname
FROM (SELECT * FROM authors) A
```

(Results abridged)

au_lname	au_fname
Bennet	Abraham
Blotchet-Halls	Reginald
Carson	Cheryl
DeFrance	Michel
del Castillo	Innes

The derived table in this query is constructed via the **SELECT * FROM authors** syntax. Any valid query could be inserted here and can contain derived tables of its own. Notice the inclusion of a table alias. This is a requirement of Transact-SQL derived tables—you must include it regardless of whether the query references other objects.

Since Transact-SQL supports nontabular SELECT statements, you can also use derived tables to construct logical tables from scratch without referencing any other database objects. Here's an example:

```
SELECT *
FROM
(SELECT 'flyweight' AS WeightClass, 0 AS LowBound, 112 AS HighBound
 UNION ALL
 SELECT 'bantamweight' AS WeightClass, 113 AS LowerBound, 118 AS HighBound
 UNION ALL
 SELECT 'featherweight' AS WeightClass, 119 AS LowerBound, 126 AS HighBound
 UNION ALL
 SELECT 'lightweight' AS WeightClass, 127 AS LowerBound, 135 AS HighBound
 UNION ALL
 SELECT 'welterweight' AS WeightClass, 136 AS LowerBound, 147 AS HighBound
 UNION ALL
 SELECT 'middleweight' AS WeightClass, 148 AS LowerBound, 160 AS HighBound
 UNION ALL
 SELECT 'light heavyweight' AS WeightClass, 161 AS LowerBound, 175 AS HighBound
 UNION ALL
 SELECT 'heavyweight' AS WeightClass, 195 AS LowerBound, 1000 AS HighBound) W
ORDER BY W.LowBound
```

WeightClass	LowBound	HighBound
flyweight	0	112
bantamweight	113	118
featherweight	119	126
lightweight	127	135
welterweight	136	147
middleweight	148	160
light heavyweight	161	175
heavyweight	195	1000

Here, we "construct" a derived table containing three columns and eight rows. Each SE-LECT represents a single row in this virtual table. The rows in the table are glued together using a series of UNIONs.

The table doesn't actually exist anywhere—it's a logical construct only. You can think of a derived table as a temporary VIEW object—it exists for the duration of the query then goes away quietly afterward. That a SELECT statement can be treated as a table is sensible given that, by definition, the result of a SQL query is itself a table—the result table. Here's a query that joins a regular table with a derived table:

```
CREATE TABLE #boxers
(Name varchar(30),
Weight float)
INSERT #boxers VALUES ('Glass Joe', 112)
INSERT #boxers VALUES ('Piston Hurricane', 176)
INSERT #boxers VALUES ('Bald Bull', 298)
INSERT #boxers VALUES ('Sugar Ray Ali', 151)
INSERT #boxers VALUES ('Leon Holmes', 119)
INSERT #boxers VALUES ('George Liston', 139)
INSERT #boxers VALUES ('Larry Leonard', 115)
INSERT #boxers VALUES ('Mike Mooncalf', 134)

SELECT B.Name, B.Weight, W.WeightClass
FROM #boxers B,
(SELECT 'flyweight' AS WeightClass, 0 AS LowBound, 112 AS HighBound
 UNION ALL
 SELECT 'bantamweight' AS WeightClass, 113 AS LowerBound, 118 AS HighBound
 UNION ALL
 SELECT 'featherweight' AS WeightClass, 119 AS LowerBound, 126 AS HighBound
 UNION ALL
 SELECT 'lightweight' AS WeightClass, 127 AS LowerBound, 135 AS HighBound
 UNION ALL
 SELECT 'welterweight' AS WeightClass, 136 AS LowerBound, 147 AS HighBound
 UNION ALL
 SELECT 'middleweight' AS WeightClass, 148 AS LowerBound, 160 AS HighBound
 UNION ALL
 SELECT 'light heavyweight' AS WeightClass, 161 AS LowerBound, 175 AS HighBound
 UNION ALL
 SELECT 'heavyweight' AS WeightClass, 195 AS LowerBound, 1000 AS HighBound) W
WHERE B.Weight BETWEEN W.LowBound and W.HighBound
ORDER BY W.LowBound
```

Name	Weight	WeightClass
Glass Joe	112.0	flyweight
Larry Leonard	115.0	bantamweight
Leon Holmes	119.0	featherweight
Mike Mooncalf	134.0	lightweight
George Liston	139.0	welterweight
Sugar Ray Ali	151.0	middleweight
Bald Bull	298.0	heavyweight

This query first constructs a table containing a list of fictional boxers and each boxer's fighting weight (our "regular" table). Next, it joins this table with the derived table introduced in the previous example to partition the list of boxers by weight class. Note that one of the boxers is omitted from the result because he doesn't fall into any of the weight classes established by the derived table.

Of course, this query could have been greatly simplified using CASE statements, but the point of the exercise was to show the power of derived tables. Here, we "created" a multirow table via UNION and some simple SELECTs without requiring a real table.

This example illustrates some of the unique abilities of derived tables. Here's an example that illustrates their necessity:

```
SELECT s.state, st.stor_name,s.totalsales,rank=COUNT(*)
FROM (SELECT t.state, t.stor_id, SUM(s.qty) AS TotalSales
   FROM sales s JOIN stores t ON (s.stor_id=t.stor_id)
   GROUP BY t.state, t.stor_id) s JOIN
   (SELECT t.state, t.stor_id, SUM(s.qty) AS TotalSales
   FROM sales s JOIN stores t ON (s.stor_id=t.stor_id)
   GROUP BY t.state, t.stor_id) t ON (s.state=t.state)
   JOIN stores st ON (s.stor_id=st.stor_id)
WHERE s.totalsales <= t.totalsales
GROUP BY s.state,st.stor_name,s.totalsales
HAVING COUNT(*) <=1
ORDER BY s.state, rank
```

```
state stor_name                                          totalsales  rank
----- -------------------------------------------------- ----------- -----------
CA    Barnum's                                           125         1
OR    Bookbeat                                           140         1
WA    Doc-U-Mat: Quality Laundry and Books               130         1
```

This query returns the store with the top sales in each state. As pointed out in the discussion of SELECT TOP *n,* it accomplishes what the TOP *n* extension is unable to—it returns a grouped top *n* result set.

In this case, a derived table is required in order to materialize the sales for each store without resorting to a VIEW object. Again, derived tables function much like inline views. Once each store's sales have been aggregated from the sales table, the derived table is joined with itself using its state column to determine the number of other stores within each store's home state that have fewer sales than it does. (Actually, we perform the inverse of this in order to give stores with more sales lower numbers, i.e., higher rankings.) This number is used to rank each store against the others in its state. The HAVING clause then uses this ranking to filter out all but the top store in each state. You could easily change the constant in the HAVING clause to include the top two stores, the top three, and so forth. The query is straightforward enough but was worth delving into in order to understand better the role derived tables play in real queries.

Of course, it would be more efficient to construct a static view to aggregate the sales for each store in advance. The query itself would be shorter and the optimizer would be more likely to be able to reuse the query plan it generates to service each aggregation:

```
CREATE VIEW SalesByState AS
SELECT s.stor_id, SUM(s.qty) AS TotalSales, t.state
FROM sales s JOIN stores t ON (s.stor_id=t.stor_id)
GROUP BY t.state, s.stor_id
```

```
SELECT s.state, st.stor_name,s.totalsales,Rank=COUNT(*)
FROM SalesByState s JOIN SalesByState t ON (s.state=t.state)
   JOIN stores st ON (s.stor_id=st.stor_id)
WHERE s.totalsales <= t.totalsales
GROUP BY s.state,st.stor_name,s.totalsales
HAVING COUNT(*) <=1
ORDER BY s.state, rank
```

Nevertheless, there are situations where constructing a view in advance isn't an option. If that's the case, a derived table may be your best option.

Joins

Chapter 1 covers the different types of joins supported by Transact-SQL in some depth, so here I'll focus on join nuances not covered there. Review Chapter 1 if you're unsure of how joins work or need a refresher on join basics.

Outer Joins and Join Order

The ordering of the clauses in an inner join doesn't affect the result set. If A=B, then certainly B=A. Inner join clauses are associative. That's not true for outer joins. The order in which tables are joined directly affects which rows are included in the result set and which values they have. That's why using the ANSI outer join syntax is so important—the legacy syntax can generate erroneous or ambiguous result sets because specifying join conditions in the WHERE clause precludes specifically ordering them.

To understand fully the effect join order has on OUTER JOINs, let's explore the effect it has on the result set a query generates. Here's a query that totals items in the Orders table of the Northwind sample database:

```
SELECT SUM(d.UnitPrice*d.Quantity) AS TotalOrdered
FROM Orders o LEFT OUTER JOIN [Order Details] d ON (o.OrderID+10=d.OrderID)
LEFT OUTER JOIN Products p ON (d.ProductID=p.ProductID)


TotalOrdered
--------------------
1339743.1900
```

I've intentionally introduced join condition failures into the query by incrementing o.OrderId by ten so that we can observe the effects of clause ordering and join failures on the result set. Now let's reorder the tables in the FROM clause and compute the same aggregate:

```
SELECT SUM(d.UnitPrice * d.Quantity) AS TotalOrdered
FROM [Order Details] d LEFT OUTER JOIN Products p ON (d.ProductID=p.ProductID)
LEFT OUTER JOIN Orders o ON (o.OrderID+10=d.OrderID)


TotalOrdered
--------------------
1354458.5900
```

See the discrepancy? The total changes based on the order of the tables. Why? Because the first query introduces mismatches between the Orders and Order Details tables *before* the Unit-Price and Quantity columns are totaled; the second query does so *afterward*. In the case of the second query, we get a total of all items listed in the Order Details table regardless of whether there's a match between it and the Orders table; in the first query, we don't. To understand this better, consider the data on which the two totals are based:

```
SELECT o.OrderDate, d.UnitPrice, d.Quantity
FROM Orders o LEFT OUTER JOIN [Order Details] d ON (o.OrderID+10=d.OrderID)
LEFT OUTER JOIN Products p ON (d.ProductID=p.ProductID)
WHERE o.OrderDate IS NULL
OR d.UnitPrice IS NULL
```

OrderDate	UnitPrice	Quantity
1998-05-04 00:00:00.000	NULL	NULL
1998-05-04 00:00:00.000	NULL	NULL
1998-05-05 00:00:00.000	NULL	NULL
1998-05-05 00:00:00.000	NULL	NULL
1998-05-05 00:00:00.000	NULL	NULL
1998-05-05 00:00:00.000	NULL	NULL
1998-05-06 00:00:00.000	NULL	NULL
1998-05-06 00:00:00.000	NULL	NULL
1998-05-06 00:00:00.000	NULL	NULL
1998-05-06 00:00:00.000	NULL	NULL

I've included a WHERE clause to pare the result set down to just those rows affected by the intentional join mismatch. Since we increment OrderNo by ten and the order numbers are sequential, ten of the OrderNo values in Orders fail to find matches in the Order Details table and, consequently, have NULL UnitPrice and Quantity fields. Here's a snapshot of the underlying data for the second query (again with a restrictive WHERE clause):

```
SELECT o.OrderDate, d.UnitPrice, d.Quantity
FROM [Order Details] d LEFT OUTER JOIN Products p ON (d.ProductID=p.ProductID)
LEFT OUTER JOIN Orders o ON (o.OrderID+10=d.OrderID)
WHERE o.OrderDate IS NULL
OR d.UnitPrice IS NULL
```

OrderDate	UnitPrice	Quantity
NULL	14.0000	12
NULL	9.8000	10
NULL	34.8000	5
NULL	18.6000	9
NULL	42.4000	40
NULL	7.7000	10
NULL	42.4000	35
NULL	16.8000	15
NULL	16.8000	6
NULL	15.6000	15
NULL	16.8000	20
NULL	64.8000	40

NULL	2.0000	25
NULL	27.2000	40
NULL	10.0000	20
NULL	14.4000	42
NULL	16.0000	40
NULL	3.6000	15
NULL	19.2000	21
NULL	8.0000	21
NULL	15.2000	20
NULL	13.9000	35
NULL	15.2000	25
NULL	44.0000	30
NULL	26.2000	15
NULL	10.4000	12
NULL	35.1000	25
NULL	14.4000	6
NULL	10.4000	15

Notice that this set is much longer—nineteen rows longer, to be exact. Why? Because twenty-nine rows were omitted from the result set of the first query due to the join mismatch, though this wasn't immediately obvious. For each broken order number link, a given number of Order Detail rows were omitted because there was a one-to-many relationship between the Orders and Order Details tables. This, of course, skewed the total reported by the query.

So the moral of the story is this: Be careful with outer join ordering, especially when the possibility of join mismatches exists.

Predicates

By definition, a predicate is an expression that returns TRUE or NOT TRUE (I'm not using "FALSE" because of the issues related to three-valued logic—sometimes we don't know whether an expression is FALSE, all we know is that it is not certainly TRUE).

Predicates are usually found in a query's WHERE or HAVING clauses, though they can be located elsewhere (e.g., in CASE expressions). Predicates can be simple logical expressions or can be composed of functions that return TRUE or NOT TRUE. Though technically *any* function can be included in a predicate expression, Transact-SQL defines a number of *predicate functions* that are specifically geared toward filtering queries and result sets. The sections that follow detail each of them.

BETWEEN

The BETWEEN predicate is probably the most often used of the Transact-SQL predicates. It indicates whether a given value falls between two other values, inclusively. Here's an example:

```
SELECT au_lname, au_fname
FROM authors
WHERE au_lname BETWEEN 'S' AND 'ZZ'
ORDER BY au_lname
```

au_lname	au_fname
Smith	Meander
Straight	Dean
Stringer	Dirk
White	Johnson
Yokomoto	Akiko

BETWEEN works with scalar ranges, so it can handle dates, numerics, and other scalar data types. It combines what would normally require two terms in the WHERE clause: a greater-than-or-equal-to expression, followed by a less-than-or-equal-to expression. **WHERE au_lname BETWEEN 'S' AND 'ZZ'** is shorthand for **WHERE au_lname >= 'S' AND au_lname <='ZZ'.**

In addition to simple constant arguments, BETWEEN accepts subquery, variable, and expression arguments. Here's an example:

```
DECLARE @au_id id
SELECT @au_id=(SELECT MAX(au_id) FROM titleauthor)

SELECT au_lname, au_fname
FROM authors
WHERE au_id BETWEEN (SELECT MIN(au_id) FROM titleauthor) AND
ISNULL(@au_id,'ZZZZZZZZZZ')
ORDER BY au_lname
```

(Results abridged)

au_lname	au_fname
Bennet	Abraham
Blotchet-Halls	Reginald
Carson	Cheryl
DeFrance	Michel
del Castillo	Innes
(...)	
White	Johnson
Yokomoto	Akiko

Since the primary purpose of the predicate is to determine whether a value lies within a given range, it's common to see BETWEEN used to determine whether one event occurs between two others. Locating overlapping events is more difficult than it first appears and its elusiveness gives rise to many false solutions.

This is best explored by way of example. Let's say we have a list of soldiers, and we need to determine which of them could have participated in the major military engagements of a given war. We'd need at least two tables—one listing the soldiers and their tours of duty and one listing each major engagement of the war with its beginning and ending dates. The idea then would be to return a result set that cross-references the soldier list with the engagement list, taking into account each time a soldier's tour of duty began or ended during a major engagement, as well as when it encompassed a major engagement. Assume we start with these tables:

```
CREATE TABLE #engagements
(Engagement varchar(30),
 EngagementStart       smalldatetime,
 EngagementEnd smalldatetime)

INSERT #engagements VALUES('Gulf of Tonkin','19640802','19640804')
INSERT #engagements VALUES('Da Nang','19650301','19650331')
INSERT #engagements VALUES('Tet Offensive','19680131','19680930')
INSERT #engagements VALUES('Bombing of Cambodia','19690301','19700331')
INSERT #engagements VALUES('Invasion of Cambodia','19700401','19700430')
INSERT #engagements VALUES('Fall of Saigon','19750430','19750430')

CREATE TABLE #soldier_tours
(Soldier     varchar(30),
 TourStartb smalldatetime,
 TourEnd     smalldatetime)

INSERT #soldier_tours VALUES('Henderson, Robert Lee','19700126','19700615')
INSERT #soldier_tours VALUES('Henderson, Kayle Dean','19690110','19690706')
INSERT #soldier_tours VALUES('Henderson, Isaac Lee','19680529','19680722')
INSERT #soldier_tours VALUES('Henderson, James D.','19660509','19670201')
INSERT #soldier_tours VALUES('Henderson, Robert Knapp','19700218','19700619')
INSERT #soldier_tours VALUES('Henderson, Rufus Q.','19670909','19680320')
INSERT #soldier_tours VALUES('Henderson, Robert Michael','19680107','19680131')
INSERT #soldier_tours VALUES('Henderson, Stephen Carl','19690102','19690914')
INSERT #soldier_tours VALUES('Henderson, Tommy Ray','19700713','19710303')
INSERT #soldier_tours VALUES('Henderson, Greg Neal','19701022','19710410')
INSERT #soldier_tours VALUES('Henderson, Charles E.','19661001','19750430')
```

Here's a preliminary solution:

```
SELECT Soldier+' served during the '+Engagement
FROM #soldier_tours, #engagements
WHERE (TourStart BETWEEN EngagementStart AND EngagementEnd)
OR (TourEnd BETWEEN EngagementStart AND EngagementEnd)
OR (EngagementStart BETWEEN TourStart AND TourEnd)

--------------------------------------------------------------------------
Henderson, Isaac Lee served during the Tet Offensive
Henderson, Rufus Q. served during the Tet Offensive
Henderson, Robert Michael served during the Tet Offensive
Henderson, Charles E. served during the Tet Offensive
Henderson, Robert Lee served during the Bombing of Cambodia
Henderson, Kayle Dean served during the Bombing of Cambodia
Henderson, Robert Knapp served during the Bombing of Cambodia
Henderson, Stephen Carl served during the Bombing of Cambodia
Henderson, Charles E. served during the Bombing of Cambodia
Henderson, Robert Lee served during the Invasion of Cambodia
Henderson, Robert Knapp served during the Invasion of Cambodia
Henderson, Charles E. served during the Invasion of Cambodia
Henderson, Charles E. served during the Fall of Saigon
```

Once the tables are created and populated, the query includes rows in the result set using three separate BETWEEN predicates: A soldier's tour began during an engagement, his tour ended during an engagement, or an engagement started during his tour. Why do we need this last check? Why do we care whether an engagement started during a soldier's tour—this would be the same as asking whether a soldier's tour ended during the engagement, wouldn't it? No, not quite. Without the third predicate expression, we aren't allowing for the possibility that an engagement could begin *and* end within a tour of duty.

Though this query works, there is a better solution. It requires considering the inverse of the problem. Rather than determining when tours of duty and major engagements overlap one another, let's determine when they don't. For a tour of duty and a major engagement *not* to coincide, one of two things must be true: Either the tour of duty ended *before* the engagement started, or it began *after* the engagement ended. Knowing this, we can greatly simplify the query and remove the BETWEEN predicates altogether, like so:

```
SELECT Soldier+' served during the '+Engagement
FROM #soldier_tours, #engagements
WHERE NOT ((TourEnd < EngagementStart) OR (TourStart > EngagementEnd))
-----------------------------------------------------------------------
Henderson, Isaac Lee served during the Tet Offensive
Henderson, Rufus Q. served during the Tet Offensive
Henderson, Robert Michael served during the Tet Offensive
Henderson, Charles E. served during the Tet Offensive
Henderson, Robert Lee served during the Bombing of Cambodia
Henderson, Kayle Dean served during the Bombing of Cambodia
Henderson, Robert Knapp served during the Bombing of Cambodia
Henderson, Stephen Carl served during the Bombing of Cambodia
Henderson, Charles E. served during the Bombing of Cambodia
Henderson, Robert Lee served during the Invasion of Cambodia
Henderson, Robert Knapp served during the Invasion of Cambodia
Henderson, Charles E. served during the Invasion of Cambodia
Henderson, Charles E. served during the Fall of Saigon
```

LIKE

LIKE tests a value for a match against a string pattern:

```
SELECT au_lname, au_fname
FROM authors
WHERE au_lname LIKE 'Green'
```

```
au_lname                                 au_fname
---------------------------------------- --------------------
Green                                    Marjorie
```

ANSI SQL specifies two pattern wildcard characters: the % (percent) character and the _ (underscore) character; % matches any number of characters, while _ matches exactly one. Here's an example:

```
SELECT au_lname, au_fname
FROM authors
WHERE au_lname LIKE 'G%'
```

```
au_lname                                  au_fname
----------------------------------------  --------------------
Green                                     Marjorie
Greene                                    Morningstar
Gringlesby                                Burt
```

Beyond those supported by ANSI SQL, Transact-SQL also supports regular expression wildcards. These wildcards allow you to test a character for membership within a set of characters. Here's an example:

```
SELECT au_lname, au_fname
FROM authors
WHERE au_lname LIKE 'Str[ai]%'
```

```
au_lname                                  au_fname
----------------------------------------  --------------------
Straight                                  Dean
Stringer                                  Dirk
```

In the example above, **[ai]** is a regular expression wildcard that matches any string with either **a** or **i** in the fourth position. To exclude strings using a regular expression, prefix its characters with a caret, like so:

```
SELECT au_lname, au_fname
FROM authors
WHERE au_lname LIKE 'Gr[^e]%'
```

```
au_lname                                  au_fname
----------------------------------------  --------------------
Gringlesby                                Burt
```

Here, we request authors whose last names begin with "Gr" and contain a character other than **e** in the third position.

There are some subtle differences between the _ and % wildcards. The _ wildcard requires at least one character; % requires none. The difference this makes is best explained by example. First, consider this query:

```
SELECT au_lname, au_fname
FROM authors
WHERE au_lname LIKE 'Green%'
```

```
au_lname                                  au_fname
----------------------------------------  --------------------
Green                                     Marjorie
Greene                                    Morningstar
```

Now consider this one:

```
SELECT au_lname, au_fname
FROM authors
WHERE au_lname LIKE 'Green_'
```

au_lname	au_fname
Greene	Morningstar

See the difference? Since _ requires at least one character, "Green_" doesn't match "Green."

Another point worth mentioning is that it's possible for a string to survive an equality test but fail a LIKE test. This is counterintuitive since LIKE would seem to be less restrictive than a plain equality test. The reason this is possible is that ANSI SQL padding rules require that two strings compared for equality be padded to the same length prior to the comparison. That's not true for LIKE. If one term is padded with blanks and the other isn't, the comparison will probably fail. Here's an example:

```
SELECT au_lname, au_fname
FROM authors
WHERE au_lname = 'Green '
```

au_lname	au_fname
Green	Marjorie

```
SELECT au_lname, au_fname
FROM authors
WHERE au_lname LIKE 'Green '
```

au_lname	au_fname

Notice that the second query doesn't return any rows due to the padding of the string constant, even though the equality test works fine.

EXISTS

EXISTS is a predicate function that takes a subquery as its lone parameter. It works very simply —if the subquery returns a result set—any result set—EXISTS returns True; otherwise it returns False.

Though EXISTS isn't defined to require parentheses per se, it does. This is necessary to avoid confusing the Transact-SQL query parser.

The subquery passed to EXISTS is usually a correlated subquery. By correlated, I mean that it references a column in the outer query in its WHERE or HAVING clause—it's joined at the hip with it. Of course, this isn't true when EXISTS is used with control-of-flow language statements such as IF and WHILE—it applies only to SELECT statements.

As a rule, you should use SELECT * in the subqueries you pass EXISTS. This allows the optimizer to select the column to use and should generally perform better.

Here's an example of a simple EXISTS predicate:

```
SELECT title
FROM titles t
WHERE EXISTS(SELECT * FROM sales s WHERE s.title_id=t.title_id)
```

(Results abridged)

```
title
--------------------------------------------------------------------------------
But Is It User Friendly?
Computer Phobic AND Non-Phobic Individuals: Behavior Variations
Cooking with Computers: Surreptitious Balance Sheets
Emotional Security: A New Algorithm
```

This query returns all titles for which sales exist in the **sales** table. Of course, this could also be written as an inner join, but more on that later.

Prefixing EXISTS with NOT negates the expression. Here's an example:

```
SELECT title
FROM titles t
WHERE NOT EXISTS(SELECT * FROM sales s WHERE s.title_id=t.title_id)
```

```
title
--------------------------------------------------------------------------------
Net Etiquette
```

This makes sense because there are no rows in the **sales** table for the Net Etiquette title.

NULLs

NULLs affect EXISTS in some interesting ways. Let's explore what happens when we introduce a NULL into the **sales** table:

```
SELECT title
FROM titles t
WHERE EXISTS(SELECT * FROM
   (SELECT * FROM sales -- Not actually needed-for illustration only
   UNION ALL
   SELECT NULL, NULL, NULL, 90, NULL, NULL) s
   WHERE s.title_id=t.title_id AND s.qty >>75)
```

```
title
--------------------------------------------------------------------------------
```

The query uses a UNION to introduce a row consisting mostly of NULL values into the **sales** table on the fly. Every field except **qty** is set to NULL. Even though the underlying columns in the **sales** table don't allow NULLs, the subquery references the *result* of the **sales**-NULL values union (ensconced in a derived table), not the table itself. Using UNION to add a "virtual" row in this manner saves us from having to modify **sales** in order to explore the effects of NULLs on EXISTS.

Even though we've introduced a row containing a **qty** with a value greater than 75, the result set is empty because that row's NULL **title_id** doesn't correlate with any in the **titles** table. Because the value of **title_id** isn't known in the NULL row, you might think that it would correlate with every row in titles, but that's not the case. Even if **titles** contained a NULL **title_id**, the two still wouldn't correlate since one NULL never equals another (this can be changed with the SET ANSI NULLS command—see Chapter 3, "Missing Values," for details). This may seem a bit odd or counterintuitive, but it's the way SQL was intended to work.

Negating the EXISTS expression produces some odd effects as well. Here's an example:

```
SELECT title
FROM titles t
WHERE NOT EXISTS(SELECT * FROM (SELECT * FROM sales
    UNION ALL
    SELECT NULL, NULL, NULL, NULL, NULL, NULL) s
  WHERE s.title_id=t.title_id)

title
--------------------------------------------------------------------------------
Net Etiquette
```

Since the server can't know whether the **title_id** for Net Etiquette matches the NULL introduced by the union, you might think that no result would be returned. With NULLs in the mix, we can't positively know that Net Etiquette's **title_id** doesn't exist; nevertheless, the query returns Net Etiquette anyway. The apparent discrepancy here comes about because of the way in which the expression is evaluated. First, SQL Server determines whether the value exists, *then* negates the expression with NOT. We are evaluating the negation of a positive predicate, *not* a negative predicate. The expression is NOT EXISTS (note the space between the keywords), not NOTEXISTS(). So, when the query gets to the **title_id** for Net Etiquette, it begins by determining whether it can establish for certain that the **title_id** exists in the UNIONed table. It can't, of course, because the ID isn't there. Therefore, the EXISTS check returns False, which satisfies the NOT negation, so the row is included in the result set, even though the fact that it does not exist in the subquery table has not been nor can be established.

EXISTS and IN

Converting an IN predicate to EXISTS has a few peculiarities of its own. For example, the first EXISTS query could be rewritten to use IN like this:

```
SELECT title
FROM titles t
WHERE t.title_id IN (SELECT title_id FROM sales)
```

(Results abridged)

```
title
--------------------------------------------------------------------------------
But Is It User Friendly?
Computer Phobic AND Non-Phobic Individuals: Behavior Variations
Cooking with Computers: Surreptitious Balance Sheets
Emotional Security: A New Algorithm
```

And here's the inverse:

```
SELECT title
FROM titles t
WHERE t.title_id NOT IN (SELECT title_id FROM sales)

title
--------------------------------------------------------------------------------
Net Etiquette
```

But look at what happens when NULLs figure into the equation:

```
SELECT title
FROM titles t
WHERE t.title_id NOT IN (SELECT title_id FROM sales UNION SELECT NULL)

title
----------------------------------------------------------------------------
```

The IN predicate provides a shorthand method of comparing a scalar value with a series of values. In this case, the subquery provides the series. Per ANSI/ISO SQL guidelines, an expression that compares a value for equality to NULL always returns NULL, so the Net Etiquette row fails the test. The other rows fail the test because they can be positively identified as being in the list and are therefore excluded by the NOT.

This behavior is different from the NOT EXISTS behavior we observed earlier and is the chief reason that converting between EXISTS and IN can be tricky when NULLs are involved.

Note that Transact-SQL's SET ANSI_NULLS command can be used to alter this behavior. When ANSI_NULLS behavior is disabled, equality comparisons to NULL are allowed, and NULL values equal one another. Since IN is shorthand for an equality comparison, it's directly affected by this setting. Here's an example:

```
SET ANSI_NULLS OFF
SELECT title
FROM titles t
WHERE t.title_id NOT IN (SELECT title_id FROM sales UNION SELECT NULL)
GO
SET ANSI_NULLS ON -- Be sure to re-enable ANSI_NULLS

title
----------------------------------------------------------------------------
Net Etiquette
```

Now that Net Etiquette's title_id can be safely compared to the NULL produced by the UNION, the IN predicate can ascertain whether it exists in the list. Since it doesn't, Net Etiquette makes it into the result set.

Joins

As I said earlier, many correlated subqueries used with EXISTS can be restated as simple inner joins. Not only are these joins easier to read, they will also tend to be faster. Furthermore, using a join instead of EXISTS allows the query to reference fields from both tables. Here's the earlier EXISTS query flattened into a join:

```
SELECT DISTINCT title
FROM titles t JOIN sales s ON (t.title_id = s.title_id)
```

(Results abridged)

```
title
----------------------------------------------------------------------------
But Is It User Friendly?
Computer Phobic AND Non-Phobic Individuals: Behavior Variations
Cooking with Computers: Surreptitious Balance Sheets
Emotional Security: A New Algorithm
```

We're forced to use DISTINCT here because there's a one-to-many relationship between **titles** and **sales.**

Result Set Emptiness

Another common use of EXISTS is to check a result set for rows. The optimizer knows that finding even a single row satisfies the expression, so this is often quite fast. Here's an example:

```
IF EXISTS(SELECT * FROM myworktable) DELETE myworktable
```

Since the query isn't qualified by a WHERE or HAVING clause, we're effectively checking the table for rows. This is much quicker than something like IF (SELECT COUNT(*) FROM myworktable)>0 and provides a speedy means of determining whether a table is empty without having to inspect system objects.

EXISTS Outside WHERE and HAVING

EXISTS, like all predicates, can do more than just restrict the rows returned by a query. EXISTS can also be used in the SELECT list within CASE expressions and in the FROM clause via derived table definitions. Here's an example:

```
SELECT CASE WHEN EXISTS(SELECT * FROM titleauthor where au_id=a.au_id) THEN
'True' ELSE 'False' END
FROM authors a


-----
True
True
True
True
True
True
True
False
True
True
True
True
True
False
True
True
True
True
False
True
False
True
True
```

Since predicates don't return values that you can use directly, your options here are more limited than they should be. That is, you can't simply SELECT the result of a predicate—it must be accessed instead via an expression or function that can handle logical values—i.e., CASE. CASE translates the logical value returned by the predicate into something the query can return.

IN

As mentioned earlier, the IN predicate provides a shorthand method of comparing a value to each member of a list. You can think of it as a series of equality comparisons between the left-side value and each of the values in the list, joined by OR. Though ANSI SQL-92 allows row values to be used with IN, Transact-SQL does not—you can specify scalar values only. The series of values searched by IN can be specified as a comma-delimited list or returned by a sub-query. Here are a couple of simple examples that use IN:

```
SELECT title
FROM titles WHERE title_id IN (SELECT title_id FROM sales)
```

(Results abridged.)

```
title
-------------------------------------------------------------------------------
But Is It User Friendly?
Computer Phobic AND Non-Phobic Individuals: Behavior Variations
Cooking with Computers: Surreptitious Balance Sheets
Emotional Security: A New Algorithm

SELECT title
FROM titles WHERE title_id NOT IN (SELECT title_id FROM sales)
title
-------------------------------------------------------------------------------
Net Etiquette
```

Note that the individual values specified aren't limited to constants—you can use expressions and subqueries, too. Here's an example:

```
SELECT title
FROM titles WHERE title_id IN ((SELECT title_id FROM sales WHERE qty>=75),
                     (SELECT title_id FROM sales WHERE qty=5),
                            'PC'+REPLICATE('8',4))
```

```
title
-------------------------------------------------------------------------------
Is Anger the Enemy?
Secrets of Silicon Valley
The Busy Executive's Database Guide
```

Optimizing IN

Though it's natural to order the terms in the value list alphabetically or numerically, it's preferable to order them instead based on frequency of occurrence since the predicate will return as soon as a single match is found. One way to do this with a subquery is to sort the subquery result set with ORDER BY. Here's an example:

```
SELECT title
FROM titles WHERE title_id IN (SELECT title_id FROM
   (SELECT TOP 100 percent title_id, COUNT(*) AS NumOccur FROM sales GROUP BY
 title_id ORDER BY NumOccur DESC) s)
```

(Results abridged)

```
title
--------------------------------------------------------------------------
Is Anger the Enemy?
The Busy Executive's Database Guide
The Gourmet Microwave
Cooking with Computers: Surreptitious Balance Sheets
```

This query uses a derived table in order to sort the sales table before handing it to the subquery. We need a derived table because we need two values—the title_id column and a count of the number of times it occurs, but only the EXISTS predicate permits a subquery to return more than one column. We sort in descending order so that title_ids with a higher degree of frequency appear first. The TOP *n* extension is required since ORDER BY isn't allowed in subqueries, derived tables, or views without it.

> **Note**
> It's likely that using IN without ordering the sales table would be more efficient in this particular example because the tables are so small. The point of the example is to show that specifically ordering a subquery result set considered by IN is sometimes more efficient than leaving it in its natural order. A sizable amount of data has to be considered before you overcome the obvious overhead associated with grouping and sorting the table.

Since a SELECT without an ORDER BY isn't guaranteed to produce rows in a particular order, a valid point that we can't trust the order of the rows in the subquery could be made. The fact that the derived table is ordered doesn't mean the subquery will be. In practice, it appears that this works as we want. To verify it, we can extract the subquery and run it separately from the main query, like so:

```
SELECT title_id
FROM (SELECT TOP 999999 title_id, COUNT(*) AS NumOccur
FROM sales GROUP BY title_id ORDER BY NumOccur DESC) s
```

(Results abridged)

```
title_id NumOccur
-------- --------
PS2091   6
BU1032   3
MC3021   2
BU1111   1
BU2075   1
BU7832   1
```

Though highly unlikely, it's still possible that the query optimizer could choose a different sort order for the subquery than the one returned by the derived table, but this is the best we can do.

ANY and ALL

The ANY and ALL predicates work exclusively with subqueries. ANY (and its synonym SOME) works similarly to IN. Here's a query expressed first using IN, then using ANY:

```
SELECT title
FROM titles WHERE title_id IN (SELECT title_id FROM sales)
```

(Results abridged)

```
title
--------------------------------------------------------------------------------
But Is It User Friendly?
Computer Phobic AND Non-Phobic Individuals: Behavior Variations
Cooking with Computers: Surreptitious Balance Sheets
Emotional Security: A New Algorithm
```

```
SELECT title
FROM titles WHERE title_id=ANY(SELECT title_id FROM sales)
```

(Results abridged)

```
title
--------------------------------------------------------------------------------
But Is It User Friendly?
Computer Phobic AND Non-Phobic Individuals: Behavior Variations
Cooking with Computers: Surreptitious Balance Sheets
Emotional Security: A New Algorithm
```

Since IN and =ANY are functionally equivalent, you might tend to think that NOT IN and <>ANY are equivalent as well, but that's not the case. Instead, <>ALL is the equivalent of NOT IN. If you think about it, this makes perfect sense. <>ANY will always return True as long as more than one value is returned by the subquery. When two or more distinct values are returned by the subquery, there will always be one that doesn't match the scalar value. By contrast, <>ALL works just like NOT IN. It returns True only when the scalar value is not equal to each and every one of the values returned by the subquery.

This brings up the interesting point that ALL is more often used with the not equal operator (<>) than with the equal operator (=). Testing a scalar value to see whether it matches every value in a list has a very limited use. The test will fail unless all the values are identical. If they're identical, why perform the test?

Subqueries

You've already been introduced to the subquery (or subselect) elsewhere in this book, particularly in the sections on predicates earlier in this chapter, but it's still instructive to delve into them a bit deeper. Subqueries are a potent tool in the Transact-SQL arsenal; they allow us to accomplish tasks that otherwise would be very difficult if not impossible. They provide a means of basing one query on another—of nesting queries—that can be both logical and speedy.

Many joins can be restated as subqueries, though this can be difficult (or even impossible) when the subquery is not used with IN or EXISTS or when it performs aggregation. As a rule, a join will be more efficient than a subquery, but this is not always the case.

Subqueries aren't limited to restricting the rows in a result set. They can be used any place in a SQL statement where an expression is valid. They can be used to provide column values, within CASE expressions, and within derived tables. (A column whose value is derived from a subquery is called a *derived column,* as we discussed earlier.) They're not limited to SELECT statements, either. Subqueries can be used with UPDATE, INSERT, and DELETE, as well.

WHERE and Subqueries

The most common use of the subquery is in the SELECT statement's WHERE clause. Here's an example:

```
SELECT SUM(qty) AS TotalSales
FROM sales
WHERE title_id=(SELECT MAX(title_id) FROM titles)


TotalSales
-----------
20
```

Here, we return the total sales for the last **title_id** in the **titles** table. Note the use of MAX function to ensure that the subquery returns only one row. Subqueries used with the equality operators (=,<>,>= and <=) may return one value only. An equality subquery that returns more than one value doesn't generate a syntax error, so be careful—you won't know about it until runtime. One way to avoid returning more than one value is to use an aggregate function, as the previous example does. Another way is to use SELECT's TOP *n* extension, like so:

```
SELECT SUM(qty) AS TotalSales
FROM sales
WHERE title_id=(SELECT TOP 1 title_id FROM titles ORDER BY title_id DESC)


TotalSales
-----------
20
```

Here, we use **TOP 1** to ensure that only one row is returned by the subquery. Just to keep the result set in line with the previous one, we sort the subquery's result set in descending order on the **title_id** column, then return the first (actually the last) one.

Make sure that subqueries used in equality comparisons return no more than one row. Code that doesn't protect against multiple subquery values is a bug waiting to happen. It can crash merely because of minor data changes in the tables it references—not a good thing.

Correlated Subqueries

A correlated subquery is a subselect that is restricted by, and very often restricts, a table in the outer query. It usually references this table via the table's alias as specified in the outer query.

In a sense, correlated subqueries behave like traditional looping constructs. For each row in the outer table, the subquery is reexecuted with a new set of parameters. On the other hand, a correlated subquery is much more efficient than the equivalent Transact-SQL looping code. It's far more efficient to iterate through a table using a correlated subquery than with, say, a WHILE loop.

Here's an example of a basic correlated subquery:

```
SELECT title
FROM titles t
WHERE (SELECT SUM(qty) AS TotalSales FROM sales WHERE title_id=t.title_id) > 30

title
-------------------------------------------------------------------------------
Is Anger the Enemy?
Onions, Leeks, and Garlic: Cooking Secrets of the Mediterranean
Secrets of Silicon Valley
The Busy Executive's Database Guide
The Gourmet Microwave
You Can Combat Computer Stress!
```

In this query, the subquery is executed for each row in **titles.** As it's executed each time, it's qualified by the **title_id** column in the outer table. This means that the SUM it returns will correspond to the current **title_id** of the outer query. This total, in turn, is used to limit the titles returned to those with sales in excess of 30 units.

Of course, this query could easily be restated as a join, but the point of the exercise is to show the way in which subqueries and their hosts can be correlated.

Note that correlated subqueries need not be restricted to the WHERE clause. Here's an example showing a correlated subquery in the SELECT list:

```
SELECT title,
(SELECT SUM(qty) FROM sales WHERE title_id=t.title_id) AS TotalSales
FROM titles t
```

(Results abridged)

```
title                                                             TotalSales
------------------------------------------------------------------ ----------
But Is It User Friendly?                                               30
Computer Phobic AND Non-Phobic Individuals: Behavior Variations        20
Cooking with Computers: Surreptitious Balance Sheets                   25
Emotional Security: A New Algorithm                                    25
```

In this example, the subquery is restricted by the outer query, but it does not affect which rows are returned by the query. The outer query depends upon the subquery in the sense that it renders one of its column values but not to the degree that it affects which rows are included in the result set.

As covered in the section on predicates, a scalar value can be compared with the result set of a subquery using special predicate functions such as IN, EXISTS, ANY, and ALL. Here's an example:

```
SELECT title
FROM titles t
WHERE title_id IN (SELECT s.title_id
                   FROM sales s
                   WHERE (t.ytd_sales+((SELECT SUM(s1.qty) FROM sales s1
                                        WHERE s1.title_id=t.title_id)*t.price))
                   > 5000)
```

```
title
----------------------------------------------------------------------------
You Can Combat Computer Stress!
The Gourmet Microwave
But Is It User Friendly?
Secrets of Silicon Valley
Fifty Years in Buckingham Palace Kitchens
```

In this example, subqueries reference two separate fields from the outer query—**ytd_sales** and **price**—in order to compute the total sales to date for each title. There are two subqueries here, one nested within the other, and both are correlated with the main query. The innermost subquery computes the total unit sales for a given title. It's necessary because **sales** is likely to contain multiple rows per title since it lists individual purchases. The outer subquery takes this total, multiplies it by the book unit price, and adds the title's year-to-date sales in order to produce a sales-to-date total for each title. Those titles with sales in excess of $5000 are then returned by the subquery and tested by the IN predicate.

As I've said, joins are often preferable to subqueries because they tend to run more efficiently. Here's the previous query rewritten as a join:

```
SELECT t.title
FROM titles t JOIN sales s ON (t.title_id=s.title_id)
GROUP BY t.title_id, t.title, t.ytd_sales, t.price
HAVING (t.ytd_sales+(SUM(s.qty)*t.price)) > 5000
```

```
title
----------------------------------------------------------------------------
You Can Combat Computer Stress!
The Gourmet Microwave
But Is It User Friendly?
Secrets of Silicon Valley
Fifty Years in Buckingham Palace Kitchens
```

Though joins are often preferable to subqueries, there are other times when a correlated subquery is the better solution. For example, consider the case of locating duplicate values among the rows in a table. Let's say that you have a list of Web domains and name servers and you want to locate each domain with the same name servers as some other domain. A domain can have no more than two name servers, so your table has three columns (ignore for the moment that these are unnormalized, repeating values). You could code this using a correlated subquery or as a self-join, but the subquery solution is better. To understand why, let's explore both methods. First, here's the self-join approach:

```
CREATE TABLE #nameservers (domain varchar(30), ns1 varchar(15), ns2 varchar(15))

INSERT #nameservers VALUES ('foolsrus.com','24.99.0.9','24.99.0.8')
INSERT #nameservers VALUES ('wewanturbuks.gov','127.0.0.2','127.0.0.3')
INSERT #nameservers VALUES ('sayhitomom.edu','127.0.0.4','24.99.0.8')
INSERT #nameservers VALUES ('knickstink.org','192.168.0.254','192.168.0.255')
INSERT #nameservers VALUES ('nukemnut.com','24.99.0.6','24.99.0.7')
INSERT #nameservers VALUES ('wedigdiablo.org','24.99.0.9','24.99.0.8')
INSERT #nameservers VALUES ('gospamurself.edu','192.168.0.255','192.168.0.254')
INSERT #nameservers VALUES ('ou812.com','100.10.0.100','100.10.0.101')
INSERT #nameservers VALUES ('rothrulz.org','100.10.0.102','24.99.0.8')

SELECT n.domain, n.ns1, n.ns2
FROM #nameservers n JOIN #nameservers a ON
   (n.domain<>a.domain AND ((n.ns1=a.ns1 AND n.ns2=a.ns2) OR (n.ns1=a.ns2 AND
n.ns2=a.ns1)))
ORDER BY 2,3,1
```

domain	ns1	ns2
knickstink.org	192.168.0.254	192.168.0.255
gospamurself.edu	192.168.0.255	192.168.0.254
foolsrus.com	24.99.0.9	24.99.0.8
wedigdiablo.org	24.99.0.9	24.99.0.8

We join with a second instance of the name server table and set up the entirety of the conditions on which we're joining in the ON clause of the JOIN. For each row in the first instance of the table, we scan the second instance for rows where a) the domain is different and b) the pair of name servers is the same. We're careful to look for domains where the name servers have been reversed as well as those that match exactly.

Now, here's the same query expressed using a subquery:

```
SELECT n.domain, n.ns1, n.ns2
FROM #nameservers n
WHERE EXISTS(SELECT a.ns1, a.ns2 FROM #nameservers a
   WHERE (a.domain<>n.domain) AND ((a.ns1=n.ns1 AND a.ns2=n.ns2) OR (a.ns1=n.ns2
   AND a.ns2=n.ns1)))
ORDER BY 2,3,1
```

domain	ns1	ns2
knickstink.org	192.168.0.254	192.168.0.255
gospamurself.edu	192.168.0.255	192.168.0.254
foolsrus.com	24.99.0.9	24.99.0.8
wedigdiablo.org	24.99.0.9	24.99.0.8

Why is this better than the self-join? Because the EXISTS predicate returns as soon as it finds a single match, regardless of how many matches there may be. The performance advantage of the subquery over the self-join will grow linearly as more duplicate name server pairs are added to the table.

As with the self-join, this approach includes rows where the name servers have been reversed. If we didn't want to consider those rows duplicates, we could streamline the query even further, like this:

```
SELECT n.domain, n.ns1, n.ns2
FROM #nameservers n
WHERE EXISTS(SELECT a.ns1, a.ns2 FROM #nameservers a
    WHERE ((a.ns1=n.ns1 AND a.ns2=n.ns2) OR (a.ns1=n.ns2 AND
    a.ns2=n.ns1))
    GROUP BY a.ns1, a.ns2
    HAVING COUNT(*)>1)
ORDER BY 2,3,1
```

```
domain                          ns1             ns2
------------------------------- --------------- ---------------
foolsrus.com                    24.99.0.9       24.99.0.8
wedigdiablo.org                 24.99.0.9       24.99.0.8
```

This query groups its results on the ns1 and ns2 columns and returns only pairs with more than one occurrence. Every pair will have one occurrence—itself. Those with two or more are duplicates of at least one other pair.

Relational Division

An area in which correlated subqueries are indispensable is relational division. In his seminal treatise on relational database theory,[1] Dr. E. F. Codd defined a relational algebra with eight basic operations: union, intersection, set difference, containment, selection, projection, join, and relational division. The last of these, relational division, is the means by which we satisfy such requests as: "Show me the students who have taken every chemistry course" or "List the customers who have purchased at least one of every item in the catalog." In relational division, you divide a dividend table by a divisor table to produce a quotient table. As you might guess, the quotient is what we're after—it's the result table of the query.

This isn't as abstruse as it might seem. Suppose we want to solve the latter of the two requests put forth above—to list the customers who have ordered at least one of every item in the sales catalog. Let's say we begin with two tables: a table listing customer orders and a catalog table. To solve the problem, we can relationally divide the customer orders table by the catalog table to return a quotient of those customers who've purchased every catalog item. And, as in regular algebraic multiplication, we can multiply the divisor table by the quotient table (using a CROSS JOIN) to produce a subset of the dividend table.

This is best explored by way of example. Below is a sample query that performs a relational divide. It makes use of the **customers, orders,** and **items** tables first introduced in Chapter 1. If you still have those tables (they should have been constructed in the GG_TS database), you'll only need to add three rows to **orders** before proceeding:

```
INSERT orders
VALUES(105,'19991111',3,1001,123.45)

INSERT orders
VALUES(106,'19991127',3,1002,678.90)

INSERT orders
VALUES(107,'19990101',1,1003,86753.09)
```

---

[1] Codd, E. F. 1970. "A Relational Model of Data for Large Shared Data Banks." *Communications of the ACM.* New York: Association for Computing Machinery.

See Chapter 1 if you need the full table definitions and the rest of the data.

Once the tables and data are in place, the following query will relationally divide the **customers** and **orders** tables to produce a quotient of the customers who've ordered at least one of every item.

```
SELECT c.LastName,c.FirstName
FROM customers c
WHERE NOT EXISTS (SELECT *
  FROM items i
  WHERE NOT EXISTS
  (SELECT *
  FROM items t JOIN orders o ON (t.ItemNumber=o.ItemNumber)
  WHERE t.ItemNumber=i.ItemNumber AND
    o.CustomerNumber=c.CustomerNumber))
```

```
LastName                        FirstName
------------------------------  ------------------------------
Doe                             John
Citizen                         John
```

This may seem a bit obscure, but it's not as bad as it first appears. Let's examine the query, piece by piece. These kinds of queries are usually best explored from the inside out, so let's start with the innermost subquery. It's correlated with both the **items** table *and* the **customers** table. The number of times it's executed is equal to the number of rows in the **items** table multiplied by the number of rows in the **customers** table. The items query iterates through the **items** table, using the subquery to find items that a) have the same item number as the current row in **items** and b) are included in orders made by the current customer in the **customers** table. Any rows meeting these criteria are discarded (via NOT EXISTS). This leaves only those rows that appear in the **items** table but not in the **orders** table. In other words, these are items that the customer has not yet ordered. The outer query—the SELECT of the **customers** table—then excludes any customer whose items subquery returns rows—that is, any customer with unordered items. The result is a quotient consisting of the customers who've ordered at least one of everything.

If we cheat a little and compare the count of the distinct items ordered by each customer with the total number of items, there are a number of other solutions to the problem. Here's one of them:

```
SELECT c.LastName, c.FirstName
FROM customers c JOIN
(SELECT CustomerNumber, COUNT(DISTINCT ItemNumber) AS NumOfItems
  FROM orders
  GROUP BY CustomerNumber) o
ON (c.CustomerNumber=o.CustomerNumber)
WHERE o.NumOfItems=(SELECT COUNT(*) FROM items)
```

```
LastName                        FirstName
------------------------------  ------------------------------
Doe                             John
Citizen                         John
```

This approach joins the **customers** table with a derived table that returns each customer number and the number of distinct items ordered. This number is then compared via a subquery on the **items** table with the total number of items on file. Those customers with the same number of ordered items as exists in the **items** table are included in the list.

Here's another rendition of the same query:

```
SELECT c.LastName, c.FirstName
FROM customers c
WHERE CustomerNumber IN (SELECT CustomerNumber FROM orders
   GROUP BY CustomerNumber
   HAVING COUNT(DISTINCT ItemNumber)=
     (SELECT COUNT(*) FROM items))
```

```
LastName                        FirstName
----------------------------    ----------------------------
Doe                             John
Citizen                         John
```

This one uses a subquery to form a list of customers whose total number of distinct ordered items is equal to the number of items in the **items** table—those that have ordered at least one of every item. It makes clever use of GROUP BY to coalesce the customer numbers in **orders** to remove duplicates and enable the use of the COUNT() aggregate in the HAVING clause. Note that even though the subquery uses GROUP BY, it doesn't compute any aggregate values. This is legal, both from an ANSI standpoint and, obviously, from a Transact-SQL perspective. The primary purpose of the GROUP BY is to allow the use of the COUNT() aggregate to filter the rows returned by the subquery. HAVING permits direct references to aggregate functions; WHERE doesn't.

Here's an approach that uses a simple join to get the job done:

```
SELECT c.LastName, c.FirstName
FROM customers c JOIN orders o ON (c.CustomerNumber=o.CustomerNumber)
JOIN items i ON (o.ItemNumber=i.ItemNumber)
GROUP BY c.LastName, c.FirstName
HAVING COUNT(DISTINCT o.ItemNumber)=(SELECT COUNT(*) FROM items)
```

```
LastName                        FirstName
----------------------------    ----------------------------
Citizen                         John
Doe                             John
```

This approach joins the **customers** and **orders** tables using their CustomerNumber columns, then pares the result set down to just those customers for whom the total number of distinct ordered items equals the number of rows in the **items** table. Again, this amounts to returning the customers who've ordered at least one of every item in the **items** table.

Aggregate Functions

Aggregate functions summarize the data in a column into a single value. They can summarize all the data for a column or they can reflect a grouped total for that data. Aggregates that summarize based on grouping columns are known as vector aggregates.

SQL Server currently supports eight aggregate functions: COUNT(), SUM(), MIN(), MAX(), STDDEV() (standard deviation), STDDEVP() (population standard deviation), VAR() (variance), and VARP() (population variance). All of these except COUNT() automatically ignore NULL values. When passed a specific column name, COUNT() ignores NULLs as well. Here's an example:

```
CREATE TABLE #testnull (c1 int null)

INSERT #testnull DEFAULT VALUES
INSERT #testnull DEFAULT VALUES

SELECT COUNT(*), COUNT(c1) FROM #testnull

----------- -----------
2           0

Warning: Null value eliminated from aggregate.
```

Each aggregate function can be passed two parameters: either the ALL or DISTINCT keyword specifying whether all values or only unique ones are to be considered (this parameter is optional and defaults to ALL) and the name of the column to aggregate. Here are some examples:

```
SELECT COUNT(DISTINCT title_id) AS TotalTitles
FROM sales
TotalTitles
-----------
17

SELECT stor_id, title_id, SUM(qty) AS TotalSold
FROM sales
GROUP BY stor_id, title_id
ORDER BY stor_id, title_id
```

(Results abridged)

```
stor_id title_id TotalSold
------- -------- -----------
6380    BU1032   5
6380    PS2091   86
7066    PC8888   50
7066    PS2091   75
7067    PS2091   10
```

In the first example, the DISTINCT keyword is included in order to yield a count of the unique **title_id**s within the table. Since the rows in the sales table are representative of individual sales, duplicate **title_id** values will definitely exist. Including the DISTINCT keyword ignores them for the purpose of counting the values in the column. Note that DISTINCT aggregates aren't available when using the CUBE or ROLLUP operators.

The second example produces a vector aggregate using the **stor_id** and **title_id** columns. In other words, the SUM() reported in each row of the result set reflects the total for a specific

stor_id/title_id combination. Since neither ALL nor DISTINCT was specified with the aggregate, all rows within each group are considered during the aggregation.

Thanks to subqueries, aggregate functions can appear almost anywhere in a SELECT statement and can also be used with INSERT, UPDATE, and DELETE. Here's an example that shows aggregate functions being used in the WHERE clause of a SELECT to restrict the rows it returns:

```
SELECT t.title
FROM titles t
WHERE (SELECT COUNT(s.title_id) FROM sales s WHERE s.title_id=t.title_id)>1

title
-------------------------------------------------------------------------------
Is Anger the Enemy?
The Busy Executive's Database Guide
The Gourmet Microwave
```

An aggregate can be referenced in the SELECT list of a query either directly via a column reference (as the earlier examples have shown) or indirectly via a subquery. Here's an example of both types of references:

```
SELECT stor_id, COUNT(DISTINCT title_id) AS titles_sold,
100*CAST(COUNT(DISTINCT title_id) AS float) / (SELECT COUNT(*) FROM titles) AS
percent_of_total
FROM sales
GROUP BY stor_id

stor_id titles_sold TotalSold
------- ----------- -------------------------------------------
6380    2           11.111111111111111
7066    2           11.111111111111111
7067    4           22.222222222222221
7131    6           33.333333333333336
7896    3           16.666666666666668
8042    5           27.777777777777779
```

Here, **COUNT(DISTINCT title_id)** is a direct reference, while **SELECT COUNT(*)** is an indirect one. As with several of the other examples, the first aggregate returns a count of the number of unique titles referenced in the **sales** table. The second aggregate is embedded in a noncorrelated subquery. It returns the total number of titles in the **titles** table so that the query can compute the percentage of the total available titles that each store sells. Naturally, it would be more efficient to store this total in a local variable and reference the variable instead—I've used the subquery here for illustration only.

Aggregates can also appear in the HAVING clause of a query. When a query has a HAVING clause, it's quite common for it to contain aggregates. Here's an example:

```
SELECT stor_id, COUNT(DISTINCT title_id) AS titles_sold,
100*CAST(COUNT(DISTINCT title_id) AS float) / (SELECT COUNT(*) FROM titles) AS
percent_of_total
FROM sales
GROUP BY stor_id
HAVING COUNT(DISTINCT title_id) > 2
```

```
stor_id titles_sold TotalSold
------- ----------- -------------------------------------------
7067    4           22.222222222222221
7131    6           33.333333333333336
7896    3           16.666666666666668
8042    5           27.777777777777779
```

This is just a rehash of the previous query, with a HAVING clause appended to it. HAVING filters the result set in the same way that WHERE filters the SELECT itself. It's common to reference an aggregate value in the HAVING clause since that value was not yet computed or available when WHERE was processed.

GROUP BY and HAVING

Closely related to the aggregate functions are the GROUP BY and HAVING clauses. GROUP BY divides a table into groups, and each group can have its own aggregate values. As I said earlier, HAVING limits the groups returned by GROUP BY.

With the exception of bit, text, ntext, and image columns, any column can participate in the GROUP BY clause. To create groups within groups, simply list more than one column. Here's a simple GROUP BY example:

```
SELECT st.stor_name, t.type, SUM(s.qty) AS TotalSold
FROM sales s JOIN titles t ON (s.title_id=t.title_id)
JOIN stores st ON (s.stor_id=st.stor_id)
GROUP BY st.stor_name, t.type
ORDER BY st.stor_name, t.type
```

```
stor_name                             type         TotalSold
------------------------------------- ------------ -----------
Barnum's                              popular_comp 50
Barnum's                              psychology   75
Bookbeat                              business     65
Bookbeat                              mod_cook     15
Bookbeat                              popular_comp 30
Bookbeat                              UNDECIDED    30
Doc-U-Mat: Quality Laundry and Books  mod_cook     25
Doc-U-Mat: Quality Laundry and Books  psychology   105
Eric the Read Books                   business     5
Eric the Read Books                   psychology   86
Fricative Bookshop                    business     50
Fricative Bookshop                    mod_cook     10
News & Brews                          psychology   10
News & Brews                          trad_cook    80
```

GROUP BY ALL generates all possible groups—even those that do not meet the query's search criteria. Aggregate values in groups that fail the search criteria are returned as NULL. Here's an example:

```
SELECT st.stor_name, t.type, SUM(s.qty) AS TotalSold
FROM sales s JOIN titles t ON (s.title_id=t.title_id)
JOIN stores st ON (s.stor_id=st.stor_id)
WHERE t.type='business'
GROUP BY ALL st.stor_name, t.type
ORDER BY st.stor_name, t.type
```

stor_name	type	TotalSold
Barnum's	popular_comp	NULL
Barnum's	psychology	NULL
Bookbeat	business	65
Bookbeat	mod_cook	NULL
Bookbeat	popular_comp	NULL
Bookbeat	UNDECIDED	NULL
Doc-U-Mat: Quality Laundry and Books	mod_cook	NULL
Doc-U-Mat: Quality Laundry and Books	psychology	NULL
Eric the Read Books	business	5
Eric the Read Books	psychology	NULL
Fricative Bookshop	business	50
Fricative Bookshop	mod_cook	NULL
News & Brews	psychology	NULL
News & Brews	trad_cook	NULL

GROUP BY ALL is incompatible with the ROLLUP and CUBE operators and with remote tables. It's also overridden by HAVING, as you might expect, in the same sense that a plain GROUP BY is overridden by it—HAVING filters what GROUP BY returns.

Notice the ORDER BY clause in the previous example. You can no longer assume that the groups returned by GROUP BY will be sorted in a particular order. This behavior differs from that of SQL Server 6.5 and earlier, so it's something to watch out for. If you require a specific order, use ORDER BY to ensure it.

Though normally used in conjunction with aggregates, GROUP BY and HAVING don't require them. Using GROUP BY without aggregates has the effect of removing duplicates from the data. It has the same effect as prefixing the grouping columns with DISTINCT in the SELECT list, and, in fact, SQL Server treats GROUP BY queries without aggregates and plain SELECTs with DISTINCT identically. This means that the same execution plan will be generated for these two queries:

```
SELECT s.title_id
FROM sales s
GROUP BY s.title_id
```

```
SELECT DISTINCT s.title_id
FROM sales s
```

(To view execution plans in Query Analyzer, press Ctrl-K or select Show Execution Plan from the Query menu before running your query.)

As we discovered in the earlier section on relational division, GROUP BY clauses without aggregate functions have a purpose beyond simulating SELECT DISTINCT queries. Including a GROUP BY clause, even one without aggregates, allows a result set to be filtered based on a direct reference to an aggregate. Unlike the WHERE clause, the HAVING clause can reference an aggregate without encapsulating it in a subquery. One of the relational division examples above uses this fact to qualify the rows returned by a subquery using an aggregate in its HAVING clause.

Pivot Tables

It's pretty common to need to reshape vertically oriented data into horizontally oriented tables suitable for reports and user interfaces. These tables are known as pivot tables or cross-tabulations (cross-tabs) and are an essential feature of any OLAP (Online Analytical Processing), EIS (Executive Information System), or DSS (Decision Support System) application.

SQL Server includes a bevy of OLAP support tools that are outside the scope of this book. Install the OLAP Services from your SQL Server CD, and view the product documentation for more information.

That said, the task of reshaping vertical data is well within the scope of this book and is fairly straightforward in Transact-SQL. Let's assume we start with this table of quarterly sales figures:

```
CREATE TABLE #crosstab (yr int, qtr int, sales money)

INSERT #crosstab VALUES (1999, 1, 44)
INSERT #crosstab VALUES (1999, 2, 50)
INSERT #crosstab VALUES (1999, 3, 52)
INSERT #crosstab VALUES (1999, 4, 49)
INSERT #crosstab VALUES (2000, 1, 50)
INSERT #crosstab VALUES (2000, 2, 51)
INSERT #crosstab VALUES (2000, 3, 48)
INSERT #crosstab VALUES (2000, 4, 45)
INSERT #crosstab VALUES (2001, 1, 46)
INSERT #crosstab VALUES (2001, 2, 53)
INSERT #crosstab VALUES (2001, 3, 54)
INSERT #crosstab VALUES (2001, 4, 47)
```

And let's say that we want to produce a cross-tab consisting of six columns: the year, a column for each quarter, and the total sales for the year. Here's a query to do the job:

```
SELECT
yr AS 'Year',
SUM(CASE qtr WHEN 1 THEN sales ELSE NULL END) AS Q1,
SUM(CASE qtr WHEN 2 THEN sales ELSE NULL END) AS Q2,
SUM(CASE qtr WHEN 3 THEN sales ELSE NULL END) AS Q3,
SUM(CASE qtr WHEN 4 THEN sales ELSE NULL END) AS Q4,
SUM(sales) AS Total
FROM #crosstab
GROUP BY yr
```

Year	Q1	Q2	Q3	Q4	Total
1999	44.0000	50.0000	52.0000	49.0000	195.0000
2000	50.0000	51.0000	48.0000	45.0000	194.0000
2001	46.0000	53.0000	54.0000	47.0000	200.0000

Note that it isn't necessary to total the Q*n* columns to produce the annual total. The query is already grouping on the **yr** column; all it has to do to summarize the annual sales is include a simple aggregate. There's no need for a subquery, derived table, or any other exotic construct, unless, of course, there are sales records that fall outside quarters 1–4, which shouldn't be possible.

The **qtr** column in the sample data made constructing the query fairly easy—almost too easy. In practice, it's pretty rare for time series data to include a quarter column—it's far more common to start with a date for each series member and compute the required temporal dimensions. Here's an example that uses the Orders table in the Northwind database to do just that. It translates the OrderDate column for each order into the appropriate temporal boundary:

```
SELECT
DATEPART(yy,OrderDate) AS 'Year',
COUNT(CASE DATEPART(qq,OrderDate) WHEN 1 THEN 1 ELSE NULL END) AS Q1,
COUNT(CASE DATEPART(qq,OrderDate) WHEN 2 THEN 1 ELSE NULL END) AS Q2,
COUNT(CASE DATEPART(qq,OrderDate) WHEN 3 THEN 1 ELSE NULL END) AS Q3,
COUNT(CASE DATEPART(qq,OrderDate) WHEN 4 THEN 1 ELSE NULL END) AS Q4,
COUNT(*) AS TotalNumberOfSales
FROM Orders
GROUP BY DATEPART(yy,OrderDate)
ORDER BY 1
```

Year	Q1	Q2	Q3	Q4	TotalNumberOfSales
1996	0	0	70	82	152
1997	92	93	103	120	408
1998	182	88	0	0	270

This query returns a count of the orders for each quarter as well as for each year. It uses the DATEPART() function to extract each date element as necessary. As the query iterates through the Orders table, the CASE functions evaluate each OrderDate to determine the quarter "bucket" into which it should go, then return either "1"—the order is counted against that particular quarter—or NULL—the order is ignored.

CUBE and ROLLUP

The GROUP BY clause's CUBE and ROLLUP operators add summary rows to result sets. CUBE produces a multidimensional cube whose dimensions are defined by the columns specified in the GROUP BY clause. This cube is an explosion of the underlying table data and is presented using every possible combination of dimensions.

ROLLUP, by contrast, presents a hierarchical summation of the underlying data. Summary rows are added to the result set based on the hierarchy of grouped columns, from left to right. Here's an example that uses the ROLLUP operator to generate subtotal and total rows:

```
SELECT CASE GROUPING(st.stor_name) WHEN 0 THEN st.stor_name ELSE 'ALL' END AS Store,
CASE GROUPING(t.type) WHEN 0 THEN t.type ELSE 'ALL TYPES' END AS Type,
SUM(s.qty) AS TotalSold
FROM sales s JOIN titles t ON (s.title_id=t.title_id)
JOIN stores st ON (s.stor_id=st.stor_id)
GROUP BY st.stor_name, t.type WITH ROLLUP
```

Store	Type	TotalSold
Barnum's	popular_comp	50
Barnum's	psychology	75
Barnum's	ALL TYPES	125
Bookbeat	business	65
Bookbeat	mod_cook	15
Bookbeat	popular_comp	30
Bookbeat	UNDECIDED	30
Bookbeat	ALL TYPES	140
Doc-U-Mat: Quality Laundry and Books	mod_cook	25
Doc-U-Mat: Quality Laundry and Books	psychology	105
Doc-U-Mat: Quality Laundry and Books	ALL TYPES	130
Eric the Read Books	business	5
Eric the Read Books	psychology	86
Eric the Read Books	ALL TYPES	91
Fricative Bookshop	business	50
Fricative Bookshop	mod_cook	10
Fricative Bookshop	ALL TYPES	60
News & Brews	psychology	10
News & Brews	trad_cook	80
News & Brews	ALL TYPES	90
ALL	ALL TYPES	636

This query has several noteworthy features. First, note the extra rows that ROLLUP inserted into the result set. Since the query groups on the **stor_name** and **type** columns, ROLLUP produces summary rows first for each **stor_name** group (ALL TYPES), then for the entire result set.

The GROUPING() function is used to translate the label assigned to each grouping column. Normally, grouping columns are returned as NULLs. By making use of GROUPING(), the query is able to translate those NULLs to something more meaningful.

Here's that same query again, this time using CUBE:

```
SELECT CASE GROUPING(st.stor_name) WHEN 0 THEN st.stor_name ELSE 'ALL' END AS Store,
CASE GROUPING(t.type) WHEN 0 THEN t.type ELSE 'ALL TYPES' END AS Type,
SUM(s.qty) AS TotalSold
FROM sales s JOIN titles t ON (s.title_id=t.title_id)
JOIN stores st ON (s.stor_id=st.stor_id)
GROUP BY st.stor_name, t.type WITH CUBE
```

Store	Type	TotalSold
Barnum's	popular_comp	50
Barnum's	psychology	75
Barnum's	ALL TYPES	125
Bookbeat	business	65
Bookbeat	mod_cook	15
Bookbeat	popular_comp	30
Bookbeat	UNDECIDED	30
Bookbeat	ALL TYPES	140
Doc-U-Mat: Quality Laundry and Books	mod_cook	25
Doc-U-Mat: Quality Laundry and Books	psychology	105
Doc-U-Mat: Quality Laundry and Books	ALL TYPES	130
Eric the Read Books	business	5

Eric the Read Books	psychology	86
Eric the Read Books	ALL TYPES	91
Fricative Bookshop	business	50
Fricative Bookshop	mod_cook	10
Fricative Bookshop	ALL TYPES	60
News & Brews	psychology	10
News & Brews	trad_cook	80
News & Brews	ALL TYPES	90
ALL	ALL TYPES	636
ALL	business	120
ALL	mod_cook	50
ALL	popular_comp	80
ALL	psychology	276
ALL	trad_cook	80
ALL	UNDECIDED	30

Note the additional rows at the end of the result set. In addition to the summary rows generated by ROLLUP, CUBE creates subtotals for each type of book as well.

Without detailed knowledge of your data, it's nearly impossible to know how many rows will be returned by CUBE. However, computing the upper limit of the number of possible rows is trivial. It's the cross product of the number of unique values +1 for each grouping column. The "+1" is for the ALL summary record generated for each attribute. In this case, there are six distinct stores and six distinct book types in the **sales** table. This means that a maximum of forty-nine rows will be returned in the CUBEd result set (6+1 * 6+1). Here, there are fewer than forty-nine rows because not every store has sold every type of book.

On a related note, you'll notice that CUBE doesn't generate zero subtotals for book types that a particular store hasn't sold. It might be useful to have these totals so that we can see what the store is and isn't selling. Having the full cube creates a result set that is dimensioned more uniformly, making it easier to create reports and charts over it. Here's a full-cube version of the last query:

```
SELECT
CASE GROUPING(st.stor_name) WHEN 0 THEN st.stor_name ELSE 'ALL' END AS Store,
CASE GROUPING(s.type) WHEN 0 THEN s.type ELSE 'ALL TYPES' END AS Type,
SUM(s.qty) AS TotalSold
FROM
    (SELECT DISTINCT st.stor_id, t.type, 0 AS qty
    FROM stores st CROSS JOIN titles t
    UNION ALL
    SELECT s.stor_id, t.type, s.qty FROM sales s JOIN titles t
    ON s.title_id=t.title_id) s
JOIN stores st ON (s.stor_id=st.stor_id)
GROUP BY st.stor_name, s.type WITH CUBE
```

Store	Type	TotalSold
Barnum's	business	0
Barnum's	mod_cook	0
Barnum's	popular_comp	50
Barnum's	psychology	75
Barnum's	trad_cook	0
Barnum's	UNDECIDED	0

Barnum's	ALL TYPES	125
Bookbeat	business	65
Bookbeat	mod_cook	15
Bookbeat	popular_comp	30
Bookbeat	psychology	0
Bookbeat	trad_cook	0
Bookbeat	UNDECIDED	30
Bookbeat	ALL TYPES	140
Doc-U-Mat: Quality Laundry and Books	business	0
Doc-U-Mat: Quality Laundry and Books	mod_cook	25
Doc-U-Mat: Quality Laundry and Books	popular_comp	0
Doc-U-Mat: Quality Laundry and Books	psychology	105
Doc-U-Mat: Quality Laundry and Books	trad_cook	0
Doc-U-Mat: Quality Laundry and Books	UNDECIDED	0
Doc-U-Mat: Quality Laundry and Books	ALL TYPES	130
Eric the Read Books	business	5
Eric the Read Books	mod_cook	0
Eric the Read Books	popular_comp	0
Eric the Read Books	psychology	86
Eric the Read Books	trad_cook	0
Eric the Read Books	UNDECIDED	0
Eric the Read Books	ALL TYPES	91
Fricative Bookshop	business	50
Fricative Bookshop	mod_cook	10
Fricative Bookshop	popular_comp	0
Fricative Bookshop	psychology	0
Fricative Bookshop	trad_cook	0
Fricative Bookshop	UNDECIDED	0
Fricative Bookshop	ALL TYPES	60
News & Brews	business	0
News & Brews	mod_cook	0
News & Brews	popular_comp	0
News & Brews	psychology	10
News & Brews	trad_cook	80
News & Brews	UNDECIDED	0
News & Brews	ALL TYPES	90
ALL	ALL TYPES	636
ALL	business	120
ALL	mod_cook	50
ALL	popular_comp	80
ALL	psychology	276
ALL	trad_cook	80
ALL	UNDECIDED	30

This query begins by creating a zero-value table of stores and book types by multiplying the stores in the stores table by the book types in the titles table using a CROSS JOIN. It then UNIONs this set with the sales table to produce a composite that includes the sales records for each store, as well as a zero value for each store–book type combo. This is then fed into the outer grouping query as a derived table. The outer query then groups and summarizes as necessary to produce the result set. Note that there are forty-nine rows in the final result set—exactly the number we predicted earlier.

There are a few caveats and limitations related to CUBE and ROLLUP of which you should be aware:

- Both operators are limited to ten dimensions.

- Both preclude the generation of DISTINCT aggregates.

- CUBE can produce huge result sets. These can take a long time to generate and can cause problems with application programs not designed to handle them.

HAVING

As I said earlier, HAVING restricts the rows returned by GROUP BY similarly to the way that WHERE restricts those returned by SELECT. It is processed after the rows are collected from the underlying table(s) and is therefore less efficient for garden-variety row selection than WHERE. In fact, behind the scenes, SQL Server implicitly converts a HAVING that would be more efficiently stated as a WHERE clause automatically. This means that the execution plans generated for the following queries are identical:

```
SELECT title_id
FROM titles
WHERE type='business'
GROUP BY title_id, type

SELECT title_id
FROM titles
GROUP BY title_id, type
HAVING type='business'
```

In the second query, HAVING doesn't do anything that WHERE couldn't do, so SQL Server converts it to a WHERE during query execution so that the number of rows processed by GROUP BY is as small as possible.

UNION

The UNION operator allows you to combine the results of two queries into a single result set. We've used UNION throughout this chapter to combine the results of various queries. UNIONs aren't complicated, but there are a few simple rules you should keep in mind when using them:

- Each query listed as a UNION term must have the same number of columns and must list them in the same order as the other queries.

- The columns returned by each SELECT must be assignment compatible or be explicitly converted to a data type that's assignment compatible with their corresponding columns in the other SELECTs.

- Combining columns that are assignment compatible but of different types produces a column with the higher type precedence of the two (e.g., combining a **smallint** and a **float** results in a **float** result column).

- The column names returned by the UNION are derived from those of the first SELECT.

- UNION ALL is faster than UNION because it doesn't remove duplicates before returning. Removing duplicates may force the server to sort the data, an expensive proposition, especially with large tables. If you aren't concerned about duplicates, use UNION ALL instead of UNION.

Here's an example of a simple UNION:

```
SELECT title_id, type
FROM titles
WHERE type='business'
UNION ALL
SELECT title_id, type
FROM titles
WHERE type='mod_cook'


title_id type
-------- ------------
BU1032    business
BU1111    business
BU2075    business
BU7832    business
MC2222    mod_cook
MC3021    mod_cook
```

This query UNIONs two separate segments of the **titles** table based on the **type** field. Since the query used UNION ALL, no sorting of the elements occurs.

As illustrated earlier in the chapter, one of the niftier features of UNION is the ability to use derived tables to create a virtual table on the fly during a query. This is handy for creating lookup tables and other types of tabular constructs that don't merit permanent storage. Here's an example:

```
SELECT title_id AS Title_ID, t.type AS Type, b.typecode AS TypeCode
FROM titles t JOIN
(SELECT 'business' AS type, 0 AS typecode
UNION ALL
SELECT 'mod_cook' AS type, 1 AS typecode
UNION ALL
SELECT 'popular_comp' AS type, 2 AS typecode
UNION ALL
SELECT 'psychology' AS type, 3 AS typecode
UNION ALL
SELECT 'trad_cook' AS type, 4 AS typecode
UNION ALL
```

```
SELECT 'UNDECIDED' AS type, 5 AS typecode) b
ON (t.type = b.type)
ORDER BY TypeCode, Title_ID
```

Title_ID	Type	TypeCode
BU1032	business	0
BU1111	business	0
BU2075	business	0
BU7832	business	0
MC2222	mod_cook	1
MC3021	mod_cook	1
PC1035	popular_comp	2
PC8888	popular_comp	2
PC9999	popular_comp	2
PS1372	psychology	3
PS2091	psychology	3
PS2106	psychology	3
PS3333	psychology	3
PS7777	psychology	3
TC3218	trad_cook	4
TC4203	trad_cook	4
TC7777	trad_cook	4
MC3026	UNDECIDED	5

The query uses Transact-SQL's ability to produce a result set without referencing a database object to construct a virtual table from a series of UNIONed SELECT statements. In this case, we use it to translate the **type** field in the **titles** table into a code. Of course, a CASE statement would be much more efficient here—we've taken the virtual table approach for purposes of illustration only.

ORDER BY

The ORDER BY clause is used to sort the data in a result set. When possible, the query optimizer will use an index to service the sort request. When this is impossible or deemed suboptimal by the optimizer, a work table is constructed to perform the sort. With large tables, this can take a while and can run tempdb out of space if it's not sized sufficiently large. This is why you shouldn't order result sets unless you actually need a specific row order—doing so wastes server resources. On the other hand, if you need a fixed sort order, be sure to include an ORDER BY clause. You can no longer rely on clauses such as GROUP BY and UNION to produce useful row ordering. This represents a departure from previous releases of SQL Server (6.5 and earlier), so watch out for it. Queries that rely on a specific row ordering without using ORDER BY may not work as expected.

Columns can be referenced in an ORDER BY clause in one of three ways: by name, by column alias, or by result set column number. Here's an example:

```
SELECT stor_id AS store, title_id AS title, qty AS sales FROM sales s
ORDER BY stor_id, 2, sales
```

```
store title  sales
----- ------ ------
6380  BU1032 5
6380  PS2091 3
6380  PS2091 30
6380  PS2091 53
7066  PC8888 50
7066  PS2091 75
7067  PS2091 10
7067  TC3218 40
7067  TC4203 20
7067  TC7777 20
7131  MC3021 25
7131  PS1372 20
7131  PS2091 20
7131  PS2106 25
7131  PS3333 15
7131  PS7777 25
7896  BU2075 35
7896  BU7832 15
7896  MC2222 10
8042  BU1032 10
8042  BU1032 30
8042  BU1111 25
8042  MC3021 15
8042  MC3026 30
8042  PC1035 30
```

This query orders the result set using all three methods, which is probably not a good idea within a single query. As with a lot of multiflavored coding techniques, there's nothing wrong with it syntactically, but doing something three different ways when one will do, needlessly obfuscates your code. Remember the law of parsimony (a.k.a. Ockham's razor)—one should neither assume nor promote the existence of more elements than are logically necessary to solve a problem.

This doesn't mean that you might not use each of these techniques at different times. The ability to reference result set columns by number is a nice shorthand way of doing so. (That said, ordering by column numbers has been deprecated in recent years, so it's advisable to name your columns and sort using column aliases instead.) Being able to use column aliases alleviates the need to repeat complex expressions in the ORDER BY clause, and referencing table columns directly allows you to order by items not in the SELECT list.

You can also include subqueries and constants in the ORDER BY clause, though this is pretty rare. Subqueries contained in the ORDER BY clause can be correlated or stand-alone.

Each column in the ORDER BY list can be optionally followed by the DESC or ASC keyword in order to sort in descending or ascending (the default) order. Here's an example:

```
SELECT st.stor_name AS Store, t.type AS Type, SUM(qty) AS Sales
FROM stores st JOIN sales s ON (st.stor_id=s.stor_id)
JOIN titles t ON (s.title_id=t.title_id)
GROUP BY st.stor_name, t.type
ORDER BY Store DESC, Type ASC
```

Store	Type	Sales
News & Brews	psychology	10
News & Brews	trad_cook	80
Fricative Bookshop	business	50
Fricative Bookshop	mod_cook	10
Eric the Read Books	business	5
Eric the Read Books	psychology	86
Doc-U-Mat: Quality Laundry and Books	mod_cook	25
Doc-U-Mat: Quality Laundry and Books	psychology	105
Bookbeat	business	65
Bookbeat	mod_cook	15
Bookbeat	popular_comp	30
Bookbeat	UNDECIDED	30
Barnum's	popular_comp	50
Barnum's	psychology	75

A few things to keep in mind regarding ORDER BY:

- You can't use ORDER BY in views, derived tables, or subqueries without also using the TOP *n* extension (see the section on TOP *n* earlier in this chapter for more information). A technique for working around this is to include a TOP 100 percent clause effectively retrieving the entire table.

- You can't sort on text, ntext, or image columns.

- If your query is a SELECT DISTINCT or combines result sets via UNION, the columns listed in the ORDER BY clause must appear in the SELECT list.

- If the SELECT includes the UNION operator, the column names and aliases you can use are limited to those of the first table in the UNION.

Summary

In this chapter, you explored the ubiquitous, omnipotent Transact-SQL SELECT statement. Mastering it is essential to becoming an adroit Transact-SQL programmer. SELECT is powerful, but that power comes at a price: complexity. While SELECT statements can be very brief and concise, they are often extremely complex in real applications.

Views

Where is the information?
Lost in the data.
Where is the data?
Lost in the #@%!& database!—Joe Celko

VIEWs are static queries that you can use as though they were tables. A VIEW consists of a SELECT statement compiled ahead of time using SQL's CREATE VIEW command and referenced in the same manner as a table. VIEW columns can consist of table columns, aggregates, constants, and expressions (computed columns). Some VIEWs are updatable; some aren't. Whether a VIEW is updatable depends largely on whether SQL Server can resolve an update to one of its rows to a single row in an underlying base table. All VIEWs must eventually reference a base table or nontabular expression (an expression that doesn't require a table—GETDATE(), for example), though VIEWs can be "nested"—meaning that a VIEW can reference other VIEWs as long as the dependence tree eventually resolves to base tables or nontabular expressions.

Restrictions

Transact-SQL doesn't support temporary VIEWs, though you can create static VIEWs in tempdb and achieve a similar effect. Also, VIEWs aren't allowed to reference temporary tables—only references to other VIEWs or permanent base tables are permitted.

As a rule, ORDER BY is not allowed in VIEWs, so the following syntax is not valid:

```
-- _Not_ valid Transact-SQL syntax
CREATE VIEW myauthors AS
SELECT * FROM authors
ORDER BY au_lname
```

There is, however, a workaround. You can use Transact-SQL's TOP 100 percent extension to allow ORDER BY in VIEWs, like this:

```
CREATE VIEW myauthors AS
SELECT TOP 100 percent *
FROM authors
ORDER BY au_lname
```

TOP 100 percent allows the use of ORDER BY within a VIEW by permitting you to request the entire table. The query below shows that the ORDER BY is in effect when we query the view:

```
SELECT au_id, au_lname, au_fname
FROM myauthors
```

au_id	au_lname	au_fname
409-56-7008	Bennet	Abraham
648-92-1872	Blotchet-Halls	Reginald
238-95-7766	Carson	Cheryl
722-51-5454	DeFrance	Michel
712-45-1867	del Castillo	Innes
427-17-2319	Dull	Ann
213-46-8915	Green	Marjorie
527-72-3246	Greene	Morningstar
472-27-2349	Gringlesby	Burt
846-92-7186	Hunter	Sheryl
756-30-7391	Karsen	Livia
486-29-1786	Locksley	Charlene
724-80-9391	MacFeather	Stearns
893-72-1158	McBadden	Heather
267-41-2394	O'Leary	Michael
807-91-6654	Panteley	Sylvia
998-72-3567	Ringer	Albert
899-46-2035	Ringer	Anne
341-22-1782	Smith	Meander
274-80-9391	Straight	Dean
724-08-9931	Stringer	Dirk
172-32-1176	White	Johnson
672-71-3249	Yokomoto	Akiko

As with stored procedures, the status of SET QUOTED_IDENTIFIER and SET ANSI_NULLS is saved with each VIEW. This means that individual session settings for these options are ignored by the VIEW when it's queried. It also means that you can localize special quoted identifier or NULL handling to a particular VIEW without affecting anything else.

DML Restrictions

An UPDATE to a VIEW is not allowed to affect more than one underlying base table at a time. If the VIEW joins two or more tables together, an UPDATE to it may alter only one of them. Likewise, an INSERT must modify only one table at a time in a multitable VIEW. This means that values can be supplied for only one table—the columns in the other table(s) must have DEFAULT constraints, allow NULLs, or otherwise be optional. DELETE can be used only with single-table VIEWs—it can't be used with multitable VIEWs of any kind.

ANSI SQL Schema VIEWs

Out of the box, SQL Server provides a number of VIEWs for accessing the system catalogs. These objects provide an ANSI SQL-92–compliant means of retrieving meta-data and otherwise querying the server for system-level information. You should use these rather than querying system catalog tables directly for two reasons: 1) the ANSI SQL-92 specification defines these VIEWs—so they should work similarly between different DBMS platforms, and 2) you can depend on them to work the same way between different releases of SQL Server, even though their underlying system tables may change from release to release. Table 7.1 lists the SQL-92–compliant VIEWs that SQL Server provides:

Table 7.1. SQL Server's ANSI SQL-92 schema VIEWs.

VIEW Name
CHECK_CONSTRAINTS
COLUMN_DOMAIN_USAGE
COLUMN_PRIVILEGES
COLUMNS
CONSTRAINT_COLUMN_USAGE
CONSTRAINT_TABLE_USAGE
DOMAIN_CONSTRAINTS
DOMAINS
KEY_COLUMN_USAGE
REFERENTIAL_CONSTRAINTS
SCHEMATA
TABLE_CONSTRAINTS
TABLES
VIEW_COLUMN_USAGE
VIEW_TABLE_USAGE
VIEWS

Note that you must refer to these objects using the INFORMATION_SCHEMA database schema. In SQL Server parlance, a schema and an owner are synonymous. This means that you must use:

```
SELECT * FROM INFORMATION_SCHEMA.TABLES
```

rather than:

```
SELECT * FROM TABLES
```

Getting a VIEW's Source Code

Unless a VIEW was created using the WITH ENCRYPTION option, you can use sp_helptext to retrieve its source code. You can also inspect and modify VIEW source code in Enterprise Manager, as well as many SQL-DMO–enabled administration tools. Here's some sample code that returns the source of the syslogins system VIEW:

```
USE master
exec sp_helptext syslogins

Text
--------------------------------------------------------------------------
CREATE VIEW syslogins AS SELECT
   suid = convert(smallint, suser_id(name)),
   sid = convert(varbinary(85), sid),
   status = convert(smallint, 8 +
        CASE WHEN (xstatus & 2)=0 THEN 1 ELSE 2 END),
     createdate = convert(datetime, xdate1),
     updatedate = convert(datetime, xdate2),
   accdate = convert(datetime, xdate1),
   totcpu = convert(int, 0),
   totio = convert(int, 0),
   spacelimit = convert(int, 0),
   timelimit = convert(int, 0),
   resultlimit = convert(int, 0),
   name = convert(varchar(30), CASE WHEN (xstatus&4)=0 THEN name
        ELSE suser_name(suser_id(name)) END),
   dbname = convert(sysname, db_name(dbid)),
   password = convert(sysname, password),
   language = convert(sysname, language),
   denylogin = convert(int, CASE WHEN (xstatus&1)=1 THEN 1 ELSE 0 END),
   hasaccess = convert(int, CASE WHEN (xstatus&2)=2 THEN 1 ELSE 0 END),
   isntname = convert(int, CASE WHEN (xstatus&4)=4 THEN 1 ELSE 0 END),
   isntgroup = convert(int, CASE WHEN (xstatus&12)=4 THEN 1 ELSE 0 END),
   isntuser = convert(int, CASE WHEN (xstatus&12)=12 THEN 1 ELSE 0 END),
   sysadmin = convert(int, CASE WHEN (xstatus&16)=16 THEN 1 ELSE 0 END),
   securityadmin = convert(int, CASE WHEN (xstatus&32)=32 THEN 1 ELSE 0 END),
   serveradmin = convert(int, CASE WHEN (xstatus&64)=64 THEN 1 ELSE 0 END),
   setupadmin = convert(int, CASE WHEN (xstatus&128)=128 THEN 1 ELSE 0 END),
   processadmin = convert(int, CASE WHEN (xstatus&256)=256 THEN 1 ELSE 0 END),
   diskadmin = convert(int, CASE WHEN (xstatus&512)=512 THEN 1 ELSE 0 END),
   dbcreator = convert(int, CASE WHEN (xstatus&1024)=1024 THEN 1 ELSE 0 END),
   loginname = convert(sysname, name)
FROM sysxlogins WHERE srvid IS NULL
```

Updatable VIEWs

As mentioned earlier, there are a number of factors affecting whether a VIEW is updatable. For a VIEW to allow updates, the following criteria must be met:

- Aggregate functions, the TOP, GROUP BY, UNION, or DISTINCT clauses or key-words are not allowed.

- Derived columns (columns constructed from complex expressions) are not updatable.

- SELECT lists consisting entirely of nontabular expressions are not allowed.

Again, the bottom line is that the server must be able to translate an update to a row in the VIEW into an update to a row in a base table. If it can't do this, you can't update the VIEW.

WITH CHECK OPTION

An updatable VIEW can be created so that it checks updates for compliance with its WHERE clause, if it has one. This prevents rows added via the VIEW from "vanishing" when the VIEW is requeried since they don't meet its selection criteria. To set up a VIEW this way, use the WITH CHECK OPTION clause when you create it, like so:

```
CREATE VIEW CALIFORNIA_AUTHORS AS
SELECT *
FROM authors
WHERE State='CA'
WITH CHECK OPTION
```

This particular example ensures that any author that's added via the VIEW resides in California. For example, this statement fails because of WITH CHECK OPTION:

```
INSERT CALIFORNIA_AUTHORS
VALUES ('867-53-09EI','Henderson','Ken',
'972 555-1212','57 Riverside','Dallas','TX','75080',1)

Server: Msg 550, Level 16, State 1, Line 1
The attempted insert or update failed because the target VIEW either specifies
WITH CHECK OPTION or spans a VIEW that specifies WITH CHECK OPTION and one or more
rows resulting from the operation did not qualify under the CHECK OPTION
constraint.
The statement has been terminated.
```

This also applies to updates. If an update you make through a VIEW that has WITH CHECK OPTION enabled would cause the row to fail the VIEW's WHERE criteria, the update will be rejected.

Derived Tables

As mentioned in Chapter 6, derived tables are SELECT statements that you embed within the FROM clause of other SELECTs in place of table references. I include coverage of them here for completeness and because they resemble implicit or automatic VIEWs. Derived tables make possible certain types of queries that previously required separate VIEW objects. Here's an example:

```
CREATE TABLE #1996_POP_ESTIMATE (Region char(7), State char(2), Population int)

INSERT #1996_POP_ESTIMATE VALUES ('West',    'CA',31878234)
INSERT #1996_POP_ESTIMATE VALUES ('South',   'TX',19128261)
INSERT #1996_POP_ESTIMATE VALUES ('North',   'NY',18184774)
INSERT #1996_POP_ESTIMATE VALUES ('South',   'FL',14399985)
INSERT #1996_POP_ESTIMATE VALUES ('North',   'NJ', 7987933)
INSERT #1996_POP_ESTIMATE VALUES ('East',    'NC', 7322870)
INSERT #1996_POP_ESTIMATE VALUES ('West',    'WA', 5532939)
INSERT #1996_POP_ESTIMATE VALUES ('Central','MO', 5358692)
INSERT #1996_POP_ESTIMATE VALUES ('East',    'MD', 5071604)
INSERT #1996_POP_ESTIMATE VALUES ('Central','OK', 3300902)

SELECT * FROM (SELECT TOP 5 WITH TIES State,
   Region, Population=Population/1000000
   FROM #1996_POP_ESTIMATE
   ORDER BY Population/1000000) p
ORDER BY Population DESC

State Region  Population
----- ------- -----------
NJ    North   7
NC    East    7
WA    West    5
MO    Central 5
MD    East    5
OK    Central 3
```

This query uses a derived table to return the five states with the lowest population among those listed in the table. It then uses an ORDER BY in the outer SELECT to sort these in descending order. Were it not for derived table support, this approach would require a separate stand-alone VIEW or a temporary table.

One subtlety worth mentioning here is the requirement for a table alias when using derived tables. Note the inclusion of the table alias in the code sample above even though it's not used. This is a requirement of derived tables, regardless of whether your code actually uses the alias.

Dynamic VIEWs

When you access a VIEW, a query plan is constructed by combining the original SELECT statement that was used to create the VIEW with the one you're using to query it. The selection criteria you specified when you built the VIEW are combined with any specified by your query and the composite is passed on to the server engine for further processing.

Most VIEWs that include selection criteria impose static criteria—the selection logic that's combined with the SELECT accessing the VIEW never changes regardless of how many times the VIEW is queried. The dynamic portion of the composite query usually comes from the user-supplied SELECT, not the VIEW. With the exception of VIEWs that use joins to link other VIEWs and tables, the criteria the VIEW supplies to filter the result set remains the same from use to use. Most of the time this is adequate, but there are times when it's handy to be able to make use of a dynamic VIEW—a VIEW whose selection criteria varies based on factors external to it.

A dynamic VIEW is simply one whose selection criteria can change based on the evaluation of the expressions in its WHERE or HAVING clauses. This is an easy concept that can come in quite handy. Rather than evaluating to constants, these expressions return different values based on environmental or session elements. The best example of such a VIEW is one that returns a result set based on a nontabular expression. Here's one that lists the sales for the current date, using the nontabular GETDATE() function:

```
CREATE VIEW DAILY_SALES AS
SELECT *
FROM sales
WHERE ord_date BETWEEN CONVERT(char(8),GETDATE(),112) AND
CONVERT(char(8),GETDATE(),112)+' 23:59:59.999'
```

You can add some rows to **sales** to see how this works:

```
INSERT sales
VALUES ('8042','QA879.1',GETDATE(),30,'Net 30','BU1032')
INSERT sales
VALUES ('6380','D4482',GETDATE(),11,'Net 60','PS2091')
INSERT sales
VALUES ('6380','D4492',GETDATE()+1,53,'Net 30','PS2091')
```

```
SELECT * FROM DAILY_SALES
```

stor_id	ord_num	ord_date	qty	payterms	title_id
6380	D4482	1999-06-24 19:14:33.657	30	Net 60	PS2091
8042	QA879.1	1999-06-24 19:13:26.230	30	Net 30	BU1032

This VIEW uses GETDATE() to limit the sales returned to those whose ord_date is today. The criteria actually processed by the server will vary based on the current date. Today, its WHERE clause will be expanded to today's date, and the first two rows that were inserted will show up. Tomorrow, it will evaluate to tomorrow's date, and the third row will show up. That's the nature of dynamic VIEWs—the criteria that are actually processed by the server change from use to use based on external factors.

Here's another example that uses CASE to make the VIEW even more dynamic. This code improves on the previous example by making it aware of weekends. Since no sales occur on weekends, this code returns the sales for either the previous Friday or the upcoming Monday when the current date falls on a weekend:

```
CREATE VIEW DAILY_SALES AS
SELECT *
FROM sales
WHERE ord_date BETWEEN
    (CASE DATEPART(DW,CONVERT(char(8),GETDATE(),112))
    WHEN 1 THEN CONVERT(char(8),GETDATE()+1,112)
    WHEN 7 THEN CONVERT(char(8),GETDATE()-1,112)
    ELSE CONVERT(char(8),GETDATE(),112)
    END)
```

```
AND  (CASE DATEPART(DW,CONVERT(char(8),GETDATE(),112))
   WHEN 1 THEN CONVERT(char(8),GETDATE()+1,112)
   WHEN 7 THEN CONVERT(char(8),GETDATE()-1,112)
   ELSE CONVERT(char(8),GETDATE(),112)
   END+' 23:59:59.999')
```

You can use other nontabular functions to create similar sliding or dynamic VIEWs. For example, SUSER_SNAME() could be used to limit the rows returned according to user name. HOST_NAME() could be used to filter based on machine name. Whatever the case, the SELECT used to query the VIEW doesn't change (in the examples above, it's always a simple **SELECT ***); only the criteria that the VIEW provides to filter the result set do.

Partitioning Data Using Views

Views are a handy mechanism for partitioning data into subsets. This partitioning can be either horizontal or vertical in nature or both. It can hide columns from inspection by unauthorized users and can group rows logically based on some predetermined criteria. Here's an example of a vertically partitioned table:

```
USE Northwind
GO
IF (OBJECT_ID('EMP_VIEW') IS NOT NULL)
   DROP VIEW EMP_VIEW
GO
CREATE VIEW EMP_VIEW AS
SELECT LastName,
       FirstName,
       Title,
       Extension
FROM employees
GO

SELECT * FROM EMP_VIEW
```

LastName	FirstName	Title	Extension
Davolio	Nancy	Sales Representative	5467
Fuller	Andrew	Vice President, Sales	3457
Leverling	Janet	Sales Representative	3355
Peacock	Margaret	Sales Representative	5176
Buchanan	Steven	Sales Manager	3453
Suyama	Michael	Sales Representative	428
King	Robert	Sales Representative	465
Callahan	Laura	Inside Sales Coordinator	2344
Dodsworth	Anne	Sales Representative	452

In this example, personal information such as the employee's home phone number and birth date is omitted from the view in order to provide a basic employee listing. Here's an example of horizontal partitioning:

```
USE Northwind
GO
IF (OBJECT_ID('USA_ORDERS') IS NOT NULL)
   DROP VIEW USA_ORDERS
GO
IF (OBJECT_ID('UK_ORDERS') IS NOT NULL)
   DROP VIEW UK_ORDERS
GO
IF (OBJECT_ID('FRENCH_ORDERS') IS NOT NULL)
   DROP VIEW FRENCH_ORDERS
GO
CREATE VIEW USA_ORDERS AS
SELECT TOP 10 EmployeeID, COUNT(*) AS NumOrdered
FROM orders
WHERE ShipCountry='USA'
GROUP BY EmployeeID
ORDER BY NumOrdered DESC
GO
CREATE VIEW UK_ORDERS AS
SELECT TOP 10 EmployeeID, COUNT(*) AS NumOrdered
FROM orders
WHERE ShipCountry='UK'
GROUP BY EmployeeID
ORDER BY NumOrdered DESC
GO
CREATE VIEW FRENCH_ORDERS AS
SELECT TOP 10 EmployeeID, COUNT(*) AS NumOrdered
FROM orders
WHERE ShipCountry='France'
GROUP BY EmployeeID
ORDER BY NumOrdered DESC
GO

PRINT 'USA ORDERS'
SELECT * FROM USA_ORDERS
GO
PRINT 'UK ORDERS'
SELECT * FROM UK_ORDERS
GO
PRINT 'FRENCH ORDERS'
SELECT * FROM FRENCH_ORDERS
GO
```

(Results)

```
USA ORDERS
EmployeeID  NumOrdered
----------  -----------
4           22
1           21
3           21
8           19
6           14
2           9
7           7
```

```
5              6
9              3
```

```
UK ORDERS
EmployeeID  NumOrdered
----------- -----------
4           12
1           9
3           8
8           6
2           5
6           5
7           5
9           4
5           2
```

```
FRENCH ORDERS
EmployeeID  NumOrdered
----------- -----------
4           14
3           13
2           11
1           9
6           9
8           8
5           5
7           5
9           3
```

Summary

You learned about VIEW objects in this chapter. VIEWs offer a powerful means of presenting data in formats that differ from the way in which it's stored in the database. They also offer an alternative to constraints and triggers for controlling data insertions and updates. SQL Server itself uses views extensively, and it's likely that you will as well if you build sophisticated applications using Transact-SQL.

8

Statistical Functions

Statistics are like a bikini. What they reveal
is suggestive, but what they conceal is vital.
—Aaron Levenstein

There's a common misconception by many developers—advanced and beginner alike—that SQL Server is unsuitable for performing complex computations. The perception is that it's really just a data retrieval facility—it's superb at storing and querying data, but any heavy calculation work must be performed in a 3GL of some sort. Though data management and retrieval are certainly its strong suit, SQL Server can perform complex calculations as well, including statistical calculations. If you know what you're doing, there are very few statistical computations beyond the reach of basic Transact-SQL.

Capabilities notwithstanding, on the surface, SQL Server may seem like an odd tool to use to compute complex statistical numbers. Just because a tool is capable of performing a task doesn't mean that it's the best choice for doing so. After all, SQL Server is a database server, right? It's an inferior choice for performing high-level mathematical operations and complex expression evaluation, right? Wrong. Transact-SQL's built-in support for statistical functions together with its orientation toward sets makes it quite adept at performing statistical computations over data stored in SQL Server databases. These two things—statistical functions and set orientation—give Transact-SQL an edge over many 3GL programming languages. Statistics need data, so what better place to extrapolate statistics from raw data than from the server storing it? If the supermarket has all the items you need at the right price, why drive all over town to get them?

Notice that I didn't mention anything about calling external functions written in traditional programming languages such as C++. You shouldn't have to resort to external functions to calculate most statistics in Transact-SQL. What Transact-SQL lacks as a programming language, it compensates for as a data language. Its orientation toward sets and its ease of working with them yield a surprising amount of computational power with a minimum of effort, as the examples later in this chapter illustrate.

Another item I've left out of the discussion is the use of stored procedures to perform complex calculations. If you ask most SQL developers how to calculate the statistical median of a column in a SQL Server table, they'll tell you that you need a stored procedure. This procedure would likely open a cursor of some sort to locate the column's middle value. While this would certainly work, it isn't necessary. As this chapter will show, you don't need stored procedures to compute most statistical values, normal SELECTs will do just fine. Iterating through tables using traditional looping techniques is an "un-SQL" approach to problem solving and is something you should avoid when possible (See Chapter 13, "Cursors," for more information). Use Transact-SQL's strengths to make your life easier, don't try to make it something it isn't. Attempting to make Transact-SQL behave like a 3GL is a mistake—it's not a 3GL. Doing this would be just as dubious and fraught with difficulty as trying to make a 3GL behave like a data language. Forcing one type of tool to behave like another is like forcing the proverbial square peg into a round hole—it probably won't work and will probably lead to little more than an acute case of frustration.

One thing to keep in mind when performing complex mathematical calculations with Transact-SQL is that SQL, as a language, does not handle floating point rounding errors. Naturally, this affects the numbers produced by queries. It can make the same query return different results based solely on the order of the data. The answer is to use fixed point types such as decimal and numeric rather than floating point types such as float and real. See the section "Floating Point Fun" in Chapter 2 for more information.

The Case for CASE

Its clunky language syntax notwithstanding, CASE is an extremely powerful weapon in the Transact-SQL arsenal. It allows us to perform complex calculations during SELECT statements that previously were the exclusive domain of arcane functions and stored procedures. Some of these solutions rely on a somewhat esoteric technique of coding Transact-SQL expressions such that the number of passes through a table is greatly reduced. This, in turn, yields better performance and code that is usually more compact than traditional coding techniques. This is best explained by way of example. Let's look at a function-based solution that creates a cross-tabulation or "pivot" table.

Assuming we have this table and data to begin with:

```
CREATE TABLE #YEARLY_SALES
(SalesYear smalldatetime,
 Sales money)
INSERT #YEARLY_SALES VALUES ('19990101',86753.09)
INSERT #YEARLY_SALES VALUES ('20000101',34231.12)
INSERT #YEARLY_SALES VALUES ('20010101',67983.56)
```

here's what a function-based pivot query would look like:

```
SELECT
   "1999"=SUM(Sales*(1-ABS(SIGN(YEAR(SalesYear)-1999)))),
   "2000"=SUM(Sales*(1-ABS(SIGN(YEAR(SalesYear)-2000)))),
   "2001"=SUM(Sales*(1-ABS(SIGN(YEAR(SalesYear)-2001))))
FROM #YEARLY_SALES
```

1999	2000	2001
86753.0900	34231.1200	67983.5600

Note the inclusion of the rarely used ABS() and SIGN() functions. This is typical of function-based solutions and is what makes them so abstruse. The term "characteristic function" was first developed by David Rozenshtein, Anatoly Abramovich, and Eugene Birger in a series of articles for the SQL Forum publication several years ago to describe such solutions. The characteristic function above is considered a "point characteristic function" for the Sales-Year column. Each instance of it returns a one when the year portion of SalesYear equals the desired year and a zero otherwise. This one or zero is then multiplied by the Sales value in each row to produce either the sales figure for that year or zero. The end result is that each column includes just the sales number for the year mentioned in the expression—exactly what we want.

Understanding how a characteristic function works within the context of a particular query requires mentally translating characteristic formulae to their logical equivalents. When characteristic functions were first "discovered," tables were published to help SQL developers through the onerous task of doing this. This translation is necessary because the problems being solved rarely lend themselves intuitively to the solutions being used. That is, pivoting a table has nothing to do with the ABS() and SIGN() functions. This is where CASE comes in.

With the advent of SQL-92 and CASE, the need for odd expressions like these to build complex inline logic has all but vanished. Instead, you should use CASE whenever possible in place of characteristic functions. CASE is easier to read, is easier to extend, and requires no mental translation to and from arcane expression tables. For example, here's the pivot query rewritten to use CASE:

```
SELECT
    "1999"=SUM(CASE WHEN YEAR(SalesYear)=1999 THEN Sales ELSE NULL END),
    "2000"=SUM(CASE WHEN YEAR(SalesYear)=2000 THEN Sales ELSE NULL END),
    "2001"=SUM(CASE WHEN YEAR(SalesYear)=2001 THEN Sales ELSE NULL END)
FROM #YEARLY_SALES
```

1999	2000	2001
86753.0900	34231.1200	67983.5600

It's vastly clearer and easier to understand than the earlier method involving SIGN() and ABS(). I also find it easier to read than:

```
SELECT
    "1999"=SUM(CASE YEAR(SalesYear) WHEN 1999 THEN Sales ELSE NULL END),
    "2000"=SUM(CASE YEAR(SalesYear) WHEN 2000 THEN Sales ELSE NULL END),
    "2001"=SUM(CASE YEAR(SalesYear) WHEN 2001 THEN Sales ELSE NULL END)
FROM #YEARLY_SALES
```

Though this solution still represents a vast improvement over the SIGN()/ABS() approach, I prefer the searched CASE approach simply because the relationship between "1999" and YEAR(SalesYear) is more explicit in the searched CASE syntax, though I'd concede that this is really a matter of preference.

Efficiency Concerns

You'll notice the liberal use of self-joins in the examples in this chapter. Techniques that involve self-joins over large tables should be viewed with a certain amount of skepticism because they can lead to serious runtime performance problems. This is also true of queries that make use of Cartesian products or cross-joins. I mention this only to forewarn you to be on the lookout for techniques that may be syntactically compact but extremely inefficient in terms of runtime performance. The key to successful SQL development is to strike a balance between the two.

Variance and Standard Deviation

Transact-SQL sports nine different aggregate functions, all of which are useful for computing statistics. Beyond the "standard" aggregate functions you see in most SQL DBMS products—SUM(), MIN(), MAX(), COUNT(), and AVG()—SQL Server provides four that are specifically related to financial and statistical calculations: STDDEV(), STDDEVP(), VAR(), VARP(). The STDDEV functions compute sample standard deviation and population standard deviation, respectively, while the VAR functions compute sample variance and population variance. These functions work just like the other aggregate functions—they ignore NULLs, can be used with GROUP BY to create vector aggregates, and so forth. Here's an example that uses Transact-SQL's built-in aggregate functions to compute some basic statistics:

```
CREATE TABLE #1996_POP_ESTIMATE (Region char(7), State char(2), Population int)
INSERT #1996_POP_ESTIMATE VALUES ('West',    'CA',31878234)
INSERT #1996_POP_ESTIMATE VALUES ('South',   'TX',19128261)
INSERT #1996_POP_ESTIMATE VALUES ('North',   'NY',18184774)
INSERT #1996_POP_ESTIMATE VALUES ('South',   'FL',14399985)
INSERT #1996_POP_ESTIMATE VALUES ('North',   'NJ', 7987933)
INSERT #1996_POP_ESTIMATE VALUES ('East',    'NC', 7322870)
INSERT #1996_POP_ESTIMATE VALUES ('West',    'WA', 5532939)
INSERT #1996_POP_ESTIMATE VALUES ('Central','MO', 5358692)
INSERT #1996_POP_ESTIMATE VALUES ('East',    'MD', 5071604)
INSERT #1996_POP_ESTIMATE VALUES ('Central','OK', 3300902)

SELECT Region, MIN(Population) AS Minimum, MAX(Population) AS Maximum,
AVG(Population) AS Average, VAR(Population) AS Variance, VARP(Population) AS
VarianceP, STDEV(Population) AS StandardDeviation, STDEVP(Population) AS
StandardDeviationP
FROM #1996_POP_ESTIMATE
GROUP BY Region
ORDER BY Maximum DESC
```

(Results abridged)

Region	Minimum	Maximum	Average	Variance
West	5532939	31878234	18705586	347037284318512.5
South	14399985	19128261	16764123	11178296966088.0
North	7987933	18184774	13086353	51987783189640.5
East	5071604	7322870	6197237	2534099301378.0
Central	3300902	5358692	4329797	2117249842050.0

Medians

Row-positioning problems—i.e., locating rows based on their physical position within a distribution—have historically been a bit of challenge in SQL. Locating a row by value is easy with a set-oriented language; locating one based on position is another matter. Medians are row-positioning problems. If there is an odd number of values in the distribution, the median value is the middle value, above and below which exist equal numbers of items. If there is an even number of values, the median is either the average of the two middle values (for financial medians) or the lesser of them (for statistical medians).

The Identity Column Technique

Row-positioning problems are greatly simplified when a unique, sequential integer key has been established for a table. When this is the case, the key becomes a virtual record number, allowing ready access to any row position in the table similarly to an array. This can allow medians to be computed almost instantly, even over distribution sets with millions of values. Here's an example:

```
SET NOCOUNT ON
USE GG_TS
IF (OBJECT_ID('financial_median') IS NOT NULL)
   DROP TABLE financial_median
GO
DECLARE @starttime datetime

SET @starttime=GETDATE()

CREATE TABLE financial_median
(
c1 float DEFAULT (
   (CASE (CAST(RAND()+.5 AS int)*-1) WHEN 0 THEN 1 ELSE -1 END)*(CAST(RAND() *
   100000 AS int) % 10000)*RAND()),
c2 int DEFAULT 0
)

-- Seed the table with 10 rows
INSERT financial_median DEFAULT VALUES
INSERT financial_median DEFAULT VALUES
INSERT financial_median DEFAULT VALUES
INSERT financial_median DEFAULT VALUES
INSERT financial_median DEFAULT VALUES
INSERT financial_median DEFAULT VALUES
INSERT financial_median DEFAULT VALUES
INSERT financial_median DEFAULT VALUES
INSERT financial_median DEFAULT VALUES
INSERT financial_median DEFAULT VALUES

-- Create a distribution of a million values
WHILE (SELECT TOP 1 rows FROM sysindexes WHERE id=OBJECT_ID('financial_median')
ORDER BY indid)< 1000000 BEGIN
   INSERT financial_median (c2) SELECT TOP 344640 c2 FROM financial_median
END
```

```
SELECT 'It took '+CAST(DATEDIFF(ss,@starttime,GETDATE()) AS varchar)+' seconds
to create and populate the table'

SET @starttime=GETDATE()
-- Sort the distribution
CREATE CLUSTERED INDEX c1 ON financial_median (c1)
ALTER TABLE financial_median ADD k1 int identity
DROP INDEX financial_median.c1
CREATE CLUSTERED INDEX k1 ON financial_median (k1)

SELECT 'It took '+CAST(DATEDIFF(ss,@starttime,GETDATE()) AS varchar)+' seconds
to sort the table'
GO

-- Compute the financial median
DECLARE @starttime datetime, @rows int
SET @starttime=GETDATE()
SET STATISTICS TIME ON
SELECT TOP 1 @rows=rows FROM sysindexes WHERE id=OBJECT_ID('financial_median')
ORDER BY indid

SELECT 'There are '+CAST(@rows AS varchar)+' rows'

SELECT AVG(c1) AS "The financial median is" FROM financial_median
WHERE k1 BETWEEN @rows / 2 AND (@rows / 2)+SIGN(@rows+1 % 2)
SET STATISTICS TIME OFF
SELECT 'It took '+CAST(DATEDIFF(ms,@starttime,GETDATE()) AS varchar)+' ms to
compute the financial median'

--------------------------------------------------------------------------------
It took 73 seconds to create and populate the table

The clustered index has been dropped.

----------------------------------------------------------------
It took 148 seconds to sort the table

---------------------------------------------------
There are 1000000 rows

The financial median is
------------------------------------------------------
-1596.1257544255732

SQL Server Execution Times:
   CPU time = 0 ms, elapsed time = 287 ms.

----------------------------------------------------------------------
It took 290 ms to compute the financial median
```

This query does several interesting things. It begins by constructing a table to hold the distribution and adding a million rows to it. Each iteration of the loop fills the c1 column with a new random number (all the rows inserted by a single operation get the same random number). The table effectively doubles in size with each pass through the loop. The top 344,640 rows are taken with each iteration in order to ensure that the set doesn't exceed a million values. The 344,640 limitation isn't significant until the final pass through the loop—until then it grabs every row in financial_median and reinserts it back into the table (after the next-to-last iteration of the loop, the table contains 655,360 rows; 344,640 = 1,000,000 − 655,360). Though this doesn't produce a random number in every row, it minimizes the time necessary to build the distribution so we can get to the real work of calculating its median.

Next, the query creates a clustered index on the table's c1 column in order to sort the values in the distribution (a required step in computing its median). It then adds an identity column to the table and switches the table's clustered index to reference it. Since the values are already sequenced when the identity column is added, they end up being numbered sequentially by it.

The final step is where the median is actually computed. The query looks up the total number of rows (so that it can determine the middle value) and returns the average of the two middle values if there's an even number of distribution values or the middle value if there's an odd number.

In a real-world scenario, it's likely that only the last step would be required to calculate the median. The distribution would already exist and be sorted using a clustered index in a typical production setup. Since the number of values in the distribution might not be known in advance, I've included a step that looks up the number of rows in the table using a small query on sysindexes. This is just for completeness—the row count is already known in this case because we're building the distribution and determining the median in the same query. You could just as easily use a MAX(k1) query to compute the number of values since you can safely assume that the k1 identity column is seeded at one and has been incremented sequentially throughout the table. Here's an example:

```
DECLARE @starttime datetime, @rows int
SET @starttime=GETDATE()
SET STATISTICS TIME ON
SELECT @rows=MAX(k1) FROM financial_median

SELECT 'There are '+CAST(@rows AS varchar)+' rows'

SELECT AVG(c1) AS "The financial median is" FROM financial_median
WHERE k1 BETWEEN @rows / 2 AND (@rows / 2)+SIGN(@rows+1 % 2)
SET STATISTICS TIME OFF
SELECT 'It took '+CAST(DATEDIFF(ms,@starttime,GETDATE()) AS varchar)+' ms to
compute the financial median'
```

Note the use of the SIGN() function in the median computation to facilitate handling an even or odd number of values using a single BETWEEN clause. The idea here is to add 1 to the index of the middle value for an even number of values and 0 for an odd number. This means that an even number of values will cause the average of the *two middle values* to be taken, while an odd number will cause the average of the *lone middle value* to be taken—the value itself. This approach allows us to use the same code for even and odd numbers of values.

Specifically, here's how this works: the SIGN() expression adds one to the number of values in the distribution set in order to switch it from odd to even or vice versa, then computes the modulus of this number and 2 (to determine whether we have an even or odd number) and returns either 1 or 0, based on its sign. So, for 1,000,000 rows, we add 1, giving us 1,000,001, then take the modulus of 2, which is 1. Next, we take the SIGN() of the number, which is 1, and add it to the number of rows (divided by 2) in order to compute the k1 value of the second middle row. This allows us to compute the AVG() of these two values in order to return the financial median. For an odd number of values, the modulus ends up being 0, resulting in a SIGN() of 0, so that both terms of the BETWEEN clause refer to the same value—the set's middle value.

The net effect of all this is that the median is computed almost instantaneously. Once the table is set up properly, the median takes less than a second to compute on the relatively scrawny 166 MHz laptop on which I'm writing this book. Considering that we're dealing with a distribution of a million rows, that's no small feat.

This is a classic example of SQL Server being able to outperform a traditional programming language because of its native access to the data. For a 3GL to compute the median value of a 1,000,000-value distribution, it would probably load the items into an array from disk and sort them. Once it had sorted the list, it could retrieve the middle one(s). This last process— that of indexing into the array—is usually quite fast. It's the loading of the data into the array in the first place that takes so long, and it's this step that SQL Server doesn't have to worry about since it can access the data natively. Moreover, if the 3GL approach loads more items than will fit in memory, some of them will be swapped to disk (virtual memory), obviously slowing down the population process and the computation of the median.

For example, consider this scenario: A 3GL function needs to compute the financial median of a distribution set. It begins by loading the entire set from a SQL Server database into an array or linked list and sorting it. Once the array is loaded and sorted, the function knows how many rows it has and indexes into or scans for the middle one(s). Foolishly, it treats the database like a flat file system. It ignores the fact that it could ask SQL Server to sort the items before returning them. It also ignores the fact that it could query the server for the number of rows before retrieving all of them, thus alleviating the need to load the entire distribution into memory just to count the number of values it contains and compute its median. These two optimizations alone—allowing the server to sort the data and asking it for the number of items in advance—are capable of reducing the memory requirements and the time needed to fill the array or list by at least half.

But SQL Server itself can do even better than this. Since the distribution is stored in a database with which the server can work directly, it doesn't need to load anything into an array or similar structure. This alone means that it could be orders of magnitude faster than the traditional 3GL approach. Since the data's already "loaded," all SQL Server has to concern itself with is locating the median value, and, as I've pointed out, having a sequential row identifier makes this a simple task.

To understand why the Transact-SQL approach is faster and better than the typical 3GL approach, think of SQL Server's storage mechanisms (B-trees, pages, extents, etc.) as a tree or linked list—a very, very smart linked list—a linked list that's capable of keeping track of its total number of items automatically, one that tracks the distribution of values within it, and one that continuously maintains a number of high-speed access paths to its values. It's a list that moves itself in and out of physical memory via a very sophisticated caching facility that constantly balances its distribution of values and that's always synchronized with a permanent disk version so there's never a reason to load or store it explicitly. It's a list that can be shared by multiple users and to which access is streamlined automatically by a built-in query optimizer. It's a list than can be transparently queried by multiple threads and processors simultaneously—that, by design, takes advantage of multiple Win32 operating system threads and multiple processors.

From a conceptual standpoint, SQL Server's storage/retrieval mechanisms and a large virtual memory–based 3GL array or linked list are not that different; it's just that SQL Server's facilities are a couple orders of magnitude more sophisticated and refined than the typical 3GL construct. Not all storage/retrieval mechanisms are created equal. SQL Server has been tuned, retuned, worked, and reworked for over ten years now. It's had plenty of time to grow up—to mature. It's benefited from fierce worldwide competition on a number of fronts throughout its entire life cycle. It has some of the best programmers in the world working year-round to enhance and speed it up. Thus it provides better data storage and retrieval facilities than 95% of the 3GL developers out there could ever build. It makes no sense to build an inferior, hackneyed version of something you get free in the SQL Server box while steadfastly and inexplicably using only a small portion of the product itself.

One thing we might consider is what to do if the distribution changes fairly often. What happens if new rows are added to it hourly, for example? The k1 identity column will cease to identify distribution values sequentially, so how could we compute the median using the identity column technique? The solution would be to drop the clustered index on k1 followed by the column itself and repeat the sort portion of the earlier query, like so:

```
DROP INDEX financial_median.k1
ALTER TABLE financial_median DROP COLUMN k1
CREATE CLUSTERED INDEX c1 ON financial_median (c1)
ALTER TABLE financial_median ADD k1 int identity
DROP INDEX financial_median.c1
CREATE CLUSTERED INDEX k1 ON financial_median (k1)
```

Obviously, this technique is impractical for large distributions that are volatile in nature. Each time the distribution is updated, it must be resorted. Large distributions updated more than, say, once a day are simply too much trouble for this approach. Instead, you should use one of the other median techniques listed below.

Note that it's actually faster overall to omit the last two steps in the sorting phase. If the clustered index on c1 is left in place, computing the median takes noticeably longer (1–2 seconds on the aforementioned laptop), but the overall process of populating, sorting, and querying the set is reduced by about 15%. I've included the steps because the most common production scenario would have the data loaded and sorted on a fairly infrequent basis—say once a day or less—while the median might be computed thousands of times daily.

The CASE Technique

Computing a median using CASE is also relatively simple. Assume we start with this table and data:

```
CREATE TABLE #dist (c1 int)
INSERT #dist VALUES (2)
INSERT #dist VALUES (3)
INSERT #dist VALUES (1)
INSERT #dist VALUES (4)
INSERT #dist VALUES (8)
```

This query returns the median value:

```
SELECT Median=d.c1
FROM #dist d CROSS JOIN #dist i
GROUP BY d.c1
HAVING COUNT(CASE WHEN i.c1 <= d.c1 THEN 1 ELSE NULL END)=(COUNT(*)+1)/2


Median
-----------
3
```

Here, we generate a cross-join of the #dist table with itself, then use a HAVING clause to filter out all but the median value. The CASE function allows us to count the number of i values that are less than or equal to each d value, then HAVING restricts the rows returned to the d value where this is exactly half the number of values in the set.

The number returned is the *statistical median* of the set of values. The statistical median of a set of values must be one of the values in the set. Given an odd number of values, this will always be the middle value. Given an even number, this will be the lesser of the two middle values. Note that it's trivial to change the example code to return the greater of the two middle values, if that's desirable:

```
CREATE TABLE #dist (c1 int)
INSERT #dist VALUES (2)
INSERT #dist VALUES (3)
INSERT #dist VALUES (1)
INSERT #dist VALUES (4)
INSERT #dist VALUES (8)
INSERT #dist VALUES (9) -- Insert an even number of values

SELECT Median=d.c1
FROM #dist d CROSS JOIN #dist i
GROUP BY d.c1
HAVING COUNT(CASE WHEN i.c1 <= d.c1 THEN 1 ELSE NULL END)=COUNT(*)/2+1


Median
-----------
4
```

A *financial median,* on the other hand, does not have to be one of the values of the set. In the case of an even number of values, the financial median is the average of the two middle values. Assuming this data:

```
CREATE TABLE #dist (c1 int)
INSERT INTO #dist VALUES (2)
INSERT INTO #dist VALUES (3)
INSERT INTO #dist VALUES (1)
INSERT INTO #dist VALUES (4)
INSERT INTO #dist VALUES (8)
INSERT INTO #dist VALUES (9)
```

here's a Transact-SQL query that computes a financial median:

```
SELECT Median=CASE COUNT(*)%2
    WHEN 0 THEN -- Even number of VALUES
       (d.c1+MIN(CASE WHEN i.c1>d.c1 THEN i.c1 ELSE NULL END))/2.0
    ELSE d.c1 END -- Odd number
FROM #dist d CROSS JOIN #dist i
GROUP BY d.c1
HAVING COUNT(CASE WHEN i.c1 <= d.c1 THEN 1 ELSE NULL END)=(COUNT(*)+1)/2

Median
-------------------
3.500000
```

The middle values of this distribution are 3 and 4, so the query above returns 3.5 as the financial median of the distribution.

Vector Medians

Since Transact-SQL doesn't include a MEDIAN() aggregate function, computing vector or partitioned medians must be done using something other than the usual GROUP BY technique. Assuming this table and data:

```
CREATE TABLE #dist (k1 int, c1 int)
INSERT #dist VALUES (1,2)
INSERT #dist VALUES (2,3)
INSERT #dist VALUES (2,1)
INSERT #dist VALUES (2,5)
INSERT #dist VALUES (5,4)
INSERT #dist VALUES (7,8)
INSERT #dist VALUES (7,9)
```

here's a modification of the first example to return a vector median:

```
SELECT d.k1, d.c1
FROM #dist d CROSS JOIN #dist i
WHERE d.k1=i.k1
GROUP BY d.k1, d.c1
HAVING COUNT(CASE WHEN i.c1<=d.c1 THEN 1 ELSE NULL END)=(COUNT(*)+1)/2
ORDER BY d.k1
```

k1	c1
1	2
2	3
5	4
7	8

"K1" is the vectoring or partitioning column in this example. If Transact-SQL had a MEDIAN() aggregate function, "k1" would be the lone item in the GROUP BY list.

Duplicate Values

A situation that none of the median queries presented thus far handles very well is the presence of duplicate values in the distribution set. In fact, in all of the examples thus far, a duplicate value near the median will cause the query to return NULL or omit the corresponding partition. The problem is that these queries group by the c1 column in the first instance of the work table. Grouping automatically combines duplicate values so that a query cannot distinguish between multiple instances of the same value. Properly handling duplicate values requires the HAVING clause to be reworked. Assuming we start with this table and data:

```
CREATE TABLE #dist (c1 int)
INSERT #dist VALUES (2)
INSERT #dist VALUES (3)
INSERT #dist VALUES (1)
INSERT #dist VALUES (3) -- Duplicate value
INSERT #dist VALUES (8)
INSERT #dist VALUES (9)
```

here's a modification of the statistical median query that handles duplicate values:

```
SELECT d.c1
FROM #dist d CROSS JOIN #dist i
GROUP BY d.c1
HAVING (COUNT(CASE WHEN i.c1 <= d.c1 THEN 1 ELSE NULL END)>=(COUNT(*)+1)/2)
AND (COUNT(CASE WHEN i.c1 >=d.c1 THEN 1 ELSE NULL END) >= COUNT(*)/2+1)

c1
-----------
3
```

Likewise, here's the financial median query modified to handle duplicate values:

```
CREATE TABLE #dist (c1 int)
INSERT #dist VALUES (2)
INSERT #dist VALUES (2)
INSERT #dist VALUES (1)
INSERT #dist VALUES (5)
INSERT #dist VALUES (5)
INSERT #dist VALUES (9)

SELECT Median=ISNULL((CASE WHEN COUNT(CASE WHEN i.c1<=d.c1 THEN 1 ELSE NULL END)
> (COUNT(*)+1)/2 THEN 1.0*d.c1 ELSE NULL END)+COUNT(*)%2,
    (d.c1+MIN((CASE WHEN i.c1>d.c1 THEN i.c1 ELSE NULL END)))/2.0)
FROM #dist d CROSS JOIN #dist i
GROUP BY d.c1
HAVING (COUNT(CASE WHEN i.c1 <= d.c1 THEN 1 ELSE NULL END)>=(COUNT(*)+1)/2)
AND (COUNT(CASE WHEN i.c1 >=d.c1 THEN 1 ELSE NULL END) >= COUNT(*)/2+1)

Median
----------------
3.5
```

As you can see, things start to get a bit complex when duplicate values enter the picture. Here's a variation of the financial median query that makes use of a key column (k1) and handles duplicates as well:

```
CREATE TABLE #dist (k1 int, c1 int)
INSERT #dist VALUES (1,2)
INSERT #dist VALUES (2,2)
INSERT #dist VALUES (3,1)
INSERT #dist VALUES (4,4)
INSERT #dist VALUES (5,5)
INSERT #dist VALUES (6,7)
INSERT #dist VALUES (7,8)
INSERT #dist VALUES (8,9)

SELECT Median=AVG(DISTINCT 1.0*c1)
FROM (SELECT d1.c1
   FROM #dist d1 CROSS JOIN #dist d2
   GROUP BY d1.k1, d1.c1
   HAVING SUM(CASE WHEN d2.c1 = d1.c1 THEN 1 ELSE 0 END) >=
   ABS(SUM(CASE WHEN d2.c1 < d1.c1 THEN 1 WHEN d2.c1 > d1.c1 THEN -1 ELSE 0 END))) d

Median
----------------------------------------
4.500000
```

Clipping

Clipping is the removal from a set of values a prefix and suffix of some predetermined size. As with medians, figuring out which values to remove is a row-positioning problem—the rows that end up being removed depend on their position in the set. Here's some sample code that illustrates how easy it is to clip values from a set:

```
CREATE TABLE #valueset (c1 int)
INSERT #valueset VALUES (2)
INSERT #valueset VALUES (3)
INSERT #valueset VALUES (1)
INSERT #valueset VALUES (4)
INSERT #valueset VALUES (8)
INSERT #valueset VALUES (9)

SELECT v.c1
FROM #valueset v CROSS JOIN #valueset a
GROUP BY v.c1
HAVING v.c1 > MIN(a.c1) AND v.c1 < MAX(a.c1)

c1
-----------
2
3
4
8
```

This code uses a cross-join and a simple HAVING clause to exclude the minimum and maximum values from the set, but what if we wanted to exclude multiple rows from the beginning or end of the set? We couldn't simply change **> MAX(a.c1)** to **> MAX(c.c1)+1** because we don't know whether the values are sequential (in fact, they aren't, in this case). Accommodating prefix /suffix sizes of more than a single row requires the HAVING clause to be reworked. Here's a new query that clips prefixes and suffixes of any size:

```
SELECT v.c1
FROM #valueset v CROSS JOIN #valueset a
GROUP BY v.c1
HAVING COUNT(CASE WHEN a.c1 <=v.c1 THEN 1 ELSE NULL END) > 2
AND COUNT(CASE WHEN a.c1 >= v.c1 THEN 1 ELSE NULL END) >2

c1
-----------
3
4
```

Note that this code is flexible enough to allow a prefix and a suffix of different sizes. The first predicate in the HAVING clause clips the prefix, and the second clause handles the suffix. The "> 2" comparison construct controls the size of the clipped region. To clip more than two rows, increase the number; to clip less, decrease it.

Returning the Top *n* Rows

In SQL Server 7.0 and later, the SELECT statement's TOP *n* extension is the most direct way to return a given number of rows from the top or bottom of a result set. TOP *n* does just what it sounds like—it restricts the rows returned to a specified number. Since you can sort the result set in descending order, TOP *n* can also return the bottommost rows from a result set. It works similarly to SET ROWCOUNT but can also handle ties and percentages. See the section "SELECT TOP" in Chapter 6 for more information.

If you're using SQL Server 6.5 or earlier or if you need more flexibility than SELECT TOP *n* provides, the code from the previous clipping example can be extended to perform a number of useful functions, including returning the topmost or bottommost rows in a result set. One obvious application is to invert it to return a prefix or suffix of a predetermined size. Here's some sample code that does just that:

```
SELECT v.c1
FROM #valueset v CROSS JOIN #valueset a
GROUP BY v.c1
HAVING COUNT(CASE WHEN a.c1 >=v.c1 THEN 1 ELSE NULL END) > COUNT(a.c1)-2

c1
-----------
1
2
```

This code returns the top two rows. As with the previous example, you can modify "-2" to return any number of rows you like. Here's the same query modified to return the bottom three rows:

```
SELECT v.c1
FROM #valueset v CROSS JOIN #valueset a
GROUP BY v.c1
HAVING COUNT(CASE WHEN a.c1 <=v.c1 THEN 1 ELSE NULL END) > COUNT(a.c1)-3

c1
-----------
4
8
9
```

This technique works but has one inherent flaw—it doesn't handle duplicates. There are a number of solutions to this problem. Here's one that uses a derived table and a correlated subquery to get the job done:

```
CREATE TABLE #valueset (c1 int)
INSERT #valueset VALUES (2)
INSERT #valueset VALUES (2) -- Duplicate value
INSERT #valueset VALUES (1)
INSERT #valueset VALUES (3)
INSERT #valueset VALUES (4)
INSERT #valueset VALUES (4) -- Duplicate value
INSERT #valueset VALUES (10)
INSERT #valueset VALUES (11)
INSERT #valueset VALUES (13)

SELECT l.c1
FROM (SELECT ranking=(SELECT COUNT(DISTINCT a.c1) FROM #valueset a
         WHERE v.c1 >= a.c1),
      v.c1
  FROM #valueset v) l
WHERE l.ranking <=3
ORDER BY l.ranking

c1
-----------
1
2
2
3
```

This technique uses a derived table and a correlated subquery rather than a cross-join to compare #valueset with itself. This, in turn, allows us to get rid of the GROUP BY clause, which caused problems with duplicates. As mentioned earlier, GROUP BY can't distinguish between multiple instances of the same value. When duplicate values exist within its grouping column(s), it combines them. The key, then, is to return all the rows in #valueset filtered by criteria that restrict them based on their rank among the other values.

The above code uses a derived table to yield a list of rankings for the values in #valueset. This derived table uses a correlated subquery to rank each value according to the number of other values in the table that are less than or equal to it. The subquery is "correlated" because it relates to (in this case, is filtered by) values in the outer table. (Note the use of **v** alias in the **SELECT COUNT(DISTINCT** query.) Those with a rank of three or better make the cut.

Note that you can easily alter this query to return the bottommost rows in the set rather than the topmost. Here's the query modified to return the bottom four rows from the table:

```
CREATE TABLE #valueset (c1 int)
INSERT #valueset VALUES (2)
INSERT #valueset VALUES (2) -- Duplicate value
INSERT #valueset VALUES (1)
INSERT #valueset VALUES (3)
INSERT #valueset VALUES (4)
INSERT #valueset VALUES (4) -- Duplicate value
INSERT #valueset VALUES (11)
INSERT #valueset VALUES (11) -- Duplicate value
INSERT #valueset VALUES (13)


SELECT l.c1
FROM (SELECT ranking=(SELECT COUNT(DISTINCT a.c1) FROM #valueset a
        WHERE v.c1 <= a.c1),
      v.c1
   FROM #valueset v) l
WHERE l.ranking <=4
ORDER BY l.ranking


c1
-----------
13
11
11
4
4
3
```

Note that both of these queries allow ties in the result set, so you may get back more rows than you request. If this is undesirable, you can use SELECT TOP or SET ROWCOUNT to limit the actual number of rows returned, as the examples that follow illustrate.

SET ROWCOUNT

Another alternative to SELECT's TOP *n* extension is the SET ROWCOUNT command. It limits the number of rows returned by a query, so you could do something like this in order to return the topmost rows from a result set:

```
SET ROWCOUNT 3
SELECT * FROM #valueset ORDER BY c1
SET ROWCOUNT 0 -- Reset to normal
```

```
c1
-----------
1
2
2
```

Returning the Bottom *n* Rows is equally simple. To return the bottommost rows instead of the topmost, change the ORDER BY to sort in descending order.

While this solution is certainly straightforward, it can't handle duplicates very flexibly. You get exactly three rows, no more, no less. Ties caused by duplicate values are not handled differently from any other value. If you request three rows and there's a tie for second place, you won't actually see the real third place row—you'll see the row that tied for second place in the third slot instead. This may be what you want, but if it isn't, there is a variation of this query that deals sensibly with ties. It takes advantage of the fact that assigning a variable using a query that returns more than one row assigns the value from the last row to the variable. This is a rarely used trick, and you should probably comment your code to indicate that it's actually what you intended to do. Here's the code:

```
CREATE TABLE #valueset (c1 int)
INSERT #valueset VALUES (2)
INSERT #valueset VALUES (2) -- Duplicate value
INSERT #valueset VALUES (1)
INSERT #valueset VALUES (3)
INSERT #valueset VALUES (4)
INSERT #valueset VALUES (4) -- Duplicate value
INSERT #valueset VALUES (11)
INSERT #valueset VALUES (11) -- Duplicate value
INSERT #valueset VALUES (13)

DECLARE @endc1 int
-- Get third distinct value
SELECT DISTINCT TOP 3 @endc1=c1 FROM #valueset ORDER BY c1
SELECT * FROM #valueset WHERE c1 <= @endc1 ORDER BY c1
```

```
c1
-----------
1
2
2
3
```

This query uses DISTINCT to avoid being fooled by duplicates. Without it, the query wouldn't handle duplicates any better than its predecessor. What we want to do here is assign the value of the third distinct value to our control variable so that we can then limit the rows returned by the ensuing SELECT to those with values less than or equal to it. So, if there are duplicates in the top three values, we'll get them. If there aren't, no harm done—the query still works as expected.

Rankings

Closely related to the Top *n* Rows problem is that of producing rankings for a set of data. In fact, you'll note that one of the Top *n* Rows solutions used a ranking column to qualify the rows it returned. Here's that query again with the ranking column included in the SELECT list:

```
CREATE TABLE #valueset (c1 int)
INSERT #valueset VALUES (2)
INSERT #valueset VALUES (2) -- Duplicate value
INSERT #valueset VALUES (1)
INSERT #valueset VALUES (3)
INSERT #valueset VALUES (4)
INSERT #valueset VALUES (4) -- Duplicate value
INSERT #valueset VALUES (11)
INSERT #valueset VALUES (11) -- Duplicate value
INSERT #valueset VALUES (13)


SELECT l.ranking, l.c1
FROM (SELECT ranking=(SELECT COUNT(DISTINCT a.c1) FROM #valueset a
        WHERE v.c1 <= a.c1),
    v.c1
  FROM #valueset v) l
ORDER BY l.ranking
```

```
ranking     c1
----------- -----------
1           13
2           11
2           11
3           4
3           4
4           3
5           2
5           2
6           1
```

This query isn't as efficient as it might be since the correlated subquery is executed for every row in #valueset. Here's a more efficient query that yields the same result:

```
SELECT Ranking=IDENTITY(int), c1
INTO #rankings
FROM #valueset
WHERE 1=0 -- Create an empty table

INSERT #rankings (c1)
SELECT c1
FROM #valueset
ORDER BY c1 DESC

SELECT * FROM #rankings ORDER BY Ranking
DROP TABLE #rankings
```

```
Ranking      c1
-----------  -----------
1            13
2            11
3            11
4            4
5            4
6            3
7            2
8            2
9            1
```

Note the use of SELECT...INTO to create the temporary working table. It uses the IDEN-TITY() function to create the table *en passant* rather than explicitly via CREATE TABLE. Though CREATE TABLE would have been syntactically more compact in this case, I think it's instructive to see how easily SELECT...INTO allows us to create work tables.

The SELECT...INTO is immediately followed by an INSERT that populates it with data. Why not perform the two operations in one pass? That is, why doesn't the SELECT...INTO move the data into the #rankings table at the same time that it creates it? There are two reasons. First, SELECT...INTO is a special nonlogged operation that can lock system tables while it runs, so initiating one that could conceivably run for an extended period of time is a bad idea. Second, SQL Server doesn't work as expected here—it hands out identity values based on the natural order of the #valueset table rather than according to the query's ORDER BY clause. So, even if locking the system tables wasn't a concern, this anomaly in SQL Server's row order-ing would prevent us from combining the two steps anyway.

This query doesn't handle ties as you might expect. Since the items in the #rankings table are numbered sequentially, values that are actually duplicates (and hence tied) are listed in se-quence as though no tie existed. If you restrict the rows returned to a given segment of the top of the list and ties are present, you won't get the results you may be expecting. For example, if you ask for four rows and there is a tie for second, you'll only see the row in first place followed by the two that tied for second and the one that placed third. You won't actually see the fourth place row. Since there's no way to know how many ties you might have, returning the top four rankings from the set is more involved than it probably should be, but modifying the query to rank the rows more sensibly is fairly easy. Here's an example:

```
SELECT Ranking=IDENTITY(int), c1
INTO #rankings
FROM #valueset
WHERE 1=2  -- Create an empty table

INSERT #rankings (c1)
SELECT c1
FROM #valueset
ORDER BY c1 DESC

SELECT a.Ranking, r.c1
FROM
```

```
   (SELECT Ranking=MIN(n.Ranking), n.c1 FROM #rankings n GROUP BY n.c1) a,
   #rankings r
WHERE r.c1=a.c1
ORDER BY a.ranking
DROP TABLE #rankings
```

```
Ranking       c1
-----------   -----------
1             13
2             11
2             11
4             4
4             4
6             3
7             2
7             2
9             1
```

In this query, ties are indicated by identical rankings. In the case of our earlier example, the two rows tied for second place would be ranked second, followed by the third row, which would be ranked fourth. This is the way that ties are often handled in official rankings; it keeps the number of values above a particular ranking manageable.

One piece of information that's missing from the above query is an indication of which rows are ties and how many ties exist for each value. Here's a modification of the query that includes this information as well:

```
SELECT a.Ranking, Ties=CAST(LEFT(CAST(a.NumWithValue AS varchar)+'-Way tie',
NULLIF(a.NumWithValue,1)*11) AS CHAR(11)), r.c1
FROM
   (SELECT Ranking=MIN(n.Ranking), NumWithValue=COUNT(*), n.c1 FROM #rankings n
GROUP BY n.c1) a,
   #rankings r
WHERE r.c1=a.c1
ORDER BY a.ranking
DROP TABLE #rankings
```

```
Ranking       Ties          c1
-----------   -----------   -----------
1             NULL          13
2             2-Way tie     11
2             2-Way tie     11
4             2-Way tie     4
4             2-Way tie     4
6             NULL          3
7             2-Way tie     2
7             2-Way tie     2
9             NULL          1
```

Modes

There are three basic ways to reflect a middle or typical value for a distribution of values: medians, means (averages), and modes. We've already covered medians and averages, so let's explore how to compute the mode of a set of values. A distribution's mode is its most common value, regardless of where the value physically appears in the set. If you have this set of values:

```
10, 10, 9, 10, 10
```

the mode is 10, the median is 9, and the mean is 9.8. The mode is 10 because it's obviously the most common value in the set. Here's a Transact-SQL query that computes the mode for a more complex set of values:

```
CREATE TABLE #valueset (c1 int)
INSERT #valueset VALUES (2)
INSERT #valueset VALUES (2)
INSERT #valueset VALUES (1)
INSERT #valueset VALUES (3)
INSERT #valueset VALUES (4)
INSERT #valueset VALUES (4)
INSERT #valueset VALUES (10)
INSERT #valueset VALUES (11)
INSERT #valueset VALUES (13)

SELECT TOP 1 WITH TIES c1, COUNT(*) AS NumInstances
FROM #valueset
GROUP BY c1
ORDER BY NumInstances DESC

c1          NumInstances
----------- ------------
2           2
4           2
```

Since a set may have more than one value with the same number of occurrences, it's possible that there may be multiple values that qualify as the set's mode. That's where SELECT's TOP n extension comes in handy. Its WITH TIES option can handle situations like this without requiring additional coding.

Histograms

The CASE function makes computing certain types of histograms quite easy, especially horizontal histograms. Using a technique similar to that in the pivoting example earlier in the chapter, we can build horizontal histogram tables with a trivial amount of Transact-SQL code. Here's an example that references the sales table in the pubs database:

```
SELECT
"Less than 10"=COUNT(CASE WHEN s.sales >=0 AND s.sales <10 THEN 1 ELSE NULL END),
"10-19"=COUNT(CASE WHEN s.sales >=10 AND s.sales <20 THEN 1 ELSE NULL END),
"20-29"=COUNT(CASE WHEN s.sales >=20 AND s.sales <30 THEN 1 ELSE NULL END),
"30-39"=COUNT(CASE WHEN s.sales >=30 AND s.sales <40 THEN 1 ELSE NULL END),
"40-49"=COUNT(CASE WHEN s.sales >=40 AND s.sales <50 THEN 1 ELSE NULL END),
"50 or more"=COUNT(CASE WHEN s.sales >=50 THEN 1 ELSE NULL END)
FROM (SELECT t.title_id, sales=ISNULL(SUM(s.qty),0) FROM titles t LEFT OUTER JOIN sales
s ON (t.title_id=s.title_id) GROUP BY t.title_id) s
```

Less than 10	10-19	20-29	30-39	40-49	50 or more
1	4	6	3	2	2

The query computes the titles that fall into each group based on their sales. Note the use of a derived table to compute the sales for each title. This is necessary because the COUNT() expressions in the SELECTs column list cannot reference other aggregates. Once the sales for each title are computed, this number is compared against the range for each group to determine its proper placement.

Histograms have a tendency to make obscure trends more obvious. This particular one illustrates that most titles have sold between ten and thirty copies.

Stratified Histograms

Beyond simple histograms, stratified histograms are crucial to comparative statistical analysis. They allow data to be compared in multiple dimensions—both horizontally and vertically. Here's a modification of the first histogram example to include a stratification column:

```
SELECT
PayTerms=isnull(s.payterms,'NA'),
"Less than 10"=COUNT(CASE WHEN s.sales >=0 AND s.sales <10 THEN 1 ELSE NULL END),
"10-19"=COUNT(CASE WHEN s.sales >=10 AND s.sales <20 THEN 1 ELSE NULL END),
"20-29"=COUNT(CASE WHEN s.sales >=20 AND s.sales <30 THEN 1 ELSE NULL END),
"30-39"=COUNT(CASE WHEN s.sales >=30 AND s.sales <40 THEN 1 ELSE NULL END),
"40-49"=COUNT(CASE WHEN s.sales >=40 AND s.sales <50 THEN 1 ELSE NULL END),
"50 or more"=COUNT(CASE WHEN s.sales >=50 THEN 1 ELSE NULL END)
FROM (SELECT t.title_id, s.payterms, sales=ISNULL(SUM(s.qty),0) FROM titles t LEFT
OUTER JOIN sales s ON (t.title_id=s.title_id) GROUP BY t.title_id, payterms) s
GROUP BY s.payterms
```

PayTerms	Less than 10	10-19	20-29	30-39	40-49	50 or more
NA	1	0	0	0	0	0
Net 30	0	0	5	2	1	1
Net 60	1	4	3	0	0	0
ON invoice	0	2	0	1	0	1

Histograms, pivot tables, and other types of OLAP constructs can also be built using SQL Server's OLAP Services module. Coverage of this suite of tools is outside the scope of this book, so you should consult the Books Online for further information.

Cumulative and Sliding Aggregates

Computing running totals in Transact-SQL is relatively straightforward. As in many of the other examples in this chapter, the technique presented here makes use of a cross-join between two copies of the source table. Here's the code:

```
CREATE TABLE #valueset (k1 int identity, c1 int)
INSERT #valueset (c1) VALUES (20)
INSERT #valueset (c1) VALUES (30)
INSERT #valueset (c1) VALUES (40)
INSERT #valueset (c1) VALUES (21)
INSERT #valueset (c1) VALUES (31)
INSERT #valueset (c1) VALUES (41)
INSERT #valueset (c1) VALUES (22)
INSERT #valueset (c1) VALUES (32)
INSERT #valueset (c1) VALUES (42)

SELECT v.c1, RunningTotal=SUM(a.c1)
FROM #valueset v CROSS JOIN #valueset a
WHERE (a.k1<=v.k1)
GROUP BY v.k1,v.c1
ORDER BY v.k1,v.c1
c1              RunningTotal
------------    ------------
20              20
30              50
40              90
21              111
31              142
41              183
22              205
32              237
42              279
```

Note the inclusion of the ORDER BY clause. It's required because the GROUP BY clause does not implicitly order the result set as it did in earlier releases of SQL Server.

Other types of running aggregates can be computed by replacing SUM() with another aggregate function. For example, to compute a running AVG(), try this:

```
SELECT v.c1, RunningAverage=AVG(a.c1)
FROM #valueset v CROSS JOIN #valueset a
WHERE (a.k1<=v.k1)
GROUP BY v.k1,v.c1
ORDER BY v.k1,v.c1

c1              RunningAverage
------------    --------------
20              20
30              25
40              30
21              27
31              28
41              30
22              29
32              29
42              31
```

To compute a running count (which produces unique row numbers), try this:

```
SELECT RowNumber=COUNT(*), v.c1
FROM #valueset v CROSS JOIN #valueset a
WHERE (a.k1<=v.k1)
GROUP BY v.k1,v.c1
ORDER BY v.k1,v.c1
```

```
RowNumber       c1
------------    ------------
1               20
2               30
3               40
4               21
5               31
6               41
7               22
8               32
9               42
```

Sliding Aggregates

A sliding aggregate differs from a cumulative aggregate in that it reflects an aggregation of a sequence of values around each value in a set. This subset "moves" or "slides" with each value, hence the term. So, for example, a sliding average might compute the average of the current value and its preceding four siblings, like so:

```
CREATE TABLE #valueset (k1 int identity, c1 int)
INSERT #valueset (c1) VALUES (20)
INSERT #valueset (c1) VALUES (30)
INSERT #valueset (c1) VALUES (40)
INSERT #valueset (c1) VALUES (21)
INSERT #valueset (c1) VALUES (31)
INSERT #valueset (c1) VALUES (41)
INSERT #valueset (c1) VALUES (22)
INSERT #valueset (c1) VALUES (32)
INSERT #valueset (c1) VALUES (42)

SELECT v.k1, SlidingAverage=AVG(1.0*a.c1)
FROM #valueset v CROSS JOIN #valueset a
WHERE (a.k1 BETWEEN v.k1-4 AND v.k1)
GROUP BY v.k1
```

```
k1              SlidingAverage
------------    --------------
1               20.000000
2               25.000000
3               30.000000
4               27.750000
5               28.400000
6               32.600000
7               31.000000
8               29.400000
9               33.600000
```

Note that the sliding averages for the first four values are returned as running averages since they don't have the required number of preceding values. Beginning with the fifth value, though, SlidingAverage reflects the mean of the current value and the four immediately before it. As with the running totals example, you can replace AVG() with different aggregate functions to compute other types of sliding aggregates.

Extremes

An *extreme,* as defined here, is the largest value among two or more columns in a given table. You can think of it as a horizontal aggregate. Oracle has functions (GREATEST() and LEAST()) to return horizontal extremes; Transact-SQL doesn't. However, retrieving a horizontal extreme value for two columns is as simple as using CASE to select between them, like so:

```
CREATE TABLE #tempsamp
(SampDate datetime,
 Temp6am int,
 Temp6pm int)

INSERT #tempsamp VALUES ('19990101',44,32)
INSERT #tempsamp VALUES ('19990201',41,39)
INSERT #tempsamp VALUES ('19990301',48,56)
INSERT #tempsamp VALUES ('19990401',65,72)
INSERT #tempsamp VALUES ('19990501',59,82)
INSERT #tempsamp VALUES ('19990601',47,84)
INSERT #tempsamp VALUES ('19990701',61,92)
INSERT #tempsamp VALUES ('19990801',56,101)
INSERT #tempsamp VALUES ('19990901',59,78)
INSERT #tempsamp VALUES ('19991001',54,74)
INSERT #tempsamp VALUES ('19991101',47,67)
INSERT #tempsamp VALUES ('19991201',32,41)

SELECT HiTemp=CASE WHEN Temp6am > Temp6pm THEN Temp6am ELSE Temp6pm END
FROM #tempsamp

HiTemp
-----------
44
41
56
72
82
84
92
101
78
74
67
41
```

You can nest CASE functions within one another if there are more than two horizontal values to consider.

Note that you can also order result sets *using* extreme values. All that's necessary is to reference the CASE function's column alias in the ORDER BY clause like this:

```
SELECT HiTemp=CASE WHEN Temp6am > Temp6pm THEN Temp6am ELSE Temp6pm END
FROM #tempsamp
ORDER BY HiTemp

HiTemp
-----------
41
41
44
56
67
72
74
78
82
84
92
101
```

If you wish to order by the extreme without actually selecting it, simply move the CASE expression from the SELECT list to the ORDER BY clause. Here's a query that returns the samples sorted by the lowest temperature on each sample date:

```
SELECT *
FROM #tempsamp
ORDER BY CASE WHEN Temp6am < Temp6pm THEN Temp6am ELSE Temp6pm END

SampDate                    Temp6am     Temp6pm
--------------------------- ----------- -----------
1999-01-01 00:00:00.000     44          32
1999-12-01 00:00:00.000     32          41
1999-02-01 00:00:00.000     41          39
1999-06-01 00:00:00.000     47          84
1999-11-01 00:00:00.000     47          67
1999-03-01 00:00:00.000     48          56
1999-10-01 00:00:00.000     54          74
1999-08-01 00:00:00.000     56          101
1999-05-01 00:00:00.000     59          82
1999-09-01 00:00:00.000     59          78
1999-07-01 00:00:00.000     61          92
1999-04-01 00:00:00.000     65          72
```

Determining Extreme Attributes

Beyond returning horizontal extreme values, a query might need to indicate which attribute actually contains the extreme value. Here's a query that does that:

```
SELECT Month=DATENAME(mm,SampDate),
   HighestTemp=CASE WHEN Temp6am > Temp6pm THEN 'Morning' ELSE 'Evening' END
FROM #tempsamp
```

```
Month                         HighestTemp
--------------------------    -----------
January                       Morning
February                      Morning
March                         Evening
April                         Evening
May                           Evening
June                          Evening
July                          Evening
August                        Evening
September                     Evening
October                       Evening
November                      Evening
December                      Evening
```

Once you've computed a horizontal extreme, you may wish to find all the rows in the table with the same extreme value. You can do this using CASE in conjunction with a subquery. Here's an example:

```
SELECT *
FROM #tempsamp
WHERE (CASE WHEN Temp6am < Temp6pm THEN Temp6am ELSE Temp6pm END)=
   (SELECT MIN(CASE WHEN Temp6am < Temp6pm THEN Temp6am ELSE Temp6pm END)
   FROM #tempsamp)

SampDate                      Temp6am     Temp6pm
--------------------------    -----------  -----------
1999-01-01 00:00:00.000       44           32
1999-12-01 00:00:00.000       32           41
```

Summary

In this chapter, you learned about computing statistical information using Transact-SQL. You learned about the built-in statistical functions as well as how to build your own. Thanks to SQL Server's set orientation and statistical functions, it's a very capable statistics calculation engine—more so, in fact, than many 3GL tools.

Runs and Sequences

*I like to remind my team that ultimately we ship
products, not specs and design documents, so we
need to remember the end game.*—Ron Soukup

Runs, regions, sequences, and series are related data constructs that usually include a minimum
of two columns: a key column that is more or less sequential and a value column that contains
the information in which we're interested. The key column of a sequence (or series) is sequential, with no gaps between identifiers. Examples of sequences include time series, invoice numbers, account numbers, and so on. A run's key column is also sequential, though there may or
may not be gaps between identifiers. Examples of runs include those of regular sequences (with
gaps, of course) as well as house numbers, version numbers, and the like. A region is a subsequence whose members all meet the same criteria. The simplest example of a region is a subsequence whose members all have the same value. An interval is the product of dividing a
sequence or run into multiple, evenly sized subsequences or subsets.

Queries to process these constructs are often quite similar to one another, and the techniques to process one type of ordered list may overlap those of another. So, the query that finds
relationships between the members of a run may also work with time series data—it just depends on what you're doing.

Sequences

Time series are probably the most ubiquitous examples of sequences. A common need with
time series is to find areas or periods within a series where values have a particular relationship
to one another. You might want to know, for example, the range of time when a stock issue was
steadily increasing in price, when prices were within a certain percentage of one another, and so
on. Here's a query that demonstrates how to do this in Transact-SQL:

```
CREATE TABLE #valueset (k1 smalldatetime, c1 int)
INSERT #valueset (k1, c1) VALUES ('19990901',28)
INSERT #valueset (k1, c1) VALUES ('19991001',25)
INSERT #valueset (k1, c1) VALUES ('19991101',13)
INSERT #valueset (k1, c1) VALUES ('19991201',15)
INSERT #valueset (k1, c1) VALUES ('20000101',35)
INSERT #valueset (k1, c1) VALUES ('20000201',38)
INSERT #valueset (k1, c1) VALUES ('20000301',16)

SELECT v.k1, v.c1
FROM #valueset v JOIN #valueset a
ON ((a.c1 >= v.c1) AND (a.k1 = DATEADD(mm,1,v.k1)))
OR ((a.c1 <= v.c1) AND (a.k1 = DATEADD(mm,-1,v.k1)))
GROUP BY v.k1, v.c1

k1                           c1
-------------------------    -----------
1999-11-01 00:00:00          13
1999-12-01 00:00:00          15
2000-01-01 00:00:00          35
2000-02-01 00:00:00          38
```

This query identifies regions within the series where values increase in succession. It uses a self-join to compare the work table with itself, then removes duplicates from the result set via a GROUP BY clause. Note the use of the DATEADD() function to refer to each data point's next and previous months.

Time Series Fluctuation

Another common need with time series data is to compute the change from one value to the next. You can use this measurement to gauge volatility from point to point within the series and to identify outlying values. Here's an example:

```
SELECT
StartTime=CAST(v.k1 AS char(12)), EndTime=CAST(a.k1 AS char(12)),
StartVal=v.c1, EndVal=a.c1,
Change=SUBSTRING('- +',SIGN(a.c1-v.c1)+2,1)+CAST(ABS(a.c1-v.c1) AS varchar)
FROM
   (SELECT k1, c1, ranking=(SELECT COUNT(DISTINCT k1) FROM #valueset u
   WHERE u.k1 <= l.k1)
   FROM #valueset l) v LEFT OUTER JOIN
   (SELECT k1, c1, ranking=(SELECT COUNT(DISTINCT k1) FROM #valueset u
   WHERE u.k1 <= l.k1)
   FROM #valueset l) a
   ON (a.ranking=v.ranking+1)
WHERE a.k1 IS NOT NULL

StartTime    EndTime      StartVal     EndVal       Change
----------   ----------   -----------  -----------  --------------------
Sep 1 1999   Oct 1 1999   28           25           -3
Oct 1 1999   Nov 1 1999   25           13           -12
Nov 1 1999   Dec 1 1999   13           15           +2
Dec 1 1999   Jan 1 2000   15           35           +20
Jan 1 2000   Feb 1 2000   35           38           +3
Feb 1 2000   Mar 1 2000   38           16           -22
```

There are several interesting elements here worth mentioning. First, note the use of derived tables to rank the values in the series against one another. Though it would be syntactically more compact to move these to a view, this approach demonstrates the viability of a single SELECT to get at the data we want.

Next, note the use of a subquery within each derived table to compute the ranking itself. It does this via a COUNT(DISTINCT) of the other values in the work table that are less than or equal to each value. Finally, note the use of the SIGN() and SUBSTRING() functions to produce a sign prefix for each change. While simply displaying **a.c1-v.c1** would have indicated negative changes via the standard "−" prefix, positive changes would have remained unsigned without the use of this technique.

Sampling Every *n*th Value

Performing calculations or computing statistics on every *n*th value is another common sequence-related task. Because the query above materializes the rankings of each item in the time series, this is relatively trivial to do. Here's the earlier query modified to sample every third value:

```
SELECT
StartTime=CAST(v.k1 AS char(12)), EndTime=CAST(a.k1 AS char(12)),
StartVal=v.c1, EndVal=a.c1,
Change=SUBSTRING('- +',SIGN(a.c1-v.c1)+2,1)+CAST(ABS(a.c1-v.c1) AS varchar)
FROM
   (SELECT k1, c1, ranking=(SELECT COUNT(DISTINCT k1) FROM #valueset u
   WHERE u.k1 <= l.k1)
   FROM #valueset l) v LEFT OUTER JOIN
   (SELECT k1, c1, ranking=(SELECT COUNT(DISTINCT k1) FROM #valueset u
   WHERE u.k1 <= l.k1)
   FROM #valueset l) a
   ON (a.ranking=v.ranking+1)
WHERE a.k1 IS NOT NULL AND v.ranking%3=0
```

StartTime	EndTime	StartVal	EndVal	Change
Nov 1 1999	Dec 1 1999	13	15	+2
Feb 1 2000	Mar 1 2000	38	16	-22

The only real change here is the use of modulus 3 to qualify the rows the query returns. Since only third rows will satisfy **v.ranking%3=0,** we get the result we're after.

Regions

The most common region-related task is identifying a region in the first place. Unlike sequences and runs, in which the presence of the construct itself is implicit, a region is defined by its values. Members of a particular region are sequential and all meet the same membership criteria. These criteria may stipulate that all members of the region have the same absolute value, that each value has the same relationship to the previous value, or that each value qualifies in some other way. Here's a technique for identifying regions within a sequence:

```
CREATE TABLE #valueset (k1 int identity, c1 int)
INSERT #valueset (c1) VALUES (20)
INSERT #valueset (c1) VALUES (30)
INSERT #valueset (c1) VALUES (0)
```

```
INSERT #valueset (c1) VALUES (0)
INSERT #valueset (c1) VALUES (0)
INSERT #valueset (c1) VALUES (41)
INSERT #valueset (c1) VALUES (0)
INSERT #valueset (c1) VALUES (32)
INSERT #valueset (c1) VALUES (42)

SELECT v.k1
FROM #valueset v JOIN #valueset a
ON (v.c1=0) AND (a.c1=0) AND (ABS(a.k1-v.k1)=1)
GROUP BY v.k1

k1
-----------
3
4
5
```

As illustrated here, the region consists of items in the sequence whose value is zero. The query's magic is performed via a self-join that's filtered for duplicates via the GROUP BY clause. The ON clause limits the values considered to 1) those whose value is zero and 2) those with an adjacent value of zero. Adjacency is determined by subtracting the value of the key column in **v** from that of **a.** An absolute value of one indicates that the key is either just before or just after the one in **v.**

Relative Condition Regions

In addition to absolute values, relative conditions are a popular criterion for establishing region membership. A relative condition identifies some relationship between the values in the sequence. A region whose values increase sequentially is an example of one based on a relative condition. Here's some Transact-SQL code that identifies a region whose values increase monotonically:

```
CREATE TABLE #valueset (k1 int, c1 int)
INSERT #valueset (k1, c1) VALUES (300,15)
INSERT #valueset (k1, c1) VALUES (340,25)
INSERT #valueset (k1, c1) VALUES (344,13)
INSERT #valueset (k1, c1) VALUES (345,14)
INSERT #valueset (k1, c1) VALUES (346,15)
INSERT #valueset (k1, c1) VALUES (347,38)
INSERT #valueset (k1, c1) VALUES (348,16)

SELECT v.k1, v.c1
FROM #valueset v JOIN #valueset a
ON ((a.c1 = v.c1+1) AND (a.k1 = v.k1+1))
OR ((a.c1 = v.c1-1) AND (a.k1 = v.k1-1))
GROUP BY v.k1, v.c1

k1          c1
----------- -----------
344         13
345         14
346         15
```

Again, we use a self-join to compare the work table with itself. The two join criteria established by the ON clause are 1) each key value in the region must be one less or one more than the value under consideration and 2) each value must be correspondingly sequential with its adjacent values.

Note that it's not difficult to modify this query to look for values that merely increase from point to point in the series—that is, ones that aren't necessarily contiguous. Here's an example:

```
SELECT v.k1, v.c1
FROM #valueset v JOIN #valueset a
ON ((a.c1 >= v.c1) AND (a.k1 = v.k1+1))
OR ((a.c1 <= v.c1) AND (a.k1 = v.k1-1))
GROUP BY v.k1, v.c1
```

```
k1           c1
-----------  -----------
344          13
345          14
346          15
347          38
```

Constraining Region Sizes

Once we've identified a region, it may be desirable to qualify it further based on size. We may not want to see within a sequence *every* region whose members have an absolute value or have a specific relationship to one another—we may want to limit the regions we consider to those of a particular size or larger. Here's some Transact-SQL code that illustrates how to constrain regions based on size:

```
CREATE TABLE #valueset(k1 int identity, c1 int)
INSERT #valueset(c1) VALUES (20)
INSERT #valueset(c1) VALUES (30)
INSERT #valueset(c1) VALUES (32)
INSERT #valueset(c1) VALUES (34)
INSERT #valueset(c1) VALUES (36)
INSERT #valueset(c1) VALUES (0)
INSERT #valueset(c1) VALUES (0)
INSERT #valueset(c1) VALUES (41)
INSERT #valueset(c1) VALUES (0)
INSERT #valueset(c1) VALUES (0)
INSERT #valueset(c1) VALUES (0)
INSERT #valueset(c1) VALUES (42)

SELECT v.k1
FROM #valueset v JOIN #valueset a ON (v.c1=0)
GROUP BY v.k1
HAVING
   (ISNULL(MIN(CASE WHEN a.k1 > v.k1 AND a.c1 !=0 THEN a.k1 ELSE null END)-1,
     MAX(CASE WHEN a.k1 > v.k1 THEN a.k1 ELSE v.k1 END))
  -
   ISNULL(MAX(CASE WHEN a.k1 < v.k1 AND a.c1 !=0 THEN a.k1 ELSE null END)+1,
     MIN(CASE WHEN a.k1 < v.k1 THEN a.k1 ELSE v.k1 END)))+1
>=3 -- Desired region size
```

```
k1
----------
9
10
11
```

The ">=3" above constrains the size of the regions listed to those of three or more elements, as the code comment indicates. Note how the first region (consisting of two zero values) in the series is ignored by the query since it's too small. Only the second one, which has the required number of members, is returned.

Beyond the use of JOIN and GROUP BY to compare the table with itself, the real work of the query is performed by the HAVING clause. Consider the first ISNULL() expression. It uses CASE to find either 1) the first key in **a** that is both less than the current key in **v** and whose value is nonzero or 2) the last key in **a** that is greater than the current key in **v**. If a key that meets the first criterion isn't found, it will always be the last key in the table. The idea is to find the nearest nonzero value following the current key in **v**. What we are attempting to do is identify the key value of the region's lower boundary—its terminator.

The second ISNULL() expression is essentially a mirror image of the first. Its purpose is to establish the identity of the first key in the region. Once the boundary keys have been identified, the upper boundary is subtracted from the lower boundary to yield the region size. This is then compared to ">=3" to filter out regions smaller than three members in size.

Though this technique works and is relatively compact from a coding standpoint, I'd be the first to concede that, at least on the surface, it appears to be a bit convoluted. For example, CASE is used to "throw" a NULL back to ISNULL()—which forces ISNULL() to evaluate its second argument—forming a crude nested if-then-else expression. Written a bit more clearly, the first ISNULL() expression might look like this:

```
CASE
   WHEN a.k1 > v.k1 AND a.c1 !=0 THEN MIN(a.k1)-1
   ELSE MAX(CASE WHEN a.k1 > v.k1 THEN a.k1 ELSE v.k1 END)
END
```

The problem with this is that the plain references to a.k1 and a.c1 aren't allowed in the HAVING clause because they aren't contained in either an aggregate or the GROUP BY clause. This is an ANSI SQL restriction and is normally a good thing—except when you're attempting complex queries with single SELECTs like this one. We can't do much about the fact that they aren't in the GROUP BY clause—we need to leave it as is to consolidate our self-join. However, we *can* nest both of these values within aggregate functions so that they conform to ANSI SQL's HAVING clause restrictions. And this is exactly what the query does—it "hides" CASE function logic within aggregates to get past limitations imposed by HAVING—and it's the main reason the logic appears somewhat tangled at first.

Region Boundaries

It's sometimes desirable to return region boundaries rather than the regions themselves. The query above used boundaries to compute region sizes in order to constrain the ones returned. Here's a variation of that query that returns the boundaries of each region it finds:

```
SELECT RegionStart=v.k1,RegionEnd=ISNULL(MIN(CASE WHEN a.k1>v.k1 AND a.c1 !=0
THEN a.k1 ELSE null END)-1,
     MAX(CASE WHEN a.k1 > v.k1 THEN a.k1 ELSE v.k1 END))
FROM #valueset v JOIN #valueset a ON (v.c1=0)
GROUP BY v.k1
HAVING
   ISNULL(MIN(CASE WHEN a.k1>v.k1 AND a.c1 !=0 THEN a.k1 ELSE null END)-1,
     MAX(CASE WHEN a.k1 > v.k1 THEN a.k1 ELSE v.k1 END)) > v.k1
AND
   ISNULL(MAX(CASE WHEN a.k1<v.k1 AND a.c1 !=0 THEN a.k1 ELSE null END)+1,
     MIN(CASE WHEN a.k1 < v.k1 THEN a.k1 ELSE v.k1 END)) = v.k1
```

```
RegionStart RegionEnd
----------- -----------
6           7
9           11
```

Runs

Like their contiguous sequence cousins, runs include a minimum of two columns: a key column and a value column. The key column is always sequential, though its values may not be contiguous.

As with sequences, the existence of a run is implicit. Examples of runs include time series with irregular entry points and numbering systems with gaps (e.g., invoice numbers, credit card numbers, house numbers, etc.).

Regions

By contrast, regions *within* runs are not implicit. As described earlier, regions exist based on membership. The Transact-SQL code required to locate regions within a run is not unlike that used to find them within sequences. Here's an example:

```
CREATE TABLE #valueset (k1 int, c1 int)
INSERT #valueset VALUES (2,0)
INSERT #valueset VALUES (3,30)
INSERT #valueset VALUES (5,0)
INSERT #valueset VALUES (9,0)
INSERT #valueset VALUES (10,0)
INSERT #valueset VALUES (11,40)
INSERT #valueset VALUES (13,0)
INSERT #valueset VALUES (14,0)
INSERT #valueset VALUES (15,42)

SELECT v.k1
FROM #valueset v JOIN #valueset a ON (v.c1=0)
GROUP BY v.k1
HAVING (MIN(CASE WHEN a.k1 > v.k1 THEN (2*(a.k1-v.k1))+CASE WHEN a.c1<>0 THEN 1
ELSE 0 END ELSE null END)%2=0)
OR (MIN(CASE WHEN a.k1 < v.k1 THEN (2*(v.k1-a.k1))+CASE WHEN a.c1<>0 THEN 1 ELSE
0 END ELSE null END)%2=0)
```

```
k1
-----------
5
9
10
13
14
```

As with many of the other queries, this query uses a self-join/GROUP BY combo to compare the work table with itself. Note the use of nested CASE expressions to effect some fairly complex logic. Also note the way in which this logic is wrapped within aggregate functions so that it complies with ANSI SQL's restrictions on the HAVING clause.

Region Boundaries

As we did with sequences, let's explore how to return the outer boundaries of run regions rather than the regions themselves. Here's some code that returns the boundaries of the regions it encounters within a run:

```
CREATE TABLE #valueset (k1 int, c1 int)
INSERT #valueset VALUES (2,20)
INSERT #valueset VALUES (3,30)
INSERT #valueset VALUES (5,0)
INSERT #valueset VALUES (9,0)
INSERT #valueset VALUES (10,0)
INSERT #valueset VALUES (11,40)
INSERT #valueset VALUES (13,0)
INSERT #valueset VALUES (15,0)
INSERT #valueset VALUES (16,42)

SELECT StartRun=v.k1, EndRun=a.k1
FROM #valueset v JOIN #valueset a ON (v.k1 < a.k1) CROSS JOIN #valueset l
GROUP BY v.k1, a.k1
HAVING
   (SUM(ABS(l.c1)*(CASE WHEN v.k1 <=l.k1 AND l.k1 <= a.k1 THEN 1 ELSE 0 END))=0)
   AND (ISNULL(MIN(CASE WHEN l.k1 > a.k1
     THEN (2*(l.k1-a.k1))+(CASE WHEN l.c1<>0 THEN 1 ELSE 0 END)
     ELSE null END),1)%2 != 0)
   AND (ISNULL(MIN(CASE WHEN l.k1 < v.k1
   THEN (2*(v.k1-l.k1))+(CASE WHEN l.c1<>0 THEN 1 ELSE 0 END)
   ELSE null END),1)
   %2 != 0)
```

```
StartRun    EndRun
----------- -----------
5           10
13          15
```

As with the previous query, this example embeds much of its work within aggregate functions in the HAVING clause. Some of this is counterintuitive. Note, for example, the HAVING clause expression:

```
(SUM(ABS(l.c1)*(CASE WHEN v.k1 <=l.k1 AND l.k1 <= a.k1 THEN 1 ELSE 0 END))=0)
```

Written more legibly, it might read:

```
((CASE WHEN v.k1 <=l.k1 AND l.k1 <= a.k1 THEN SUM(ABS(l.c1)) ELSE 0 END)=0)
```

However, as mentioned before, v.k1 and l.k1 must either also appear in the GROUP BY clause or be wrapped in an aggregate function in order to be used in the HAVING clause, so this syntax won't work. Instead, we return either one or zero from the CASE expression and then multiply SUM(ABS(l.c1)) by it, achieving the same result.

Another interesting characteristic of this query is the use of three instances of the work table. The fact that the run's key values may not be sequential causes some additional work that requires a third instance of the table to be performed, even though no columns are returned from it by the query.

Constrained Regions

As mentioned in the sequence examples, the need to constrain regions based on size is a common one. Here's a Transact-SQL query that scans a run for regions consisting of three or more members with values less than 10:

```
CREATE TABLE #valueset (k1 int, c1 int)
INSERT #valueset VALUES (2,20)
INSERT #valueset VALUES (3,30)
INSERT #valueset VALUES (5,0)
INSERT #valueset VALUES (9,4)
INSERT #valueset VALUES (10,8)
INSERT #valueset VALUES (11,40)
INSERT #valueset VALUES (13,0)
INSERT #valueset VALUES (15,12)
INSERT #valueset VALUES (16,42)

SELECT
   StartRun=v.k1,
   StartRunV=v.c1,
   EndRun=a.k1,
   EndRunV=a.c1,
   RunSize=COUNT(CASE WHEN v.k1 <= l.k1 AND l.k1 <= a.k1 THEN 1 ELSE null END),
   RunAvg=AVG(CASE WHEN v.k1 <= l.k1 AND l.k1 <= a.k1 THEN l.c1 ELSE null END)
FROM #valueset v JOIN #valueset a ON (v.k1 < a.k1) CROSS JOIN #valueset l
GROUP BY v.k1, v.c1, a.k1, a.c1
HAVING (COUNT(CASE WHEN v.k1 <= l.k1 AND l.k1 <= a.k1 THEN 1 ELSE NULL END)>=3)
-- 3 = Desired Run size
AND (COUNT((CASE WHEN l.c1 >=10 THEN 1 ELSE NULL END)*(CASE WHEN v.k1 <= l.k1
AND l.k1 <= a.k1 THEN 1 ELSE NULL END))=0)
AND (ISNULL(MIN((CASE WHEN l.k1 > a.k1 THEN (2*(l.k1-a.k1))+(CASE WHEN l.c1>=10
THEN 1 ELSE 0 END) ELSE null END)),1)%2 != 0)
AND (ISNULL(MIN((CASE WHEN l.k1 < v.k1 THEN (2*(v.k1-l.k1))+(CASE WHEN l.c1>=10
THEN 1 ELSE 0 END) ELSE null END)),1)%2 != 0)
```

StartRun	StartRunV	EndRun	EndRunV	RunSize	RunAvg
5	0	10	8	3	4

This query also requires three instances of the work table to get the job done. It self-joins the first two, then cross-joins the third and removes the resulting duplicates using a GROUP BY clause. Beyond that, most of the logic controlling which rows make it into the result set is contained in the HAVING clause. As in many of the examples presented thus far, much of the selection logic is embedded in aggregate functions so that it conforms to the restrictions imposed by HAVING.

Intervals

An interval is an ordered subsequence of values of a particular size. The ability to split a sequence into a given number of equally sized intervals has lots of business applications—everything from stratifying customer lists to breaking sample sequences into more manageable chunks. Assuming we start with the following table:

```
CREATE TABLE #valueset (c1 int)
INSERT #valueset VALUES (20)
INSERT #valueset VALUES (30)
INSERT #valueset VALUES (40)
INSERT #valueset VALUES (21)
INSERT #valueset VALUES (31)
INSERT #valueset VALUES (41)
INSERT #valueset VALUES (22)
INSERT #valueset VALUES (32)
INSERT #valueset VALUES (42)
```

here's a Transact-SQL SELECT statement that breaks the sequence into three intervals, returning the end point of each one:

```
SELECT v.c1
FROM #valueset v CROSS JOIN #valueset a
GROUP BY v.c1
HAVING COUNT(CASE WHEN a.c1 <= v.c1 THEN 1 ELSE null END)%(COUNT(*)/3)=0

c1
-----------
22
32
42
```

Here again we use the JOIN/GROUP BY combo to compare the table with itself. And, again, the query's selection logic is embedded in its HAVING clause. The "/3" in the HAVING clause indicates the interval size we seek. The HAVING clause works by counting the number of items in **a** that are less than or equal to the current item in **v,** then checking that number modulus the total number of rows divided by the desired interval size. If the modulus is zero, we have an interval end point that will be returned by the query.

Note that it's trivial to return the position of each end point as well. Here's the code:

```
SELECT
IntervalEnd=v.c1,
IntervalPos=COUNT(CASE WHEN a.c1 <= v.c1 THEN 1 ELSE null END)
FROM #valueset v CROSS JOIN #valueset a
GROUP BY v.c1
HAVING COUNT(CASE WHEN a.c1 <= v.c1 THEN 1 ELSE null END)%(COUNT(*)/3)=0


IntervalEnd IntervalPos
----------- -----------
22          3
32          6
42          9
```

To get the start points rather than the end points of each interval, change the modulus check to "1," like this:

```
SELECT v.c1
FROM #valueset v CROSS JOIN #valueset a
GROUP BY v.c1
HAVING COUNT(CASE WHEN a.c1 <= v.c1 THEN 1 ELSE null END)%(COUNT(*)/3)=1


c1
-----------
20
30
40
```

Partitioned Intervals

Rather than computing intervals over an entire sequence, it's often desirable to compute them in a sectioned or partitioned fashion. That is, instead of seeing all the partitions across an entire table, we might want to see them grouped based on a particular column—a GROUP BY column (or columns), if you will. Since Transact-SQL has no INTERVAL_BEGIN()- or INTERVAL_END()-type aggregate functions, performing a vector computation such as this requires a nontraditional approach. As with most of the solutions presented in this chapter, the technique presented here uses the Cartesian product of two instances of the work table, together with GROUP BY and HAVING to return the data we seek. Here's a Transact-SQL routine that returns a partitioned listing of interval information:

```
CREATE TABLE #valueset (k1 int, c1 int)
INSERT #valueset VALUES (1,20)
INSERT #valueset VALUES (1,21)
INSERT #valueset VALUES (1,22)
INSERT #valueset VALUES (1,24)
INSERT #valueset VALUES (1,28)
INSERT #valueset VALUES (2,31)
INSERT #valueset VALUES (2,32)
INSERT #valueset VALUES (2,40)
INSERT #valueset VALUES (2,41)
INSERT #valueset VALUES (3,52)
```

```
INSERT #valueset VALUES (3,53)
INSERT #valueset VALUES (3,56)
INSERT #valueset VALUES (3,58)
INSERT #valueset VALUES (3,59)
INSERT #valueset VALUES (4,60)
INSERT #valueset VALUES (4,61)
INSERT #valueset VALUES (4,62)

SELECT v.k1, v.c1
FROM #valueset v JOIN #valueset a ON (v.k1=a.k1)
GROUP BY v.k1, v.c1
HAVING
   COUNT(CASE WHEN a.c1 <= v.c1 THEN 1 ELSE null END)
   BETWEEN (COUNT(*)/4) AND (COUNT(*)/4)*2
```

k1	c1
1	20
1	21
2	31
2	32
3	52
3	53

This code partitions, or groups, the rows in the table using the k1 column into intervals of four. It then returns the top two values from each interval. This would be useful, for example, if you needed to return the top *n* salespeople from each region or the top *n* students within each class, but you wanted to constrain the list to intervals of a particular size to filter out salespeople in regions with no competition or students in classes with few other students.

Summary

Sequences, series, runs, and regions are similar data constructs that typically include at least two columns: a sequential (though not necessarily contiguous) key column and a value column. Sequences and series are synonymous. A sequence's key column values are sequential, with no gaps between them. A run's key column values are also sequential, though they may not be contiguous. A region is a portion of a sequence or run whose members meet a given set of criteria. Intervals are produced by dividing a sequence or run into multiple, evenly sized subsequences or subsets.

In this chapter, you learned how to use self-joins and cross-joins to identify complex data trends and data relationships within tables. Using the example code included in this chapter, you should be able to solve most types of run- and sequence-related problems without resorting to control-of-flow language statements such as loops.

10

Arrays

Init, Use, Destroy. Three procedure calls, six possible sequences, five of them wrong. I am quietly impressed that any nontrivial applications ever work.
—Thomas L. Holaday

Because there's no built-in array data type, there's really no direct way to store or work with true arrays in Transact-SQL. There are a couple of alternatives that are fairly array-like, but since they really aren't arrays in the 3GL sense of the word, they're less than ideal.

The two most obvious ways to simulate an array in Transact-SQL are setting up a table that mimics an array (with columns simulating dimensions) and using a single column to store multiple values (with special indexing routines to flatten or compose the array elements). The first approach has the advantage of being more relational and extensible. Adding a dimension is as simple as adding a column. The second approach has the advantage of simplicity and intuitiveness. Having a column that stores multiple values is not far removed from having one that can store an array—it's largely a question of semantics and syntax.

Note that arrays, by their very nature, violate the basic rules of normalization. For a table to be even first normal form compliant, it must be free of repeating values. Repeating values can take the form of multiple columns used to store instances of the same type of value or multiple values within a single column. These repeating values must be removed if a table is to be considered normalized. Storing arrays—even "virtual" arrays like the ones discussed in this chapter—is a form of denormalization that you should undertake only in special circumstances.

Arrays as Big Strings

Storing arrays as large character strings is not a new concept. In fact, in the 1980s, the Advanced Revelation DBMS garnered quite a following through its support of "multivalued" columns—essentially string fields with multiple values and special routines to manipulate them. Even today, many DBMSs that support array columns store them internally as simple buffers and provide SQL extensions that insulate the developer from having to know or deal with this. Here's a sample query that demonstrates the multivalued column approach in Transact-SQL:

```
CREATE TABLE #array (k1 int identity, arraycol varchar(8000))

INSERT #array (arraycol) VALUES ('LES PAUL        '+
                                 'BUDDY GUY       '+
                                 'JEFF BECK       ')
INSERT #array (arraycol) VALUES ('STEVE MILLER    '+
                                 'EDDIE VAN HALEN'+
                                 'TOM SCHOLZ      ')
INSERT #array (arraycol) VALUES ('STEVE VAI       '+
                                 'ERIC CLAPTON    '+
                                 'SLASH           ')
SELECT Element1=SUBSTRING(arraycol,(0*15)+1,15),
   Element2=SUBSTRING(arraycol,(1*15)+1,15),
   Element3=SUBSTRING(arraycol,(2*15)+1,15)
FROM #array a

Element1         Element2         Element3
--------------- --------------- ---------------
LES PAUL        BUDDY GUY       JEFF BECK
STEVE MILLER    EDDIE VAN HALEN TOM SCHOLZ
STEVE VAI       ERIC CLAPTON    SLASH
```

This technique stores multiple values in the work table's arraycol column. These values emulate a single-dimensional array, which is the easiest type to work with using this approach. Multidimensional arrays are feasible as well, but they're geometrically more complex to deal with. Rather than building multidimensional arrays into a single row, another way to accomplish the same thing is to spread the dimensions of the array over the entire table, with each record representing just one row in that array.

Note the use of varchar(8000) to define the array column. With the advent of SQL Server's large character data types, we can now store a reasonably sized array using this approach. In the case of an array whose elements are fifteen bytes long, we can store up to 533 items *in each array column, in each row.* That's plenty for most applications.

Also note that virtually any type of data can be stored in this type of virtual array, not just strings. Of course, anything stored in a character column must be converted to a string first, but that's a minor concern. The only prerequisite is that each item must be uniformly sized, regardless of its original data type.

The INSERT statements used to populate the table are intentionally split over multiple lines to mimic filling an array. Though it's unnecessary, you should consider doing this as well if you decide to use this approach. It's more readable and also helps with keeping each element sized appropriately—an essential for the technique to work correctly.

Note the use of the expression **(n*s)+1** to calculate each array element's index. Here, **n** represents the element number (assuming a base of zero) you wish to access, and **s** represents the element size. Though it would be easier to code

```
SUBSTRING(arraycol,1,15)
```

using the expression establishes the relationship between the element you seek and the string stored in the varchar column. It makes accessing any element as trivial as supplying its array index.

This technique does not require that the number of elements be uniform between rows in the table. Here's an example that shows how to implement "jagged" or unevenly sized arrays:

```
CREATE TABLE #array (k1 int identity, arraycol varchar(8000))
INSERT #array (arraycol) VALUES ('LES PAUL         '+
                                 'BUDDY GUY        '+
                                 'JEFF BECK        '+
                                 'JOE SATRIANI     ')
INSERT #array (arraycol) VALUES ('STEVE MILLER     '+
                                 'EDDIE VAN HALEN'+
                                 'TOM SCHOLZ       ')
INSERT #array (arraycol) VALUES ('STEVE VAI        '+
                                 'ERIC CLAPTON     '+
                                 'SLASH            '+
                                 'JIMI HENDRIX     '+
                                 'JASON BECKER     '+
                                 'MICHAEL HARTMAN')
SELECT
   Element1=SUBSTRING(arraycol,(0*15)+1,15),
   Element2=SUBSTRING(arraycol,(1*15)+1,15),
   Element3=SUBSTRING(arraycol,(2*15)+1,15),
   Element4=SUBSTRING(arraycol,(3*15)+1,15),
   Element5=SUBSTRING(arraycol,(4*15)+1,15),
   Element6=SUBSTRING(arraycol,(5*15)+1,15)
FROM #array a
```

Element1	Element2	Element3	Element4	Element5	Element6
LES PAUL	BUDDY GUY	JEFF BECK	JOE SATRIANI		
STEVE MILLER	EDDIE VAN HALEN	TOM SCHOLZ			
STEVE VAI	ERIC CLAPTON	SLASH	JIMI HENDRIX	JASON BECKER	MICHAEL HARTMAN

The only thing that's really different here is the data. Since SUBSTRING() returns an empty string when passed an invalid starting point, we don't need special handling for arrays with fewer than six elements.

The example above is limited to arrays with six or fewer elements. What if we want to support arrays of sixty elements? What if we need arrays with hundreds of elements? Are we forced to include a separate column in the result set for each one? The technique would be rather limited if we had to set up a separate result set column for every element. That would get cumbersome in a hurry. Here's some code that demonstrates how to handle arrays of any size without coding static result set columns for each element:

```
DECLARE @arrayvar varchar(8000)
DECLARE @i int, @l int
DECLARE c CURSOR FOR SELECT arraycol FROM #array

OPEN c
FETCH c INTO @arrayvar

WHILE (@@FETCH_STATUS=0) BEGIN
   SET @i=0
   SET @l=DATALENGTH(@arrayvar)/15

   WHILE (@i<@l) BEGIN
     SELECT 'Guitarist'=SUBSTRING(@arrayvar,(@i*15)+1,15)
     SET @i=@i+1
   END
   FETCH c INTO @arrayvar
END
```

```
CLOSE c
DEALLOCATE c

Guitarist
---------------
LES PAUL

Guitarist
---------------
BUDDY GUY

Guitarist
---------------
JEFF BECK

Guitarist
---------------
JOE SATRIANI

Guitarist
---------------
STEVE MILLER

Guitarist
---------------
EDDIE VAN HALEN

Guitarist
---------------
TOM SCHOLZ

Guitarist
---------------
STEVE VAI

Guitarist
---------------
ERIC CLAPTON

Guitarist
---------------
SLASH

Guitarist
---------------
JIMI HENDRIX

Guitarist
---------------
JASON BECKER

Guitarist
---------------
MICHAEL HARTMAN
```

This code opens a cursor on the work table, then iterates through the array in each row. It uses the DATALENGTH() function to determine the length of each array and a loop to SELECT each element from the array using the indexing expression introduced in the previous query.

Though this technique is flexible in that it allows us to process as many array elements as we want with a minimum of code, it suffers from one fundamental flaw: It returns multiple result sets. Many front ends don't know how to handle multiple result sets and will balk at query output such as this. There are a couple of ways around this. Here's one approach:

```
CREATE TABLE #results (Guitarist varchar(15))

DECLARE @arrayvar varchar(8000)
DECLARE @i int, @l int
DECLARE c CURSOR FOR SELECT arraycol FROM #array

OPEN c
FETCH c INTO @arrayvar

WHILE (@@FETCH_STATUS=0) BEGIN
   SET @i=0
   SET @l=DATALENGTH(@arrayvar)/15
   WHILE (@i<@l) BEGIN
     INSERT #results SELECT SUBSTRING(@arrayvar,(@i*15)+1,15)
     SET @i=@i+1
   END
   FETCH c INTO @arrayvar
END
CLOSE c
DEALLOCATE c

SELECT * FROM #results
DROP TABLE #results

Guitarist
---------------
LES PAUL
BUDDY GUY
JEFF BECK
JOE SATRIANI
STEVE MILLER
EDDIE VAN HALEN
TOM SCHOLZ
STEVE VAI
ERIC CLAPTON
SLASH
JIMI HENDRIX
JASON BECKER
MICHAEL HARTMAN
```

Here, we use a temporary table to store each array element as it's processed by the query. Once processing completes, the contents of the table are returned as a single result set and the temporary table is dropped. A variation on this would be to move the code to a stored procedure and return a pointer to the cursor via an output parameter. Then the caller could process the array at its convenience.

Another, though slightly more limited, way to process the array is to generate a SELECT statement as the array is processed and execute it afterward. Here's an example:

```
DECLARE @arrayvar varchar(8000), @select_stmnt varchar(8000)
DECLARE @k int, @i int, @l int, @c int
DECLARE c CURSOR FOR SELECT * FROM #array

SET @select_stmnt='SELECT '
SET @c=0

OPEN c
FETCH c INTO @k, @arrayvar

WHILE (@@FETCH_STATUS=0) BEGIN
   SET @i=0
   SET @l=DATALENGTH(@arrayvar)/15
   WHILE (@i<@l) BEGIN
     SELECT @select_stmnt=@select_stmnt+'Guitarist'+CAST(@c as
     varchar)+'='+QUOTENAME(RTRIM(SUBSTRING(@arrayvar,(@i*15)+1,15)),'"')+','
     SET @i=@i+1
     SET @c=@c+1
   END
   FETCH c INTO @k, @arrayvar
END
CLOSE c
DEALLOCATE c

SELECT @select_stmnt=LEFT(@select_stmnt,DATALENGTH(@select_stmnt)-1)

EXEC(@select_stmnt)
```

(Results abridged)

```
Guitarist0 Guitarist1 Guitarist2 Guitarist3    Guitarist4    Guitarist5
---------- ---------- ---------- ------------   ------------  ---------------
LES PAUL   BUDDY GUY  JEFF BECK  JOE SATRIANI   STEVE MILLER  EDDIE VAN HALEN
```

Note the use of the QUOTENAME() function to surround each array value with quotes so that it can be returned by the SELECT statement. The default quote delimiters are '[' and ']' but, as the example shows, you can specify others.

This routine is more limited than the temporary table solution because it's restricted by the maximum size of varchar. That is, since the SELECT statement that we build is stored in a variable of type varchar, it can't exceed 8000 bytes. While the other techniques allot 8000 bytes *for each row's* array, this one limits the sum length of the arrays *in all records* to just 8000 bytes. Given that this string must also store a column name for each element (most front ends have trouble processing unnamed columns), this is a significant limitation.

Nevertheless, the fact that this approach builds SQL that it then executes is interesting in and of itself. You can probably think of other applications for this technique such as variably sized cross-tabs, run and sequence flattening, and so on.

Modifying Array Elements

One inherent weakness of storing arrays as strings is revealed when we attempt to make modifications to element values. Unless you're making the most basic kind of change, updating either a single value or an entire dimension is not a straightforward process. Clearing the array in a given row is simple—we just do something like this:

```
UPDATE #array SET arraycol = '' WHERE k1=1
```

If you think of the array in each record as a row in a larger array (which spans the entire table), you can think of this as clearing a single row.

What if we wanted to clear just the second element in each record's array? We'd need something like this:

```
UPDATE #array
SET arraycol =
LEFT(arraycol,1*15)+SPACE(1*15)+RIGHT(arraycol,DATALENGTH(arraycol)-(2*15))
```

(Results abridged)

Element1	Element2	Element3	Element4	Element5
LES PAUL		JEFF BECK	JOE SATRIANI	
STEVE MILLER		TOM SCHOLZ		
STEVE VAI		SLASH	JIMI HENDRIX	JASON BECKER

This involves a few somewhat abstruse computations that depend on the element size to work correctly. As with the earlier queries, this code multiplies an array index by the element size in order to access the array. Though it's certainly more compact to use SPACE(15) rather than SPACE(1*15), using the expression is more flexible in that it's easily reusable with other elements.

Note that we could use this technique to *set* the value of a particular dimension rather than simply clearing it. For example, to fill the third element in each row's array with a specific value, we would use code like this:

```
UPDATE #array
SET arraycol =
LEFT(arraycol,(2*15))+'MUDDY WATERS '+RIGHT(arraycol,DATALENGTH(arraycol)-(3*15))
```

To limit the change to a particular record, include a WHERE clause that restricts the UPDATE, like this:

```
UPDATE #array
SET arraycol =
LEFT(arraycol,(3*15))+'MUDDY WATERS   '+
RIGHT(arraycol,CASE WHEN (DATALENGTH(arraycol)-(4*15))<0 THEN 0 ELSE
DATALENGTH(arraycol)-(4*15) END)
WHERE k1=2
```

As you can see, things can get pretty convoluted considering all we want to do is change an array element. Naturally, things would be much simpler if Transact-SQL supported arrays directly.

Arrays as Tables

Implementing a virtual array using a simple table is also a viable alternative to native array support. This technique uses one or more columns as array indexes. If the array is single-dimensional, there's just one index column. If it's multidimensional, there may be several. Here's an example:

```
CREATE TABLE #array (k1 int identity (0,1), guitarist varchar(15))

INSERT #array (guitarist) VALUES('LES PAUL');
INSERT #array (guitarist) VALUES('BUDDY GUY');
INSERT #array (guitarist) VALUES('JEFF BECK');
INSERT #array (guitarist) VALUES('JOE SATRIANI');
INSERT #array (guitarist) VALUES('STEVE MILLER');
INSERT #array (guitarist) VALUES('EDDIE VAN HALEN');
INSERT #array (guitarist) VALUES('TOM SCHOLZ');
INSERT #array (guitarist) VALUES('STEVE VAI');
INSERT #array (guitarist) VALUES('ERIC CLAPTON');
INSERT #array (guitarist) VALUES('SLASH');
INSERT #array (guitarist) VALUES('JIMI HENDRIX');
INSERT #array (guitarist) VALUES('JASON BECKER');
INSERT #array (guitarist) VALUES('MICHAEL HARTMAN');

-- To set the third element in the array
UPDATE #array
SET guitarist='JOHN GMUENDER'
WHERE k1=2

SELECT guitarist
FROM #array

guitarist
---------------
LES PAUL
BUDDY GUY
JOHN GMUENDER
JOE SATRIANI
STEVE MILLER
EDDIE VAN HALEN
TOM SCHOLZ
STEVE VAI
ERIC CLAPTON
SLASH
JIMI HENDRIX
JASON BECKER
MICHAEL HARTMAN
```

This code illustrates a simple way to emulate a single-dimensional array using a table. Note the use of a seed value for the identity column in order to construct a zero-based array, as we did in the string array examples. Transact-SQL requires that you also specify an increment value whenever you specify a seed value, so we specified an increment of one.

This code changes the value of the third element (which has an index value of two). Removing the WHERE clause would allow the entire virtual array to be set or cleared.

Sorting

Unlike the varchar array technique, sorting a virtual table array is as simple as supplying an ORDER BY clause. Deleting elements is simple, too—all you need is a DELETE statement qualified by a WHERE clause. Inserting a new element (as opposed to appending one) is more difficult since we're using an identity column as the array index. However, it's still doable—either via SET IDENTITY_INSERT or by changing the index column to a nonidentity type.

Adding a dimension is as straightforward as adding a column. Here's an example:

```
CREATE TABLE #array (band int, single int, title varchar(50))

INSERT #array VALUES(0,0,'LITTLE BIT O'' LOVE');
INSERT #array VALUES(0,1,'FIRE AND WATER');
INSERT #array VALUES(0,2,'THE FARMER HAD A DAUGHTER');
INSERT #array VALUES(0,3,'ALL RIGHT NOW');
INSERT #array VALUES(1,0,'BAD COMPANY');
INSERT #array VALUES(1,1,'SHOOTING STAR');
INSERT #array VALUES(1,2,'FEEL LIKE MAKIN'' LOVE');
INSERT #array VALUES(1,3,'ROCK AND ROLL FANTASY');
INSERT #array VALUES(2,0,'SATISFACTION GUARANTEED');
INSERT #array VALUES(2,1,'RADIOACTIVE');
INSERT #array VALUES(2,2,'MONEY CAN''T BUY');
INSERT #array VALUES(2,3,'TOGETHER');
INSERT #array VALUES(3,0,'GOOD MORNING LITTLE SCHOOLGIRL');
INSERT #array VALUES(3,1,'HOOCHIE-COOCHIE MAN');
INSERT #array VALUES(3,2,'MUDDY WATER BLUES');
INSERT #array VALUES(3,3,'THE HUNTER');

-- To set the third element in the fourth row of the array
UPDATE #array
SET title='BORN UNDER A BAD SIGN'
WHERE band=3 AND single=2

SELECT title

FROM #array
```

(Results)

```
title
--------------------------------------------------
LITTLE BIT O' LOVE
FIRE AND WATER
THE FARMER HAD A DAUGHTER
ALL RIGHT NOW
BAD COMPANY
SHOOTING STAR
FEEL LIKE MAKIN' LOVE
ROCK AND ROLL FANTASY
SATISFACTION GUARANTEED
RADIOACTIVE
MONEY CAN'T BUY
TOGETHER
GOOD MORNING LITTLE SCHOOLGIRL
HOOCHIE-COOCHIE MAN
BORN UNDER A BAD SIGN
THE HUNTER
```

This code sets up a two-dimensional array, then changes the third element in its fourth row. Because its indexes are simple integer columns, the SQL necessary to manipulate the array is much more intuitive. For example, clearing a given dimension in the array is trivial:

```
UPDATE #array
SET title=''
WHERE band=2


SELECT *
FROM #array


band          single          title
----------- -----------    -------------------------------------------------------------
0             0               LITTLE BIT O' LOVE
0             1               FIRE AND WATER
0             2               THE FARMER HAD A DAUGHTER
0             3               ALL RIGHT NOW
1             0               BAD COMPANY
1             1               SHOOTING STAR
1             2               FEEL LIKE MAKIN' LOVE
1             3               ROCK AND ROLL FANTASY
2             0
2             1
2             2
2             3
3             0               GOOD MORNING LITTLE SCHOOLGIRL
3             1               HOOCHIE-COOCHIE MAN
3             2               MUDDY WATER BLUES
3             3               THE HUNTER
```

This code uses a simple UPDATE statement qualified by a WHERE clause to clear the array's third dimension.

Another nifty feature of this approach is that row and column totals are easy to produce using basic aggregate functions and the GROUP BY clause. Here's a query that performs a variety of aggregations using the array's indexes as grouping columns:

```
CREATE TABLE #array (band int, single int, title varchar(50))

INSERT #array VALUES(0,0,'LITTLE BIT O'' LOVE');
INSERT #array VALUES(0,1,'FIRE AND WATER');
INSERT #array VALUES(0,2,'ALL RIGHT NOW');
INSERT #array VALUES(1,0,'BAD COMPANY');
INSERT #array VALUES(1,1,'SHOOTING STAR');
INSERT #array VALUES(1,2,'FEEL LIKE MAKIN'' LOVE');
INSERT #array VALUES(1,3,'ROCK AND ROLL FANTASY');
INSERT #array VALUES(1,4,'BURNING SKY');
INSERT #array VALUES(2,0,'SATISFACTION GUARANTEED');
INSERT #array VALUES(2,1,'RADIOACTIVE');
INSERT #array VALUES(2,2,'MONEY CAN''T BUY');
INSERT #array VALUES(2,3,'TOGETHER');
INSERT #array VALUES(3,0,'GOOD MORNING LITTLE SCHOOLGIRL');
INSERT #array VALUES(3,1,'HOOCHIE-COOCHIE MAN');
INSERT #array VALUES(3,2,'MUDDY WATER BLUES');
INSERT #array VALUES(3,3,'THE HUNTER');
```

```
SELECT Band, NumberOfSongsPerBand=COUNT(single)
FROM #array
GROUP BY Band

SELECT Band, "Last Song (Alphabetically)"=MAX(title)
FROM #array
GROUP BY Band
ORDER BY 2

SELECT Single, NumberOfBandsPerSingle=COUNT(Band)
FROM #array
GROUP BY Single
```

```
Band          NumberOfSongsPerBand
-----------   --------------------
0             3
1             5
2             4
3             4


Band          Last Song (Alphabetically)
-----------   ------------------------------------------------
0             LITTLE BIT O' LOVE
1             SHOOTING STAR
3             THE HUNTER
2             TOGETHER


Single        NumberOfBandsPerSingle
-----------   ------------------------------------------------
0             4
1             4
2             4
3             3
4             1
```

Keep in mind that the index columns used with this approach can be data types other than integers since we access them via the WHERE clause. Datetime types, GUIDs, and bit types are popular indexes as well. Also, these indexes can be accessed via more complex expressions than the diminutive "=i" where i is an array index. The LIKE, BETWEEN, IN, and EXISTS predicates, as well as subqueries, can also be used to traverse the array.

Transposing Dimensions

Swapping array dimensions is also relatively trivial with this approach. For example, assume we have a two-dimensional array, and we want to swap its rows and columns. How would we do it? With the varchar array approach, this could get quite involved. However, it's fairly straight-forward using the table array approach and a feature of the UPDATE statement. Here's the code:

```
DECLARE @i int

UPDATE #array SET @i=Band, Band=Single, Single=@i

SELECT *
FROM #array
ORDER BY Band, Single
```

```
band           single         title
-----------    -----------    -----------------------------------------------------
0              0              LITTLE BIT O' LOVE
0              1              BAD COMPANY
0              2              SATISFACTION GUARANTEED
0              3              GOOD MORNING LITTLE SCHOOLGIRL
1              0              FIRE AND WATER
1              1              SHOOTING STAR
1              2              RADIOACTIVE
1              3              HOOCHIE-COOCHIE MAN
2              0              ALL RIGHT NOW
2              1              FEEL LIKE MAKIN' LOVE
2              2              MONEY CAN'T BUY
2              3              MUDDY WATER BLUES
3              1              ROCK AND ROLL FANTASY
3              2              TOGETHER
3              3              THE HUNTER
4              1              BURNING SKY
```

Since Transact-SQL is processed left to right, we're able to set **@i** to store the value of **band** so that we may swap **band** and **single.** The ability to set a local variable via UPDATE was originally intended as a performance enhancement to shorten the time locks were held. It was designed to combine the functionality of performing an UPDATE, then immediately SELECTing a value from the same table into a local variable for further processing. In our case, we're using this feature, along with Transact-SQL's left-to-right execution, to swap one column with another.

It's possible that Transact-SQL's ability to reuse variables set by an UPDATE within the UPDATE itself might change someday since it's not specifically documented. As with all undocumented features, you should use it only when necessary and with due caution. It might not be supported in a future release, so be wary of becoming too dependent upon it.

Note that if you only want to swap the dimensions *in the result set* (rather than changing the array itself), that's easy enough to do:

```
SELECT Band=single, Single=Band, Title
FROM #array
ORDER BY 1, 2
```

```
Band           Single         Title
-----------    -----------    -----------------------------------------------------
0              0              LITTLE BIT O' LOVE
0              1              BAD COMPANY
0              2              SATISFACTION GUARANTEED
0              3              GOOD MORNING LITTLE SCHOOLGIRL
1              0              FIRE AND WATER
1              1              SHOOTING STAR
1              2              RADIOACTIVE
1              3              HOOCHIE-COOCHIE MAN
2              0              ALL RIGHT NOW
2              1              FEEL LIKE MAKIN' LOVE
2              2              MONEY CAN'T BUY
2              3              MUDDY WATER BLUES
3              1              ROCK AND ROLL FANTASY
3              2              TOGETHER
3              3              THE HUNTER
4              1              BURNING SKY
```

We get the same results as the previous query, but the array itself remains unmodified. A VIEW object is ideal in this situation if you need to swap an array's dimensions on a regular basis.

Ensuring Array Integrity

There are a couple of nifty ways to ensure the veracity of the array index values you store. One is to create unique constraints on them. You can do this via PRIMARY KEY or UNIQUE KEY constraints on the appropriate columns. For example, we might modify the CREATE TABLE statement above like so:

```
CREATE TABLE #array (band int, single int, title varchar(50)
PRIMARY KEY (band, single))
```

This ensures that no duplicate indexes are allowed into the table, which is what you want. It also creates an index over the array indexes—which will probably benefit performance.

Reshaping the Array

Many of the techniques that were used to reshape or flatten the varchar array work with table arrays as well. The most flexible of those presented is the technique that reshapes the array by populating a temporary table with values. However, table arrays give us another option that requires far less code and is much easier to follow:

```
SELECT Free=MAX(CASE band WHEN 0 THEN title ELSE NULL END),
    BadCompany=MAX(CASE band WHEN 1 THEN title ELSE NULL END),
    TheFirm=MAX(CASE band WHEN 2 THEN title ELSE NULL END),
    Solo=MAX(CASE band WHEN 3 THEN title ELSE NULL END)
FROM #array a
GROUP BY a.single
```

Free	BadCompany	TheFirm	Solo
LITTLE BIT O' LOVE	BAD COMPANY	SATISFACTION GUARANTEED	GOOD MORNING LITTLE SCHOOLGIRL
FIRE AND WATER	SHOOTING STAR	RADIOACTIVE	HOOCHIE-COOCHIE MAN
ALL RIGHT NOW	FEEL LIKE MAKIN' LOVE	MONEY CAN'T BUY	MUDDY WATER BLUES
NULL	ROCK AND ROLL FANTASY	TOGETHER	THE HUNTER
NULL	BURNING SKY	NULL	NULL

This technique uses an aggregate to "hide" the selection of the **title** column for each **band** so that it can use GROUP BY to flatten the result set. It groups on the **single** column because **single** provides the type of unique identifier we need to coalesce the array elements. To understand this, it's instructive to view what the result set would look like without the MAX()/ GROUP BY combo:

```
SELECT Free=(CASE band WHEN 0 THEN title ELSE NULL END),
    BadCompany=(CASE band WHEN 1 THEN title ELSE NULL END),
    TheFirm=(CASE band WHEN 2 THEN title ELSE NULL END),
    Solo=(CASE band WHEN 3 THEN title ELSE NULL END)
FROM #array
```

Free	BadCompany	TheFirm	Solo
LITTLE BIT O' LOVE	NULL	NULL	NULL
FIRE AND WATER	NULL	NULL	NULL
ALL RIGHT NOW	NULL	NULL	NULL
NULL	BAD COMPANY	NULL	NULL
NULL	SHOOTING STAR	NULL	NULL
NULL	FEEL LIKE MAKIN' LOVE	NULL	NULL
NULL	ROCK AND ROLL FANTASY	NULL	NULL
NULL	BURNING SKY	NULL	NULL
NULL	NULL	SATISFACTION GUARANTEED	NULL
NULL	NULL	RADIOACTIVE	NULL
NULL	NULL	MONEY CAN'T BUY	NULL
NULL	NULL	TOGETHER	NULL
NULL	NULL	NULL	GOOD MORNING LITTLE SCHOOLGIRL
NULL	NULL	NULL	HOOCHIE-COOCHIE MAN
NULL	NULL	NULL	MUDDY WATER BLUES
NULL	NULL	NULL	THE HUNTER

As the query traverses the table, it can fill only one column of our flattened array (actually just a simple cross-tab) at a time. Each column's CASE expression establishes that. This means that for each row in the initial result set, every column will be NULL except one. This is where the MAX()/GROUP BY duo comes to the rescue. Grouping on **single** allows us to coalesce the values in each column so that these extraneous NULLs are removed. Using MAX() allows us to select each column while grouping (all nongrouping columns in the SELECT list must either be aggregates or constants when GROUP BY is present). Note that MIN() would have worked equally well. All we really need is an aggregate that can return the **title** column—the aggregate merely serves to support the use of GROUP BY—which is the opposite of how we usually think of the aggregate–GROUP BY relationship. Since MIN() and MAX() are the only two aggregates capable of returning character fields, we're limited to using one of them.

Comparing Arrays

It's sometimes desirable to compare two arrays or two subsets of the same array with one another. This can be tricky because comparing arrays involves ordering the elements, whereas comparing plain sets does not. Here's a modification of the previous code sample that checks elements of the table array against one another for equality:

```
CREATE TABLE #array (band int, single int, title varchar(30))

INSERT #array VALUES(0,0,'LITTLE BIT O'' LOVE');
INSERT #array VALUES(0,1,'FIRE AND WATER');
INSERT #array VALUES(0,2,'ALL RIGHT NOW');
INSERT #array VALUES(0,3,'THE HUNTER');
INSERT #array VALUES(1,0,'BAD COMPANY');
INSERT #array VALUES(1,1,'SHOOTING STAR');
INSERT #array VALUES(1,2,'FEEL LIKE MAKIN'' LOVE');
INSERT #array VALUES(1,3,'ROCK AND ROLL FANTASY');
INSERT #array VALUES(1,4,'BURNING SKY');
INSERT #array VALUES(2,0,'SATISFACTION GUARANTEED');
INSERT #array VALUES(2,1,'RADIOACTIVE');
INSERT #array VALUES(2,2,'MONEY CAN''T BUY');
INSERT #array VALUES(2,3,'TOGETHER');
```

```
INSERT #array VALUES(3,0,'GOOD MORNING LITTLE SCHOOLGIRL');
INSERT #array VALUES(3,1,'HOOCHIE-COOCHIE MAN');
INSERT #array VALUES(3,2,'MUDDY WATER BLUES');
INSERT #array VALUES(3,3,'THE HUNTER');

SELECT * FROM
(SELECT Free=MAX(CASE band WHEN 0 THEN title ELSE NULL END),
   BadCompany=MAX(CASE band WHEN 1 THEN title ELSE NULL END),
   TheFirm=MAX(CASE band WHEN 2 THEN title ELSE NULL END),
   Solo=MAX(CASE band WHEN 3 THEN title ELSE NULL END)
   FROM #array
   GROUP BY single) a
WHERE Free=BadCompany
OR Free=TheFirm
OR Free=Solo
OR BadCompany=TheFirm
OR BadCompany=Solo
OR TheFirm=Solo
```

Free	BadCompany	TheFirm	Solo
THE HUNTER	ROCK AND ROLL FANTASY	TOGETHER	THE HUNTER

This technique turns the earlier array flattening query into a derived table, which it then qualifies with a WHERE clause. (As mentioned in Chapter 7, you can think of a derived table as an implicit or inline VIEW.) It then returns all rows where the title of one band's single is identical to that of another.

One problem with this approach is that it returns data we don't need. The entries in the middle two columns are extraneous—all we really care about is that bands zero and three have singles with the same title. This could mean that one plagiarized the other, that the songwriters for one of the bands weren't terribly original, or, perhaps, that the same lead singer sang for both.

Efficiency is another problem with this technique. The derived table selects every row in the #array table before handing it back to the outer query to pare down. Though the query optimizer will look at combining the two queries into one, the way that CASE is used here would probably confuse it. It would likely be more efficient to filter the rows returned as they're selected rather than afterward. Here's a code refinement that does that:

```
SELECT
Free=MAX(CASE a.band WHEN 0 THEN a.title ELSE NULL END),
BadCompany=MAX(CASE a.band WHEN 1 THEN a.title ELSE NULL END),
TheFirm=MAX(CASE a.band WHEN 2 THEN a.title ELSE NULL END),
Solo=MAX(CASE a.band WHEN 3 THEN a.title ELSE NULL END)
FROM #array a LEFT JOIN #array b ON (a.title=b.title)
   WHERE NOT (a.band=b.band AND a.single=b.single)
   GROUP BY a.single
```

Free	BadCompany	TheFirm	Solo
THE HUNTER	NULL	NULL	THE HUNTER

The technique joins the array table with itself to locate duplicate elements. The query's WHERE clause ensures that it doesn't make the mistake of matching an element with itself.

Since this approach filters the rows it returns as it processes them, it should be more efficient than the derived table approach. However, the introduction of a self-join may cancel out any performance gains achieved. Whether this technique is more efficient than the first one in a particular situation depends on the exact circumstances and data involved.

Note that this approach has the side effect of removing the extraneous values from the middle columns. Doing that with the derived table approach would be much more involved since it would basically amount to encoding the search criteria in two places: in the WHERE clause as well as in the SELECT list (via CASE expressions).

Summary

Since Transact-SQL doesn't directly support arrays, they must be simulated using other constructs. The two most popular means of emulating arrays are to store them as large character fields and to set up table columns that mimic array dimensions. Using large strings for arrays is practical for single-dimensional constructs, but the table column approach is better for multi-dimensional arrays. Whatever type of faux array you elect to use, keep in mind that storing repeating values in a table row is a form a denormalization. Be sure that's what you intend before you begin redesigning your database.

In this chapter, you learned to manipulate both types of pseudoarrays. You learned to add elements, to delete them, and to add and clear whole dimensions. You learned how to flatten simulated arrays into cross-tabs and to return array elements as result sets.

11

Sets

*Servile flattery—the kind made mostly of lies—
will endear a lot of different kinds of people to you.
Sycophancy wins friends and influences people. But
I've never known anyone—and certainly none of the
people I call "hero"—who chased after an elusive
dream—one that required sacrifice, courage, resolve,
or just plain mettle—and seized it through unctuous
flattery. Edison, Jefferson, Lincoln, Einstein, Twain,
Socrates, Confucius, Poe, Da Vinci, King—none of
them fawned his way into history. Instead, they waged
war against the toadies and trucklers of the world.
They left indelible handprints on the past because
they had the audacity to be honest and because they
knew the difference between loyalty and servility.*
—Trace Ambraise

Given that the relational model is based on sets of tuples, it should come as no surprise that SQL Server provides a rich suite of tools for working with sets of rows. The set is the focal point of work in SQL Server—the server resolves the queries you pass it by returning sets—result sets. It stores sets of rows together in tables (or *bags*) and relates sets to one another via Declarative Referential Integrity and joins. That it provides such comprehensive set support is to be expected—sets are the life's blood of relational databases.

The ANSI SQL-92 set operation keywords—UNION, EXCEPT, and INTERCEPT—are used to determine set union, difference, and intersection, respectively (sets are assumed to be collections of rows). Though Transact-SQL supports only one of these directly—UNION—it's straightforward to perform the other operations using simple coding techniques. SQL is a set-oriented language; working with sets of records is what it does best.

Unions

Performing a set union is trivial in Transact-SQL thanks to the inclusion of the UNION keyword. Here's some sample code that combines two sets using the UNION operator:

```
CREATE TABLE #set1 (col1 int, col2 int)
CREATE TABLE #set2 (col3 int, col4 int)

INSERT #set1 VALUES (1,1)
INSERT #set1 VALUES (2,2)
INSERT #set1 VALUES (3,3)
INSERT #set1 VALUES (4,4)
INSERT #set1 VALUES (5,5)

INSERT #set2 VALUES (1,1)
INSERT #set2 VALUES (2,2)
INSERT #set2 VALUES (5,5)

SELECT * FROM #set1
UNION
SELECT * FROM #set2
```

```
col1          col2
-----------   -----------
3             3
2             2
1             1
5             5
4             4
```

Note that the column names of the two tables differ in this example. All that's required of SELECT statements joined via UNION is that they have the same number of columns and that each column's data type either matches its counterpart or is capable of being implicitly converted to it. The SELECT statements themselves can be as complex as necessary, though they may not include COMPUTE, ORDER BY, or FOR BROWSE. You can use COMPUTE and ORDER BY with the result set returned by the UNION operation but not with any of its individual SELECT statements. Conversely, GROUP BY and HAVING can be used by individual SELECT statements but not by the entire result set. This is a pretty serious limitation, but fortunately there's a workaround. Here's some code that shows a way of using GROUP BY and HAVING with result sets created by UNION:

```
SELECT col1, Num=COUNT(*)
FROM (SELECT * FROM #set1
   UNION ALL
   SELECT * FROM #set2) s
GROUP BY col1
HAVING (COUNT(*) > 1)
```

```
col1          Num
-----------   -----------
1             2
2             2
5             2
```

This approach uses a derived table to wrap the UNION result set, then groups and qualifies it using GROUP BY and HAVING. An alternative would be to encapsulate the UNION operation in a view, but the illustrated approach is more expedient since it doesn't involve the creation of a separate object.

Note the use of UNION ALL in the example code. Normally, UNION removes duplicates from its result set by sorting or hashing them. Obviously, this can take time. If you know your result set is already free of duplicates or if you don't care whether it contains duplicates, UNION ALL can be a much faster way of combining tables. It simply combines the results of its component SELECTs and returns them—there's no sorting or duplicate elimination. It's needed by the query above because we want to apply a HAVING clause that filters the result set according to the number of instances of each **col1** value. Obviously, we can't do that if UNION removes all duplicates, effectively restricting the number of instances of each value to just one. So, we use UNION ALL within the derived table, then remove duplicates and aggregate our results using the GROUP BY of the outer SELECT.

> **Caution**
> Avoid mixing UNION and UNION ALL if you can. If duplicates are removed in some cases but not in others, you may end up with a result set that is difficult to interpret. The individual SELECT statements composing a compound UNION operation cease to be associative when UNION and UNION ALL are mixed. This means, by extension, that Transact-SQL's left-to-right order of execution will affect the result set.

Transact-SQL provides a nifty enhancement to SQL's standard UNION syntax that allows a table to be created *en passant*. To do this, you include an INTO *tablename* clause in the *first* SELECT statement of those included in the UNION operation, like so:

```
SELECT * INTO #tempset FROM #set1
UNION ALL
SELECT * FROM #set2

SELECT col1, Num=COUNT(*) FROM #tempset
GROUP BY col1
HAVING (COUNT(*) > 1)

col1        Num
----------- -----------
1           2
2           2
5           2
```

This code first creates a table via the UNION construct, then queries it via a separate SELECT statement. This technique is better than the derived table approach if you need to process the UNION result set further following the operation.

Differences

ANSI SQL-92 defines the EXCEPT keyword for returning a result set consisting of the difference between two sets. Most SQL vendors, including Microsoft, have yet to implement this keyword (Oracle has the MINUS synonym), but since Transact-SQL is a set-oriented language at heart, determining the difference between two sets isn't a difficult task.

The most obvious way to determine the rows that exist in one set but not in another is via the EXISTS predicate. Here's a code sample that returns the rows in one table that do not exist in another:

```
CREATE TABLE #set1 (col1 int, col2 int)
CREATE TABLE #set2 (col1 int, col2 int)

INSERT #set1 VALUES (1,1)
INSERT #set1 VALUES (2,2)
INSERT #set1 VALUES (3,3)
INSERT #set1 VALUES (4,4)
INSERT #set1 VALUES (5,5)

INSERT #set2 VALUES (1,1)
INSERT #set2 VALUES (2,2)
INSERT #set2 VALUES (5,5)

SELECT * FROM #set1 s1
WHERE NOT EXISTS(SELECT * FROM #set2 s2 WHERE s2.col1=s1.col1 AND
        s2.col2=s1.col1)


col1        col2
----------- -----------
3           3
4           4
```

This method uses a correlated subquery to find the rows in **#set1** that do not exist in **#set2.** Note that this method requires each column in each table to be matched up individually. This can quickly become very cumbersome when dealing with tables with lots of columns.

Unlike the ANSI SQL EXCEPT construct, this solution returns duplicate rows if they exist in the first table. To remedy this, insert the DISTINCT keyword in the outer SELECT.

A more efficient way to return the difference between two sets is to use a simple OUTER join. This alleviates the need for a correlated subquery, so it's not only faster but also easier to read:

```
SELECT s1.*
FROM #set1 s1 LEFT OUTER JOIN #set2 s2
  ON (s1.col1=s2.col1 AND s1.col2=s2.col2)
WHERE s2.col1 IS NULL


col1        col2
----------- -----------
3           3
4           4
```

The approach works by virtue of the fact that a left outer join returns columns from the rightmost table as NULL when the join condition fails. The query simply limits the rows it returns to those where this occurs. In other words, it restricts the rows returned from the leftmost table to those that don't exist in the right-side table. As in the previous example, this technique requires that every column in the first set be compared with its counterpart in the second set, which gets tedious with lots of columns.

One type of set that neither of these approaches handles very well is one containing duplicates. Codd's relational model and basic set theory prohibit duplicate set elements, but ANSI/ISO SQL permits them and so does Transact-SQL. That's why tables are sometimes referred to as "multisets"—they may contain multiple sets that individually contain unique elements.

The issues that arise when duplicates are present in a set are many and varied. If the first set contains two instances of a given row, but the second contains just one, what should we do? One could make the case that a result set that shows the difference between the two sets should include duplicate rows from the first set that have no matches in the second set. It shouldn't exclude the row from the result set simply because there's a match for an earlier duplicate in the second set.

Unfortunately, neither of the techniques presented thus far can handle this situation. Regardless of how many times a given row appears in the first set, if it occurs even once in the second set, it's not included in the difference set. Here's a query that ensures that each set has at least as many copies of a given row as the other set before a match is assumed (I've altered the sets to include duplicate rows):

```
CREATE TABLE #set1 (col1 int, col2 int)
CREATE TABLE #set2 (col1 int, col2 int)

INSERT #set1 VALUES (1,1)
INSERT #set1 VALUES (1,1)
INSERT #set1 VALUES (2,2)
INSERT #set1 VALUES (3,3)
INSERT #set1 VALUES (4,4)
INSERT #set1 VALUES (5,5)

INSERT #set2 VALUES (1,1)
INSERT #set2 VALUES (2,2)
INSERT #set2 VALUES (5,5)
INSERT #set2 VALUES (5,5)

SELECT col1, col2
FROM (SELECT col1,
      col2,
      Num1=COUNT(*),
      Num2=(SELECT COUNT(*) FROM #set2 ss2 WHERE col1=ss1.col1 AND col2=ss1.col2)
    FROM #set1 ss1
    GROUP BY col1, col2) s1
GROUP BY col1, col2
HAVING (ABS(SUM(Num1)-SUM(Num2))>0)
```

```
col1        col2
----------- -----------
1           1
3           3
4           4
5           5
```

Even though row (1,1) appears in both sets, this query returns the row in the difference set because it appears more times in the first set than in the second. Similarly, even though (5,5) appears in both sets, it appears more times in the second set than in the first, so it's included in the result set.

Intersections

As with set differences, returning simple set intersections is easy using the EXISTS predicate. Here's an example:

```
CREATE TABLE #set1 (col1 int, col2 int)
CREATE TABLE #set2 (col1 int, col2 int)

INSERT #set1 VALUES (1,1)
INSERT #set1 VALUES (2,2)
INSERT #set1 VALUES (3,3)
INSERT #set1 VALUES (4,4)
INSERT #set1 VALUES (5,5)

INSERT #set2 VALUES (1,1)
INSERT #set2 VALUES (2,2)
INSERT #set2 VALUES (5,5)

SELECT * FROM #set1 s1
WHERE EXISTS(SELECT * FROM #set2 s2 WHERE s2.col1=s1.col1 AND s2.col2=s1.col1)
```

```
col1          col2
-----------   -----------
1             1
2             2
5             5
```

Like the initial set difference query, this one requires that each field in the first set be compared with its counterpart in the second. Each row in the first set whose columns match those of the second is then returned by the query. The result is the intersection of the two sets—those rows contained in both sets.

A more efficient way to return the intersection of two sets is simply to join them. An inner join works nicely for this since it omits rows without matches. Here's an example:

```
SELECT s1.*
FROM #set1 s1 INNER JOIN #set2 s2
   ON (s1.col1=s2.col1 AND s1.col2=s2.col2)
```

```
col1          col2
-----------   -----------
1             1
2             2
5             5
```

It's syntactically more compact and faster and is the most common way that set intersections are returned in SQL.

As with the set difference techniques, both of these techniques are unable to handle duplicates correctly. A single row in the second set may match up two or more rows in the first set—there's no provision for ensuring that a row appears the same number of times in each set before a match is assumed. Here's a query that addresses this:

```
CREATE TABLE #set1 (col1 int, col2 int)
CREATE TABLE #set2 (col1 int, col2 int)
```

```
INSERT #set1 VALUES (1,1)
INSERT #set1 VALUES (1,1)
INSERT #set1 VALUES (2,2)
INSERT #set1 VALUES (3,3)
INSERT #set1 VALUES (4,4)
INSERT #set1 VALUES (5,5)

INSERT #set2 VALUES (1,1)
INSERT #set2 VALUES (2,2)
INSERT #set2 VALUES (2,2)
INSERT #set2 VALUES (4,4)
INSERT #set2 VALUES (5,5)

SELECT col1, col2
FROM (SELECT col1,
     col2,
     Num1=COUNT(*),
     Num2=(SELECT COUNT(*) FROM #set2 ss2 WHERE col1=ss1.col1 AND col2=ss1.col2)
   FROM #set1 ss1
   GROUP BY col1, col2) s1
GROUP BY col1, col2
HAVING SUM(Num1)=SUM(Num2)

col1        col2
----------- -----------
4           4
5           5
```

This approach uses a derived table and a subquery to count the number of rows that appear in each set for each pair of values. It then restricts the rows it returns to those that appear the same number of times in each set. In this case, (1,1) is excluded because it appears twice in the first set but only once in the second. Likewise, (2,2) is excluded because it appears twice in the second set but only once in the first.

Determining set intersection based on the number of times a row appears may amount to nothing more than an academic exercise in many cases. You may not care that the counts are different—you may want to know only when the two sets share a common value. If that's the case, the first two techniques presented will accomplish the task with a minimum of code.

Subsets

Of course, the easiest way to locate a portion of a set—a subset—is with a SELECT statement and a WHERE clause. That's the most direct route and the one most often traveled.

Beyond that, though, what if you need something that, at least on the surface, appears to be too difficult for the WHERE clause? Take the problem of returning the top *n* rows in a set. What's the best way to do this?

There are a number of approaches to this problem. Some of them are presented elsewhere in this book (e.g., see the section "Returning the Top *n* Rows" in Chapter 8), so I won't bother going into them here. Though it's also covered adequately elsewhere in the book, the TOP *n* extension to the SELECT command is worth mentioning here in the context of sets and subsets. By far the most straightforward way to return the top portion of a set is via the TOP *n* clause, like this:

```
CREATE TABLE #1996_POP_ESTIMATE (Region char(7), State char(2), Population int)

INSERT #1996_POP_ESTIMATE VALUES ('West',     'CA',31878234)
INSERT #1996_POP_ESTIMATE VALUES ('South',    'TX',19128261)
INSERT #1996_POP_ESTIMATE VALUES ('North',    'NY',18184774)
INSERT #1996_POP_ESTIMATE VALUES ('South',    'FL',14399985)
INSERT #1996_POP_ESTIMATE VALUES ('North',    'NJ', 7987933)
INSERT #1996_POP_ESTIMATE VALUES ('East',     'NC', 7322870)
INSERT #1996_POP_ESTIMATE VALUES ('West',     'WA', 5532939)
INSERT #1996_POP_ESTIMATE VALUES ('Central','MO', 5358692)
INSERT #1996_POP_ESTIMATE VALUES ('East',     'MD', 5071604)
INSERT #1996_POP_ESTIMATE VALUES ('Central','OK', 3300902)

SELECT TOP 3 State, Region, Population
FROM #1996_POP_ESTIMATE
ORDER BY Population DESC

State Region  Population
----- ------- -----------
CA    West    31878234
TX    South   19128261
NY    North   18184774
```

SET ROWCOUNT also works nicely for this, though, at least for SELECTs, TOP *n* is preferable because it doesn't require a separate SQL statement. Here's a version of the previous query that uses SET ROWCOUNT:

```
SET ROWCOUNT 3

SELECT State, Region, Population
FROM #1996_POP_ESTIMATE
ORDER BY Population DESC
SET ROWCOUNT 0 -- Reset ROWCOUNT
```

One distinct advantage the TOP *n* approach has over SET ROWCOUNT is in its ability to handle ties. The WITH TIES clause allows TOP *n* to include ties in the result set when an ORDER BY clause is used. Consider this variation on the earlier query:

```
SELECT TOP 5 State, Region, Population=Population/1000000
FROM #1996_POP_ESTIMATE
ORDER BY Population/1000000 DESC

State Region  Population
----- ------- -----------
CA    West    31
TX    South   19
NY    North   18
FL    South   14
NJ    North   7
```

It lists the top five states in population based on millions of people. Only whole millions are considered—fractional parts are truncated. Without the TIES option, the query can't recognize the fact that there's actually a tie for fifth place. New Jersey and North Carolina each had a population in excess of 7 million people in 1996. Here's the query with the TIES option in place, along with its result set:

```
SELECT TOP 5 WITH TIES State, Region, Population=Population/1000000
FROM #1996_POP_ESTIMATE
ORDER BY Population/1000000 DESC
```

```
State Region  Population
----- ------- -----------
CA    West    31
TX    South   19
NY    North   18
FL    South   14
NJ    North   7
NC    East    7
```

Because ORDER BY supports both ascending and descending sorts, TOP *n* can be used to retrieve the bottommost rows from a set as well, like so:

```
SELECT TOP 5 WITH TIES State, Region, Population=Population/1000000
FROM #1996_POP_ESTIMATE
ORDER BY Population/1000000
```

```
State Region  Population
----- ------- -----------
OK    Central 3
WA    West    5
MO    Central 5
MD    East    5
NJ    North   7
NC    East    7
```

If you wish to order the result set returned by TOP *n* differently (let's say you'd like the result set above in descending order, for example), you can easily embed it within a derived table and sort it using a separate ORDER BY clause, like so:

```
SELECT * FROM (SELECT TOP 5 WITH TIES State,
   Region, Population=Population/1000000
   FROM #1996_POP_ESTIMATE
   ORDER BY Population/1000000) p
ORDER BY Population DESC
```

```
State Region  Population
----- ------- -----------
NJ    North   7
NC    East    7
WA    West    5
MO    Central 5
MD    East    5
OK    Central 3
```

Returning Every *n*th Row

Beyond lopping off the rows at the extremities of a set, you may wish to extract them based on position. For example, you may wish to pull the odd- or even-numbered items from a set or, perhaps, every third item or every fifth and so on. This is the same basic problem as returning an interval from a sequence or run. The examples in Chapter 9, "Runs and Sequences," illustrate how to return intervals that are larger than one row in size and that can have other complex criteria attached to them. For the time being, here's a query that illustrates how to return all the even-numbered items in a set:

```
CREATE TABLE #set1 (k1 int identity)

INSERT #set1 DEFAULT VALUES
INSERT #set1 DEFAULT VALUES
INSERT #set1 DEFAULT VALUES
INSERT #set1 DEFAULT VALUES
INSERT #set1 DEFAULT VALUES
INSERT #set1 DEFAULT VALUES
INSERT #set1 DEFAULT VALUES
INSERT #set1 DEFAULT VALUES
INSERT #set1 DEFAULT VALUES
INSERT #set1 DEFAULT VALUES

SELECT s1.k1
FROM #set1 s1 JOIN #set1 s2 ON (s1.k1 >= s2.k1)
GROUP BY s1.k1
HAVING (COUNT(*) % 2) = 0

k1
-----------
2
4
6
8
10
```

This approach uses the familiar self-JOIN/GROUP BY technique, introduced earlier in this book, to compare the table with itself. It then uses the modulus operator (%) to restrict the rows it returns to even-numbered ones. Of course, you could change the **=0** to **=1** in order to return the odd-numbered rows, like so:

```
SELECT s1.k1
FROM #set1 s1 JOIN #set1 s2 ON (s1.k1 >= s2.k1)
GROUP BY s1.k1
HAVING (COUNT(*) % 2) = 1

k1
-----------
1
3
5
7
9
```

Summary

Transact-SQL is a set-oriented language. This is one of its strengths as a query tool and one of the chief advantages it holds over traditional programming languages. It was designed from the start to work with data in sets. Even though only one set-oriented operator is supported directly by Transact-SQL, finding the union, difference, or intersection between two sets is trivial compared to 3GL-based solutions. The relational model on which SQL Server is based makes these kinds of tasks quite straightforward.

12

Hierarchies

If you think education is expensive, try ignorance.
—Derek Bok, former president of Harvard.

A hierarchy is special kind of data structure made up of nodes connected to one another via one-way relationships known as edges. These nodes exist at multiple levels and roughly resemble a tree—in fact, you'll often hear the terms "hierarchy" and "tree" used interchangeably. Out of the box, Transact-SQL provides only meager support for hierarchies and trees. Other products such as Oracle have decent tree support, but Transact-SQL is strangely lacking here. This isn't the limitation that it might seem, though, because there are a number of straightforward techniques that make displaying and manipulating hierarchies fairly simple in Transact-SQL.

There are a number of common programming problems that have to do with traversing and manipulating trees. The one that comes immediately to mind is the task of displaying an organizational chart based on a personnel table. Each employee occupies one row in the table and each row contains a pointer to the employee's manager, which can itself be another row in the table. These types of hierarchies are usually established using just one database table.

By contrast, the Bill of Materials problem (which involves determining all the individual parts that make up an item) is usually a two-table problem. This is because, unlike an organizational chart, the node or leaf level members of a parts explosion can appear multiple times in a tree. For example, a given widget may be a component of several items within a BOM schematic. Using a second table keeps the database normalized and allows a part to appear more than once in the hierarchy.

Simple Hierarchies

If you're interested only in one-level-deep hierarchies, the SQL needed to produce them is fairly straightforward. Here's some code that lists a single-level organizational chart:

```
CREATE TABLE staff (employee int PRIMARY KEY, employee_name varchar(10),
supervisor int NULL REFERENCES staff (employee))

INSERT staff VALUES (1,'GROUCHO',1)
INSERT staff VALUES (2,'CHICO',1)
```

```
INSERT staff VALUES (3,'HARPO',2)
INSERT staff VALUES (4,'ZEPPO',2)
INSERT staff VALUES (5,'MOE',1)
INSERT staff VALUES (6,'LARRY',5)
INSERT staff VALUES (7,'CURLY',5)
INSERT staff VALUES (8,'SHEMP',5)
INSERT staff VALUES (9,'JOE',8)
INSERT staff VALUES (10,'CURLY JOE',9)

SELECT t.employee_name, supervises='supervises', s.employee_name
FROM staff s INNER JOIN staff t ON (s.supervisor=t.employee)
WHERE s.supervisor<>s.employee
ORDER BY s.employee, s.supervisor

employee_name supervises employee_name
------------- ---------- -------------
GROUCHO       supervises CHICO
CHICO         supervises HARPO
CHICO         supervises ZEPPO
GROUCHO       supervises MOE
MOE           supervises LARRY
MOE           supervises CURLY
MOE           supervises SHEMP
SHEMP         supervises JOE
JOE           supervises CURLY JOE
```

You could order these results a number of ways; the code above takes advantage of the fact that the rows were entered in the desired display sequence in order to sort them aesthetically.

Multilevel Hierarchies

A tree that's only one level deep isn't really a hierarchy at all. After all, the head pointy-haired boss at a company lords his authority over the entire staff, not just those who immediately report to him. A company's organizational chart is normally several levels deep for a reason—everyone technically reports to everyone above her in the chart, not just to her immediate supervisor. Getting at this chain of command requires a more sophisticated approach than the simple one presented above. What we need to do is somehow iterate through the base table, collecting not only each employee's boss but also his boss's boss, and her boss's boss, and so on, all the way up to the CEO. Here's a query that does just that:

```
SELECT chartdepth=1, employee=o2.employee, supervisor=o1.employee
INTO #org_chart
FROM staff o1 JOIN staff o2 ON (o1.employee=o2.supervisor)

INSERT INTO #org_chart
SELECT DISTINCT o1.chartdepth+1, o2.employee, o1.supervisor
FROM #org_chart o1 JOIN #org_chart o2 ON (o1.employee=o2.supervisor)
WHERE o1.chartdepth=(SELECT MAX(chartdepth) FROM #org_chart)

INSERT INTO #org_chart
SELECT DISTINCT o1.chartdepth+1, o2.employee, o1.supervisor
FROM #org_chart o1 JOIN #org_chart o2 ON (o1.employee=o2.supervisor)
WHERE o1.chartdepth=(SELECT MAX(chartdepth) FROM #org_chart)
```

```
INSERT INTO #org_chart
SELECT DISTINCT o1.chartdepth+1, o2.employee, o1.supervisor
FROM #org_chart o1 JOIN #org_chart o2 ON (o1.employee=o2.supervisor)
WHERE o1.chartdepth=(SELECT MAX(chartdepth) FROM #org_chart)


INSERT INTO #org_chart
SELECT DISTINCT o1.chartdepth+1, o2.employee, o1.supervisor
FROM #org_chart o1 JOIN #org_chart o2 ON (o1.employee=o2.supervisor)
WHERE o1.chartdepth=(SELECT MAX(chartdepth) FROM #org_chart)


INSERT INTO #org_chart
SELECT DISTINCT o1.chartdepth+1, o2.employee, o1.supervisor
FROM #org_chart o1 JOIN #org_chart o2 ON (o1.employee=o2.supervisor)
WHERE o1.chartdepth=(SELECT MAX(chartdepth) FROM #org_chart)


INSERT INTO #org_chart
SELECT DISTINCT o1.chartdepth+1, o2.employee, o1.supervisor
FROM #org_chart o1 JOIN #org_chart o2 ON (o1.employee=o2.supervisor)
WHERE o1.chartdepth=(SELECT MAX(chartdepth) FROM #org_chart)


INSERT INTO #org_chart
SELECT DISTINCT o1.chartdepth+1, o2.employee, o1.supervisor
FROM #org_chart o1 JOIN #org_chart o2 ON (o1.employee=o2.supervisor)
WHERE o1.chartdepth=(SELECT MAX(chartdepth) FROM #org_chart)


SELECT s.employee_name, supervises='supervises', e.employee_name
FROM #org_chart o JOIN staff s ON (o.supervisor=s.employee)
INNER JOIN staff e ON (o.employee=e.employee)
WHERE o.supervisor<>o.employee
GROUP BY o.supervisor, o.employee, s.employee_name, e.employee_name
ORDER BY o.supervisor, o.employee, s.employee_name, e.employee_name


employee_name supervises employee_name
------------- ---------- -------------
GROUCHO       supervises CHICO
GROUCHO       supervises HARPO
GROUCHO       supervises ZEPPO
GROUCHO       supervises MOE
GROUCHO       supervises LARRY
GROUCHO       supervises CURLY
GROUCHO       supervises SHEMP
GROUCHO       supervises JOE
GROUCHO       supervises CURLY JOE
CHICO         supervises HARPO
CHICO         supervises ZEPPO
MOE           supervises LARRY
MOE           supervises CURLY
MOE           supervises SHEMP
MOE           supervises JOE
MOE           supervises CURLY JOE
SHEMP         supervises JOE
SHEMP         supervises CURLY JOE
JOE           supervises CURLY JOE
```

This query constructs a temporary table containing the path between every supervisor and every employee under him or her. It does this by requiring that you execute a separate INSERT statement for each level you want to include. Naturally, this requires that you know how many levels your hierarchy has in advance—not an optimal solution. Here's a better one:

```
SELECT chartdepth=1, employee=o2.employee, supervisor=o1.employee
INTO #org_chart
FROM staff o1 INNER JOIN staff o2 ON (o1.employee=o2.supervisor)

WHILE (@@rowcount > 0) BEGIN
   INSERT #org_chart (chartdepth, employee, supervisor)
   SELECT DISTINCT o1.chartdepth+1, o2.employee, o1.supervisor
   FROM #org_chart o1 JOIN #org_chart o2 ON (o1.employee=o2.supervisor)
   WHERE o1.chartdepth=(SELECT MAX(chartdepth) FROM #org_chart)
   AND o1.supervisor<>o1.employee
END

SELECT s.employee_name, supervises='supervises', e.employee_name
FROM #org_chart o JOIN staff s ON (o.supervisor=s.employee)
INNER JOIN staff e ON (o.employee=e.employee)
WHERE o.supervisor<>o.employee
GROUP BY o.supervisor, o.employee, s.employee_name, e.employee_name
ORDER BY o.supervisor, o.employee, s.employee_name, e.employee_name
```

```
employee_name supervises employee_name
------------- ---------- -------------
GROUCHO        supervises CHICO
GROUCHO        supervises HARPO
GROUCHO        supervises ZEPPO
GROUCHO        supervises MOE
GROUCHO        supervises LARRY
GROUCHO        supervises CURLY
GROUCHO        supervises SHEMP
GROUCHO        supervises JOE
GROUCHO        supervises CURLY JOE
CHICO          supervises HARPO
CHICO          supervises ZEPPO
MOE            supervises LARRY
MOE            supervises CURLY
MOE            supervises SHEMP
MOE            supervises JOE
MOE            supervises CURLY JOE
SHEMP          supervises JOE
SHEMP          supervises CURLY JOE
JOE            supervises CURLY JOE
```

This approach uses a WHILE loop to repeat the INSERT as many times as necessary to process all levels. It works for any number of levels and doesn't require that you know how many you have in advance.

Like the first query, this approach uses the fact that the employee records were inserted in the desired order to sort them logically. This might not always be possible. The CEO may be employee number 340—obviously you can't depend on employees being added to the database in order of job level. Here's a variation on the preceding routine that doesn't make any assumptions about the initial row insertion order:

```
SELECT seq=IDENTITY(int), chartdepth=1, employee=o2.employee,
supervisor=o1.employee
INTO #org_chart
FROM staff o1 JOIN staff o2 ON (o1.employee=o2.supervisor)

WHILE (@@rowcount > 0) BEGIN
  INSERT #org_chart (chartdepth, employee, supervisor)
  SELECT DISTINCT o1.chartdepth+1, o2.employee, o1.supervisor
  FROM #org_chart o1 JOIN #org_chart o2 ON (o1.employee=o2.supervisor)
  WHERE o1.chartdepth=(SELECT MAX(chartdepth) FROM #org_chart)
  AND o1.supervisor<>o1.employee
END

SELECT s.employee_name, supervises='supervises', e.employee_name
FROM #org_chart o JOIN staff s ON (o.supervisor=s.employee)
INNER JOIN staff e ON (o.employee=e.employee)
WHERE o.supervisor<>o.employee
ORDER BY seq
```

```
employee_name supervises employee_name
------------- ---------- -------------
GROUCHO       supervises CHICO
CHICO         supervises HARPO
CHICO         supervises ZEPPO
GROUCHO       supervises MOE
MOE           supervises LARRY
MOE           supervises CURLY
MOE           supervises SHEMP
SHEMP         supervises JOE
JOE           supervises CURLY JOE
GROUCHO       supervises HARPO
GROUCHO       supervises ZEPPO
GROUCHO       supervises LARRY
GROUCHO       supervises CURLY
GROUCHO       supervises SHEMP
MOE           supervises JOE
SHEMP         supervises CURLY JOE
GROUCHO       supervises JOE
GROUCHO       supervises CURLY JOE
MOE           supervises CURLY JOE
GROUCHO       supervises CURLY JOE
```

This approach uses the IDENTITY() function with SELECT...INTO to add an identity column to the work table. It then uses this column to sort the result set when returning it.

Indenting a Hierarchy

A common need with hierarchies is to indent them according to level. Since the previous routine already tracks the chart level of each row, indenting the result set is simple. Here's a stored procedure that indents the result set by level:

```
SET ANSI_NULLS OFF
USE tempdb
IF OBJECT_ID('populate_hierarchy') IS NOT NULL DROP PROC populate_hierarchy
GO
CREATE PROC populate_hierarchy @supervisor int AS
DECLARE @employee int
DECLARE stf CURSOR LOCAL FOR SELECT employee FROM staff WHERE supervisor=@supervisor
OPEN stf
FETCH stf INTO @employee
WHILE (@@FETCH_STATUS=0) BEGIN
    INSERT #org_chart (chartdepth, employee, supervisor) VALUES (@@NESTLEVEL, @employee,
    @supervisor)  -- Use @@NESTLEVEL to track chart depth (hierarchy level)
    IF EXISTS (SELECT s.employee, o.employee FROM staff s LEFT OUTER JOIN #org_chart
    o ON (s.employee=o.employee)
                WHERE s.supervisor=@employee AND o.employee IS NULL) EXEC
                populate_hierarchy @employee
    FETCH stf INTO @employee
END
GO
IF OBJECT_ID('staff') IS NOT NULL DROP TABLE staff
CREATE TABLE staff (employee int NOT NULL PRIMARY KEY, employee_name varchar(10) NULL,
supervisor int NULL)
GO
INSERT staff(employee, employee_name, supervisor) VALUES(1,'GROUCHO',NULL)
INSERT staff(employee, employee_name, supervisor) VALUES(2,'CHICO',1)
INSERT staff(employee, employee_name, supervisor) VALUES(3,'HARPO',2)
INSERT staff(employee, employee_name, supervisor) VALUES(4,'ZEPPO',5)
INSERT staff(employee, employee_name, supervisor) VALUES(5,'MOE',1)
INSERT staff(employee, employee_name, supervisor) VALUES(6,'LARRY',5)
INSERT staff(employee, employee_name, supervisor) VALUES(7,'CURLY',5)
INSERT staff(employee, employee_name, supervisor) VALUES(8,'SHEMP',5)
INSERT staff(employee, employee_name, supervisor) VALUES(9,'JOE',8)
INSERT staff(employee, employee_name, supervisor) VALUES(10,'CURLY JOE',9)
GO
IF OBJECT_ID('#org_chart') IS NOT NULL DROP TABLE #org_chart
CREATE TABLE #org_chart (seq int identity PRIMARY KEY,chartdepth int,employee
int,supervisor int)
GO
DECLARE @supervisor int SET @supervisor=NULL
EXEC populate_hierarchy @supervisor
SELECT OrgChart=CONVERT(VARCHAR(50),REPLICATE(CHAR(9),chartdepth-1)+s.employee_name)
FROM (SELECT employee, seq=MIN(seq), chartdepth=MAX(chartdepth) FROM #org_chart
GROUP BY employee) o INNER JOIN staff s ON (o.employee=s.employee) ORDER BY o.seq
```

This technique uses the REPLICATE() function to generate a string of tab characters corresponding to the **chartdepth** of each row. It also uses a derived table and some aggregate tricks to remove duplicates from the result set before returning it. The derived table is necessary because we don't want to have to encapsulate the references to the **employee_name** and **chartdepth** columns in aggregate functions in order to GROUP BY the **employee** column. We need to GROUP BY **employee** or **employee_name** in order to remove duplicates from the result set. If we include **chartdepth** in the GROUP BY clause, some of the duplicates remain, differentiated only by **chartdepth.**

Another Approach

There's certainly more than one way to expand a tree in Transact-SQL. Another way of doing so is to loop through the base table, processing each node separately and using a temporary table to track which nodes have been processed. Here's a code sample that uses this technique to display a multilevel hierarchy:

```
CREATE TABLE DINOSAURS (OrderNo int PRIMARY KEY, OrderName varchar(30),
PredecessorNo int NULL REFERENCES DINOSAURS (OrderNo))

INSERT DINOSAURS VALUES (1,'Amphibia',1)
INSERT DINOSAURS VALUES (2,'Cotylosauri',1)
INSERT DINOSAURS VALUES (3,'Pelycosauria',2)
INSERT DINOSAURS VALUES (4,'Therapsida',2)
INSERT DINOSAURS VALUES (5,'Chelonia',3)
INSERT DINOSAURS VALUES (6,'Sauropterygia',3)
INSERT DINOSAURS VALUES (7,'Ichthyosauria',3)
INSERT DINOSAURS VALUES (8,'Squamata',3)
INSERT DINOSAURS VALUES (9,'Thecodontia',3)
INSERT DINOSAURS VALUES (10,'Crocodilia',9)
INSERT DINOSAURS VALUES (11,'Pterosauria',9)
INSERT DINOSAURS VALUES (12,'Saurichia',9)
INSERT DINOSAURS VALUES (13,'Ornithischia',9)

CREATE TABLE #work (lvl int, OrderNo int)
CREATE TABLE #DINOSAURS (seq int identity, lvl int, OrderNo int)

DECLARE @lvl int, @curr int
SELECT TOP 1 @lvl=1, @curr=OrderNo FROM DINOSAURS WHERE OrderNo=PredecessorNo

INSERT INTO #work (lvl, OrderNo) VALUES (@lvl, @curr)
WHILE (@lvl > 0) BEGIN
   IF EXISTS(SELECT * FROM #work WHERE lvl=@lvl) BEGIN
      SELECT TOP 1 @curr=OrderNo FROM #work
      WHERE lvl=@lvl

      INSERT #DINOSAURS (lvl, OrderNo) VALUES (@lvl, @curr)

      DELETE #work
      WHERE lvl=@lvl and OrderNo=@curr

      INSERT #work
      SELECT @lvl+1, OrderNo
      FROM DINOSAURS
      WHERE PredecessorNo=@curr
      AND PredecessorNo <> OrderNo

      IF (@@ROWCOUNT > 0) SET @lvl=@lvl+1
   END ELSE
      SET @lvl=@lvl-1
END

SELECT 'Dinosaur Orders'=
REPLICATE(CHAR(9),lvl)+i.OrderName
```

```
FROM #DINOSAURS d JOIN DINOSAURS i ON (d.OrderNo=i.OrderNo)
ORDER BY seq

Dinosaur Orders:
---------------------------------------------------------------------------
    Amphibia
       Cotylosauri
          Pelycosauria
             Chelonia
             Sauropterygia
             Ichthyosauria
             Squamata
             Thecodontia
                Crocodilia
                Pterosauria
                Saurichia
                Ornithischia
          Therapsida
```

      This technique loops through the rows in the base table, placing each node it encounters into one temporary table and the children of that node into another. When the loop cycles, the first child in this work table is checked to see whether it has children of its own, and the process repeats itself. Each node is removed from the work table once it's processed. This iteration continues until all nodes have been expanded.

      As with the earlier queries, this routine uses an identity column to sequence itself. It also makes use of REPLICATE(CHAR(9)) to format its result set.

      I don't like this approach as much as those earlier in the chapter because, if for no other reason, it requires significantly more code. However, it may be more efficient since it doesn't require a GROUP BY clause. The base table would have to be much larger than it is in these examples for there to be an appreciable difference in performance between any of the approaches presented here.

Listing Leaf Nodes

Rather than returning an entire hierarchy, you may wish to list its leaf nodes only. A node is
a leaf node if it has no children. Given that all you have to do is find the nodes that aren't listed as the parent of any of the other nodes, locating leaf nodes is easy enough. Here's an example:

```
SELECT Grunts=s.employee_name
FROM staff s
WHERE NOT EXISTS
   (SELECT * FROM staff t WHERE t.supervisor=s.employee)

Grunts
----------
HARPO
ZEPPO
LARRY
CURLY
CURLY JOE
```

Indented Lists

Though not quite the same thing as a tree or hierarchy, an indented list provides a pseudohierarchy via its formatting. Though its uses are mostly simplistic, understanding the tools available to you for result set formatting is always handy, regardless of whether you end up using all of them. Here's a code sample that returns an indented list of first and last names from the **authors** table in the **pubs** sample database:

```
SELECT authors=
    CASE WHEN au_fname=(SELECT MIN(au_fname) FROM authors WHERE au_lname=a.au_lname)
        THEN au_lname
    ELSE "
    END+CHAR(13)+CHAR(9)+au_fname
FROM authors a

authors
------------------------------------------------------------
Bennet
    Abraham
Blotchet-Halls
    Reginald
Carson
    Cheryl
DeFrance
    Michel
del Castillo
    Innes
Dull
    Ann
Green
    Marjorie
Greene
    Morningstar
Gringlesby
    Burt
Hunter
    Sheryl
Karsen
    Livia
Locksley
    Charlene
MacFeather
    Stearns
McBadden
    Heather
O'Leary
    Michael
Panteley
    Sylvia
Ringer
    Albert
    Anne
```

```
Smith
    Meander
Straight
    Dean
Stringer
    Dirk
White
    Johnson
Yokomoto
    Akiko
```

Note the use of the CASE function to limit the inclusion of each last name to one occurrence. For example, the Ringer surname has two corresponding authors—Albert and Anne— but the surname itself is listed just once. Also note the use of both CHAR(13) (carriage return) and CHAR(9) (tab) to create new lines and indent the result set. You can use CHAR() to great effect when formatting result sets. By coupling it with CASE, you can perform the same type of basic formatting that was previously the exclusive domain of report writers and external development tools.

Summary

Though Transact-SQL provides no direct support for hierarchies, you can still produce hierarchical result sets with a minimum of code. Self-joins and creative use of the CHAR() and REPLICATE() functions provide ample means of generating basic hierarchical listings.

Cursors

Bandwagon jumpers make choices based not on merit or value but on brand names, slogans, and tag lines. As long as there are people willing to part with their hard-earned cash for gimmickry, the world will continue to be a place where marketing is more important than what's marketed.—H. W. Kenton

A cursor is a mechanism for accessing the rows in a table or result set on a piecemeal basis—one at a time. They run counter to SQL Server's normal way of doing things by parceling result sets into individual rows; fetching a row from a cursor is analogous to returning a single row via a SELECT statement. Unlike a traditional result set, a cursor keeps track of its position automatically and provides a wealth of facilities for scrolling around in the underlying result set. Cursors also provide a handy means of updating the underlying result set in a positional fashion and of returning result set pointers via variables.

The advice I usually give people who are thinking about using cursors is not to. If you can solve a problem using Transact-SQL's many set-oriented tools, do so. It's rare (but not impossible) for a cursor-based solution to outperform a set-based approach. SQL Server's standard result sets (also known as "firehose" cursors) have been used to solve a myriad of distinct kinds of computing problems for years—there aren't many conventional database challenges that actually *require* a cursor, though some are certainly more suited to cursors than to set handling.

On Cursors and ISAMs

People porting ISAM or local database applications to SQL Server are often tempted to perform shallow ports—to make no more changes than absolutely necessary to get the app working on the new DBMS. This usually involves shortcuts like replacing ISAM record navigation (e.g., xBase SKIP) with Transact-SQL cursor loops. ISAM records and SQL Server cursors aren't synonymous, and any effort to treat a relational DBMS like an ISAM product is likely to go down in flames.

Some time ago, I had the misfortune of assuming the task of porting an ISAM database application to a full-blown SQL Server app. I was trying to get the company to move to client/server RDBMS technology, and, after months of ambivalence, they finally decided that they wanted to convert their flagship application from an ISAM product to SQL Server as a kind of proof of concept. Since, in spite of my best efforts, the intrinsic benefits of RDBMSs weren't apparent to them, I was inclined to accept the challenge in order to prove the viability of the technology. This was despite the fact that I would much rather have started with a new app than with an existing, vitally important product.

With my guardian angel in silent verbal assault and without having investigated the code much, I accepted the task, naively believing that the developers had built the app in a reasonably relational and logical manner. Having nothing to suggest otherwise, I assumed that they were processing records in sets where possible in order to save time and code, because even the puny local DBMS on which the app was built supported a fair amount of set-oriented access (including its own basic SQL dialect). Of course, I didn't expect the code to be perfect, but I guess I assumed they'd used their tools more or less as they were intended to be used. In talking with the app's authors, that's certainly the impression they gave me, and I quickly rushed in where angels fear to tread.

After two to three weeks of wading through some of the worst application code I'd ever seen, of having the application block *itself* from server resources due to its dreadful design, and of having one bowling ball after another roll out of the top of the proverbial closet and hit me in the head, I finally pulled the plug on the SQL Server conversion.

The app broke virtually every basic tenet of sensible database application design. It used application code to loop through tables rather than processing rows in sets. What minimal relational and data integrity it had was implemented in a hodgepodge of application code and database constraints and was far from airtight. It used a fatuous table versioning scheme that had never been finished or used consistently and gave no thought to uniform naming conventions or name casing, so database objects had arcane names that were impossible to remember and incongruous with one another. The same attribute in multiple tables often had different names, and different attributes among multiple tables often had the same name. Tables were denormalized throughout the database, not for performance but because the developers didn't know any better. There'd been no attempt to provide for concurrency, and the app was by design (or by the lack of it) strictly a single-user contrivance. In short, it was a complete disaster from an architectural standpoint, and the fact that it had ever worked at all, even on the ISAM product, was more a testament to the developers' tenacity than to the robustness of the app.

So, shortly after this joyous experience, I began rewriting the application. Of course, I could have taken the "easy" way out and merely performed a shallow port of the app to SQL Server, essentially turning the server into a glorified ISAM database server. I could have reused as much of the existing code as possible, regardless of how poorly designed it was. Every row-by-row access in the app could have been translated to an equivalent cursor operation on SQL Server. I could have used SQL Server in ways it was never intended to be used, and I could have refrained from fixing the many relational and other problems in the app, madly bolting the various disparate pieces together into a misshapen, software-borne Frankenstein. I could have done that—it certainly would have been faster in the short run and would have made management happier—but I just couldn't bring myself to. It's been my experience that there's usually an optimal way to build software—and all my instincts, training, and knowledge told me that this wasn't it.

Instead, it was apparent to me that the app would have to be redesigned from the ground up if it was to have a prayer of working properly on SQL Server or on any other RDBMS. The acute need for a rewrite was as much due to the radical differences between ISAM products and RDBMSs as it was to poor design and coding in the application to begin with. The fact that software *appears* to work properly doesn't mean that it's been constructed properly any more than the fact that a house *appears* to be sound means that it won't fall into the ground the first time you try to build on to it. There is more to application design than whether the app meets immediate customer requirements. Making customers happy is paramount, but it should not come completely at the expense of long-term concerns such as extensibility, interoperability, performance, scalability, concurrency, and supportability.

These may seem like technology-centric concerns, but customers care about these things, too, whether they know it or not. They're certainly affected by them indirectly—if not directly. A feature request that might seem trivial to the typical user—converting a single-user app to a multiuser app, for example—can be difficult if not impossible if the app was designed incorrectly to begin with. If the app's designer gave no thought to concurrency when she was building it, the app will likely have to be rewritten in order to accommodate multiple users. This rewrite translates into delayed releases and users having to wait for the features they need. Application design affects real people in real ways. Beauty is not in the eye of the beholder—it's in the eye of the designer.

The really ironic thing about the whole experience was that many of the problem application's design decisions didn't make any more sense on the ISAM database platform than they would have on SQL Server. It's just that SQL Server would have exposed many of these defects to the light of day. It would have forced the app to clean up its act or go elsewhere. Because of their emphasis on robustness and performance, relational DBMSs tend to be less forgiving of application misbehavior than ISAM products. I don't lament this—I think it's a good thing. Developers shouldn't build shoddy applications regardless of the back end.

Porting ISAM applications to SQL Server is not a menial task, even for properly designed applications. Quickly performing a shallow port by doing things like replacing ISAM access with SQL Server cursors is almost never the right approach. It takes a good amount of moral fortitude and a stiff spine to say, "This port is going to take some work; the app will have to be redesigned or rewritten," but that's often the best approach. Reinventing the wheel is fine—even necessary—if the wheel you're "reinventing" was a square one to begin with. Do deep ports when moving applications to SQL Server—think of it as the foundation on which your applications should stand, not as just another service they use. Shallow ports are for those who, as Ron Soukup says, "believe that there's never time to do the port right but there's always time to do it over."

Types of Cursors

There are four types of cursors supported by Transact-SQL: FORWARD_ONLY, DYNAMIC, STATIC, and KEYSET. The primary difference between these types is in the ability to detect changes to their underlying data while the cursor is being traversed and in the resources (locks, tempdb space, etc.) they use.

Depending on the type of cursor you create, changes made to its underlying data may or may not be shown while traversing the cursor. In addition to new column values, these changes

Table 13.1. The types of cursors Transact-SQL supports and their attributes.

Type	Scrollable	Membership/ Order	Column Values
FORWARD_ONLY (default)	No	Dynamic	Dynamic
DYNAMIC / SENSITIVE	Yes	Dynamic	Dynamic
STATIC / INSENSITIVE	Yes	Fixed	Fixed
KEYSET	Yes	Fixed	Dynamic

can affect which rows are returned by the cursor (membership), as well as the ordering of those rows. Also, opening the cursor may cause the entirety of its result set (or their keys) to be placed in a temporary table, possibly causing resource contention problems in tempdb. Table 13.1 summarizes the different cursor types and their attributes.

Forward-Only Cursors

A forward-only cursor (the default) returns rows sequentially from the database. It does not require space in tempdb, and changes made to the underlying data are visible as soon as they're reached. Here's an example:

```
CREATE TABLE #temp (k1 int identity, c1 int NULL)

INSERT #temp DEFAULT VALUES
INSERT #temp DEFAULT VALUES
INSERT #temp DEFAULT VALUES
INSERT #temp DEFAULT VALUES

DECLARE c CURSOR FORWARD_ONLY
FOR SELECT k1, c1 FROM #temp

OPEN c

FETCH c

UPDATE #temp
SET c1=2
WHERE k1=3

FETCH c
FETCH c

SELECT * FROM #temp

CLOSE c
DEALLOCATE c
GO
DROP TABLE #temp
```

```
k1          c1
----------- -----------
1           NULL

k1          c1
----------- -----------
2           NULL

k1          c1
----------- -----------
3           2

k1          c1
----------- -----------
1           NULL
2           NULL
3           2
4           NULL
```

Dynamic Cursors

As with forward-only cursors, dynamic cursors reflect changes to their underlying rows as those rows are reached. No extra tempdb space is required. Unlike forward-only cursors, dynamic cursors are inherently scrollable—you aren't limited to accessing their rows sequentially. They're sometimes referred to as *sensitive* cursors because of their sensitivity to source data changes. Here's an example:

```
CREATE TABLE #temp (k1 int identity, c1 int NULL)

INSERT #temp DEFAULT VALUES
INSERT #temp DEFAULT VALUES
INSERT #temp DEFAULT VALUES
INSERT #temp DEFAULT VALUES

DECLARE c CURSOR DYNAMIC
FOR SELECT k1, c1 FROM #temp

OPEN c

FETCH c

UPDATE #temp
SET c1=2
WHERE k1=1

FETCH c
FETCH PRIOR FROM c

SELECT * FROM #temp

CLOSE c
DEALLOCATE c
GO
DROP TABLE #temp
```

```
k1            c1
-----------   -----------
1             NULL

k1            c1
-----------   -----------
2             NULL

k1            c1
-----------   -----------
1             2

k1            c1
-----------   -----------
1             2
2             NULL
3             NULL
4             NULL
```

Here, we fetch a row, then update it, fetch another, and then refetch the first row. When we fetch the first row for the second time, we see the change made via the UPDATE, even though the UPDATE didn't use the cursor to make its change.

Static Cursors

A static cursor returns a read-only result set that's impervious to changes to the underlying data. It's the opposite of a dynamic cursor, though it's still completely scrollable. Once a static cursor is opened, changes made to its source data are not reflected by the cursor. This is because the entirety of its result set is copied to tempdb when it's first opened. Static cursors are sometimes called *snapshot* or *insensitive* cursors because they aren't sensitive to changes made to their source data. Here's an example:

```
CREATE TABLE #temp (k1 int identity, c1 int NULL)

INSERT #temp DEFAULT VALUES
INSERT #temp DEFAULT VALUES
INSERT #temp DEFAULT VALUES
INSERT #temp DEFAULT VALUES

DECLARE c CURSOR STATIC
FOR SELECT k1, c1 FROM #temp

OPEN c -- The entire result set is copied to tempdb

UPDATE #temp
SET c1=2
WHERE k1=1

FETCH c -- This doesn't reflect the change made by the UPDATE

SELECT * FROM #temp -- But the change is indeed there
```

```
CLOSE c
DEALLOCATE c
GO
DROP TABLE #temp
```

k1	c1
1	NULL

k1	c1
1	2
2	NULL
3	NULL
4	NULL

Here, we open the cursor and immediately make a change to the first row in its underlying table. This change isn't reflected when we fetch that row from the cursor because the row is actually coming from tempdb. A subsequent SELECT from the underlying table shows the change to be intact even though it's not reflected by the cursor.

Keyset Cursors

Opening a keyset cursor returns a fully scrollable result set whose membership and order are fixed. As with forward-only and static cursors, changes to the values in its underlying data (except for keyset columns) are reflected when they're accessed; however, new row insertions are *not* reflected by the cursor. As with a static cursor, the set of unique key values for the cursor's rows are copied to a table in tempdb (hence the term *keyset*) when the cursor is opened. That's why membership in the cursor is fixed. If the underlying table doesn't have a primary or unique key, the entire set of candidate key columns is copied to the keyset table. Since changes to keyset columns aren't reflected by the cursor, failing to define a unique key of some type for the underlying data results in a keyset that doesn't reflect changes to *any* of its candidate key columns. Here's a simple keyset example:

```
CREATE TABLE #temp (k1 int identity PRIMARY KEY, c1 int NULL)

INSERT #temp DEFAULT VALUES
INSERT #temp DEFAULT VALUES
INSERT #temp DEFAULT VALUES
INSERT #temp DEFAULT VALUES

DECLARE c CURSOR KEYSET
FOR SELECT k1, c1 FROM #temp

OPEN c -- The keyset is copied to tempdb

UPDATE #temp
SET c1=2
WHERE k1=1

INSERT #temp VALUES (3) -- won't be visible to cursor (can safely omit identity column)
```

```
FETCH c -- Change is visible
FETCH LAST FROM c -- New row isn't

SELECT * FROM #temp

CLOSE c
DEALLOCATE c
GO
DROP TABLE #temp
```

```
k1           c1
-----------  -----------
1            2


k1           c1
-----------  -----------
4            NULL


k1           c1
-----------  -----------
1            2
2            NULL
3            NULL
4            NULL
5            3
```

Here, once the keyset cursor is opened, a change is made to its first row before the row is fetched from the cursor. Another row is then inserted into the underlying table. Once the routine begins fetching rows from the cursor, the first change we made shows up, but the new row doesn't. This is because membership in a keyset cursor doesn't change once it's opened.

Note the inclusion of a PRIMARY KEY constraint in the work table. Without it, changes to the table's **c1** column aren't visible to the cursor, even though the cursor has an identity column. Why? Because, in and of themselves, identity columns aren't guaranteed to be unique. You could always use SET IDENTITY_INSERT to add duplicate identity values or reset the identity seed to have the server add them for you. To ensure uniqueness, a PRIMARY or UNIQUE KEY constraint is required. Without a unique key, the server copies the entirety of the candidate keys for each row to the keyset cursor's temporary table.

Appropriate Cursor Use

A word of advice: Use cursors only when you have to. That may seem a little simplistic or overly broad, but I think most seasoned Transact-SQL developers would agree that using cursors should be near the bottom of your list of coding techniques. Instead, try to find a solution that leverages Transact-SQL's ability to work with sets of data to solve your problems. That's what it was designed to do; that's what it does best. Though cursors are an easy concept for beginners to grasp, cursor overuse/misuse is a common source of performance problems with most relational DBMSs, including SQL Server.

This isn't to say that cursor use is taboo or that all cursor users are headed for a fiery after-life. If you program long enough in Transact-SQL, you'll use cursors sooner or later. Some kinds of development require them extensively. As in many things, your degree of success will depend largely on your mindset. *Use* cursors when it makes sense—just be careful not to *mis-use* them.

Some examples of situations where cursor use is appropriate are dynamic queries, row-oriented operations, and scrollable forms. Dynamic queries build and execute Transact-SQL code at runtime. Row-oriented operations are multistatement routines that are too complex or otherwise unsuitable for single statement operations such as SELECT or UPDATE. Scrollable forms typically feature a facility (sometimes listing multiple rows) that allows users to navigate within a result set. Scrollable cursors make setting up this functionality as straightforward as possible for the developer.

Dynamic Queries

Cursors come in handy with dynamic queries because they allow you to construct executable Transact-SQL code based on a result set. For example, suppose we want to construct a cross-tab (pivot table) over a series of values. Let's assume that there are three columns in the series —a key, a subkey, and the value column itself. We want a cross-tab featuring the keys on its x-axis and the subkeys on its y-axis, with the values listed at each intersection. Each key may have a different number of subkeys, and these subkeys may or may not be consecutive. Here's an approach that uses a cursor to construct dynamic T-SQL to render the cross-tab:

```
CREATE TABLE #series
(key1 int,
 key2 int,
 value1 decimal(6,2) DEFAULT (
(CASE (CAST(RAND()+.5 AS int)*-1) WHEN 0 THEN 1 ELSE -1 END)*(CONVERT(int,
 RAND() * 100000) % 10000)*RAND()
)
)

INSERT #series (key1, key2) VALUES (1,1)
INSERT #series (key1, key2) VALUES (1,2)
INSERT #series (key1, key2) VALUES (1,3)
INSERT #series (key1, key2) VALUES (1,4)
INSERT #series (key1, key2) VALUES (1,5)
INSERT #series (key1, key2) VALUES (1,6)
INSERT #series (key1, key2) VALUES (2,1)
INSERT #series (key1, key2) VALUES (2,2)
INSERT #series (key1, key2) VALUES (2,3)
INSERT #series (key1, key2) VALUES (2,4)
INSERT #series (key1, key2) VALUES (2,5)
INSERT #series (key1, key2) VALUES (2,6)
INSERT #series (key1, key2) VALUES (2,7)
INSERT #series (key1, key2) VALUES (3,1)
INSERT #series (key1, key2) VALUES (3,2)
INSERT #series (key1, key2) VALUES (3,3)
```

```
DECLARE s CURSOR
FOR
SELECT DISTINCT key2 FROM #series ORDER BY key2


DECLARE @key2 int, @key2str varchar(10), @sql varchar(8000)


OPEN s
FETCH s INTO @key2
SET @sql=''
WHILE (@@FETCH_STATUS=0) BEGIN
   SET @key2str=CAST(@key2 AS varchar)
   SET @sql=@sql+',SUM(CASE WHEN key2='+@key2str+' THEN value1 ELSE NULL END)
   ['+@key2str+']'
   FETCH s INTO @key2
END


SET @sql='SELECT key1'+@sql+' FROM #series GROUP BY key1'
EXEC(@sql)


CLOSE s
DEALLOCATE s
DROP TABLE #series
```

key1	1	2	3	4	5	6	7
1	212.74	-1608.59	1825.29	690.48	1863.44	5302.54	NULL
2	-7531.42	1848.63	-3746.60	-54.37	-2263.63	-1013.01	5453.57
3	126.13	-10.41	205.35	NULL	NULL	NULL	NULL

To best understand how this works, it's instructive to examine the dynamic query itself. Here's what @sql looks like just prior to execution:

```
SELECT key1,SUM(CASE WHEN key2=1 THEN value1 ELSE NULL END) [1],
SUM(CASE WHEN key2=2 THEN value1 ELSE NULL END) [2],
SUM(CASE WHEN key2=3 THEN value1 ELSE NULL END) [3],
SUM(CASE WHEN key2=4 THEN value1 ELSE NULL END) [4],
SUM(CASE WHEN key2=5 THEN value1 ELSE NULL END) [5],
SUM(CASE WHEN key2=6 THEN value1 ELSE NULL END) [6],
SUM(CASE WHEN key2=7 THEN value1 ELSE NULL END) [7]
FROM #series GROUP BY key1
```

The cursor returns a row for each unique subkey in the series. Regardless of the key that contains it, if a subkey appears in the table, the cursor's SELECT DISTINCT returns an instance of it. The CASE statement that's constructed for each cross-tab column returns the **value1** column when the subkey matches up with its column and NULL otherwise. The GROUP BY flattens the rows returned by the query such that each key appears exactly once. To understand this better, let's look at the cross-tab without the GROUP BY:

key1	1	2	3	4	5	6	7
1	212.74	NULL	NULL	NULL	NULL	NULL	NULL
1	NULL	-1608.59	NULL	NULL	NULL	NULL	NULL
1	NULL	NULL	1825.29	NULL	NULL	NULL	NULL
1	NULL	NULL	NULL	690.48	NULL	NULL	NULL
1	NULL	NULL	NULL	NULL	5302.54	NULL	NULL
1	NULL	NULL	NULL	NULL	NULL	5302.54	NULL
2	-7531.42	NULL	NULL	NULL	NULL	NULL	NULL
2	NULL	1848.63	NULL	NULL	NULL	NULL	NULL
2	NULL	NULL	-3746.60	NULL	NULL	NULL	NULL
2	NULL	NULL	NULL	-54.37	NULL	NULL	NULL
2	NULL	NULL	NULL	NULL	-2263.63	NULL	NULL
2	NULL	NULL	NULL	NULL	NULL	-1013.01	NULL
2	NULL	NULL	NULL	NULL	NULL	NULL	5453.57
3	126.13	NULL	NULL	NULL	NULL	NULL	NULL
3	NULL	-10.41	NULL	NULL	NULL	NULL	NULL
3	NULL	NULL	205.35	NULL	NULL	NULL	NULL

Due to the characteristics of the original series data, only one subkey column in each key row has a value. The rest of the columns are set to NULL by their respective CASE expressions. The GROUP BY clause minimizes these NULLs, summarizing the pivot table such that each series value appears in its respective subkey column when present.

Row-Oriented Operations

Another good use of cursors is in row-oriented operations. A row-oriented operation is one that exceeds the capabilities of single-statement processing (e.g., SELECT). Some characteristic of it requires more power or more flexibility than a single-statement solution can provide. Here's an example of a row-oriented operation that lists the source code for the triggers attached to each table in a database:

```
USE pubs
DECLARE objects CURSOR
FOR
SELECT name, deltrig, instrig, updtrig
FROM sysobjects WHERE type='U' AND deltrig+instrig+updtrig>0

DECLARE @objname sysname, @deltrig int, @instrig int, @updtrig int,
   @deltrigname sysname, @instrigname sysname, @updtrigname sysname

OPEN objects
FETCH objects INTO @objname, @deltrig, @instrig, @updtrig
WHILE (@@FETCH_STATUS=0) BEGIN
  PRINT 'Triggers for object: '+@objname
  SELECT @deltrigname=OBJECT_NAME(@deltrig), @instrigname=OBJECT_NAME(@instrig),
      @updtrigname=OBJECT_NAME(@updtrig)
  IF @deltrigname IS NOT NULL BEGIN
    PRINT 'Table: '+@objname+' Delete Trigger: '+@deltrigname
    EXEC sp_helptext @deltrigname
  END
```

```
   IF @instrigname IS NOT NULL BEGIN
      PRINT 'Table: '+@objname+' Insert Trigger: '+@instrigname
      EXEC sp_helptext @instrigname
   END
   IF @updtrigname IS NOT NULL BEGIN
      PRINT 'Table: '+@objname+' Update Trigger: '+@updtrigname
      EXEC sp_helptext @updtrigname
   END
   FETCH objects INTO @objname, @deltrig, @instrig, @updtrig
END

CLOSE objects
DEALLOCATE objects
```

(Results)

```
Triggers for object: employee
Table: employee Insert Trigger: employee_insupd
Text
--------------------------------------------------------------------------------
CREATE TRIGGER employee_insupd
ON employee
FOR insert, UPDATE
AS
-- Get the range of level for this job type from the jobs table.
declare @min_lvl tinyint,
   @max_lvl tinyint,
   @emp_lvl tinyint,
   @job_id smallint
select @min_lvl = min_lvl,
   @max_lvl = max_lvl,
   @emp_lvl = i.job_lvl,
   @job_id = i.job_id
from employee e, jobs j, inserted i
where e.emp_id = i.emp_id AND i.job_id = j.job_id
IF (@job_id = 1) and (@emp_lvl <> 10)
begin
   raiserror ('Job id 1 expects the default level of 10.',16,1)
   ROLLBACK TRANSACTION
end
ELSE
IF NOT (@emp_lvl BETWEEN @min_lvl AND @max_lvl)
begin
   raiserror ('The level for job_id:%d should be between %d and %d.',
      16, 1, @job_id, @min_lvl, @max_lvl)
   ROLLBACK TRANSACTION
end

Table: employee Update Trigger: employee_insupd
Text
--------------------------------------------------------------------------------
CREATE TRIGGER employee_insupd
ON employee
FOR insert, UPDATE
```

```
AS
-- Get the range of level for this job type from the jobs table.
declare @min_lvl tinyint,
   @max_lvl tinyint,
   @emp_lvl tinyint,
   @job_id smallint
select @min_lvl = min_lvl,
   @max_lvl = max_lvl,
   @emp_lvl = i.job_lvl,
   @job_id = i.job_id
from employee e, jobs j, inserted i
where e.emp_id = i.emp_id AND i.job_id = j.job_id
IF (@job_id = 1) and (@emp_lvl <> 10)
begin
   raiserror ('Job id 1 expects the default level of 10.',16,1)
   ROLLBACK TRANSACTION
end
ELSE
IF NOT (@emp_lvl BETWEEN @min_lvl AND @max_lvl)
begin
   raiserror ('The level for job_id:%d should be between %d and %d.',
      16, 1, @job_id, @min_lvl, @max_lvl)
   ROLLBACK TRANSACTION
end
```

Of course, we could query the syscomments table directly and join it with the sysobjects table to render the same information, but the result set wouldn't be formatted suitably. By iterating through the table one row at a time, we can format the output for each table and its triggers however we like.

Scrollable Forms

Whether you should use a cursor to service a scrollable form depends largely on how much data the form might require. Since Transact-SQL cursors reside on the server and return only fetched rows, they can save lots of time and resources when dealing with large result sets. You wouldn't want to return 100,000 rows over a network to a client application. On the other hand, cursors are unnecessary with smaller result sets and probably not worth the trouble. Other factors to consider when determining whether a cursor is appropriate for a scrollable form are whether the form is updatable and whether you want changes by other users to show up immediately. If the form is read-only or you're not concerned with showing changes by other users, you may be able to avoid using a cursor.

T-SQL Cursor Syntax

There are a number of commands and functions that relate to cursors. Table 13.2 summarizes them.

The following sections cover these commands in more detail.

Table 13.2. Transact-SQL cursor syntax.

Command or Function	Purpose
DECLARE CURSOR	Defines a cursor
OPEN	Opens a cursor so that data may be retrieved from it
FETCH	Fetches a single row from the cursor
CLOSE	Closes the cursor, leaving intact the internal structures that service it
DEALLOCATE	Frees the cursor's internal structures
@@CURSOR_ROWS	Returns the number of rows exposed by the cursor
@@FETCH_STATUS	Indicates the success or failure of the last FETCH
CURSOR_STATUS()	Reports status info for cursors and cursor variables

DECLARE CURSOR

DECLARE CURSOR defines cursors. There are two basic versions of the DECLARE CUR-
SOR command—the ANSI/ISO SQL 92–compliant syntax and Transact-SQL's extended syntax. The ANSI/ISO syntax looks like this:

```
DECLARE name [INSENSITIVE][SCROLL] CURSOR
FOR select
[FOR {READ ONLY | UPDATE [OF column [,...n]]}]
```

Transact-SQL's extended syntax follows this form:

```
DECLARE name CURSOR
[LOCAL | GLOBAL]
[FORWARD_ONLY | SCROLL]
[STATIC | KEYSET | DYNAMIC | FAST_FORWARD]
[READ_ONLY | SCROLL_LOCKS | OPTIMISTIC]
[TYPE_WARNING]
FOR select
[FOR {READ ONLY | UPDATE [OF column [,...n]]}]
```

The *select* component of the command is a standard SELECT statement that defines what data
the cursor returns. It is not permitted to contain the keyword COMPUTE [BY], FOR BROWSE,
or INTO. The s*elect* component affects whether a cursor is read-only. For example, if you include the FOR UPDATE clause but specify a *select* that inherently prohibits updates (e.g., one
that includes GROUP BY or DISTINCT), your cursor will be implicitly converted to a read-
only (or static) cursor. The server converts cursors to static cursors that, by their very nature,
cannot be updated. These types of automatic conversions are known as *implicit cursor conversions*. There are a number of criteria that affect implicit cursor conversions; see the Books
Online for more information.

The corollary to this is that you don't have to specify FOR UPDATE in order to update a
cursor if its SELECT statement is inherently updatable. Again, unless specified otherwise, the
characteristics of the SELECT statement determine whether the cursor is updatable. Here's an
example:

```
CREATE TABLE #temp (k1 int identity, c1 int NULL)

INSERT #temp DEFAULT VALUES
INSERT #temp DEFAULT VALUES
INSERT #temp DEFAULT VALUES
INSERT #temp DEFAULT VALUES

DECLARE c CURSOR
FOR SELECT k1, c1 FROM #temp

OPEN c
FETCH c
UPDATE #temp
SET c1=2
WHERE CURRENT OF c

SELECT * FROM #temp
CLOSE c
DEALLOCATE c
GO
DROP TABLE #temp

k1           c1
----------- -----------
1            NULL

k1           c1
----------- -----------
1            2
2            NULL
3            NULL
4            NULL
```

Even though this cursor isn't specifically defined as an updatable cursor, it's updatable by virtue of the fact that its SELECT statement is updatable—that is, the server can readily translate an update to the cursor into an update to a specific row in the underlying table.

If you specify the FOR UPDATE clause and include a column list, the column(s) you update must appear in that list. If you attempt to update a column not in the list using UPDATE's WHERE CURRENT OF clause, SQL Server will reject the change and generate an error message. Here's an example:

```
CREATE TABLE #temp (k1 int identity, c1 int NULL, c2 int NULL)

INSERT #temp DEFAULT VALUES
INSERT #temp DEFAULT VALUES
INSERT #temp DEFAULT VALUES
INSERT #temp DEFAULT VALUES

DECLARE c CURSOR
FOR SELECT k1, c1, c2 FROM #temp
FOR UPDATE OF c1
```

```
OPEN c
FETCH c

-- BAD T-SQL -- This UPDATE attempts to change a column not in the FOR UPDATE
OF -- list
UPDATE #temp
SET c2=2
WHERE CURRENT OF c
```

```
k1           c1           c2
----------   ----------   ----------
1            NULL         NULL
```

```
Server: Msg 16932, Level 16, State 1, Line 18
The cursor has a FOR UPDATE list and the requested column to be updated is not
in this list.
The statement has been terminated.
```

If *select* references a variable, the variable is resolved when the cursor is declared, *not* when it's opened. This is significant in that you must assign values to variables before you declare a cursor that uses them. You can't declare a cursor first, then assign a value to a variable that it depends on and expect the cursor to work properly. Here's an example:

```
-- In case these remain from the previous example
DEALLOCATE c
DROP TABLE #temp
GO

CREATE TABLE #temp (k1 int identity, c1 int NULL)

INSERT #temp DEFAULT VALUES
INSERT #temp DEFAULT VALUES
INSERT #temp DEFAULT VALUES
INSERT #temp DEFAULT VALUES

DECLARE @k1 int

DECLARE c CURSOR
FOR SELECT k1, c1 FROM #temp WHERE k1<@k1 -- Won't work -- @k1 is NULL here

SET @k1=3 -- Need to move this before the DECLARE CURSOR
OPEN c
FETCH c

UPDATE #temp
SET c1=2
WHERE CURRENT OF c

SELECT * FROM #temp
CLOSE c
DEALLOCATE c
GO
DROP TABLE #temp
```

```
k1              c1
----------- -----------

Server: Msg 16930, Level 16, State 1, Line 18
The requested row is not in the fetch buffer.
The statement has been terminated.
k1              c1
----------- -----------
1               NULL
2               NULL
3               NULL
4               NULL
```

Global vs. Local Cursors

A global cursor is visible outside the batch, stored procedure, or trigger that created it and persists until it's explicitly deallocated or until its host connection disconnects. A local cursor is visible only within the code module that created it unless it's returned via an output parameter. Local cursors are implicitly deallocated when they go out of scope.

For compatibility with earlier releases, SQL Server creates global cursors by default, but you can override the default behavior by explicitly specifying the GLOBAL or LOCAL keyword when you declare a cursor. Note that you can have global and local cursors with identical names, though this is an ill-advised coding practice. For example, this code runs without error:

```
DECLARE Darryl CURSOR        -- My brother Darryl
LOCAL
FOR SELECT stor_id, title_id, qty FROM sales

DECLARE Darryl CURSOR        -- My other brother Darryl
GLOBAL
FOR SELECT au_lname, au_fname FROM authors

OPEN GLOBAL Darryl
OPEN Darryl

FETCH GLOBAL Darryl
FETCH Darryl

CLOSE GLOBAL Darryl
CLOSE Darryl

DEALLOCATE GLOBAL Darryl
DEALLOCATE Darryl
```

(Results)

```
au_lname                                au_fname
--------------------------------------- --------------------
White                                   Johnson

stor_id title_id qty
------- -------- ------
6380    BU1032   5
```

You can change whether SQL Server creates global cursors when the scope is unspecified via the **sp_dboption** system procedure (see the following section "Configuring Cursors" for more information).

OPEN

OPEN makes a cursor's rows accessible via FETCH. If the cursor is an INSENSITIVE or STATIC cursor, OPEN copies the entirety of its result set to a temporary table. If it's a KEYSET cursor, OPEN copies its set of unique key values (or the entirety of all candidate key columns if no unique key exists) to a temporary table. OPEN can indicate the scope of the cursor by including the optional GLOBAL keyword. If there are both a local and a global cursor with the same name (something you should avoid when possible), use GLOBAL to indicate the one you want to open. (The **default to local cursor** database option determines whether you get a global or local cursor when neither is explicitly specified. See the following section on configuring cursors for more information.)

Use the @@CURSOR_ROWS automatic variable to determine how many rows are in the cursor. Here's a simple OPEN example:

```
CREATE TABLE #temp (k1 int identity PRIMARY KEY, c1 int NULL)

INSERT #temp DEFAULT VALUES
INSERT #temp DEFAULT VALUES
INSERT #temp DEFAULT VALUES
INSERT #temp DEFAULT VALUES

DECLARE GlobalCursor CURSOR STATIC -- Declare a GLOBAL cursor
GLOBAL
FOR SELECT k1, c1 FROM #temp

DECLARE LocalCursor CURSOR STATIC -- Declare a LOCAL cursor
LOCAL
FOR SELECT k1, c1 FROM #temp WHERE k1<4 -- Only returns three rows

OPEN GLOBAL GlobalCursor
SELECT @@CURSOR_ROWS AS NumberOfGLOBALCursorRows

OPEN LocalCursor
SELECT @@CURSOR_ROWS AS NumberOfLOCALCursorRows
CLOSE GLOBAL GlobalCursor
DEALLOCATE GLOBAL GlobalCursor
CLOSE LocalCursor
DEALLOCATE LocalCursor
GO
DROP TABLE #temp

NumberOfGLOBALCursorRows
-----------------------
4


NumberOfLOCALCursorRows
-----------------------
3
```

For dynamic cursors, @@CURSOR_ROWS returns –1 since new row additions could change the number of rows returned by the cursor at any time. If the cursor is being populated asynchronously (see the "Configuring Cursors" section), @@CURSOR_ROWS returns a negative number whose absolute value indicates the number of rows currently in the cursor.

FETCH

FETCH is the means by which you retrieve data from a cursor. Think of it as a special SELECT that returns just one row from a predetermined result set. Typically, FETCH is called within a loop that uses @@FETCH_STATUS as its control variable, with each successive FETCH returning the cursor's next row.

Scrollable cursors (DYNAMIC, STATIC, and KEYSET cursors, or those declared using the SCROLL option) allow FETCH to retrieve rows other than the cursor's next row. In addition to retrieving the next row, scrollable cursors allow FETCH to retrieve a cursor's previous row, its first row, its last row, an absolute row number, and a row relative to the current row. Here's a simple example:

```
SET NOCOUNT ON
CREATE TABLE #cursortest (k1 int identity)

INSERT #cursortest DEFAULT VALUES
INSERT #cursortest DEFAULT VALUES
INSERT #cursortest DEFAULT VALUES
INSERT #cursortest DEFAULT VALUES
INSERT #cursortest DEFAULT VALUES
INSERT #cursortest DEFAULT VALUES
INSERT #cursortest DEFAULT VALUES
INSERT #cursortest DEFAULT VALUES
INSERT #cursortest DEFAULT VALUES
INSERT #cursortest DEFAULT VALUES

DECLARE c CURSOR SCROLL
FOR SELECT * FROM #cursortest

OPEN c

FETCH c -- Gets the first row
FETCH ABSOLUTE 4 FROM c -- Gets the 4th row
FETCH RELATIVE -1 FROM c -- Gets the 3rd row
FETCH LAST FROM c -- Gets the last row
FETCH FIRST FROM c -- Gets the first row

CLOSE c
DEALLOCATE c
GO
DROP TABLE #cursortest

k1
-----------
1
```

```
k1
-----------
4

k1
-----------
3

k1
-----------
10

k1
-----------
1
```

FETCH can be used to return a result set of its own, but usually it's used to fill local variables with table data. FETCH's INTO clause allows retrieved values to be assigned to local variables. Here's an example:

```
SET NOCOUNT ON
CREATE TABLE #cursortest (k1 int identity)

INSERT #cursortest DEFAULT VALUES
INSERT #cursortest DEFAULT VALUES
INSERT #cursortest DEFAULT VALUES
INSERT #cursortest DEFAULT VALUES
INSERT #cursortest DEFAULT VALUES
INSERT #cursortest DEFAULT VALUES
INSERT #cursortest DEFAULT VALUES
INSERT #cursortest DEFAULT VALUES
INSERT #cursortest DEFAULT VALUES
INSERT #cursortest DEFAULT VALUES

DECLARE c CURSOR SCROLL
FOR SELECT * FROM #cursortest

DECLARE @k int

OPEN c
FETCH c INTO @k
WHILE (@@FETCH_STATUS=0) BEGIN
   SELECT @k
   FETCH c INTO @k
END

CLOSE c
DEALLOCATE c
GO
DROP TABLE #cursortest
```

(Results)

```
-----------
1
```

```
-----------
2

-----------
3

-----------
4

-----------
5

-----------
6

-----------
7

-----------
8          /

-----------
9

-----------
10
```

NEXT is the default fetch operation, so if you don't specify what type of fetch you want, you'll retrieve the cursor's next row. For fetch operations other than NEXT, the FROM keyword is required.

FETCH RELATIVE 0 can be used to refresh the current record. This allows you to accommodate changes made to the current row while the cursor is being traversed. Here's an example:

```
USE pubs
SET CURSOR_CLOSE_ON_COMMIT OFF -- In case it's been turned on previously
SET NOCOUNT ON

DECLARE c CURSOR SCROLL
FOR SELECT title_id, qty FROM sales ORDER BY qty

OPEN c

BEGIN TRAN -- So that we can undo the changes we make

PRINT 'Before image'

FETCH c

UPDATE sales
SET qty=4
WHERE qty=3 -- We happen to know that only one row qualifies, the first one

PRINT 'After image'
FETCH RELATIVE 0 FROM c
```

```
ROLLBACK TRAN -- Reverse the UPDATE

CLOSE c
DEALLOCATE c

Before image
title_id qty
-------- ------
PS2091   3

After image
title_id qty
-------- ------
PS2091   4
```

CLOSE

CLOSE frees the current cursor result set and releases any locks being held by the cursor. (Prior to version 7.0, SQL Server retained *all* locks until the current transaction completed, including cursor locks. With 7.0 and later, cursor locks are handled independently of other kinds of locks.) The cursor's data structures themselves are left in place so that the cursor may be reopened if necessary. Specify the GLOBAL keyword to indicate that you're closing a GLOBAL cursor.

DEALLOCATE

When you're finished with a cursor, you should always deallocate it. A cursor takes up space in the procedure cache that can be used for other things if you get rid of it when it's no longer needed. Even though deallocating a cursor automatically closes it, it's considered poor form to deallocate a cursor without first closing it with the CLOSE command.

Configuring Cursors

In addition to configuring cursors through declaration options, Transact-SQL provides commands and configuration options that can modify cursor behavior as well. The procedures **sp_configure** and **sp_dboption** and the **SET** command can be used to configure how cursors are created and the way that they behave once created.

Asynchronous Cursors

By default, SQL Server generates all keysets synchronously—that is, the call to OPEN doesn't return until the cursor's result set has been fully materialized. This may not be optimal for large data sets, and you can change it via the **sp_configure 'cursor threshold'** configuration option (**cursor threshold** is an advanced option; enable advanced options via **sp_configure 'show advanced options'** in order to access it). Here's an example that illustrates the difference rendering a cursor asynchronously can make:

```
-- Turn on advanced options so that 'cursor threshold' can be configured
EXEC sp_configure 'show advanced options',1
RECONFIGURE WITH OVERRIDE

USE northwind
```

```
DECLARE c CURSOR STATIC -- Force rows to be copied to tempdb
FOR SELECT OrderID, ProductID FROM [Order Details]

DECLARE @start datetime
SET @start=getdate()

-- First try it with a synchronous cursor
OPEN c

PRINT CHAR(13) -- Pretty up the display
SELECT DATEDIFF(ms,@start,getdate()) AS [Milliseconds elapsed for Synchronous cursor]

SELECT @@CURSOR_ROWS AS [Number of rows in Synchronous cursor]

CLOSE c

-- Now reconfigure 'cursor threshold' and force an asynch cursor
EXEC sp_configure 'cursor threshold', 1000 -- Asynchronous for cursors > 1000 rows
RECONFIGURE WITH OVERRIDE
PRINT CHAR(13) -- Pretty up the display

SET @start=getdate()
OPEN c -- Opens an asynch cursor since there are over 1000 rows in the table

-- OPEN comes back immediately because the cursor is being populated asynchronously
SELECT DATEDIFF(ms,@start,getdate()) AS [Milliseconds elapsed for Asynchronous cursor]

SELECT @@CURSOR_ROWS AS [Number of rows in Asynchronous cursor]

CLOSE c

DEALLOCATE c
GO
EXEC sp_configure 'cursor threshold', -1 -- Back to synchronous
RECONFIGURE WITH OVERRIDE
```

(Results)

```
DBCC execution completed. If DBCC printed error messages, contact your system administrator.
Configuration option changed. Run the RECONFIGURE statement to install.

Milliseconds elapsed for Synchronous cursor
-------------------------------------------
70

Number of rows in Synchronous cursor
------------------------------------
2155

DBCC execution completed. If DBCC printed error messages, contact your system administrator.
Configuration option changed. Run the RECONFIGURE statement to install.

Milliseconds elapsed for Asynchronous cursor
--------------------------------------------
0

Number of rows in Asynchronous cursor
-------------------------------------
-1

DBCC execution completed. If DBCC printed error messages, contact your system administrator.
Configuration option changed. Run the RECONFIGURE statement to install.
```

ANSI/ISO Automatic Cursor Closing

The ANSI/ISO SQL-92 specification calls for cursors to be closed automatically when a transaction is committed. This doesn't make a lot of sense for the types of apps where cursors would most often be used (those with scrollable forms, for example), so SQL Server doesn't comply with the standard out of the box. By default, a SQL Server cursor remains open until explicitly closed or until the connection that created it disconnects. To force SQL Server to close cursors when a transaction is committed, use the SET CURSOR_CLOSE_ON_COMMIT command. Here's an example:

```
CREATE TABLE #temp (k1 int identity PRIMARY KEY, c1 int NULL)

INSERT #temp DEFAULT VALUES
INSERT #temp DEFAULT VALUES
INSERT #temp DEFAULT VALUES
INSERT #temp DEFAULT VALUES

DECLARE c CURSOR DYNAMIC
FOR SELECT k1, c1 FROM #temp

OPEN c
SET CURSOR_CLOSE_ON_COMMIT ON
BEGIN TRAN

UPDATE #temp
SET c1=2
WHERE k1=1

COMMIT TRAN

-- These FETCHes will fail because the cursor was closed by the COMMIT
FETCH c
FETCH LAST FROM c

-- This CLOSE will fail because the cursor was closed by the COMMIT
CLOSE c
DEALLOCATE c
GO
DROP TABLE #temp
SET CURSOR_CLOSE_ON_COMMIT OFF
```

```
Server: Msg 16917, Level 16, State 2, Line 0
Cursor is not open.
Server: Msg 16917, Level 16, State 2, Line 26
Cursor is not open.
Server: Msg 16917, Level 16, State 1, Line 29
Cursor is not open.
```

Contrary to the Books Online, rolling back a transaction does *not* close updatable cursors when CLOSE_CURSOR_ON_COMMIT is disabled. The actual behavior following a ROLLBACK differs significantly from the documentation and more closely follows what happens when a transaction is committed. Basically, ROLLBACK doesn't close cursors unless CLOSE_CURSOR_ON_COMMIT has been enabled. Here's an example:

```
USE pubs
SET CURSOR_CLOSE_ON_COMMIT ON
BEGIN TRAN

DECLARE c CURSOR DYNAMIC
FOR SELECT qty FROM sales

OPEN c

FETCH c

UPDATE sales
SET qty=qty+1
WHERE CURRENT OF c

ROLLBACK TRAN

-- These FETCHes will fail because the cursor was closed by the ROLLBACK
FETCH c
FETCH LAST FROM c

-- This CLOSE will fail because the cursor was closed by the ROLLBACK
CLOSE c
DEALLOCATE c
GO
SET CURSOR_CLOSE_ON_COMMIT OFF

qty
------
5

Server: Msg 16917, Level 16, State 2, Line 21
Cursor is not open.
Server: Msg 16917, Level 16, State 2, Line 22
Cursor is not open.
Server: Msg 16917, Level 16, State 1, Line 25
Cursor is not open.
```

Now let's disable CURSOR_CLOSE_ON_COMMIT and run the query again:

```
SET CURSOR_CLOSE_ON_COMMIT OFF
BEGIN TRAN

DECLARE c CURSOR DYNAMIC
FOR SELECT qty FROM sales

OPEN c
FETCH c

UPDATE sales
SET qty=qty+1
WHERE CURRENT OF c

ROLLBACK TRAN
```

```
-- These FETCHes will succeed because the cursor was left open in spite of the
-- ROLLBACK
FETCH c
FETCH LAST FROM c

-- This CLOSE will succeed because the cursor was left open in spite of the
-- ROLLBACK
CLOSE c
DEALLOCATE c

qty
------
5

qty
------
3

qty
------
30
```

Despite the fact that a transaction is rolled back while our dynamic cursor is open, the cursor is unaffected. This contradicts the way the server is documented to behave.

Defaulting to Global or Local Cursors

Out of the box, SQL Server creates global cursors by default. This is in keeping with previous versions of the server that did not support local cursors. If you'd like to change this, set the **default to local cursor** database option to true using **sp_dboption.**

Updating Cursors

The WHERE CURRENT OF clause of the UPDATE and DELETE commands allows you to update and delete rows via a cursor. An update or delete performed via a cursor is known as a *positioned* modification. Here's an example:

```
USE pubs
SET CURSOR_CLOSE_ON_COMMIT OFF

SET NOCOUNT ON
DECLARE c CURSOR DYNAMIC
FOR SELECT * FROM sales

OPEN c

FETCH c

BEGIN TRAN -- Start a transaction so that we can reverse our changes
-- A positioned UPDATE
UPDATE sales SET qty=qty+1 WHERE CURRENT OF c
```

```
FETCH RELATIVE 0 FROM c

FETCH c

-- A positioned DELETE
DELETE sales WHERE CURRENT OF c

SELECT * FROM sales WHERE qty=3

ROLLBACK TRAN -- Throw away our changes

SELECT * FROM sales WHERE qty=3 -- The deleted row comes back

CLOSE c
DEALLOCATE c
```

stor_id	ord_num	ord_date	qty	payterms	title_id
6380	6871	1994-09-14 00:00:00.000	5	Net 60	BU1032

stor_id	ord_num	ord_date	qty	payterms	title_id
6380	6871	1994-09-14 00:00:00.000	6	Net 60	BU1032

stor_id	ord_num	ord_date	qty	payterms	title_id
6380	722a	1994-09-13 00:00:00.000	3	Net 60	PS2091

stor_id	ord_num	ord_date	qty	payterms	title_id

stor_id	ord_num	ord_date	qty	payterms	title_id
6380	722a	1994-09-13 00:00:00.000	3	Net 60	PS2091

Cursor Variables

Transact-SQL allows you to define variables that contain pointers to cursors via its **cursor** data type. The OPEN, FETCH, CLOSE, and DEALLOCATE commands can reference cursor variables as well as cursor names. You can set up variables within stored procedures that store cursor definitions, and you can return a cursor created by a stored procedure via an output parameter. Several of SQL Server's own procedures use this capability to return results to their callers in an efficient, modular fashion (e.g., sp_cursor_list, sp_describe_cursor, sp_fulltext_tables_cursor). Note that you can't pass a cursor via an input parameter into a procedure—you can return cursors only via output parameters. You also cannot define table columns using the **cursor** data type—only variables are allowed—nor can you assign a cursor variable using the SELECT statement (as with scalar variables)—you must use SET.

Cursor output parameters represent an improvement over the traditional result set approach in that they give the caller more control over how to deal with the rows a procedure returns. You can process the cursor immediately if you want—treating it just like a traditional result set—or you can retain it for later use. Before the advent of cursor variables, the only way to achieve this same degree of flexibility was to trap the stored procedure's result set in a table, then process the table as needed. This worked okay for simple, small result sets but could be problematic with larger ones.

You can use the CURSOR_STATUS() function to check a cursor output parameter to see whether it references an open cursor and to determine the number of rows it exposes. Here's an example that features cursor variables, output parameters, and the CURSOR_STATUS() function:

```
CREATE PROC listsales_cur @title_id tid, @salescursor cursor varying OUT
AS
-- Declare a LOCAL cursor so it's automatically freed when it
-- goes out of scope
DECLARE c CURSOR DYNAMIC
LOCAL
FOR SELECT * FROM sales WHERE title_id LIKE @title_id

DECLARE @sc cursor          -- A local cursor variable
SET @sc=c                -- Now we have two references to the cursor

OPEN c

FETCH @sc

SET @salescursor=@sc       -- Return the cursor via the output parm
RETURN 0
GO
SET NOCOUNT ON
-- Define a local cursor variable to receive the output parm
DECLARE @mycursor cursor

EXEC listsales_cur 'BU1032', @mycursor OUT -- Call the procedure

-- Make sure the returned cursor is open and has at least one row
IF (CURSOR_STATUS('variable','@mycursor')=1) BEGIN
   FETCH @mycursor
   WHILE (@@FETCH_STATUS=0) BEGIN
     FETCH @mycursor
   END
END

CLOSE @mycursor
DEALLOCATE @mycursor
```

(Results)

stor_id	ord_num	ord_date	qty	payterms	title_id
6380	6871	1994-09-14 00:00:00.000	5	Net 60	BU1032

stor_id	ord_num	ord_date	qty	payterms	title_id
8042	423LL930	1994-09-14 00:00:00.000	10	ON invoice	BU1032

stor_id	ord_num	ord_date	qty	payterms	title_id
-------	----------------	-------------------------	------	------------	--------
8042	QA879.1	1999-06-24 19:13:26.230	30	Net 30	BU1032

stor_id	ord_num	ord_date	qty	payterms	title_id
-------	----------------	-------------------------	------	------------	--------

Notice the way example code references the cursor using three different variables as well as its original name. For every command except DEALLOCATE, referencing a cursor variable is synonymous with referencing the cursor by name. If you OPEN the cursor, regardless of whether you reference it using a cursor variable or the cursor name itself, the cursor is opened, and you can FETCH rows using any variable that references it. DEALLOCATE differs in that it doesn't actually deallocate the cursor unless it's the last reference to it. It does, however, prevent future access using the specified cursor identifier. So if you have a cursor named **foo** and a cursor variable named **foovar** to which **foo** has been assigned, deallocating **foo** will do nothing except prohibit access to the cursor via **foo**—**foovar** remains intact.

Cursor Stored Procedures

SQL Server provides a number of cursor-related stored procedures with which you should familiarize yourself if you expect to work with cursors much. Table 13.3 provides a brief list of them, along with a description of each.

Each of these returns its result via a cursor output parameter, so you'll need to supply a local cursor variable in order to process them.

Optimizing Cursor Performance

The best performance improvement technique for cursors is not to use them at all if you can avoid it. As I've said, SQL Server works much better with sets of data than with individual rows. It's a relational database, and single-row access has never been the strong suit of relational DBMSs. That said, there are times when using a cursor is unavoidable, so here are a few tips for optimizing them:

- Don't use static/insensitive cursors unless you need them. Opening a static cursor causes all of its rows to be copied to a temporary table. That's why it's insensitive

Table 13.3. Stored procedures that relate to cursors.

Procedure	Function
sp_cursor_list	Returns a list of the cursors and their attributes that have been opened by a connection
sp_describe_cursor	Lists the attributes of an individual cursor
sp_describe_cursor_columns	Lists the columns (and their attributes) returned by a cursor
sp_describe_cursor_tables	Returns a list of the tables referenced by a cursor

to changes—it's actually referencing a copy of the table in tempdb. Naturally, the larger the result set, the more likely declaring a static cursor over it will cause resource contention issues in tempdb.

- Don't use keyset cursors unless you really need them. As with static cursors, opening a keyset cursor creates a temporary table. Though this table contains only key values from the underlying table (unless no unique key exists), it can still be quite substantial when dealing with large result sets.

- Use the FAST_FORWARD cursor option in lieu of FORWARD_ONLY when working with unidirectional, read-only result sets. Using FAST_FORWARD defines a FORWARD_ONLY, READ_ONLY cursor with a number of internal performance optimizations.

- Define read-only cursors using the READ_ONLY keyword. This prevents you from making accidental changes and lets the server know that the cursor will not alter the rows it traverses.

- Be careful with modifying large numbers of rows via a cursor loop that's contained within a transaction. Depending on the transaction isolation level, those rows may remain locked until the transaction is committed or rolled back, possibly causing resource contention on the server.

- Be careful with updating dynamic cursors, especially those constructed over tables with nonunique clustered index keys, because they can cause the "Halloween Problem"—repetitive, erroneous updates of the same row or rows. Because SQL Server forces nonunique clustered index keys to be unique internally by suffixing them with a sequence number, it's possible that you could update a row's key to a value that already exists and force the server to append a suffix that would move it later in the result set. As you fetched through the remainder of the result set, you'd encounter the row again, and the process would repeat itself, resulting in an infinite loop. Here's an example that illustrates this problem:

```
-- This code creates a cursor that exhibits the Halloween Problem.
-- Don't run it unless you find infinite loops intriguing.
SET NOCOUNT ON
CREATE TABLE #temp (k1 int identity, c1 int NULL)
CREATE CLUSTERED INDEX c1 ON #temp(c1)

INSERT #temp VALUES (8)
INSERT #temp VALUES (6)
INSERT #temp VALUES (7)
INSERT #temp VALUES (5)
INSERT #temp VALUES (3)
INSERT #temp VALUES (0)
INSERT #temp VALUES (9)

DECLARE c CURSOR DYNAMIC
FOR SELECT k1, c1 FROM #temp

OPEN c
```

```
FETCH c

WHILE (@@FETCH_STATUS=0) BEGIN
  UPDATE #temp
  SET c1=c1+1
  WHERE CURRENT OF c
  FETCH c
  SELECT * FROM #temp ORDER BY k1
END

CLOSE c
DEALLOCATE c
GO
DROP TABLE #temp
```

- Consider using asynchronous cursors with large result sets in order to return control to the caller as quickly as possible. Asynchronous cursors are especially useful when returning a sizable result set to a scrollable form because they allow the application to begin displaying rows almost immediately.

Summary

In this chapter, you learned about the different types of cursors that Transact-SQL supports and how to create and manage them and about some potential pitfalls and performance optimizations to be aware of as you use them. Cursors are not the recommended way to solve most problems, and they can cause serious performance headaches when used improperly.

14

Transactions

*I think I am motivated mostly by dread, by fear of a
miserable life. Certainly I am troubled by worries of
obsolescence, of incompetence, of unemployability.
I would probably be happier if I were motivated by
positives, by goals to be attained and rewards to be
enjoyed.*—Thomas L. Holaday

An in-depth discussion of transaction management is outside the scope of this book. There are
a number of books out there that cover the internals of SQL Server transaction management in
detail. The Books Online is also a good source of information for exploring the mechanics of
SQL Server transactions.

Transactions Defined

SQL Server's transaction management facilities help ensure the integrity and recoverability of
the data stored in its databases. A transaction is a set of one or more database operations that
are treated as a single unit—either they all occur or none of them do. As such, a transaction is
a database's basic operational metric—its fundamental unit of work.

SQL Server transactions ensure data recoverability and consistency in spite of any hardware,
operating system, application, or SQL Server errors that may occur. They ensure that multiple
commands performed within a transaction are performed either completely or not at all and that
a single command that alters multiple rows changes either all of them or none of them.

The ACID Test

SQL Server transactions are often described as having the *ACID* properties or "passing the
ACID test," where *ACID* is an acronym for atomic, consistent, isolated, and durable. Transactional adherence to the ACID tenets is commonplace in modern DBMSs and is a prerequisite
for ensuring the safety and reliability of data.

Atomicity

A transaction is atomic if it's an all-or-nothing proposition. When the transaction succeeds, all of its changes are stored permanently; when it fails, they're completely reversed. So, for example, if a transaction includes ten DELETE commands and the last one fails, rolling back the transaction will reverse the previous nine. Likewise, if a single command attempts ten row deletions and one of them fails, the entire operation fails.

Consistency

A transaction is consistent if it ensures that its underlying data never appears in an interim or illogical state—that is, if it never appears to be inconsistent. So, the data affected by an UPDATE command that changes ten rows will never appear to the outside world in an intermediate state—all rows will appear in either their initial state or their final state. This prevents one user from inadvertently interfering with another user's work in progress. Consistency is usually implied by the other ACID properties.

Isolation

A transaction is isolated if it is not affected by, nor affects, other concurrent transactions on the same data. The extent to which a transaction is isolated from other transactions is controlled by its transaction isolation level (specified via the SET TRANSACTION ISOLATION LEVEL command). These TILs range from no isolation at all—during which transactions can read uncommitted data and cannot exclusively lock resources—to serializable isolation—which locks the entire data set and prevents users from modifying it in any way until the transaction completes. (See the following section, "Transaction Isolation Levels," for more information.) The trade-off with each isolation level is one of concurrency (concurrent access and modification of a data set by multiple users) vs. consistency. The more airtight the isolation, the higher the degree of data consistency. The higher the consistency, the lower the concurrency. This is because SQL Server locks resources to ensure data consistency. More locks means fewer simultaneous data modifications and reduced accessibility overall.

Isolation prevents a transaction from retrieving illogical or incomplete snapshots of data currently under modification by another transaction. For example, if a transaction is inserting a number of rows into a table, isolation prevents other transactions from seeing those rows until the transaction is committed. SQL Server's TILs allow you to balance your data accessibility needs with your data integrity requirements.

Durability

A transaction is considered durable if it can complete despite a system failure or, in the case of uncommitted transactions, if it can be completely reversed following a system failure. SQL Server's write-ahead logging and the database recovery process ensure that transactions committed but not yet stored in the database are written to the database following a system failure (rolled forward) and that transactions in progress are reversed (rolled back).

How SQL Server Transactions Work

SQL Server transactions are similar to command batches in that they usually consist of multiple Transact-SQL statements that are executed as a group. They differ in that a command batch is a client-side concept—it's a mechanism for sending groups of commands to the server—while a transaction is a server-side concept—it controls what SQL Server considers completed and in-progress work.

There's a many-to-many relationship between command batches and transactions. Command batches can contain multiple transactions, and a single transaction can span multiple batches. As a rule, you want to avoid transactions that span lengthy command batches because of the concurrency and performance problems that such transactions can cause.

Any time a data modification occurs, SQL Server writes a record of the change to the transaction log. This occurs before the change itself is performed and is the reason SQL Server is described as having a "write-ahead" log—log records are written ahead of their corresponding data changes. Failing to do this could result in data changes that would not be rolled back if the server failed before the log record was written.

Modifications are never made directly to disk. Instead, SQL Server reads data pages into a buffer area as they're needed and changes them in memory. Before it changes a page in memory, the server ensures that the change is recorded in the transaction log. Since the transaction log is also cached, these changes are initially made in memory as well. Write-ahead logging ensures that the lazywriter process does not write modified data pages ("dirty" pages) to disk before their corresponding log records.

No permanent changes are made to a database until a transaction is committed. The exact timing of this varies based on the type of transaction. Once a transaction is committed, its changes are written to the database and cannot be rolled back.

Transactions and Nonlogged Operations

Regardless of whether an operation is logged or nonlogged, terminating it before it's been committed results in the operation being rolled back completely. This is possible with nonlogged operations because page allocations are recorded in the transaction log.

Transactions and Triggers

Triggers behave as though they were nested one level deep. If a transaction that contains a trigger is rolled back, so is the trigger. If the trigger is rolled back, so is any transaction that encompasses it.

Types of Transactions

SQL Server supports four basic types of transactions: automatic, implicit, user-defined, and distributed. Each has its own nuances, so I'll discuss each one separately.

Automatic Transactions

By default, each Transact-SQL command is its own transaction. These are known as automatic (or autocommit) transactions. They are begun and committed by the server automatically. A DML command that's executed outside a transaction (and while implicit transactions are disabled) is an example of an automatic transaction. You can think of an automatic transaction as a Transact-SQL statement that's ensconced between a BEGIN TRAN and a COMMIT TRAN. If the statement succeeds, it's committed. If not, it's rolled back.

Implicit Transactions

Implicit transactions are ANSI SQL-92–compliant automatic transactions. They're initiated automatically when any of numerous DDL or DML commands is executed. They continue until explicitly committed by the user. To toggle implicit transaction support, use the SET IMPLICIT_TRANSACTIONS command. By default, OLEDB and ODBC connections enable the ANSI_DEFAULTS switch, which, in turn, enables implicit transactions. However, they then immediately disable implicit transactions because of the grief mismanaged transactions can cause applications. Enabling implicit transactions is like rigging your car doors to lock automatically every time you shut them. It costs more time than it saves, and, sooner or later, you're going to leave your keys in the ignition.

User-Defined Transactions

User-defined transactions are the chief means of managing transactions in SQL Server applications. A user-defined transaction is user-defined in that you control when it begins and when it ends. The BEGIN TRAN, COMMIT TRAN, and ROLLBACK TRAN commands are used to control user-defined transactions. Here's an example:

```
SELECT TOP 5 title_id, stor_id FROM sales ORDER BY title_id, stor_id
BEGIN TRAN
DELETE sales
SELECT TOP 5 title_id, stor_id FROM sales ORDER BY title_id, stor_id
GO
ROLLBACK TRAN
SELECT TOP 5 title_id, stor_id FROM sales ORDER BY title_id, stor_id

title_id stor_id
-------- -------
BU1032   6380
BU1032   8042
BU1032   8042
BU1111   8042
BU2075   7896

(5 row(s) affected)

(25 row(s) affected)

title_id stor_id
-------- -------

(0 row(s) affected)

title_id stor_id
-------- -------
BU1032   6380
BU1032   8042
BU1032   8042
BU1111   8042
BU2075   7896

(5 row(s) affected)
```

Distributed Transactions

Transactions that span multiple servers are known as distributed transactions. These transactions are administered by a central manager application that coordinates the activities of the involved servers. SQL Server can participate in distributed transactions coordinated by manager applications that support the X/Open XA specification for Distributed Transaction Processing, such as the Microsoft Distributed Transaction Coordinator (DTC). You can initiate a distributed transaction in Transact-SQL using the BEGIN DISTRIBUTED TRANSACTION command.

Avoiding Transactions Altogether

Other than avoiding making database modifications, there's really no way to disable transaction logging completely. Some operations generate a minimum of log information, but there's no configuration option that turns off logging altogether.

Commands That Minimize Logging

The BULK INSERT, TRUNCATE TABLE, SELECT...INTO, and WRITETEXT/ UPDATE-TEXT commands minimize transaction logging by causing only page operations to be logged (BULK INSERT can, depending on the circumstances, create regular detail log records). Contrary to a popular misconception, these operations *are* logged—it's just that they don't generate *detail* transaction log information. That's why the Books Online refers to them as *nonlogged* operations—they're nonlogged in that they don't generate row-level log records.

Nonlogged operations tend to be much faster than fully logged operations. And since they generate page allocation log records, they can be rolled back (but not forward) just like other operations. The price you pay for using them is transaction log recovery. Once you've executed a nonlogged command in a database, you can no longer back up the database's transaction log—you must perform a full or differential database backup instead.

Read-Only and Single-User Databases

One obvious way of avoiding logging as well as resource blocks and deadlocks in a database is by making the database read-only. Naturally, if the database can't be changed, there's no need for transaction logging or resource blocks. Making the database single-user even alleviates the need for read locks, avoiding the possibility of an application blocking itself.

Though reducing a database's accessibility in order to minimize transaction management issues might sound a little like not driving your car in order to keep it from breaking down, you sometimes see this in real applications. For example, it's fairly common for DSS (Decision Support System) applications to make use of read-only databases. These databases can be updated off-hours (e.g., overnight or on weekends), then returned to read-only status for use during normal working hours. Obviously, transaction management issues are greatly simplified when a database is modifiable only by one user at a time, is changed only *en masse,* or can't be changed at all.

Read-only databases can also be very functional as members of partitioned data banks. Sometimes an application can be spread across multiple databases—one containing static data that doesn't change much (and can therefore be set to read-only) and one containing more dynamic data that must submit to at least nominal transaction management.

Automatic Transaction Management

SQL Server provides a number of facilities for automating transaction management. The most prominent example of these is the automatic transaction (autocommit) facility. As mentioned earlier, an automatic transaction is begun and committed or rolled back implicitly by the server. There's no need for explicit BEGIN TRAN or COMMIT/ ROLLBACK TRAN statements. The server initiates a transaction when a modification command begins and, depending on the command's success, commits or rolls it back afterward. Automatic transaction mode is SQL Server's default mode but is disabled when implicit or user-defined transactions are enabled.

Implicit transactions offer another type of automated transaction management. Whenever certain commands (ALTER TABLE, FETCH, REVOKE, CREATE, GRANT, SELECT, DELETE, INSERT, TRUNCATE TABLE, DROP, OPEN, UPDATE) are executed, a transaction is automatically started. In a sense, implicit transactions offer an automated alternative to explicit transactions—a facility falling somewhere between autocommit transactions and user-defined transactions in terms of functionality. These transactions are only semiautomated, though, since an explicit ROLLBACK TRAN or COMMIT TRAN is required to close them. Only the first part of the process is automated—the initiation of the transaction. Its termination must still be performed explicitly. Transact-SQL's SET IMPLICIT_TRANSACTIONS command is used to toggle implicit transaction mode.

SET XACT_ABORT toggles whether a transaction is aborted when a command raises a runtime error. The error can be a system-generated error condition or a user-generated one. It's essentially equivalent to checking @@ERROR after every statement and rolling back the transaction if an error is detected. Note that the command is a bit of misnomer. When XACT_ABORT is enabled and a runtime error occurs, not only is the current transaction aborted, but the entire batch is as well. For example, consider this code:

```
SET XACT_ABORT ON
SELECT TOP 5 au_lname, au_fname FROM authors ORDER BY au_lname, au_fname
BEGIN TRAN
DELETE authors
DELETE sales
SELECT TOP 5 au_lname, au_fname FROM authors ORDER BY au_lname, au_fname
ROLLBACK TRAN
PRINT 'End of batch -- never makes it here'
GO
SELECT TOP 5 au_lname, au_fname FROM authors ORDER BY au_lname, au_fname
SET XACT_ABORT ON
```

(Results)

```
au_lname                                    au_fname
----------------------------------------    --------------------
Bennet                                      Abraham
Blotchet-Halls                              Reginald
Carson                                      Cheryl
DeFrance                                    Michel
del Castillo                                Innes

(5 row(s) affected)
```

```
Server: Msg 547, Level 16, State 1, Line 1
DELETE statement conflicted with COLUMN REFERENCE constraint
'FK__titleauth__au_id__164452B1'. The conflict occurred in database 'pubs',
table 'titleauthor', column 'au_id'.
au_lname                                   au_fname
---------------------------------------    --------------------
Bennet                                     Abraham
Blotchet-Halls                             Reginald
Carson                                     Cheryl
DeFrance                                   Michel
del Castillo                               Innes

(5 row(s) affected)
```

Execution never reaches the PRINT statement because the constraint violation generated by attempting to empty the **authors** table aborts the entire command batch (the statements before the GO). This is in spite of the fact that a ROLLBACK TRAN immediately precedes the PRINT.

The fact that the entire command batch is aborted is what makes checking @@ERROR after each data modification preferable to enabling SET XACT_ABORT. This is particularly true when calling a stored procedure within a transaction. If the procedure causes a runtime error, the statements following it in the command batch are aborted, affording no opportunity to handle the error condition.

Transaction Isolation Levels

SQL Server supports four transaction isolation levels. As mentioned earlier, a transaction's isolation level controls how it affects, and is affected by, other transactions. The trade-off is always one of data consistency vs. concurrency. Selecting a more restrictive TIL increases data consistency at the expense of accessibility. Selecting a less restrictive TIL increases concurrency at the expense of data consistency. The trick is to balance these opposing interests so that the needs of your application are met.

Use the SET TRANSACTION ISOLATION LEVEL command to set a transaction's isolation level. Valid TILs include READ UNCOMMITTED, READ COMMITTED, REPEATABLE READ, and SERIALIZABLE.

READ UNCOMMITTED

Specifying READ UNCOMMITTED is essentially the same as using the NOLOCK hint with every table referenced in a transaction. It is the least restrictive of SQL Server's four TILs. It permits dirty reads (reads of uncommitted changes by other transactions) and nonrepeatable reads (data that changes between reads during a transaction). To see how READ UNCOMMITTED permits dirty and nonrepeatable reads, run the following queries simultaneously:

```
-- Query 1
SELECT TOP 5 title_id, qty FROM sales ORDER BY title_id, stor_id
BEGIN TRAN
UPDATE sales SET qty=0
SELECT TOP 5 title_id, qty FROM sales ORDER BY title_id, stor_id
WAITFOR DELAY '00:00:05'
ROLLBACK TRAN
SELECT TOP 5 title_id, qty FROM sales ORDER BY title_id, stor_id
```

```
-- Query 2
SET TRANSACTION ISOLATION LEVEL READ UNCOMMITTED
PRINT 'Now you see it...'
SELECT TOP 5 title_id, qty FROM sales
WHERE qty=0
ORDER BY title_id, stor_id
IF @@ROWCOUNT>0 BEGIN
   WAITFOR DELAY '00:00:05'

   PRINT '...now you don''t'
   SELECT TOP 5 title_id, qty FROM sales
   WHERE qty=0
   ORDER BY title_id, stor_id
END
```

(Results)

```
Now you see it...
title_id qty
-------- ------
BU1032   0
BU1032   0
BU1032   0
BU1111   0
BU2075   0

(5 row(s) affected)

...now you don't
title_id qty
-------- ------

(0 row(s) affected)
```

While the first query is running (you have five seconds), fire off the second one, and you'll see that it's able to access the uncommitted data modifications of the first query. It then waits for the first transaction to finish and attempts to read the same data again. Since the modifications were rolled back, the data has vanished, leaving the second query with a nonrepeatable read.

READ COMMITTED

READ COMMITTED is SQL Server's default TIL, so if you don't specify otherwise, you'll get READ COMMITTED. READ COMMITTED avoids dirty reads by initiating share locks on accessed data but permits changes to underlying data during the transaction, possibly resulting in nonrepeatable reads and/or phantom data. To see how this works, run the following queries simultaneously:

```
-- Query 1
SET TRANSACTION ISOLATION LEVEL READ COMMITTED
BEGIN TRAN
PRINT 'Now you see it...'
SELECT TOP 5 title_id, qty FROM sales ORDER BY title_id, stor_id
WAITFOR DELAY '00:00:05'
PRINT '...now you don''t'
SELECT TOP 5 title_id, qty FROM sales ORDER BY title_id, stor_id
```

```
GO
ROLLBACK TRAN

-- Query 2
SET TRANSACTION ISOLATION LEVEL READ COMMITTED
UPDATE sales SET qty=6 WHERE qty=5
```

(Results)

```
Now you see it...
title_id qty
-------- ------
BU1032   5
BU1032   10
BU1032   30
BU1111   25
BU2075   35

...now you don't
title_id qty
-------- ------
BU1032   6
BU1032   10
BU1032   30
BU1111   25
BU2075   35
```

As in the previous example, start the first query, then quickly run the second one simultaneously (you have five seconds).

In this example, the value of the **qty** column in the first row of the **sales** table changes between reads during the first query—a classic nonrepeatable read.

REPEATABLE READ

REPEATABLE READ initiates locks to prevent other users from changing the data a transaction accesses but doesn't prevent new rows from being inserted, possibly resulting in phantom rows appearing between reads during the transaction. Here's an example (as with the other examples, start the first query; then run the second one simultaneously—you have five seconds to start the second query):

```
-- Query 1
SET TRANSACTION ISOLATION LEVEL REPEATABLE READ
BEGIN TRAN
PRINT 'Nothing up my sleeve...'
SELECT TOP 5 title_id, qty FROM sales ORDER BY qty
WAITFOR DELAY '00:00:05'
PRINT '...except this rabbit'
SELECT TOP 5 title_id, qty FROM sales ORDER BY qty
GO
ROLLBACK TRAN

-- Query 2
SET TRANSACTION ISOLATION LEVEL REPEATABLE READ
INSERT sales VALUES (6380,9999999,GETDATE(),2,'USG-Whenever','PS2091')
```

(Results)

```
Nothing up my sleeve...
title_id qty
-------- ------
PS2091   3
BU1032   5
PS2091   10
MC2222   10
BU1032   10

...except this rabbit
title_id qty
-------- ------
PS2091   2
PS2091   3
BU1032   5
PS2091   10
MC2222   10
```

As you can see, a new row appears between the first and second reads of the **sales** table, even though REPEATABLE READ has been specified. Though REPEATABLE READ prevents changes to data it has already accessed, it doesn't prevent the addition of new data, thus introducing the possibility of phantom rows.

SERIALIZABLE

SERIALIZABLE prevents dirty reads and phantom rows by placing a range lock on the data it accesses. It is the most restrictive of SQL Server's four TILs. It's equivalent to using the HOLDLOCK hint with every table a transaction references. Here's an example (delete the row you added in the previous example before running this code):

```
-- Query 1
SET TRANSACTION ISOLATION LEVEL SERIALIZABLE
BEGIN TRAN
PRINT 'Nothing up my sleeve...'
SELECT TOP 5 title_id, qty FROM sales ORDER BY qty
WAITFOR DELAY '00:00:05'
PRINT '...or in my hat'
SELECT TOP 5 title_id, qty FROM sales ORDER BY qty
ROLLBACK TRAN

-- Query 2
BEGIN TRAN
SET TRANSACTION ISOLATION LEVEL SERIALIZABLE
-- This INSERT will be delayed until the first transaction completes
INSERT sales VALUES (6380,9999999,GETDATE(),2,'USG-Whenever','PS2091')
ROLLBACK TRAN
```

(Results)

```
Nothing up my sleeve...
title_id qty
-------- ------
PS2091   3
BU1032   5
```

```
PS2091    10
MC2222    10
BU1032    10

...or in my hat
title_id qty
-------- ------
PS2091    3
BU1032    5
PS2091    10
MC2222    10
BU1032    10
```

In this example, the locks initiated by the SERIALIZABLE isolation level prevent the second query from running until after the first one finishes. While this provides airtight data consistency, it does so at a cost of greatly reduced concurrency.

Transaction Commands and Syntax

As I said earlier, the BEGIN TRAN, COMMIT TRAN, and ROLLBACK TRAN commands are used to manage transactions in Transact-SQL (the sp_xxxx_xact system stored procedures are legacy code that was used in the past with DB-Library two-phase commit applications, and you should not use them). The exact syntax used to begin a transaction is:

```
BEGIN TRAN[SACTION] [name|@TranNameVar]
```

To commit a transaction, use:

```
COMMIT TRAN[SACTION] [name|@TranNameVar]
```

And to roll back a transaction, use:

```
ROLLBACK TRAN[SACTION] [name|@TranNameVar]
```

You can also use the COMMIT WORK and ROLLBACK WORK synonyms in lieu of COMMIT TRANSACTION and ROLLBACK TRANSACTION, though you cannot use transaction names with them.

Nested Transactions

Transact-SQL allows you to nest transaction operations by issuing nested BEGIN TRAN commands. The @@TRANCOUNT automatic variable can be queried to determine the level of nesting—0 indicates no nesting, 1 indicates nesting one level deep, and so forth. Batches and stored procedures that are nesting sensitive should query @@TRANCOUNT when first executed and respond accordingly.

Though on the surface it appears otherwise, SQL Server doesn't support truly nested transactions. A COMMIT issued against any transaction except the outermost one doesn't commit any changes to disk—it merely decrements the @@TRANCOUNT automatic variable. A ROLLBACK, on the other hand, works regardless of the level at which it is issued, but rolls back all transactions, regardless of the nesting level. Though this is counterintuitive, there's a very good reason for it. If a nested COMMIT actually wrote changes permanently to disk, an outer ROLLBACK wouldn't be able to reverse those changes since they would already be recorded permanently. Likewise, if ROLLBACK didn't reverse all changes at all levels, calling it from within stored procedures and triggers would be vastly more complicated since the caller would have to check return values and the transaction nesting level when the routine returned in order to determine whether it needed to roll back pending transactions. Here's an example that illustrates some of the nuances of nested transactions:

```
SELECT 'Before BEGIN TRAN',@@TRANCOUNT
BEGIN TRAN
   SELECT 'After BEGIN TRAN',@@TRANCOUNT
   DELETE sales
   BEGIN TRAN nested
      SELECT 'After BEGIN TRAN nested',@@TRANCOUNT
      DELETE titleauthor
   COMMIT TRAN nested -- Does nothing except decrement @@TRANCOUNT
   SELECT 'After COMMIT TRAN nested',@@TRANCOUNT
GO -- When possible, it's a good idea to place ROLLBACK TRAN in a separate batch
   -- to prevent batch errors from leaving open transactions
ROLLBACK TRAN
SELECT 'After ROLLBACK TRAN',@@TRANCOUNT
SELECT TOP 5 au_id FROM titleauthor
```

   (Results)

```
---------------- ----------
Before BEGIN TRAN 0

---------------- ----------
After BEGIN TRAN 1

----------------------- ----------
After BEGIN TRAN nested 2

------------------------ ----------
After COMMIT TRAN nested 1

------------------- ----------
After ROLLBACK TRAN 0

au_id
-----------
213-46-8915
409-56-7008
267-41-2394
724-80-9391
213-46-8915
```

   In this example, we see that despite the nested COMMIT TRAN, the outer ROLLBACK still reverses the effects of the DELETE **titleauthor** command. Here's another nested transaction example:

```
SELECT 'Before BEGIN TRAN',@@TRANCOUNT
BEGIN TRAN
   SELECT 'After BEGIN TRAN',@@TRANCOUNT
   DELETE sales
   BEGIN TRAN nested
     SELECT 'After BEGIN TRAN nested',@@TRANCOUNT
     DELETE titleauthor
```

```
   ROLLBACK TRAN
   SELECT 'After ROLLBACK TRAN',@@TRANCOUNT
IF @@TRANCOUNT>0 BEGIN
   COMMIT TRAN -- Never makes it here because of the ROLLBACK
   SELECT 'After COMMIT TRAN',@@TRANCOUNT
END

SELECT TOP 5 au_id FROM titleauthor
```

(Results)

```
---------------- ----------
Before BEGIN TRAN 0

---------------- ----------
After BEGIN TRAN 1

---------------------- ----------
After BEGIN TRAN nested 2

------------------- ----------
After ROLLBACK TRAN 0

au_id
-----------
213-46-8915
409-56-7008
267-41-2394
724-80-9391
213-46-8915
```

In this example, execution never reaches the outer COMMIT TRAN because the ROLLBACK TRAN reverses all transactions currently in progress and sets @@TRANCOUNT to zero.

Note that we can't ROLLBACK the nested transaction. ROLLBACK can reverse a named transaction only when it's the outermost transaction. Attempting to roll back our nested transaction yields the message:

```
Server: Msg 6401, Level 16, State 1, Line 10
Cannot roll back nested. No transaction or savepoint of that name was found.
```

The error message notwithstanding, the problem isn't that no transaction exists with the specified name. It's that ROLLBACK can reference a transaction by name only when it is also the outermost transaction. Here's an example that illustrates using ROLLBACK TRAN with transaction names:

```
SELECT 'Before BEGIN TRAN main',@@TRANCOUNT
BEGIN TRAN main
   SELECT 'After BEGIN TRAN main',@@TRANCOUNT
   DELETE sales
   BEGIN TRAN nested
      SELECT 'After BEGIN TRAN nested',@@TRANCOUNT
      DELETE titleauthor
   ROLLBACK TRAN main
   SELECT 'After ROLLBACK TRAN main',@@TRANCOUNT
IF @@TRANCOUNT>0 BEGIN
   ROLLBACK TRAN      -- Never makes it here because of the earlier ROLLBACK
   SELECT 'After ROLLBACK TRAN',@@TRANCOUNT
END
```

```
SELECT TOP 5 au_id FROM titleauthor
```

(Results)

```
---------------------- ----------
Before BEGIN TRAN main 0

--------------------- ----------
After BEGIN TRAN main 1

----------------------- ----------
After BEGIN TRAN nested 2

------------------------ ----------
After ROLLBACK TRAN main 0

au_id
-----------
213-46-8915
409-56-7008
267-41-2394
724-80-9391
213-46-8915
```

Here, we named the outermost transaction "main" and then referenced it by name with ROLLBACK TRAN. Note that a transaction name is never required by ROLLBACK TRAN, regardless of whether the transaction is initiated with a name. For this reason, many developers avoid using transaction names with ROLLBACK altogether, since they serve no real purpose. This is largely a matter of personal choice and works acceptably well either way as long as you understand it. Unless called with a save point (see below), ROLLBACK TRAN always rolls back all transactions and sets @@TRANCOUNT to zero, regardless of the context in which it's called.

SAVE TRAN and Save Points

You can control how much work ROLLBACK reverses via the SAVE TRAN command. SAVE TRAN creates a save point to which you can roll back if you wish. Syntactically, you just pass the name of the save point to the ROLLBACK TRAN command. Here's an example:

```
SELECT 'Before BEGIN TRAN main',@@TRANCOUNT
BEGIN TRAN main
   SELECT 'After BEGIN TRAN main',@@TRANCOUNT
   DELETE sales
   SAVE TRAN sales    -- Mark a save point
   SELECT 'After SAVE TRAN sales',@@TRANCOUNT -- @@TRANCOUNT is unchanged
   BEGIN TRAN nested
      SELECT 'After BEGIN TRAN nested',@@TRANCOUNT
      DELETE titleauthor
      SAVE TRAN titleauthor -- Mark a save point
      SELECT 'After SAVE TRAN titleauthor',@@TRANCOUNT -- @@TRANCOUNT is unchanged
   ROLLBACK TRAN sales
   SELECT 'After ROLLBACK TRAN sales',@@TRANCOUNT -- @@TRANCOUNT is unchanged
   SELECT TOP 5 au_id FROM titleauthor
IF @@TRANCOUNT>0 BEGIN
   ROLLBACK TRAN
   SELECT 'After ROLLBACK TRAN',@@TRANCOUNT
END
```

```
SELECT TOP 5 au_id FROM titleauthor
```

(Results)

```
---------------------- ----------
Before BEGIN TRAN main 0

-------------------- ----------
After BEGIN TRAN main 1

-------------------- ----------
After SAVE TRAN sales 1

---------------------- ----------
After BEGIN TRAN nested 2

------------------------- ----------
After SAVE TRAN titleauthor 2

------------------------- ----------
After ROLLBACK TRAN sales 2

au_id
-----------
213-46-8915
409-56-7008
267-41-2394
724-80-9391
213-46-8915

------------------- ----------
After ROLLBACK TRAN 0

au_id
-----------
213-46-8915
409-56-7008
267-41-2394
724-80-9391
213-46-8915
```

As with version 6.5, SQL Server 7.0 allows you to reuse a save point name if you wish, but if you do so, only the last save point is retained. Rolling back using the save point name will roll the transaction back to the save point's last reference.

Avoid Accidental ROLLBACKs

Since ROLLBACK TRAN reverses all transactions in progress, it's important not to inadvertently nest calls to it. Once it's been called a single time, there's no need (nor are you allowed) to call it again until a new transaction is initiated. For example, consider this code:

```
SELECT 'Before BEGIN TRAN',@@TRANCOUNT
BEGIN TRAN
    SELECT 'After BEGIN TRAN',@@TRANCOUNT
    DELETE sales
```

```
   BEGIN TRAN nested
      SELECT 'After BEGIN TRAN nested',@@TRANCOUNT
      DELETE titleauthor
   IF @@ROWCOUNT > 1000
      COMMIT TRAN nested
   ELSE BEGIN
      ROLLBACK TRAN -- Completely rolls back both transactions
      SELECT 'After ROLLBACK TRAN',@@TRANCOUNT
   END
   SELECT TOP 5 au_id FROM titleauthor
ROLLBACK TRAN -- This is an error -- there's no transaction to rollback
SELECT 'After ROLLBACK TRAN',@@TRANCOUNT

SELECT TOP 5 au_id FROM titleauthor
```

(Results)

```
------------------ ----------
Before BEGIN TRAN 0

---------------- ----------
After BEGIN TRAN 1

----------------------- ----------
After BEGIN TRAN nested 2

-------------------- ----------
After ROLLBACK TRAN 0

au_id
-----------
213-46-8915
409-56-7008
267-41-2394
724-80-9391
213-46-8915

Server: Msg 3903, Level 16, State 1, Line 17
The ROLLBACK TRANSACTION request has no corresponding BEGIN TRANSACTION.

-------------------- ----------
After ROLLBACK TRAN 0

au_id
-----------
213-46-8915
409-56-7008
267-41-2394
724-80-9391
213-46-8915
```

Note the error message that's generated by the second ROLLBACK TRAN. Since the first ROLLBACK TRAN reverses both transactions, there's no transaction for the second to reverse. This situation is best handled by querying @@TRANCOUNT first, like this:

```
IF @@TRANCOUNT>0 BEGIN
   ROLLBACK TRAN
   SELECT 'After ROLLBACK TRAN',@@TRANCOUNT
END
```

Invalid T-SQL Syntax in Transactions

Some normally valid Transact-SQL syntax is prohibited while a transaction is active. For example, you can't use sp_dboption to change database options or call any other stored procedure that modifies the **master** database from within a transaction. Also, a number of Transact-SQL commands are illegal inside transactions: ALTER DATABASE, DROP DATABASE, RECONFIGURE, BACKUP LOG, DUMP TRANSACTION, RESTORE DATABASE, CREATE DATABASE, LOAD DATABASE, RESTORE LOG, DISK INIT, LOAD TRANSACTION, and UPDATE STATISTICS.

Debugging Transactions

Two DBCC (database consistency checker) commands come in very handy when debugging transaction-related problems. The first is DBCC OPENTRAN(). It allows you to retrieve the oldest active transaction in a database. Since only the inactive portion of a log is backed up and truncated, a malevolent or zombie transaction can cause the log to fill prematurely. You can use DBCC OPENTRAN()to identify the offending process so that it may be terminated if necessary. Here's an example:

```
DBCC OPENTRAN(pubs)
Transaction information for database 'pubs'.

Oldest active transaction:
   SPID (server process ID) : 15
   UID (user ID) : 1
   Name            : user_transaction
   LSN             : (57:376:596)
   Start time      : Aug 5 1999 5:54:46:713AM
```

Another handy command for tracking down transaction-related problems is the DBCC LOG command. DBCC LOG lists the database transaction log. You can use it to look under the hood and see what operations are being carried out on your data. Here's an example:

```
CREATE TABLE #logrecs
(CurrentLSN varchar(30),
 Operation varchar(20),
 Context varchar(20),
 TransactionID varchar(20))

INSERT #logrecs
EXEC('DBCC LOG(''pubs'')')

SELECT * FROM #logrecs
GO
DROP TABLE #logrecs
```

(Results abridged)

CurrentLSN	Operation	Context	TransactionID
00000035:00000144:0001	LOP_BEGIN_CKPT	LCX_NULL	0000:00000000
00000035:00000145:0001	LOP_END_CKPT	LCX_NULL	0000:00000000
00000035:00000146:0001	LOP_MODIFY_ROW	LCX_SCHEMA_VERSION	0000:00000000
00000035:00000146:0002	LOP_BEGIN_XACT	LCX_NULL	0000:000020e0
00000035:00000146:0003	LOP_MARK_DDL	LCX_NULL	0000:000020e0
00000035:00000146:0004	LOP_COMMIT_XACT	LCX_NULL	0000:000020e0
00000035:00000147:0001	LOP_MODIFY_ROW	LCX_SCHEMA_VERSION	0000:00000000
00000035:00000147:0002	LOP_BEGIN_XACT	LCX_NULL	0000:000020e1
00000035:00000147:0003	LOP_MARK_DDL	LCX_NULL	0000:000020e1

No discussion of SQL Server transaction debugging would be complete without covering the @@TRANCOUNT automatic variable. Though we've already covered it elsewhere in this chapter, @@TRANCOUNT is a frequent target of PRINT statements and debugger watches because it reports the current transaction nesting level. When debugging complex nested transactions, it's common to insert SELECT or PRINT statements throughout the code to determine the current nesting level at various procedural junctures.

Finally, don't forget about the Windows NT Performance Monitor. It sports numerous objects and counters related to transaction management and performance. In particular, the **SQL Server:Databases** object provides a wealth of transaction- and transaction log–related counters.

Optimizing Transactional Code

There are a number of general guidelines for writing efficient transaction-oriented T-SQL. Here are a few of them:

- Keep transactions as short as possible. Once you've determined what data modifications need to be made, initiate your transaction, perform those modifications, and end the transaction as soon as possible. Try not to initiate transactions prematurely.

- Limit transactions to data modification statements when practical. Don't initiate a transaction while scanning data if you can avoid it. Though transactions certainly affect reading data as well as writing it (e.g., dirty and nonrepeatable reads, phantom rows, etc.), it's often possible to limit them to just those statements that modify data, especially if you do not need to reread data within a transaction.

- Don't require user input during a transaction. Doing so could allow a slow user to tie up server resources indefinitely. It could also cause the transaction log to fill prematurely since active transactions cannot be cleared from it.

- Try to use optimistic concurrency control when possible. That is, rather than explicitly locking every object your application may change, allow the server to determine when a row has been changed by another user. You may find that user change conflicts occur so little in practice (perhaps the app is naturally partitioned, or, once entered, rows are rarely updated, etc.) that improving performance at the expense of consistency is a worthwhile trade-off.

- Use nonlogged operations wisely. As I've pointed out, nonlogged operations preclude normal transaction log backups. This may or may not be a showstopper, but, when allowable, nonlogged operations can turbocharge an application. They can often reduce processing time for large amounts of data by orders of magnitude and virtually eliminate a number of common transaction management headaches. Keep in mind that this increase in performance sometimes comes at a cost. SELECT...INTO, for example, can lock system tables until it completes.

- Try to use lower (less restrictive) TILs when possible. READ COMMITTED, the default, is suitable for most applications and will provide better concurrency than REPEATABLE READ or SERIALIZABLE.

- Attempt to keep the amount of data you change within a transaction to a minimum. Don't indiscriminately attempt to change millions of rows in a table and expect concurrency and resource utilization to take care of themselves magically. Database modifications require resources and locks, and these locks by definition affect other users. Unless your app is a single-user app, it pays to be mindful of operations that could negatively affect concurrency.

- Don't use implicit transactions unless you really need them, and, even then, watch them very closely. Because implicit transactions are initiated by nearly any primary Transact-SQL command (including SELECT), they can be started when you least expect them, potentially lowering concurrency and causing transaction log problems. It's nearly always better to manage transactions explicitly with BEGIN TRAN, COMMIT TRAN, and ROLLBACK TRAN than to use implicit transactions. When you manage transactions yourself, you know exactly when they're started and stopped—you have full control over what happens.

Summary

Transactions are SQL Server's basic unit of work. They ensure that a data modification operation is carried out either completely or not at all. Atomicity, consistency, isolation, and durability —the so-called ACID properties—characterize SQL Server transactions and help guard your data against incomplete or lost updates.

The current transaction isolation level (TIL) governs transaction isolation. You set the TIL via the SET TRANSACTION ISOLATION LEVEL command. Each TIL represents a trade-off between concurrency and consistency.

In this chapter, you became acquainted with SQL Server transactions and explored the various Transact-SQL commands that relate to transaction management. You learned about autocommit and implicit transactions, as well as user-defined and distributed transactions. You also explored some common transaction-related pitfalls, and you learned methods for avoiding them.

Stored Procedures and Triggers

Programming without an overall architecture or design in mind is like exploring a cave with only a flashlight: You don't know where you've been, you don't know where you're going, and you don't know quite where you are.—Danny Thorpe

A stored procedure is a batch of SQL that's stored permanently on the server and compiled when used. It's not compiled in the sense of being translated to machine code or even Java byte codes—it's pseudocompiled to speed execution. You create stored procedures using the Trans-act-SQL CREATE PROCEDURE command. All that really happens when you create a procedure is the insertion of its source code into the syscomments system table. The procedure isn't compiled until it's executed for the first time (and in certain other circumstances—see the following section, "Internals," for more information). Despite the name, syscomments stores far more than comments—it's the repository for the source code for stored procedures, views, triggers, rules, and defaults. If you delete the source code for an object from syscomments, the object will no longer be accessible.

You can list the source code to a procedure, view, trigger, rule, or default using the sp_help-text system procedure. If the object is not encrypted, sp_helptext will list its source, formatted similarly to the way you entered it. Here's an example:

```
EXEC sp_helptext 'sp_hexstring'

Text
--------------------------------------------------------------------------------
CREATE PROC dbo.sp_hexstring @int varchar(10)=NULL, @hexstring varchar(30)=NULL OUT
/*
Object: sp_hexstring
Description: Return an integer as a hexadecimal string

Usage: sp_hexstring @int=Integer to convert, @hexstring=OUTPUT parm to receive hex string

Returns: (None)
```

```
Created by: Ken Henderson. Email: khen@khen.com

Version: 1.0

Example: sp_hexstring 23, @myhex OUT

Created: 1999-08-02. Last changed: 1999-08-15.
*/
AS
IF (@int IS NULL) OR (@int = '/?') GOTO Help
DECLARE @i int, @vb varbinary(30)
SELECT @i=CAST(@int as int), @vb=CAST(@i as varbinary)
EXEC master..xp_varbintohexstr @vb, @hexstring OUT
RETURN 0
Help:
EXEC sp_usage @objectname='sp_hexstring',
   @desc='Return an integer as a hexadecimal string',
   @parameters='@int=Integer to convert, @hexstring=OUTPUT parm to receive hex string',
   @example='sp_hexstring "23", @myhex OUT',
   @author='Ken Henderson',
   @email='khen@khen.com',
   @version='1', @revision='0',
   @datecreated='19990802', @datelastchanged='19990815'
RETURN -1
```

Stored Procedure Advantages

There are several advantages to using stored procedures; here are a few of them:

- They allow business rules and policies to be encapsulated and changed in one place.

- They allow sharing of application logic by different applications.

- They can facilitate data modification, ensuring that all applications update data consistently.

- They can simplify parameterized queries, easily facilitating running the same query repetitively with different sets of parameters.

- Autostart procedures can automate startup routines, executing each time the server is cycled.

- They can modularize an application, organizing it into manageable pieces.

- They can provide security mechanisms, allowing users controlled access to database objects they could not otherwise use.

- They can reduce network bandwidth use by greatly lessening the amount of Transact-SQL code that must traverse the network in order to accomplish tasks.

- Since their execution plans are retained by the server for reuse, they can improve application performance considerably.

Internals

There are four major steps involved with using stored procedures:

1. Creation—where you initially create the procedure with CREATE PROC

2. User execution—where you execute it with EXEC

3. Compilation—where the server compiles and optimizes the procedure during an EXEC

4. Server execution—where the server runs its compiled execution plan during an EXEC

Creation

The creation step is where you use the CREATE PROCEDURE command to construct the procedure on the server. Each time you successfully create a new procedure, its name and other vital information are recorded in sysobjects, and its source code is stored in syscomments. Objects referenced by the procedure are not resolved until you execute it.

User Execution

The first time you execute a newly created procedure (or the server recompiles it), it's read from syscomments, and its object references are resolved. During this process, the command processor constructs what's known as a *sequence tree* or *query tree* that will be passed to the query optimizer for compilation and optimization.

Compilation

Once the query tree has been successfully created, the SQL Server query optimizer compiles the entire batch, optimizes it, and checks access privileges.

During the optimization phase, the optimizer scans the query tree and develops what it believes is the optimal plan for accessing the data the procedure is after. The following criteria are considered during this step:

- The presence of the GROUP BY, ORDER BY, and UNION clauses

- The amount of data the procedure will retrieve

- The use of joins to link tables together

- The characteristics of the indexes built over referenced tables

- The degree of data distribution in each index's key columns

- The use of comparison operators and values in WHERE and HAVING clauses within the procedure

An execution plan is the result of this process, and it's placed in the procedure cache when the optimizer finishes building it. This execution plan consists of the following:

- The steps required to carry out the work of the stored procedure

- The steps necessary to enforce constraints

- The steps needed to branch to any triggers fired by the stored procedure

Execution plans in SQL Server 7.0 and later are reentrant and read-only. This differs from previous releases, where each connection received its own copy of the execution plan for a given procedure.

Server Execution

The execution phase is where the execution plan is processed sequentially and each step is dispatched to an appropriate internal manager process. There are a number of internal managers— the DDL and DML managers, the transaction manager, the ODSOLE manager (for processing the OLE automation procedures such as sp_OAcreate), the stored procedure manager, the utility manager, the T-SQL manager, etc. These managers are called repeatedly until all steps in the execution plan have been processed.

Execution plans are never stored on disk. The only portion of the stored procedure that's stored permanently is its source code (in syscomments). Since they're kept in memory, cycling the server disposes of all current execution plans (as does the undocumented DBCC FREEPROCCACHE() command).

SQL Server will automatically recreate a procedure's execution plan when:

- The procedure's execution environment differs significantly from its creation environment (see the following section, "Environmental Concerns," for more information).

- The sysobjects **schema_ver** column changes for any of the objects the procedure references. The **schema_ver** and **base_schema_ver** columns are updated any time the schema information for a table changes. This includes column additions and deletions, data type changes, constraint additions and deletions, as well as rule and default bindings.

- The statistics have changed for any of the objects the procedure references.

- An index that was referenced by the procedure's execution plan is dropped.

- A copy of the procedure's execution plan is not available in the cache. Execution plans are removed from the cache to make room for new plans using an LRU (least recently used) algorithm.

Additionally, you can force a procedure's execution plan to be recompiled using these three methods:

1. Creating the procedure using the WITH RECOMPILE option (and then executing it)

2. Executing the procedure using the WITH RECOMPILE option

3. Flagging any of the tables the procedure references with the sp_recompile procedure (sp_recompile merely updates sysobjects' schema_ver column) and then executing it

A nifty way to load execution plans into the cache at system startup is to execute them via an autostart procedure. Rather than execute each procedure itself as an autostart routine, you should call the procedures you want to load into the cache from a single autostart procedure in order to conserve execution threads (each autostart routine gets its own thread).

Once an execution plan is in the cache, subsequent calls to the procedure can reuse the plan without rebuilding the query tree or recompiling the plan. This eliminates two of the three steps that occur when you execute a stored procedure and is the chief performance advantage stored procedures give you over plain SQL batches.

Creating Stored Procedures

You create stored procedures using the CREATE PROCEDURE command; you alter them with ALTER PROCEDURE. The advantage to using ALTER PROC rather than CREATE PROC to change a stored procedure is that it preserves access permissions, whereas CREATE PROC doesn't. A key difference between them is that ALTER PROC requires the use of the same encryption and recompile options as the original CREATE PROC. Other than that, the semantics of using the two commands are exactly the same.

A procedure can contain any valid Transact-SQL command except these: CREATE DEFAULT, CREATE PROC, CREATE RULE, CREATE SCHEMA, CREATE TRIGGER, and CREATE VIEW. Procedures *can* create databases, tables, and indexes but not other procedures, defaults, rules, schemas, triggers, or views.

Note
GO is not a Transact-SQL command. It's a command batch terminator, which is to say, it tells tools like Query Analyzer and OSQL where one batch of SQL ends and another begins. As such, it's never allowed within a stored procedure—attempting this simply terminates the procedure. One rather odd aspect of the fact that GO is not a Transact-SQL command comes into play with comments. You can't comment out GO using the /* */ comments. If GO is the leftmost item on its line, it will terminate the command batch regardless of the comment markers. Since this will prevent the closing comment marker from being reached, you'll get an error message about a missing end comment marker. The solution? Use the "--" comment style, delete the GO altogether, or remove its "G."

To execute CREATE PROC you must be a member of the sysadmin role, the db_owner role, or the db_ddladmin_role. You can also execute CREATE PROC if you've been explicitly granted permission by a member of either the sysadmin or db_owner role.

The maximum stored procedure size is the lesser of 65,536 * the network packet size (which defaults to 4096 bytes) and 250 megabytes. The maximum number of parameters a procedure may receive is 1024.

Creation Tips

- Include a comment header with each procedure that identifies its author, purpose, creation date and revision history, the parameters it receives, and so on. You can place this comment block after the CREATE PROC statement itself (but before the rest of the procedure) in order to ensure that it's stored in syscomments and is visible from tools like Enterprise Manager that can access stored procedure source code directly via syscomments. Here's a system procedure that generates comment headers for you:

```
USE master
GO
IF OBJECT_ID('dbo.sp_object_script_comments') IS NOT NULL
   DROP PROC dbo.sp_object_script_comments
GO
CREATE PROCEDURE dbo.sp_object_script_comments
     -- Required parameters
     @objectname sysname=NULL,
     @desc sysname=NULL,

     -- Optional parameters
     @parameters varchar(8000)=NULL,
     @example varchar(8000)=NULL,
     @author sysname=NULL,
     @email sysname='(none)',
     @version sysname=NULL,
     @revision sysname='0',
     @datecreated smalldatetime=NULL,
     @datelastchanged smalldatetime=NULL
/*

Object: sp_object_script_comments
Description: Generates comment headers for object-creation SQL scripts

Usage: sp_object_script_comments @objectname="ObjectName", @desc="Description
of object",@parameters="param1[,param2...]"

Created by: Ken Henderson. Email: khen@khen.com

Version: 3.1

Example usage: sp_object_script_comments @objectname="sp_who", @desc="Returns
a list of currently running jobs", @parameters=[@loginname]

Created: 1992-04-03. Last changed: 1999-07-01 01:13:00.
```

```
*/
AS

IF (@objectname+@desc) IS NULL GOTO Help

PRINT '/*'
PRINT CHAR(13)
EXEC sp_usage @objectname=@objectname,
   @desc=@desc,
   @parameters=@parameters,
   @example=@example,
   @author=@author,
   @email=@email,
   @version=@version, @revision=@revision,
   @datecreated=@datecreated, @datelastchanged=@datelastchanged
PRINT CHAR(13)+'*/'

RETURN 0

Help:
EXEC sp_usage @objectname='sp_object_script_comments',
   @desc='Generates comment headers for SQL scripts',
   @parameters='@objectname="ObjectName", @desc="Description of
   object",@parameters="param1[,param2...]"',
   @example='sp_object_script_comments @objectname="sp_who", @desc="Returns
   a list of currently running jobs", @parameters=[@loginname]',
   @author='Ken Henderson',
   @email='khen@khen.com',
   @version='3', @revision='1',
   @datecreated='19920403', @datelastchanged='19990701'
RETURN -1
```

This procedure generates comment header information for a stored procedure by calling the sp_usage procedure detailed below. It can be executed from any database by any procedure.

- Allow an optional single parameter to be passed into every procedure that tells the caller how to use the procedure (e.g., '/?'). You can place this usage information at the end of the procedure in order to keep it from crowding your display and to locate it consistently from procedure to procedure. The best way to do this is to set up and call a separate procedure whose whole purpose is to report usage information. Here's a script that creates the sp_usage procedure that's used throughout this book for that very purpose:

```
USE master
GO
IF OBJECT_ID('dbo.sp_usage') IS NOT NULL
   DROP PROC dbo.sp_usage
GO
CREATE PROCEDURE dbo.sp_usage
     -- Required parameters
     @objectname sysname=NULL,
     @desc sysname=NULL,
```

```
      -- Optional parameters
      @parameters varchar(8000)=NULL,
      @returns varchar(8000)='(None)',
      @example varchar(8000)=NULL,
      @author sysname=NULL,
      @email sysname='(none)',
      @version sysname=NULL,
      @revision sysname='0',
      @datecreated smalldatetime=NULL,
      @datelastchanged smalldatetime=NULL
/*

Object: sp_usage
Description: Provides usage information for stored procedures and descriptions of
other types of objects

Usage: sp_usage @objectname="ObjectName", @desc="Description of object"
      [, @parameters="param1,param2..."]
      [, @example="Example of usage"]
      [, @author="Object author"]
      [, @email="Author email"]
      [, @version="Version number or info"]
      [, @revision="Revision number or info"]
      [, @datecreated="Date created"]
      [, @datelastchanged="Date last changed"]


Returns: (None)


Created by: Ken Henderson. Email: khen@khen.com


Version: 3.1


Example: sp_usage @objectname="sp_who", @desc="Returns a list of currently
running jobs", @parameters=[@loginname]


Created: 1992-04-03. Last changed: 1999-07-01.


*/
AS
SET NOCOUNT ON
IF (@objectname+@desc IS NULL) GOTO Help

PRINT 'Object: '+@objectname
PRINT 'Description: '+@desc

IF (OBJECTPROPERTY(OBJECT_ID(@objectname),'IsProcedure')=1)
OR (OBJECTPROPERTY(OBJECT_ID(@objectname),'IsExtendedProc')=1)
OR (OBJECTPROPERTY(OBJECT_ID(@objectname),'IsReplProc')=1)
OR (LOWER(LEFT(@objectname,3))='sp_') BEGIN -- Special handling for system
procedures
    PRINT CHAR(13)+'Usage: '+@objectname+' '+@parameters
    PRINT CHAR(13)+'Returns: '+@returns
END
```

```
IF (@author IS NOT NULL)
   PRINT CHAR(13)+'Created by: '+@author+'. Email: '+@email
IF (@version IS NOT NULL)
   PRINT CHAR(13)+'Version: '+@version+'.'+@revision
IF (@example IS NOT NULL)
   PRINT CHAR(13)+'Example: '+@example
IF (@datecreated IS NOT NULL) BEGIN -- Crop time if it's midnight
   DECLARE @datefmt varchar(8000), @dc varchar(30), @lc varchar(30)
   SET @dc=CONVERT(varchar(30), @datecreated, 120)
   SET @lc=CONVERT(varchar(30), @datelastchanged, 120)
   PRINT CHAR(13)+'Created: '+CASE
DATEDIFF(ss,CONVERT(char(8),@datecreated,108),'00:00:00') WHEN 0 THEN LEFT(@dc,10)
ELSE @dc END
+'. Last changed: '+CASE
DATEDIFF(ss,CONVERT(char(8),@datelastchanged,108),'00:00:00') WHEN 0 THEN
LEFT(@lc,10) ELSE @lc END+'.'
END

RETURN 0

Help:
EXEC sp_usage @objectname='sp_usage',              -- Recursive call
   @desc='Provides usage information for stored procedures and descriptions of
   other types of objects',
   @parameters='@objectname="ObjectName", @desc="Description of object"
      [, @parameters="param1,param2..."]
      [, @example="Example of usage"]
      [, @author="Object author"]
      [, @email="Author email"]
      [, @version="Version number or info"]
      [, @revision="Revision number or info"]
      [, @datecreated="Date created"]
      [, @datelastchanged="Date last changed"]',
   @example='sp_usage @objectname="sp_who", @desc="Returns a list of currently
   running jobs", @parameters=[@loginname]',
   @author='Ken Henderson',
   @email='khen@khen.com',
   @version='3', @revision='1',
   @datecreated='4/3/92', @datelastchanged='7/1/99'
RETURN -1
```

You can call sp_usage to report usage info for any procedure. In fact, sp_usage calls itself to do just that. (That's the source of the message "Cannot add rows to sysdepends for the current stored procedure because it depends on the missing object 'sp_usage'." The stored procedure will still be created.) Note the use of a GOTO label to place the usage info at the end of the procedure. Since Transact-SQL doesn't support subroutines, this is unfortunately necessary. It allows code at the start of the procedure to check for invalid parameter values and quickly jump to the usage routine if necessary.

- Set any environment options (QUOTED_IDENTIFIER, ANSI_DEFAULTS, etc.) that materially affect the procedure early in it. It's a good practice to set them immediately on entrance to the procedure so that their presence is obvious to other developers.

- Avoid situations where the owner of a stored procedure and the owner of its referenced tables differ. The best way to do this is by specifying the dbo user as the owner of every object you create. Having multiple objects with the same name but different owners adds a layer of obfuscation to the database that nobody needs. While perhaps plausible during development, it's definitely something to avoid on production servers. Allow database users besides dbo to own objects only in very special circumstances.

- Don't use the **sp_** prefix for anything but system procedures that reside in the master database. Don't create procedures in user databases with the **sp_** prefix, and don't create nonsystem procedures in master.

- For procedures that must be created in a specific database (e.g., system procedures), include USE *dbname*, where *dbname* is the name of the target database, at the top of the script that creates the procedure. This ensures that the procedure winds up where you want it and alleviates having to remember to change the current database in your query tool before executing the script.

- Keep stored procedures as simple and modular as possible. Each stored procedure should accomplish a single task or a small group of closely related tasks.

- Use SET NOCOUNT ON to minimize network traffic from stored procedures. As a rule, it should be the first statement in every stored procedure you create. (Note that SET NOCOUNT ON can cause problems with some applications—e.g., some versions of Microsoft Access.)

- Create a procedure using the WITH ENCRYPTION option if you want to hide its source code from users. Don't delete it from syscomments—doing so will render the procedure unable to execute, and you'll have to drop and recreate it.

Temporary Procedures

Temporary procedures are created the same way temporary tables are created—a prefix of one pound sign (#) creates a local temporary procedure that's visible only to the current connection, while a prefix of two pound signs (##) creates a global temporary procedure that's visible to all connections.

System Procedures

System procedures are procedures that reside in the master database and are prefixed with **sp_**. System procedures are executable from any database. When executed from a database other than master, the system procedure assumes the context of the database in which it's running. So, for example, if it references the sysobjects table, which exists in every database, it will access the one in the database that's current when it's executed, not the one in master. Here's an example of a simple system procedure:

```
USE master
IF OBJECT_ID('dbo.sp_created') IS NOT NULL
   DROP PROC dbo.sp_created
GO
CREATE PROC dbo.sp_created @objname sysname=NULL
/*
Object: sp_created
Description: Lists the creation date(s) for the specified object(s)

Usage: sp_created @objname="Object name or mask you want to display"

Returns: (None)

Created by: Ken Henderson. Email: khen@khen.com

Version: 1.0

Example: sp_created @objname="myprocs%"

Created: 1999-08-01. Last changed: 1999-08-15.
*/
AS
IF (@objname IS NULL) or (@objname='/?') GOTO Help
SELECT name, crdate FROM sysobjects
WHERE name like @objname
RETURN 0

Help:
EXEC sp_usage @objectname='sp_created',
   @desc='Lists the creation date(s) for the specified object(s)',
   @parameters='@objname="Object name or mask you want to display"',
   @example='sp_created @objname="myprocs%"',
   @author='Ken Henderson',
   @email='khen@khen.com',
   @version='1', @revision='0',
   @datecreated='19990801', @datelastchanged='19990815'
RETURN -1

USE pubs
EXEC sp_created '%author%'
```

(Results)

```
name                          crdate
---------------------------   ---------------------------
authors                       1998-11-13 03:10:48.470
CK__authors__au_id__08EA5793  1998-11-13 03:10:48.657
CK__authors__zip__0AD2A005    1998-11-13 03:10:48.657
DF__authors__phone__09DE7BCC  1998-11-13 03:10:48.657
titleauthor  1998-11-13 03:10:49.220
```

This procedure lists the names and creation dates of the objects that match a mask.

Here's an example that uses one of SQL Server's own system stored procedures. Like the procedure above, it can be run from any database to retrieve info on that database:

```
USE pubs
EXEC sp_spaceused
```

```
database_name      database_size       unallocated space
---------------    ------------------  ------------------
pubs               4.13 MB             2.30 MB

reserved           data                index_size          unused
------------------ ------------------  ------------------  ------------------
1864 KB            816 KB              696 KB              352 KB
```

Sp_spaceused queries various system tables to create the report it returns. Even though it resides in the master database, it automatically reflects the context of the current database because it's a system procedure.

Note that you can trick system procedures into running in the context of any database (regardless of the current database) by prefixing them with the target database as though they resided in that database. Here's an example:

```
USE pubs
EXEC northwind..sp_spaceused

database_name      database_size       unallocated space
---------------    ------------------  ------------------
Northwind          23.88 MB            21.01 MB

reserved           data                index_size          unused
------------------ ------------------  ------------------  ------------------
2936 KB            1240 KB             1336 KB             360 KB
```

Here, even though sp_spaceused resides in master, and despite the fact that the current database is pubs, sp_spaceused reports space utilization info for the Northwind database because we've prefixed its name with Northwind. Even though sp_spaceused doesn't reside in Northwind, SQL Server correctly locates it in master and runs it within the Northwind database context.

A system procedure that's created by a user is listed as a user object in Enterprise Manager. This is because the system bit of its status column in sysobjects (0xC0000000) isn't set by default. You can change this by calling the undocumented procedure sp_MS_marksystemobject. The procedure takes one argument—the name of the object whose system bit you want to set. Several undocumented functions and DBCC command verbs do not work properly unless called from a system object (see Chapter 20, "Undocumented T-SQL," for more information). You can determine whether an object's system bit has been set via the OBJECTPROPERTY() function's IsMSShipped property.

Extended Procedures

Extended procedures are routines that reside in DLLs (Dynamic Link Libraries) that look and work like regular stored procedures. They receive parameters and return results via the Open Data Services framework and are normally written in C or C++. They reside in the master database (you cannot create them elsewhere) and run within the SQL Server process space.

Note that there's nothing about extended procedures that requires them to be written in C or C++, but if you intend to write them in another language, you'll first have to complete the formidable task of translating the Microsoft-provided ODS header files into that language. I've personally written extended procedures using Delphi and a couple of other tools, so this can be done, but it's not for the timid.

Another possibility for calling routines written in languages besides C/C++ is to create "wrapper" routines using a C++ compiler and the ODS headers and call your routines (which reside in some other DLL) from them. Then you get the best of both worlds—you create procedures in the language you prefer, and you're not forced to translate a bevy of constants, function declarations, and the like to another language.

Note that, unlike SQL Server 6.5 and earlier, extended procedure names are not case sensitive. Prior to version 7.0, extended procedure calls had to match the case of the underlying routine as it existed in its DLL, regardless of the case-sensitivity setting on the server. With version 7.0 and later, the server will find the underlying routine regardless of the case used.

Calls to extended procedures do not work like system procedures. They aren't automatically located in master when referenced from other databases, and they don't assume the context of the current database when run. If you want to execute an extended procedure from a database other than master, you'll have to qualify the reference (e.g., EXEC master..xp_cmdshell 'dir') fully.

A common technique of making extended procedures a bit handier is to wrap them in system stored procedures. This allows them to be called from any database without requiring the "master.." prefix. You see this in a number of SQL Server's own routines—many undocumented extended procedures are wrapped within system stored procedures. Here's an example of a wrapped call to an extended procedure:

```
USE master
IF (OBJECT_ID('dbo.sp_hexstring') IS NOT NULL)
   DROP PROC dbo.sp_hexstring
GO
CREATE PROC dbo.sp_hexstring @int varchar(10)=NULL, @hexstring varchar(30)=NULL OUT
/*
Object: sp_hexstring
Description: Return an integer as a hexadecimal string

Usage: sp_hexstring @int=Integer to convert, @hexstring=OUTPUT parm to receive hex
string

Returns: (None)

Created by: Ken Henderson. Email: khen@khen.com

Version: 1.0

Example: sp_hexstring 23, @myhex OUT

Created: 1999-08-02. Last changed: 1999-08-15.
*/
AS
IF (@int IS NULL) OR (@int = '/?') GOTO Help
DECLARE @i int, @vb varbinary(30)
SELECT @i=CAST(@int as int), @vb=CAST(@i as varbinary)
EXEC master..xp_varbintohexstr @vb, @hexstring OUT
RETURN 0
```

```
Help:
EXEC sp_usage @objectname='sp_hexstring',
    @desc='Return an integer as a hexadecimal string',
    @parameters='@int=Integer to convert, @hexstring=OUTPUT parm to receive hex string',
    @example='sp_hexstring "23", @myhex OUT',
    @author='Ken Henderson',
    @email='khen@khen.com',
    @version='1', @revision='0',
    @datecreated='19990802', @datelastchanged='19990815'
RETURN -1

GO

DECLARE @hex varchar(30)
EXEC sp_hexstring 10, @hex OUT
SELECT @hex
```

    (Results)

```
----------------------------
0x0000000A
```

All this procedure really does is clean up the parameters to be passed to the extended procedure xp_varbintohexstr before calling it. Because it's a system procedure, it can be called from any database without referencing the extended procedure directly.

Faux Procedures

There are a number of system-supplied stored procedures that are neither true system procedures nor extended procedures—they're implemented internally by the server itself. Examples of these include sp_executesql, sp_prepare, most of the sp_cursorXXXX routines, sp_reset_connection, etc. These routines have stubs in master..sysobjects, and are listed as extended procedures but are, in fact, implemented internally by the server, not within an external ODS-based DLL. You can't list their source code because it's part of the server itself, and you can't trace into them with a T-SQL debugger because they're not written in Transact-SQL.

Executing Stored Procedures

Executing a stored procedure can be as easy as listing it on a line by itself in a T-SQL batch, like this:

```
sp_who
```

You should make a habit of prefixing all stored procedure calls with the EXEC keyword. Stored procedures without EXEC must be the first command in a command batch. Even if that were the case initially, inserting additional lines before the procedure call at some later date would break your code.

You can specify the WITH RECOMPILE option when calling a stored procedure (with or without EXEC) in order to force the recreation of its execution plan. This is handy when you know that factors related to the execution plan creation have changed enough that performance would benefit from rebuilding the plan.

INSERT and EXEC

The INSERT command supports calling a stored procedure in order to supply rows for insertion into a table. Here's an example:

```
CREATE TABLE #locks (spid int, dbid int, objid int, objectname sysname NULL,
indid int, type char(4), resource char(15), mode char(10), status char(6))
INSERT #locks (spid, dbid, objid, indid, type, resource, mode, status)
EXEC sp_lock
```

This is a handy way of trapping the output of a stored procedure in a table so that you can manipulate it or retain it for later use. Prior to the advent of cursor OUTPUT parameters, this was the only way to perform further work on a stored procedure's result set within Transact-SQL.

Note that INSERT...EXEC works with extended procedures that return result sets as well. Here's a simple example:

```
CREATE TABLE #cmd_result (output varchar(8000))
INSERT #cmd_result
EXEC master..xp_cmdshell 'copy errorlog.1 *.sav'
```

Environmental Concerns

A number of SQL Server environmental settings affect the execution of stored procedures. They're specified via the SET command and control the way that stored procedures handle quotes, nulls, cursors, BLOB fields, etc. The status of two of these — QUOTED_IDENTIFIER and ANSI_NULLS—is actually recorded in each procedure's status field in sysobjects. QUOTED_IDENTIFIER controls whether strings within double quotes are interpreted as object identifiers, and ANSI_NULLS controls whether non-ANSI equality comparisons with NULLs are allowed. Here's an example that features a quoted identifier:

```
USE pubs
SET QUOTED_IDENTIFIER ON
GO
IF OBJECT_ID('TABLE') IS NOT NULL
   DROP PROC "TABLE"
GO
CREATE PROC "TABLE" @tableclause varchar(8000),
@columnclause varchar(8000)='*',
@whereclause varchar(8000)=NULL,
@groupbyclause varchar(8000)=NULL,
@havingclause varchar(8000)=NULL,
@orderbyclause varchar(8000)=NULL,
@computeclause varchar(8000)=NULL
AS
DECLARE @execstr varchar(8000)
SET @execstr='SELECT '+@columnclause+' FROM '+@tableclause
+ISNULL(' WHERE '+@whereclause,' ')
+ISNULL(' GROUP BY '+@groupbyclause,' ')
+ISNULL(' HAVING '+@havingclause,' ')
+ISNULL(' ORDER BY '+@orderbyclause,' ')
+ISNULL(' COMPUTE '+@computeclause,")
```

```
EXEC(@execstr)
GO
SET QUOTED_IDENTIFIER OFF
GO
```

Thanks to SET QUOTED_IDENTIFIER, we can use a reserved word, TABLE, as the name of the procedure. It allows us to build our own version of the ANSI/ISO SQL **TABLE** command, which Transact-SQL does not implement. Since it's named using a reserved word, executing such a procedure requires SET QUOTED_IDENTIFIER as well:

```
SET QUOTED_IDENTIFIER ON
GO
"TABLE" 'sales','title_id, SUM(qty) AS
sales','title_id<>''PS2091''','title_id',DEFAULT,'2 DESC'
GO
SET QUOTED_IDENTIFIER OFF
GO
```

(Results abridged)

```
title_id sales
-------- -----------
PC8888   50
BU1032   45
MC3021   40
TC3218   40
BU2075   35
```

Note that I don't recommend you use reserved words for object identifiers. In my opinion, this adds needless confusion to your code. It is, however, something you should be aware of because other developers sometimes do it.

Rather than allowing developers to name procedures with reserved words, the more common use of SET QUOTED_IDENTIFIER with stored procedures is to facilitate references to objects whose names contain reserved words, spaces, or other normally disallowed characters. Here's an example:

```
USE Northwind
SET QUOTED_IDENTIFIER ON
GO
IF OBJECT_ID('dbo.listorders') IS NOT NULL
   DROP PROC dbo.listorders
GO
CREATE PROC dbo.listorders
AS
SELECT * FROM "Order Details"
GO
SET QUOTED_IDENTIFIER OFF
GO

EXEC listorders
```

(Results abridged)

OrderID	ProductID	UnitPrice	Quantity	Discount
10248	11	14.0000	12	0.0
10248	42	9.8000	10	0.0
10248	72	34.8000	5	0.0
10249	14	18.6000	9	0.0
10249	51	42.4000	40	0.0
10250	41	7.7000	10	0.0

The table name "Order Details" (from the Northwind sample database) contains both a reserved word and a space, so it can't be referenced without special handling. In this case, we turned on quoted identifier support and enclosed the table name in double quotes, but a better way would be to enclose it in square brackets (e.g., **[Order Details]**) because this alleviates the need to change any settings. Note that square bracket delimiters are a SQL Server extension—they're not a part of the ANSI/ISO SQL standard.

The ANSI_NULLS setting is equally important to stored procedures. It controls whether non-ANSI equality comparisons with NULLs are allowed. This is particularly important with stored procedure parameters that can allow NULLs. Here's an example:

```
USE Northwind
IF (OBJECT_ID('dbo.ListRegionalEmployees') IS NOT NULL)
   DROP PROC dbo.ListRegionalEmployees
GO
SET ANSI_NULLS OFF
GO
CREATE PROC dbo.ListRegionalEmployees @region nvarchar(30)
AS

SELECT EmployeeID, LastName, FirstName, Region FROM employees
WHERE Region=@region

GO
SET ANSI_NULLS ON
GO

EXEC listregionalemployees NULL
```

EmployeeID	LastName	FirstName	Region
5	Buchanan	Steven	NULL
6	Suyama	Michael	NULL
7	King	Robert	NULL
9	Dodsworth	Anne	NULL

If not for SET ANSI_NULLS, the procedure would be unable to compare a NULL @region successfully with the Region column in the Northwind Employees table. The query would never return any rows because, according to the ANSI spec, one NULL value never equals another. The handiness of this becomes more obvious when a procedure defines a number of

NULLable parameters like @region. Without the ability to test NULL values for equality in a manner identical to non-NULL values, each NULLable parameter would require its own special IS NULL handling, perhaps multiplying the amount of code necessary to implement the query.

The fact that the QUOTED_IDENTIFIER and ANSI_NULLS settings are saved with each stored procedure means that you can count on them to have their original values when the procedure is executed. SQL Server restores them to the values they had when the procedure was created each time it's executed and then resets them afterward. So, if we have this code:

```
SET ANSI_NULLS ON
EXEC listregionalemployees NULL
```

the stored procedure still executes as though ANSI_NULLS is set to OFF. Note that you can check the saved status of a procedure's QUOTED_IDENTIFIER and ANSI_NULLS settings via the OBJECTPROPERTY() function. Here's an example:

```
USE pubs
SELECT OBJECTPROPERTY(OBJECT_ID('table'),'ExecIsQuotedIdentOn') AS 'QuotedIdent'

USE Northwind
SELECT OBJECTPROPERTY(OBJECT_ID('listregionalemployees'),'ExecIsAnsiNullsOn') AS 'AnsiNulls'

QuotedIdent
-----------
1

AnsiNulls
-----------
0
```

There are numerous other commands that affect how Transact-SQL code—both within and outside stored procedures—executes. Commands like SET TEXTSIZE, SET CURSOR_CLOSE_ON_COMMIT, and SET IMPLICIT_TRANSACTIONS all affect how a stored procedure's code carries out its duties. If you have procedure code that relies on a SET command to have a particular setting, the wise thing to do is establish that setting as early as possible in the procedure and document why it's necessary via comments.

Parameters

Parameters can be passed to stored procedures by name or by position. Here's an example of each method:

```
EXEC sp_msforeachtable @command1='sp_help "?"', @replacechar = '?'

EXEC sp_msforeachtable 'sp_help "?"', '?'
```

The obvious advantage to referencing parameters by name is that they can be specified out of order.

You can force a parameter for which a default value has been defined to use that default by omitting it altogether or by passing it the DEFAULT keyword, like so:

```
EXEC sp_msforeachtable @command1='sp_help "?"', @replacechar = DEFAULT
```

You can specify NULL to supply individual parameters with NULL values. That's sometimes handy for procedures that expose special features when parameters are omitted or set to NULL. Here's an example:

```
EXEC sp_who @loginame=NULL
```

(Results abridged)

spid	status	loginame
1	sleeping	sa
2	background	sa
3	background	sa
6	background	sa
7	sleeping	CALIGULA\KHEN
8	sleeping	CALIGULA\KHEN
9	sleeping	CALIGULA\KHEN

In this example, sp_who returns a list of all active connections because its lone parameter is NULL. When a valid login name is specified, sp_who returns just those connections established by the specified login name. When the @loginame parameter is NULL, all connections are listed. The same thing would happen if @loginame was omitted altogether. I've specified NULL here for illustration purposes.

Output Parameters

Output parameters allow values to be returned from stored procedures. These parameters can be integers, character strings, dates, and even cursors. Here's an example:

```
USE pubs
IF OBJECT_ID('dbo.listsales') IS NOT NULL
   DROP PROC dbo.listsales
GO
CREATE PROC dbo.listsales @bestseller tid OUT, @topsales int OUT,
        @salescursor cursor varying OUT
AS

SELECT @bestseller=bestseller, @topsales=totalsales
FROM (
     SELECT TOP 1 title_id AS bestseller, SUM(qty) AS totalsales
     FROM sales
     GROUP BY title_id
     ORDER BY 2 DESC) bestsellers

DECLARE s CURSOR
LOCAL
FOR SELECT * FROM sales
```

```
OPEN s

SET @salescursor=s
RETURN(0)

DECLARE @topsales int, @bestseller tid, @salescursor cursor
EXEC listsales @bestseller OUT, @topsales OUT, @salescursor OUT
SELECT @bestseller, @topsales

FETCH @salescursor
CLOSE @salescursor
DEALLOCATE @salescursor


------ -----------
PS2091 191

stor_id ord_num        ord_date                qty    payterms  title_id
------- ---------------- ------------------------ ------ --------- --------
6380    6871            1994-09-14 00:00:00.000  5      Net 60    BU1032
```

Output parameters are identified with the OUTPUT keyword (which can be abbreviated as "OUT"). Notice the use of the OUT keyword in the procedure definition as well as in the EXEC parameter list. Both the procedure and its caller must specify which parameters are output parameters.

Cursor output parameters are a sensible means of returning a result set to a caller. Notice the use of the **varying** keyword with the cursor parameter in the procedure definition. This keyword is required with cursor parameters and indicates that the return value is nonscalar—that is, it returns more than a single value. Cursor parameters can only be output parameters, so the OUT keyword is required as well.

Result Codes

Procedures return result codes via the RETURN command. A return code of 0 indicates success, values -1 through -14 indicate different types of failures, and values -15 through -99 are reserved for future use. Table 15.1 lists the meaning of codes -1 through -14:

Table 15.1. Stock return codes and their meanings.

Code	Meaning
-1	Object missing
-2	Data type error occurred
-3	Process chosen as deadlock victim
-4	Permission error
-5	Syntax error
-6	Miscellaneous user error
-7	Resource error
-8	Nonfatal internal error
-9	System limit reached
-10	Fatal internal inconsistency error
-11	Fatal internal inconsistency error
-12	Corrupt table or index
-13	Corrupt database
-14	Hardware error

You can access a procedure's return code by assigning it to an integer value, like this:

```
DECLARE @res int
EXEC @res=sp_who
```

Listing Procedure Parameters

You can list a procedure's parameters (which include its return code—considered parameter 0) using the undocumented procedure sp_procedure_params_rowset. Here's an example:

```
EXEC sp_procedure_params_rowset 'sp_MSforeachtable'
```

(Results abridged)

PROCEDURE_CATALOG	PROCEDURE_SCHEMA	PROCEDURE_NAME	PARAMETER_NAME	ORDINAL_POSITION	PARAMETER_TYPE
master	dbo	sp_MSforeachtable;1	RETURN_VALUE	0	4
master	dbo	sp_MSforeachtable;1	@command1	1	1
master	dbo	sp_MSforeachtable;1	@replacechar	2	1
master	dbo	sp_MSforeachtable;1	@command2	3	1
master	dbo	sp_MSforeachtable;1	@command3	4	1
master	dbo	sp_MSforeachtable;1	@whereand	5	1
master	dbo	sp_MSforeachtable;1	@precommand	6	1
master	dbo	sp_MSforeachtable;1	@postcommand	7	1

General Parameter Notes

- Provide default values for parameters when it makes sense. Parameter defaults are limited to constants and the NULL value.

- Check parameters for invalid or missing values early in your stored procedures.

- Use human-friendly parameter names so that parameters can be passed by name easily.

- Parameter names are local to stored procedures. You can use the same name in multiple procedures.

- You can find stored procedure parameter information in the syscolumns system table (that's where sp_procedure_params_rowset gets its info).

- Stored procedures support up to 1024 parameters. The number of stored procedure local variables is limited only by available memory.

Important Automatic Variables

By their very nature, automatic variables (what the Books Online now call "functions") are usually accessed from within stored procedures. This makes most of them relevant in some way to stored procedures. However, a few of them are more relevant to stored procedure use than the others. Table 15.2 summarizes them.

Table 15.2. Stored procedure–related automatic variables.

Variable Name	Returns
@@NESTLEVEL	The current procedure nesting level (see "Nesting" later)
@@OPTIONS	A bitmap of the currently specified user options
@@PROCID	The object ID of the current procedure
@@SPID	The process ID of the current process
@@TRANCOUNT	The current transaction nesting level

Flow Control Language

No discussion of stored procedures would be complete without covering control-of-flow language statements. These are referred to as "flow control" or "control-of-flow" statements because they control the flow of execution through a stored procedure or batch. Transact-SQL flow control language statements include IF...ELSE, WHILE, GOTO, RETURN, WAITFOR, BREAK, CONTINUE, and BEGIN..END. Without repeating what's already covered quite adequately by the Books Online, here's a simple procedure that illustrates all of them:

```
USE pubs
IF OBJECT_ID('dbo.listsales') IS NOT NULL
   DROP PROC dbo.listsales
GO
CREATE PROC dbo.listsales @title_id tid=NULL
AS

IF (@title_id='/?') GOTO Help     -- Here's a basic IF

-- Here's one with a BEGIN..END block
IF NOT EXISTS(SELECT * FROM titles WHERE title_id=@title_id) BEGIN
   PRINT 'Invalid title_id'
   WAITFOR DELAY '00:00:03' -- Delay 3 secs to view message
   RETURN -1
END

IF NOT EXISTS(SELECT * FROM sales WHERE title_id=@title_id) BEGIN
   PRINT 'No sales for this title'
   WAITFOR DELAY '00:00:03' -- Delay 3 secs to view message
   RETURN -2
END

DECLARE @qty int, @totalsales int
SET @totalsales=0

DECLARE c CURSOR
FOR SELECT qty FROM sales WHERE title_id=@title_id

OPEN c

FETCH c INTO @qty
```

```
WHILE (@@FETCH_STATUS=0) BEGIN      -- Here's a WHILE loop
   IF (@qty<0) BEGIN
      Print 'Bad quantity encountered'
      BREAK     -- Exit the loop immediately
   END ELSE IF (@qty IS NULL) BEGIN
      Print 'NULL quantity encountered -- skipping'
      FETCH c INTO @qty
      CONTINUE -- Continue with the next iteration of the loop
   END
   SET @totalsales=@totalsales+@qty
   FETCH c INTO @qty
END

CLOSE c
DEALLOCATE c

SELECT @title_id AS 'TitleID', @totalsales AS 'TotalSales'
RETURN 0      -- Return from the procedure indicating success

Help:
EXEC sp_usage @objectname='listsales',
   @desc='Lists the total sales for a title',
   @parameters='@title_id="ID of the title you want to check"',
   @example='EXEC listsales "PS2091"',
   @author='Ken Henderson',
   @email='khen@khen.com',
   @version='1', @revision='0',
   @datecreated='19990803', @datelastchanged='19990818'
WAITFOR DELAY '00:00:03' -- Delay 3 secs to view message
RETURN -1
GO

EXEC listsales 'PS2091'
EXEC listsales 'badone'
EXEC listsales 'PC9999'


TitleID TotalSales
------- -----------
PS2091  191

Invalid title_id
No sales for this title
```

Errors

Stored procedures report errors via return codes and the RAISERROR command. RAISERROR doesn't change the flow of the procedure, it merely displays an error message (optionally writing it to the SQL Server error log and the NT application event log) and sets the @@ERROR automatic variable. RAISERROR can reference predefined error messages that reside in the sysmessages table (you create these with sp_addmessage), or you can supply it with a custom message string of your own. If you supply a message during the call to RAISERROR, the error number is set to 50,000. RAISERROR can format messages similarly to the C printf() function, allowing you to supply your own arguments for the messages it displays.

RAISERROR allows both a severity and a state to be specified with each message. Severity values less than 16 produce informational messages in the system event log (when logged), a severity of 16 produces a warning message in the event log, and severity values greater than 16 produce error messages in the event log. Severity values up through 18 can be specified by any user; severity values 19–25 are reserved for members of the sysadmin role and require the use of the WITH LOG option. Note that severity values over 20 are considered fatal and cause the client connection to be terminated.

State is an informational value that you can use to indicate state information to your front-end application—it has no predefined meaning to SQL Server. Raising an error with a state of 127 will cause the ISQL and OSQL utilities to set the operating system ERRORLEVEL value to the error number returned by RAISERROR. Note that, unlike releases prior to 7.0, the ISQL utility no longer exits immediately when a state of 127 is used—it merely sets ERRORLEVEL; OSQL, by contrast, exits immediately. So if we have this SQL batch:

```
RAISERROR('Setting the OS ERRORLEVEL variable',16,127) WITH NOWAIT
PRINT 'Prior to 7.0, execution would never make it here in ISQL'
```

and we execute it from this operating system command batch:

```
@ECHO OFF
isql -Usa -P -iraiserror01.sql
ECHO %ERRORLEVEL%
osql -Usa -P -iraiserror01.sql
ECHO %ERRORLEVEL%
```

here's what happens:

```
D:\>RAISERROR
1> 2> 3> Msg 50000, Level 16, State 127, Server CALIGULA, Line 1
Setting the OS ERRORLEVEL variable
Prior to 7.0, execution would never make it here in ISQL
50000
1> 2> 3> Msg 50000, Level 16, State 127, Server CALIGULA, Procedure , Line 1
[Microsoft][ODBC SQL Server Driver][SQL Server]Setting the OS ERRORLEVEL
variable
50000
```

This is handy for exiting a command batch immediately without causing undue alarm or generating unnecessary entries in the system event log. Though you could raise a message with a high severity level to terminate the connection, that creates log entries and potentially raises a red flag over something that's completely normal: aborting a batch before processing it completely. And though you could also abort the batch with the EXIT command, the operating system ERRORLEVEL wouldn't be set, so you'd have no way of knowing why the batch exited.

RAISERROR supports a handful of options that affect its behavior. The WITH LOG option copies the error message to the NT event log (assuming SQL Server is running on Windows NT) and the SQL Server error log regardless of whether the message was defined using the **with_log** option of sp_addmessage. The WITH NOWAIT option causes the message to be returned immediately to the client. The WITH SETERROR option forces the automatic

@@ERROR variable to return the last error number raised, regardless of the severity of the error message.

The system procedure sp_addmessage is used to add messages to the sysmessages table that RAISERROR can then use. User messages should have error numbers of 50,000 or higher. The chief advantage of using SQL Server's system messages facility is that it's language independent. Because you specify a language with each message you add, you can have several messages with the same error number but with different language indicators. Then, based on the language setting the user chooses when installing SQL Server, the appropriate message will be displayed when your code calls RAISERROR.

Because RAISERROR can display a message and set the @@ERROR variable in one fell swoop, it's sometimes used for tasks other than displaying error messages. Its printf()-like formatting ability makes it ideal for formatting strings other than error messages. Here's an example that features RAISERROR used to list a table:

```
DECLARE c CURSOR
FOR SELECT title_id, SUM(qty) as sales FROM sales GROUP BY title_id

DECLARE @title_id tid, @qty int

OPEN c

RAISERROR('Starting loop',1,1) -- Seed @@ERROR
WHILE (@@ERROR<=1) BEGIN
   FETCH c INTO @title_id, @qty
   IF (@@FETCH_STATUS=0)
     RAISERROR('Title ID %s has sold %d units',1,1,@title_id,@qty)
   ELSE
     BREAK
END

CLOSE c

DEALLOCATE c
```

(Results)

```
Msg 50000, Level 1, State 50000
Starting loop
Msg 50000, Level 1, State 50000
Title ID BU1032 has sold 45 units
Msg 50000, Level 1, State 50000
Title ID BU1111 has sold 25 units
Msg 50000, Level 1, State 50000
Title ID BU2075 has sold 35 units
Msg 50000, Level 1, State 50000
Title ID BU7832 has sold 15 units
Msg 50000, Level 1, State 50000
Title ID MC2222 has sold 10 units
Msg 50000, Level 1, State 50000
Title ID MC3021 has sold 40 units
Msg 50000, Level 1, State 50000
Title ID MC3026 has sold 30 units
Msg 50000, Level 1, State 50000
Title ID PC1035 has sold 30 units
```

```
Msg 50000, Level 1, State 50000
Title ID PC8888 has sold 50 units
Msg 50000, Level 1, State 50000
Title ID PS1372 has sold 20 units
Msg 50000, Level 1, State 50000
Title ID PS2091 has sold 191 units
Msg 50000, Level 1, State 50000
Title ID PS2106 has sold 25 units
Msg 50000, Level 1, State 50000
Title ID PS3333 has sold 15 units
Msg 50000, Level 1, State 50000
Title ID PS7777 has sold 25 units
Msg 50000, Level 1, State 50000
Title ID TC3218 has sold 40 units
Msg 50000, Level 1, State 50000
Title ID TC4203 has sold 20 units
Msg 50000, Level 1, State 50000
Title ID TC7777 has sold 20 units
```

Of course, the obligatory "Msg..." lines would be a bit of an annoyance, but you could strip these out in your front-end application if you decided to use this approach.

@@ERROR

Make a habit of checking @@ERROR after significant code in your procedures, especially after data modification operations. The hallmark of robust code is thorough error checking, and until Transact-SQL supports structured exception handling, @@ERROR is the best way to accomplish this.

xp_logevent

You can use the xp_logevent system procedure to add a message to the SQL Server error log or the NT event log. The main difference between this approach and calling RAISERROR is that no error message is sent to the client. The message number or string you pass to xp_logevent is silently logged without client notification.

Nesting

Stored procedures can be nested up to 32 levels deep. The @@NESTLEVEL automatic variable indicates the level of nesting at any given time. A nesting level of 0 is returned at the command batch level, 1 within each stored procedure called from level 0 (and from first-level triggers), 2 for each proc called from level 1, and so forth. Objects (including temporary tables) and cursors created within a stored procedure are visible to all objects it calls. Objects and cursors created at level 0 are visible to all objects.

Recursion

Transact-SQL supports recursion. Recursion can be defined as a method of solving a problem wherein the solution is arrived at by repetitively applying it to subsets of the problem. An obvious use of recursion is in creating parsers and performing numeric computations that lend themselves to repetitive evaluation by the same processing logic. Here's a an example that features a stored procedure that calculates the factorial of a number:

```
SET NOCOUNT ON
USE master
IF OBJECT_ID('dbo.sp_calcfactorial') IS NOT NULL
    DROP PROC dbo.sp_calcfactorial

DECLARE @typestr varchar(20)
SET @typestr='decimal('+CAST(@@MAX_PRECISION AS varchar(2))+',0)'
IF TYPEPROPERTY('bigd','precision') IS NOT NULL
    EXEC sp_droptype 'bigd'

EXEC sp_addtype 'bigd',@typestr -- Add a custom type corresponding to the @@MAX_PRECISION variable

GO
CREATE PROC dbo.sp_calcfactorial @base_number bigd, @factorial bigd OUT
AS
SET NOCOUNT ON
DECLARE @previous_number bigd

IF ((@base_number>26) and (@@MAX_PRECISION<38)) OR (@base_number>32) BEGIN
    RAISERROR('Computing this factorial would exceed the server''s max. numeric precision of %d or
    the max. procedure nesting level of 32',16,10,@@MAX_PRECISION)
    RETURN(-1)
END

IF (@base_number<0) BEGIN
    RAISERROR('Can''t calculate negative factorials',16,10)
    RETURN(-1)
END

IF (@base_number<2) SET @factorial=1 -- Factorial of 0 or 1=1
ELSE BEGIN
    SET @previous_number=@base_number-1
    EXEC sp_calcfactorial @previous_number, @factorial OUT -- Recursive call
    IF (@factorial=-1) RETURN(-1) -- Got an error, return
    SET @factorial=@factorial*@base_number
    IF (@@ERROR<>0) RETURN(-1) -- Got an error, return
END
RETURN(0)
GO

DECLARE @factorial bigd
EXEC sp_calcfactorial 26, @factorial OUT
SELECT @factorial
```

(Results)

```
Type added.

Cannot add rows to sysdepends for the current stored procedure because it depends on
the missing object 'sp_calcfactorial'. The stored procedure will still be created.

-------------------------------
403291461126605635584000000
```

The first thing this procedure does is create a decimal-based user-defined data type that matches the @@MAX_PRECISION automatic variable. This allows the procedure to use as large a number as the server can handle. Next, the procedure checks to make sure it has been passed a valid number for which to compute a factorial. It then recursively calls itself to perform the computation. As you can see, with the default maximum numeric precision of 28, SQL Server can handle numbers in excess of 400 *septillion!* [1]

Autostart Procedures

Autostart procedures have lots of practical uses. You can use them to perform start-up processes and other administrative work. You can use them to load commonly used procedures into the procedure cache with each server boot. You use the sp_procoption stored procedure to flag a stored procedure as an autostart routine, like so:

```
EXEC sp_procoption 'sp_databases','startup',true
```

Some notes about autostart procedures:

- They must reside in the master database.
- They must be owned by a member of the sysadmin role.
- They cannot require any parameters.
- They cannot return a result set.
- You can pass trace flag 4022 (-T4022) on the SQL Server command line to prevent autostart routines from executing.

Encryption

You can encrypt the source code that's stored in syscomments for a stored procedure, view, or trigger using the WITH ENCRYPTION option when you create the object. This prevents users from viewing your source code with tools such as Enterprise Manager, but it also thwarts stored procedure debuggers, like the one included with the Enterprise Edition of Visual Studio. Encrypted objects have the third bit of the texttype column in syscomments set.

Note that once you've encrypted an object, there's no supported way of decrypting it. You can't view it, nor can members of the sysadmin role or anyone else.

Triggers

A trigger is a special type of stored procedure that executes when a specified DML operation (an INSERT, DELETE, or UPDATE or any combination of them) occurs. Triggers are constructed via the CREATE TRIGGER command and are attached to tables. When its host table is dropped, so is the trigger.

Most of the details of stored procedure programming apply equally well to triggers. In fact, since you can call a stored procedure from a trigger, you can effectively do anything in a trigger

---

[1] This assumes the definition of septillion as used in the United States: 1 followed by 24 zeros. In Great Britain and Germany, a septillion is equal to 1 followed by 42 zeros.

that a stored procedure can do. One thing that triggers don't normally do is return result sets. Most front ends have no way of handling trigger-generated result sets, so you just don't see it in production code. Note that SQL Server doesn't permit triggers to return result codes.

Triggers fire once per statement, not per row, regardless of the number of rows changed by a given DML statement. You can set up as many triggers as you want (well, up to 2 billion per database, anyway) for a table—triggers associated with the same DML statement will fire in succession in no particular order.

DRI (declarative referential integrity) constraints have precedence over triggers. This means that a violation of a DRI constraint by a DML command will prevent triggers from executing.

Inside triggers, you can check which columns are being updated by a DML operation via the UPDATE() and COLUMNS_UPDATE() functions. The UPDATE() function returns true or false based on whether the value of a specified column is being set (regardless of whether it's actually changing). COLUMNS_UPDATED() returns a bitmap representing which columns are being set.

Triggers can cause other triggers to fire if the **nested triggers** option has been enabled with sp_configure. Triggers can fire themselves recursively if the **recursive triggers** database option has been enabled. The @@NESTLEVEL automatic variable returns 1 within a first-level trigger, 2 within one it causes to fire, 3 for any it causes to fire, and so forth.

When a user transaction is not active, a trigger and the DML operation that fired it are considered a single transaction. When a trigger generates a fatal error or executes a ROLLBACK TRANSACTION, the currently active transaction is rolled back and the current command batch is canceled.

SQL Server exposes special logical tables for use by triggers: the **inserted** and **deleted** tables. For INSERT operations, the inserted table lists the row(s) about to be appended to the table. For DELETE operations, the deleted table lists the row(s) about to be removed from the table. For UPDATE operations, the deleted table lists the old version of the row(s) about to be updated, and the inserted table lists the new version. You can query these tables to allow or prevent database modifications based on the columns or data the operations are attempting to modify. Rolling back the current transaction is normally the way that triggers are aborted since SQL Server's Transact-SQL doesn't support a ROLLBACK TRIGGER command (à la Sybase). Note that you can't modify these logical tables—they're for inspection only.

Nonlogged operations (operations that do not generate row modification log records) do not fire triggers. So, for example, even though TRUNCATE TABLE deletes all the rows in a table, those row deletions aren't logged individually and therefore do not fire any delete triggers that may have been defined for the table.

You can disable a trigger via the ALTER TABLE...DISABLE TRIGGER command. Disabled triggers can be reenabled using ALTER TABLE...ENABLE TRIGGER. Here are a few examples:

```
ALTER TABLE sales
DISABLE TRIGGER SalesQty_INSERT_UPDATE

ALTER TABLE sales
ENABLE TRIGGER SalesQty_INSERT_UPDATE

ALTER TABLE sales
DISABLE TRIGGER ALL

ALTER TABLE sales
ENABLE TRIGGER ALL
```

Triggers fire just after the work has been completed by the DML statement but before it has been committed to the database. A DML statement's execution plan branches to any triggers it fires just before returning. If the trigger permits the operation to proceed, and if no user transaction is present, any changes made by the DML statement are then committed to the database.

Here are a few trigger examples:

```
SET NOCOUNT ON
USE pubs
DROP TRIGGER SalesQty_INSERT_UPDATE
GO
CREATE TRIGGER SalesQty_INSERT_UPDATE ON sales FOR INSERT, UPDATE AS

IF @@ROWCOUNT=0 RETURN -- No rows affected, exit immediately

IF (UPDATE(qty)) AND (SELECT MIN(qty) FROM inserted)<10 BEGIN
   RAISERROR('Minimum order is 10 units',16,10)
   ROLLBACK TRAN
   RETURN
END
GO


-- Test a single-row INSERT
BEGIN TRAN
   INSERT sales VALUES (6380,'ORD9997',GETDATE(),5,'Net 60','BU1032')
IF @@TRANCOUNT>0 ROLLBACK TRAN
GO


-- Test a multirow INSERT
BEGIN TRAN
   INSERT sales
   SELECT stor_id, ord_num+'A', ord_date, 5, payterms, title_id FROM sales
IF @@TRANCOUNT>0 ROLLBACK TRAN
GO


DROP TRIGGER Sales_DELETE
GO
CREATE TRIGGER Sales_DELETE ON sales FOR DELETE AS

IF @@ROWCOUNT=0 RETURN -- No rows affected, exit immediately

IF (@@ROWCOUNT>1) BEGIN
   RAISERROR('Deletions of more than one row at a time are not permitted',16,10)
   ROLLBACK TRAN
   RETURN
END
GO
BEGIN TRAN
   DELETE sales
IF @@TRANCOUNT>0 ROLLBACK TRAN
GO


DROP TRIGGER Salesord_date_qty_UPDATE
GO
CREATE TRIGGER Salesord_date_qty_UPDATE ON sales FOR INSERT, UPDATE AS
```

```
IF @@ROWCOUNT=0 RETURN -- No rows affected, exit immediately

-- Check to see whether the 3rd and 4th columns are being updated simultaneously
IF (COLUMNS_UPDATED() & (POWER(2,3-1) | POWER(2,4-1)))=12 BEGIN

UPDATE s SET payterms='Cash'
FROM sales s JOIN inserted i ON (s.stor_id=i.stor_id AND s.ord_num=i.ord_num)

IF (@@ERROR<>0) -- UPDATE generated an error, rollback transaction
   ROLLBACK TRANSACTION
RETURN

END
GO

-- Test with a single-row UPDATE
BEGIN TRAN
   UPDATE sales SET ord_date=GETDATE(), qty=15
   WHERE stor_id=7066 and ord_num='A2976'

   SELECT * FROM sales
   WHERE stor_id=7066 and ord_num='A2976'
IF @@TRANCOUNT>0 ROLLBACK TRAN
GO

-- Test with a multirow UPDATE
BEGIN TRAN
   UPDATE sales SET ord_date=GETDATE(), qty=15
   WHERE stor_id=7066

   SELECT * FROM sales
   WHERE stor_id=7066
IF @@TRANCOUNT>0 ROLLBACK TRAN
```

(Results)

```
Server: Msg 50000, Level 16, State 10, Procedure CheckSalesQty, Line 3
Minimum order is 10 units
Server: Msg 50000, Level 16, State 10, Procedure CheckSalesQty, Line 3
Minimum order is 10 units
Server: Msg 50000, Level 16, State 10, Procedure CheckSalesDelete, Line 3
Deletions of more than one row at a time are not permitted
```

stor_id	ord_num	ord_date	qty	payterms	title_id
7066	A2976	1999-06-13 01:10:16.193	15	Cash	PC8888

stor_id	ord_num	ord_date	qty	payterms	title_id
7066	A2976	1999-06-13 01:10:16.243	15	Cash	PC8888
7066	QA7442.3	1999-06-13 01:10:16.243	15	Cash	PS2091

Some general trigger notes:

- Make sure your triggers allow for the possibility that more than one row could be altered at once. Triggers that work fine with single-row operations often break when multirow operations come their way. Not allowing for multirow updates is the single most common error that trigger neophytes make.

• Begin each trigger by checking @@ROWCOUNT to see whether any rows have changed. If none have, exit immediately since there's nothing for the trigger to do.

• Use the UPDATE() and COLUMNS_UPDATED() functions to ensure the values you're wanting to verify have actually changed.

• Never wait for user input or any other user event within a trigger.

• Check for errors after significant operations within your triggers, especially DML operations. The admonition regarding checking for errors after DML operations in stored procedures applies to triggers as well.

• Keep operations within a trigger to a minimum. Triggers should execute as quickly as possible to keep from adversely affecting system performance.

• Provide descriptive error messages without being loquacious. Return user messages rather than obscure system error messages when possible.

• Modularize your triggers by locating code that's executed by multiple triggers or that's lengthy or complex in separate stored procedures.

• Check triggers that enforce referential integrity for robustness. Try every combination of columnar updates to be sure all scenarios are covered.

• Write a test script for every trigger you build. Make sure it tests every situation the trigger is supposed to handle.

Debugging Procedures

The Enterprise Edition of Visual Studio, as well as various third-party tools, allows Transact-SQL stored procedures to be debugged. This means that you can step into stored procedures called from Visual Studio projects such as VB and VC++ applications. You can set breakpoints, establish watches, and generally do what debuggers are designed to do—debug code.

The interface by which this occurs is known as the SQL Server Debug Interface, or SDI for short. It was originally introduced with SQL Server 6.5 and has now been completely integrated with Visual Studio.

Some notes on debugging Transact-SQL with the SDI:

• SDI is implemented via the sp_sdidebug pseudo procedure (see the section "Faux Procedures" earlier in the chapter for more information on "pseudo" procedures).

• You should run SQL Server under a user account, not the LocalSystem account, when debugging because running under LocalSystem disables breakpoints.

• When debugging on the same machine as your server, run the server under the same user context as the debugger.

- Ensure that you can run SQL Server as a console app rather than a service.

- On Windows NT, SDI messages are written to the Application event log under MSDEVSDI.

Summary

In this chapter, you explored many of the nuances and idiosyncrasies of building stored procedures and triggers. You learned how to construct user as well as system procedures and how to pass parameters to and from the procedures you create. You became familiar with some of the internals of the stored procedure execution process, and you learned how triggers work. You became acquainted with debugging stored procedures, and you learned about fringe elements of stored procedure creation such as encryption and execution plan recompilation.

16

Transact-SQL Performance Tuning

Good engineering is the difference between code running in eight minutes or eight hours. It affects real people in real ways. It's not a "matter of opinion" any more than a bird taking flight is a "matter of opinion."
—H. W. Kenton

General SQL Server performance tuning is outside the scope of this book. That subject alone could easily fill several volumes on its own. Instead, the focus of this chapter is on tuning the performance of Transact-SQL queries. The options are many and the tools are sometimes complex, but there are a number of specific techniques you can employ to write optimal Transact-SQL code and to improve the performance of queries that don't perform acceptably well.

General Performance Guidelines

- The best thing you can do to ensure the code you write performs optimally is to deepen the level of expertise on your development team. Good developers write good code. It pays to grow development talent through aggressive training. None of us was born knowing what a correlated subquery is. Investment in people often yields long-term benefits that are difficult if not impossible to obtain otherwise.

- Identify and thoroughly investigate your application's key database operations and transactions as early in the development process as possible. Knowing these well early on and addressing them as soon as possible can mean the difference between a successful release and a fiasco.

- Go into every project you build—from small ones to mammoth ones—assuming that no amount of performance tuning will rectify poor application or database design. It's essential to get these right up front.

- Define performance requirements in terms of peak usage. Making a general statement like "The system must handle five hundred users" is not terribly useful. First, will all these users be logged in simultaneously? What's the peak number of users? Second, what will they be doing? When is the server likely to have to work hardest? When it comes to predicting real-world application performance, TPS benchmark numbers are relative indicators at best. Being as intimate as possible with the real stress points of your application is the key to success. The devil is in the details.

- Keep in mind that sometimes perception dictates reality. This is particularly true with interactive applications. Sometimes it's more important to return control to an application quickly than to perform a query as efficiently as possible. The SELECT statement's FAST *n* hint allows you to return control quickly to the calling application, though using it may actually cause the query to take longer to run to completion. Using asynchronous cursors is another way to return quickly from a query (see Chapter 13, "Cursors," for more information). And remember that you can use the SET LOCK_TIMEOUT command to configure how long a query waits on a locked resource before timing out. This can prevent an app from appearing to hang while it waits on a resource. Even though a query may take longer overall to execute, returning control to the user in an expeditious manner can sometimes head off client machine reboots born of impatience or frustration. These reboots can affect performance themselves—especially if SQL Server and the application reside on the same machine. Thus perception directly affects reality.

- Be sure to gauge performance extensively and often throughout the development process. Application performance testing is not a separable step that you can wait until after development to begin. It has to be an ongoing, fluid process that tracks the development effort closely. Application components should be prototyped, demonstrated, and benchmarked throughout the development process. It's better to know early on that a user finds performance unacceptable than to find out when you ship.

- Thoroughly load test your app before shipping it. Load more data than your largest customer will require before you burn your first CD. If time permits, take your load testing to the next logical step and stress test the app—find out the magic values for data load, user connections, memory, and so on that cause it to fail or that exceed its capacity.

Database Design Performance Tips

- Table row and key lengths should be as short as sensible. Be efficient, but don't be a miser. Trimming one byte per row isn't much of a savings if you have only a few rows, or, worse yet, you end up needing that one byte. The reason for narrow rows is obvious—the less work the server has to do to satisfy a query, the quicker it finishes. Using shorter rows allows more rows per page and more data in the same amount of cache space. This is also true for index pages—narrow keys allow more rows per page than wider ones.

- Keeping clustered index keys as narrow as possible will help reduce the size of nonclustered indexes since they now reference the clustered index (if one exists) rather than referencing the table directly.

- Begin by normalizing every database you build at least to third normal form. You can denormalize the design later if the need arises. See the "Denormalization" section later in this chapter for further information.

- Use Declarative Referential Integrity constraints to ensure relational integrity when possible because they're generally faster than triggers and stored procedures. DRI constraints cause highly optimized native machine code internal to SQL Server to run. Triggers and stored procedures, by contrast, consist of pseudocompiled Transact-SQL code. All other things being equal, native machine code is clearly the better performer of the two.

- Use fixed-length character data types when the length of a column's data doesn't vary significantly throughout a table. Processing variable-length columns requires more processing resources than handling fixed-length columns.

- Disallow NULLs when possible—handling NULLs adds extra overhead to storage and query processing. It's not unheard of for developers to avoid NULLs altogether, using placeholders to signify missing values as necessary.

- Consider using filegroups to distribute large tables over multiple drives and to separate indexes from data. If possible, locate the transaction log on a separate drive or drives from the filegroups that compose the database, and separate key tables from one another. This is especially appropriate for very large database (VLDB) implementations.

- If the primary key for a given table is sequential (e.g., an identity column), consider making it a nonclustered primary key. A clustered index on a monotonically increasing key is less than optimal since you probably won't ever query the table for a range of key values or use the primary key column(s) with ORDER BY. A clustered sequential primary key can cause users to contend for the same area of the database as they add rows to the table, creating what's known as a "hotspot." Avoid this if you can by using clustered keys that sort the data more evenly across the table.

- If a table frequently experiences severe contention, especially when multiple users are attempting to insert new rows, page locks may be at fault. Consider using the sp_indexoptions system stored procedure to disable page locks on the suspect table. Disabling page locks forces the server to use row locks and table locks. This will prevent the automatic escalation of row locks to page locks from reducing concurrency.

- Use computed columns to render common column calculations rather than deriving them via SQL each time you query a table. This is syntactically more compact, reduces the work required to generate an execution plan, and cuts down on the SQL that must traverse the network for routine queries.

- Test your database with different row volumes in order to get a feel for the amount of data the design will support. This will let you know early on what the capacity of your model is, possibly pointing out serious problems in the design. A database that works fine for a few thousand rows may collapse miserably under the weight of a few million.

- When all else fails, consider limited database denormalization to improve performance. See the "Denormalization" section later in this chapter for more information.

Index Performance Tips

- Create indexes the query optimizer can use. Generally speaking, clustered indexes are best for range selections and ordered queries. Clustered indexes are also appropriate for keys with a high density (those with many duplicate values). Since rows are physically sorted, queries that search using these nonunique values will find them with a minimum number of I/O operations. Nonclustered indexes are better for singleton selects and individual row lookups.

- Make nonclustered indexes as highly selective (i.e., with as low densities) as possible. Index selectivity can be calculated using the formula **Selectivity = # of Unique Keys / # of Rows.** Nonclustered indexes with a selectivity less than 0.1 are not efficient, and the optimizer will refuse to use them. Nonclustered indexes are best used to find single rows. Obviously, duplicate keys force the server to work harder to locate a particular row.

- Along the lines of making indexes highly selective, order the key columns in a multicolumn index by selectivity, placing more selective columns first. As the server traverses the index tree to find a given key column value, the use of highly selective key columns means that it will have to perform fewer I/Os to reach the leaf level of the index, resulting in a faster query.

- Keep key database operations and transactions in mind as you construct indexes. Build indexes that the query optimizer can use to service your more crucial transactions.

- Consider creating indexes to service popular join conditions. If you frequently join two tables on a set of columns, consider building an index to speed the join.

- Drop indexes that aren't being used. If you inspect the execution plans for the queries that should be using an index and find that the index can't be used as is, consider getting rid of it. Redesign it if that makes sense, or simply omit it— whatever works best in your particular situation.

- Consider creating indexes on foreign key references. Foreign keys require a unique key index on the referenced table but make no index stipulations on the table making the reference. Creating an index on the dependent table can speed up foreign key integrity checks that result from modifications to the referenced table and can improve join performance between the two tables.

- Create temporary indexes to service infrequent reports and user queries. A report that's run only annually or semiannually may not merit an index that has to be maintained year-round. Consider creating the index just before you run the report and dropping it afterward if that's faster than running the report without the index.

- It may be advantageous to drop and recreate indexes during BULK INSERT operations. BULK INSERT operations, especially those involving multiple clients, will generally be faster when indexes aren't present. This is no longer the maxim it once was, but common sense tells us the less work that has to occur during a bulk load, the faster it should be.

- If the optimizer can retrieve all the data it needs from a nonclustered index without having to reference the underlying table, it will do so. This is called *index covering,* and indexes that facilitate it are known as *covered indexes.* If adding a small column or columns to an existing nonclustered index would give it all the data a popular query needs, you may find that it speeds up the query significantly. Covered indexes are the closest you'll get to having multiple clustered indexes on the same table.

- Allow SQL Server to maintain index statistic information for your databases automatically. This helps ensure that it's kept reasonably up to date and alleviates the need by most apps to rebuild index statistics manually.

- Because SQL Server's automatic statistics facility uses sampling to generate statistical info as quickly as possible, it may not be as representative of your data as it could be. If the query optimizer elects not to use indexes that you think it should be using, try updating the statistics for the index manually using UPDATE STATISTICS...WITH FULLSCAN.

- You can use DBCC DBREINDEX() to rebuild the indexes on a table. This is one way of removing dead space from a table or changing the FILLFACTOR of one of its indexes. Here's an example:

```
DBCC DBREINDEX('Customers','PK_Customers')
DBCC DBREINDEX('Customers','',100)
```

Both of these examples cause all indexes on the Northwind Customers table to be rebuilt. In the first example, we pass the name of the clustered index into DBREINDEX. Rebuilding its clustered index rebuilds a table's nonclustered indexes as well. In the second example, we pass an empty string for the index name. This also causes all indexes on the table to be rebuilt.

The nice thing about DBREINDEX is that it's atomic—either the specified index or indexes are all dropped and recreated or none of them are. This includes indexes set up by the server to maintain constraints, such as primary and unique keys. In fact, DBREINDEX is the only way to rebuild primary and unique key indexes without first dropping their associated constraints. Since other tables may depend upon a table's primary or unique key, this can get quite complicated. Fortunately, DBREINDEX takes care of it automatically—it can drop and recreate any of a table's indexes regardless of dependent tables and constraints.

- You can use DBCC SHOWCONTIG to list fragmentation information for a table and its indexes. You can use this info to decide whether to reorganize the table by rebuilding its clustered index.

- As mentioned in the section "Database Design Performance Tips," if an index regularly experiences a significant level of contention during inserts by multiple users, page locking may be the culprit. Consider using the sp_indexoptions system procedure to disable page locks for the index. Disabling page locks forces the server to use row locks and table locks. As long as row locks do not escalate to table locks inordinately often, this should result in improved concurrency.

- Thanks to the query optimizer's use of multiple indexes on a single table, multiple single-key indexes can yield better overall performance than a compound-key index. This is because the optimizer can query the indexes separately and then merge them to return a result set. This is more flexible than using a compound-key index because the single-column index keys can be specified in any combination. That's not true with a compound key—you must use compound-key columns in a left-to-right order.

- Use the Index Tuning Wizard to suggest the optimal indexes for queries. This is a sophisticated tool that can scan SQL Profiler trace files to recommend indexes that may improve performance. You can access it via the Management|Index Tuning Wizard option on the Tools|Wizards menu in Enterprise Manager or the Perform Index Analysis option on the Query menu in Query Analyzer.

SELECT Performance Tips

- Match query search columns with those leftmost in the index when possible. An index on stor_id, ord_num will not be of any help to a query that filters results on the ord_num column.

- Construct WHERE clauses that the query optimizer can recognize and use as search arguments. See the "SARGs" section later for more information.

- Don't use DISTINCT or ORDER BY "just in case." Use them if you need to remove duplicates or if you need to guarantee a particular result set order, respectively. Unless the optimizer can locate an index to service them, they can force the creation of an intermediate work table, which can be expensive in terms of performance.

- Use UNION ALL rather than UNION when you don't care about removing duplicates from a UNIONed result set. Because it removes duplicates, UNION must sort or hash the result set before returning it. Obviously, if you can avoid this, you can improve performance—sometimes dramatically.

- As mentioned earlier, you can use SET LOCK_TIMEOUT to control the amount of time a connection waits on a blocked resource. At session startup, @@LOCK_TIMEOUT returns –1, which means that no timeout value has been set yet. You can set LOCK_TIMEOUT to a positive integer to control the number of milliseconds a query will wait on a blocked resource before timing out. In highly contentious environments, this is sometimes necessary to prevent applications from appearing to hang.

- If a query includes an IN predicate that contains a list of constant values (rather than a subquery), order the values based on frequency of occurrence in the outer query, if you know the bias of your data well enough. A common approach is to order the values alphabetically or numerically, but that may not be optimal. Since the predicate returns true as soon as any of its values match, moving those that appear more often to the first of the list should speed up the query, especially if the column being searched is not indexed.

- Give preference to joins over nested subqueries. A subquery can require a nested iteration—a loop within a loop. During a nested iteration, the rows in the inner table are scanned for each row in the outer table. This works fine for smaller tables and was the only join strategy supported by SQL Server until version 7.0. However, as tables grow larger, this approach becomes less and less efficient. It's far better to perform normal joins between tables and let the optimizer decide how best to process them. The optimizer will usually take care of flattening unnecessary subqueries into joins, but it's always better to write efficient code in the first place.

- Avoid CROSS JOINs if you can. Unless you actually need the cross product of two tables, use a more succinct join form to relate one table to another. Returning an unintentional Cartesian product and then removing the duplicates it generates using DISTINCT or GROUP BY are a common problem among beginners and a frequent cause of serious query performance problems.

- You can use the TOP *n* extension to restrict the number of rows returned by a query. This is particularly handy when assigning variables using a SELECT statement because you may wish to see values from the first row of a table only.

- You can use the OPTION clause of a SELECT statement to influence the query optimizer directly through query hints. You can also specify hints for specific tables and joins. As a rule, you should allow the optimizer to optimize your queries, but you may run into situations where the execution plan it selects is less than ideal. Using query, table, and join hints, you can force a particular type of join, group, or union, the use of a particular index and so on. The section on the Transact-SQL SELECT statement in the Books Online documents the available hints and their effects on queries.

- If you are benchmarking one query against another to determine the most efficient way to access data, be sure to keep SQL Server's caching mechanisms from skewing your test results. One way to do this is to cycle the server between query runs. Another is to use undocumented DBCC command verbs to clear out the relevant caches. DBCC FREEPROCCACHE frees the procedure cache; DBCC DROPCLEANBUFFERS clears all caches.

INSERT Performance Tips

- Because individual row inserts aren't logged, SELECT...INTO is often many times faster than a regular logged INSERT. It can lock system tables, so use it with care. If you use SELECT...INTO to create a large table, other users may be unable to create objects in your database until the SELECT...INTO completes. This has particularly serious implications for tempdb because it can prevent users from creating temporary objects that might very well wreak havoc with your apps, lead to angry mobs with torches, and cause all sorts of panic and mayhem. That's not to say that you shouldn't use SELECT...INTO—just be careful not to monopolize a database when you do.

- BULK INSERT is faster than INSERT for loading external data, even when fully logged, because it operates at a lower level within the server. Use it rather than lengthy INSERT scripts to load large quantities of data onto the server.

Bulk Copy Performance Tips

- Use the new BULK INSERT command rather than the bcp utility to perform bulk load operations. Though, at the lowest level, they use the same facility that's been in SQL Server since its inception, data loaded via BULK INSERT doesn't navigate the Tabular Data Stream protocol, go through Open Data Services, or traverse the network. It's sent directly to SQL Server as an OLE-DB rowset. The upside of this is that it's much faster—sometimes twice as fast—as the bcp utility. The downside is that the data file being loaded must be accessible over the network *by the machine on which SQL Server is running*. This can present problems over a WAN (wide area network) where different segments of the network may be isolated from one another but where you can still access SQL Server via a routable protocol such as TCP/IP.

- If possible, lock tables during bulk load operations (e.g., BULK INSERT). This can significantly increase load speed by reducing lock contention on the table. The best way to do this is to enable the **table lock on bulk load** option via the sp_tableoption system procedure, though you can also force table locks for specific bulk load operations via the TABLOCK hint.

- Four criteria must be met in order to enable the minimally logged mode of the BULK INSERT command:

1. The table must be lockable (see the sp_tableoption recommendation).

2. The **select/into bulk copy** option must be turned on in the target database.

3. The table cannot be marked for replication.

4. If the table has indexes, they must also be empty.

Minimally logged (or "nonlogged" in Books Online parlance) bulk load operations are usually faster than logged operations, sometimes very much so, but even a logged BULK INSERT is faster than a series of INSERT statements. I call these operations minimally logged because page and extent allocations are logged regardless of the mode in which a bulk load operation runs (which is what allows it to be rolled back).

- You can bulk load data simultaneously from multiple clients provided that the following criteria are met:

  1. The table can have no indexes.

  2. The **select/into bulk copy** option must be enabled for the database.

  3. The target table must be locked (as mentioned, sp_tableoption is the best way of setting this up).

  Parallel bulk loading requires the ODBC version of the bulk data API, so DB-Library–based bulk loaders (such as the **bcp** utility from SQL Server 6.5) cannot participate. As with any mostly serial operation, running small pieces of it in parallel can yield remarkable performance gains. You can specify contiguous FIRSTROW/LASTROW sets to break a large input file into multiple BULK INSERT sets.

- Consider directing bulk inserts to a staging area when possible, preferably to a separate database. Since the minimally logged version of BULK INSERT prohibits indexes on the target table (including those created as a result of a PRIMARY KEY constraint), it's sensible to set up staging tables whose whole purpose is to receive data as quickly as possible from BULK INSERT. By placing these tables in a separate database, you avoid invalidating the transaction log in your other databases during bulk load operations. In fact, you might not have to enable **select into/bulkcopy** in any database except the staging area. Once the data is loaded into the staging area, you can then use stored procedures to move it in batches from one database to another.

- When bulk loading data, especially when you wish to do so from multiple clients simultaneously, consider dropping the target table's indexes before the operation and recreating them afterward. Since nonclustered indexes now reference the clustered index (when one is present) rather than the table itself, the constant shuffling and reshuffling of nonclustered index keys that was once characteristic of bulk load operations are mostly a thing of the past. In fact, dropping your indexes before a bulk load operation may not yield any perceptible performance gain. As with most of the recommendations in this chapter, trial and error should have the final word. Try it both ways and see which one performs better. There are situations where dropping indexes before a bulk load operation can improve performance by orders of magnitude, so it's worth your time to investigate.

- Consider breaking large BULK INSERT operations into batches via the BATCH-SIZE parameter. This lessens the load on the transaction log since each batch is committed separately. The upside is that this can speed up extremely large insert operations and improve concurrency considerably. The downside is that the target table will be left in an interim state if the operation is aborted for any reason. The batch that was being loaded when the operation aborted will be rolled back; however, all batches up to that point will remain in the database. With this in mind, it's wise to maintain a small LoadNumber column in your target table to help identify the rows appended by each bulk load operation.

DELETE and UPDATE Performance Tips

- Because individual row deletions aren't logged, TRUNCATE TABLE is usually many times faster than a logged DELETE. Like all minimally logged operations, it invalidates the transaction log, so use it with care.

- DELETE and UPDATE statements are normally qualified by a WHERE clause, so the admonitions regarding establishing search arguments for SELECT statements apply to them as well. The faster the engine can find the rows you want to modify, the faster it can process them.

Cursor Performance Tips

- Use cursors parsimoniously and only when absolutely necessary (perhaps at gunpoint or when your mother-in-law comes to visit). Try to find a noncursor approach to solving problems. You'll be surprised at how many problems you can solve with the diversely adept SELECT statement.

- Consider asynchronous cursors for extremely large result sets. Returning a cursor asynchronously allows you to continue processing while the cursor is being populated. OPEN can return almost immediately when used with an asynchronous cursor. See Chapter 13, "Cursors," for more information on asynchronous cursors.

- Don't use static or keyset cursors unless you really need their unique features. Opening a static or keyset cursor causes a temporary table to be created so that a second copy of its rows or keys can be referenced by the cursor. Obviously, you want to avoid this if you can.

- If you don't need to change the data a cursor returns, define it using the READ_ONLY keyword. This alleviates the possibility of accidental changes and notifies the server that the rows the cursor traverses won't be changed.

- Use the FAST_FORWARD cursor option rather than FORWARD_ONLY when setting up read-only, forward-only result sets. FAST_FORWARD creates a FORWARD_ONLY, READ_ONLY cursor with a number of built-in performance optimizations.

- Be wary of updating key columns via dynamic cursors on tables with nonunique clustered index keys because this can result in the "Halloween Problem." SQL Server forces nonunique clustered index keys to be unique internally by suffixing them with a sequence number. If you update one of these keys, it's possible that you could cause a value that already exists to be generated and force the server to append a suffix that would move it later in the result set (if the cursor was ordered by the clustered index). Since the cursor is dynamic, fetching through the remainder of the result set would yield the row again, and the process would repeat itself, resulting in an infinite loop.

- Avoid modifying a large number of rows using a cursor loop contained within a transaction because each row you change may remain locked until the end of the transaction, depending on the transaction isolation level.

Stored Procedure Performance Tips

- Use stored procedures rather than ad hoc queries whenever possible. For the cached execution plan of an ad hoc SQL statement to be reused, a subsequent query will have to match it exactly and must fully qualify every object it references. If anything about a subsequent use of the query is different—parameters, object names, key elements of the SET environment—anything—the plan won't be reused. A good workaround for the limitations of ad hoc queries is to use the sp_executesql system stored procedure. It covers the middle ground between rigid stored procedures and ad hoc Transact-SQL queries by allowing you to execute ad hoc queries with replaceable parameters. This facilitates reusing ad hoc execution plans without requiring exact textual matches.

- If you know that a small portion of a stored procedure needs to have its query plan rebuilt with each execution (e.g., due to data changes that render the plan suboptimal) but don't want to incur the overhead of rebuilding the plan for the entire procedure each time, you should try moving it to its own procedure. This allows its execution plan to be rebuilt each time you run it without affecting the larger procedure. If this isn't possible, try using the EXEC() function to call the suspect code from the main procedure, essentially creating a poor man's subroutine. Since it's built dynamically, this subroutine can have a new plan generated with each execution without affecting the query plan for the stored procedure as a whole.

- Use stored procedure output parameters rather than result sets when possible. If you need to return the result of a computation or to locate a single value in a table, return it as a stored procedure output parameter rather than a singleton result set. Even if you're returning multiple columns, stored procedure output parameters are far more efficient than full-fledged result sets.

- Consider using cursor output parameters rather than "firehose" cursors (result sets) when you need to return a set of rows from one stored procedure to another. This is more flexible and can allow the second procedure to return more quickly since no result set processing occurs. The caller can then process the rows returned by the cursor at its leisure.

- Minimize the number of network round-trips between clients and the server. One very effective way to do this is to disable DONE_IN_PROC messages. You can disable them at the procedure level via SET NOCOUNT or at the server level with the trace flag 3640. Especially over relatively slow networks such as WANs, this can make a huge performance difference. If you elect not to use trace flag 3640, SET NOCOUNT ON should be near the top of every stored procedure you write.

- Use DBCC PROCCACHE to list info about the procedure cache when tuning queries. Use DBCC FREEPROCCACHE to clear the procedure cache in order to keep multiple executions of a given procedure from skewing benchmark results. Use DBCC FLUSHPROCINDB to force the recreation of all procedure execution plans for a given database.

- You can query the syscacheobjects table in the master database to list caching information for procedures, triggers, and other objects. One key piece of information that's reported by syscacheobjects is the number of plans in the cache for a particular object. This can help you determine whether a plan is being reused when you execute a procedure. Syscacheobjects is a pseudotable—it does not actually exist—the server materializes it each time you query it (you can execute **SELECT OBJECTPROPERTY(OBJECT_ID('syscacheobjects'), 'TableIsFake')** to verify this). Here's a stored procedure that reports on the procedure cache and queries syscacheobjects for you:

```
USE master
IF OBJECT_ID('sp_helpproccache') IS NOT NULL
   DROP PROC sp_helpproccache
GO
CREATE PROCEDURE sp_helpproccache @dbname sysname = NULL,
   @procsonly varchar(3)='NO',
   @executableonly varchar(3)='NO'
/*
Object: sp_helpproccache
Description: Lists information about the procedure cache

Usage: sp_helpproccache @dbname=name of database to list; pass ALL to list
all,
   @procsonly=[yes|NO] list stored procedures only,
   @executableonly=[yes|NO] list executable plans only

Returns: (None)
```

```
Created by: Ken Henderson. Email: khen@khen.com

Version: 1.3

Example: EXEC sp_helpproccache "ALL", @proconly="YES"

Created: 1999-06-02. Last changed: 1999-08-11.
*/
AS
SET NOCOUNT ON
DECLARE @sqlstr varchar(8000)

IF (@dbname='/?') GOTO Help
DBCC PROCCACHE
PRINT ''

SET @sqlstr=
"SELECT LEFT(o.name,30) AS 'Procedure',
    LEFT(cacheobjtype,30) AS 'Type of Plan',
    COUNT(*) AS 'Number of Plans'
FROM master..syscacheobjects c JOIN ?..sysobjects o ON (c.objid=o.id)
WHERE dbid = db_id('?')"+
  CASE @procsonly WHEN 'YES' THEN ' and objtype = "Proc" ' ELSE ' ' END+
  CASE @executableonly WHEN 'YES' THEN
    ' and cacheobjtype = "Executable Plan" ' ELSE ' ' END+
  "GROUP BY o.name, cacheobjtype
  ORDER BY o.name, cacheobjtype"

IF (@dbname='ALL')
    EXEC sp_MSforeachdb @command1="PRINT '***Displaying the procedure cache for
    database: ?'",
    @command2='PRINT ""', @command3=@sqlstr
ELSE BEGIN
  PRINT '***Displaying the procedure cache for database: '+DB_NAME()
  PRINT ''
  SET @sqlstr=REPLACE(@sqlstr,'?',DB_NAME())
  EXEC(@sqlstr)
END
RETURN 0

Help:
EXEC sp_usage @objectname='sp_helproccache',
    @desc='Lists information about the procedure cache',
    @parameters='@dbname=name of database to list; pass ALL to list all,
    @procsonly=[yes|NO] list stored procedures only,
    @executableonly=[yes|NO] list executable plans only',
    @example='EXEC sp_helpproccache "ALL", @proconly="YES"',
    @author='Ken Henderson',
    @email='khen@khen.com',
    @version='1', @revision='3',
    @datecreated='6/2/99', @datelastchanged='8/11/99'
RETURN -1

GO
EXEC sp_helpproccache 'ALL'
```

(Results abridged)

num proc buffs	num proc buffs used	num proc buffs active	proc cache size	proc cache used
574	574	162	617	617

***Displaying the procedure cache for database: master

Procedure	Type of Plan	Number of Plans
sp_databases	Compiled Plan	1
sp_dir	Compiled Plan	3
sp_dir	Executable Plan	3
sp_executesql	Extended Proc	1
sp_helpproccache	Compiled Plan	1
sp_MSforeach_worker	Compiled Plan	1
sp_MSforeachdb	Compiled Plan	1
sp_table	Compiled Plan	1
sp_table	Executable Plan	1
sp_usage	Compiled Plan	1
sp_usage	Executable Plan	1
syscomments	Parse Tree	1

***Displaying the procedure cache for database: msdb

Procedure	Type of Plan	Number of Plans
sysindexes	Parse Tree	1
sysobjects	Parse Tree	1
systypes	Parse Tree	1

***Displaying the procedure cache for database: Northwind

Procedure	Type of Plan	Number of Plans
syscolumns	Parse Tree	1
sysindexes	Parse Tree	1
sysobjects	Parse Tree	1
systypes	Parse Tree	1

***Displaying the procedure cache for database: pubs

Procedure	Type of Plan	Number of Plans
author_crosstab	Compiled Plan	1
author_crosstab	Executable Plan	1
CK__authors__au_id__08EA5793	Parse Tree	1
sysindexes	Parse Tree	1
sysobjects	Parse Tree	1
systypes	Parse Tree	1

```
***Displaying the procedure cache for database: SCW_TS

Procedure                        Type of Plan      Number of Plans
------------------------------   ----------------  ---------------

***Displaying the procedure cache for database: tempdb

Procedure                        Type of Plan      Number of Plans
------------------------------   ----------------  ---------------
```

SARGs

Strive to construct queries that are "SARGable." A SARG, or search argument, is a clause in a query that the optimizer can potentially use in conjunction with an index to limit the results returned by the query. SARGs have the form:

```
Column op Constant/Variable
```

(the terms can be reversed) where **Column** is a table column; **op** is one of the following inclusive operators: $=, >=, <=, >, <$, BETWEEN, and LIKE (some LIKE clauses qualify as SARGs; some don't—see below for details); and **Constant/Variable** is a constant value or variable reference.

SARGs can be joined together with AND to form compound clauses. The rule of thumb for identifying SARGs is that a clause can be a useful search argument if the optimizer can detect that it's a comparison between an index key value and a constant or variable. A clause that compares two columns or one that compares two expressions is not a SARG clause. A common beginner's error is to wrap a column in a function or expression when comparing it with a constant or variable. This prevents the clause from being a SARG because the optimizer doesn't know what the expression is actually evaluating—it's not known until runtime. Here's an example of such a query.

```
-- Don't do this -- Bad T-SQL
SELECT city, state, zip FROM authors
WHERE au_lname+', '+au_fname='Dull, Ann'

city                 state zip
-------------------- ----- -----
Palo Alto            CA    94301
```

Better written, this query might look like this:

```
SELECT city, state, zip
FROM authors
WHERE au_lname='Dull'
AND au_fname='Ann'
```

To see the difference this small change makes, let's look at the execution plan generated by each. To enable execution plan viewing in Query Analyzer, press Ctrl-K or select Show Execution Plan from the Query menu and run the query. Figure 16.1 shows the execution plan for the first query, and Figure 16.2 shows the plan for the second query.

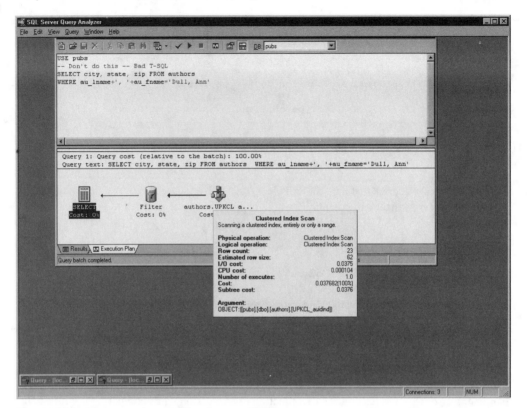

Figure 16.1. The execution plan for the non-SARG query.

You can view details for a particular execution plan step by resting your mouse pointer over it. Execution plans read from right to left, so start with the rightmost node and work your way to the left. See the difference? The concatenation of the au_lname and au_fname columns in the first query prevents the use of the aunmind index—whose keys feature both columns. Instead, the first query must use the table's clustered index, whose key is the au_id column, not terribly useful for locating an author by name (it's effectively a table scan). By contrast, the second query is able to use the author name index because it correctly avoids confusing the optimizer with unnecessary string concatenation.

Let's consider some additional queries and determine whether they're "SARGable." We'll begin by adding a few indexes for the sake of comparison. Run the following script to set up some additional secondary indexes:

```
USE pubs
CREATE INDEX qty ON sales (qty)
CREATE INDEX pub_name ON publishers (pub_name)
CREATE INDEX hirange ON roysched (hirange)
USE Northwind
CREATE INDEX ContactName ON Customers (ContactName)
```

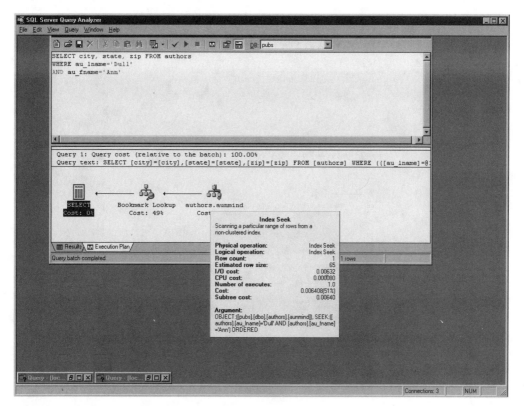

Figure 16.2. The execution plan for the SARG query.

Here's a query that selects rows from the pubs sales table based on the qty column:

```
SELECT *
FROM sales
WHERE qty+1 > 10
```

Does the WHERE clause contain a SARG? Let's look at the execution plan (Figure 16.3).
The optimizer has chosen a clustered index scan—essentially a sequential read of the entire table—even though there's an index on the qty column. Why? Because the qty column in the query is involved in an expression. As mentioned before, enclosing a table column in an expression prevents it from being useful to the optimizer as a SARG. Let's rewrite the query's WHERE clause such that the qty column stands alone (Figure 16.4):

```
SELECT *
FROM sales
WHERE qty > 9
```

Since an unfettered qty is now being compared with a constant, the optimizer elects to use the index we added earlier.

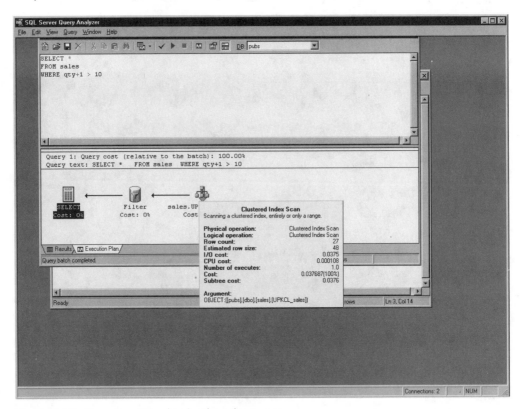

Figure 16.3. The execution plan for the sales query.

Here's another example (Figure 16.5):

```
SELECT * FROM authors
WHERE au_lname LIKE '%Gr%'
```

Once again, the optimizer has elected to do a clustered index scan rather than use the non-clustered index that's built on the au_lname column. The reason for this is simple—it can't translate the LIKE mask into a usable SARG. Let's rewrite the query to make it SARGable (Figure 16.6):

```
SELECT au_lname, au_fname
FROM authors
WHERE au_lname LIKE 'Gr%'
```

Figure 16.4. The new, improved execution plan for the sales query.

> **Note**
> In addition to their obvious syntactical differences, the LIKE masks of the two
> queries differ functionally as well. Strictly speaking, they don't ask quite the
> same question. I'm assuming here that the query author *intended* to ask for
> all names beginning with 'Gr' even though the first mask is prefixed with a
> wildcard.

Now the optimizer elects to use the nonclustered index on the table that includes au_lname
as its high-order key. Internally, the optimizer translates

```
au_lname LIKE 'Gr%'
```

to

```
au_lname > 'GQ_' AND au_lname < 'GS'
```

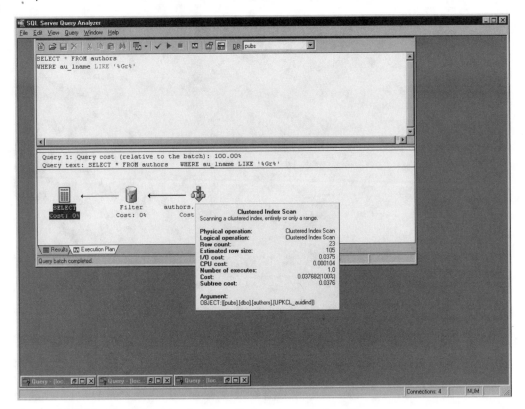

Figure 16.5. The execution plan for the authors query.

This allows specific key values in the index to be referenced. Value 'GQ_' can be located in the index (or its closest matching key) and the keys following it read sequentially until 'GS' is reached. The '_' character has the ASCII value of 254, so 'GQ_' is two values before 'Gr' followed by any character. This ensures that the first value beginning with 'Gr' is located.

Let's look at a similar query with two wildcards:

```
SELECT *
FROM publishers
WHERE pub_name LIKE 'New%Moon%'
```

And here's the execution plan (notice the internal translation of the WHERE clause similar to the previous example) (Figure 16.7).

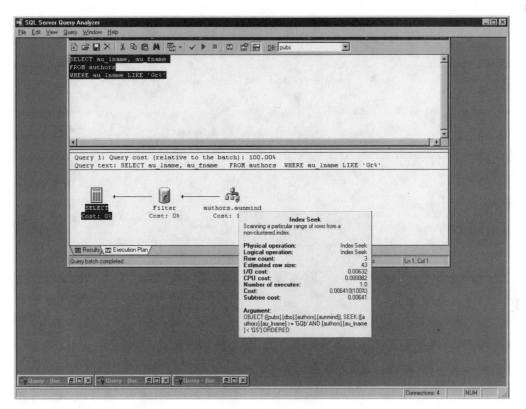

Figure 16.6. The execution plan for the improved authors query.

LIKE expressions that can be restated in terms of "x is greater than value y and less than value z" are useful to the optimizer as SARGs—otherwise they aren't.

Here's another query that references the qty column in the pubs sales table (Figure 16.8):

```
SELECT *
FROM sales
WHERE qty BETWEEN 20 AND 30
```

Again, the query optimizer translates the WHERE clause into a pair of expressions it finds more useful. It converts the BETWEEN clause into a compound SARG that uses the simpler >= and <= operators to implement BETWEEN's inclusive search behavior.

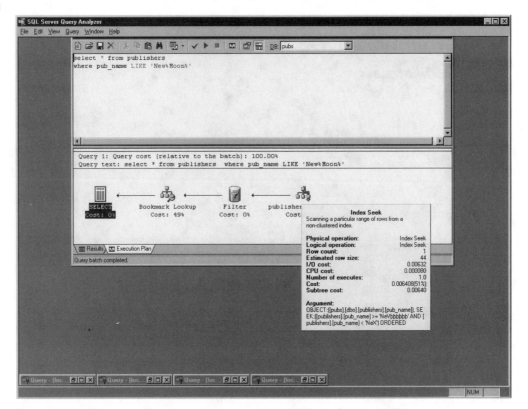

Figure 16.7. When possible, the optimizer translates LIKE clauses into SARGs.

Here's an example that places the constant on the left of the operator (Figure 16.9):

```
SELECT * FROM roysched
WHERE 5000 < hirange
```

As you can see, the ordering of the terms doesn't matter—the SARG is still correctly identified and matched with the appropriate index.

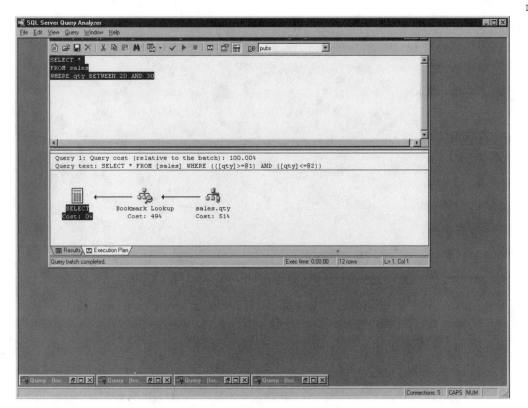

Figure 16.8. The query optimizer translates BETWEEN into a compound SARG clause.

Let's look at another query on the sales table. This one involves a search on two columns:

```
SELECT * FROM sales
WHERE qty > 40 OR stor_id=6380
```

Prior to SQL Server 7.0, the server would use only one index per table, regardless of how many columns from the same table you listed in the WHERE clause. That's no longer the case, and, as you can see from the query's execution plan, the table's clustered index and the nonclustered index we built on the qty column earlier are used to populate the result set. Since we joined the two SARG clauses via OR, they're processed in parallel using the appropriate index and then combined using a "hash match" operation just before being returned as a result set (Figure 16.10).

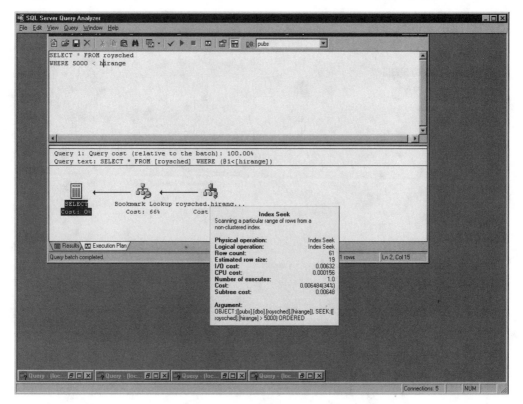

Figure 16.9. The query optimizer correctly identifies constant-first SARGs.

In the past, inequalities were the Achilles heel of the query optimizer—it didn't know how to translate them into index key values and consequently would perform a full scan of the table in order to service them. That's still true on some DBMSs but not SQL Server. For example, consider this query:

```
SELECT *
FROM sales
WHERE qty != 0
```

Figure 16.11 shows the execution plan we get.

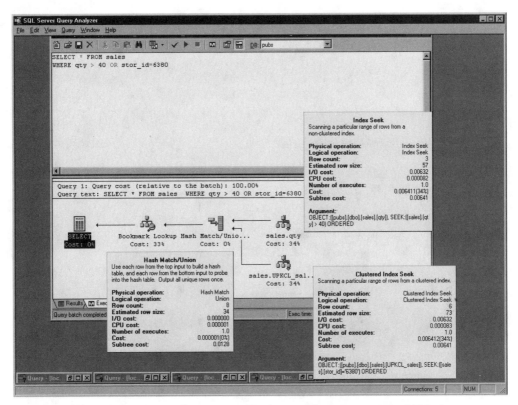

Figure 16.10. This execution plan features a "hash match" of two separate SARG clauses.

The optimizer translates

```
qty !=0
```

to

```
qty < 0 OR qty > 0
```

This allows comparisons with specific index key values and facilitates the use of the index we built earlier, as the execution plan shows.

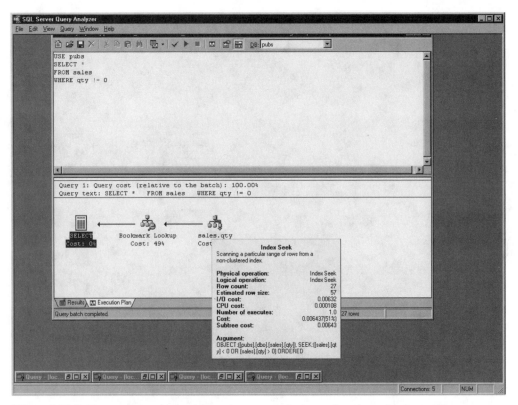

Figure 16.11. The query optimizer knows how to optimize comparisons for inequality.

Here's an example that filters the result set based on parts of a date column—a common need and an area rife with common pitfalls:

```
USE Northwind
SELECT * FROM Orders
WHERE DATEPART(mm,OrderDate)=5
AND DATEPART(yy,OrderDate)=1998
AND (DATEPART(dd,OrderDate) BETWEEN 1 AND 3)
```

This query requests the orders for the first three days of a specified month. Figure 16.12 shows the execution plan it produces.

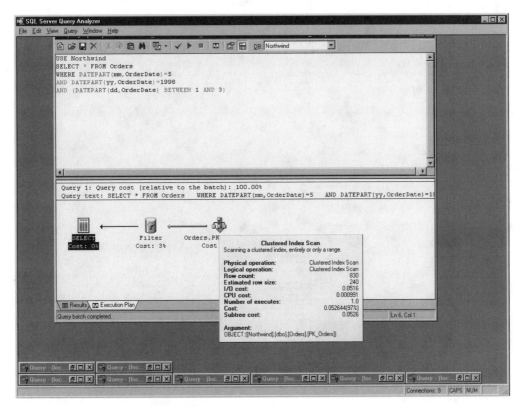

Figure 16.12. The execution plan for the first rendition of the date query.

This execution plan performs a sequential scan of the clustered index and then filters the result according to the WHERE clause criteria. Is the query optimizer able to use any of the WHERE clause criteria as SARGs? No. Once again, table columns are ensconced in expressions—the optimizer has no way of knowing what those expressions actually render. Here's the query rewritten such that it allows the optimizer to recognize SARGs (Figure 16.13):

```
USE Northwind
SELECT * FROM Orders
WHERE OrderDate BETWEEN '19980501' AND '19980503'
```

As you can see, the optimizer now properly recognizes and uses the SARGs in the WHERE clause to filter the query. It translates the BETWEEN clause into a compound SARG that uses the OrderDate index of the Orders table.

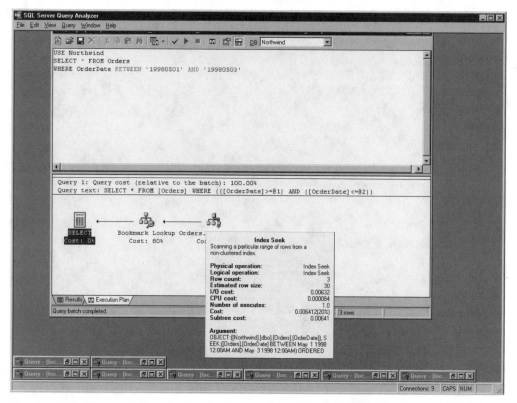

Figure 16.13. The execution plan for the improved version of the date query.

What happens if we want more than three days of data? What if we want the whole month? Here's the first query rewritten to request an entire month's worth of data (Figure 16.14):

```
USE Northwind
SELECT * FROM Orders
WHERE DATEPART(mm,OrderDate)=5
AND DATEPART(yy,OrderDate)=1998
```

And here's the improved version of the query, similarly modified (Figure 16.15):

```
USE Northwind
SELECT * FROM Orders
WHERE OrderDate BETWEEN '19980501' AND '19980531'
```

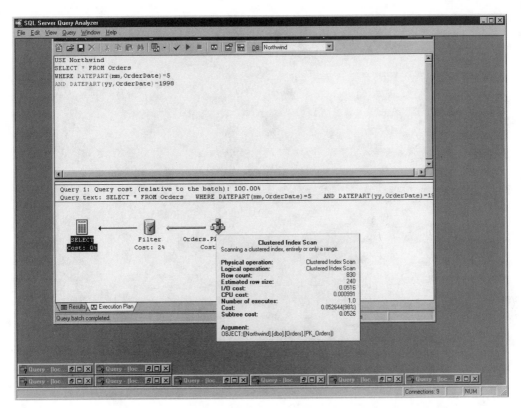

Figure 16.14. The original query still performs a sequential scan of the clustered index.

Interestingly, the improved query now scans the clustered index as well. Why? The amount of data being returned is the key. The optimizer has estimated that it's less expensive to scan the entire table and filter results sequentially than to use the nonclustered index because each row located via the index must then be looked up in the clustered index (or underlying table if no clustered index exists) in order to retrieve the other columns the query requests.

The step in the execution plan where this occurs is called the "Bookmark lookup" step (see Figure 16.13 for an example). An execution plan that locates rows using a nonclustered index must include a Bookmark lookup step if it returns columns other than those in the index. In this case, the optimizer has estimated that the overhead of this additional step is sufficient to warrant a full clustered index scan. In the original query, this step accounted for 80% of the execution plan's total work, so this makes sense. We've now multiplied the number of rows being returned several times over, so this step has become so lengthy that it's actually more efficient just to read the entire table.

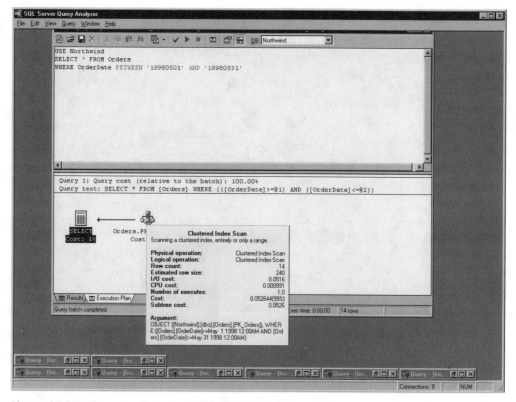

Figure 16.15. The execution plan of the SARGable date query.

There are a couple of ways around this. We've already explored one of them—returning less data. In fact, the threshold at which the optimizer decides it's more efficient to perform a sequential scan is at five days' worth of Orders data—returning five or more days results in a clustered index scan. Another way around this would be to eliminate the Bookmark lookup step altogether by satisfying the query with a nonclustered index. To do this, we'd either have to create a nonclustered index containing the columns we want to return (the wider the index key becomes, the more expensive using it becomes in terms of I/O) or narrow the columns we request to those already in a nonclustered index. In this case, that would mean requesting only the OrderDate column from the table since that's the lone key column of the nonclustered index we're using (by virtue of the WHERE clause criteria). Here's the query revised to request only the OrderDate column and its accompanying execution plan (Figure 16.16):

```
USE Northwind
SELECT OrderDate FROM Orders
WHERE OrderDate BETWEEN '19980501' AND '19980531'
```

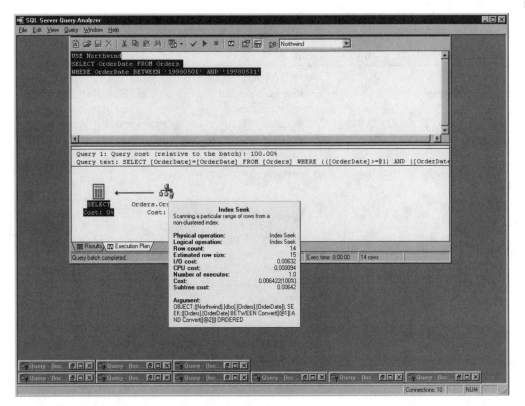

Figure 16.16. The execution plan of the covered date query.

Now, neither the clustered index nor the Bookmark lookup step is needed. As mentioned earlier, this is called *index covering,* meaning that the nonclustered index covers the query—it's able to satisfy it—without referencing the underlying table or its clustered index.

Practically speaking, it's pretty rare that you'll find a nonclustered index whose key columns satisfy a query completely. However, you'll often find that adding a column or two to the nonclustered index used by a query allows it to cover the query without becoming excessively expensive. Keep in mind that widening nonclustered index key columns results in slower updates, because they must be kept up to date, and slower query processing, because they're physically larger—they require more I/O and more memory to process.

Table 16.1 lists some examples of SARGable and non-SARGable clauses.

Table 16.1. SARGs and non-SARGs.

Clause	SARG-able?	Reason	Should be
qty+1 > 10	No	Column involved in expression	qty > 9
au_lname LIKE '%Gr%'	No	Optimizer must scan all rows for a match	au_lname LIKE 'Gr%' (if seeking names beginning with "Gr")
pub_name LIKE 'New Moon%'	Yes	Optimizer can gen code to seek to 'New Moon'	
qty BETWEEN 20 AND 30	Yes	Optimizer can gen code to seek to 20	
5000 < hirange	Yes	Optimizer can gen code to seek to 5000	
ContactName='Hanna Moos'	Yes	Optimizer can gen code to seek literal value	
qty > 40 OR stor_id=6380	Yes	Optimizer can gen code to perform a Hash Match using two separate indexes	
qty != 0	Yes	Optimizer translates to **qty <0 OR qty >0**	
DATEPART(mm, OrderDate)=5 AND DATEPART(yy, OrderDate)=2000	No	Column involved in expression	BETWEEN '20000501' AND '20000531'
LEFT(au_lname, 2) = 'Gr'	No	Column involved in expression	au_lname LIKE 'Gr%'
au_lname LIKE 'S%'	Yes	Optimizer translates to au_lname > 'R_' and au_lname < 'T'	

Denormalization

Especially among developers new to relational databases, there's sometimes a temptation to attribute poor database design to "denormalization for performance." You can't know for certain whether denormalizing a database is necessary until you've first normalized it and tested performance thoroughly. Even then, denormalizing shouldn't be your first option—it should be near the bottom of the list. I wouldn't recommend denormalization as the first method of fixing a performance problem any more than I'd recommend brain surgery for a headache. As a rule, garden-variety applications' development does not require database denormalization. If it did, the database design standards that have been forged and refined over the last thirty years wouldn't be worth much—what good is a standard if you have to break it in order to do anything useful?

That said, denormalization is a fairly common method of improving query performance—especially in high-performance and high-throughput systems. Eliminating a single join operation from a query that processes millions of rows can yield real dividends.

Understand that there's no absolute standard of measurement by which a database either is or isn't normalized. There are different degrees of normalization, but even the best database designers build databases that fail to measure up in some way to someone else's concept of normalization.

Basic Guidelines

- Know your database. Be sure you understand how it's organized from a logical standpoint, and be sure you know how applications use it. Have a good understanding of the database's data integrity setup. Introducing redundant data into the system makes maintaining data integrity more difficult and more expensive in terms of performance. It's therefore crucial to understand the *frequency* of data modifications. If the database serves a high-throughput OLTP application, you may find that the performance gains you achieved through denormalization are offset by the performance problems its creates in maintaining data integrity.

- Don't denormalize the entire database at once. Start small, working with logically separable pieces.

- Ascertain early on whether computed or contrived columns would address your performance needs. You may find that SQL Server's computed columns provide the performance your app requires without having to resort to large-scale denormalization.

- Become intimate with the data volume and the transaction types underlying the parts of your application having performance problems. You will probably find that you can further tune your queries or the server and resolve those problems without having to redesign the database.

- Become acquainted with the material resources of your server machine. Increasing the physical memory in the machine or the amount that's allocated to the SQL Server process may improve query performance dramatically. Adding or upgrading processors may help—especially if you have key queries that are CPU-bound. The biggest gains in terms of system performance usually come from hard drive–related optimizations. Using a speedier hard drive or more of them may improve performance by orders of magnitude. For example, you may find that using RAID in conjunction with filegroups can resolve your performance problems without having to denormalize.

Basic Techniques

A number of techniques that you can use to denormalize a database and hopefully improve performance exist:

- Creating contrived or virtual columns
- Maintaining redundant copies of data

- Keeping summary tables

- Partitioning data horizontally or vertically

Contrived Columns

A contrived or virtual column is one that's composed of the values from other columns. SQL Server includes direct support for contrived columns through its computed column support. Setting up a computed column saves you from having to include its underlying expression each time you query the table. It's syntactically more compact and makes the expression's result readily available to anyone who uses the table. You define computed columns with the CREATE TABLE or ALTER TABLE command. Here's an example:

```
USE Northwind
GO
ALTER TABLE Orders ADD DaysToShip AS CASE WHEN ShippedDate IS NULL THEN
DATEDIFF(dd,OrderDate,RequiredDate) ELSE NULL END
GO
SELECT OrderId, CONVERT(char(10),OrderDate,101) AS OrderDate,
   CONVERT(char(10),RequiredDate,101) AS RequiredDate,
   CONVERT(char(10),ShippedDate,101) AS ShippedDate,
   DaysToShip FROM Orders
GO
ALTER TABLE Orders DROP COLUMN DaysToShip
GO
```

(Results abridged)

OrderId	OrderDate	RequiredDate	ShippedDate	DaysToShip
11058	04/29/1998	05/27/1998	NULL	28
11059	04/29/1998	06/10/1998	NULL	42
11060	04/30/1998	05/28/1998	05/04/1998	NULL
11061	04/30/1998	06/11/1998	NULL	42
11062	04/30/1998	05/28/1998	NULL	28
11063	04/30/1998	05/28/1998	05/06/1998	NULL
11064	05/01/1998	05/29/1998	05/04/1998	NULL
11065	05/01/1998	05/29/1998	NULL	28

Redundant Data

A common denormalization technique is to maintain multiple copies of the same data. For example, you may find that it's worthwhile to look up and store join values in advance. This cuts down on the work necessary to return useful information when you query a table. A variation on this duplicates foreign key values so that they don't have to be referenced across tables. Of course, you'll want to be careful with this because it adds additional overhead to maintaining data integrity. The more copies of data you have, the more work required to keep it up to date and the more likely a mishap can compromise database integrity. The corollary to this is the essence of the relational model: The fewer copies of nonkey data you have, the easier it is to maintain and the less likely its integrity is to be damaged in the event of problems.

Here's an example that adds columns for the first and last names of authors to the pubs titleauthor table:

```
ALTER TABLE titleauthor ADD au_lname varchar(40) NULL, au_fname varchar(20)
NULL
GO
UPDATE t
  SET au_lname=a.au_lname,
    au_fname=a.au_fname
FROM titleauthor t JOIN authors a ON (t.au_id=a.au_id)
GO
SELECT * FROM titleauthor
GO
ALTER TABLE titleauthor DROP COLUMN au_lname
ALTER TABLE titleauthor DROP COLUMN au_fname
```

au_id	title_id	au_ord	royaltyper	au_lname	au_fname
172-32-1176	PS3333	1	100	White	Johnson
213-46-8915	BU1032	2	40	Green	Marjorie
213-46-8915	BU2075	1	100	Green	Marjorie
238-95-7766	PC1035	1	100	Carson	Cheryl

By adding these redundant columns to titleauthor, we've eliminated one of the joins that must be performed in order to return useful information from the table. For a query processing millions of rows, this can make a significant difference in performance. Of course, a mechanism similar to the UPDATE featured in the example must be used to ensure that these redundant values are properly maintained.

Summary Tables

An increasingly common method of denormalizing for performance involves the creation of summary tables—tables that summarize detail data from other tables. The technique has become so popular, in fact, that some DBMS vendors offer built-in support for summary tables.

Building a summary table typically consists of running a popular query (that perhaps takes an extended period of time to run) ahead of time and storing its results in a summary table. When applications need access to the data, they access this static table. Then—during off-peak periods or whenever it's convenient—the summary query can be rerun and the table updated with the latest info. This works well and is a viable alternative to executing lengthy queries repetitively.

One problem with this approach is in administration. Setting up a summary table counterpart for a detail table doubles the administrative work on that table. If you had ten stored procedures on the original table, you are likely to need twenty now. Everything you did for the detail table in terms of administration must now be done redundantly—all triggers, constraints, etc. must be maintained in two places now rather than one. The more summary tables you have, the more headaches you have.

An option that solves the administrative dilemma while providing the query performance gains of summary tables is what I call *inline summarization*. Inline summarization involves changing the original detail table slightly so that it can store summary as well as detail data, then summarizing a portion of it and inserting that summary data back into the table itself, optionally removing or archiving the original detail rows. One of the benefits of this approach is that summary and detail data can be easily queried together or separately—in fact, queries over the table normally don't know whether they're working with detail or summary data. Subtle clues can indicate which rows are summary rows, but they are otherwise indistinguishable from their detail siblings. Note that, strictly speaking, if you remove the detail data, you also avoid the problems that accompany keeping redundant data. Another benefit of this approach is that you don't have the redundant administration hassles that accompany the separate table approach. All the foreign key references, triggers, constraints, views, query batches, and stored procedures that worked with the detail data work automatically with summary data, too.

This is best explored by way of example. Here's a query that performs inline summarization on the Orders table in the Northwind sample database:

```
USE Northwind
GO
ALTER TABLE Orders ADD NumberOfOrders int DEFAULT 1 -- Add summary column
GO
UPDATE Orders SET NumberOfOrders=DEFAULT -- Force current rows to contain DEFAULT value
GO
-- Insert summary info
INSERT Orders (CustomerID, EmployeeID, OrderDate, RequiredDate, ShippedDate,
    ShipVia, Freight, ShipName, ShipAddress, ShipCity,
    ShipRegion, ShipPostalCode, ShipCountry, NumberOfOrders)
SELECT NULL, EmployeeID, CONVERT(char(6), OrderDate, 112)+'01',
    '19000101', '19000101',1,0,'','','','','','',COUNT(*) -- Summarize rows
FROM Orders
WHERE OrderDate < '19980101'
GROUP BY EmployeeID, CONVERT(char(6), OrderDate, 112)+'01'

-- Delete Order Details rows corresponding to summarized rows
DELETE d
FROM [Order Details] d JOIN Orders o ON d.OrderID=o.OrderID
WHERE o.OrderDate <'19980101' AND RequiredDate > '19000101'
-- Use RequiredDate to leave summary rows

-- Delete nonsummary versions of rows that were summarized
DELETE Orders
WHERE OrderDate < '19980101' AND RequiredDate > '19000101'
-- Use RequiredDate to leave summary rows
```

This query begins by adding a new column to the Orders table, NumberOfOrders. In the past, determining the number of orders on file involved using COUNT(*). Inline summarization changes that. It uses NumberOfOrders to indicate the number of orders a given row represents. In the case of detail tables, this is always "1"—hence the DEFAULT constraint. In the case of summary rows, this could be any number up to the maximum **int** can store. So, to aggregate the number of orders, we simply sum the NumberOfOrders column. Regardless of whether the rows summed are detail or summary rows, this works as we expect.

What this means is that instead of running this query to list the number of orders per month:

```
SELECT CONVERT(char(6), OrderDate, 112) AS OrderMonth,
COUNT(*) AS TotalNumberOfOrders -- Use COUNT() to count the number of orders
FROM Orders
GROUP BY CONVERT(char(6), OrderDate, 112)
ORDER BY OrderMonth
```

(Results)

```
OrderMonth TotalNumberOfOrders
---------- -------------------
199607     22
199608     25
199609     23
199610     26
199611     25
199612     31
199701     33
199702     29
199703     30
199704     31
199705     32
199706     30
199707     33
199708     33
199709     37
199710     38
199711     34
199712     48
199801     55
199802     54
199803     73
199804     74
199805     14
```

we run this one:

```
SELECT CONVERT(char(6), OrderDate, 112) AS OrderMonth,
SUM(NumberOfOrders) AS TotalNumberOfOrders -- Use SUM to return the order count
FROM Orders
GROUP BY CONVERT(char(6), OrderDate, 112)
ORDER BY OrderMonth
```

(Results)

```
OrderMonth TotalNumberOfOrders
---------- -------------------
199607     22
199608     25
199609     23
199610     26
199611     25
199612     31
199701     33
199702     29
199703     30
199704     31
199705     32
199706     30
199707     33
199708     33
199709     37
199710     38
199711     34
```

```
199712      48
199801      55
199802      54
199803      73
199804      74
199805      14
```

It's perhaps helpful to look at the data itself. Here's a small sample of it:

```
SELECT CustomerID, EmployeeID, OrderDate, RequiredDate, NumberOfOrders
FROM Orders
WHERE OrderDate BETWEEN '19971201' AND '19980101'
ORDER BY OrderDate, EmployeeID
```

(Results)

```
CustomerID EmployeeID  OrderDate                RequiredDate             NumberOfOrders
---------- ----------- ------------------------ ------------------------ --------------
NULL       1           1997-12-01 00:00:00.000  1900-01-01 00:00:00.000  7
NULL       2           1997-12-01 00:00:00.000  1900-01-01 00:00:00.000  5
NULL       3           1997-12-01 00:00:00.000  1900-01-01 00:00:00.000  11
NULL       4           1997-12-01 00:00:00.000  1900-01-01 00:00:00.000  10
NULL       5           1997-12-01 00:00:00.000  1900-01-01 00:00:00.000  1
NULL       6           1997-12-01 00:00:00.000  1900-01-01 00:00:00.000  5
NULL       7           1997-12-01 00:00:00.000  1900-01-01 00:00:00.000  3
NULL       8           1997-12-01 00:00:00.000  1900-01-01 00:00:00.000  3
NULL       9           1997-12-01 00:00:00.000  1900-01-01 00:00:00.000  3
OLDWO      2           1998-01-01 00:00:00.000  1998-01-29 00:00:00.000  1
LAUGB      2           1998-01-01 00:00:00.000  1998-01-29 00:00:00.000  1
WELLI      7           1998-01-01 00:00:00.000  1998-01-29 00:00:00.000  1
```

Notice that the CustomerID column is NULL in summary rows because we summed on EmployeeID and OrderMonth. This is one way to distinguish summary rows from detail rows. Another way is to inspect the RequireDate column—it's always set to 01/01/1900—SQL Server's base date—in summary rows.

Vertical Partitioning

Since SQL Server uses a fixed database page size of 8KB and a single row cannot span pages, the number of rows that will fit on a page is determined by row width. The wider a row, the fewer rows that fit on each page. Physically splitting a table vertically into multiple tables allows more rows to fit on a page, potentially increasing query performance. Here's an example that vertically partitions the Orders table in the Northwind sample database:

```
SET NOCOUNT ON
USE Northwind
BEGIN TRAN -- So we can undo all this

DECLARE @pagebin binary(6), @file int, @page int

-- Get the first page of the table (usually)
SELECT TOP 1 @pagebin=first
FROM sysindexes
WHERE id=OBJECT_ID('Orders')
ORDER BY indid
```

```
-- Translate first into a file and page number
EXEC sp_decodepagebin @pagebin, @file OUT, @page OUT

-- Show the first file and page in the table
-- Look at the m_slotCnt column in the page header to determine
-- the number of row/page for this page.
DBCC TRACEON(3604)
PRINT CHAR(13)
PRINT '***Dumping the first page of Orders BEFORE the partitioning'
DBCC PAGE('Northwind',@file,@page,0,1)

-- Run a query so we can check the cost of the query
-- before the partitioning
SELECT *
INTO #ordertmp1
FROM Orders

-- Now partition the table vertically into two separate tables

-- Create a table to hold the primary order information
SELECT OrderID, CustomerID, EmployeeID, OrderDate, RequiredDate
INTO OrdersMain
FROM Orders

-- Add a clustered primary key
ALTER TABLE OrdersMain ADD CONSTRAINT PK_OrdersMain PRIMARY KEY (OrderID)

-- Create a table that will store shipping info only
SELECT OrderID, Freight, ShipVia, ShipName, ShipAddress, ShipCity, ShipRegion,
ShipPostalCode, ShipCountry
INTO OrdersShipping
FROM Orders

-- Add a clustered primary key
ALTER TABLE OrdersShipping ADD CONSTRAINT PK_OrdersShipping PRIMARY KEY (OrderID)

-- Now check the number of rows/page in the first of the new tables.
-- Vertically partitioning Orders has increased the number of rows/page
-- and should speed up queries
SELECT TOP 1 @pagebin=first
FROM sysindexes
WHERE id=OBJECT_ID('OrdersMain')
ORDER BY indid

EXEC sp_decodepagebin @pagebin, @file OUT, @page OUT

PRINT CHAR(13)
PRINT '***Dumping the first page of OrdersMain AFTER the partitioning'
DBCC PAGE('Northwind',@file,@page,0,1)

-- Run a query so we can check the cost of the query
-- after the partitioning
SELECT *
INTO #ordertmp2
FROM OrdersMain
```

```
-- Check the number of rows/page in the second table.
SELECT TOP 1 @pagebin=first
FROM sysindexes
WHERE id=OBJECT_ID('OrdersShipping')
ORDER BY indid

EXEC sp_decodepagebin @pagebin, @file OUT, @page OUT

PRINT CHAR(13)
PRINT '***Dumping the first page of OrdersShipping AFTER the partitioning'
DBCC PAGE('Northwind',@file,@page,0,1)
DBCC TRACEOFF(3604)

DROP TABLE #ordertmp1
DROP TABLE #ordertmp2

GO
ROLLBACK TRAN -- Undo it all
***Dumping the first page of Orders BEFORE the partitioning


PAGE:


BUFFER:


BUF @0x11B3B000
---------------
bpage = 0x1FD90000     bhash = 0x00000000     bpageno = (1:143)
bdbid = 6              breferences = 8        bkeep = 1
bstat = 0x9            bspin = 0              bnext = 0x00000000


PAGE HEADER:


Page @0x1FD90000
----------------
m_pageId = (1:143)    m_headerVersion = 1    m_type = 1
m_typeFlagBits = 0x0  m_level = 0            m_flagBits = 0x0
m_objId = 357576312   m_indexId = 0          m_prevPage = (0:0)
m_nextPage = (1:291)  pminlen = 58           m_slotCnt = 42
m_freeCnt = 146       m_freeData = 7962      m_reservedCnt = 0
m_lsn = (18:151:6)    m_xactReserved = 0     m_xactId = (0:0)
m_ghostRecCnt = 0     m_tornBits = 81921
GAM (1:2) ALLOCATED, SGAM (1:3) NOT ALLOCATED, PFS (1:1) 0x60 MIXED_EXT ALLOCATED
0_PCT_FULL

DBCC execution completed. If DBCC printed error messages, contact your system
administrator.

***Dumping the first page of OrdersMain AFTER the partitioning


PAGE:


BUFFER:
```

```
BUF @0x11B37EC0
---------------
bpage = 0x1FC06000 bhash = 0x00000000 bpageno = (1:424)
bdbid = 6          breferences = 0    bkeep = 1
bstat = 0x9        bspin = 0          bnext = 0x00000000

PAGE HEADER:

Page @0x1FC06000
----------------
m_pageId = (1:424)   m_headerVersion = 1  m_type = 1
m_typeFlagBits = 0x0 m_level = 0          m_flagBits = 0x4
m_objId = 2005582183 m_indexId = 0        m_prevPage = (0:0)
m_nextPage = (1:425) pminlen = 38         m_slotCnt = 188
m_freeCnt = 12       m_freeData = 7804    m_reservedCnt = 0
m_lsn = (28:144:24)  m_xactReserved = 0   m_xactId = (0:0)
m_ghostRecCnt = 0    m_tornBits = 0
GAM (1:2) ALLOCATED, SGAM (1:3) NOT ALLOCATED, PFS (1:1) 0x40 ALLOCATED 0_PCT_FULL

DBCC execution completed. If DBCC printed error messages, contact your system
administrator.

***Dumping the first page of OrdersShipping AFTER the partitioning

PAGE:

BUFFER:

BUF @0x11B49E80
---------------
bpage = 0x20504000 bhash = 0x00000000 bpageno = (1:488)
bdbid = 6          breferences = 0    bkeep = 1
bstat = 0x9        bspin = 0          bnext = 0x00000000

PAGE HEADER:

Page @0x20504000
----------------
m_pageId = (1:488)   m_headerVersion = 1  m_type = 1
m_typeFlagBits = 0x0 m_level = 0          m_flagBits = 0x0
m_objId = 2037582297 m_indexId = 0        m_prevPage = (0:0)
m_nextPage = (1:489) pminlen = 12         m_slotCnt = 55
m_freeCnt = 43       m_freeData = 8039    m_reservedCnt = 0
m_lsn = (28:179:24)  m_xactReserved = 0   m_xactId = (0:0)
m_ghostRecCnt = 0    m_tornBits = 0
GAM (1:2) ALLOCATED, SGAM (1:3) NOT ALLOCATED, PFS (1:1) 0x40 ALLOCATED 0_PCT_FULL
```

The steps this query goes through are as follows:

1. Start a transaction so that all changes can be rolled back when we're done.

2. Show the first page of the Orders table as it appears before we partition it. This tells us how many rows are being stored on the page (see the m_slotcnt field in the page header).

3. Run a query that traverses the entire table so that we can compare the costs of querying the data before and after partitioning.

4. Partition Orders into two news tables using SELECT...INTO. Put primary order-related columns in one table; put shipping-related columns in the other.

5. Show the first page of the first new table. This tells us how many rows are being stored on the first page of the new table.

6. Run the earlier query against the first of the new tables so we can compare query costs.

7. Dump the first page of the second new table. This tells us how many rows fit on its first page.

8. Drop the temporary tables created by the cost queries.

9. Roll back the transaction.

When you run the query, inspect the m_slotcnt field in the page header of each set of DBCC PAGE output. This field indicates how many row slots there are on the listed page. You'll notice that it increases substantially from the original Orders table to the OrdersMain table. In fact, it should be roughly four times as high in the new table. What does this mean? It means that a query retrieving rows from OrdersMain will be roughly four times more efficient than one pulling them from Orders. Even if these pages are in the cache, this could obviously make a huge difference.

Understand that the actual number of rows on each page is not constant. That is, even though the first page of the new table may hold, say, 100 rows, the second page may not. This is due to a number of factors. First, SQL Server doesn't maintain the table's FILLFACTOR over time. Data modifications can change the number of rows on a given page. Second, if a table contains variable-length columns, the length of each row can vary to the point of changing how many rows fit on a given page. Also, the default FILLFACTOR (0) doesn't force pages to be completely full—it's not the same as a FILLFACTOR of 100. A FILLFACTOR of 0 is similar to 100 in that it creates clustered indexes with full data pages and nonclustered indexes with full leaf pages. However, it differs in that it reserves space in the upper portion of the index tree and in the non-leaf-level index pages for the maximum size of one index entry.

This query makes use of the sp_decodepagebin stored procedure. The sp_decodepagebin procedure converts binary file/page numbers such as those in the **first, root,** and **FirstIAM** columns of the sysindexes system table to integers that can be used with DBCC PAGE. When passed a binary(6) value, like those in sysindexes, it returns two output parameters containing the file and page number encoded in the value. Here's its source code:

```
USE master
IF OBJECT_ID('sp_decodepagebin') IS NOT NULL
   DROP PROC sp_decodepagebin
GO
CREATE PROC sp_decodepagebin @pagebin varchar(12), @file int=NULL OUT,
   @page int=NULL OUT
/*
Object: sp_decodepagebin
Description: Translates binary file/page numbers (like those in the sysindexes
root, first, and FirstIAM columns) into integers
```

```
Usage: sp_decodepagebin @pagebin=binary(6) file/page number, @file=OUTPUT parm
for file number, @page=OUTPUT parm for page number

Returns: (None)

Created by: Ken Henderson. Email: khen@khen.com

Version: 1.2

Example: EXEC sp_decodepagebin "0x050000000100", @myfile OUT, @mypage OUT

Created: 1999-06-13. Last changed: 1999-08-05.
*/
AS
DECLARE @inbin binary(6)
IF (@pagebin='/?') GOTO Help
SET @inbin=CAST(@pagebin AS binary(6))
SELECT @file=(CAST(SUBSTRING(@inbin,6,1) AS
int)*POWER(2,8))+(CAST(SUBSTRING(@inbin,5,1) AS int)),
   @page=(CAST(SUBSTRING(@inbin,4,1) AS int)*POWER(2,24)) +
   (CAST(SUBSTRING(@inbin,3,1) AS int)*POWER(2,16)) +
   (CAST(SUBSTRING(@inbin,2,1) AS int)*POWER(2,8)) +
   (CAST(SUBSTRING(@inbin,1,1) AS int))
from sysindexes
RETURN 0

Help:
EXEC sp_usage @objectname='sp_decodepagebin',
   @desc='Translates binary file/page numbers (like those in the sysindexes
   root, first, and FirstIAM columns) into integers',
   @parameters='@pagebin=binary(6) file/page number, @file=OUTPUT parm for file
   number, @page=OUTPUT parm for page number',
   @example='EXEC sp_decodepagebin "0x050000000100", @myfile OUT, @mypage OUT',
   @author='Ken Henderson',
   @email='khen@khen.com',
   @version='1', @revision='2',
   @datecreated='6/13/99', @datelastchanged='8/5/99'
RETURN -1
```

This procedure is necessary because the **first, root,** and **FirstIAM** pages are not useful in their native format. We need to access **first** in order to access the table's starting page (though **first** isn't guaranteed to reference the table's initial page by the server, it's unfortunately the best access we have). In order to convert the binary(6) value that's stored in **first** into a usable file and page number, we need to swap the bytes in the number and then convert the values from hexadecimal to decimal. Once swapped, the initial two bytes of the **first** column reference its page; the last four identify its page number. By using sp_decodepagebin, we're spared the details of producing these.

The example code executed a SELECT * query before and after the table partitioning in order to test the effect of the partitioning on query costing. Let's look at the execution plan of the before and after instances of the query in Figures 16.17 and 16.18.

The most striking difference between the two execution plans is the estimated row size. It drops from 240 in the first query to 41 in the second. Naturally, this means that more rows fit on a given page and more will be retrieved with each page read.

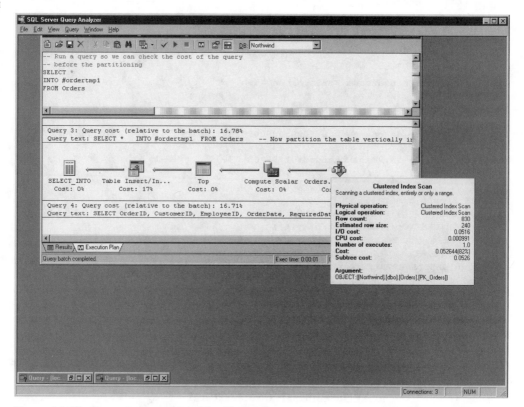

Figure 16.17. The execution plan of the "before" query.

Horizontal Partitioning

Despite having tuned a given table thoroughly, you may find that it's just too large to support the type of performance you need. As rows are added to a table, the infrastructure required to support it grows in size. Eventually, it gets so large that index navigation alone is an expensive and time-consuming proposition. Traversing an index B-tree that contains millions of keys can require more time than accessing the data itself.

One answer to this is to partition the table horizontally—to break it into multiple tables based on the value of some column or columns. Then, the number of rows any one query will have to navigate is far less.

Horizontal partitioning is especially handy when a subset of a table is considerably more active than the rest of the table. By putting it in its own partition, you allow queries that reference it to avoid wading through lots of data they don't need.

Unlike vertically partitioned tables, horizontal partitions contain identical columns. Here's an example that horizontally partitions the Orders table in the Northwind sample database by month based on the OrderDate column:

```
USE Northwind
BEGIN TRAN -- So we can undo all this
```

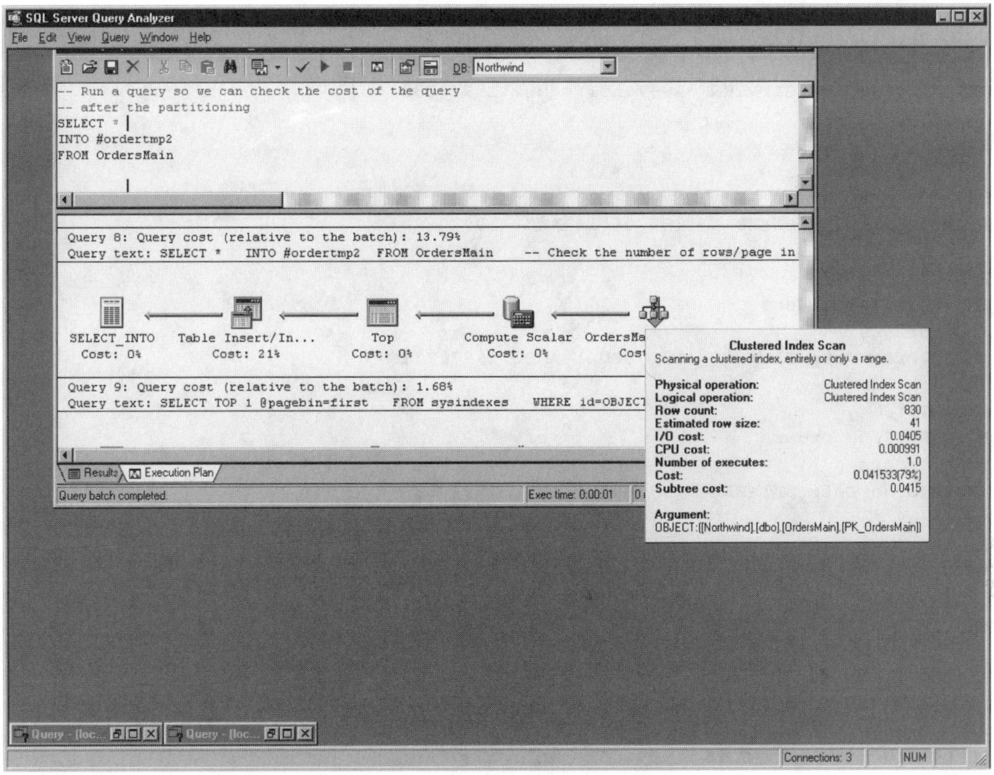

Figure 16.18. The execution plan of the "after" query.

```
-- Drop the index so we can see the effects of paritioning more easily
DROP INDEX Orders.OrderDate

SELECT *
INTO P199701_Orders
FROM Orders
WHERE OrderDate BETWEEN '19970101' AND '19970131'

SELECT *
INTO P199702_Orders
FROM Orders
WHERE OrderDate BETWEEN '19970201' AND '19970228'

SELECT *
INTO P199703_Orders
FROM Orders
WHERE OrderDate BETWEEN '19970301' AND '19970331'

SELECT *
INTO P199704_Orders
FROM Orders
WHERE OrderDate BETWEEN '19970401' AND '19970430'
```

```
SELECT *
INTO P199705_Orders
FROM Orders
WHERE OrderDate BETWEEN '19970501' AND '19970531'

SELECT *
INTO P199706_Orders
FROM Orders
WHERE OrderDate BETWEEN '19970601' AND '19970630'

SELECT *
INTO P199707_Orders
FROM Orders
WHERE OrderDate BETWEEN '19970701' AND '19970731'

SELECT *
INTO P199708_Orders
FROM Orders
WHERE OrderDate BETWEEN '19970801' AND '19970831'

SELECT *
INTO P199709_Orders
FROM Orders
WHERE OrderDate BETWEEN '19970901' AND '19970930'

SELECT *
INTO P199710_Orders
FROM Orders
WHERE OrderDate BETWEEN '19971001' AND '19971031'

SELECT *
INTO P199711_Orders
FROM Orders
WHERE OrderDate BETWEEN '19971101' AND '19971130'

SELECT *
INTO P199712_Orders
FROM Orders
WHERE OrderDate BETWEEN '19971201' AND '19971231'

-- Now let's run a couple queries to see the effects of the partitioning
SELECT CONVERT(char(6), OrderDate, 112) OrderMonth, COUNT(*) NumOrders
FROM Orders
WHERE OrderDate BETWEEN '19970701' AND '19970731'
GROUP BY CONVERT(char(6), OrderDate, 112)
ORDER BY OrderMonth

ALTER TABLE P199707_Orders ADD CONSTRAINT PK_P199707_Orders PRIMARY KEY (OrderID)

SELECT CONVERT(char(6), OrderDate, 112) OrderMonth, COUNT(*) NumOrders
FROM P199707_Orders
WHERE OrderDate BETWEEN '19970701' AND '19970731'
GROUP BY CONVERT(char(6), OrderDate, 112)
ORDER BY OrderMonth
```

```
OrderMonth NumOrders
---------- -----------
199707     33
```

```
OrderMonth NumOrders
---------- -----------
199707     33
```

To see the effect partitioning the table has had on performance, let's examine the execution plans of the two grouped SELECTs in the query—Figures 16.19 and 16.20.

The query against the partitioned table is 28% more efficient in terms of I/O cost and 89% more efficient in terms of CPU cost. Obviously, traversing a subset of a table is quicker than traversing the entire table.

Among the drawbacks of horizontal partitioning is increased query complexity. Queries that span more than one partition become linearly more complicated. You can alleviate some of this by using views to merge partitions via UNIONs, but this is only marginally effective. Some degree of additional complexity is unavoidable. Also, self-referencing constraints are at a disadvantage when horizontal partitions are present. If a table needs to reference itself to check the validity of a value, the presence of partitions may force it to have to check several other tables.

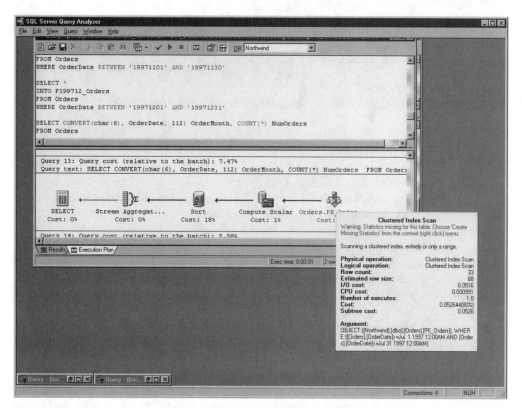

Figure 16.19. The execution plan for the query against the entire Orders table.

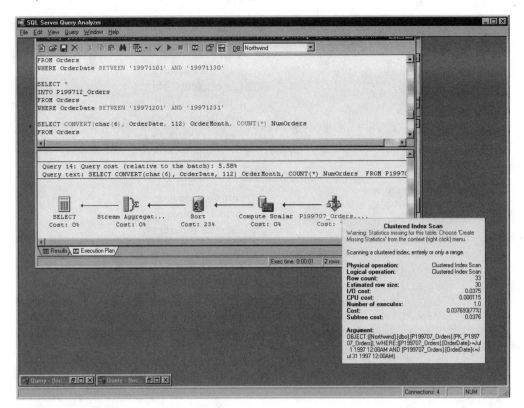

Figure 16.20. The execution plan for the query against the partitioned table.

The Query Optimizer

One of the strengths of modern relational DBMSs is server-based query optimization. It's an area where client/server systems have a distinct advantage over flat-file databases. Without a server, there's little opportunity for optimizing queries submitted by applications, especially multiuser applications. For example, there's no chance of reusing the execution plan of a query run by one user with one run by another user. There's no opportunity to cache database objects accessed by multiple users in a manner beyond simplistic file system–based caching because nothing but the database drivers knows anything about the database. To the operating system, it's just another file or files. To the application, it's a resource accessed by way of a special driver, usually a DLL. In short, no one's in charge—no one's minding the store as far as making sure access to the database is consistent and efficient across all the clients using it.

Client/server DBMSs have changed this by making the server an equal partner with the developer in ensuring database access is as efficient as possible. The science behind query optimization has evolved over the years to the point that the optimizer is usually able to tune a query better and more quickly than a human counterpart. A modern optimizer can leverage one of the things computers do best—iteration. It can quickly loop through an assortment of potential query solutions in order to select the best one.

DBMSs take a variety of approaches to optimizing queries. Some optimize based on heuristics—internally reordering and reorganizing queries based on a predefined set of algebraic rules. Query trees are dissected, and associative and commutative rules are applied in a predetermined order until a plan for satisfying the entire query emerges.

Some DBMSs optimize queries based on syntactic elements. This places the real burden of optimization on the user because WHERE clause predicates and join criteria are not reordered —they generate the same execution plan with each run. Because the user becomes the real optimizer, intimate knowledge of the database is essential for good query performance.

Semantic optimization is a theoretical technique that assumes the optimizer knows the database schema and can infer optimization potential through constraint definitions. Several vendors are exploring this area of query optimization as a means of allowing a database designer or modeler a direct means of controlling the optimization process.

The most prevalent means of query optimization, and, I think, the most effective, is cost-based optimization. Cost-based optimization weighs several different methods of satisfying a query against one another and selects the one that will execute in the shortest time. A cost-based optimizer bases this determination on estimates of I/O, CPU utilization, and other factors that affect query performance. This is the approach that SQL Server takes, and its implementation is among the most advanced in the industry.

I've already touched briefly on the query optimizer and some of its features elsewhere in this chapter, but I think it's essential to have a good understanding of how it works in order to write optimal T-SQL code and to tune queries properly.

The optimizer goes through several steps in order to optimize a query. It analyzes the query, identifying SARGs and OR clauses, locating joins, etc. It compares different ways of performing any necessary joins and evaluates the best indexes to use with the query. Since the optimizer is cost-based, it selects the method of satisfying the query with the least cost. Usually, it makes the right choice, but sometimes it needs a little help.

Join Optimizations

Releases 7.0 and later of SQL Server support join types beyond the simple nested loop (or nested iteration) joins of earlier releases. This flexibility allows the optimizer to find the best way of linking one table with another using all the information at its disposal.

Nested Loops

Nested loop joins consist of a loop within a loop. They designate one table in the join as the outer loop and the other as the inner loop. For each iteration of the outer loop, the entire inner loop is traversed. This works fine for small to medium-sized tables, but as the loops grow larger, this strategy becomes increasingly inefficient. Figure 16.21 illustrates a nested loop query and its execution plan.

Merge Joins

Merge joins perform much more efficiently with large data sets than nested loop joins. A row from each table in the join is retrieved and compared. Both tables must be sorted on the merge column for the join to work. The optimizer usually opts for a merge join when working with a large data set and when the comparison columns in both tables are already sorted. Figure 16.22 illustrates a query that the optimizer processes using a merge join.

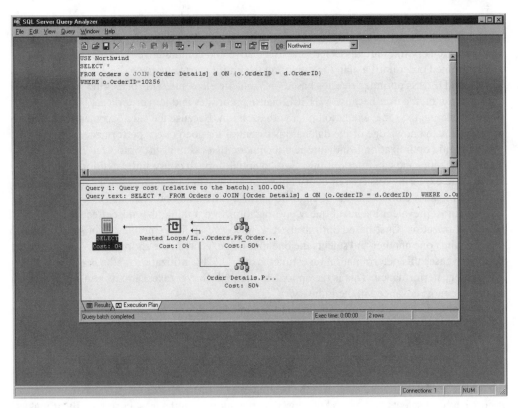

Figure 16.21. A nested loop join.

Hash Joins

Hash joins are also more efficient with large data sets than nested loop joins. Additionally, they work well with tables that are not sorted on the merge column(s). The server performs hash joins by hashing the rows from the smaller of the two tables (designated the "build" table), inserting them into a hash table, processing the larger table (the "probe" table) a row at a time, and scanning the hash table for matches. Because the smaller of the two tables supplies the values in the hash table, the table size is kept to a minimum, and because hashed values rather than real values are used, comparisons can be made between the tables very quickly.

Hash joins are a variation on the concept of hashed indexes that have been available in a handful of advanced DBMS products for several years. With hashed indexes, the hash table is stored permanently—it *is* the index. Data is hashed into slots that have the same hashing value. If the index has a unique contiguous key, what is known as a *minimal perfect hashing function* exists—every value hashes to its own slot and there are no gaps between slots in the index. If the index is unique but noncontiguous, the next best thing—a *perfect hashing function*—can exist wherein every value hashes to its own slot, but potentially there are gaps between them. Figure 16.23 illustrates a hash join.

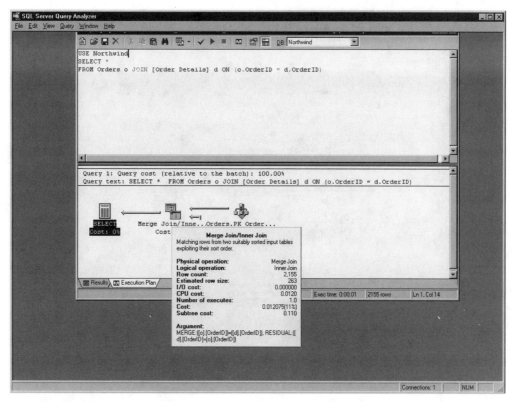

Figure 16.22. The optimizer chooses a merge join when both tables are suitably sorted.

Index Optimizations

In addition to identifying search arguments and using indexes to service them, the query optimizer can make use of indexes in other ways to streamline query processing. A number of these are made possible by the optimizer's ability to make use of multiple indexes on the same table.

Index Joins

As mentioned elsewhere in this chapter, index covering is the process whereby the optimizer uses a nonclustered index to satisfy a query rather than referencing the underlying table or clustered index. It requires that the columns requested by the query exist as keys in a nonclustered index. An execution plan that uses a nonclustered index to retrieve data but does not include a Bookmark lookup step is making use of index covering. SQL Server can join multiple nonclustered indexes to create covered indexes on the fly. This is often faster than using the indexes separately and certainly quicker than sequentially scanning the table itself. Figure 16.24 shows a query that the optimizer translates into a join between two nonclustered indexes.

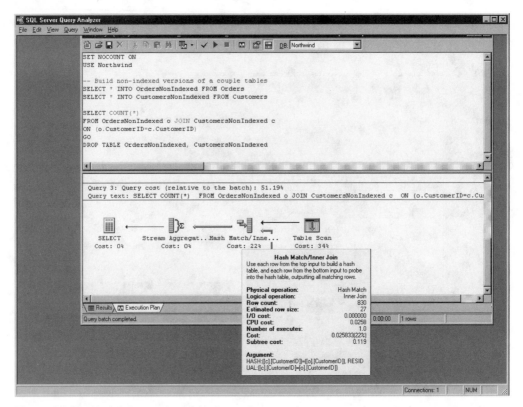

Figure 16.23. Hash joins work well for large data sets that may not be sorted.

SQL Server's ability to join nonclustered indexes in this fashion has some ramifications for physical database design. Prior to the advent of index joins, the common technique for setting up index covering was to add a column or two to an existing index in order to allow it to cover a given query or queries. Now that the optimizer can join indexes, it may be more sensible to split these keys into multiple indexes and allow the optimizer to join them as necessary. This allows the optimizer to use them individually as well, which wouldn't be the case with a compound key index. This isn't to say that you should abandon compound index keys altogether, but splitting them into separate indexes is certainly something to consider.

Index Merging and Intersection

Similar to index joins is the optimizer's ability to merge and intersect indexes. This allows it to merge the matching keys in multiple indexes into a set of key values that it may then look up in the clustered index or underlying table in order to retrieve columns not found in the indexes. Figure 16.25 illustrates an index merge/intersection query and execution plan.

Notice that the execution plan includes a Bookmark lookup step. This means that the query isn't being covered by nonclustered indexes. They are, however, intersected to help service it.

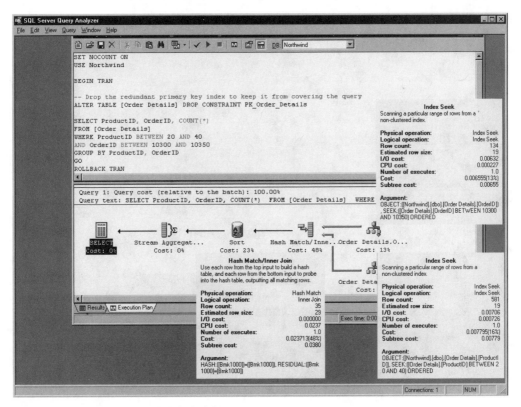

Figure 16.24. The server can join indexes to cover a query.

Data Warehouse Optimizations

In addition to the data warehousing and OLAP tools that ship with SQL Server, the query optimizer can recognize star schema layouts and perform special optimizations for queries that join fact and dimension tables. Since dimension tables tend to be microscopic compared with fact tables, the query optimizer can generate an execution plan that first cross-joins the dimension tables in a query with each other and then joins the result with the fact table. The end result is a smaller number of joins than with traditional methods of combining these types of tables.

This is best understood by way of example. For the sake of discussion, assume we have three tables—two dimension tables and one fact table. The dimension tables have ten rows each, and the fact table has a million rows. If you join the fact table to the two dimension tables with inner joins and the optimizer performs no additional optimizations, two million joins will be performed (one million for the join between the fact table and the first dimension table and one million for the join with the second dimension table). If, instead, you cross-join the two dimension tables, then join the fact table with the result, you reduce the number of joins by nearly half:

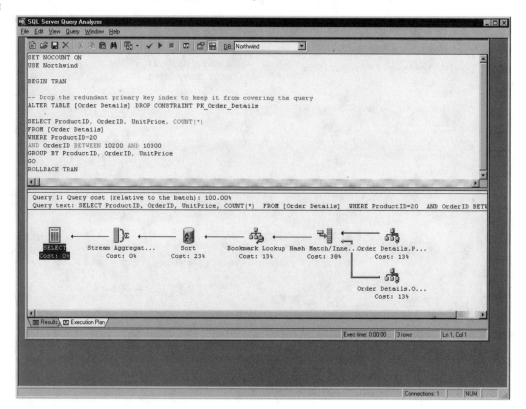

Figure 16.25. The server can intersect indexes to service a query.

$$10 \times 10 \quad \text{dimension rows} = 100 \text{ joins}$$
$$+ \; 1{,}000{,}000 \quad \text{joins between the fact table and the dimension composite}$$
$$= \; 1{,}000{,}100 \quad \text{total joins}$$

The following SQL script illustrates a typical star schema join. It first constructs the dimension and fact tables described earlier and then joins the fact table with the two dimension tables.

> ### Note
> Don't run this query with Show Execution Plan enabled in Query Analyzer—each row insertion will get its own section in the graphical execution plan, which will take an eternity to run and not be terribly useful. If you want to see the join query's execution plan for yourself, highlight the portion of the script up to the join and press Ctrl-E in Query Analyzer to run it. This will create the tables and populate them with data. Next, press Ctrl-K to turn on the graphical execution plan display; highlight the join itself and run it.

```
SET NOCOUNT ON

CREATE TABLE #dim1 (dim1 int identity PRIMARY KEY, dim1val int)
CREATE TABLE #dim2 (dim2 int identity PRIMARY KEY, dim2val int)
CREATE TABLE #facttable (k1 int identity PRIMARY KEY, dim1 int, dim2 int)

DECLARE @loop INT
SET @loop=1

WHILE @loop<=10 BEGIN
   INSERT #dim1 VALUES (@loop*50)
   INSERT #dim2 VALUES (@loop*25)
   SET @loop=@loop+1
END

SET @loop=1

WHILE @loop<=1000000 BEGIN
   INSERT #facttable VALUES ((@loop / 100000)+1,10-(@loop / 100000))
   SET @loop=@loop+1
END

SELECT COUNT(*)
FROM #facttable f JOIN #dim1 d ON (f.dim1=d.dim1)
JOIN #dim2 i ON (f.dim2=i.dim2)
```

Figure 16.26 shows the query's execution plan.

Semijoins

When the fact table in a star schema relationship contains indexes on the dimension columns used in a join, the optimizer will use those indexes to perform index intersections with the dimension tables. Each dimension table will be joined with an appropriate index on the fact table, and the results of those joins will be intersected before retrieving rows from the fact table. This strategy allows the optimizer to return rows from the fact table when it's most efficient to do so—after membership in the result set has been pared down by the index intersections.

Grouping Optimizations

The normal order of events when GROUP BY is present in a query containing joins is to perform the joins before grouping the data. Sometimes, however, it's faster to group the data first, especially when working with a huge number of rows that will be coalesced into a relatively small number of groups. In the past, Transact-SQL developers had to perform this optimization by hand, usually via a stored procedure and some temporary tables. Now, the optimizer can potentially recognize situations where grouping first would be beneficial and act accordingly.

Predicate Clause Optimizations

The optimizer can detect when predicate clauses are associative and eliminate unnecessary join steps. Here's a query that illustrates:

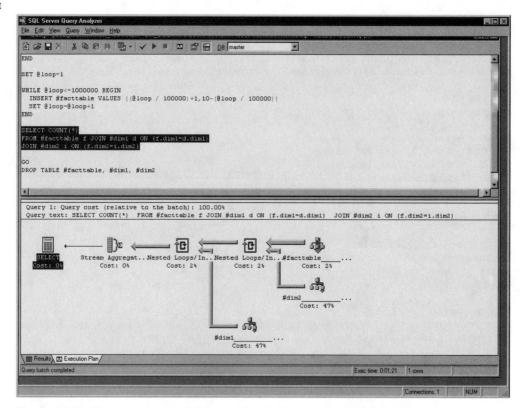

Figure 16.26. The server can perform special optimizations on star schema queries.

```
SET NOCOUNT ON
CREATE TABLE #tmp1 (k1 int identity PRIMARY KEY)
CREATE TABLE #tmp2 (k1 int identity PRIMARY KEY)
CREATE TABLE #tmp3 (k1 int identity PRIMARY KEY)

DECLARE @loop int
SET @loop=1

WHILE @loop<=10 BEGIN
   INSERT #tmp1 DEFAULT VALUES
   INSERT #tmp2 DEFAULT VALUES
   INSERT #tmp3 DEFAULT VALUES
   SET @loop=@loop+1
END

SELECT COUNT(*)
FROM #tmp1 t1, #tmp2 t2, #tmp3 t3
WHERE t1.k1=t2.k1 AND t2.k1=t3.k1
GO
DROP TABLE #tmp1, #tmp2, #tmp3
```

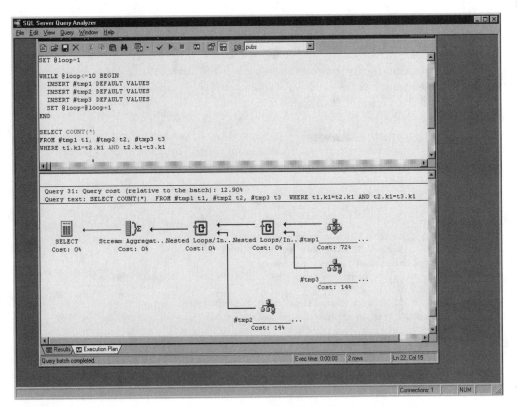

Figure 16.27. The optimizer can detect associative predicate clauses.

Note

I'm using old-style joins here to underscore the associative properties of predicate clauses. The concept applies equally well to ANSI joins.

This query first populates three temporary tables and joins all three of them on the same column. Normally, the flow of execution would be to join #tmp1 and #tmp2, then join #tmp2 and #tmp3, and then join the results of the first to joins. If all three tables are joined on the same column(s), the query optimizer can eliminate one of these three steps by joining #tmp1 and #tmp3 and then joining the result with #tmp2. The execution plan for the example code shows this is indeed what happens (Figure 16.27). As you can see, the plan begins with #tmp1 and #tmp3 being joined using a nested loop. The result of this operation is then joined with #tmp2 to form the result set.

The Index Tuning Wizard

SQL Server provides a nice facility for helping you determine the indexes you need to service anything from a specific query to an entire application. You can access the Index Tuning Wizard via the Query I Perform Index Analysis menu option in Query Analyzer or the Tools I Wizards I Management I Index Tuning Wizard option in Enterprise Manager. Both facilities use the same engine internally.

Query Analyzer's Perform Index Analysis option can be used to suggest (and optionally to create) indexes to improve the performance of a given query. To explore this, let's create non-indexed versions of the Orders, Order Details, and Customers tables in the Northwind sample database and join them together:

```
SET NOCOUNT ON
USE Northwind
SELECT * INTO OrdersNI FROM Orders
SELECT * INTO OrderDetailsNI FROM [Order Details]
SELECT * INTO CustomersNI FROM Customers
SELECT o.OrderDate, c.CompanyName, SUM(d.UnitPrice * d.Quantity) AS
BeforeDiscount
FROM OrdersNI o JOIN OrderDetailsNI d ON (o.OrderID=d.OrderID)
JOIN CustomersNI c ON (o.CustomerID=c.CustomerID)
GROUP BY o.OrderDate, c.CompanyName
ORDER BY o.OrderDate, c.CompanyName
```

(Results abridged)

```
OrderDate                CompanyName                          BeforeDiscount
----------------------   ----------------------------------   --------------------
1996-07-04 00:00:00.000  Vins et alcools Chevalier            440.0000
1996-07-05 00:00:00.000  Toms Spezialitäten                   1863.4000
1996-07-08 00:00:00.000  Hanari Carnes                        1813.0000
1996-07-08 00:00:00.000  Victuailles en stock                 670.8000
1996-07-09 00:00:00.000  Suprêmes délices                     3730.0000
```

Once the tables are created, highlight the join query and press Ctrl-I to instruct Query Analyzer to analyze the indexes used by the query. It will recommend two new nonclustered indexes—one on the OrdersNI table and one on OrderDetailsNI. Figure 16.28 illustrates.

Curiously, the analyzer doesn't recommend an index for the CustomersNI table. This is probably due to the fact that it believes the query is just as efficient using a table scan on CustomerNI as it would be with an index over the table.

The Index Tuning Wizard in Enterprise Manager works similarly, but it's designed to work with entire databases or database objects rather than specific queries. To use it, follow these steps:

1. Start the Profiler tool and begin a trace that traps Transact-SQL statement execution.

2. Run your application, focusing on areas that are not performing as well as they need to.

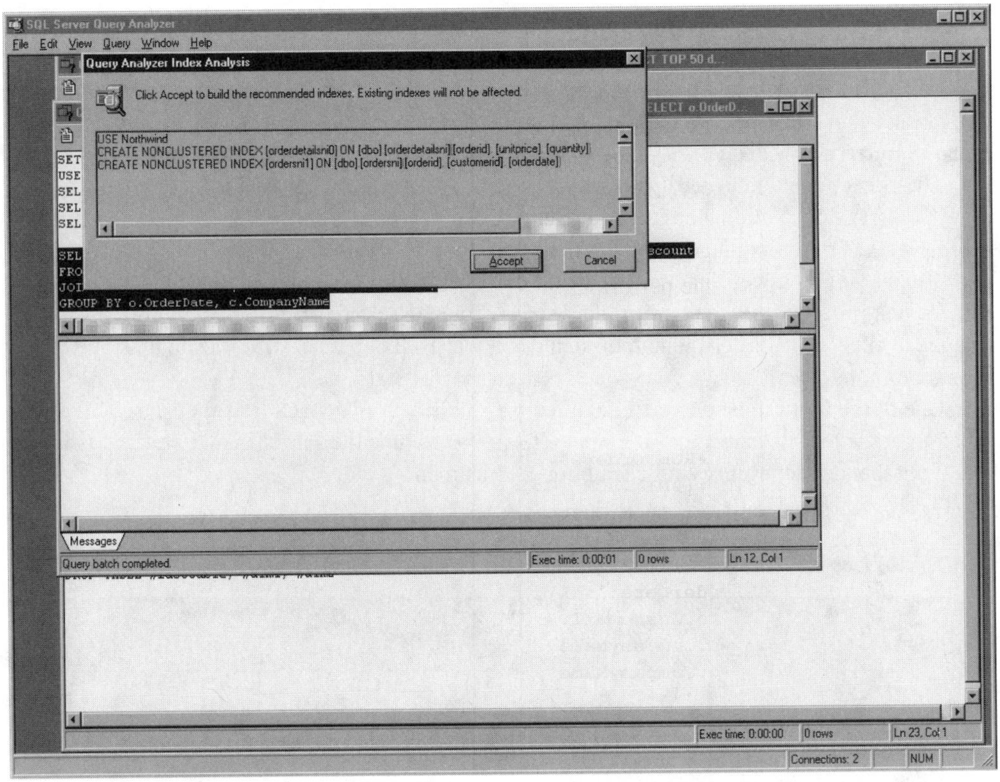

Figure 16.28. The Perform Index Analysis option in Query Analyzer can suggest indexes.

3. Save the trace information in Profile to a file.

4. Start the Index Tuning Wizard in Enterprise Manager.

5. Opt to perform a complete analysis unless the database is so large that that's impractical.

6. Select your database and include all objects in the analysis unless you know for certain that a given object isn't used.

7. Supply the workload file you saved earlier in Profiler as the input for the tuning process.

8. The wizard will then recommend indexes based on the workload you specified.

9. Click the Analysis button to gain insight into the wizard's recommendations. You can view a number of reports and save them to disk.

Profiler

The Profiler tool allows you to set up traces that watch server activity for particular events such as Transact-SQL statement execution. You can find it in the SQL Server folder or on the Tools menu in Enterprise Manager.

The concept behind using Profiler to tune your system is to capture events emitted from the server's storage or relational engine, then tune the server, query, database, and so on, and replay those events in order to gauge the success of your tuning efforts.

You can set up traces that identity worst-performing queries, queries that cause deadlocks, queries that produce long table scans, and so on. You can set up private traces as well as those that are available to all users. The tool includes a wizard that assists with setting up some of the more common traces.

One of the tool's most powerful features is its ability to play back traced events. This is what gives the tool its name, and it's what allows you to tune the server in an iterative fashion, replaying the suspect events with each tuning adjustment.

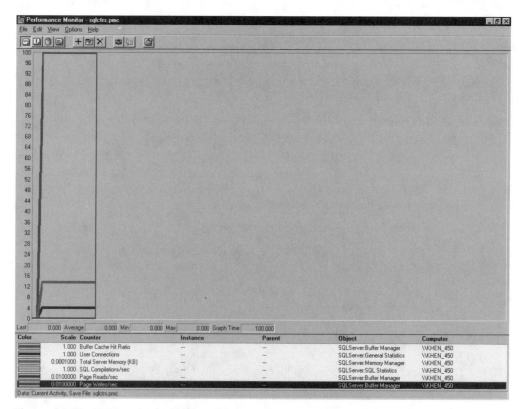

Figure 16.29. Starting the Perfmon tool from Profiler enables several SQL Server counters.

Perfmon

The Windows NT Performance Monitor allows a myriad of operational and performance statistics to be tracked for SQL Server. You can find it in the SQL Server folder as well as in the NT Administrative tools folder. It's also available from the toolbar of the Profiler tool.

Normally, you'll want to start Perfmon from Profiler or the SQL Server group because doing so automatically enables a number of SQL Server–related counters, as illustrated by Figure 16.29.

Perfmon can display performance counters in a variety of formats, but the most popular is the default histogram format. The chart is updated every three seconds and graphically depicts the values for the currently selected counters.

The most popular Perfmon counters are the Buffer Cache:Buffer Cache Hit Ratio, General Statistics:SQL Cache Memory(KB), and the Databases:Percent Log Used counters. Some counters, including Percent Log Used, require you to select a database, as Figure 16.30 illustrates.

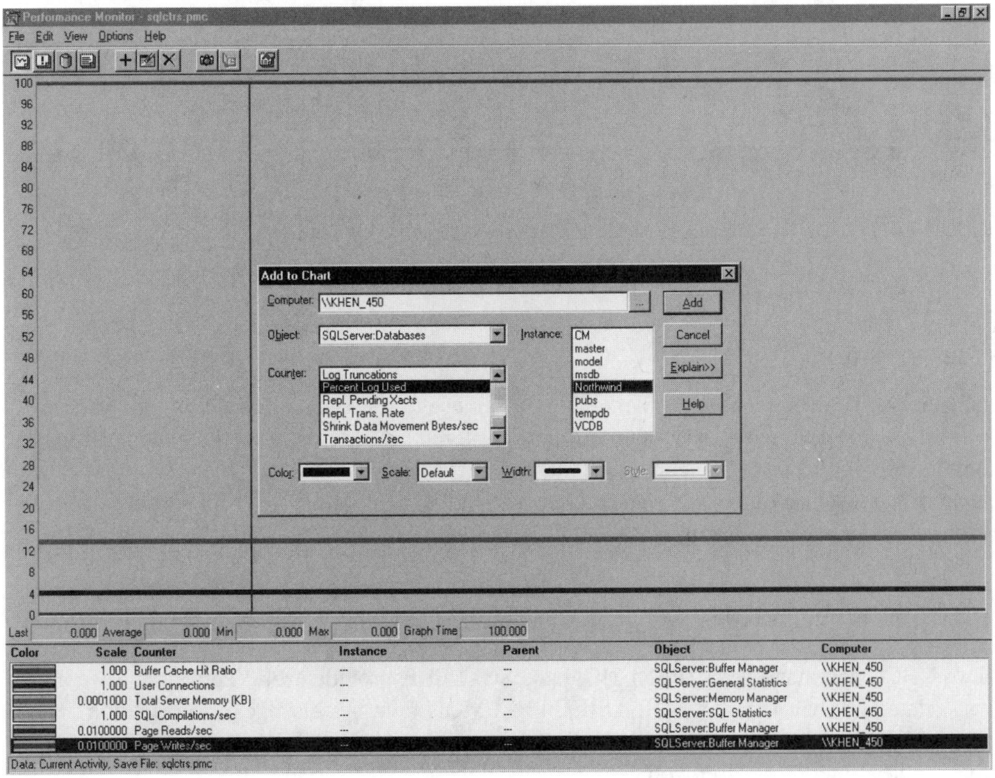

Figure 16.30. Some Perfmon counters require a database instance to be selected.

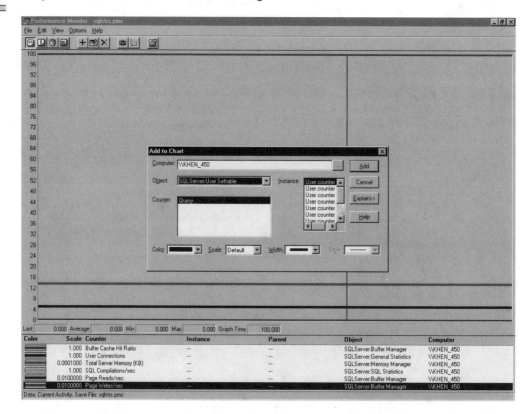

Figure 16.31. You can set up user-defined counters in Perfmon and set them in your apps.

User Counters

SQL Server defines ten user counters that you can use to track performance in your own applications. You use the sp_user_counterN system stored procedures to set these values from within your application. You can watch them in Perfmon by setting the Query counter of the appropriate instance of the SQLServer:User Settable object. Figure 16.31 illustrates setting a user-defined counter in Perfmon.

Perfmon-Related DBCC Commands

Two DBCC command verbs, PERFMON and SQLPERF, provide useful Performance Monitor–related info via Transact-SQL. DBCC PERFMON returns a barrage of information in text form that's also reported graphically by Perfmon itself, and DBCC SQLPERF (LOGSPACE) returns the Percent Log Used counter for each database on the server.

Summary

Transact-SQL provides a wealth of query tuning techniques. Properly designing your databases and constructing queries to take advantage of your design are at the top of the list. Sound database designs and optimal queries work in harmony with one another.

Performance tuning is a complex topic that could easily fill several books all by itself. The key to successful tuning is to know your tools, know how the server works, and have the tenacity to work through performance problems in an iterative fashion.

17

Administrative Transact-SQL

Thinking is the hardest work there is, which is probably the reason so few engage in it.—Henry Ford

While database administration itself is beyond the scope of this book, we can still delve into administrative Transact-SQL in some depth. In many shops, the line between database programmer and database administrator is a gray one indeed, so, regardless of whether you're a DBA, it's handy to have a working knowledge of administrative Transact-SQL commands and syntax.

It's common for shops to author custom stored procedures and Transact-SQL batches to perform administrative functions. Backups, index statistic refreshes, and data warehouse updates are examples of the types of tasks these routines usually perform. Using the SQL Server Agent service, they can be set up to run when system utilization is relatively low.

Oscar Wilde said, "Dullness is the coming of age of seriousness." Oftentimes, database administration is the "coming of age" of database application development. Once an app is built, someone has to feed and care for it, including its database. This is usually a dreary task and a thankless job, so it makes sense to use scripts and stored procedures to automate it whenever possible.

GUI Administration

There was a time when the first response of old-timers to SQL Server management issues was to fire up ISQL, the venerable predecessor of Query Analyzer. Since I started working with the product when it had little in the way of real administration tools, this has been my default, gut reaction for years. The tools that shipped with SQL Server (and its look-alike cousin, Sybase) were poor enough (remember the execrable SAF utility?) that there was little other choice. However, with SQL Server's increasing complexity and the steady improvement of its graphical tools, this isn't the necessity it once was. No matter how adept you are with Transact-SQL, your best bet for administrating SQL Server is to use the many nice graphical tools that come with it. Enterprise Manager, with its many built-in facilities and utilities, is a very capable administration tool. Gone are the days when the administrator was forced to resort to a mixed bag of

Transact-SQL and third-party tools to get the job done. In fact, with all the functionality now present in the product, managing SQL Server using only Transact-SQL would be difficult if not impossible. Furthermore, Enterprise Manager has matured to the point that it has greatly diminished the need for third-party tools. The product offers a rich assortment of management facilities that's coherent and easy to use. Before you go to the trouble of writing lots of elaborate custom procedures using Transact-SQL syntax that is at times rather obscure, check out what comes free in the box.

System Stored Procedures

On that note, your first move in deciding what administrative tasks to automate and how to automate them is to peruse the system procedures that ship with SQL Server. There are a number of handy routines that come with SQL Server out of the box. They supplement Transact-SQL with useful functionality not found in the language itself, ranging from the simple listing of meta-data to specifying database option settings and configuring the server. The procedures included in Table 17.1 aren't listed in order of importance, nor is the list anywhere near complete. They're intended to spur your interest in the canned routines that come with the product so that you'll get to know them for yourself.

Administrative Transact-SQL Commands

In addition to the bevy of administration-related procedures that ship with SQL Server, there are a number of Transact-SQL commands that have to do with system and database administration. Table 17.2 lists some of the more pertinent ones.

As with the earlier list, this one is far from complete. It's worth your time to scan the entirety of the Transact-SQL language for commands and syntax that can lessen your administrative workload.

Administrative System Functions

There are also several Transact-SQL functions that relate to database administration. Technically, most of the functions in Transact-SQL play a role in server administration at one time or another since they end up in the stored procedures and scripts used to perform administrative tasks. Some of them you may be familiar with, some you might not be. Table 17.3 lists a few of the more important ones.

Administrative Automatic Variables

Automatic variables are predefined, read-only variables that have the prefix "@@." The SQL Server Books Online usually refers to them as "functions," but they aren't really functions in the normal sense of the term (e.g., unlike functions, they can be passed as parameters to stored

Table 17.1. Administration-related stored procedures.

Procedure	Purpose
Catalog stored procedures such as sp_tables, sp_columns, sp_stored_procedures, sp_statistics, etc.	Provide catalog-level information about database objects. As with the ANSI SQL-92 information schema views, these can be used in lieu of direct system table references to avoid system schema dependencies.
sp_add_job, sp_add_jobschedule, sp_add_jobserver, sp_addjobstep	Used to manage SQL Server Agent automated tasks.
sp_autostats	Used to toggle the automatic maintenance of index statistics for a given index or indexes.
sp_create_removable	Creates a removable database.
sp_cycle_errorlog	Recreates the error log as though the server had been shut down and restarted.
sp_dboption	Sets database-wide options such as **select into/bulk copy, trunc. log on chkpt.**, etc.
sp_dbremove	Drops a database and all files associated with it.
sp_lock	Lists detailed information about object locks, who holds them, etc.
sp_makewebtask	Creates a job that produces HTML from query result sets.
sp_manage_jobs_by_login	Allows the jobs belonging to a specific login to be reassigned or deleted.
sp_monitor	Reports server-wide performance information.
sp_processmail	Executes queries contained in mail sent to SQL Server and returns the results as email replies.
sp_procoption	Configures (or displays) a procedure's autostartup status.
sp_refreshview	Rebuilds the catalog info for a view so that it reflects changes to underlying objects.
sp_server_info	Returns attributes and capability information for the current server, a database gateway, or data source (analogous to ODBC's SQLGetInfo function).
sp_serveroption	Allows options for remote and linked servers to be specified.
sp_spaceused	Reports on the physical space used by a database or database object.
sp_tableoption	Sets table-level options (e.g., **table lock on bulk load**).
sp_updatestats	Updates the index statistics for all user-defined indexes in the current database.
sp_validname	Checks to see whether an identifier is a valid SQL Server name.
sp_who	Reports on current user activity.
xp_cmdshell	Executes an operating system command.
xp_printf, xp_sscanf	Allows string variables to be formatted similarly to the C printf() and scanf() functions.

Table 17.2. Administration-related Transact-SQL commands.

Command	Purpose
BACKUP/RESTORE	Allows databases and transaction logs to be backed up and restored
BULK INSERT	Loads data from an operating system file into a table
CHECKPOINT	Forces dirty pages to be written to disk
CREATE DATABASE	Creates a new database
CREATE SCHEMA	Creates a series of database objects in one fell swoop
CREATE STATISTICS	Creates an index histogram over a selection of columns in a table
DBCC CHECK...	Checks databases and related structures for errors
DBCC OPENTRAN	Returns information on the oldest running transaction in a database
DBCC SHRINKDATABASE	Shrinks the size of the specified database
DBCC SQLPERF	Returns transaction log usage information
GRANT and DENY	Permits or prevents access to database objects and commands
KILL	Stops a currently connected process
RECONFIGURE	Makes server configuration changes permanent
SHUTDOWN	Shuts the server down

Table 17.3. Administration-related Transact-SQL functions.

Function	Purpose
DATABASEPROPERTY(), OBJECTPROPERTY(), INDEXPROPERTY(), TYPEPROPERTY(), COLUMNPROPERTY()	Return meta-data info from the system catalogs
FILE_ID(), FILE_NAME(), FILEGROUP_ID(), FILEGROUP_NAME(), FILEGROUPPROPERTY()	Return information on files and filegroups
OBJECT_ID(), OBJECT_NAME()	Return object identification information
PERMISSIONS()	Returns a bitmask indicating the rights a user has to a given object or column
USER_NAME, SUSER_SNAME(), USER_ID(), SUSER_SID()	Return user identification information

procedures). Throughout this book, you'll see them referred to as "automatic variables." Because they're global in scope—that is, they're available from any database—many of them by nature relate to database or system administration. Table 17.4 lists the more prominent ones.

Where's the Beef?

While getting familiar with administrative Transact-SQL syntax is certainly worthwhile, using it to build real-world procedures and scripts is far more interesting. Throughout the rest of the chapter, I'll present a variety of stored procedures and scripts that utilize the Transact-SQL ele-

Table 17.4. Administration-related automatic variables.

Variable	Purpose
@@CONNECTIONS, @@MAX_CONNECTIONS	Returns the number of connections since the server was started and the maximum allowed connections
@@CPU_BUSY, @@IDLE, @@IO_BUSY	Reports on server resource utilization
@@ERROR	Returns the error number of the last command
@@MAX_PRECISION	Returns on the maximum floating point precision supported by the server (can be changed via **/p** command line option)
@@OPTIONS	Reports on the default user options in effect. These are set via **sp_configure 'user options'.**
@@PACK_SENT, @@PACK_RECEIVED, @@PACK_ERRORS	Reports packet transmission statistics
@@SERVERNAME, @@REMSERVER, @@SERVICENAME	Returns server identification information
@@SPID, @@PROCID	Identifies the current user and stored procedure, respectively
@@TOTAL_ERRORS, @@TOTAL_READ, @@TOTAL_WRITE	Reports disk read/write statistics
@@VERSION	Returns the server version string

ments highlighted thus far for server and database administration. You can use these routines in your own work to provide functionality that's missing or inconvenient to access in Enterprise Manager.

Status Routines

Status routines report on the status of the server, the users connected to it, the jobs running on it, etc. These types of routines are surprisingly valuable to the administrator. Database administrators like to know what's going on. Keeping a finger on the pulse of the servers and databases under her care helps the DBA avoid unpleasant surprises like blocked processes, inaccessible objects, disgruntled users, and angry mobs. Here are a few of the more valuable status routines I've used over the years.

sp_active_processes

This routine tracks system activity over a period of time. Unlike sp_who, it benchmarks what's going on at one point in time against what's happening at another. It provides a number of useful statistics related to system CPU utilization, logical I/O, and physical I/O. It lets you see what type of work the server is doing at a particular time and who's doing it. Here's the code:

```
USE MASTER
GO
IF OBJECT_ID('sp_active_processes') IS NOT NULL
   DROP PROC sp_active_processes
GO
CREATE PROC sp_active_processes
   @loginame varchar(30)=NULL,  --  'ACTIVEONLY' | spid | login name
   @duration int=5              --  seconds to sample
/*

Object: sp_active_processes
Description: Shows system activity over a period of time
Usage: sp_active_processes [@loginame=login name | "ACTIVEONLY" | spid][,
@duration=seconds to monitor]

Returns: (None)

Created by: Ken Henderson. Email: khen@khen.com

Version: 4.2

Example usage:
   sp_active_processes @duration=10  --  Monitors all processes for 10 seconds
   sp_active_processes "ACTIVEONLY",30  --  Monitors all processes for 30 seconds,
   but only lists active ones
   sp_active_processes 34,5  --  Monitors spid 34 for 5 seconds

Created: 1991-05-11. Last changed: 1999-07-02.

*/
AS
SET NOCOUNT ON

DECLARE @before datetime,
        @after datetime,
        @lowlogin sysname,
        @highlogin sysname,
        @spidlow int,
        @spidhigh int

SELECT @lowlogin='',
       @highlogin=REPLICATE('z',TYPEPROPERTY('sysname','Precision')),
       @spidlow=0,
       @spidhigh=32767

-- Crack @loginame
IF (@loginame<>'ACTIVEONLY') AND (@loginame IS NOT NULL) BEGIN
   SELECT @lowlogin=@loginame,
          @highlogin=@loginame
   IF SUSER_SID(@lowlogin) IS NULL BEGIN
      IF @loginame LIKE "[0-9]%"
         SELECT @spidlow=CAST(@loginame AS int),
                @spidhigh=CAST(@loginame AS int),
                @lowlogin='',
                @highlogin=REPLICATE('z',TYPEPROPERTY('sysname','Precision'))
```

```
        ELSE BEGIN
           PRINT 'Invalid loginame'
           PRINT CHAR(13)
           GOTO Help
        END
   END
END

-- Get locks
SELECT spid,'L1'=COUNT(*),'L2'=0 INTO #LCKS FROM master..syslocks WHERE spid BETWEEN
@spidlow AND @spidhigh GROUP BY spid

-- Save off time
SELECT @before=CURRENT_TIMESTAMP

-- Get processes
SELECT SPID,LOGINAME,C1=CPU,C2=0,I1=PHYSICAL_IO,I2=0,CM1=CMD,CM2=CAST(' LOGGED OFF' AS
CHAR(16)),S1=CAST(STATUS AS CHAR(16)),S2=SPACE(16),B2=0,dbid=0,HOSTNAME=SPACE(10)
INTO #PRCS FROM master..sysprocesses WHERE loginame BETWEEN @lowlogin AND @highlogin
AND spid BETWEEN @spidlow AND @spidhigh

-- Wait for duration specified
DECLARE @WAITFORSTR varchar(30)
SET @WAITFORSTR='WAITFOR DELAY
"'+CONVERT(char(8),DATEADD(ss,@duration,'19000101'),108)+'"'
EXEC(@WAITFORSTR)

-- Get the locks again
INSERT #LCKS SELECT DISTINCT spid,0,COUNT(*) FROM master..syslocks WHERE spid BETWEEN
@spidlow AND @spidhigh GROUP BY spid

-- Save off the time again
SELECT @after=CURRENT_TIMESTAMP

-- Get the processes a second time
INSERT #PRCS SELECT spid,loginame,0,CPU,0,PHYSICAL_IO,' ',CMD,'
',STATUS,BLOCKED,DBID,HOSTNAME FROM master..sysprocesses
WHERE loginame BETWEEN @lowlogin AND @highlogin AND spid BETWEEN @spidlow AND @spidhigh

-- Put an entry for every process in the locks work table
INSERT #LCKS SELECT DISTINCT spid,0,0 FROM #PRCS

-- Grab the blockers out of the process and lock work tables
SELECT SPID=B2,BLKING=STR(COUNT(*),4)
INTO #BLK
FROM #PRCS WHERE B2<>0 GROUP BY B2

INSERT #BLK
SELECT DISTINCT l.spid,STR(0,4) FROM #LCKS l LEFT OUTER JOIN #BLK b ON (l.spid<>b.spid)
WHERE b.spid IS NULL

-- Print report header
PRINT 'STATISTICS FOR '+@@SERVERNAME+' AS OF '+CAST(CURRENT_TIMESTAMP AS varchar)
PRINT 'ACTIVITY OF '+CASE WHEN @lowlogin=@highlogin THEN 'LOGIN '+@loginame ELSE
UPPER(LEFT(ISNULL(@loginame,'ALL'),6))+' LOGINS' END+' FOR THE PAST
'+CAST(DATEDIFF(SS,@before,@after) AS varchar)+' SECOND(S)'
PRINT CHAR(13)
```

```
-- Print report body
SELECT ' A'=CASE WHEN P.spid=@@spid THEN '*' ELSE ' ' END+
   CASE WHEN (L.L2<>L.L1)
        OR (P.C2<>P.C1)
        OR (P.I2<>P.I1)
        OR (P.CM1<>P.CM2)
        OR (P.S1<>P.S2)
      THEN 'A'
      ELSE 'I'
      END,
   SPID=STR(P.spid, 5),
   LOGIN=LEFT(P.loginame,20),
   HOST=P.HOSTNAME,
   --C1, C2, I1, I2, L1, L2, CM1, CM2, S1, S2,
   LOG_IO=STR(P.C2,10),
   ' +/-'=SUBSTRING('- +',SIGN(P.C2-P.C1)+2,1)+LTRIM(STR(P.C2  - P.C1,6)),
   '%Chg'=STR(CASE WHEN P.C1<>0 THEN (1.0*(P.C2-P.C1)/P.C1) ELSE 0 END*100,6,1),
   PHYS_IO=STR(P.I2,10),
   ' +/-'=SUBSTRING('- +',SIGN(P.I2-P.I1)+2,1)+LTRIM(STR(P.I2  - P.I1,6)),
   '%Chg'=STR(CASE WHEN P.I1<>0 THEN (1.0*(P.I2-P.I1)/P.I1) ELSE 0 END*100,6,1),
   LCKS=STR(L.L2,5),
   ' +/-'=SUBSTRING('- +',SIGN(L.L2-L.L1)+2,1)+LTRIM(STR(L.L2  - L.L1,6)),
   '%Chg'=STR(CASE WHEN L.L1<>0 THEN (1.0*(L.L2-L.L1)/L.L1) ELSE 0 END*100,6,1),
   BLK=STR(P.B2 ,4),
   BLKCNT=B.BLKING,
   COMMAND=P.CM2,
   STATUS=LEFT(P.S2,10),
   DB=DB_NAME(P.DBID)
FROM (SELECT spid,
   loginame=MAX(loginame),
   C1=SUM(C1),
   C2=SUM(C2),
   I1=SUM(I1),
   I2=SUM(I2),
   CM1=MAX(CM1),
   CM2=MAX(CM2),
   S1=MAX(S1),
   S2=MAX(S2),
   B2=MAX(B2),
   dbid=MAX(DBID),
   hostname=MAX(HOSTNAME)
   FROM #PRCS
   GROUP BY spid) P,
   (SELECT spid,
   L1=SUM(L1),
   L2=SUM(L2)
   FROM #LCKS
   GROUP BY spid) L,
   #BLK B
WHERE P.spid=L.spid
AND    P.spid=B.spid
AND    (@loginame<>'ACTIVEONLY'
OR     @loginame IS NULL
OR     L.L2<>L.L1
OR     P.C2<>P.C1
```

```
OR      P.I2<>P.I1
OR      P.CM1<>P.CM2
OR      P.S1<>P.S2)

-- Print report footer
PRINT CHAR(13)+'TOTAL PROCESSES: '+CAST(@@ROWCOUNT AS varchar)+CHAR(13)+'(A -
ACTIVE, I - INACTIVE, * - THIS PROCESS.)'

-- Delete work tables
DROP TABLE #LCKS
DROP TABLE #PRCS
DROP TABLE #BLK
RETURN 0

Help:
EXEC sp_usage @objectname='sp_active_processes', @desc='Shows system activity
over a period of time',
    @parameters='[@loginame=login name | "ACTIVEONLY" | spid][, @duration=seconds
    to monitor]',
    @example='
sp_active_processes @duration=10  --  Monitors all processes for 10 seconds
sp_active_processes "ACTIVEONLY",30  --  Monitors all processes for 30 seconds,
but only lists active ones
sp_active_processes 34,5  --  Monitors spid 34 for 5 seconds',
    @author='Ken Henderson',@email='khen@khen.com',
    @version='4',@revision='2',
    @datecreated='19910511',@datelastchanged='19990702'
RETURN -1

GO

sp_active_processes
```

(Results abridged)

```
STATISTICS FOR KH AS OF Jul 5 1999 12:39AM
ACTIVITY OF ALL LOGINS FOR THE PAST 5 SECOND(S)

A   SPID LOGIN HOST   LOG_IO   +/-  %Chg  PHYS_IO  +/-  %Chg  LCKS  +/-  %Chg
--- ---- ----- ------ -------- ---- ----- -------- ---- ----- ----- ---- -----
I   1    sa            0        0    0.0   0        0    0.0   1     0    0.0
I   2    sa            0        0    0.0   0        0    0.0   0     0    0.0
I   3    sa            0        0    0.0   0        0    0.0   0     0    0.0
I   4    sa            0        0    0.0   0        0    0.0   0     0    0.0
I   5    sa            0        0    0.0   0        0    0.0   0     0    0.0
I   6    sa            0        0    0.0   64       0    0.0   1     0    0.0
I   7    KH\KH KH      0        0    0.0   3        0    0.0   1     0
*A  8    KH\KH KH      0        0    0.0   57       +12  26.7  6     +1   20.0

TOTAL PROCESSES: 8(A - ACTIVE, I - INACTIVE, * - THIS PROCESS.)
```

This routine simulates sp_who in many ways, but it's vastly improved over it in that you get a feel for actual system *activity* rather than just a basic report listing who's logged in.

The code itself exhibits a couple of noteworthy elements. First, note the use of derived tables to embed the final process and blocking queries. This cuts down on the number of steps within the query itself, simplifying and shortening the code somewhat. Also, note the use of the CHAR() function to format the report delivered by PRINT. You can use CHAR() to perform lots of menial formatting tasks. Here, we use it to embed a carriage return in the string we're about to display in order to ensure that there's a line break between it and the line just printed. Doing this saves an extra call to PRINT. Curiously, placing CHAR(13) at the *end* of a PRINT statement doesn't have the same effect. PRINT seems insistent on including one—and only one—carriage return at the end of each string it displays.

> ### Note
> The stored procedures and scripts in this chapter rely on various ancillary procedures not listed here. For example, the stored procedure sp_usage is used by the procedures in this book to list usage help when '/?' is passed as the first argument or when invalid parameter values are specified. You can find these routines detailed in Chapter 15, "Stored Procedures and Triggers," and you can find their source code on the CD accompanying this book. I've included the source code in multiple places on the CD in order to make it easy to find.

sp_pss

Sp_pss returns detailed information about running processes. It allows you to spy on your users to an extent by displaying detailed process information, including the input and output buffers, for each connection. It uses DBCC PSS() to access this info from the server's internal process-tracking facilities.

You can optionally set the @buffersonly parameter to "YES" to limit the procedure's report to the input and output buffers of each process. As you may have guessed, these buffers constitute the last SQL batch submitted and the last results returned, respectively, for each connection. When you specify this option, sp_pss uses DBCC INPUTBUFFER() and DBCC OUTPUTBUFFER() rather than DBCC PSS() in order to construct its report. Note that these functions offer a subset of what DBCC PSS() itself provides. DBCC PSS() returns the buffers for a connection via its **psrvproc->m_pwchLangBuff** and **psrvproc->srvio.outbuff** columns, along with lots of other useful information.

Here's the source to sp_pss:

```
USE master
go
IF OBJECT_ID('sp_pss') IS NOT NULL
   DROP PROC SP_PSS
go
CREATE PROC sp_pss
     @spid varchar(10)='%',
     @buffersonly varchar(3)='NO'
/*
Object: sp_pss
Description: Lists detail info for running processes
```

```
Usage: sp_pss [@spid=process id to list] (Defaults to all
processes)[,@buffersonly=YES|NO] -
determines whether the report is limited to the input/output buffers for each process

Returns: (None)

Created by: Ken Henderson. Email: khen@khen.com

Version: 4.2

Example usage: sp_pss 8

Created: 1991-01-28. Last changed: 1999-06-02.
*/
AS
SET NOCOUNT ON

IF (@spid='/?') OR NOT EXISTS(SELECT * FROM sysprocesses WHERE spid LIKE @spid) GOTO
Help

SET @buffersonly=UPPER(@buffersonly)

DECLARE @sp int, @lname sysname

DECLARE Processes CURSOR
FOR SELECT spid, loginame FROM master..sysprocesses
WHERE spid LIKE @spid
AND HostProcess IS NOT NULL
AND HostProcess <> ''

OPEN Processes

DBCC TRACEON(3604)

FETCH Processes INTO @sp, @lname
WHILE (@@FETCH_STATUS=0) BEGIN
   IF (@buffersonly='NO') BEGIN
      PRINT CHAR(13)+'Retrieving PSS info for spid: '+CAST(@sp AS varchar)+' user:
      '+@lname
      DBCC PSS(0,@sp)
   END ELSE BEGIN
      PRINT CHAR(13)+'Retrieving the input buffer for spid: '+CAST(@sp AS varchar)+'
      user: '+@lname
      PRINT CHAR(13)
      DBCC INPUTBUFFER(@sp)
      PRINT CHAR(13)+'Retrieving the output buffer for spid: '+CAST(@sp AS varchar)+'
      user: '+@lname
      PRINT CHAR(13)
      DBCC OUTPUTBUFFER(@sp)
   END
   FETCH Processes INTO @sp, @lname
END
```

```
DBCC TRACEOFF(3604)
CLOSE Processes
DEALLOCATE Processes
RETURN 0


Help:
EXEC sp_usage @objectname='sp_pss',@desc='Lists detail info for running processes',
   @parameters='[@spid=process id to list] (Defaults to all
processes)[,@buffersonly=YES|NO] -
determines whether the report is limited to the input/output buffers for each process',
   @author='Ken Henderson', @email='khen@khen.com',
   @version='4', @revision='2',
   @example='sp_pss 8
sp_pss @buffersonly="YES"',
   @datecreated='19910128', @datelastchanged='19990602'
RETURN -1


GO
sp_pss 14
```

   (Results abridged)

```
DBCC execution completed. If DBCC printed error messages, contact your system
administrator.

Retrieving PSS info for spid: 14 user: KHEN_450\KHEN
PSS:


PSS @0x1FF350E4
---------------
pspid = 14 m_dwLoginFlags = 0x83e0 plsid = 15
pbackground = 0
pbSid
-----
    0: 01050000 00000005 15000000 0a423635   .............B65
    10: ff313668 ff47202c ff030000         .16h.G ,....


sSecFlags = 0x1e         pdeadlockpri = 0         poffsets = 0x0
pss_stats = 0x20         ptickcount = 105934285
pcputickcount = 47488887255395                    ploginstamp = 73
ptimestamp = 1999-07-07 14:35:15.273              prowcount = 23
plangid = 0              pdateformat = 1           pdatefirst = 7
Language = us_english    RemServer =               UserName = KHEN_450\KHEN
HostName = KHEN_450      poptions = 0x20000020     poptions2 = 0x1f038
pline = 1                pcurstepno = 0            prowcount = 23
pstatlist = 0            pcurcmd = 253             pseqstat = 0
ptextsize = 64512        pretstat = 0
pslastbatchstarttime = 1900-01-01 00:00:00.000    pmemusage = 0
hLicense = 0             tpFlags = 0x1             isolation_level = 0
fips_flag = 0x0          sSaveSecFlags = 0x0       psavedb = 0
pfetchstat = 0           pcrsrows = 0
pslastbatchtime = 1999-07-07 14:35:23.777         pNtUser = KHEN
pNtDomain = KHEN_450     pubexecdb = 0             finReplicatedProcExec = 0
pdelimitor =             pxcb = 0x1fffa028         pxcb->xcb_xactcnt = 0
pxcb_lock_recursion = 0  pdlckseq = 0              presSemCount = [0]8646092
```

```
pressSemCount = [0]8646092 pcputot = 0            pcputotstart = 0
pcpucmdstart = 0           pbufread = 0           pbufreadstart = 0
plogbufread = 42           plogbufreadstart = 40  pbufwrite = 0
pbufwritestart = 0         pLockTimeout = 4294967295
pec
---
ecid = 0                   ec_stat = 0x0          pcurdb = 5
ec_curckptdb = 0x0         ec_lasterror = 0       ec_preverror = 0
ec_cpucur = 201229         ec_cmderrs = 0         ec_timeslice = 16
ec_dbtable = 0x1f718028    ec_reswait = 0x0       ec_dbindex = -1
psrvproc->eclClient = 2    psrvproc->status = 128 psrvproc->bNewPacket = 0
psrvproc->pmo = 0x21e80028
psrvproc->ums_context = 0xe45c90
psrvproc->pV7LoginRec
---------------------
00000000:  b2000000 00000070 00100000 00000006   .......p........
00000010:  01010000 00000000 e0830000 e0010000   ................
00000020:  09040000 56000800 00000000 00000000   ....V...........
00000030:  66001500 90000700 00000000 9e000400   f...............
00000040:  a6000000 a6000600 00500404 4a190000   .........P..J...
00000050:  0000b200 00004b00                      ......K.


psrvproc->m_pwchLangBuff
------------------------
00000000:  73006500 6c006500 63007400 20002a00   s.e.l.e.c.t. .*.
00000010:  20006600 72006f00 6d002000 61007500   .f.r.o.m. .a.u.
00000020:  74006800 6f007200 73000d00 0a00        t.h.o.r.s.....


psrvproc->srvio.outbuff
-----------------------
00000000:  04010877 00000000 81090001 010800a7   ...w............
00000010:  0b000561 0075005f 00690064 00000008   ...a.u._.i.d....
00000020:  00a72800 08610075 005f006c 006e0061   ..(..a.u._.l.n.a
00000030:  006d0065 00000008 00a71400 08610075   .m.e.........a.u
00000040:  005f0066 006e0061 006d0065 00000008   ._.f.n.a.m.e....
00000050:  00af0c00 05700068 006f006e 00650000   .....p.h.o.n.e..
00000060:  000900a7 28000761 00640064 00720065   ....(..a.d.d.r.e
00000070:  00730073 00000009 00a71400 04630069   .s.s.........c.i
00000080:  00740079 00000009 00af0200 05730074   .t.y.........s.t
00000090:  00610074 00650000 000900af 0500037a   .a.t.e.........z
000000a0:  00690070 00000008 00320863 006f006e   .i.p.....2.c.o.n
000000b0:  00740072 00610063 007400d1 0b003137   .t.r.a.c.t....17
000000c0:  322d3332 2d313137 36050057 68697465   2-32-1176..White
000000d0:  07004a6f 686e736f 6e0c0034 30382034   ..Johnson..408 4
000000e0:  39362d37 3232330f 00313039 33322042   96-7223..10932 B
000000f0:  69676765 2052642e 0a004d65 6e6c6f20   igge Rd...Menlo
00000100:  5061726b 02004341 05003934 30323501   Park..CA..94025.
00000110:  d10b0032 31332d34 362d3839 31350500   ...213-46-8915..
00000120:  47726565 6e08004d 61726a6f 7269650c   Green..Marjorie.
00000130:  00343135 20393836 2d373032 30110033   .415 986-7020..3
00000140:  30392036 33726420 53742e20 23343131   09 63rd St. #411
00000150:  07004f61 6b6c616e 64020043 41050039   ..Oakland..CA..9
00000160:  34363138 01d10b00 3233382d 39352d37   4618....238-95-7
00000170:  37363606 00436172 736f6e06 00436865   766..Carson..Che
00000180:  72796c0c 00343135 20353438 2d373732   ryl..415 548-772
```

```
00000190:   330e0035 38392044 61727769 6e204c6e   3..589 Darwin Ln
000001a0:   2e080042 65726b65 6c657902 00434105   ...Berkeley..CA.
000001b0:   00393437 303501d1 0b003236 372d3431   .94705....267-41
000001c0:   2d323339 3407004f 274c6561 72790700   -2394..O'Leary..
000001d0:   4d696368 61656c0c 00343038 20323836   Michael..408 286
000001e0:   2d323432 38140032 3220436c 6576656c   -2428..22 Clevel
000001f0:   616e6420 41762e20 23313408 0053616e   and Av. #14..San
00000200:   204a6f73 65020043 41050039 35313238   Jose..CA..95128
various psrvproc flags = 0x00000100
```

**DBCC execution completed. If DBCC printed error messages, contact your system
administrator.**

The routine itself isn't very complex because all the real work is done by DBCC. It gets the
job done by opening a cursor on sysprocesses, looping through the table, and calling the appropriate DBCC function for each process.

sp_find_root_blocker

When one process blocks another from accessing an object, it's often because yet another
process is blocking it. This situation can produce a virtual chain of resource blocks that is difficult to trace. It creates a veritable "whodunit" for the DBA—a mystery that requires tracking
down the prime offenders—the processes that block others but are not blocked themselves.

The best tool for the sleuth in this case isn't a magnifying glass or meerschaum pipe—it's
a stored procedure that traces process blocks back to their originators. That's what sp_find_
root_blocker does. Here's the code:

```
USE master
GO
IF OBJECT_ID('sp_find_root_blocker') IS NOT NULL
   DROP PROC sp_find_root_blocker
GO

CREATE PROCEDURE sp_find_root_blocker @help char(2)=NULL
/*

Object: sp_find_root_blocker
Description: Finds the root offender(s) in the chain(s) of blocked processes

Usage: sp_find_root_blocker

Returns: spid of the root blocking process (returns the last one if there are multiple)

Created by: Ken Henderson. Email: khen@khen.com

Version: 6.0

Example: sp_find_root_blocker

Created: 1992-11-03. Last changed: 1999-07-05.

*/
AS
IF (@help='/?') GOTO Help
```

```
IF EXISTS (SELECT * FROM master..sysprocesses p1 JOIN master..sysprocesses p2 ON
(p1.spid=p2.blocked)) BEGIN
   DECLARE @spid int

   SELECT @spid=p1.spid -- Get the _last_ prime offender
   FROM master..sysprocesses p1 JOIN master..sysprocesses p2 ON (p1.spid=p2.blocked)
   WHERE p1.blocked=0

   SELECT p1.spid,
      p1.status,
      loginame=LEFT(p1.loginame,20),
      hostname=substring(p1.hostname,1,20),
      blk=CONVERT(char(3),p1.blocked),
      db=LEFT(db_name(p1.dbid),10),
      p1.cmd,
      p1.waittype
   FROM master..sysprocesses p1 JOIN master..sysprocesses p2 ON (p1.spid=p2.blocked)
   WHERE p1.blocked=0
   RETURN(@spid) -- Return the last root blocker
END ELSE BEGIN
   PRINT 'No processes are currently blocking others.'
   RETURN(0)
END

RETURN 0

Help:
EXEC sp_usage @objectname='sp_find_root_blocker', @desc='Finds the root offender(s) in
the chain(s) of blocked processes',
@parameters='', @returns='spid of the root blocking process (returns the last one if
there are multiple)',
@author='Ken Henderson', @email='khen@khen.com',
@version='6', @revision='0',
@datecreated='19921103', @datelastchanged='19990705',
@example='sp_find_root_blocker'

RETURN -1

GO

sp_find_root_blocker
```

(Results abridged)

spid	status	loginame	hostname	blk	db	cmd
7	runnable	SLUK_CREW\KHEN	SLUK_CREW	0	pubs	SELECT

This routine simply performs a self-join of sysprocesses with itself to locate those processes that block others but are not themselves blocked. It then returns a result set of the prime offenders. Note the assignment of the @spid return variable. Using a SELECT that returns more than one row to assign a local variable results in the variable receiving the last value returned. This means that @spid will return the last prime blocker if there is more than one of them.

sp_lock_verbose

SQL Server includes a stored procedure, sp_lock, which returns useful info regarding re-source locks. Unfortunately, it's not as useful as it might be due to its inexplicable terseness. For example, rather than returning the name of an object that's locked, sp_lock reports its object ID. Rather than listing the database name of each locked object, it reports its database ID only. And the report is completely void of any reference to the user actually maintaining the lock—it lists only the spid of the locking process, which is meaningless without cross-referencing the sysprocesses system table.

The normal course of action for the DBA is to run sp_lock and then translate the IDs of interest into their corresponding names using the appropriate functions and table references. This is tedious and shouldn't be necessary. Here's a stored procedure that provides those details for you:

```
USE master
GO
IF OBJECT_ID('sp_lock_verbose') IS NOT NULL
   DROP PROC sp_lock_verbose
GO
CREATE PROC sp_lock_verbose @spid1 varchar(10)=NULL, @spid2 varchar(10)=NULL
/*
Object: sp_lock_verbose
Description: A more verbose version of sp_lock

Usage: sp_lock_verbose [@spid1=first spid to check][,@spid2=second spid to check]

Returns: (None)

Created by: Ken Henderson. Email: khen@khen.com

Version: 4.2

Example usage: sp_lock_verbose 18,25 -- checks spid's 18 and 25

Created: 1994-11-18. Last changed: 1999-06-01.

*/
AS
SET NOCOUNT ON

IF (@spid1='/?') GOTO Help

DECLARE @dbid varchar(20), @dbname sysname, @objname sysname, @objid int, @execstr
varchar(8000), @nexecstr nvarchar(4000)
CREATE TABLE #locks (spid int, dbid int, objid int, objectname sysname NULL,
indid int, type char(4), resource char(15), mode char(10), status char(6))

-- Get basic locking info from sp_lock
INSERT #locks (spid, dbid, objid, indid, type, resource, mode, status)
EXEC sp_lock @spid1, @spid2

-- Loop through the work table and translate each object id into an object name
DECLARE DBs CURSOR FOR SELECT DISTINCT dbid=CAST(dbid AS varchar) FROM #locks
```

```
OPEN DBs
FETCH DBs INTO @dbid
WHILE ((@@FETCH_STATUS=0) BEGIN
   SET @dbname=DB_NAME(@dbid)
   EXEC master..xp_sprintf @execstr OUTPUT, 'UPDATE #locks SET objectname=o.name FROM
   %s..sysobjects o WHERE (#locks.type=''TAB'' OR #locks.type=''PAG'') AND dbid=%s AND
   #locks.objid=o.id', @dbname, @dbid
      EXEC(@execstr)
   EXEC master..xp_sprintf @execstr OUTPUT, 'UPDATE #locks SET objectname=i.name FROM
   %s..sysindexes i WHERE (#locks.type=''IDX'' OR #locks.type=''KEY'') AND dbid=%s AND
   #locks.objid=i.id AND #locks.indid=i.indid', @dbname, @dbid
      EXEC(@execstr)
   EXEC master..xp_sprintf @execstr OUTPUT, 'UPDATE #locks SET objectname=f.name FROM
   %s..sysfiles f WHERE #locks.type=''FIL'' AND dbid=%s AND #locks.objid=f.fileid',
   @dbname, @dbid
      EXEC(@execstr)
   FETCH DBs INTO @dbid
END
CLOSE DBs
DEALLOCATE DBs

-- Return the result set
SELECT login=LEFT(p.loginame,20), db=LEFT(DB_NAME(l.dbid),30), l.type, object=CASE WHEN
l.type='DB' THEN LEFT(DB_NAME(l.dbid),30) ELSE LEFT(objectname,30) END, l.resource,
l.mode, l.status, l.objid, l.indid, l.spid
FROM #locks l JOIN sysprocesses p ON (l.spid=p.spid)
ORDER BY 1,2,3,4,5,6,7

DROP TABLE #locks

RETURN 0

Help:
EXEC sp_usage @objectname='sp_lock_verbose', @desc='A more verbose version of sp_lock',
@parameters='[@spid1=first spid to check][,@spid2=second spid to check]',
@author='Ken Henderson',@email='khen@khen.com',
@version='4',@revision='2',
@datecreated='19941118', @datelastchanged='19990601',
@example="sp_lock_verbose 18,25 -- checks spid's 18 and 25"
RETURN -1

GO
sp_lock_verbose
```

(Results abridged)

login	db	type	object	resource
KHEN_450\KHEN	master	DB	master	
KHEN_450\KHEN	master	DB	master	
KHEN_450\KHEN	master	DB	master	
KHEN_450\KHEN	master	TAB	spt_values	
KHEN_450\KHEN	Northwind	DB	Northwind	
KHEN_450\KHEN	pubs	DB	pubs	
KHEN_450\KHEN	pubs	DB	pubs	

KHEN_450\KHEN	pubs	DB	pubs	
KHEN_450\KHEN	pubs	DB	pubs	
KHEN_450\KHEN	pubs	DB	pubs	
KHEN_450\KHEN	pubs	KEY	aunmind	(08079ef3ee55)
KHEN_450\KHEN	pubs	KEY	aunmind	(08079ef3ee55)
KHEN_450\KHEN	pubs	KEY	UPKCL_auidind	(28024f0bec4e)
KHEN_450\KHEN	pubs	KEY	UPKCL_auidind	(28024f0bec4e)
KHEN_450\KHEN	pubs	KEY	UPKCL_auidind	(28024f0bec4e)
KHEN_450\KHEN	pubs	KEY	UPKCL_auidind	(28024f0bec4e)
KHEN_450\KHEN	pubs	KEY	UPKCL_auidind	(28024f0bec4e)
KHEN_450\KHEN	pubs	PAG	authors	1:110
KHEN_450\KHEN	pubs	PAG	authors	1:110
KHEN_450\KHEN	pubs	PAG	authors	1:110
KHEN_450\KHEN	pubs	PAG	authors	1:110
KHEN_450\KHEN	pubs	PAG	authors	1:128
KHEN_450\KHEN	pubs	PAG	authors	1:128
KHEN_450\KHEN	pubs	TAB	authors	
KHEN_450\KHEN	pubs	TAB	authors	
KHEN_450\KHEN	pubs	TAB	authors	
KHEN_450\KHEN	pubs	TAB	authors	
KHEN_450\KHEN	pubs	TAB	authors	
KHEN_450\KHEN	tempdb	DB	tempdb	
KHEN_450\KHEN	tempdb	DB	tempdb	
KHEN_450\KHEN	tempdb	DB	tempdb	
KHEN_450\KHEN	tempdb	TAB	#locks_____	
NT AUTHORITY\SYSTEM	msdb	DB	msdb	
NT AUTHORITY\SYSTEM	msdb	DB	msdb	
sa	master	DB	master	
sa	master	DB	master	

The execution path for this query is fairly straightforward. First, it runs sp_lock and "traps" its output in a temporary table using INSERT...EXEC. Next, it iterates through the temporary table and updates the objectname column based on the **type** of lock. Last, it returns the lock report as a result set, translating any remaining IDs as necessary.

You may be wondering why we don't just use the OBJECT_NAME() function rather than query the system tables directly to translate the object IDs returned by sp_lock. The reason this is necessary is that OBJECT_NAME() doesn't work across databases. That is, if the current database focus is **pubs** and you pass OBJECT_NAME() an ID from **Northwind,** you'll get a NULL result unless that ID also happens to be used in **pubs.** So, we have to find a way to take the database context into account when looking up the object name. One way to do this would be to prefix the SQL we issue via the EXEC() function with 'USE *dbname;*' where *db-name* is the name of the database we want to change to. Syntactically, this works but doesn't return the result we want. OBJECT_NAME() still returns NULL for object IDs outside the current database.

Also, since the INFORMATION_SCHEMA views do not include object identifiers, we can't use them to avoid querying the system tables directly. We receive only an object ID from sp_lock, so we must cross-reference a table or view that itself includes object IDs, such as the sysobjects, sysindexes, and sysfiles tables.

Catalog Procedures

Catalog procedures return meta-data about objects stored by the server. SQL Server ships with a number of these, but you may find that you need more information than they provide or that you need it in a different format. When possible, you should avoid querying system catalog tables directly and use either the INFORMATION_SCHEMA views or the catalog procedures instead. Referencing the system tables indirectly will prevent your code from breaking should their exact layout change in a future release of SQL Server.

sp_table

SQL Server provides several methods of getting at the columns contained in a table or view, but none of them is particularly handy. Sp_help, for example, provides a wealth of information, but its formatting is far from ideal. First, it returns the various elements of table meta-data as separate result sets. A single table may generate half a dozen result sets. Second, it doesn't support wildcards, so you're forced to inspect each table separately. Last, it doesn't bother to trim the columns it displays, so many of them require the maximum width of **sysname** (128 characters) in screen real estate to display. You have to pan several screens just to view a basic column specification.

The COLUMNS view in INFORMATION_SCHEMA suffers from many of the same defects, as well as some of its own. The procedures below were written to address many of these shortcomings. Perhaps they have flaws of their own, but at least they are different flaws. Here's sp_table:

```
USE master
GO
IF OBJECT_ID('sp_table') IS NOT NULL
   DROP PROC sp_table
GO
CREATE PROC sp_table @objectname sysname = '%'
/*

Object: sp_table
Description: Lists the columns in a table

Usage: sp_table [@objectname]=Name of table or view to list catalog info for
(defaults to '%')

Returns: (None)

Created by: Ken Henderson. Email: khen@khen.com

Version: 4.2

Example: sp_table "authors"

Created: 1994-02-04. Last changed: 1999-04-11.
*/
AS
SET NOCOUNT ON
```

```
IF (@objectname='/?') GOTO HELP
DECLARE Objects CURSOR FOR
   SELECT name
   FROM sysobjects
   WHERE name like @objectname
   AND type in ('U','S','V')
OPEN Objects
FETCH Objects INTO @objectname
IF (@@FETCH_STATUS<>0) BEGIN -- No matching objects
   CLOSE Objects
   DEALLOCATE Objects
   PRINT 'No table(s) or view(s) were found that match "'+@objectname+'"'
   GOTO Help
END

WHILE (@@FETCH_STATUS=0) BEGIN
   PRINT 'Name: '+@objectname
   PRINT 'Type: '+CASE WHEN OBJECTPROPERTY(OBJECT_ID(@objectname),'IsUserTable')=1 THEN
   'Table'
      WHEN OBJECTPROPERTY(OBJECT_ID(@objectname),'IsSystemTable')=1 THEN 'System Table'
      WHEN OBJECTPROPERTY(OBJECT_ID(@objectname),'IsView')=1 THEN 'View' END
   PRINT CHAR(13)
   SELECT
      'No.'=C.colid,
      'Name'=LEFT(C.name,30),
      'Type'=LEFT(CASE WHEN (T.name IN ('char','varchar','nchar','nvarchar')) THEN
      T.name+'('+LTRIM(RTRIM(STR(C.length)))+')'
         ELSE t.name END,30)+' '+CASE C.status WHEN 1 THEN 'NULL' ELSE 'NOT NULL' END
   FROM syscolumns c JOIN sysobjects o ON (c.id = o.id)
      JOIN systypes t ON (c.xusertype = t.xusertype)
   WHERE o.name = @objectname
   ORDER BY C.colid
   FETCH Objects INTO @objectname
END
CLOSE Objects
DEALLOCATE Objects

RETURN 0

Help:
   EXEC sp_usage @objectname='sp_table', @desc='Lists the columns in a table',
   @parameters='[@objectname]=Name of table or view to list catalog info for (defaults
   to ''%'')',
   @example='sp_table "authors"',
   @author='Ken Henderson', @email='khen@khen.com',
   @version='4', @revision='2',
   @datecreated='19940204', @datelastchanged='19990411'
   RETURN -1
GO
```

(Results)

```
sp_table 'authors'

Name: authors

Type: Table
```

No.	Name	Type
1	au_id	id NOT NULL
2	au_lname	varchar(40) NOT NULL
3	au_fname	varchar(20) NOT NULL
4	phone	char(12) NOT NULL
5	address	varchar(40) NOT NULL
6	city	varchar(20) NOT NULL
7	state	char(2) NOT NULL
8	zip	char(5) NOT NULL
9	contract	bit NOT NULL

This routine provides a simple listing of the columns in a view or table by querying syscolumns, sysobjects, and systypes and truncating the data it displays to a reasonable length. It's formatted similarly to the Oracle DESC command and provides a quick view of what columns are exposed by the object.

The query doesn't do anything that's particularly fancy. It doesn't decode user-defined data types and doesn't bother to report ancillary information such as constraints, indexes, or triggers. Its primary goal is to provide a quick snapshot of a table or view schema. It accepts wildcards, so you can list multiple tables at once from a given database.

sp_dir

Stand-alone database objects include tables, views, stored procedures, triggers, default objects, rule objects, and user-defined data types. Out of the box, SQL Server lacks a procedure or view that can list all of them at once. There's no easy way to get a listing of all the objects you've created in a database without resorting to custom system table queries. That's why sp_dir was written. It provides a listing similar to the operating system DIR command and includes all the objects matching a mask you specify. Here's the code:

```
USE master
GO
IF OBJECT_ID('sp_dir') IS NOT NULL
   DROP PROC sp_dir
GO
CREATE PROCEDURE sp_dir @mask varchar(30) = '%',
   @obtype varchar(2) = 'U',
   @orderby varchar(8000)='/N'
/*

Object: sp_dir
Description: Lists object catalog information similar to the OS DIR command.

Usage: sp_dir [@mask=name mask][,@obtype=object type][,@orderby=order switch[ ASC|DESC]]

@mask = pattern of object names to list (supports SQL wildcards); defaults to all objects
@obtype = type of objects to list (supports SQL wildcards); default to user tables

The following object types are supported:
```

```
U  = User tables
S  = System tables
V  = Views
P  = Stored procedures
X  = Extended procedures
RF = Replication filter stored procedures
TR = Triggers
D  = Default objects
R  = Rule objects
T  = User-defined data types

@orderby = column on which to sort listing.
Can also include ASC or DESC to specify ascending/descending order.

The following orderings are supported:

/N = by Name
/R = by number of rows
/S = by total object size
/D = by date created
/A = by total size of data pages
/X = by total size of index pages
/U = by total size of unused pages
/L = by maximum row length
/O = by owner


Returns: (None)


Created by: Ken Henderson. Email: khen@khen.com


Version: 7.0

Example usage:
   Parameters can be specified positionally, like so:

sp_dir 'TRA%','U','/S'

or by name, like so:

sp_dir @mask='TRA%',@obtype='U',@orderby='/S DESC'

You can also specify additional ordering columns with @orderby, like so:

sp_dir @mask='TRA%',@obtype='U',@orderby='/S DESC, row_count, date_created DESC'

All parameters are optional. If no parameters are specified, the following
command is executed:

sp_dir '%','U','/N'

Created: 1992-06-12. Last changed: 1999-07-02.

*/
AS
SET NOCOUNT ON
```

```
IF (@mask='/?') GOTO Help

SELECT @orderby=UPPER(@orderby)

DECLARE @execstr varchar(8000)

SET @execstr=
"SELECT -- Get regular objects
' '=' ',
name=LEFT(o.name,30),
o.type,
date_created=o.crdate,
row_count=ISNULL(rows,0),
row_len_in_bytes=
   ISNULL((SELECT SUM(length) FROM syscolumns WHERE id=o.id AND o.type in ('U','S')),0),
total_size_in_KB=
   ISNULL((SELECT SUM(reserved) FROM sysindexes WHERE indid in (0, 1, 255) AND id =
   o.id),0)*2,
data_space_in_KB=
   ISNULL(((SELECT SUM(dpages) FROM sysindexes WHERE indid > 2 AND id = o.id)+
   (SELECT ISNULL(SUM(used), 0) FROM sysindexes WHERE indid = 255 AND id = o.id)),0)*2,
index_space_in_KB=
   ISNULL(((SELECT SUM(used) FROM sysindexes WHERE indid in (0, 1, 255) AND id = o.id) -
   ((SELECT SUM(dpages) FROM sysindexes WHERE indid > 2 AND id = o.id)+
   (SELECT ISNULL(SUM(used), 0) FROM sysindexes WHERE indid = 255 AND id = o.id))),0)*2,
unused_space_in_KB=
   ISNULL(((SELECT SUM(reserved) FROM sysindexes WHERE indid in (0,1,255) AND id = o.id) -
   (SELECT SUM(used) FROM sysindexes WHERE indid in (0, 1, 255) AND id = o.id)),0)*2,
owner=USER_NAME(o.uid)
FROM sysobjects o,
sysindexes i
WHERE o.name like '"+@mask+"' AND o.type LIKE '"+@obtype+"'AND o.id*=i.id
AND i.indid>=1
UNION ALL -- Get user-defined data types
SELECT ' ', LEFT(name,30), 'T', NULL, NULL, NULL, NULL, NULL, NULL, NULL, USER_NAME(uid)
FROM systypes
WHERE (usertype & 256)<>0
AND name LIKE '"+@mask
+"'AND 'T' LIKE '"+@obtype
+"' UNION ALL -- Get totals
SELECT
'*',
'{TOTAL}',
     NULL,
     NULL,
     SUM(row_count),
     NULL,
     SUM(total_size_in_KB),
     SUM(data_space_in_KB),
     SUM(index_space_in_KB),
     SUM(unused_space_in_KB),
     NULL
```

```
FROM
(SELECT
 row_count=ISNULL(rows,0),
 total_size_in_KB=
   ISNULL((SELECT SUM(reserved) FROM sysindexes WHERE indid in (0, 1, 255) AND id =
   o.id),0)*2,
data_space_in_KB=
   ISNULL(((SELECT SUM(dpages) FROM sysindexes
      WHERE indid > 2 AND id=o.id)+(SELECT ISNULL(SUM(used), 0)
      FROM sysindexes WHERE indid = 255 AND id = o.id)),0)*2,
 index_space_in_KB=
   ISNULL(((SELECT SUM(used) FROM sysindexes WHERE indid in (0, 1, 255) AND id = o.id) -
   ((SELECT SUM(dpages) FROM sysindexes WHERE indid > 2 AND id = o.id)+
    (SELECT ISNULL(SUM(used), 0) FROM sysindexes WHERE indid = 255 AND id = o.id))),0)*2,
 unused_space_in_KB=
   ISNULL(((SELECT SUM(reserved) FROM sysindexes WHERE indid in (0, 1, 255) AND id =
   o.id)-
   (SELECT SUM(used) FROM sysindexes WHERE indid in (0, 1, 255) AND id = o.id)),0)*2
FROM sysobjects o,
     sysindexes i
WHERE o.name like '"+@mask+"' AND o.type LIKE '"+@obtype+"' AND o.id*=i.id
AND i.indid>=1) O
ORDER BY ' ',"+ -- Ensure that totals sort last
   CASE LEFT(@orderby,2)
   WHEN '/N' THEN 'name'+SUBSTRING(@orderby,3,8000) -- Include ASC/DESC flag if there is
   one
   ELSE
     CASE LEFT(@orderby,2)
     WHEN '/D' THEN 'date_created'
     WHEN '/S' THEN 'total_size_in_KB '
     WHEN '/R' THEN 'row_count'
     WHEN '/A' THEN 'data_space_in_KB'
     WHEN '/X' THEN 'index_space_in_KB'
     WHEN '/U' THEN 'unused_space_in_KB'
     WHEN '/L' THEN 'row_len_in_bytes'
     WHEN '/O' THEN 'owner'
   END+SUBSTRING(@orderby,3,8000)+',name' -- Include name as secondary sort to resolve
   ties
   END


EXEC(@execstr)

RETURN 0

Help:
   EXEC sp_usage @objectname='sp_dir',
     @desc='Lists object catalog information similar to the OS DIR command.',
     @parameters='[@mask=name mask][,@obtype=object type][,@orderby=order switch[
     ASC|DESC]]

@mask = pattern of object names to list (supports SQL wildcards); defaults to all objects
@obtype = type of objects to list (supports SQL wildcards); default to user tables
```

The following object types are supported:

```
U  = User tables
S  = System tables
V  = Views
P  = Stored procedures
X  = Extended procedures
RF = Replication filter stored procedures
TR = Triggers
D  = Default objects
R  = Rule objects
T  = User-defined data types
```

@orderby = column on which to sort listing.
Can also include ASC or DESC to specify ascending/descending order.

The following orderings are supported:

```
/N = by Name
/R = by number of rows
/S = by total object size
/D = by date created
/A = by total size of data pages
/X = by total size of index pages
/U = by total size of unused pages
/L = by maximum row length
/O = by owner',
@example="
    Parameters can be specified positionally, like so:

    sp_dir 'TRA%','U','/S'

    or by name, like so:

    sp_dir @mask='TRA%',@obtype='U',@orderby='/S DESC'

    You can also specify additional ordering columns with @orderby, like so:

    sp_dir @mask='TRA%',@obtype='U',@orderby='/S DESC, row_count, date_created DESC'

    All parameters are optional. If no parameters are specified, the following
    command is executed:

    sp_dir '%','U','/N'",
@author='Ken Henderson', @email='khen@khen.com',
@version='7', @revision='0',
@datecreated='19920612', @datelastchanged='19990702'
RETURN -1

GO

sp_dir 't%'
```

(Results abridged)

```
     name                   type  date_created                  row_count  row_len_in_bytes
---- ---------------------  ----  -------------------------     ---------  ----------------
     temp_authors           U     1999-06-17 23:33:19.120       23         151
     testident              U     1999-05-19 17:52:29.570       132        14
     testtxt                U     1999-05-28 16:43:08.683       0          16
     tid                    T     NULL                          NULL       NULL
     titleauthor            U     1998-11-13 03:10:49.220       25         22
     titleauthor2           U     1999-05-28 16:10:34.153       25         22
     titles                 U     1998-11-13 03:10:48.970       18         334
*    {TOTAL}                NULL  NULL                          223        NULL
```

The routine returns a number of useful object meta-data elements. It can be qualified by object name and type and can be sequenced by any of the columns it returns (including combinations of them).

As you can see from the result set fragment, user-defined data types are returned along with other types of objects despite the fact that they reside in a different system table than those objects. Developers tend to think of user-defined data types as of equal stature with other types of objects, so the procedure treats them uniformly.

There are a couple of features of the code itself that are worth mentioning. First, note that the procedure doesn't use looping or control-flow syntax to generate its report. A single, rather large SELECT statement generates the result set returned by the procedure. The statement uses UNION ALL to aggregate the objects from sysobjects, systypes, and the table-related totals from sysobjects. This is more for syntactical amusement than anything else—storing each of the UNION terms separately in a temporary table and listing the table would work equally well and might well be more efficient since the totals query could reference the temporary table rather than sysobjects.

UNION ALL is used rather than UNION because it's more efficient in situations where you aren't worried about duplicates. UNION removes duplicates from its result set before returning it; UNION ALL doesn't. Here, the object names that come from sysobjects are guaranteed to be unique by the system anyway, and we wouldn't want to remove duplicates between the systypes and sysobjects tables, so we use UNION ALL because it's faster.

Another noteworthy feature of the query is its use of a dummy column to sequence the result set. We want the totals row to be the last row of the report, but we also want to allow sorting of the other rows. Remember that you can't count on the natural order of a table—if you want a specific order, you must specify it with an ORDER BY clause. This makes the problem a little more difficult than simply placing the rows in a temporary table in the order in which we want to list them. The solution used here makes use of a pseudocolumn at the left of the report that contains either blanks for nontotals or an asterisk for totals and uses that column as the first term in the ORDER BY clause, regardless of the sort order selected by the user. Since the value for this column is the same for all nontotal rows, the real sorting of those rows is controlled by the other ordering columns we specify, not the pseudocolumn.

One final point worth mentioning is the flexibility the procedure provides in ordering the result set. Beyond the simple mnemonics that can be passed to @orderby to specify a sort order, the procedure allows the DESC and ASC keywords of the Transact-SQL ORDER BY clause to be specified as well. Other ordering columns can also be specified, so '/D DESC, owner ASC' could be specified to sort the report in descending order by date created, then in ascending order by owner. This is made possible by the fact that the procedure uses the EXEC() function to execute a query that it constructs dynamically at runtime. Any ORDER BY terms passed into the procedure are simply appended to the end of the query following the pseudocolumn reference.

sp_object

As of SQL Server 7.0, Transact-SQL includes a collection of system functions that are useful for accessing system meta-data. Getting at this catalog information previously required spelunking around in the system tables and translating lots of arcane bitmaps and fossilized column values. That's no longer the case—Transact-SQL's meta-functions make accessing system-level info much easier than it once was. The OBJECTPROPERTY(), TYPEPROPERTY(), COLUMNPROPERTY(), INDEXPROPERTY(), and DATABASEPROPERTY() functions are particularly handy in this regard.

The stored procedure that follows uses these functions, with some help from the system tables, to interrogate the object meta-data stored in a database. This amounts to providing textual descriptions of an object's defining characteristics by examining its catalog info. There's a wealth of available data there if you know where to look.

Similarly to sp_dir, sp_object lists detail-level information for an object or objects. It lists regular objects as well as user-defined data types and uses the ...PROPERTY() functions to yield the pertinent details of each. Here's the source code to sp_object:

```
USE master
GO
DROP PROC sp_object
GO
CREATE PROC sp_object @objectname sysname='%', @orderby
varchar(8000)='1,2,3,4,5,6'
/*

Object: sp_object
Description: Returns detailed object info

Usage: sp_object [@objectname=name or mask of object(s) to list][,@orderby=ORDER
BY clause for query]

Returns: (None)

Created by: Ken Henderson. Email: khen@khen.com

Version: 7.0

Example: sp_object 'authors'

Created: 1994-06-29. Last changed: 1999-07-01.

*/
AS

IF (@objectname='/?') GOTO Help
```

```
EXEC("
SELECT Object=LEFT(O.Object,30), O.Type, 'SubType'=
CAST(CASE O.Type
   WHEN 'Constraint' THEN
      CASE WHEN OBJECTPROPERTY(id,'IsCheckCnst')=1 THEN 'Check Constraint'
         WHEN OBJECTPROPERTY(id,'IsForeignKey')=1 THEN 'Foreign Key Constraint'
         WHEN OBJECTPROPERTY(id,'IsPrimaryKey')=1 THEN 'Primary Key Constraint'
         WHEN OBJECTPROPERTY(id,'IsDefaultCnst')=1 THEN 'Default Constraint'
         WHEN OBJECTPROPERTY(id,'IsUniqueCnst')=1 THEN 'Unique Constraint'
END
   WHEN 'Table' THEN
      CASE  WHEN OBJECTPROPERTY(id,'TableIsFake')=1 THEN 'Virtual'
            WHEN OBJECTPROPERTY(id,'IsSystemTable')=1 THEN 'System'
            WHEN OBJECTPROPERTY(id,'IsUserTable')=1 THEN 'User'
      END
   WHEN 'Trigger' THEN
   (SELECT ISNULL(SUBSTRING('Insert ', OBJECTPROPERTY(id,'ExecIsInsertTrigger'),7),'')+
   ISNULL(SUBSTRING('Delete ', OBJECTPROPERTY(id,'ExecIsDeleteTrigger'),7),'')+
   ISNULL(SUBSTRING('Update ', OBJECTPROPERTY(id,'ExecIsUpdateTrigger'),7),'')+
   ISNULL(SUBSTRING('(Disabled) ', OBJECTPROPERTY(id,'ExecIsTriggerDisabled'),11),''))

   WHEN 'Stored Procedure' THEN
      CASE  WHEN OBJECTPROPERTY(id,'IsExtendedProc')=1 THEN 'Extended'
            WHEN OBJECTPROPERTY(id,'IsReplProc')=1 THEN 'Replication'
            ELSE 'User'
      END
   WHEN 'View' THEN
      CASE  WHEN OBJECTPROPERTY(id,'OwnerId')=3 THEN 'ANSI SQL-92'
            WHEN OBJECTPROPERTY(id, 'IsMSShipped')=1 THEN 'System'
      ELSE 'User'
      END
   WHEN 'User-defined Data Type' THEN
      (SELECT name+
      CASE WHEN name in ('char','varchar','nchar','nvarchar') THEN
      '('+CAST(TYPEPROPERTY(Object,'Precision') AS varchar)+')'
      WHEN name in ('float','numeric','decimal','real','money','smallmoney') THEN
      '('+CAST(TYPEPROPERTY(Object,'Precision') AS varchar)+ ','+
      CAST(ISNULL(TYPEPROPERTY(Object,'Scale'),0) AS varchar)+')'
      ELSE ''
      END
      FROM systypes WHERE (type=id) AND (usertype & 256)=0 AND
      (name<>'sysname') AND
      prec=(SELECT MAX(prec) FROM systypes WHERE type=id))
   END
AS varchar(25)),
Owner=LEFT(USER_NAME(uid),25),
'System-Supplied'=
   CASE Type
   WHEN 'User-defined Data Type' THEN 'NO' -- Can't be, by definition
   ELSE
   CASE OBJECTPROPERTY(id,'IsMSShipped') WHEN 0 THEN 'NO' ELSE 'YES' END
   END,
```

```
Description=
SUBSTRING(
   CASE WHEN O.Type='Constraint' THEN
      (SELECT ISNULL(SUBSTRING(',Clustered Key,', OBJECTPROPERTY(id,
      'CnstIsClustKey'),30),'')+
      ISNULL(SUBSTRING(',Column Constraint,',OBJECTPROPERTY(id,'CnstIsColumn'),30),'')+
      ISNULL(SUBSTRING(',Disabled,',OBJECTPROPERTY(id,'CnstIsDisabled'),30),'')+
      ISNULL(SUBSTRING(',Non-clustered key,', OBJECTPROPERTY(id,
      'CnstIsNonClustKey'),30),'')+ISNULL(SUBSTRING(',NOT FOR
      REPLICATION,',OBJECTPROPERTY(id,'CnstIsNotRepl'),30),''))
   WHEN O.Type='Table' THEN
      (SELECT CASE
      WHEN OBJECTPROPERTY(id,'TableHasDeleteTrigger')=1 THEN
      ',# DELETE trig.:'+CAST(OBJECTPROPERTY(id,
      'TableDeleteTriggerCount') AS varchar) ELSE '' END+
      CASE WHEN OBJECTPROPERTY(id,'TableHasInsertTrigger')=1 THEN
      ',# INSERT trig.:'+ CAST(OBJECTPROPERTY(id,
      'TableInsertTriggerCount') AS varchar) ELSE '' END+
      CASE WHEN OBJECTPROPERTY(id,'TableHasUpdateTrigger')=1 THEN
      ',# UPDATE trig.:'+CAST(OBJECTPROPERTY(id,
      'TableUpdateTriggerCount') AS varchar) ELSE '' END+
      ',Full-text index?:'+RTRIM(SUBSTRING('NO YES', (OBJECTPROPERTY(id,
      'TableHasActiveFulltextIndex')*3)+1,3))+
      (CASE WHEN OBJECTPROPERTY(id, 'TableHasActiveFullTextIndex')=1
      THEN ',Full-text catalog ID: '+ISNULL(CAST(OBJECTPROPERTY(id,
      'FulltextCatalogID') AS varchar),'(None)')+
      ',Full-text key column: '+
      ISNULL((SELECT name FROM syscolumns WHERE id=id and
      colid=OBJECTPROPERTY(id,'TableFulltextKeyColumn')),'(None)')
      ELSE '' END)+
      ',Primary key?:'+RTRIM(SUBSTRING('NO YES',(OBJECTPROPERTY(id,
      'TableHasPrimaryKey')*3)+1,3))+
      ',Check cnst?:'+RTRIM(SUBSTRING('NO YES',(OBJECTPROPERTY(id,
      'TableHasCheckCnst')*3)+1,3))+
      ',Default cnst?:'+RTRIM(SUBSTRING('NO YES', (OBJECTPROPERTY(id,
      'TableHasDefaultCnst')*3)+1,3))+
      ',Foreign key?:'+RTRIM(SUBSTRING('NO YES',( OBJECTPROPERTY(id,
      'TableHasForeignKey')*3)+1,3))+
      ',Foreign key ref?:'+RTRIM(SUBSTRING('NO YES',(OBJECTPROPERTY(id,
      'TableHasForeignRef')*3)+1,3))+
      ',Unique cnst?:'+RTRIM(SUBSTRING('NO YES',(OBJECTPROPERTY(id,
      'TableHasUniqueCnst')*3)+1,3))+
      ',Indexed?:'+RTRIM(SUBSTRING('NO YES',(OBJECTPROPERTY(id,
      'TableHasIndex')*3)+1,3))+
      ',Clust. idx?:'+RTRIM(SUBSTRING('NO YES',(OBJECTPROPERTY(id,
      'TableHasClustIndex')*3)+1,3))+
      ',Non-clust. idx?:'+RTRIM(SUBSTRING('NO YES',(OBJECTPROPERTY(id,
      'TableHasNonclustIndex')*3)+1,3))+
      ',Identity?:'+RTRIM(SUBSTRING('NO YES',(OBJECTPROPERTY(id,
      'TableHasIdentity')*3)+1,3))+
      ',ROWGUIDCOL?:'+RTRIM(SUBSTRING('NO YES',(OBJECTPROPERTY(id,
      'TableHasRowGUIDCol')*3)+1,3))+
      ',Text col.?:'+RTRIM(SUBSTRING('NO YES',(OBJECTPROPERTY(id,
```

```
            'TableHasTextImage')*3)+1,3))+
            ',Timestamp?:'+RTRIM(SUBSTRING('NO YES',(OBJECTPROPERTY(id,
            'TableHasTimestamp')*3)+1,3))+
            ',Pinned?:'+RTRIM(SUBSTRING('NO YES',(OBJECTPROPERTY(id,
            'TableIsPinned')*3)+1,3)))
        WHEN O.Type='User-defined Data Type' THEN
            (SELECT ',Allows NULLs?:'+RTRIM(SUBSTRING('NO YES',
            (TYPEPROPERTY(Object,'AllowsNull')*3)+1,3))+
            ISNULL(',Uses ANSI trim?:'+RTRIM(SUBSTRING('NO YES',
            (TYPEPROPERTY(Object,'UsesANSITrim')*3)+1,3)),''))
        WHEN O.Type IN ('Trigger','Stored Procedure','View') THEN
            (SELECT ',ANSI NULLS='+RTRIM(SUBSTRING('OFFON ',
            (OBJECTPROPERTY(id,'ExecIsAnsiNullsOn')*3)+1,3))+
            ',Startup='+RTRIM(SUBSTRING('FALSETRUE ',
            (OBJECTPROPERTY(id,'ExecIsStartUp')*5)+1,5))+
            ',QuotedIdent='+RTRIM(SUBSTRING('FALSETRUE ',(OBJECTPROPERTY(id,
            'ExecIsQuotedIdentOn')*5)+1,5)))
    END
,2,4000)
FROM (
SELECT Object=name,
    'Type'=
    CASE
    WHEN OBJECTPROPERTY(id,'IsConstraint')=1 THEN 'Constraint'
    WHEN OBJECTPROPERTY(id,'IsDefault')=1 THEN 'Default Object'
    WHEN OBJECTPROPERTY(id,'IsProcedure')=1 OR
         OBJECTPROPERTY(id,'IsExtendedProc')=1 OR
         OBJECTPROPERTY(id,'IsReplProc')=1 THEN 'Stored Procedure'
    WHEN OBJECTPROPERTY(id,'IsRule')=1 THEN 'Rule Object'
    WHEN OBJECTPROPERTY(id,'IsTable')=1 THEN 'Table'
    WHEN OBJECTPROPERTY(id,'IsTrigger')=1 THEN 'Trigger'
    WHEN OBJECTPROPERTY(id,'IsView')=1 THEN 'View'
    ELSE 'Unknown'
    END,
id,
uid
FROM sysobjects
WHERE name LIKE '"+@objectname+"'
UNION ALL
SELECT name, 'User-defined Data Type',
type,
uid
FROM systypes
WHERE (usertype & 256)<>0
AND name LIKE '"+@objectname+"'
) O
ORDER BY "+@orderby
)

RETURN 0

Help:
EXEC sp_usage @objectname='sp_object', @desc='Returns detailed object info',
@parameters='[@objectname=name or mask of object(s) to list][,@orderby=ORDER BY clause
for query]',
```

```
@author='Ken Henderson',@email='khen@khen.com',
@version='7',@revision='0',
@datecreated='19940629',@datelastchanged='19990701',
@example='sp_object ''authors'' '

RETURN -1

GO

sp_object 'authors'
```

(Results abridged)

Object	Type	SubType	Owner	System-Supplied	Description
authors	Table	User	dbo	NO	Full-text index?:NO,Primary key?:YES,Check cn

```
sp_object 'ti%'
```

(Results abridged)

Object	Type	SubType	Owner	System-Supplied	Description
tid	User-defined Data Type	varchar(6)	dbo	NO	Allows NULLs?:NO,Uses ANSI tr
titleauthor	Table	User	dbo	NO	Full-text index?:NO,Primary k
titleauthor2	Table	User	dbo	NO	Full-text index?:NO,Primary k
titles	Table	User	dbo	NO	Full-text index?:NO,Primary k
titleview	View	User	dbo	NO	ANSI NULLS=OFF,Startup=FALSE,

This procedure uses Transact-SQL's meta-data functions to probe the object-level information stored in the system catalogs. It accepts wildcards and lists each object's name, type, subtype, owner, and origin, along with a free-form description field further depicting the object's makeup.

As with sp_dir, sp_object uses UNION ALL to combine the objects found in the sysobjects and systypes tables. Since it doesn't generate report totals, sp_dir's second UNION—used solely to compute totals—isn't needed. Also like sp_dir, this routine constructs at runtime a query that it then executes. This allows the ORDER BY criteria to be specified directly by the user.

Note the use of a derived table to simplify the query. The derived table allows us to use the values it yields to qualify the outer query. That is, rather than coding **CASE OBJECTPROP-ERTY(id, 'IsTable')** in the outer query, we can code **CASE Type WHEN 'Table'** **...** instead. This is much more readable and helps modularize the code to an extent.

Note the use of the expression:

```
RTRIM(SUBSTRING('NO YES',(OBJECTPROPERTY(id,'TableHasPrimaryKey')*3)+1,3))
```

to translate the 1 or 0 returned by OBJECTPROPERTY() into "YES" or "NO." This is functionally equivalent to:

```
CASE OBJECTPROPERTY('TableHasPrimaryKey') WHEN 0 THEN 'No' ELSE 'Yes' END
```

I used this technique because there are already dozens of examples of CASE in the procedure and it's good to be aware of the other options available to you for translating integers into string tokens. Also, the sheer number of CASE expressions in the query can be a bit overwhelming at first—breaking it up with deviations like this helps alleviate some of the monotony without really affecting performance.

The code used to decode user-defined data types is also of interest. The subquery:

```
(SELECT name+
CASE WHEN name in ('char','varchar','nchar','nvarchar') THEN
'('+CAST(TYPEPROPERTY(Object,'Precision') AS varchar)+')'
WHEN name in ('float','numeric','decimal','real','money','smallmoney') THEN
'('+CAST(TYPEPROPERTY(Object,'Precision') AS varchar)+ ','+
CAST(ISNULL(TYPEPROPERTY(Object,'Scale'),0) AS varchar)+')'
ELSE ''
END
FROM systypes WHERE (type=id) AND (usertype & 256)=0 AND
(name<>'sysname') AND
prec=(SELECT MAX(prec) FROM systypes WHERE type=id))
```

determines the underlying base type of a UDDT by scanning the systypes system table for the largest base type (**usertype** & 256 = 0) whose **type** field matches the **id** column exposed by the query. We scan for the largest type because our subquery is allowed to return only one value. It's entirely possible that there's more than one base type with the same type ID. For character data types, this will always be the case due to the inclusion of their Unicode versions. Returning only the largest types means that nchar and nvarchar will be ignored since they have less precision (4000 characters vs. 8000 characters) than their non-Unicode siblings.

Maintenance Routines

Automating the maintenance of the system is probably the single most common use of administrative Transact-SQL. Most people, even DBAs, don't like to spend their time manually maintaining and keeping their systems tuned. Few subscribe to Marguerite Duras's assertion that "the best way to fill time is to waste it." Most people have better things to do.

To that end, below you'll find an assortment of maintenance procedures and scripts that I've used in my own work to make life easier as it relates to database and system administration. Many of these are the types of routines that you can schedule via the SQL Server Agent service. Most of them perform tasks that you'll want to complete on a regular basis, so it's sensible to schedule them to run automatically when possible.

sp_update_stats_all

Regardless of whether you allow SQL Server automatically to maintain the statistics that it uses to optimize queries, you may still need to update these statistics manually on an occasional basis. There are a couple of reasons for this. First, the server uses sampling techniques to minimize the time spent automatically generating statistics. Sometimes these samples aren't representative of a table's overall data and prevent the optimizer from properly optimizing queries. In that case, you may have to help the server a bit by creating the statistics yourself using CREATE STATISTICS or UPDATE STATISTICS.

Another reason you may wish to update statistics manually is that you may be forced to disable automatic statistics generation for performance reasons. When autogeneration is enabled, the server ages and rebuilds statistics as needed when it optimizes queries that use those statistics. This process costs a certain amount of resources and processor time. In high-volume transactional environments, you may find that it's more efficient to update statistics manually once a day or once a week than to allow them to be maintained automatically by the server. The trade-off here is similar to the one you face when deciding whether to drop nonclustered indexes before bulk data operations—you may find that it's more efficient to "buy now and pay later" with index statistics than to "pay as you go."

The following is a stored procedure that updates the statistics for all the tables in the database or databases you specify. It accepts wildcards and simply calls the SQL Server system procedure sp_updatestats to update the statistics in each database. Here's the code:

```
USE master
IF OBJECT_ID('sp_updatestats_all') IS NOT NULL
   DROP PROC sp_updatestats_all
GO
CREATE PROC sp_updatestats_all @dbname sysname='%'
/*

Object: sp_updatestats_all
Description: Updates index statistics for a given database or databases

Usage: sp_updatestats_all [@dbname=Name of database to update (Default: "%")]

Returns: (None)

Created by: Ken Henderson. Email: khen@khen.com

Version: 4.2

Example: sp_updatestats_all "pubs"

Created: 1991-09-12. Last changed: 1999-05-03.

*/
AS
SET NOCOUNT ON
IF (@dbname='/?') GOTO Help
DECLARE Databases CURSOR FOR
   SELECT CATALOG_NAME
   FROM INFORMATION_SCHEMA.SCHEMATA
   WHERE NOT
   (CATALOG_NAME IN ('tempdb','master','msdb','model')) -- Omit system DBs
   AND CATALOG_NAME LIKE @dbname
DECLARE @execstr varchar(8000)

OPEN Databases
```

```
FETCH Databases INTO @dbname
IF (@@FETCH_STATUS<>0) BEGIN -- No matching databases
   CLOSE Databases
   DEALLOCATE Databases
   PRINT 'No databases were found that match "'+@dbname+'"'
   GOTO Help
END

WHILE (@@FETCH_STATUS=0) BEGIN
   PRINT CHAR(13)+'Updating statistics information for database: '+@dbname
   -- Prefixing the DB name temporarily changes the current DB
   SET @execstr='EXEC '+@dbname+'..sp_updatestats'
   EXEC(@execstr)
   FETCH Databases INTO @dbname
END
CLOSE Databases
DEALLOCATE Databases
RETURN 0

Help:
EXEC sp_usage @objectname='sp_updatestats_all', @desc='Updates index statistics
for a given database or databases',
@parameters='[@dbname=Name of database to update (Default: "%")]',
@author='Ken Henderson', @email='khen@khen.com',
@version='4', @revision='2',
@datecreated='19910912', @datelastchanged='19990503',
@example='sp_updatestats_all "pubs"'
RETURN -1

sp_updatestats_all
```

(Results)

```
Updating statistics information for database: Northwind
Updating dbo.employees
Updating dbo.categories
Updating dbo.customers
Updating dbo.dtproperties
Updating dbo.shippers
Updating dbo.suppliers
Updating dbo.orders
Updating dbo.products
Updating dbo.order details
Updating dbo.customercustomerdemo
Updating dbo.customerdemographics
Updating dbo.region
Updating dbo.territories
Updating dbo.employeeterritories

Statistics for all tables have been updated.

Updating statistics information for database: pubs
Updating dbo.authors
Updating dbo.publishers
Updating dbo.titles
```

```
Updating dbo.titleauthor
Updating dbo.stores
Updating dbo.sales
Updating dbo.roysched
Updating dbo.discounts
Updating dbo.jobs
Updating dbo.pub_info
Updating dbo.employee
Updating dbo.bets
Updating dbo.testident
Updating dbo.dtproperties
Updating dbo.titleauthor2
Updating dbo.authors2
Updating dbo.testtxt
Updating dbo.authors22
Updating dbo.temp_authors
Statistics for all tables have been updated.
```

This routine isn't terribly complicated. It opens a cursor on the SCHEMATA view and iterates through the databases listed by it, executing sp_updatestats for each one. Note that the query could have queried sysdatabases instead, but using an INFORMATION_SCHEMA view is always preferable when one that meets your needs is available.

The actual call to sp_updatestats uses the trick, demonstrated earlier in the chapter and elsewhere in this book, of prefixing the system procedure name with the name of the database in order to change the database context temporarily:

```
EXEC dbname..sp_updatestats
```

This causes the procedure to run in the context of the database *dbname,* as though a USE *dbname* had immediately preceded the call to EXEC.

sp_updateusage_all

Like sp_updatestats_all, sp_updateusage_all iterates through the databases on the current server to update system-level information. Specifically, it executes DBCC UPDATEUSAGE() to correct errors in sysindexes that can cause inaccuracies in the object sizes listed by stored procedures such as sp_spaceused and sp_dir. Here's the code:

```
USE master
IF OBJECT_ID('sp_updateusage_all') IS NOT NULL
   DROP PROC sp_updateusage_all
GO
CREATE PROC sp_updateusage_all @dbname sysname='%'
/*
Object: sp_updateusage_all
Description: Corrects usage errors in sysindexes

Usage: sp_updateusage_all [@dbname=Name of database to update (Default: "%")]

Returns: (None)

Created by: Ken Henderson. Email: khen@khen.com
```

```
Version: 4.2

Example: sp_updateusage_all "pubs"

Created: 1991-09-12. Last changed: 1999-05-03.

*/
AS
SET NOCOUNT ON

IF (@dbname='/?') GOTO Help
DECLARE Databases CURSOR FOR
   SELECT CATALOG_NAME
   FROM INFORMATION_SCHEMA.SCHEMATA
   -- Omit system DBs
   WHERE NOT (CATALOG_NAME IN ('tempdb','master','msdb','model'))
   AND CATALOG_NAME LIKE @dbname
DECLARE @execstr varchar(8000)
OPEN Databases

FETCH Databases INTO @dbname
IF (@@FETCH_STATUS<>0) BEGIN -- No matching databases
   CLOSE Databases
   DEALLOCATE Databases
   PRINT 'No databases were found that match "'+@dbname+'"'
   GOTO Help
END

WHILE (@@FETCH_STATUS=0) BEGIN
   PRINT CHAR(13)+
     'Updating sysindexes usage information for database: '+@dbname
   SET @execstr='DBCC UPDATEUSAGE('+@dbname+') WITH COUNT_ROWS, NO_INFOMSGS'
   EXEC(@execstr)
   FETCH Databases INTO @dbname
END
CLOSE Databases
DEALLOCATE Databases
RETURN 0

Help:
EXEC sp_usage @objectname='sp_updateusage_all', @desc='Corrects usage errors in
sysindexes',
@parameters='[@dbname=Name of database to update (Default: "%")]',
@author='Ken Henderson', @email='khen@khen.com',
@version='4', @revision='2',
@datecreated='19910912', @datelastchanged='19990503',
@example='sp_updateusage_all "pubs"'
RETURN -1
```

If no errors are found in sysindexes, DBCC UPDATEUSAGE() returns no output, so you'll often see nothing but the "Updating sysindexes information for database..." message that the procedure generates for each database. Also, DBCC UPDATEUSAGE() can take some time to run for large tables. You should issue sp_updateusage_all with care and preferably when system utilization is low.

sp_rebuildindexes_all

There are times when you'll need to rebuild all the indexes for a given table or tables. Bulk data loads, nightly posts, and other types of massive data updates are examples of operations that can necessitate index rebuilds. The procedure below uses DBCC DBREINDEX() to rebuild the indexes on all the tables in the databases you specify. Rebuilding indexes in this way allows the indexes that service PRIMARY KEY and UNIQUE constraints to be rebuilt without having to recreate those constraints manually. It also allows a table's indexes to be rebuilt without knowing anything about the table.

Because DBCC DBREINDEX() can rebuild all the indexes on a table in a single statement, it is inherently atomic, which means that either all the index creations will occur or none of them will. Comparable DROP INDEX and CREATE INDEX statements would have to be encapsulated in a transaction in order to achieve the same effect. Also, DBCC DBREINDEX() is easier for the server to optimize than a query featuring analogous DROP and CREATE INDEX statements. Here's the source to sp_rebuildindexes_all:

```
USE master
IF OBJECT_ID('sp_rebuildindexes_all') IS NOT NULL
   DROP PROC sp_rebuildindexes_all
GO
IF OBJECT_ID('sp_rebuildindexes') IS NOT NULL
   DROP PROC sp_rebuildindexes
GO

CREATE PROC sp_rebuildindexes @tablename sysname='%'
AS
SET NOCOUNT ON

DECLARE @execstr varchar(8000)
DECLARE Tables CURSOR FOR
   -- Tried to use INFORMATION_SCHEMA.TABLES here but it refused to work
   SELECT name
   FROM sysobjects
   -- Exclude views and system tables
   WHERE OBJECTPROPERTY(OBJECT_ID(name),'IsUserTable')=1
   AND name LIKE @tablename
OPEN Tables
FETCH Tables INTO @tablename
WHILE (@@FETCH_STATUS=0) BEGIN
   PRINT CHAR(13)+'Rebuilding indexes for: '+@tablename
   SET @execstr='DBCC DBREINDEX('+@tablename+')'
   EXEC(@execstr)
   FETCH Tables INTO @tablename
END
CLOSE Tables
DEALLOCATE Tables
RETURN 0
GO
```

```
CREATE PROC sp_rebuildindexes_all @dbname sysname='%'
/*

Object: sp_rebuildindexes_all
Description: Rebuilds the indexes for all tables in a given database or databases

Usage: sp_rebuildindexes_all [@dbname=Name of database to update (Default: "%")]

Returns: (None)

Created by: Ken Henderson. Email: khen@khen.com

Version: 4.2

Example: sp_rebuildindexes_all "pubs"

Created: 1991-09-12. Last changed: 1999-05-03.

*/
AS
SET NOCOUNT ON
IF (@dbname='/?') GOTO Help
DECLARE Databases CURSOR FOR
   SELECT CATALOG_NAME
   FROM INFORMATION_SCHEMA.SCHEMATA
   WHERE NOT (CATALOG_NAME IN ('tempdb','master','msdb','model')) -- Omit system DBs
   AND CATALOG_NAME LIKE @dbname
DECLARE        @execstr varchar(8000), @tablename sysname

OPEN Databases

FETCH Databases INTO @dbname
IF (@@FETCH_STATUS<>0) BEGIN -- No matching databases
   CLOSE Databases
   DEALLOCATE Databases
   PRINT 'No databases were found that match "'+@dbname+'"'
   GOTO Help
END

WHILE (@@FETCH_STATUS=0) BEGIN
   PRINT CHAR(13)+'Rebuilding indexes in database: '+@dbname
   PRINT CHAR(13)
   -- Prefixing DB name temporarily changes current DB
   SET @execstr='EXEC '+@dbname+'..sp_rebuildindexes'
   EXEC(@execstr)
   FETCH Databases INTO @dbname
END
CLOSE Databases
DEALLOCATE Databases
RETURN 0

Help:
EXEC sp_usage @objectname='sp_rebuildindexes_all',
@desc='Rebuilds the indexes for all tables in a given database or databases',
@parameters='[@dbname=Name of database to update (Default: "%")]',
@author='Ken Henderson', @email='khen@khen.com',
```

```
@version='4', @revision='2',
@datecreated='19910912', @datelastchanged='19990503',
@example='sp_rebuildindexes_all "pubs"'
RETURN -1

GO

sp_rebuildindexes_all
```

(Results abridged)

```
Rebuilding indexes for: authors
Index (ID = 1) is being rebuilt.
Index (ID = 2) is being rebuilt.
DBCC execution completed. If DBCC printed error messages, contact your system
administrator.

Rebuilding indexes for: jobs
Index (ID = 1) is being rebuilt.
DBCC execution completed. If DBCC printed error messages, contact your system
administrator.

Rebuilding indexes for: publishers
Index (ID = 1) is being rebuilt.
DBCC execution completed. If DBCC printed error messages, contact your system
administrator.

Rebuilding indexes for: roysched
Index (ID = 2) is being rebuilt.
DBCC execution completed. If DBCC printed error messages, contact your system
administrator.

Rebuilding indexes for: sales
Index (ID = 1) is being rebuilt.
Index (ID = 2) is being rebuilt.
Index (ID = 3) is being rebuilt.
DBCC execution completed. If DBCC printed error messages, contact your system
administrator.

Rebuilding indexes for: stores
Index (ID = 1) is being rebuilt.
DBCC execution completed. If DBCC printed error messages, contact your system
administrator.

Rebuilding indexes for: titleauthor
Index (ID = 1) is being rebuilt.
Index (ID = 2) is being rebuilt.
Index (ID = 3) is being rebuilt.
DBCC execution completed. If DBCC printed error messages, contact your system
administrator.

Rebuilding indexes for: titles
Index (ID = 1) is being rebuilt.
Index (ID = 2) is being rebuilt.
Index (ID = 3) is being rebuilt.
DBCC execution completed. If DBCC printed error messages, contact your system
administrator.
```

Note the use of the sp_rebuildindexes stored procedure to call DBCC DBREINDEX() Why is this? Why didn't we just call DBREINDEX() from the main procedure? Why do we need a second routine? We need sp_rebuildindexes in order to change the database context temporarily so that the Transact-SQL actually performing the reindex runs in the correct database. Prefixing a call to a system procedure (one beginning with "sp_" and residing in the master database) with a database name—any database name—changes the database context for the duration of the procedure, as I've mentioned before. It's tantamount to issuing a **USE dbname** just prior to calling the procedure and then returning to the original database afterward.

sp_dbbackup

Enterprise Manager includes a nice facility for scheduling and managing database backups. Since scheduled jobs can also be run ad hoc, you should normally use this facility to execute and manage your backups.

That said, there may be times when you want to perform backups using Transact-SQL. You may have other code that needs to execute immediately prior to the backup, you might need to create backups on alternate media or with different options, or you may have some other compelling reason for making backups this way—there are a number of situations where this might be the case. Here's a procedure that automates the task of backing up all the databases on a server:

```
USE master
GO

IF OBJECT_ID('sp_dbbackup') IS NOT NULL
   DROP PROC sp_dbbackup
GO
CREATE PROC sp_dbbackup @dbname sysname='%',
   @server sysname='(local)', @username sysname=NULL, @password sysname="
/*

Object: sp_dbbackup
Description: Backups up one or more databases, creating backup devices as needed

Usage: sp_dbbackup [@dbname=database name or mask to backup (Default: '%')],
[,@server="server name"][, @username="user name"][, @password="password"]

Returns: (None)

Created by: Ken Henderson. Email: khen@khen.com

Version: 7.01

Example: sp_dbbackup 'm%' -- Backs up all databases whose names begin with 'm'

Created: 1990-01-07. Last changed: 1999-07-03.

*/
AS
SET NOCOUNT ON
IF (@dbname='/?') GOTO Help
```

```
IF (@username IS NULL) SET @username=SUSER_SNAME()


-- Create backup devices and backup each database (except tempdb)


DECLARE @rootpath sysname, @devname sysname, @execstr varchar(8000), @logmessage
varchar(8000)
-- Get SQL Server root installation path
EXEC sp_getSQLregistry @regkey='SQLRootPath', @regvalue=@rootpath OUTPUT,
@server=@server,
   @username=@username, @password=@password


DECLARE Databases CURSOR FOR
   SELECT CATALOG_NAME
   FROM INFORMATION_SCHEMA.SCHEMATA
   WHERE CATALOG_NAME <> 'tempdb' -- Omit system DBs
   AND CATALOG_NAME LIKE @dbname
   ORDER BY CATALOG_NAME


OPEN Databases


FETCH Databases INTO @dbname
SET @devname=@dbname+'back'
WHILE (@@FETCH_STATUS=0) BEGIN
   IF NOT EXISTS(
     SELECT * FROM master..sysdevices WHERE name = @dbname+'back')
   BEGIN
     -- Create the data backup device
     PRINT CHAR(13)+'Adding the data backup device for: '+@dbname
     SET @execstr='EXEC sp_addumpdevice ''disk'',"'+@dbname+'back'+'", "'+
     @rootpath+'\backup\'+@dbname+'back.dmp"'
     EXEC(@execstr)
   END


   -- Backup the database
   PRINT CHAR(13)+'Backing up database '+@dbname
   BACKUP DATABASE @dbname TO @devname
   SET @logmessage='Backup of database '+@dbname+' complete'
   EXEC master..xp_logevent 60000, @logmessage, 'INFORMATIONAL'


   -- Backup its log
   IF (@dbname<>'master') AND (DATABASEPROPERTY(@dbname,'IsTruncLog')=0)
   BEGIN
    IF NOT
     EXISTS(SELECT * FROM master..sysdevices WHERE name = @dbname+'back')
     BEGIN
       -- Create the log backup device
       PRINT 'Adding the log backup device for: '+@dbname
       SET @execstr='EXEC sp_addumpdevice ''disk'', "'+ @dbname +
       'logback'+'", "'
       +@rootpath+'\backup\'+@dbname+'logback.dmp"'
       EXEC(@execstr)
     END
```

```
   PRINT 'Backing up the transaction log for: '+@dbname
   SET @devname=@dbname+'logback'
   BACKUP LOG @dbname TO @devname
   SET @logmessage='Backup of the transaction log for database '+
   @dbname+' complete'
   EXEC master..xp_logevent 60000, @logmessage, 'INFORMATIONAL'
  END

  FETCH Databases INTO @dbname
  SET @devname=@dbname+'back'
END
CLOSE Databases
DEALLOCATE Databases

PRINT CHAR(13)+'Backup operation successfully completed'
RETURN 0

Help:
EXEC sp_usage @objectname='sp_dbbackup', @desc='Backups up one or more databases,
creating backup devices as needed',
@parameters='[@dbname=database name or mask to backup (Default: ''%'')]
[,@server="server name"][, @username="user name"][, @password="password"]',
@author='Ken Henderson', @email='khen@khen.com',
@version='7',@revision='01',
@datecreated='19900107', @datelastchanged='19990703',
@example='sp_dbbackup ''m%'' -- Backs up all databases whose names begin with ''m'' '
RETURN -1

GO

sp_dbbackup

Backing up database GVM
Processed 824 pages for database 'GVM', file 'GVM_Data' on file 30.
Processed 1 pages for database 'GVM', file 'GVM_Log' on file 30.
Backup or restore operation successfully processed 825 pages in 2.468 seconds
(2.735 MB/sec).
Backing up the transaction log for: GVM
Processed 1 pages for database 'GVM', file 'GVM_Log' on file 14.
Backup or restore operation successfully processed 1 pages in 0.086 seconds
(0.011 MB/sec).

Backing up database master
Processed 1264 pages for database 'master', file 'master' on file 21.
Processed 1 pages for database 'master', file 'mastlog' on file 21.
Backup or restore operation successfully processed 1265 pages in 3.302 seconds
(3.136 MB/sec).

Backing up database model
Processed 96 pages for database 'model', file 'modeldev' on file 18.
Processed 1 pages for database 'model', file 'modellog' on file 18.
Backup or restore operation successfully processed 97 pages in 0.433 seconds
(1.818 MB/sec).
```

```
Backing up database msdb
Processed 936 pages for database 'msdb', file 'MSDBData' on file 17.
Processed 1 pages for database 'msdb', file 'MSDBLog' on file 17.
Backup or restore operation successfully processed 937 pages in 2.369 seconds
(3.237 MB/sec).

Backing up database Northwind
Processed 392 pages for database 'Northwind', file 'Northwind' on file 17.
Processed 1 pages for database 'Northwind', file 'Northwind_log' on file 17.
Backup or restore operation successfully processed 393 pages in 1.113 seconds
(2.886 MB/sec).

Adding the data backup device for: Northwind2
'Disk' device added.

Backing up database Northwind2
Processed 112 pages for database 'Northwind2', file 'Northwind2sys' on file 1.
Processed 16 pages for database 'Northwind2', file 'Northwind2data' on file 1.
Processed 1 pages for database 'Northwind2', file 'Northwind2log' on file 1.
Backup or restore operation successfully processed 129 pages in 0.591 seconds
(1.775 MB/sec).

Backing up database pubs
Processed 248 pages for database 'pubs', file 'pubs' on file 18.
Processed 1 pages for database 'pubs', file 'pubs_log' on file 18.
Backup or restore operation successfully processed 249 pages in 0.770 seconds
(2.639 MB/sec).

Backup operation successfully completed
```

The procedure does a couple of interesting things. First, it not only performs backups but also creates backup devices as needed. It uses the sp_getSQLregistry procedure (introduced in Chapter 19) to query the system registry for SQL Server's root path and constructs a physical device location using this path. The fact that it automatically creates devices is one advantage this routine has over a backup scheduled via Enterprise Manager.

Another interesting element of the procedure is the use of DATABASEPROPERTY() to determine whether a database has been configured with the **trunc. log on chkpt** option. It needs to know this in order to avoid attempting to back up such a database's transaction log, since this would result in an error. Backing up a transaction log that has been truncated by the system would be nonsensical—the backup would be useless—and the server will prohibit you from doing so. Once **trunc. log on chkpt** is enabled, your only option for backing up a database is to back up the entire database.

sp_copyfile

The ability to execute operating system commands is a very powerful extension to the Transact-SQL language. This, coupled with its OLE automation support, allows Transact-SQL to perform the kinds of tasks normally reserved for traditional programming languages. The procedure below uses the extended procedure xp_cmdshell to copy an operating system file. It accepts operating system wildcards, so it can copy more than one file at a time. Here's the code:

```
USE master
IF OBJECT_ID('sp_copyfile') IS NOT NULL
    DROP PROC sp_copyfile
GO
CREATE PROCEDURE sp_copyfile @sourcefilepath sysname, @targetfilepath sysname=NULL
/*

Object: sp_copyfile
Description: Copies an operating system file

Usage: sp_copyfile @sourcefilepath=full source file path, @targetfilepath=target file
path and/or filename

Returns: (None)

Created by: Ken Henderson. Email: khen@khen.com
Version: 6.0

Example: sp_copyfile 'c:\mssql7\backup\masterback.dmp'
'c:\mssql7\backup\masterback.dmp.copy'
sp_copyfile 'c:\mssql7\backup\masterback.dmp' '\\archiveserver\d$\backups'
sp_copyfile 'c:\mssql8\backup\*.dmp' 'g:\databasedumps'

Created: 1995-12-19. Last changed: 1999-06-02.

*/
AS
SET NOCOUNT ON
IF (@sourcefilepath='/?') OR (@targetfilepath IS NULL) GOTO Help

DECLARE @cmdstr varchar(8000)

CREATE TABLE #cmd_result (output varchar(8000))

EXEC master..xp_sprintf @cmdstr OUTPUT, 'copy %s %s',@sourcefilepath, @targetfilepath

INSERT #cmd_result
EXEC master..xp_cmdshell @cmdstr

SELECT * FROM #cmd_result
IF EXISTS(SELECT * FROM #cmd_result WHERE output like '%file(s) copied%') BEGIN
    SET @cmdstr='The file copy operation "'+@cmdstr+'" was successful (at least one file
    was copied)'
    PRINT @cmdstr
    EXEC master..xp_logevent 60000, @cmdstr, 'INFORMATIONAL'
END ELSE RAISERROR('File copy failed',16,1)

DROP TABLE #cmd_result
RETURN 0

Help:
EXEC sp_usage @objectname='sp_copyfile',@desc='Copies an operating system file',
@parameters='@sourcefilepath=full source file path, @targetfilepath=target file path
and/or filename',
@author='Ken Henderson', @email='khen@khen.com',
@version='6',@revision='0',
```

```
@datecreated='19951219',@datelastchanged='19990602',
@example='sp_copyfile ''c:\mssql7\backup\masterback.dmp''
''c:\mssql7\backup\masterback.dmp.copy''
sp_copyfile ''c:\mssql7\backup\masterback.dmp'' ''\\archiveserver\d$\backups''
sp_copyfile ''c:\mssql8\backup\*.dmp'' ''g:\databasedumps'' '

GO
```

(Results)

```
sp_copyfile 'c:\mssql7\log\errorlog', 'c:\mssql7\log\errorlog.sav'
---------------------------------------------------------------------------
        1 file(s) copied.

The file copy operation "copy c:\mssql7\log\errorlog
c:\mssql7\log\errorlog.sav"
was successful (at least one file was copied)
```

This routine uses xp_sprintf to set up the operating system COPY command before executing it. We could have created the command through simple string concatenation, but I've used xp_sprintf here to highlight its availability and usefulness. It provides functionality very similar to that of the C/C++ sprintf() function and can come in quite handy, especially when your formatting needs are more complex than those presented here. Unfortunately, it supports only string arguments at present, but you can cast other types of variables as strings in order to pass them to it.

Note the use of the database prefix on both the call to xp_sprintf and the call to xp_cmdshell. This is mandatory because, unlike regular system procedures, extended procedures aren't automatically located across databases. Failing to qualify fully a call to an extended procedure will result in that call failing from any database except **master.**

Unless its **no_output** option is specified, xp_cmdshell returns a result set containing the output of the operating system command(s) it executes. In this case, sp_copyfile uses INSERT ...EXEC to place this output in a table so that it can be scanned to see whether the operation succeeded. We need to find the string "file(s) copied" in order to ensure that at least one file was successfully copied. The routine uses the EXISTS predicate to determine whether the string appears in the xp_cmdshell output and displays the appropriate message.

sp_make_portable

The need for portable databases has grown increasingly over the last few years. Networks have gotten faster, hard drives have gotten bigger, and machines have gotten cheaper to the point that it's common to see file transfers and email attachments of several megabytes in size. It's not uncommon to see a whole database attached to an email.

SQL Server provides the sp_create_removable stored procedure for the express purpose of creating portable—that is, movable—databases. Sp_make_portable uses this procedure to automate the process of making a portable copy of an existing database. You pass in a database name, and sp_make_portable creates a portable database containing the same objects as the original (without data). This database can then be taken off line and copied onto removable media, emailed, transferred to another server, and so on. Here's the code:

```
USE master
IF OBJECT_ID('sp_make_portable') IS NOT NULL
   DROP PROC sp_make_portable
GO
```

```
CREATE PROC sp_make_portable @dbname sysname=NULL, @newdbname sysname=NULL, @objectname
sysname='%',
@username sysname=NULL, @password sysname='', @server sysname='(local)'
/*

Object: sp_make_portable
Description: Makes a portable copy of an existing database (schema only - no data)

Usage: sp_make_portable @newdbname=name of new database to create
[,@dbname=database to copy (Default: DB_NAME())]
[,@objectname=mask specifying which objects to copy (Default "%")]
[,@username=user account to use for SQL-DMO (Default: SUSER_SNAME()]
[,@password=password for DMO user account (Default: "")]
[,@server=server to log into (Default: "(local)")]

Returns: (None)

Created by: Ken Henderson. Email: khen@khen.com

Version: 7.0

Example: sp_make_portable @dbname="northwind", @newdbname="northwind2", @user="sa"

Created: 1996-08-03. Last changed: 1999-07-03.

*/
AS
SET NOCOUNT ON

IF (@dbname='/?') OR (@newdbname='/?') OR (@newdbname IS NULL) GOTO Help

DECLARE @workstr varchar(8000), @sqlpath varchar(8000), @scriptfile sysname, @res int,
@sysdevp sysname, @datadevp sysname, @logdevp sysname,
@sysdevl sysname, @datadevl sysname, @logdevl sysname
-- Default to copying the current database
IF (@dbname IS NULL) SET @dbname=DB_NAME()
-- Use the current user's login name for DMO
IF (@username IS NULL) SET @username=SUSER_SNAME()

IF (DB_ID(@dbname) IS NULL) GOTO Help       -- Invalid source database name

EXEC @res=sp_validname @newdbname,0         -- Very rudimentary -- doesn't do much
IF (@res=1) GOTO Help

-- Get rid of target database if it already exists
IF (DB_ID(@newdbname) IS NOT NULL)
   EXEC sp_dbremove @newdbname,DROPDEV

-- Get SQL Server's default installation path
EXEC sp_getSQLregistry 'SQLRootPath',@sqlpath OUTPUT,
   @username=@username, @password=@password, @server=@server
EXEC master..xp_sprintf @workstr OUTPUT, 'DEL %s\\data\\%s.*',
   @sqlpath,@newdbname
-- Delete the operating system files for the target DB
EXEC master..xp_cmdshell @workstr, no_output

SET @sysdevl=@newdbname+'sys'      -- Define logical and physical device names
SET @datadevl=@newdbname+'data'    -- based on the name of the new database
SET @logdevl=@newdbname+'log'
```

```
SET @sysdevp=@sqlpath+'\data\'+@newdbname+'.sdf'
SET @datadevp=@sqlpath+'\data\'+@newdbname+'.mdf'
SET @logdevp=@sqlpath+'\data\'+@newdbname+'.ldf'

EXEC master..sp_create_removable              -- Build the new database
   @dbname=@newdbname,
   @syslogical=@sysdevl,
   @sysphysical=@sysdevp,
   @syssize=1,
   @loglogical=@logdevl,
   @logphysical=@logdevp,
   @logsize=1,
   @datalogical1=@datadevl,
   @dataphysical1=@datadevp,
   @datasize1=3

/*
-- Commented out because sp_certify_removable is (7/3/99, SQL 7 SP1) apparently broken.
It reports:
-- Server: Msg 208, Level 16, State 1, Procedure sp_check_portable, Line 18
-- Invalid object name 'sysdatabases'.
-- when called in the following manner:

EXEC @res=master..sp_certify_removable @newdbname, auto     -- Ensure that the
new DB is portable
IF (@res<>0) BEGIN
   RAISERROR('Error creating portable database. Database files
   sp_certify_removable check',16,1)
   DECLARE @filename sysname
   SET @filename = 'CertifyR_['+@newdbname+'].txt'
   EXEC sp_readtextfile @filename
   RETURN -1
END

EXEC master..sp_dboption @newdbname,'offline',false -- Set database back online
*/

EXEC master..xp_sprintf @workstr OUTPUT,'EXEC %s..sp_generate_script @objectname="%s",
@outputname="%s\%sTEMP.SQL",
   @resultset="NO", @username="%s", @password="%s", @server="%s"',
   @dbname,@objectname,@sqlpath,@newdbname, @username, @password, @server
EXEC(@workstr)          -- Generate a script for the old database

EXEC master..xp_sprintf @workstr OUTPUT,'osql -U%s -P%s -S%s -d%s -
i%s\%sTEMP.SQL -o%s\%sTEMP.OUT',
   @username,@password,@server,@newdbname,@sqlpath, @newdbname, @sqlpath, @newdbname
-- Run the script _in the new database_
EXEC master..xp_cmdshell @workstr, no_output

PRINT REPLICATE('-',256)+CHAR(13)+
   'Removable database '+@newdbname+' successfully created'
RETURN 0

Help:
EXEC sp_usage @objectname='sp_make_portable',
@desc='Makes a portable copy of an existing database (schema only - no data)',
```

```
@parameters='@newdbname=name of new database to create
[,@dbname=database to copy (Default: DB_NAME())]
[,@objectname=mask specifying which objects to copy]
[,@username=user account to use for SQL-DMO (Default: SUSER_SNAME())]
[,@password=password for DMO user account (Default: "")]
[,@server=server to log into (Default: "(local)")]',
@author='Ken Henderson', @email='khen@khen.com',@version='7',@revision='0',
@datecreated='19960803', @datelastchanged='19990703',
@example='sp_make_portable @dbname="northwind", @newdbname="northwind2", @user="sa"'
RETURN -1

GO

sp_make_portable @dbname='Northwind', @newdbname='Northwind2'
```

(Results)

```
The CREATE DATABASE process is allocating 1.00 MB on disk 'Northwind2sys'.
The CREATE DATABASE process is allocating 1.00 MB on disk 'Northwind2log'.
Extending database by 3.00 MB on disk 'Northwind2data'.
The filegroup property 'DEFAULT' has been set.
```

The first step in building the new database is to determine where SQL Server is installed so that we can build the names of the physical devices that will host it. Next, we call sp_create_removable to build the database. Once this happens, we call sp_generate_script (covered later in this chapter) to generate a SQL script for the entire source database; then we call OSQL (via xp_cmdshell) to execute it. We use OSQL's **-d** command-line option to execute the script within the context of the new database instead of the original database. This ensures that the objects created by the script end up in the new database.

The end result of all this is a database that's portable. Once your portable database is constructed, you can use sp_dboption to take it off line so that you can copy its operating system files elsewhere. You could even use sp_copyfile to copy them.

The system procedure sp_attach_db is used to make a portable database accessible from a new server. This is perfect for installing ready-made databases from removable media such as CD-ROMs. It presents a viable alternative to using scripts and backups to deploy databases with your applications.

INIT_SERVER.SQL

One task that it pays to standardize and streamline as much as possible is that of setting up new servers. DBAs who set up database servers on a regular basis usually get the whole process down to a well-oiled routine. They're able to do it in their sleep if they must (and sometimes they must).

The script presented below presents a template from which you can construct such a routine of your own. It's certainly not comprehensive—it's likely that each shop will have its own setup requirements and needs. The template isn't provided as a stored procedure because the first thing you'd have to do to with a stored procedure is load a script on the new server to create it. Given that server initialization is usually a one-time thing, you might as well just use a script in the first place.

The kinds of things that you typically find in server initialization scripts are:

- Dump device construction
- Creation of user databases and/or restore operations to populate them

- Custom stored procedure installation

- Autostartup procedure specification

- Template database (model) setup

- Maintenance job scheduling

- User account and security setup

- Database and database option configuration

- Server configuration

Getting the server set up correctly to begin with is essential if you want it to behave itself down the road. Even though the DBA's workload has been reduced with each successive release of SQL Server, planning is everything. Even moderately used systems require some degree of management.

Here's an example of a server initialization script:

```
/*

Object: INIT_SERVER.SQL
Description: Server initialization script

Created by: Ken Henderson. Email: khen@khen.com

Version: 7.0

Created: 1990-02-06. Last changed: 1999-07-05.

*/
SET NOCOUNT ON
GO
USE master
GO

DECLARE @username sysname, @password sysname, @server sysname
SET @username='sa'                   -- Put the login you want to use here
SET @password="                      -- Put your password here (be sure this
                                     -- script is stored in a secure location!)
SET @server='(local)'                -- Put your server name here

-- Set template database options
PRINT 'Setting template database options'
EXEC master..sp_dboption 'model','auto update statistics',true
EXEC master..sp_dboption 'model','autoshrink',true
EXEC master..sp_dboption 'model','select into/bulkcopy',true
EXEC master..sp_dboption 'model','torn page detection',true

-- Add tempdate data types
PRINT 'Adding template data types'
IF EXISTS(SELECT * FROM model..systypes WHERE name = 'd')
   EXEC model..sp_droptype 'd'
EXEC model..sp_addtype 'd', 'decimal(10,2)','NULL'
```

```
-- Create backup devices and job steps for every database except tempdb
PRINT 'Creating backup devices and job steps for every database except tempdb'

DECLARE @rootpath sysname, @execstr varchar(8000), @dbname sysname, @job_id
uniqueidentifier, @step_id int
-- Get SQL Server root installation path
EXEC sp_getSQLregistry @regkey='SQLRootPath', @regvalue=@rootpath OUTPUT,
@username=@username, @password=@password, @server=@server

-- Delete the operator if it already exists
IF EXISTS(SELECT * FROM msdb..sysoperators WHERE name = 'Puck Feet')
   EXEC msdb..sp_delete_operator 'Puck Feet'

-- Add the operator
PRINT 'Setting up the job operator.'
EXEC msdb..sp_add_operator @name = 'Puck Feet',
   @enabled = 1,
   @email_address ='[SMTP:puckfeet@dastard.com]',
   @pager_address = '8675309@pagerpros.com',
   @weekday_pager_start_time = 090000,
   @weekday_pager_end_time = 210000,
   @pager_days = 127,
   @netsend_address='NOT_HOCKEY'

-- Delete the job if it already exists
SELECT @job_id = job_id FROM msdb..sysjobs WHERE name='DailyBackup'
IF (@job_id IS NOT NULL) BEGIN
   -- Don't delete if it's a multi-server job
   IF (EXISTS (SELECT * FROM msdb..sysjobservers WHERE (job_id=@job_id) AND (server_id
   <> 0))) BEGIN
      RAISERROR ('Unable to create job because there is already a multi-server job with
      the same name.',16,1)
   END ELSE -- Delete the job
      EXECUTE msdb..sp_delete_job @job_id=@job_id
   END

-- Add the backup job
PRINT 'Adding the backup job'
EXEC msdb..sp_add_job @job_name = 'DailyBackup',
   @enabled = 1,
   @description = 'Daily backup of all databases',
   @owner_login_name = 'sa',
   @notify_level_eventlog = 2,
   @notify_level_netsend = 2,
   @notify_netsend_operator_name='Puck Feet',
   @delete_level = 0

-- Schedule the job
PRINT 'Scheduling the job'
EXEC msdb..sp_add_jobschedule @job_name = 'DailyBackup',
   @name = 'ScheduledBackup',
   @freq_type = 4, -- everyday
   @freq_interval = 1,
   @active_start_time = 101600
```

```
DECLARE Databases CURSOR FOR
   SELECT CATALOG_NAME
   FROM INFORMATION_SCHEMA.SCHEMATA
   WHERE CATALOG_NAME <> 'tempdb' -- Omit system DBs
   ORDER BY CATALOG_NAME
OPEN Databases

FETCH Databases INTO @dbname
SET @step_id=0
WHILE (@@FETCH_STATUS=0) BEGIN
   IF NOT EXISTS(SELECT * FROM master..sysdevices WHERE name =
   @dbname+'back') BEGIN
      -- Create the data backup device
      PRINT 'Adding the data backup device for '+@dbname
      SET @execstr='EXEC sp_addumpdevice ''disk'', "'+@dbname+'back'+'",
      "'+@rootpath+'\backup\'+@dbname+'back.dmp"'
      EXEC(@execstr)
   END

   -- Add a job step to backup the database
   PRINT 'Adding the database backup job step for '+@dbname
   SET @execstr='EXEC msdb..sp_add_jobstep @job_name = ''DailyBackup'',
   @step_name = "'+'Backup of database: '+@dbname+'",
   @subsystem = ''TSQL'',
   @command = ''BACKUP DATABASE '+@dbname+' TO '+@dbname+'back'',
   @on_success_action=3'
   EXEC(@execstr)
   SET @step_id=@step_id+1

   -- Add one to backup its log
   IF (@dbname<>'master') AND (DATABASEPROPERTY(@dbname,'IsTruncLog')=0)
   BEGIN
      IF NOT EXISTS(SELECT * FROM master..sysdevices
         WHERE name = @dbname+'back') BEGIN
         -- Create the log backup device
         PRINT 'Adding the log backup device for '+@dbname
         SET @execstr='EXEC sp_addumpdevice ''disk'',
         "'+@dbname+'logback'+'", "'
         +@rootpath+'\backup\'+@dbname+'logback.dmp"'
         EXEC(@execstr)
      END

      PRINT 'Adding the log backup job step for '+@dbname
      SET @execstr='EXEC msdb..sp_add_jobstep @job_name = ''DailyBackup'',
         @step_name = "'+'Backup of log for database: '+@dbname+'",
         @subsystem = ''TSQL'',
         @command = ''BACKUP LOG '+@dbname+' TO '+@dbname+'logback'',
         @on_success_action=3'
      EXEC(@execstr)
      SET @step_id=@step_id+1
   END

   FETCH Databases INTO @dbname
END
CLOSE Databases
DEALLOCATE Databases
```

```
-- Set the last job step to quit with success
EXEC msdb..sp_update_jobstep @job_name='DailyBackup', @step_id=@step_id,
@on_success_action=1

-- Associate the job with the job server
EXEC msdb..sp_add_jobserver @job_name='DailyBackup'

PRINT CHAR(13)+'Successfully initialized server'

GO
```

(Results)

```
Setting template database options
Checkpointing database that was changed.

DBCC execution completed. If DBCC printed error messages, contact your system
administrator.

Checkpointing database that was changed.

DBCC execution completed. If DBCC printed error messages, contact your system
administrator.

Checkpointing database that was changed.

DBCC execution completed. If DBCC printed error messages, contact your system
administrator.

Checkpointing database that was changed.

DBCC execution completed. If DBCC printed error messages, contact your system
administrator.

Adding template data types

Type has been dropped.

Type added.

Creating backup devices and job steps for every database except tempdb

Setting up the job operator

Adding the backup job

Scheduling the job

Adding the database backup job step for CM

Adding the log backup job step for CM

Adding the database backup job step for master

Adding the database backup job step for model

Adding the database backup job step for msdb
```

```
Adding the database backup job step for Northwind

Adding the database backup job step for Northwind2

Adding the database backup job step for PM

Adding the database backup job step for PO

Adding the database backup job step for pubs

Adding the database backup job step for VCDB

Successfully initialized server
```

This script does a number of interesting things. First, it sets up the **model** database, specifying a template set of data types and options. These parameters will be used for new databases when they're created. They'll also be used for **tempdb** when it's rebuilt each time the server is cycled. So, for example, you could enable **select into/bulk copy** in **model** if you want it enabled in **tempdb** when the server starts. That said, an autostart custom procedure is probably a better option because it averts the risk of enabling **select/into bulk copy** by accident in other newly created databases.

Next, the script uses sp_getSQLregistry to find SQL Server's installation path, then builds backup devices as necessary using this path. It then sets up a SQL Server Agent job to back up each database (and its log, as appropriate), along with an operator and a schedule on which to run the job.

Each SQL Server Agent job is composed of job steps. A simple job might have just one step; more complex ones will have many. Here, we add a separate step to back up each database and each database's log. We specify a default **on_success_action** of **3,** which tells the Agent to proceed with the next step when a job step completes successfully. This doesn't work for the final step of the job since there is no next step. Thus the script includes a call to sp_update_jobstep that tells the final job step simply to terminate the job when it successfully completes.

Note the call to sp_add_jobserver. This associates the newly created job with the local job server. Failing to do this results in a job that never runs. One would think that simply adding the job via sp_add_job would establish this link, but that's not the case. The flexibility here—the separation of jobs from job servers—allows you to schedule jobs on other servers, a feature that's quite useful to administrators managing multiserver environments. However, the cost of this flexibility is that you must remember to link your job with your job server when scheduling jobs via Transact-SQL. This is another good argument for using the GUI tools. You don't have to worry about details like this when using Enterprise Manager to schedule jobs—it defaults to scheduling jobs on the local server.

sp_readtextfile

Text files are so ubiquitous in system administration that it's no surprise that DBAs often need to be able to access them from SQL Server. Processing the output from operating system commands and SQL Server's command-line utilities, perusing the error log, and loading SQL script files are just a few examples of the many dealings DBAs commonly have with text files. To that end, below is a procedure that reads a text file and returns it as a result set. Using IN-SERT...EXEC, you can place its output in a table for further processing or simply return it as a result set of your own, as the sp_generate_script procedure below demonstrates. Here's the source code to sp_readtextfile:

```
USE master
IF OBJECT_ID('sp_readtextfile') IS NOT NULL
   DROP PROC sp_readtextfile
GO
CREATE PROC sp_readtextfile @textfilename sysname
/*

Object: sp_readtextfile
Description: Reads the contents of a text file into a SQL result set

Usage: sp_readtextfile @textfilename=name of file to read

Returns: (None)

Created by: Ken Henderson. Email: khen@khen.com

Version: 7.0

Example: sp_readtextfile 'D:\MSSQL7\LOGS\errorlog'

Created: 1996-05-01. Last changed: 1999-06-14.

*/
AS
SET NOCOUNT ON

IF (@textfilename='/?') GOTO Help

CREATE TABLE #lines (line varchar(8000))

EXEC('BULK INSERT #lines FROM "'+@textfilename+'"')

SELECT * FROM #lines

DROP TABLE #lines
RETURN 0

Help:
EXEC sp_usage @objectname='sp_readtextfile',
@desc='Reads the contents of a text file into a SQL result set',
@parameters='@textfilename=name of file to read',
@author='Ken Henderson', @email='khen@khen.com',
@version='7',@revision='0',
@datecreated='19960501', @datelastchanged='19990614',
@example='sp_readtextfile ''D:\MSSQL7\LOGS\errorlog'' '
RETURN -1

EXEC sp_readtextfile 'c:\mssql7\log\errorlog.sav'
```

(Results abridged)

```
line
--------------------------------------------------------------------------------
1999-07-06 09:10:41.14 kernel  Microsoft SQL Server 7.00 - 7.00.699 (Intel X86)
   May 21 1999 14:08:18
   Copyright (c) 1988-1998 Microsoft Corporation
   Desktop Edition on Windows NT 4.0 (Build 1381: Service Pack 4)
```

```
1999-07-06 09:10:41.25 kernel   Copyright (C) 1988-1997 Microsoft Corporation.
1999-07-06 09:10:41.25 kernel   All rights reserved.
1999-07-06 09:10:41.25 kernel   Logging SQL Server messages in file
                                'd:\MSSQL7\log\ERRORLOG'.
1999-07-06 09:10:41.56 kernel   initconfig: Number of user connections limited to 32767.
1999-07-06 09:10:41.56 kernel   SQL Server is starting at priority class 'normal'(1 CPU
                                detected).
1999-07-06 09:10:41.70 kernel   User Mode Scheduler configured for thread processing
1999-07-06 09:10:43.34 server   Directory Size: 16215
1999-07-06 09:10:43.45 spid1    Using dynamic lock allocation. [500] Lock Blocks, [1000]
                                Lock Owner Blocks
1999-07-06 09:10:43.49 spid1    Starting up database 'master'.
1999-07-06 09:10:43.49 spid1    Opening file d:\MSSQL7\data\master.mdf.
1999-07-06 09:10:43.73 spid1    Opening file d:\MSSQL7\data\mastlog.ldf.
1999-07-06 09:10:44.23 spid1    Loading SQL Server's Unicode collation.
1999-07-06 09:10:44.28 spid1    Loading SQL Server's non-Unicode sort order and
                                character set.
1999-07-06 09:10:45.36 spid1    107 transactions rolled forward in database 'master' (1).
1999-07-06 09:10:45.37 spid1    0 transactions rolled back in database 'master' (1).
1999-07-06 09:10:51.28 spid1    Recovery complete.
1999-07-06 09:10:51.28 spid1    SQL Server's Unicode collation is:
1999-07-06 09:10:51.28 spid1          'English' (ID = 1033).
1999-07-06 09:10:51.28 spid1          comparison style = 196609.
1999-07-06 09:10:51.28 spid1    SQL Server's non-Unicode sort order is:
1999-07-06 09:10:51.28 spid1          'nocase_iso' (ID = 52).
1999-07-06 09:10:51.28 spid1    SQL Server's non-Unicode character set is:
1999-07-06 09:10:51.28 spid1          'iso_1' (ID = 1).
```

The internal workings of this routine are pretty straightforward. It first loads the file supplied to it into a temporary table via BULK INSERT. Next, it issues a **SELECT *** against the temporary table to return its contents as a result set. The end result is that the caller receives the text file as a SQL Server result set.

Note

There's a bug in the initial shipping version of SQL 7.0 that prevents sp_readtext from being called by routines that use the OLE Automation sp_OAxxxx procedures. Sp_readtext uses the Transact-SQL BULK INSERT command to load its text file into a temporary table, which it then returns as a result set. BULK INSERT is marked as a free threaded OLE provider. With the ODSOLE facility (the sp_OAxxxx procedures), COM is initialized using the single-apartment model. When BULK INSERT is called by a thread already initialized as a single apartment, the conflict between the two models causes the instantiation of the OLE-DB Stream provider to fail—BULK INSERT can't read the operating system file that's been passed to it.

The workaround requires modifying the system registry. Follow these steps to allow BULK INSERT to be called from procedures and scripts using the single-apartment COM model:

1. Run regedit.exe or regedt32.exe.

2. Drill down into HKEY_CLASSES_ROOT\CLSID\{F3A18EEA-D34B-11d2-88D7-00C04F68DC44}\InprocServer32\ThreadingModel.

3. Replace **Free** with **Both**.

Scripting Routines

A common administrative need is to be able to generate scripts for database objects. DBAs sometimes want these for extra backups, for making a duplicate of a database or an object, or for searching for some unusual coding technique or object definition.

Enterprise Manager provides a nice facility for scripting database objects, and it should be your tool of choice for doing so. It performs its magic by accessing SQL Server's SQL-DMO (Distributed Management Objects) facility, a COM interface that provides server management facilities to applications. Since Transact-SQL provides access to COM servers via its ODSOLE facility (the sp_Oaxxx procedures), we can access SQL-DMO directly from SQL without going through Enterprise Manager. (Refer to Chapter 19 for more details on this technique.) Here's a procedure that scripts objects directly from Transact-SQL:

```
USE master
GO
IF OBJECT_ID('sp_generate_script') IS NOT NULL
   DROP PROC sp_generate_script
GO
CREATE PROC sp_generate_script
   @objectname sysname=NULL,   -- Object mask to copy
   @outputname sysname=NULL,   -- Output file to create (default: @objectname+'.SQL')
   @scriptoptions int=NULL,     -- Options bitmask for Transfer
   @resultset varchar(3)="YES",      -- Determines whether the script is returned as a result set
   @server sysname='(local)',        -- Name of the server to connect to
   @username sysname='sa',           -- Name of the user to connect as (defaults to 'sa')
   @password sysname=NULL            -- User's password
/*

Object: sp_generate_script
Description: Generates a creation script for an object or collection of objects

Usage: sp_generate_script [@objectname="Object name or mask (defaults to all object in current
database)"]
   [,@outputname="Output file name" (Default: @objectname+".SQL", or GENERATED_SCRIPT.SQL for
   entire database)]
   [,@scriptoptions=bitmask specifying script generation options]
   [,@resultset="YES"|"NO" -- determines whether to return the script as a result set (Default:
   "YES")]
   [,@server="server name"][, @username="user name"][, @password="password"]

Returns: (None)

Created by: Ken Henderson. Email: khen@khen.com

Version: 2.0

Created: 1996-12-01. Last changed: 1999-06-06.

*/
AS
/* SQL-DMO constant variables omitted for brevity. They are included in the CD version.*/
DECLARE @dbname sysname,
   @sqlobject int, -- SQL Server object
   @object int,    -- Work variable for accessing COM objects
   @hr int,        -- Contains HRESULT returned by COM
   @tfobject int   -- Stores pointer to Transfer object
```

```
IF (@objectname='/?') GOTO Help

SET @resultset=UPPER(@resultset)

IF (@objectname IS NOT NULL) AND (CHARINDEX('%',@objectname)=0) AND
(CHARINDEX('_',@objectname)=0) BEGIN
   SET @dbname=ISNULL(PARSENAME(@objectname,3),DB_NAME()) -- Extract the DB
   name; default to current
   SET @objectname=PARSENAME(@objectname,1)      -- Remove extraneous stuff from table name
   IF (@objectname IS NULL) BEGIN
      RAISERROR('Invalid object name.',16,1)
      RETURN -1
   END
   IF (@outputname IS NULL)
      SET @outputname=@objectname+'.SQL'
END ELSE BEGIN
   SET @dbname=DB_NAME()
   IF (@outputname IS NULL)
      SET @outputname='GENERATED_SCRIPT.SQL'
END


-- Create a SQLServer object
EXEC @hr=sp_OACreate 'SQLDMO.SQLServer', @sqlobject OUTPUT
IF (@hr <> 0) BEGIN
   EXEC sp_displayoaerrorinfo @sqlobject, @hr
   RETURN
END


-- Create a Transfer object
EXEC @hr=sp_OACreate 'SQLDMO.Transfer', @tfobject OUTPUT
IF (@hr <> 0) BEGIN
   EXEC sp_displayoaerrorinfo @tfobject, @hr
   RETURN
END


-- Set Transfer's CopyData property
EXEC @hr = sp_OASetProperty @tfobject, 'CopyData', 0
IF (@hr <> 0) BEGIN
   EXEC sp_displayoaerrorinfo @tfobject, @hr
   RETURN
END


-- Tell Transfer to copy the schema
EXEC @hr = sp_OASetProperty @tfobject, 'CopySchema', 1
IF (@hr <> 0) BEGIN
   EXEC sp_displayoaerrorinfo @tfobject, @hr
   RETURN
END
IF (@objectname IS NULL) BEGIN -- Get all objects in the database

   -- Tell Transfer to copy all objects
   EXEC @hr = sp_OASetProperty @tfobject, 'CopyAllObjects', 1
   IF (@hr <> 0) BEGIN
      EXEC sp_displayoaerrorinfo @tfobject, @hr
      RETURN
   END

   -- Tell Transfer to get groups as well
   EXEC @hr = sp_OASetProperty @tfobject, 'IncludeGroups', 1
```

```
   IF (@hr <> 0) BEGIN
      EXEC sp_displayoaerrorinfo @tfobject, @hr
      RETURN
   END

   -- Tell it to include users
   EXEC @hr = sp_OASetProperty @tfobject, 'IncludeUsers', 1
   IF (@hr <> 0) BEGIN
      EXEC sp_displayoaerrorinfo @tfobject, @hr
      RETURN
   END

   -- Tell it to include logins
   EXEC @hr = sp_OASetProperty @tfobject, 'IncludeLogins', 1
   IF (@hr <> 0) BEGIN
      EXEC sp_displayoaerrorinfo @tfobject, @hr
      RETURN
   END

   -- Include object dependencies, too
   EXEC @hr = sp_OASetProperty @tfobject, 'IncludeDependencies', 1
   IF (@hr <> 0) BEGIN
      EXEC sp_displayoaerrorinfo @tfobject, @hr
      RETURN
   END

   IF (@scriptoptions IS NULL)
      SET @scriptoptions=@SQLDMOScript_OwnerQualify | @SQLDMOScript_Default |
         @SQLDMOScript_Triggers | @SQLDMOScript_Bindings |
         @SQLDMOScript_DatabasePermissions | @SQLDMOScript_Permissions |
         @SQLDMOScript_ObjectPermissions | @SQLDMOScript_ClusteredIndexes |
         @SQLDMOScript_Indexes | @SQLDMOScript_Aliases | @SQLDMOScript_DRI_All |
         @SQLDMOScript_IncludeHeaders

END ELSE BEGIN
   DECLARE @obname sysname,
      @obtype varchar(2),
      @obowner sysname,
      @OBJECT_TYPES varchar(30),
      @obcode int

-- Used to translate sysobjects.type into the bitmap that Transfer requires
SET @OBJECT_TYPES='T     V  U  P    D  R  TR '

   -- Find all the objects that match the mask and add them to Transfer's
   -- list of objects to script
   DECLARE ObjectList CURSOR FOR
        SELECT name,type,USER_NAME(uid) FROM sysobjects
        WHERE (name LIKE @objectname)
      AND (CHARINDEX(type+' ',@OBJECT_TYPES)<>0)
      AND (OBJECTPROPERTY(id,'IsSystemTable')=0)
      AND (status>0)
         UNION ALL   -- Include user-defined data types
         SELECT name,'T',USER_NAME(uid)
         FROM SYSTYPES
         WHERE (usertype & 256)<>0
         AND (name LIKE @objectname)
```

```
OPEN ObjectList

FETCH ObjectList INTO @obname, @obtype, @obowner WHILE (@@FETCH_STATUS=0) BEGIN
    SET @obcode=POWER(2,(CHARINDEX(@obtype+' ',@OBJECT_TYPES)/3))

        EXEC @hr = sp_OAMethod @tfobject, 'AddObjectByName', NULL, @obname, @obcode, @obowner
        IF (@hr <> 0) BEGIN
          EXEC sp_displayoaerrorinfo @tfobject, @hr
          RETURN
        END
        FETCH ObjectList INTO @obname, @obtype, @obowner END
    CLOSE ObjectList
    DEALLOCATE ObjectList

    IF (@scriptoptions IS NULL)
       -- Keep it simple when not scripting the entire database
       SET @scriptoptions=@SQLDMOScript_Default
END


-- Set Transfer's ScriptType property
EXEC @hr = sp_OASetProperty @tfobject, 'ScriptType', @scriptoptions
IF (@hr <> 0) BEGIN
   EXEC sp_displayoaerrorinfo @tfobject, @hr
   RETURN
END


-- Connect to the server
IF (@password IS NOT NULL) AND (@password<>'')
   EXEC @hr = sp_OAMethod @sqlobject, 'Connect', NULL, @server, @username, @password
ELSE
   EXEC @hr = sp_OAMethod @sqlobject, 'Connect', NULL, @server, @username
IF (@hr <> 0) BEGIN
   EXEC sp_displayoaerrorinfo @sqlobject, @hr
   RETURN
END


-- Get a pointer to the SQLServer object's Databases collection
EXEC @hr = sp_OAGetProperty @sqlobject, 'Databases', @object OUT
IF @hr <> 0 BEGIN
   EXEC sp_displayoaerrorinfo @sqlobject, @hr
   RETURN
END


-- Get a pointer from the Databases collection for the specified database
EXEC @hr = sp_OAMethod @object, 'Item', @object OUT, @dbname
IF @hr <> 0 BEGIN
   EXEC sp_displayoaerrorinfo @object, @hr
   RETURN
END


PRINT 'Ignore the code displayed below. It's a remnant of the SQL-DMO method used to produce
the script file'

-- Call the Database object's ScriptTransfer method to create the script
EXEC @hr = sp_OAMethod @object, 'ScriptTransfer',NULL, @tfobject, 2, @outputname
```

```
IF @hr <> 0 BEGIN
   EXEC sp_displayoaerrorinfo @object, @hr
   RETURN
END


EXEC sp_OADestroy @sqlobject       -- For cleanliness
EXEC sp_OADestroy @tfobject         -- For cleanliness


IF (@resultset="YES") EXEC sp_readtextfile @outputname

RETURN 0

Help:
EXEC sp_usage @objectname='sp_generate_script',@desc='Generates a creation script for an
object or collection of objects',
@parameters='[@objectname="Object name or mask (defaults to all object in current
database)"][,@outputname="Output file name" (Default: @objectname+".SQL", or
GENERATED_SCRIPT.SQL for entire database)]
[,@scriptoptions=bitmask specifying script generation options]
[,@server="server name"][, @username="user name"][, @password="password"]',
@author='Ken Henderson', @email='khen@khen.com',
@version='7', @revision='0',
@datecreated='19980401', @datelastchanged='19990702',
@example='sp_generate_script @objectname=''authors'', @outputname=''authors.sql'' '
RETURN -1

GO


EXEC sp_generate_script 'authors'

line
-------------------------------------------------------------------------------------------
set quoted_identifier OFF
GO
NULL
CREATE TABLE [authors] (
   [au_id] [id] NOT NULL ,
   [au_lname] [varchar] (40) NOT NULL ,
   [au_fname] [varchar] (20) NOT NULL ,
   [phone] [char] (12) NOT NULL CONSTRAINT [DF__authors__phone__09DE7BCC] DEFAULT ('UNKNOWN'),
   [address] [varchar] (40) NULL ,
   [city] [varchar] (20) NULL ,
   [state] [char] (2) NULL ,
   [zip] [char] (5) NULL ,
   [contract] [bit] NOT NULL ,
   CONSTRAINT [UPKCL_auidind] PRIMARY KEY CLUSTERED
   (
      [au_id]
   )  ON [PRIMARY] ,
   CHECK (([au_id] like '[0-9][0-9][0-9]-[0-9][0-9]-[0-9][0-9][0-9][0-9]')),
   CHECK (([zip] like '[0-9][0-9][0-9][0-9][0-9]'))
)
```

This code exhibits a number of interesting techniques. Let's go through a few of them.

The procedure begins by instantiating the DMO SQLServer and Transfer objects. DMO's SQLServer object is its root level access path—you use it to connect to the server and to access other objects on the server. The Transfer object encapsulates DMO's server-to-server or server-to-file object and data transfer facility. Sp_generate_script uses it to generate SQL scripts.

Once Transfer is created, the procedure determines whether the user wants to script the entire database or only selected objects. This distinction is important because DMO lists objects in order of dependency when scripting an entire database. If only a subset of the objects in a database is to be scripted, the procedure opens a cursor on the sysobjects and systypes tables (via UNION ALL) and calls Transfer's AddObjectByName method to set them up for scripting, one by one.

The procedure next uses the SQLServer object to locate the database housing objects it needs to script. It finds this database by accessing the object's Databases collection. DMO objects often expose collections of other objects. Items in these collections can be accessed by name or by ordinal index. In the case of sp_generate_script, collection items are always accessed by name.

Once the procedure retrieves a pointer to the correct database, it calls that database's ScriptTransfer method, passing it the previously created Transfer object as a parameter. This generates a SQL script containing the objects we've specified.

The final step in the procedure is to return the script as a result set. Usually, the caller will expect to see the script immediately. If **@resultset** = "YES" (the default), sp_generate_script calls sp_readtextfile to return the newly generated script file to the caller via a result set. A useful variation of this would be to return a cursor pointer to the script.

Summary

Though it was sometimes the only method for getting the job done in earlier releases of SQL Server, the need to use Transact-SQL to perform administrative tasks has lessened as the GUI tools have improved. This means that you should make using the GUI tools your default mode of operation for managing your servers. That said, there may be times when your needs exceed the capabilities of Enterprise Manager and the other GUI tools. When that happens, you can use the routines presented in this chapter, along with procedures and scripts you write yourself, to fill in the gaps left by the other tools.

18

Full-Text Search

While there is certainly an artistic element to engineering, nobody cares what color the bridge was that collapsed and killed fifty people.
—H. W. Kenton

The ability to search character and text fields is nothing new in the world of SQL databases. For years, DBMSs have provided facilities for searching character strings and fields for other strings. However, these facilities are usually rudimentary at best. Historically, SQL Server's built-in text searching tools have been of the garden-variety type—just beyond ANSI compliance, but nothing to write home about. You could perform equality tests using character strings (as with all data types), and you could search for a pattern within a string (using LIKE and PATINDEX()), but you couldn't do anything sophisticated such as search by word proximity or inflectional usage.

The recent addition of native full-text indexing support has changed this. Traditionally, database architects who wanted advanced text searching had to rely on database gateways, operating system files, and technologies external to SQL Server. That's no longer the case. The Microsoft Search service provides the functionality of a full-blown text search engine such as Microsoft Index Server (an operating system file-based search engine) within the SQL Server environment. It's used to build the meta-data necessary to support full-text searching and to process full-text search queries. The service itself runs only on Windows NT Server (but not in a Windows NT Server Enterprise Edition clustering environment) and can be accessed by SQL Server clients on NT Workstation and Windows 9x.

The data maintained by Microsoft Search—the full-text indexes and catalog information it uses to service queries—is not stored in regular system tables and can't be accessed directly from SQL Server. It's stored in operating system files and is accessible only by the service itself and by NT administrators. You can think of Microsoft Search as a *text* server in the same way that SQL Server is a *SQL* or *database* server—it receives queries and instructions related to full-text searching and returns results appropriately. Its one client is SQL Server, which is how you access it.

> **Note**
> To install Microsoft Search, make sure the Full-Text Search option is selected in the Select Components dialog of the SQL Server installation program (this option is available only on Windows NT Server). Once installed, the service must be started and full-text searching must be enabled separately at the database, table, and column levels.

Setting up full-text indexes is not a one-step process. With increased flexibility often comes increased complexity. The process required to set up a specific table column so that it's available to full-text search syntax such as the CONTAINS() predicate and the FREETEXTTABLE() rowset function includes six steps. They are as follows:

1. Full-text indexing must be enabled in the host database.

2. Full-text catalogs must be created for the database.

3. Full-text indexing must then be enabled for the host table and associated with a full-text catalog.

4. The column must then be added to the table's full-text index.

5. This full-text index must then be activated.

6. The full-text catalog must then be populated. This population can be a full or incremental population. Of course, the initial population of a full-text index is always a full population. Subsequent populations can be incremental if the table contains a **timestamp** column and if its meta-data hasn't changed since the last population.

As with most SQL Server administrative tasks, the best tool for creating full-text indexes is Enterprise Manager. The process required is too tedious to do by hand frequently. That said, this book isn't about Enterprise Manager or the GUI tools, so here's some sample code that illustrates how to set up a full-text search column using nothing but Transact-SQL (I've numbered the steps in the code to correspond to the list above):

```
USE pubs
DECLARE @tablename sysname, @catalogname sysname, @indexname sysname,
@columnname sysname

SET @tablename='pub_info'
SET @catalogname='pubsCatalog'
SET @indexname='UPKCL_pubinfo'
SET @columnname='pr_info'

-- STEP 1: Enable FTS for the database
EXEC sp_fulltext_database 'enable'

-- STEP 2: Create a full-text catalog
EXEC sp_fulltext_catalog @catalogname, 'create'
```

```
-- STEP 3: Create a full-text index for the table
EXEC sp_fulltext_table @tablename,'create',@catalogname,@indexname

-- STEP 4: Add the column to it
EXEC sp_fulltext_column @tablename, @columnname, 'add'

-- STEP 5: Activate the newly created FT index
EXEC sp_fulltext_table @tablename,'activate'

-- STEP 6: Populate the newly created FT catalog
EXEC sp_fulltext_catalog @catalogname, 'start_full'
```

This code sets up full-text indexing on the pr_info column in pubs.pub_info. Pr_info is a text column, so it's a good candidate for full-text indexing. For simplicity's sake, the routine makes a number of assumptions that may not be valid in the real world. For example, it doesn't check to see whether the full-text catalog exists before attempting to create it. If the catalog already exists, the statement and the batch will fail. The same is true of the full-text index on the pub_info table. Each table can have just one full-text index. Attempting to create a second full-text index or recreate an existing one results in an error. The routine serves merely to demonstrate the basics of setting up full-text indexing using Transact-SQL.

Much of the information that we need to check before calling the full-text stored procedures can be accessed via meta-data functions. For example, you can use the FULLTEXT-CATALOGPROPERTY() function to determine whether a given catalog exists (it returns NULL when passed a nonexistent name). You can determine whether a table has a full-text index via the OBJECTPROPERTY() function and whether a column has been added to a full-text index using the COLUMNPROPERTY() function. Here's a stored procedure that makes use of these functions and a few others to set up a column for full-text indexing in a much more reliable fashion. It's significantly more robust than the earlier example and much safer to use in the real world:

```
USE master
GO
IF OBJECT_ID('sp_enable_fulltext') IS NOT NULL
   DROP PROC sp_enable_fulltext
GO
CREATE PROC sp_enable_fulltext @tablename sysname, @columnname sysname=NULL,
@catalogname sysname=NULL, @startserver varchar(3)='NO'
/*

Object: sp_enable_fulltext
Description: Enables full-text indexing for a specified column

Usage: sp_enable_fulltext @tablename=name of host table, @columnname=column to set up,
[,@catalogname=name of full-text catalog to use (Default:
DB_NAME()+"Catalog")][,@startsrever=YES|NO specifies whether to start the
Microsoft Search service on this machine prior to setting up the column (Default: YES)]

Returns: (None)

Created by: Ken Henderson. Email: khen@khen.com
```

```
Example: EXEC sp_enable_fulltext "pubs..pub_info","pr_info",DEFAULT,"YES"

Created: 1999-06-14. Last changed: 1999-07-14.

*/
AS
SET NOCOUNT ON

IF (@tablename='/?') OR (@columnname IS NULL) OR (OBJECT_ID(@tablename) IS NULL) GOTO
Help

IF (FULLTEXTSERVICEPROPERTY('IsFulltextInstalled')=0) BEGIN -- Search engine's not
installed
   RAISERROR('The Microsoft Search service is not installed on server
   %s',16,10,@@SERVERNAME)
   RETURN -1
END

DECLARE @catalogstatus int, @indexname sysname

IF (UPPER(@startserver)='YES')
   EXEC master..xp_cmdshell 'NET START mssearch', no_output

IF (@catalogname IS NULL)
   SET @catalogname=DB_NAME()+'Catalog'

CREATE TABLE #indexes (     -- Used to located a unique index for use with FTS
Qualifier      sysname NULL,
Owner          sysname NULL,
TableName      sysname NULL,
NonUnique      smallint NULL,
IndexQualifier     sysname NULL,
IndexName      sysname NULL,
Type           smallint NULL,
PositionInIndex    smallint NULL,
ColumnName     sysname NULL,
Collation      char(1) NULL,
Cardinality    int NULL,
Pages          int NULL,
FilterCondition    sysname NULL)

INSERT #indexes
EXEC sp_statistics @tablename

SELECT @indexname=IndexName FROM #indexes WHERE NonUnique=0   -- Get a unique index on
the table (gets LAST if multiple)

DROP TABLE #indexes

IF (@indexname IS NULL) BEGIN -- If no unique indexes, abort
   RAISERROR('No suitable unique index found on table %s',16,10,@tablename)
   RETURN -1
END
```

```
IF (DATABASEPROPERTY(DB_NAME(),'IsFulltextEnabled')<>1) -- Enable FTS for the database
   EXEC sp_fulltext_database 'enable'

SET @catalogstatus=FULLTEXTCATALOGPROPERTY(@catalogname,'PopulateStatus')

IF (@catalogstatus IS NULL)              --  Doesn't yet exist
   EXEC sp_fulltext_catalog @catalogname, 'create'
ELSE IF (@catalogstatus IN (0,1,3,4,6,7)) -- Population in progress, Throttled,
Recovering, Incremental Population in Progress or Updating Index
   EXEC sp_fulltext_catalog @catalogname, 'stop'

IF (OBJECTPROPERTY(OBJECT_ID(@tablename), 'TableHasActiveFullTextIndex')=0) -- Create
full text index if not already present
   EXEC sp_fulltext_table @tablename,'create',@catalogname,@indexname
ELSE
   EXEC sp_fulltext_table @tablename,'deactivate' -- Deactivate it so we can make
   changes to it

IF (COLUMNPROPERTY(OBJECT_ID(@tablename),@columnname,'IsFulltextIndexed')=0) BEGIN --
Add the column to the index
   EXEC sp_fulltext_column @tablename, @columnname, 'add'
   PRINT 'Successfully added a fulltext index for '+@tablename+'.'+@columnname+' in
   database '+DB_NAME()
END ELSE
   PRINT 'Column '+@columnname+' in table '+DB_NAME()+'.'+@tablename+' is already full-
   text indexed'

EXEC sp_fulltext_table @tablename,'activate'

EXEC sp_fulltext_catalog @catalogname, 'start_full'
RETURN 0

Help:
EXEC sp_usage @objectname='sp_enable_fulltext',@desc='Enables full-text indexing for a
specified column',
@parameters='@tablename=name of host table, @columnname=column to set up,
[,@catalogname=name of full-text catalog to use (Default:
DB_NAME()+"Catalog")][,@startsrever=YES|NO specifies whether to start the
Microsoft Search service on this machine prior to setting up the column (Default:
YES)]',
@author='Ken Henderson', @email='khen@khen.com',
@datecreated='19990614',@datelastchanged='19990714',
@example='EXEC sp_enable_fulltext "pubs..pub_info","pr_info",DEFAULT,"YES"'
RETURN -1

sp_enable_fulltext 'pub_info','pr_info'

Successfully added a fulltext index for pub_info.pr_info in database pubs
```

This procedure does a number of interesting things. It begins by checking to see whether the Microsoft Search service has been installed. If it hasn't, the procedure aborts immediately. Next, it uses xp_cmdshell to start the Microsoft Search service if asked to do so (the command has no effect if the service is already running). This is done via the **NET START mssearch** operating system command. **NET START** is the Windows NT command syntax for starting a service, and **mssearch** is the internal name of the Microsoft Search service. (You can also start the server via Enterprise Manager, the Services applet in the Windows NT Control Panel, and the SQL Server Services Manager.)

The procedure next retrieves a unique key table index for the specified table. Adding a full-text index to a table requires a unique key index. Here, the procedure traps the output of sp_statistics (which lists a table's indexes) in a temporary table via INSERT...EXEC and then scans that table for a unique index on the table. If it doesn't find one, it aborts immediately.

Next, the procedure checks to see whether the database is enabled for full-text indexing. If not, it enables it. The code next checks the status of the full-text catalog. If it's nonexistent, the routine creates it. If it's active, it shuts the catalog down so that changes can be made to it. This is step 2 in the list above.

Once the full-text catalog is in place, the routine creates a full-text index for the table after checking with OBJECTPROPERTY() to ensure that a full-text index doesn't already exist. This is where the unique index that the routine located earlier is used.

After the full-text index has been set up, the routine adds the specified column to it. The procedure takes the name of the column that was passed into it and adds it to the table's full-text index using sp_fulltext_column. This tells the server that you want to build an index to track advanced search info for the specified column but doesn't actually activate the index or populate it with data. That comes next.

The routine finishes up by calling sp_fulltext_table and sp_fulltext_catalog to activate the new full-text index and populate it with data. Once these processes complete, you're ready to begin using full-text predicates and rowset functions in your code.

Full-Text Predicates

A predicate is a logical construct that returns True or Not True (I'll avoid False here because of the issues related to three-value logic). In SQL, these usually take the form of functions and reside in the WHERE clause. LIKE and EXISTS are examples of WHERE clause predicates.

When full-text searching is enabled, two additional predicates are available in Transact-SQL: CONTAINS() and FREETEXT(). CONTAINS() provides support for both exact and inexact string matches, word proximity–based searches, word inflection searches, and weighted searches. FREETEXT(), by contrast, is used to find words or phrases with the same basic *meaning* as those in the search term.

Before we begin exploring these functions via code, let's enable full-text searching on the Employees table in the Northwind database. Employees includes a Notes text column that's ideal for full-text searching. You can use the sp_enable_fulltext procedure you just created to set it up, like so:

```
EXEC northwind..sp_enable_fulltext 'Employees','notes'
```

This should create the necessary meta-data and indexing information to allow the full-text search functions to work properly.

The CONTAINS() Predicate

CONTAINS() locates rows that contain a word or words or variations of them. It can perform exact and inexact word locations, word proximity searches, and inflectional searches. You can think of it as the LIKE predicate on steroids. Here's an example that uses CONTAINS() to find all the people in the Employees table whose Notes fields mention the word "English":

```
SELECT LastName, FirstName, Notes
FROM EMPLOYEES
WHERE CONTAINS(Notes,'English')
```

(Results abridged)

```
LastName           FirstName Notes
----------------   --------- -------------------------------------------------
Peacock            Margaret  Margaret holds a BA in English literature from
Dodsworth          Anne      Anne has a BA degree in English from St.
King               Robert    ...completing his degree in English
```

Note that since we're searching all the full-text index columns in Employees (there's only one), we could have substituted "*" for the column name and achieved the same result, like this:

```
SELECT LastName, FirstName, Notes
FROM EMPLOYEES
WHERE CONTAINS(*,'English')
```

CONTAINS() supports word proximity searches, as well. Here's a refinement of the last example that narrows the employees listed to those whose Notes field contains the word "degree" located near the word "English":

```
SELECT LastName, FirstName, Notes
FROM EMPLOYEES
WHERE CONTAINS(*,'degree NEAR English')
```

(Results abridged)

```
LastName           FirstName Notes
----------------   --------- -------------------------------------------------
Dodsworth          Anne      Anne has a BA degree in English from St.
King               Robert    ...completing his degree in English
```

This time, only two rows are listed because Margaret Peacock's Notes field doesn't contain the word "degree" at all. Note that the tilde character ("~") is synonymous with NEAR, so you rewrite the previous example like this:

```
SELECT LastName, FirstName, Notes
FROM EMPLOYEES
WHERE CONTAINS(*,'degree ~ English')
```

The search condition string also supports Boolean expressions and wildcards. Here are some examples:

```
SELECT LastName, FirstName, Notes
FROM EMPLOYEES
WHERE CONTAINS(Notes,'English OR German')
```

(Results abridged)

```
LastName          FirstName Notes
----------------- --------- ------------------------------------------------
Peacock           Margaret  Margaret holds a BA in English literature from
Dodsworth         Anne      Anne has a BA degree in English from St.
Fuller            Andrew    ...and reads German
King              Robert    ...completing his degree in English
```

This query returns the rows containing the words "English" and "German." The exact or relative positions of the words are unimportant—if either of the words appears anywhere in the Notes column, the row is returned.

In this use, CONTAINS() behaves similarly to LIKE, but there's one important difference—CONTAINS() is sensitive to word boundaries; LIKE isn't. For example, here's the query rewritten to use LIKE:

```
SELECT LastName, FirstName, Notes
FROM EMPLOYEES
WHERE Notes LIKE '%English%'
OR Notes LIKE '%German%'
```

It looks similar, but this query doesn't really ask the same question as the CONTAINS() query. It will find matches with variations of the search words and even with words that happen to contain them (e.g., Germantown, Englishman, Germanic, Burgerman). The CONTAINS() query, by contrast, is word-savvy—it knows the difference between English and Englishman and is smart enough to return only what you ask for.

CONTAINS() also supports prefix-based wildcards. Unfortunately, they're more like operating system wildcards than standard SQL wildcards. Here's an example:

```
SELECT LastName, FirstName, Notes
FROM EMPLOYEES
WHERE CONTAINS(*,'"psy*" OR "chem*"')
```

(Result abridged)

```
LastName          FirstName Notes
----------------- --------- ------------------------------------------------
Leverling         Janet     Janet has a BS degree in chemistry from Boston
Davolio           Nancy     Education includes a BA in psychology from
Callahan          Laura     Laura received a BA in psychology from the
```

This query locates all rows with Notes fields containing words that begin with "psy" or "chem." Note that suffix-based wildcards and single-character wildcards aren't supported.

Quotes are used within the condition string to delineate search strings from one another. When wildcards and multiple terms are present in the search criteria string, quotes are required, and omitting them will cause the query to fail.

A really powerful aspect of CONTAINS() is its support for inflectional searches. The ability to search based on word forms is a potent and often very useful addition to the Transact-SQL repertoire. Here's an example that illustrates how to search for the forms of a word:

```
SELECT LastName, FirstName, Notes
FROM EMPLOYEES
WHERE CONTAINS(*,'FORMSOF(INFLECTIONAL,complete)')
```

(Results abridged)

```
LastName          FirstName Notes
----------------- --------- -----------------------------------------------
Leverling         Janet     ...completed a certificate program in food
Davolio           Nancy     ...She also completed "The Art of the Cold
King              Robert    ...completing his degree in English at the
Buchanan          Steven    ...has completed the courses
Callahan          Laura     ...completed a course in business French.
```

You can use the FORMSOF() clause to locate the difference tenses of a verb, as well as the singular and plural forms of a noun. In this case, the code finds five rows that contain forms of the word "complete" including "completed" and "completing."

The FREETEXT() Predicate

FREETEXT() is useful for locating rows containing words that have the same basic meaning as those in a search string. Unlike CONTAINS(), FREETEXT() allows you to specify a series of terms that are then weighted internally and matched with values in the full-text column(s). Here's an example that locates employees with college degrees, especially bachelor's degrees:

```
SELECT LastName, FirstName, Notes
FROM EMPLOYEES
WHERE FREETEXT(Notes,'BA BTS BS BSC degree')
```

(Results abridged)

```
LastName            FirstName Notes
------------------- --------- ------------------------------------------------
Leverling           Janet     Janet has a BS degree in chemistry from Boston
Davolio             Nancy     Education includes a BA in psychology
Peacock             Margaret  Margaret holds a BA in English literature from
Dodsworth           Anne      Anne has a BA degree in English from St.
Fuller              Andrew    Andrew received his BTS commercial in 1974 and
King                Robert    Robert King [completed] his degree in English at
Buchanan            Steven    Steven Buchanan graduated with a BSC degree in
Callahan            Laura     Laura received a BA in psychology from the
```

Here, any row containing any of the terms or similar words are returned. As with CONTAINS(), "*" is used to signify all full-text indexed columns in the table.

Rowset Functions

Transact-SQL defines a special class of functions called *rowset* functions that can be used in place of tables in the FROM clauses of queries. Rowset functions return result sets in a fashion similar to a derived table and can be joined with real tables, summarized, grouped, and so on.

There are two rowset functions related to full-text searching: CONTAINSTABLE() and FREE-TEXTTABLE(). These are rowset versions of the predicates discussed earlier in the chapter. Rather than being used in the WHERE clause, these functions typically appear in the FROM clause of a SELECT statement. They return a result set consisting of index key values and row rankings.

The CONTAINSTABLE() Rowset Function

In addition to the fact that it's a rowset function rather than a predicate, the CONTAINSTABLE() function works similarly to CONTAINS(), as its name would suggest. It supports exactly the same search string criteria as CONTAINS() and requires one parameter—the name of the underlying table—in addition to those required by the predicate. Here's an example that uses CONTAINSTABLE() to produce a list of key values and search rankings:

```
SELECT *
FROM CONTAINSTABLE(Employees,*,'English OR French OR Italian OR German OR Flemish')
ORDER BY RANK DESC

KEY         RANK
---------   ---------
8           64
2           64
4           48
7           48
9           48
6           32
5           32
```

CONTAINSTABLE() returns two columns: the key value of the row from the underlying table and a ranking of each row. In this example, we use the RANK column to sequence the rows logically such that higher rankings are listed first. The key value can be used to join back to the original table in order to translate the key into something a bit more meaningful, as you'll see in a moment.

The rankings returned by the RANK column can be tailored to your needs using the IS-ABOUT() function of the search criteria string. Here's an example:

```
SELECT *
FROM CONTAINSTABLE(Employees,*,'ISABOUT(English weight(0.8), French weight(0.1),
Italian weight(0.2), German weight(0.4), Flemish weight(0.0))')
ORDER BY RANK DESC

KEY         RANK
---------   ---------
9           85
2           54
4           47
7           47
8           7
6           3
5           3
```

In this example, weights are assigned for each language skill specifically indicated by an employee's Notes entry, ranging from zero for Flemish to 0.8 for English. Valid weights range from 0.0 to 1.0. As in the previous example, we use the RANK column to sequence the rows such that higher rankings are listed first. ISABOUT() is also available with the CONTAINS() predicate but has no effect since its only purpose is to alter the RANK column that is not used by the predicate.

To generate results that are truly meaningful, you need to join the result set returned by CONTAINSTABLE() with its underlying table. The key values and rankings returned by the function itself aren't terribly useful without some correlation to the original data. Here's an example:

```
SELECT R.RANK, E.LastName, E.FirstName, E.Notes
FROM Employees AS E JOIN
CONTAINSTABLE(Employees,*,'ISABOUT(English weight(0.8), French weight(0.1),
Italian weight(0.2), German weight(0.4), Flemish weight(0.0))') AS R ON
(E.EmployeeId=R.[KEY])
ORDER BY R.RANK DESC
```

(Results abridged)

RANK	LastName	FirstName	Notes
85	Dodsworth	Anne	...is fluent in French and German.
54	Fuller	Andrew	...fluent in French and Italian and reads German
47	Peacock	Margaret	Margaret holds a BA in English literature
47	King	Robert	...before completing his degree in English
7	Callahan	Laura	...reads and writes French
3	Suyama	Michael	...can read and write French, Portuguese, and
3	Buchanan	Steven	...is fluent in French

A simple inner join using the Employee table's EmployeeID column and the KEY column from the CONTAINSTABLE() function is all that's required to link the two tables. KEY contains the value of the EmployeeID column in the rows returned by CONTAINSTABLE(), so this makes sense.

As with the earlier examples, this query sequences its result set using the RANK column returned by CONTAINSTABLE(). Note the use of brackets ("[]") around the reference to the **KEY** column returned by CONTAINSTABLE(). Inexplicably, SQL Server uses **KEY** as a column name for CONTAINSTABLE(), even though it's a reserved word. This necessitates surrounding it with brackets (or double quotes if the QUOTED_IDENTIFIER setting is enabled) any time you reference it directly.

To see the effect of the rank weighting, let's revise the query to use the default ranking returned by Microsoft Search:

```
SELECT R.RANK, E.LastName, E.FirstName, E.Notes
FROM Employees AS E JOIN
CONTAINSTABLE(Employees,*,'English OR French OR Italian OR German OR Flemish') AS R ON
(E.EmployeeId=R.[KEY])
ORDER BY R.RANK DESC
```

(Results abridged)

RANK	LastName	FirstName	Notes
64	Fuller	Andrew	...fluent in French and Italian and reads German
64	Callahan	Laura	...reads and writes French
48	Peacock	Margaret	Margaret holds a BA in English literature
48	King	Robert	...before completing his degree in English
48	Dodsworth	Anne	...is fluent in French and German.
32	Suyama	Michael	...can read and write French, Portuguese, and
32	Buchanan	Steven	...is fluent in French

As you can see, the custom weighting we supplied makes a huge difference. It completely changes the order in which the rows are listed.

The FREETEXTTABLE() Rowset Function

As with its predicate cousin, FREETEXTTABLE() locates rows containing words with the same basic meaning as those specified in the search criteria. The format of its search criteria string is open-ended ("free") and has no specific syntax. The search engine extracts each word from the string and assigns it a weight and locates rows accordingly. Here's the earlier example that locates employees with bachelor's degrees rewritten to use FREETEXTTABLE():

```
SELECT R.RANK, E.LastName, E.FirstName, E.Notes
FROM Employees AS E JOIN
FREETEXTTABLE(Employees,*,'BA BTS BS BCS degree') AS R ON (E.EmployeeId=R.[KEY])
ORDER BY R.RANK DESC
```

RANK	LastName	FirstName	Notes
24	Leverling	Janet	Janet has a BS degree in chemistry
10	Fuller	Andrew	Andrew received his BTS commercial
16	Dodsworth	Anne	Anne has a BA degree in English
from 8	Peacock	Margaret	Margaret holds a BA in English
8	Callahan	Laura	Laura received a BA in psychology
8	Davolio	Nancy	Education includes a BA in
8	King	Robert	Robert King completing his degree
in 8	Buchanan	Steven	with a BSC degree in 1976. Upon

With such a broad criteria string, the query returns all but one row in the Employees table. Each of these has some form of one of the words listed in the search criteria string.

Summary

SQL Server's full-text searching facility is a potent tool that provides most of the functionality of stand-alone file-based search engines. Enabling columns for text searching is nontrivial, and you should use Enterprise Manager or the sp_enable_fulltext stored procedure (included in this chapter) to set them up. Once a column has been set up for full-text searches, the CONTAINS() and FREETEXT() predicates, as well as the CONTAINSTABLE() and FREETEXTTABLE() rowset functions, become available for use with it. They offer a powerful alternative to commonplace search implements such as LIKE and PATINDEX().

19

OLE Automation

The paperless office is about as likely as the paperless bathroom.—Joe Celko

SQL Server provides a set of stored procedures whose purpose is to work with automation (formerly known as OLE automation) objects. Automation provides a language-independent means of controlling and using objects exposed by other programs. For example, you can use automation to instruct Word to spell check a document or Excel to compute a formula. A good number of programs and tools expose pieces of themselves to the outside world through automation objects. If you have access to an automation controller, you can make use of those objects to manipulate the host application. Fortunately, you do have access to such a controller—SQL Server's ODSOLE facility, which is exposed via a set of system procedures that you can call from Transact-SQL.

The Transact-SQL stored procedures that relate to automation are named using the convention sp_OA*Function* where *Function* indicates what the procedure does (e.g., sp_OACreate instantiates automation objects, sp_OAMethod calls an automation method, sp_OAGetProperty and sp_OASetProperty get and set properties). This facility adds a considerable amount of power to the Transact-SQL language. Anything you can get at via an automation interface, you can manipulate with Transact-SQL.

To illustrate how this works, I'll show you a stored procedure that uses automation to fill a gap in the Transact-SQL arsenal. You may recall that Transact-SQL has a BULK INSERT command. Its purpose is to bulk load an operating system file via SQL Server's bulk copy interface. Unfortunately, there's no reciprocating syntax for exporting data. You'd think they would have provided a BULK EXPORT command for exporting data to operating system files, but that's not the case. Of course, there are a number of ways around this that don't involve Transact-SQL. For example, you could use the **bcp.exe** command-line utility to perform data exports. You could build an automation controller using a traditional development tool such as Visual Basic or Delphi. You could even use Enterprise Manager to perform your exports. But none of these alternatives would be nearly as much fun as exporting data directly from Transact-SQL vis-à-vis BULK INSERT.

The examples that follow will illustrate how to use the automation stored procedures to automate objects exposed by the server itself—the Distributed Management Objects (SQL-DMO).

These objects provide much of Enterprise Manager's underlying functionality and are a handy way of managing the server via program code. Note that you aren't limited to accessing automation objects exposed by SQL Server—you can manipulate automation objects exposed by any application—Access, Visio, Visual C++, etc.

sp_exporttable

Given that SQL Server provides a robust automation interface to the bulk copy facility in SQL-DMO, we can build Transact-SQL code that performs bulk exports using Transact-SQL and the automation procedures mentioned above. Here's a script that builds a stored procedure to do just that:

```
USE master
GO
IF (OBJECT_ID('sp_exporttable') IS NOT NULL)
   DROP PROC sp_exporttable
GO
CREATE PROC sp_exporttable
   @table varchar(128),              -- Table to export
   @outputpath varchar(128)=NULL,    -- Output directory, terminate with a "\"
   @outputname varchar(128)=NULL,    -- Output filename (default @table+'.BCP')
   @server varchar(128)='(local)',   -- Name of the server to connect to
   @username varchar(128)='sa',      -- User name to use (defaults to 'sa')
   @password varchar(128)=NULL       -- User's password
/*
Object: sp_exporttable
Description: Exports a table in a manner similar to BULK INSERT

Usage: sp_exporttable
   @table varchar(128),              -- Table to export
   @outputpath varchar(128)=NULL,    -- Output directory, terminate with a '\'
   @outputname varchar(128)=NULL,    -- Output filename (default @table+'.BCP')
   @server varchar(128)='(local)',   -- Name of the server to connect to
   @username varchar(128)='sa',      -- User name to use (defaults to 'sa')
   @password varchar(128)=NULL       -- User's password

Returns: Number of rows exported

Created by: Ken Henderson. Email: khen@khen.com

Example: EXEC sp_exporttable "authors"

Created: 1999-06-14. Last changed: 1999-07-14.
*/
AS
IF (@table='/?') OR (@outputpath IS NULL) GOTO Help
DECLARE @object int,         -- Work variable for instantiating automation objects
   @hr int,                  -- Contains HRESULT returned by automation
   @bcobject int,            -- Stores pointer to BulkCopy object
   @TAB_DELIMITED int,       -- Will store a constant for tab-delimited output
   @logname varchar(128),    -- Name of the log file
   @errname varchar(128),    -- Name of the error file
   @dbname varchar(128),     -- Name of the database
   @rowsexported int         -- Number of rows exported
```

```
SET @TAB_DELIMITED=2                              -- SQL-DMO constant for tab-delimited
                                                     exports
SET @dbname=ISNULL(PARSENAME(@table,3),DB_NAME()) -- Extract the DB name; default to current
SET @table=PARSENAME(@table,1)                    -- Remove extraneous stuff from table name
IF (@table IS NULL) BEGIN
   RAISERROR('Invalid table name.',16,1)
   GOTO Help
END
IF (RIGHT(@outputpath,1)<>'\')
   SET @outputpath=@outputpath+'\'        -- Append a "\" if necessary
SET @logname=@outputpath+@table+'.LOG' -- Construct the log file name
SET @errname=@outputpath+@table+'.ERR' -- Construct the error file name

IF (@outputname IS NULL)-- Construct the output name based on export table
   SET @outputname=@outputpath+@table+'.BCP'
ELSE
   IF (CHARINDEX('\',@outputname)=0)
      SET @outputname=@outputpath+@outputname

-- Create a SQLServer object
EXEC @hr=sp_OACreate 'SQLDMO.SQLServer', @object OUTPUT
IF (@hr <> 0) BEGIN
   EXEC sp_displayoaerrorinfo @object, @hr
   RETURN
END


-- Create a BulkCopy object
EXEC @hr=sp_OACreate 'SQLDMO.BulkCopy', @bcobject OUTPUT
IF (@hr <> 0) BEGIN
   EXEC sp_displayoaerrorinfo @bcobject, @hr
   RETURN
END


-- Set BulkCopy's DataFilePath property to the output file name
EXEC @hr = sp_OASetProperty @bcobject, 'DataFilePath', @outputname
IF (@hr <> 0) BEGIN
   EXEC sp_displayoaerrorinfo @bcobject, @hr
   RETURN
END


-- Tell BulkCopy to create tab-delimited files
EXEC @hr = sp_OASetProperty @bcobject, 'DataFileType', @TAB_DELIMITED
IF (@hr <> 0) BEGIN
   EXEC sp_displayoaerrorinfo @bcobject, @hr
   RETURN
END


-- Set BulkCopy's LogFilePath property to the log file name
EXEC @hr = sp_OASetProperty @bcobject, 'LogFilePath', @logname
IF (@hr <> 0) BEGIN
   EXEC sp_displayoaerrorinfo @bcobject, @hr
   RETURN
END


-- Set BulkCopy's ErrorFilePath property to the error file name
EXEC @hr = sp_OASetProperty @bcobject, 'ErrorFilePath', @errname
IF (@hr <> 0) BEGIN
   EXEC sp_displayoaerrorinfo @bcobject, @hr
   RETURN
END
```

```
-- Connect to the server
IF (@password IS NOT NULL)
    EXEC @hr = sp_OAMethod @object, 'Connect', NULL, @server, @username, @password
ELSE
    EXEC @hr = sp_OAMethod @object, 'Connect', NULL, @server, @username
IF (@hr <> 0) BEGIN
    EXEC sp_displayoaerrorinfo @object, @hr
    RETURN
END

-- Get a pointer to the SQLServer object's Databases collection
EXEC @hr = sp_OAGetProperty @object, 'Databases', @object OUT
IF @hr <> 0 BEGIN
    EXEC sp_displayoaerrorinfo @object, @hr
    RETURN
END

-- Get a pointer from the Databases collection for the specified database
EXEC @hr = sp_OAMethod @object, 'Item', @object OUT, @dbname
IF @hr <> 0 BEGIN
    EXEC sp_displayoaerrorinfo @object, @hr
    RETURN
END

-- Get a pointer from the Database object's Tables collection for the table
IF (OBJECTPROPERTY(OBJECT_ID(@table),'IsTable')=1) BEGIN
    EXEC @hr = sp_OAMethod @object, 'Tables', @object OUT, @table
    IF @hr <> 0 BEGIN
        EXEC sp_displayoaerrorinfo @object, @hr
        RETURN
    END
END ELSE
IF (OBJECTPROPERTY(OBJECT_ID(@table),'IsView')=1) BEGIN
    EXEC @hr = sp_OAMethod @object, 'Views', @object OUT, @table
    IF @hr <> 0 BEGIN
        EXEC sp_displayoaerrorinfo @object, @hr
        RETURN
    END
END ELSE BEGIN
    RAISERROR('Source object must be either a table or view.',16,1)
    RETURN -1
END

-- Call the object's ExportData method to export the table/view using BulkCopy
EXEC @hr = sp_OAMethod @object, 'ExportData', @rowsexported OUT, @bcobject
IF @hr <> 0 BEGIN
    EXEC sp_displayoaerrorinfo @object, @hr
    RETURN
END

RETURN @rowsexported

Help:

EXEC sp_usage @objectname='sp_exporttable',
@desc='Exports a table in a manner similar to BULK INSERT',
@parameters="
    @table varchar(128),            -- Table to export
    @outputpath varchar(128)=NULL,  -- Output directory, terminate with a '\'
```

```
    @outputname varchar(128)=NULL,   -- Output filename (default @table+'.BCP')
    @server varchar(128)='(local)',  -- Name of the server to connect to
    @username varchar(128)='sa',     -- User name to use (defaults to 'sa')
    @password varchar(128)=NULL      -- User's password
",
@author='Ken Henderson', @email='khen@khen.com',
@datecreated='19990614',@datelastchanged='19990714',
@example='EXEC sp_exporttable "authors", "C:\TEMP\"',
@returns='Number of rows exported'
RETURN -1
GO
```

Follow the comments in the source code to see how the procedure works—it's fairly straightforward. Once the procedure is created, you can run it using this syntax:

```
DECLARE @rc int
EXEC @rc=pubs..sp_exporttable @table='pubs..authors',
@outputpath='d:\_temp\bcp\'
SELECT RowsExported=@rc


RowsExported
------------
23
```

Note the use of the "pubs.." prefix when calling the stored procedure. The stored procedure makes use of the OBJECTPROPERTY() function, which does not work across databases. Therefore, for the procedure to work correctly with objects in other databases, you need to change the current database context temporarily to match the one passed in via @table. As mentioned elsewhere in this book, prefixing a system procedure call with a database name temporarily changes the database context. The call to sp_exporttable above is the functional equivalent of:

```
USE pubs
GO
EXEC @rc=sp_exporttable @table='pubs..authors', @outputpath='d:\_temp\bcp\'
GO
USE master -- or some other database
GO
```

Also note the use of the sp_displayoaerrorinfo system procedure. This procedure isn't created by default, but you can find the source to it in the Books Online. It relies on sp_hexadecimal, which is also available in the Books Online. See the topic "OLE Automation Return Codes and Error Information" under the sp_OAGetErrorInfo stored procedure in the Books Online for the source code to both procedures.

The tasks the procedure must accomplish are as follows:

1. Create a SQLServer object and log into the server. All communication with the server via SQL-DMO happens through this connection.

2. Create a BulkCopy object and set its properties to reflect the type of bulk copy operation we want to perform. We'll call the Table object's ExportData method to do the actual data export, but it requires a BulkCopy object in order to perform the operation.

3. Locate the source database by extracting its name from @table and looking it up in the SQLServer object's Databases collection.

4. Locate the source table/view by looking it up in the Database object's Tables or Views collection.

5. Call the object's ExportData method, passing it the BulkCopy object that was previously created.

6. Return an integer indicating the number of rows exported. Return −1 in case of an error.

Using automation, the procedure is able to perform all these tasks with relative ease. The amount of Transact-SQL code required to do this is no more than that required by a comparable Delphi or Visual Basic program.

sp_importtable

Even though Transact-SQL provides the BULK INSERT command for bulk loading data, for completeness, here's the bulk load counterpart to sp_exporttable:

```
USE master
GO
IF (OBJECT_ID('sp_importtable') IS NOT NULL)
   DROP PROC sp_importtable
GO
CREATE PROC sp_importtable
   @table varchar(128),            -- Table to import
   @inputpath varchar(128)=NULL,   -- input directory, terminate with a "\"
   @inputname varchar(128)=NULL,   -- input filename (defaults to @table+'.BCP')
   @server varchar(128)='(local)', -- Name of the server to connect to
   @username varchar(128)='sa',    -- Name of the user to connect as (defaults to 'sa')
   @password varchar(128)=NULL     -- User's password
/*
Object: sp_importtable
Description: Imports a table similarly to BULK INSERT

Usage: sp_importtable
   @table varchar(128),            -- Table to import
   @inputpath varchar(128)=NULL,   -- input directory, terminate with a '\'
   @inputname varchar(128)=NULL,   -- input filename (defaults to @table+'.BCP')
   @server varchar(128)='(local)', -- Name of the server to connect to
   @username varchar(128)='sa',    -- Name of the user to connect as (defaults to 'sa')
   @password varchar(128)=NULL     -- User's password

Returns: Number of rows imported

Created by: Ken Henderson. Email: khen@khen.com

Example: EXEC importtable "authors", "C:\TEMP\"

Created: 1999-06-14. Last changed: 1999-07-14.
*/
AS
```

```
IF (@table='/?') OR (@inputpath IS NULL) GOTO Help
DECLARE @object int,       -- Work variable for instantiating automation objects
   @hr int,                -- Contains HRESULT returned by automation
   @bcobject int,          -- Stores pointer to BulkCopy object
   @TAB_DELIMITED int,     -- Will store a constant for tab-delimited input
   @logname varchar(128),  -- Name of the log file
   @errname varchar(128),  -- Name of the error file
   @dbname varchar(128),   -- Name of the database
   @rowsimported int       -- Number of rows imported

SET @TAB_DELIMITED=2                                  -- SQL-DMO constant for tab-delimited
                                                         imports
SET @dbname=ISNULL(PARSENAME(@table,3),DB_NAME()) -- Extract the DB name; default to current
SET @table=PARSENAME(@table,1)                        -- Remove extraneous stuff from table name
IF (@table IS NULL) BEGIN
   RAISERROR('Invalid table name.',16,1)
   RETURN -1
END
IF (RIGHT(@inputpath,1)<>'\')
   SET @inputpath=@inputpath+'\'       -- Append a "\" if necessary
SET @logname=@inputpath+@table+'.LOG' -- Construct the log file name
SET @errname=@inputpath+@table+'.ERR' -- Construct the error file name

IF (@inputname IS NULL)
   SET @inputname=@inputpath+@table+'.BCP' -- Construct the input name based on import table
ELSE
   SET @inputname=@inputpath+@inputname    -- Prefix source path


-- Create a SQLServer object
EXEC @hr=sp_OACreate 'SQLDMO.SQLServer', @object OUT
IF (@hr <> 0) BEGIN
   EXEC sp_displayoaerrorinfo @object, @hr
   RETURN
END
-- Create a BulkCopy object
EXEC @hr=sp_OACreate 'SQLDMO.BulkCopy', @bcobject OUT
IF (@hr <> 0) BEGIN
   EXEC sp_displayoaerrorinfo @bcobject, @hr
   RETURN
END


-- Set BulkCopy's DataFilePath property to the input file name
EXEC @hr = sp_OASetProperty @bcobject, 'DataFilePath', @inputname
IF (@hr <> 0) BEGIN
   EXEC sp_displayoaerrorinfo @bcobject, @hr
   RETURN
END


-- Tell BulkCopy to create tab-delimited files
EXEC @hr = sp_OASetProperty @bcobject, 'DataFileType', @TAB_DELIMITED
IF (@hr <> 0) BEGIN
   EXEC sp_displayoaerrorinfo @bcobject, @hr
   RETURN
END


-- Set BulkCopy's LogFilePath property to the log file name
EXEC @hr = sp_OASetProperty @bcobject, 'LogFilePath', @logname
```

```
IF (@hr <> 0) BEGIN
   EXEC sp_displayoaerrorinfo @bcobject, @hr
   RETURN
END

-- Set BulkCopy's ErrorFilePath property to the error file name
EXEC @hr = sp_OASetProperty @bcobject, 'ErrorFilePath', @errname
IF (@hr <> 0) BEGIN
   EXEC sp_displayoaerrorinfo @bcobject, @hr
   RETURN
END

-- Set BulkCopy's UseServerSideBCP property to true
EXEC @hr = sp_OASetProperty @bcobject, 'UseServerSideBCP', 1
IF (@hr <> 0) BEGIN
   EXEC sp_displayoaerrorinfo @bcobject, @hr
   RETURN
END

-- Connect to the server
IF (@password IS NOT NULL)
EXEC @hr = sp_OAMethod @object, 'Connect', NULL, @server, @username, @password
ELSE
   EXEC @hr = sp_OAMethod @object, 'Connect', NULL, @server, @username
IF (@hr <> 0) BEGIN
   EXEC sp_displayoaerrorinfo @object, @hr
   RETURN
END

-- Get a pointer to the SQLServer object's Databases collection
EXEC @hr = sp_OAGetProperty @object, 'Databases', @object OUT
IF @hr <> 0 BEGIN
   EXEC sp_displayoaerrorinfo @object, @hr
   RETURN
END

-- Get a pointer from the Databases collection for the specified database
EXEC @hr = sp_OAMethod @object, 'Item', @object OUT, @dbname
IF @hr <> 0 BEGIN
   EXEC sp_displayoaerrorinfo @object, @hr
   RETURN
END

-- Get a pointer from the Database object's Tables collection for the specified table
IF (OBJECTPROPERTY(OBJECT_ID(@table),'IsTable')<>1) BEGIN
   RAISERROR('Target object must be a table.',16,1)
   RETURN -1
END BEGIN
   EXEC @hr = sp_OAMethod @object, 'Tables', @object OUT, @table
   IF @hr <> 0 BEGIN
      EXEC sp_displayoaerrorinfo @object, @hr
      RETURN
   END
END

-- Call the Table object's importData method to import the table using BulkCopy
EXEC @hr = sp_OAMethod @object, 'ImportData', @rowsimported OUT, @bcobject
IF @hr <> 0 BEGIN
```

```
        EXEC sp_displayoaerrorinfo @object, @hr
        RETURN
END

RETURN @rowsimported

Help:

EXEC sp_usage @objectname='sp_importtable',
@desc='Imports a table similarly to BULK INSERT',
@parameters="
    @table varchar(128),              -- Table to import
    @inputpath varchar(128)=NULL,     -- input directory, terminate with a '\'
    @inputname varchar(128)=NULL,     -- input filename (defaults to @table+'.BCP')
    @server varchar(128)='(local)',   -- Name of the server to connect to
    @username varchar(128)='sa',      -- Name of the user to connect as (defaults to 'sa')
    @password varchar(128)=NULL       -- User's password
",
@author='Ken Henderson', @email='khen@khen.com',
@datecreated='19990614',@datelastchanged='19990714',
@example='EXEC importtable "authors", "C:\TEMP\"',
@returns='Number of rows imported'
RETURN -1
GO
```

Like BULK INSERT, sp_importtable loads operating system files into tables. As with sp_exporttable, it makes certain assumptions about the format of the file that you may change if you wish. Here's a code sample that uses sp_exporttable and sp_importtable together:

```
SET NOCOUNT ON
USE pubs
DECLARE @rc int

-- First, export the rows
EXEC @rc=pubs..sp_exporttable @table='pubs..authors', @outputpath='d:\_temp\bcp\'
SELECT @rc AS RowsExported

-- Second, create a new table to store the rows
SELECT * INTO authorsimp FROM authors WHERE 1=0

-- Third, import the exported rows
EXEC pubs..sp_importtable @table='authorsimp',
@inputpath='d:\_temp\bcp\',@inputname='authors.bcp'

SELECT COUNT(*) AS RowsLoaded FROM authorsimp
GO
DROP TABLE authorsimp
```

This script begins by exporting the authors table from the pubs sample database. It then creates an empty copy of the table and imports the exported rows using sp_importtable. As with BULK INSERT, the file it loads must be directly accessible by the machine on which SQL Server is running.

sp_getSQLregistry

In addition to bulk load operations, SQL Server's SQL-DMO interface provides access to a wealth of administration services and server information. Much of this is exposed via automation objects. One such object is the Registry object. It provides access to the portion of the system registry controlled by SQL Server. You can use it to access such things as the currently installed character set, the default SQL Mail login name, the number of processors, the amount of memory installed on the server computer, and so on. Here's a stored procedure that gives you access to the bevy of information provided by the Registry object:

```
USE master
GO
IF OBJECT_ID('sp_getSQLregistry') IS NOT NULL
   DROP PROC sp_getSQLregistry
GO
CREATE PROC sp_getSQLregistry
   @regkey varchar(128),              -- Registry key to extract
   @regvalue varchar(8000)=NULL OUTPUT, -- Value from SQL Server registry tree for key
   @server varchar(128)='(local)',    -- Name of the server to connect to
   @username varchar(128)='sa',       -- Name of the user to connect as (defaults to 'sa')
   @password varchar(128)=NULL        -- User's password
/*

Object: sp_getSQLregistry
Description: Retrieves a value from the SQL Server branch in the system registry

Usage: sp_getSQLregistry
   @regkey varchar(128),              -- Registry key to extract
   @regvalue varchar(8000) OUTPUT,    -- Value from SQL Server registry tree for key
   @server varchar(128)="(local)",    -- Name of the server to connect to
   @username varchar(128)="sa",       -- Name of the user to connect as (Default: "sa")
   @password varchar(128)=NULL        -- User's password

Returns: Data length of registry value

Created by: Ken Henderson. Email: khen@khen.com

Version: 6.4

Example: sp_getSQLregistry "SQLRootPath", @sqlpath OUTPUT

Created: 1996-09-03. Last changed: 1999-07-01.

*/
AS
SET NOCOUNT ON
IF (@regkey='/?') GOTO Help

DECLARE @object int, -- Work variable for instantiating automation objects
   @hr int              -- Contains HRESULT returned by automation

-- Create a SQLServer object
EXEC @hr=sp_OACreate 'SQLDMO.SQLServer', @object OUTPUT
IF (@hr <> 0) BEGIN
   EXEC sp_displayoaerrorinfo @object, @hr
   RETURN
END
```

```
-- Connect to the server
IF (@password IS NOT NULL) AND (@password<>'')
   EXEC @hr = sp_OAMethod @object, 'Connect', NULL, @server, @username, @password
ELSE
   EXEC @hr = sp_OAMethod @object, 'Connect', NULL, @server, @username
IF (@hr <> 0) BEGIN
   EXEC sp_displayoaerrorinfo @object, @hr
   RETURN
END


-- Get a pointer to the SQLServer object's Registry object
EXEC @hr = sp_OAGetProperty @object, 'Registry', @object OUT
IF @hr <> 0 BEGIN
   EXEC sp_displayoaerrorinfo @object, @hr
   RETURN
END


-- Get a pointer to the SQLServer object's Databases collection
EXEC @hr = sp_OAGetProperty @object, @regkey, @regvalue OUT
IF @hr <> 0 BEGIN
   EXEC sp_displayoaerrorinfo @object, @hr
   RETURN
END


RETURN datalength(@regvalue)


Help:
EXEC sp_usage @objectname='sp_getSQLregistry',
@desc='Retrieves a value from the SQL Server branch in the system registry',
@parameters='
   @regkey varchar(128),         -- Registry key to extract
   @regvalue varchar(8000) OUTPUT, -- Value from SQL Server registry tree for key
   @server varchar(128)="(local)", -- Name of the server to connect to
   @username varchar(128)="sa",     -- Name of the user to connect as (Default: "sa")
   @password varchar(128)=NULL      -- User'' password',
@author='Ken Henderson', @email='khen@khen.com',
@datecreated='19960903', @datelastchanged='19990701',
@version='6', @revision='4',
@returns='Data length of registry value',
@example='sp_getSQLregistry "SQLRootPath", @sqlpath OUTPUT'

GO
```

Here's a script that uses sp_getSQLregistry to access key system information:

```
SET NOCOUNT ON
DECLARE @numprocs varchar(10), @installedmemory varchar(20), @rootpath varchar(8000)

EXEC sp_getSQLregistry 'PhysicalMemory', @installedmemory OUT
EXEC sp_getSQLregistry 'NumberOfProcessors', @numprocs OUT
EXEC sp_getSQLregistry 'SQLRootPath', @rootpath OUT

SELECT @numprocs AS NumberOfProcessors, @installedmemory AS InstalledRAM, @rootpath AS
RootPath

DECLARE @charset varchar(100), @sortorder varchar(100)
EXEC sp_getSQLregistry 'CharacterSet', @charset OUT
```

```
SELECT @charset AS CharacterSet

EXEC sp_getSQLregistry 'SortOrder', @sortorder OUT

SELECT @sortorder AS SortOrder

NumberOfProcessors InstalledRAM      RootPath
------------------ ----------------- ------------------------------------
1                  79                c:\MSSQL7

CharacterSet
---------------------------------------------------------------------------
Character Set = 1, iso_1  ISO 8859-1 (Latin-1)  -- Western European 8-bit character set.

SortOrder
--------------------------------------------------------------------------
Sort Order = 52, nocase_iso   Case-insensitive dictionary sort order for use with
several We
```

Summary

Transact-SQL's ability to interface with automation objects allows it to perform the kinds of tasks usually reserved for traditional development tools such as Delphi and Visual Basic. In this chapter, you explored manipulating automation objects that the server itself exposes—the Distributed Management Objects—but Transact-SQL's automation procedures (sp_OAxxxx) aren't limited to automation objects exposed by SQL Server. You can automate Excel, Word, Visio, or any application that provides an automation interface—all from within Transact-SQL.

20

Undocumented T-SQL

An ounce of technique is worth a pound of technology.
—Danny Thorpe

I can't stress enough how important it is to avoid relying on undocumented routines unless absolutely necessary. They're undocumented for a reason. As a rule, the functions, DBCC command verbs, stored procedures, and trace flags that have been omitted from the SQL Server documentation have been left out because Microsoft doesn't want you to use them. They can be dangerous —possibly even catastrophic—if used improperly. Wanton misuse of a DBMS's undocumented features is a fast ticket to lost data and apathy from the vendor.

So be careful with the commands and syntax that follow. Use them sparingly and, even then, with due caution. A mangled server quickly extinguishes the joy you get from using this or that gadget simply because you've just learned that it exists.

If you decide to use undocumented routines in your own code, go into it with the full expectation that those routines may change in a future release of the product. The PWDENCRYPT() function below, for example, changed between releases 6.5 and 7.0 of SQL Server, and people who wrote code that relied on it ran into trouble when they migrated to 7.0.

Don't expect vendor support for undocumented routines. When you see the word "undocumented," read "unsupported." Leaving a feature undocumented frees the vendor to change it at will without having to be concerned about breaking customer code. If you decide to base mission-critical code on undocumented aspects of the product, you do so at your own risk.

Defining Undocumented

Undocumented Transact-SQL, as defined here, refers to commands, functions, trace flags, DBCC command verbs, and stored procedures not listed in the SQL Server Books Online. Some of these routines are found in other publicly available Microsoft documentation; some aren't. For this chapter, the bottom line is this: If it isn't in the BOL, it isn't documented.

Undocumented DBCC Commands

The DBCC (database consistency checker) command originally housed a small collection of database maintenance routines that were outside the realm and syntax of traditional Transact-SQL. The idea was to group these routines under an easy-to-remember, easy-to-use command "toolbox," out of the way of normal queries. This worked well and was basically a good idea.

Since that time, Sybase and Microsoft have expanded DBCC's original mission to include loads of functionality not foreseen by the original designers. The verb list for the command has grown to include dozens of things not related to database error checking—to the point of being extremely unwieldy and bordering a bit on the ridiculous. These days, DBCC does everything from checking databases for consistency to wrangling full-text indexes, from managing server caches to interacting with Performance Manager. It's practically a language unto itself.

Many of these command verbs are not documented—some for very good reasons. Why some of them were not made separate Transact-SQL commands, only the vendors know.

Before we delve into DBCC's undocumented command verbs, there are a few pointers to be aware of. First, include the WITH NO_INFOMSGS option to limit DBCC output to error messages. This makes the output from some loquacious commands like DBCC CHECKALLOC much more manageable without losing anything of real importance. Second, use DBCC HELP(*commandverb*) to list built-in help on DBCC command verbs. Most of the undocumented commands aren't displayed by the command, but it never hurts to check. Last, use DBCC TRACEON(3604) to route DBCC output to your client connection rather than the system error log. Many of the undocumented commands send their output to the error log by default, so keep this in mind. If you execute one of the commands below and receive nothing back from the server, it's likely that the command's output went to the error log, and you need to use trace flag 3604 to route it to you instead.

DBCC ADDEXTENDEDPROC(procname,DLL)

This command adds an extended procedure to the list maintained by the server. It has the same basic functionality as the sp_addextendedproc stored procedure and is, in fact, called by the procedure. The **procname** parameter is the name of the extended procedure, and **DLL** is the name of the DLL in which it resides.

```
DBCC ADDEXTENDEDPROC('xp_computemode','xp_stats.dll')
```

DBCC ADDINSTANCE(object,instance)

This command adds an object instance to track in Performance Monitor. Stored procedures that initialize Performance Monitor counters use this to set up various areas of SQL Server for performance tracking. **Object** is the name of the object that contains the instance (e.g., "SQL Replication Agents"), and **instance** is the name of the instance to add (e.g., "Logreader").

```
DBCC ADDINSTANCE("SQL Replication Agents", "Snapshot")
```

DBCC BCPTABLOCK(dbid, tabid, setflag)

This command sets the **table lock on bulk load** option for a table and can improve performance for bulk inserts since it avoids setting a row lock for every inserted row. **Dbid** is the database ID, **tabid** is the table's object ID, and **setflag** is a 1 or 0 indicating whether to set the option.

```
DECLARE @dbid int, @objid int
SELECT @dbid=DB_ID('pubs'), @objid=OBJECT_ID('titles')
DBCC BCPTABLOCK(@dbid,@objid,1)
```

DBCC BUFFER(dbid[,objid][,numberofbuffers][,printopt {0 | 1 | 2}])

This command is used to dump the contents of SQL Server memory buffers. Buffers can be listed for a specific object or for an entire database.

```
DECLARE @dbid int, @objid int
SELECT @dbid=DB_ID('pubs'), @objid=OBJECT_ID('pubs..titles')
SELECT COUNT(*) FROM pubs..titles -- Load up the buffers
DBCC BUFFER(@dbid,@objid,1,2)
```

(Results abridged)

```
BUFFERS (in MRU to LRU order):

BUFFER:

BUF @0x11B38300
---------------
bpage = 0x1FC28000     bhash = 0x00000000     bpageno = (1:122)
bdbid = 5              breferences = 8        bkeep = 0
bstat = 0x9            bspin = 0              bnext = 0x00000000

PAGE HEADER:

Page @0x1FC28000
----------------
m_pageId = (1:122)       m_headerVersion = 1     m_type = 2
m_typeFlagBits = 0x0     m_level = 0             m_flagBits = 0x0
m_objId = 261575970      m_indexId = 7          m_prevPage = (0:0)
m_nextPage = (0:0)       pminlen = 13           m_slotCnt = 18
m_freeCnt = 7592         m_freeData = 564       m_reservedCnt = 0
m_lsn = (50:302:9)       m_xactReserved = 0     m_xactId = (0:0)
m_ghostRecCnt = 0        m_tornBits = 0

DATA:

Memory Dump @0x1FC28060
-----------------------
1fc28060: 36627573 696e6573 73202020 20020000 6business    ...
1fc28070: 01001a00 42553130 33323662 7573696e ....BU10326busin
1fc28080: 65737320 20202002 00000100 1a004255 ess       .......BU
1fc28090: 31313131 36627573 696e6573 73202020 11116business
1fc280a0: 20020000 01001a00 42553230 37353662 .......BU20756b
1fc280b0: 7573696e 65737320 20202002 00000100 usiness       .....
```

DBCC BYTES(startingaddress,length)

This command lists the contents of the memory area beginning at **startingaddress** for **length** bytes. The address specified must be a valid address within the SQL Server process space.

```
DBCC BYTES(0014767000,50)

00e15398: 00000000 00000000 690b1808 00000000 ...........i....
00e153a8: 00000000 00000000 00000000 00000000 ...............
00e153b8: 00000000 00000008 00000000 00000000 ...............
00e153c8:     0000                             ..
```

DBCC CALLFULLTEXT(funcid[,catid][,objid])

This command is used to perform a variety of full-text-related functions. **Funcid** specifies what function to perform and what parameters are valid. **Catid** is the full-text catalog ID, and **objid** is the object ID of the affected object. Note that CALLFULLTEXT is valid only within a system stored procedure. This procedure must have its system bit set (see the undocumented procedure sp_MS_marksystemobject below for more info), and its name must begin with "sp_fulltext_." Table 20.1 lists the supported functions:

Table 20.1. DBCC CALLFULLTEXT() functions.

Funcid	Function	Parameters
1	Creates a catalog	Catalog ID, path
2	Drops a catalog	Catalog ID
3	Populates a catalog	Catalog ID, 0=full, 1=incremental
4	Stops a catalog population	Catalog ID
5	Adds table for FT indexing	Catalog ID, Object ID
6	Removes table from FT indexing	Catalog ID, Object ID
7	Drops all catalogs	Database ID
8	Performs catalog clean-up	
9	Specifies the level of CPU resources allocated to Microsoft Search	Resource value (1–5; 1=background, 5=dedicated—default: 3)
10	Sets FT connection timeout	Timeout value in seconds (1–32767)

```
USE master
GO
IF OBJECT_ID('sp_fulltext_resource') IS NOT NULL
   DROP PROC sp_fulltext_resource
GO
CREATE PROC sp_fulltext_resource @value int -- value for 'resource_usage'
AS
   DBCC CALLFULLTEXT(9,@value)               -- FTSetResource (@value)
   IF (@@error<>0) RETURN 1
   -- SUCCESS --
RETURN 0  -- sp_fulltext_resource
GO

EXEC sp_MS_marksystemobject 'sp_fulltext_resource'
EXEC sp_fulltext_resource 3
```

DBCC DBCONTROL(dbname,option)

This command sets database options. It performs many of the functions of sp_dboption and is, in fact, called by the procedure. **Dbname** is the name of the database, and **option** is a token specifying the option to set. Table 20.2 lists the valid values for **option:**

Table 20.2. Valid option values for DBCC DBCONTROL().

Option	Description
multi	Specifies multiuser mode
offline	Takes database off line
online	Brings database back on line
readonly	Makes database readonly
readwrite	Makes database readwrite
single	Specifies single-user mode

```
DBCC DBCONTROL('pubs',multi)
```

DBCC DBINFO(dbname)

This command lists system-level information about the specified database, including its creation date, ID, status, next timestamp value, etc.

```
DBCC DBINFO('pubs')

DBINFO STRUCTURE:

DBINFO @0x0690F998
------------------
dbi_dbid = 5             dbi_status = 4194436        dbi_nextid = 1810821513
dbi_dbname = pubs        dbi_maxDbTimestamp = 2000 dbi_version = 515
dbi_createVersion = 515 dbi_nextseqnum = 1900-01-01 00:00:00.000
dbi_crdate = 1998-11-13 03:10:45.610              dbi_filegeneration = 1


dbi_checkptLSN
--------------
m_fSeqNo = 65  m_blockOffset = 340    m_slotId = 1

dbi_dbbackupLSN
---------------
m_fSeqNo = 43  m_blockOffset = 326    m_slotId = 1

dbi_lastdbbackupLSN
-------------------
m_fSeqNo = 43  m_blockOffset = 332    m_slotId = 1

dbi_createIndexLSN
------------------
m_fSeqNo = 0             m_blockOffset = 0 m_slotId = 0
dbi_sortord = 52         dbi_charset = 1    dbi_LcidCfg = 1033
dbi_CompFlagsCfg = 196609 dbi_maxLogSpaceUsed = 3828736
```

DBCC DBRECOVER(dbname)

This command manually recovers a database. Normally, databases are recovered at system startup. If this did not occur—due to an error or the disabling of recovery (see trace flags 3607 and 3608 below)—DBCC DBRECOVER can be used to attempt a manual recovery. **Dbname** is the name of the database to recover.

```
DBCC DBRECOVER('pubs')
```

DBCC DBTABLE(dbid)

This command lists DBT (DB Table) and FCB (File Control Block) information for the specified database.

```
DECLARE @dbid int
SET @dbid=DB_ID('pubs')
DBCC DBTABLE(@dbid)

DBTABLES:

DBTABLE @0x1FA05914
-------------------
dbt_dbid = 5             dbt_dbname = pubs        dbt_spid = 0
dbt_cmptlevel = 70       dbt_crtime = 1999-01-26 15:36:50.723
dbt_dbdes = 0x374b7de0   dbt_next = 0x1f9bd418    dbt_protstamp = 0
dbt_nextid = 1810821513  dbt_dbname = pubs        dbt_stat = 0x400004
dbt_stat2 = 0x100000     dbt_relstat = 0x41000000 dbt_maxDbTimestamp = 2000
dbt_dbTimestamp = 2000   dbt_dbVersion = 515      dbt_repltrans = 0
dbt_replcount = 0        dbt_replrate = 0.000000  dbt_repllatency = 0.000000
dbt_logmgr = 0x1f9d3eb8  dbt_backupmgr = 0x0      distbeginlsn = (0:0:0)
distendlsn = (0:0:0)     replbeginlsn = (0:0:0)   replendlsn = (0:0:0)

FCB @0x1FA4A448
---------------
fcb_hdl = 0x3f0                  fcb_dbid = 5             fcb_fileid = 1
fcb_name = d:\MSSQL7\DATA\pubs.mdf                        fcb_lname = pubs
fcb_nwrt = 0                     fcb_nread = 0            m_status = 51380611
m_size = 272                     m_maxSize = 4294967295 m_minSize = 96
m_allocSize = 272                m_growth = 10            m_perf = 0
m_FormattedSectorSize = 512                              m_ActualSectorSize = 512

FCB @0x1FA4AE48
---------------
fcb_hdl = 0x3f8                      fcb_dbid = 5             fcb_fileid = 2
fcb_name = d:\MSSQL7\DATA\pubs_log.ldf                       fcb_lname = pubs_log
fcb_nwrt = 0                         fcb_nread = 0            m_status = 51429698
m_size = 528                         m_maxSize = 4294967295 m_minSize = 63
m_allocSize = 528                    m_growth = 10            m_perf = 0
m_FormattedSectorSize = 512                                  m_ActualSectorSize = 512
```

DBCC DELETEINSTANCE(object,instance)

This command deletes a Performance Monitor object instance previously set up with DBCC ADDINSTANCE. **Object** is the name of the Performance Monitor object, and **instance** is the name of the instance to delete. Specify a wildcard for **instance** to delete multiple instances.

```
DBCC DELETEINSTANCE("SQL Replication Merge", "%")
```

DBCC DES(dbid,objid)

This command lists system-level descriptive information for the specified object.

```
DECLARE @dbid int, @objid int
SELECT @dbid=DB_ID('pubs'), @objid=OBJECT_ID('authors')
DBCC DES(@dbid, @objid)

DESs:

DES @0x374B74E0
---------------
dhash = 0x374b53e0          dNavCnt = 0              dindex = 0x1f9b23f8
dmaxrow = 183               dopen = 0                dobjstat.objid = 117575457
dobjstat.objsysstat = 0x3903                         ddbid = 5
dstatus = 0x20              ddbptr = 0x1fa05914 ddbdes = 0x374b73e0
dminlen = 24                dtscolid = 0             dtsoff = 0
decwait = 0x0               dobjid = 117575457       dobjtype = 8277
dobjrepl = 0                dschema = 102            dobjcols = 9
```

DBCC DETACHDB(dbname)

This command detaches a database from the server. The database can then be moved to another server and reattached with sp_attach_db. This function is called by the sp_detach_db stored procedure.

```
DBCC DETACHDB('northwind2')
```

DBCC DROPCLEANBUFFERS

This command flushes all data from memory. This is useful if you're running benchmarks and don't want caching to skew test results.

```
DBCC DROPCLEANBUFFERS
```

DBCC DROPEXTENDEDPROC(procname)

This command drops an extended procedure. It's called by sp_dropextendedprocedure.

```
USE master
DBCC DROPEXTENDEDPROC('xp_computemode')
```

DBCC ERRORLOG

This command closes the current error log and starts another one, cycling the file extensions similarly to a server restart. It's called by the sp_cycle_errorlog stored procedure.

```
DBCC ERRORLOG
```

DBCC EXTENTINFO(dbname, tablename, indid)

This command lists extent information for all the extents belonging to an object. **Dbname** is the name of the database, **tablename** is the name of the table, and **indid** is the index ID of the index to list.

```
DBCC EXTENTINFO('pubs','titles',1)
```

file_id	page_id	pg_alloc	ext_size	obj_id	index_id	pfs_bytes	avg_used
1	120	1	1	261575970	1	0x6000000000000000	25
1	132	1	1	261575970	1	0x6000000000000000	25

DBCC FLUSHPROCINDB(dbid)

This command forces a recompile of all the stored procedures in a database. **Dbid** is the database ID of the target database. This is handy when you've changed an option in the database that would materially affect the queries generated for its stored procedures. Sp_dboption, for example, uses DBCC FLUSHPROCINDB to ensure that changes to compile-time options are accommodated by a database's stored procs.

```
DECLARE @dbid int
SET @dbid=DB_ID('pubs')
DBCC FLUSHPROCINDB(@dbid)
```

DBCC FREEPROCCACHE

This command flushes the procedure cache. This is handy when you need to eliminate the effects of procedure caching on benchmark tests or when you want procedure execution plans to take new configuration values into account.

```
DBCC FREEPROCCACHE
```

DBCC IND(dbid, objid[,indid])

This command lists system-level index information for the specified object.

```
DECLARE @dbid int, @objid int
SELECT @dbid=DB_ID('pubs'), @objid=OBJECT_ID('pubs..authors')
DBCC IND(@dbid,@objid, 1)
```

PageFID	PagePID	IAMFID	IAMPID	ObjectID	IndexID	PageType	IndexLevel	NextPageFID
1	101	NULL	NULL	117575457	1	10	0	0
1	100	1	101	117575457	0	1	0	0
1	127	1	101	117575457	1	2	0	0

DBCC LOCKOBJECTSCHEMA (objname)

This command blocks schema changes by other connections until the caller commits the current transaction. It also increments the schema_ver column in sysobjects. This command has no effect if executed outside a transaction.

```
USE pubs
BEGIN TRAN

DBCC LOCKOBJECTSCHEMA('titleauthor')

-- Comment out the COMMIT below and try a DDL modification to titleauthor
-- from another connection. Your new connection will wait until this one
-- commits.

COMMIT TRAN
```

DBCC LOG(dbid)

This command displays log record information from the current database's transaction log. You can use INSERT..EXEC() to trap this output in a table for further processing.

```
CREATE TABLE #logrecs
(CurrentLSN varchar(30),
 Operation varchar(20),
 Context varchar(20),
 TransactionID varchar(20))

INSERT #logrecs
EXEC('DBCC LOG(''ubs''')

SELECT * FROM #logrecs
GO
DROP TABLE #logrecs
```

(Results abridged)

CurrentLSN	Operation	Context	TransactionID
00000035:00000144:0001	LOP_BEGIN_CKPT	LCX_NULL	0000:00000000
00000035:00000145:0001	LOP_END_CKPT	LCX_NULL	0000:00000000
00000035:00000146:0001	LOP_MODIFY_ROW	LCX_SCHEMA_VERSION	0000:00000000
00000035:00000146:0002	LOP_BEGIN_XACT	LCX_NULL	0000:000020e0
00000035:00000146:0003	LOP_MARK_DDL	LCX_NULL	0000:000020e0
00000035:00000146:0004	LOP_COMMIT_XACT	LCX_NULL	0000:000020e0
00000035:00000147:0001	LOP_MODIFY_ROW	LCX_SCHEMA_VERSION	0000:00000000
00000035:00000147:0002	LOP_BEGIN_XACT	LCX_NULL	0000:000020e1
00000035:00000147:0003	LOP_MARK_DDL	LCX_NULL	0000:000020e1

DBCC PAGE (dbid|dbname, filenum, pagenum [,printopt])

This command dumps the contents of a specific database page. **Dbid|dbname** is the ID or name of the database, **filenum** is the database file number containing the page, **pagenum** is the number of the page, and **printopt** specifies what to print.

Table 20.3 lists the valid values for **printopt**:

Table 20.3. Valid printopt values.

Value	Meaning
0	(Default)—print the page and buffer headers
1	Print the page and buffer headers, each row of the table, and the row offset table
2	Print the page and buffer headers, the page itself, and the row offset table

Note that this command requires DBCC TRACEON(3604) in order to direct its output to your client connection.

```
DBCC TRACEON(3604)
GO
DBCC PAGE('pubs',1,70,2,0)
GO
DBCC TRACEOFF(3604)
GO
```

(Results abridged)

```
PAGE:

BUFFER:

BUF @0x11BB1E80
---------------
bpage = 0x1F6E4000    bhash = 0x00000000    bpageno = (1:70)
bdbid = 5             breferences = 1       bkeep = 1
bstat = 0x9           bspin = 0             bnext = 0x00000000

PAGE HEADER:

Page @0x1F6E4000
----------------
m_pageId = (1:70)     m_headerVersion = 1 m_type = 10
m_typeFlagBits = 0x0 m_level = 0           m_flagBits = 0x2
m_objId = 19          m_indexId = 1        m_prevPage = (0:0)
m_nextPage = (0:0)    pminlen = 90         m_slotCnt = 2
m_freeCnt = 4         m_freeData = 8184    m_reservedCnt = 0
m_lsn = (1:324:11)    m_xactReserved = 0   m_xactId = (0:0)
m_ghostRecCnt = 0     m_tornBits = 0
GAM (1:2) ALLOCATED, SGAM (1:3) NOT ALLOCATED, PFS (1:1) 0x70 IAM_PG MIXED_EXT
ALLOCATED 0_PCT_FULL
```

```
DATA:
Memory Dump @0x1F6E4060
-----------------------
1f6e4060: 00005e00 00000000 00000000 00000000  ..^.............
1f6e4070: 00000000 00000000 00000000 00000000  ................
```

DBCC PRTIPAGE(dbid, objid, indexid[, printopt {0 | 1 | 2}])

This command lists page information for the specified index.

```
DECLARE @dbid int, @pagebin varchar(12), @pageid int, @fileid int, @objid int
SELECT TOP 1 @dbid=DB_ID('pubs'), @objid=id, @pagebin=first
FROM pubs..sysindexes WHERE id=OBJECT_ID('pubs..authors')

EXEC sp_decodepagebin @pagebin, @fileid OUT, @pageid OUT

DBCC PRTIPAGE(@dbid, @objid, 2, @pageid)
```

(Results abridged)

FileId	PageId	Row	Level	au_lname	au_fname
1	228	0	0	Bennet	Abraham
1	228	1	0	Blotchet-Halls	Reginald
1	228	2	0	Carson	Cheryl
1	228	3	0	DeFrance	Michel
1	228	4	0	del Castillo	Innes
1	228	5	0	Dull	Ann
1	228	6	0	Green	Marjorie
1	228	7	0	Greene	Morningstar
1	228	8	0	Gringlesby	Burt
1	228	9	0	Hunter	Sheryl

DBCC RESOURCE

This command lists resource utilization information for the server.

```
DBCC TRACEON(3604)
DBCC resource
DBCC TRACEOFF(3604)
```

```
RESOURCE:

RESOURCE @0x007D8228
--------------------
rdbtab = 531005480        rdes = 927695072         *rdeshash = 927671776
rdescount = 128           *prpssarray = 528654468   rprocihash = 0x3747053c
rprocnhash = 0x3749053c   rprocmemused = 78         rflag1 = 144
rflag2 = 0                rprocnum = 32             rdump = 0
rMSversion = 117441211    rbufsteals = 0            rpsytab = 927665708
rlangcache = 528558048    rlangfree = 0             rbinaryversion = 515
rservername = KHEN_450    servicename = MSSQLServer rnls = 14848
```

```
ropen_objmsgs = 0        pPerfStats = 8658600        pBufGStats = 8659488
pResLock = 927379360     LoginMode = 0               rsaspid = 0
DefaultLogin = guest     AuditLevel = 0              ckpt_status = 0
DefaultDomain = KHEN_450 SetHostName = 0             MapChars[0] '_' =
MapChars[1] '$' =        MapChars[2] '#' =           MaxConnections = 32767
MaxCPUs = 2              fDBCSNonCase = TRUE         bpool = 8224800
pbuffreewait = 0         pHandlers = 0               article_cache = 528647120
pResLockFree = 927662120 MaxSubProcesses = 32767     CurSubProcesses = 0
pesExprSrv = 0x1f81c3e8  replmem = 0x1f826028

PERFMON @0x007D8260
--------------------
pcputicks = 0            pioticks = 0                pidlticks = 0
pbs_rpck = 683           pbs_spck = 0                pbs_rbyt = 90854
pbs_sbyt = 0            pbs_conn = 36                pbs_errors = 0
pblk_rd = 932           pblk_wr = 1568               pblk_errors = 0
pblk_outstanding_rd = 0 pblk_outstanding_wr = 0 psiteconns = 0
LRU_cnt = 0             BUFLNK_cnt = 0               DATASERV_cnt = 0

DS_CONFIG @0x007D9060
--------------------
cconfsz = 8             cmajor = 6                   cminor = 0
crevision = 14         cbootsource = 2               crestimeout = 10
crecinterval = 0       ccatalogupdates = 1           cmbSrvMemMin = 0
cmbSrvMemMax = 2147483647 cusrconnections = 0       cnetworkpcksize = 4096
ckbIndexMem = 0        cfillfactor = 0               cavetimeslice = 100
cextendedmemory_MB = 0 ctapreten = 0                 cwritestatus = 0
cspinctr = 0           cfgpriorityboost = 0x0 cfgexposeadvparm = 0x1
cfglogintime = 5       cfgpss = 0                    cfgpad = 4096
cfgxdes = 16           cfgaffinitymask = 0           cfgbuf = 4362
cfgdes = 0             cfglocks = 0                  cfgquerytime = 0
cstacksz = 0           cfgcursorthrsh = -1           cnblkmax = 32
cfgrmttimeout = 10     cfg_dtc_rpcs = 0              cclkrate = 31250
cfg_max_text_repl_size = 65536                       cfgupddate = 36386
cfgupdtime = 15525951  fRemoteAccess = 1             cfgbufminfree = 331
cnestedtriggers = 0x1  cfgworkingset = 0x0           ccaseless = 0
cdeflang = 0           cnlanginfo = 3                cold_sortord = 0x34
cold_charset = 0x1     csortord = 0x34               ccharset = 0x1
lcidCfg = 0x409        lcidCfgOld = 0x409            dwCompFlagsCfg = 0x30001
dwCompFlagsCfgOld = 0x30001                          cfgCutoffYear = 2049
cfgLangNeutralFT = 0   csysdbstart = 0               cfglogsleep = 0
maxworkthreads = 255   minworkthreads = 32           minnetworkthreads = 32
threadtimeout = 15     connectsperthread = 0         cusroptions = 0
exchcostthreshold = 5  maxdop = 0                     cchecksum = 770
rWrkExtCache = Used     Cache Entry = Iam (1:86), Extent (1:112)
 Cache Entry = Iam (1:104), Extent (1:96)
 Cache Entry = Iam (0:0), Extent (0:0)
```

DBCC SETINSTANCE(object,counter,instance,val)

This command sets the value of a Performance Monitor instance counter. You can use this when benchmarking query and stored procedure performance to set a user-definable counter inside Performance Monitor. In fact, this is how the sp_user_counter*nn* procedures work—they call DBCC SETINSTANCE. **Object** is the name of the Performance Monitor object, **instance** is the name of the object's instance to adjust, **counter** is the name of the performance counter to change, and **val** is the new value of the counter.

```
DBCC SETINSTANCE('SQLServer:User Settable', 'Query', 'User counter 1', 3)
```

DBCC TAB(dbid,objid[,printopt {0 | 1 | 2}}])

This command lists system-level information for the specified table.

```
DECLARE @dbid int, @objid int
SELECT @dbid=DB_ID('pubs'), @objid=OBJECT_ID('pubs..authors')
DBCC TAB(@dbid, @objid, 2)
```

PageFID	PagePID	IAMFID	IAMPID	ObjectID	IndexID	PageType	IndexLevel	NextPageFID	NextPagePID
1	101	NULL	NULL	117575457	1	10	0	0	0
1	100	1	101	117575457	0	1	0	0	0
1	127	1	101	117575457	1	2	0	0	0
1	229	NULL	NULL	117575457	2	10	0	0	0
1	228	1	229	117575457	2	2	0	0	0

DBCC UPGRADEDB(dbname)

This command upgrades the system objects in the specified database to the current version of the database engine.

```
DBCC UPGRADEDB('oldpubs')
```

Undocumented Functions and Variables

As I said earlier, undocumented Transact-SQL elements, including functions, are usually not documented for a reason. They can be dangerous or even catastrophic if improperly used. They may also change between releases. So, use good judgment when you decide whether to use these functions in your own code.

ENCRYPT(string)

This command encrypts a string. It's used internally by the server to encrypt Transact-SQL code stored in syscomments (when WITH ENCRYPTION is specified).

```
SELECT ENCRYPT('VALET')
-------------------------------------------------------
0x594F55415245415348414D454C4553535359434F5048414E54
```

GET_SID(username)

This command returns the current NT system ID for a specified user or group name as a **varbinary(85).** Prefix username with \U to search for an NT user ID; prefix it with \G to search for an NT group ID. Note that this function works only within system-stored procedures that have their system bit set—see the undocumented procedure sp_MS_marksystemobject below for more information.

```
USE master
GO
IF (OBJECT_ID('sp_get_sid') IS NOT NULL)
   DROP PROC sp_get_sid
GO
CREATE PROCEDURE sp_get_sid
   @loginame sysname
AS
DECLARE @sid varbinary(85)

IF (charindex('\', @loginame) = 0)
   SELECT SUSER_SID(@loginame) AS 'SQL User ID'
ELSE BEGIN
   SELECT @sid=get_sid('\U'+@loginame, NULL)
   IF @sid IS NULL
      SELECT @sid=get_sid('\G'+@loginame, NULL) -- Maybe it's a group
   IF @sid IS NULL BEGIN
      RAISERROR('Couldn't find an ID for the specified loginame',16,10)
         RETURN -1
      END ELSE SELECT @sid AS 'NT User ID'
      RETURN 0
END
GO
EXEC sp_MS_marksystemobject 'sp_get_sid'
EXEC sp_get_sid 'LEX_TALIONIS\KHEN'


NT User ID
--------------------------------------------------------------------------------
0x010500000000000515000000A423635BE3136688847202CE8030000
```

OBJECT_ID(..,'local')

While the OBJECT_ID() function itself is, of course, documented, its optional second parameter isn't. Since you can pass a fully qualified object name as the first argument, OBJECT_ID() can return ID numbers for objects that reside in databases other than the current one. There may be times when you want to prevent this. For example, if you're performing a task on an object that requires access to catalog information in the current database, you may need to ensure not only that the object name translates to a valid object ID but also that it's a local object. Pass 'local' as OBJECT_ID()'s second parameter in order to ensure that it sees objects in the current database only, like so:

```
USE pubs
SELECT OBJECT_ID('Northwind..Orders'), OBJECT_ID('Northwind..Orders','local')


---------  --------------------------------------------------------------------
357576312 NULL
```

PWDCOMPARE(str,pwd,oldenc)

This command compares a string with an encrypted password. **Str** is the string to compare, **pwd** is the encrypted password to use, and **oldenc** is a 1 or 0 indicating whether old-style encryption was used to encrypt **pwd.** You can retrieve an encrypted password directly from the sysxlogins password column, or you can use the undocumented PWDENCRYPT() function to create one from a string (see below).

```
SELECT PWDCOMPARE('enmity', password, (CASE WHEN xstatus&2048=2048 THEN 1 ELSE 0 END))
FROM sysxlogins
WHERE name='k_reapr'

-----------
1
```

PWDENCRYPT(str)

This command encrypts a string using SQL Server's password encryption algorithm. Stored procedures that manage SQL Server passwords use this function to encrypt user passwords. You can use the undocumented PWDCOMPARE() function to compare an unencrypted string with the return value of PWDENCRYPT().

```
SELECT PWDENCRYPT('vengeance') AS EncryptedString,PWDCOMPARE('vengeance',
PWDENCRYPT('vengeance'), 0) AS EncryptedCompare
EncryptedString EncryptedCompare

EncryptedString  EncryptedCompare
---------------- ----------------
    _____         1
```

TSEQUAL(ts1,ts2)

This command compares two timestamp values—returning 1 if they're identical and raising an error if they're not. The TSEQUAL() function has been around for years—it dates back to the days when Microsoft SQL Server was merely an OS/2 port of Sybase SQL Server. It's not used as often any more, mainly because it's no longer necessary. You can compare two timestamp columns directly and decide for yourself whether to raise an error. There's also no performance advantage to using TSEQUAL rather than a simple equality comparison. Still, it's not documented in the Books Online, so I'm compelled to include it here.

```
USE tempdb
CREATE TABLE #testts
(k1 int identity,
timestamp timestamp)

DECLARE @ts1 timestamp, @ts2 timestamp

SELECT @ts1=@@DBTS, @ts2=@ts1

SELECT CASE WHEN TSEQUAL(@ts1, @ts2) THEN 'Equal' ELSE 'Not Equal' END

INSERT #testts DEFAULT VALUES

SET @ts2=@@DBTS
```

```
SELECT CASE WHEN TSEQUAL(@ts1, @ts2) THEN 'Equal' ELSE 'Not Equal' END
GO
DROP TABLE #testts
```

```
---------
Equal
```

```
Server: Msg 532, Level 16, State 2, Line 16
The timestamp (changed to 0x0000000000000093) shows that the row has been updated by
another user.
```

@@MICROSOFTVERSION

This automatic variable returns an internal tracking number used by Microsoft.

```
SELECT @@MICROSOFTVERSION
```
```
-----------
117441211
```

Undocumented Trace Flags

Trace flags are special server settings that you can configure primarily by calling DBCC
TRACEON() or via the −T server command-line option. Some options make sense only on a
server-wide basis, so they're best specified on the server command line. Most, however, are
specified via DBCC TRACEON(*flagnum*), where *flagnum* is the flag you want to set. To set
more than one flag at a time, separate them with commas.

Use DBCC TRACESTATUS(*flagnum*) to list whether a flag is enabled. Pass a −1 to return a list of all flags currently set. Here's a simple DBCC TRACEON() / TRACESTATUS()
example:

```
EXEC master..xp_logevent 99999,'CHECKPOINT before setting flag
3502',informational
CHECKPOINT
DBCC TRACEON(3604,3502)
DBCC TRACESTATUS(-1)
EXEC master..xp_logevent 99999,'CHECKPOINT after setting flag
3502',informational
CHECKPOINT
DBCC TRACEOFF(3604,3502)
DBCC TRACESTATUS(-1)
```

Here's what the error log looks like as a result of these commands (trace flag 3502 enables
extra CHECKPOINT log information):

```
1999-07-27 19:57:20.06 spid11 Error: 99999, Severity: 10, State: 1
1999-07-27 19:57:20.06 spid11 CHECKPOINT before setting flag 3502.
1999-07-27 19:57:20.06 spid11 DBCC TRACEON 3604, server process ID (SPID) 11.
1999-07-27 19:57:20.06 spid11 DBCC TRACEON 3502, server process ID (SPID) 11.
1999-07-27 19:57:20.07 spid11 Error: 99999, Severity: 10, State: 1
1999-07-27 19:57:20.07 spid11 CHECKPOINT after setting flag 3502.
1999-07-27 19:57:20.07 spid11 Ckpt dbid 4 started (100000)
1999-07-27 19:57:20.07 spid11 Ckpt dbid 4 phase 1 ended (100000)
```

Table 20.4. A few of SQL Server's undocumented trace flags.

Flag	Purpose
1200	Displays verbose locking info
1206	Complements flag 1204 by displaying the other locks held by deadlock parties
2509	Used in conjunction with DBCC CHECKTABLE to see the total count of ghost records in a table
3502	Logs extra information to the system error log each time a checkpoint occurs
3607	Skips automatic recovery of all databases
3608	Skips automatic recovery of all databases except master
3609	Skips the creation of tempdb at system startup
8687	Disables query parallelism

```
1999-07-27 19:57:20.07 spid11 Ckpt dbid 4 complete
1999-07-27 19:57:20.07 spid11 DBCC TRACEOFF 3604, server process ID (SPID) 11.
1999-07-27 19:57:20.07 spid11 DBCC TRACEOFF 3502, server process ID (SPID) 11.
```

Table 20.4 lists some of the many undocumented SQL Server trace flags. (See the Books Online for a list of documented flags.) This list is not comprehensive—there are many undocumented flags not included here.

Undocumented Procedures

There are scads of undocumented procedures. By my count, there are nearly a hundred of them, not counting replication routines. I've listed most of them in Table 20.5. I haven't included all of them here for a number of reasons. First, there are simply too many to cover with any sort of adequacy. That's why I've intentionally omitted the undocumented routines related to replication. Also, some undocumented routines are so dangerous and add so little value to the Transact-SQL command set that they are best left undocumented. As they say, some things are better left unsaid. Last, some of the undocumented routines behave so erratically or are so reliant on code external to the server (e.g., in Enterprise Manager or SQL-DMO) that they are either unusable or of dubious value to the Transact-SQL developer. The idea here is to provide thorough coverage without being excessive

Table 20.5. Undocumented system and extended stored procedures.

Procedure	Purpose	Example
sp_checknames [@mode]	Checks key system tables for non-ASCII names.	sp_checknames @mode='silent'
sp_delete_backuphistory @oldest_date	Clears system backup history prior to a given date.	msdb..sp_delete_backuphistory @oldest_date datetime
sp_enumerrorlogs	Enumerates the current server error log files.	master..sp_enumerrorlogs

(continues)

Table 20.5. *Continued.*

Procedure	Purpose	Example
sp_enumoledbdatasources	Enumerates the OLEDB data providers visible to the server.	sp_enumoledbdatasources
sp_fixindex @dbname, @tabname, @indid	Allows indexes on system tables to be dropped/recreated.	USE northwind EXEC sp_dboption 'northwind','single',true EXEC sp_fixindex 'northwind', 'sysobjects', 2 EXEC sp_dboption 'northwind','single',false
sp_gettypestring @tabid, @colid, @typestring output	Renders a textual description of a column's data type.	declare @tabid int, @typestr varchar(30) SET @tabid=OBJECT_ID('authors') EXEC sp_gettypestring @tabid, 1, @typestr OUT
sp_MS_marksystemobject @objname	Sets an object's system bit (0xC0000000). Several functions and DBCC command verbs do not work properly unless executed from a system object. Setting this bit will cause the IsMSShipped object property to return 1.	sp_Ms_marksystemobject 'sp_dir'
Sp_MSaddguidcol @source_owner, @source_table	Adds a ROWGUIDCOL column to a table. Also marks the table for replication (use EXEC sp_MSunmarkreplinfo to reverse this).	sp_MSaddguidcolumn dbo,testguid
sp_MSaddguidindex @source_owner, @source_table	Creates an index on a table's ROWGUIDCOL column.	sp_MSaddguidindex dbo,testuid
sp_MSaddlogin_implicit_ntlogin @loginame	Adds a SQL Server login that corresponds to an existing NT login.	sp_MSaddlogin_implicit_ntlogin 'GoofyTingler'
sp_MSadduser_implicit_ntlogin @ntname	Adds a database user that corresponds to an existing NT login.	sp_MSadduser_implicit_ntlogin 'GoofyTingler'
sp_MScheck_uid_owns_anything @uid	Returns 1 when a user owns any objects in the current database.	DECLARE @res int, @uid int SELECT @uid=SUSER_ID() EXEC @res=sp_MScheck_uid_owns_anything @uid
sp_MSdbuseraccess @mode='perm'l'db', @qual'db name mask	Returns a list of databases a user can access and a bitmap representing the access in each.	sp_MSdbuseraccess @mode='db'
sp_MSdbuserpriv @mode ='perm'l'serv'l'ver'l'role'	Returns a bitmap representing user privileges.	sp_MSdbuserpriv @mode='role'

(continue

Table 20.5. *Continued.*

Procedure	Purpose	Example
sp_MSdependencies @objname, @objtype, @flags int, @objlist	Shows object dependencies.	sp_MSdependencies @objname = 'titleauthor'
sp_MSdrop_object [@object_id] [,@object_name] [,@object_owner]	Generically drops a table, view, trigger, or procedure.	sp_MSdrop_object @object_name='authors2'
sp_MSexists_file @full_path, @filename	Checks for the existence of an operating system file.	DECLARE @res int EXEC @res=sp_MSexists_file 'd:\readme.txt'
sp_MSforeachdb @command1 @replacechar = '?' [,@command2] [,@command3] [,@precommand] [,@postcommand]	Executes up to three commands for every database on the system. @replacechar will be replaced with the name of each database. @precommand and @postcommand can be used to direct commands to a single result set.	EXEC sp_MSforeachdb 'DBCC CHECKDB(?)' EXEC sp_MSforeachdb @command1='PRINT "Listing ?"', @command2='USE ?; EXEC sp_dir'
sp_msforeachtable @command1 @replacechar = '?' [,@command2] [,@command3] [,@whereand] [,@precommand] [,@postcommand]	Executes up to three commands for every table in a database (optionally matching the @whereand clause). @replacechar will be replaced with the name of each table. @precommand and @postcommand can be used to direct commands to a single result set.	EXEC sp_MSforeachtable @command1='EXEC sp_help [?]' EXEC sp_MSforeachtable @command1='PRINT "Listing ?=', @command2='SELECT * FROM ?',@whereand=' AND name like "title%"'
sp_MSget_oledbinfo @server [,@infotype] [,@login] [,@password]	Returns OLEDB provider information for a linked server.	sp_MSget_oledbinfo @server='pythia', @login='sa'
sp_MSget_qualified_name @object_id, @qualified_name OUT	Translates an object ID into a fully qualified object name.	DECLARE @oid int, @obname sysname SET @oid=OBJECT_ID('titles') EXEC sp_MSget_qualified_name @oid, @obname OUT
sp_MSget_type @tabid, @colid, @colname OUT, @type OUT	Returns the name and type of a table column.	DECLARE @tabid int, @colname sysname, @type nvarchar(4000) SET @tabid=OBJECT_ID('authors') EXEC sp_MSget_type @tabid, 1, @colname OUT, @type OUT

(continues)

Table 20.5. *Continued.*

Procedure	Purpose	Example
sp_MSguidtostr @guid, @mystr OUT	Returns a uniqueidentifier as a string.	DECLARE @guid uniqueidentifier, @guidstr sysname SET @guid=NEWID() EXEC sp_MSguidtostr @guid, @guidstr OUT
sp_MShelpindex @tablename [,@indexname] [,@flags]	Lists index catalog info.	sp_MShelpindex 'titles'
sp_MShelptype [@typename] [,@flags='sdt'l'uddt' |NULL]	List data type catalog info.	EXEC sp_MShelptype 'id' EXEC sp_MShelptype 'int','sdt' EXEC sp_MShelptype
sp_MSindexspace @tablename [,@index_name]	Lists index size info.	EXEC sp_MSindexspace 'titles'
sp_MSis_pk_col @source_table, @colname, @indid	Checks a column to see whether it's a primary key.	DECLARE @res int EXEC @res=sp_MSis_pk_col 'titles','title_id',1
sp_MSkilldb @dbname	Uses DBCC DBREPAIR to drop a database (even if the database isn't damaged).	sp_MSkilldb 'northwind2'
sp_MSloginmappings @loginname	Lists login, database, user, and alias mappings.	sp_MSloginmappings
sp_MStable_has_unique_ index @tabid	Checks a table for a unique index.	DECLARE @objid int, @res int SET @objid=OBJECT_ID('titles') EXEC @res=sp_MStable_has_unique_index @objid
sp_MStablekeys [tablename] [,@colname] [,@type] [,@keyname] [,@flags]	Lists a table's keys.	sp_MStablekeys 'titles'
sp_Mstablerefs @tablename,@type= N'actualtables', @direction = N'primary', @reftable	Lists the objects a table refer- ences or that reference it.	sp_MStablerefs 'titleauthor'
sp_MStablespace [@name]	Lists table space information.	sp_MStablespace 'titleauthor'

(continues)

Table 20.5. *Continued.*

Procedure	Purpose	Example
sp_MSunc_to_drive @unc_path, @local_server, @local_path OUT	Converts a UNC path to a drive.	DECLARE @path sysname EXEC sp_MSunc_to_drive '\\PYTHIA\C$\', 'PYTHIA',@path OUT
sp_MSuniquecolname table_name, @base_colname, @unique_colname OUT	Generates a unique column name for a specified table using a base name.	DECLARE @uniquename sysname EXEC sp_MSuniquecolname 'titles','title_id',@uniquename OUT
sp_Msuniquename @seed, @start	Returns a result set containing a unique object name for the current database using a specified seed name and start value.	sp_MSuniquename 'titles',3
sp_Msuniqueobjectname @name_in, @name_out OUT	Generates a unique object name for the current database.	DECLARE @outname sysname SET @outname='' -- Can't be NULL EXEC sp_MSuniqueobjectname 'titles',@outname OUT
sp_Msuniquetempname @name_in, @name_out OUT	Generates a unique temporary object (tempdb) name using a base name.	CREATE TABLE tempdb..test (c1 int) DECLARE @outname sysname EXEC sp_MSuniquetempname 'test',@outname OUT
sp_readerrorlog [@lognum]	Lists the system error log corresponding to lognum. Omit lognum to list the current error log.	sp_readerrorlog
sp_remove_tempdb_file @filename	Removes a file on which tempdb is based.	master..sp_remove_tempdb_file 'tempdev02'
sp_set_local_time [@server_name] [,@adjustment_in_ minutes] (for Win9x)	Synchronize the computer's local time with another server (if supplied).	msdb..sp_set_local_time
Sp_tempdbspace	Returns space usage info for tempdb.	sp_tempdbspace
xp_dirtree 'rootpath'	Completely lists all the sub-directories (and their sub-directories) of a given path, including the node level of each directory.	master..xp_dirtree 'c:\'
xp_dsninfo @systemdsn	Lists ODBC DSN information for the specified system datasource.	master..xp_dsninfo 'pubsdsn'

(continues)

Table 20.5. *Continued.*

Procedure	Purpose	Example
xp_enum_oledb_providers	Enumerates the OLEDB providers available on the server machine.	master..xp_enum_oledb_providers
xp_enumdsn	Enumerates the system ODBC datasources available on the server machine.	master..xp_enumdsn
xp_enumerrorlogs	Enumerates (lists) the current server error log files.	master..xp_enumerrorlogs
xp_fileexist 'filename'	Returns a result set indicating whether a file exists.	master..xp_fileexist 'd:\mssql7\install\readme.txt'
xp_fixeddrives	Returns a result set listing the fixed drives on the server machine.	master..xp_fixeddrives
xp_get_MAPI_default_profile	Returns the default MAPI mail profile.	master..xp_get_MAPI_default_profile
xp_get_MAPI_profiles	Returns a result set listing the system's MAPI profiles.	master..xp_get_MAPI_profiles
xp_getfiledetails 'filename'	Returns a result set listing file details for the specified file.	master..xp_getfiledetails 'd:\mssql7\install\readme.txt'
xp_getnetname	Returns the network name of the server computer.	master..xp_getnetname
xp_oledbinfo @providername, @datasource, @location, @providerstring, @catalog, @login, @password, @infotype	Returns a result set listing detailed OLEDB information about a specific linked server.	master..xp_oledbinfo 'SQLOLEDB', 'PYTHIA', NULL, NULL, NULL, 'sa', 'drkildare', NULL
xp_readerrorlog [lognum]	Returns a result set (c1 char(255) c2 int) containing the error log specified by lognum (omit to get the current error log).	master..xp_readerrorlog
xp_regaddmultistr xp_regdeletekey xp_regdeletevalue xp_regenumvalues xp_regread xp_regremovemultistring xp_regwrite	Allows addition, modification, and deletion of registry keys and key values.	EXEC master..xp_regenumvalues 'HKEY_LOCAL_MACHINE', 'SOFTWARE\Microsoft\MSSQLServer\MSSQLServer' DECLARE @df nvarchar(64) EXECUTE master.dbo.xp_regread N'HKEY_CURRENT_USER', N'Control Panel\International', N'sShortDate', @df OUT, N'no_output'

(continues)

Table 20.5. *Continued.*

Procedure	Purpose	Example
xp_subdirs	Returns a result set containing a directory's immediate subdirectories.	master..xp_subdirs 'D:\MSSQL7'
xp_test_MAPI_profile 'profile'	Tests the specified MAPI profile that ensure that it's valid and can be connected to.	master..xp_test_MAPI_profile 'SQL'
xp_varbintohexstr	Converts a varbinary variable to a hexadecimal string.	CREATE PROC sp_hex @i int, @hx varchar(30) OUT AS DECLARE @vb varbinary(30) SET @vb=CAST(@i as varbinary) EXEC master..xp_varbintohexstr @vb, @hx OUT GO DECLARE @hex varchar(30) EXEC sp_hex 343, @hex OUT

Summary

This chapter explored a number of SQL Server trace flags, DBCC commands, functions, variables, and stored procedures that are not documented in the Books Online. If you decide to use them in your own work, you should do so with care and with the expectation that they may change in a future release of the product. And don't expect any support from Microsoft—that's the whole idea of not documenting something—you don't have to support it, and you can change it at will. Using the undocumented features of any product—SQL Server included—is generally inadvisable. You shouldn't do it unless absolutely necessary.

21

Potpourri

Intolerance is the root of all evil—or at least many kinds of it. That could have been my son or your son that was beaten to death and tied to a barbed-wire fence because of his sexual preference. Or it could have been your brother or my brother that was dragged behind a pickup truck until his head came off. Or it could have been you or me. If you want to rid the world of evil, start with intolerance.
—H. W. Kenton

This chapter is the catchall of this book. Here, you'll find an assortment of odds and ends that didn't seem to fit elsewhere. Banishment to this chapter doesn't necessarily make a topic a second-class citizen. You may find some of the techniques presented here quite useful. Being a misfit doesn't necessarily make one a miscreant.

Obscure Functions

Each new release of SQL Server has introduced new functions to the Transact-SQL language. There are now over fifty of them. With so many functions, it's no surprise that the casual developer might miss a few. Though the goal of this book is not to supplant SQL Server's Books Online, a few of these bear mentioning because they can save you real work if you know about them.

Status Functions

Status functions tell us something about the work environment. SQL Server has a number of these. You're probably familiar with some of them; some of them you may not be. Here are a few that stand out from the rest in terms of rarity and usefulness:

GETANSINULL() allows you to determine default nullability for a database. Default nullability is controlled by the **ANSI null default** option of each database (set via sp_dboption), as

well as the SET ANSI_NULL_DFLT_ON/SET ANSI_NULL_DFLT_OFF session-level commands. GETANSINULL() can optionally receive a single parameter—the database you'd like
to check.

Here's some code that uses GETANSINULL():

```
DECLARE @ansinull int

-- Save it off so that we can restore it later
SET @ansinull=GETANSINULL('tempdb')

IF (@ansinull=0)
   SET ANSI_NULL_DFLT_ON ON

CREATE TABLE #nulltest (c1 int)
INSERT #nulltest (c1) VALUES (NULL)
SELECT * FROM #nulltest

IF (@ansinull=0) -- Reverse the setting above
   SET ANSI_NULL_DFLT_ON OFF
```

This code uses GETANSINULL() to determine the status of **ANSI null default** before
changing the setting. It then creates a temporary table consisting of a single column whose
NULLability is unspecified and inserts a NULL value into it. Afterwards, it restores the setting
to its original value.

HOST_NAME(), GETDATE(), and **USER_NAME()** are also handy environmental status
functions. Frequently, you'll see them used to establish column defaults, though they can also
be featured in SELECT lists, as this code illustrates:

```
SELECT HOST_NAME()
--------------------------------------------------------------------------------
PUCK_FEET
```

Here, HOST_NAME() is used to return the current workstation name.

Another common use of these functions is as column default values. Here's an example:

```
CREATE TABLE #REPORT_LOG
(ReportLogId int identity PRIMARY KEY,
 ReportDate datetime DEFAULT GETDATE(),
 ReportUser varchar(30) DEFAULT USER_NAME(),
 ReportMachine varchar(30) DEFAULT HOST_NAME(),
 ReportName varchar(30) DEFAULT 'UNKNOWN')

INSERT #REPORT_LOG DEFAULT VALUES
SELECT * FROM #REPORT_LOG
```

(Results abridged)

ReportLogId	ReportDate	ReportUser	ReportMachine
1	1999-06-17 02:10:03.617	dbo	PUCK_FEET

Note the use of INSERT...DEFAULT VALUES to add a row to the table using nothing but
default values. Nullable columns without default values are inserted with NULL as their value;
nonnullable columns without defaults cause an error to be generated.

Note that you could have used the ANSI SQL-92 CURRENT_TIMESTAMP and CURRENT_USER niladic functions in place of GETDATE() and USER_NAME(), respectively. USER and SESSION_USER are synonyms for CURRENT_USER. Interestingly, ANSI-92 niladic functions such as these may also be featured in SELECT lists, like so:

```
SELECT CURRENT_TIMESTAMP, CURRENT_USER
```

```
-------------------------- ----------------------------------------------------
1999-06-17 02:32:13.600    dbo
```

The **SUSER_NAME()** and **SUSER_SNAME()** functions come in handy if you prefer to default a column to the current user's login name rather than his or her database user name (SYSTEM_USER is the ANSI SQL equivalent). If your app always logs in as 'sa' and doesn't use database user names, storing the current database user name in a table isn't likely to be terribly useful. It will always be "dbo." Storing the user's login name will permit you to track user activity without forcing you to set up separate database logins for each user.

SUSER_NAME() is included in the latest release of SQL Server for backward compatibility only—you should use SUSER_SNAME(), instead. SUSER_NAME() no longer maps directly to the SQL Server security model, so there's a notable performance penalty for using it.

Property Functions

Property functions return information about objects in the database. Usually, this info is in the form of "meta-data"—data about data. There was a time when getting at even basic meta-data on SQL Server required spelunking through system tables. Fortunately, enough functions have been added that that's no longer the case. What follows are some of the more interesting ones.

COLUMNPROPERTY() returns useful info about table columns and stored procedure parameters. It takes three parameters—the object ID of the table or stored procedure (you can use OBJECT_ID() to get this), the name of the column or parameter, and a string expression indicating the exact info you're after. You can refer to the Books Online for more information, but some of the more interesting uses of COLUMNPROPERTY() are illustrated below:

```
CREATE TABLE #testfunc
(k1 int identity PRIMARY KEY, c1 decimal(10,2), c3 AS k1*c1)

USE tempdb
SELECT COLUMNPROPERTY(OBJECT_ID('#testfunc'),'k1','IsIdentity'),
COLUMNPROPERTY(OBJECT_ID('#testfunc'),'c1','Scale'),
COLUMNPROPERTY(OBJECT_ID('#testfunc'),'c3','IsComputed'),
COLUMNPROPERTY(OBJECT_ID('#testfunc'),'k1','AllowsNull')
```

```
---------- ---------- ---------- ----------
1          2          1          0
```

Note the **USE tempdb** immediately preceding the calls to COLUMNPROPERTY(). It's necessary because the object in question resides in tempdb and COLUMNPROPERTY() can't deal with cross-database references.

DATABASEPROPERTY() is similar to COLUMNPROPERTY() in that it returns property-level info about an object—in this case, a database. It takes two parameters—the name of the database and the property you're after. Here are some examples that use DATABASEPROPERTY():

```
SELECT
   DATABASEPROPERTY('pubs','IsBulkCopy'),
   DATABASEPROPERTY('pubs','Version'),
   DATABASEPROPERTY('pubs','IsAnsiNullsEnabled'),
   DATABASEPROPERTY('pubs','IsSuspect'),
   DATABASEPROPERTY('pubs','IsTruncLog')
```

```
---------- ---------- ---------- ---------- ----------
1          515        0          0          1
```

In the old days, you had to query master..sysdatabases and translate cryptic bit masks in order to get this information. Now, Transact-SQL makes the job much easier, completely insulating the developer from the underlying implementation details.

TYPEPROPERTY() returns property-level information about data types. It takes two parameters—the name of the data type you want to inspect and a string expression indicating the property in which you're interested. The data type you supply can be either a system-supplied type or a user-defined data type. Here's a query that uses TYPEPROPERTY():

```
SELECT TYPEPROPERTY('id','AllowsNull')
-----------
0
```

Identifier Functions

IDENT_SEED() and **IDENT_INCR**() return the seed and increment settings for identity columns. Each function takes a single parameter—a string expression that specifies the name of the table you want to inspect (you specify a table rather than a column because each table is limited to one identity column).

IDENTITYCOL is a niladic function that returns the value of a table's identity column. You can use it in SELECT statements to return an identity column's value without referencing the column by name, like so:

```
CREATE TABLE #testident (k1 int identity, c1 int DEFAULT 0)

INSERT #testident DEFAULT VALUES
INSERT #testident DEFAULT VALUES
INSERT #testident DEFAULT VALUES

SELECT IDENTITYCOL FROM #testident
```

This is handy for writing generic routines that copy data from table to table, for example. If you establish a convention of always keying your tables using an identity column, IDENTITYCOL provides a generic way of referencing each table's primary key without having to know it in advance.

The **IDENTITY**() function allows you to create tables, using SELECT..INTO, that contain new identity columns. Previously, this required adding the identity column after the table was created using ALTER...TABLE. Here's an example that features IDENTITY():

```
SELECT AuthorId=IDENTITY(int), au_lname, au_fname INTO #testident FROM authors

USE tempdb
SELECT COLUMNPROPERTY(OBJECT_ID('#testident'),'AuthorId','IsIdentity')

-----------
1
```

Though, technically speaking, it doesn't have anything to do with identity columns, **NEWID()** is similar to IDENTITY() in that it generates unique identifiers. It returns a value of type uniqueidentifier and is most often used to supply a default value for a column. Here's an example:

```
CREATE TABLE #testuid (k1 uniqueidentifier DEFAULT NEWID(), k2 int identity)

INSERT #testuid DEFAULT VALUES
INSERT #testuid DEFAULT VALUES
INSERT #testuid DEFAULT VALUES
INSERT #testuid DEFAULT VALUES

SELECT * FROM #testuid

k1                                      k2
------------------------------------    ----------
F4F407B5-244F-11D3-934F-005004044A19    1
F4F407B6-244F-11D3-934F-005004044A19    2
F4F407B7-244F-11D3-934F-005004044A19    3
F4F407B8-244F-11D3-934F-005004044A19    4
```

The uniqueidentifier data type corresponds to the Windows GUID type. It's a unique value that is guaranteed to be unique across all networked computers in the world. You can use the **ROWGUIDCOL** keyword to designate a single uniqueidentifier column in each table as a global row identifier. Once you've done this, you can use ROWGUIDCOL analogously to IDENTITYCOL to return a table's uniqueidentifier column without referencing it directly, like so:

```
CREATE TABLE #testguid
(k1 uniqueidentifier ROWGUIDCOL DEFAULT NEWID(), k2 int identity)

INSERT #testguid DEFAULT VALUES
INSERT #testguid DEFAULT VALUES
INSERT #testguid DEFAULT VALUES
INSERT #testguid DEFAULT VALUES

SELECT ROWGUIDCOL FROM #testguid
```

Index Functions

INDEX_COL() returns the column name of a particular index key column. You can use it to iterate through a table's indexes, displaying each set of key columns as you go. Here's a code sample that illustrates how to use INDEX_COL():

```
SELECT TableName=OBJECT_NAME(id), IndexName=name,
KeyName=INDEX_COL(OBJECT_NAME(id),indid,1) -- Just get the first key
FROM sysindexes
```

(Results abridged)

```
TableName          IndexName            KeyName
--------------     --------------       -------------------------------
authors            UPKCL_auidind        au_id
authors            aunmind              au_lname
publishers         UPKCL_pubind         pub_id
titles             UPKCL_titleidind     title_id
titles             titleind             title
titleauthor        UPKCL_taind          au_id
titleauthor        auidind              au_id
titleauthor        titleidind           title_id
stores             UPK_storeid          stor_id
sales              UPKCL_sales          stor_id
sales              titleidind           title_id
sales              _WA_Sys_payterms_1A1 payterms
```

Note that the INFORMATION_SCHEMA.KEY_COLUMN_USAGE system schema view provides the same information. Querying KEY_COLUMN_USAGE is the ANSI SQL-compliant method of accessing index column schema information. It also has the advantage of being immune to changes in the underlying system tables between releases of SQL Server.

The **INDEXPROPERTY()** function, like the COLUMNPROPERTY() and DATABASE-PROPERTY() functions, returns schema-level information. Like COLUMNPROPERTY(), it takes three arguments—the ID of the index's host table, the name of the index, and a string expression indicating what info you'd like. Here's a query that uses INDEXPROPERTY():

```
SELECT
   TableName=CAST(OBJECT_NAME(id) AS varchar(15)),
   IndexName=CAST(name AS VARCHAR(20)),
   KeyName=CAST(INDEX_COL(OBJECT_NAME(id),indid,1) AS VARCHAR(30)),
   "Clustered?"=CASE INDEXPROPERTY(id,name,'IsClustered') WHEN 1 THEN 'Yes' ELSE 'No' END,
   "Unique?"=CASE INDEXPROPERTY(id,name,'IsUnique') WHEN 1 THEN 'Yes' ELSE 'No' END
FROM sysindexes
```

(Results abridged)

TableName	IndexName	KeyName	Clustered?	Unique?
authors	UPKCL_auidind	au_id	Yes	Yes
authors	aunmind	au_lname	No	No
publishers	UPKCL_pubind	pub_id	Yes	Yes
titles	UPKCL_titleidind	title_id	Yes	Yes
titles	titleind	title	No	No
titleauthor	UPKCL_taind	au_id	Yes	Yes
titleauthor	auidind	au_id	No	No
titleauthor	titleidind	title_id	No	No
stores	UPK_storeid	stor_id	Yes	Yes
sales	UPKCL_sales	stor_id	Yes	Yes
sales	titleidind	title_id	No	No
sales	_WA_Sys_payterms_1A1	payterms	No	No

Again, it's preferable to use the KEY_COLUMN_USAGE system view to get this type of information rather than querying sysindexes directly.

STATS_DATE() returns the date the index statistics were last updated for a particular index. This is handy for determining when to issue UPDATE STATISTICS for the indexes in a database. You could easily write a query that checks each index's last statistics date and issues UPDATE STATISTICS commands for those considered out of date. Here's a query that does just that:

```
DECLARE c CURSOR FOR
SELECT
   TableName=OBJECT_NAME(id),
   IndexName=name,
   StatsUpdated=STATS_DATE(id, indid)
FROM sysindexes
WHERE
OBJECTPROPERTY(id,'IsSystemTable')=0
AND indid>0
AND indid<255

DECLARE @tname varchar(30),
   @iname varchar(30),
   @dateupd datetime

OPEN c
FETCH c INTO @tname, @iname, @dateupd

WHILE (@@FETCH_STATUS=0) BEGIN
   IF (SELECT DATEDIFF(dd,ISNULL(@dateupd,'19000101'),GETDATE()))>30 BEGIN
     PRINT 'UPDATE STATISTICS '+@tname+' '+@iname
     EXEC('UPDATE STATISTICS '+@tname+' '+@iname)
   END
   FETCH c INTO @tname, @iname, @dateupd
END

CLOSE c
DEALLOCATE c
```

(Results abridged)

```
UPDATE STATISTICS authors UPKCL_auidind
UPDATE STATISTICS authors aunmind
UPDATE STATISTICS publishers UPKCL_pubind
UPDATE STATISTICS titles UPKCL_titleidind
UPDATE STATISTICS titles titleind
UPDATE STATISTICS titleauthor UPKCL_taind
UPDATE STATISTICS titleauthor auidind
UPDATE STATISTICS titleauthor titleidind
UPDATE STATISTICS stores UPK_storeid
UPDATE STATISTICS sales UPKCL_sales
UPDATE STATISTICS sales titleidind
```

Of course, you could get the same basic functionality with the sp_updatestats system procedure—it updates the statistics of every index on every table in a database, but you might not want to update all of them—you might want to be a bit more selective. Updating statistics can take a long time on large tables, so you'll want to run it only against tables it actually benefits and when system utilization is low. Also, keep in mind that SQL Server can maintain index statistics information for you automatically, alleviating much of the need for UPDATE STATISTICS. You can turn automatic statistic generation on for a given table via sp_autostats or for the entire database via sp_dboption.

Data Functions

ISDATE() and **ISNUMERIC()** return 1 or 0 based on whether a given expression evaluates to a date or numeric value, respectively. These can be handy for data scrubbing operations where you need to convert a character column to a date or numeric but need to check it first for invalid entries. Here's a query that searches for bad dates in a character field:

```
CREATE TABLE #testis (c1 char(8) NULL)
INSERT #testis VALUES ('19990131')
INSERT #testis VALUES ('20000131')
INSERT #testis VALUES ('19990229')
INSERT #testis VALUES ('20000229')
INSERT #testis VALUES ('19990331')
INSERT #testis VALUES ('20000331')

SELECT *
FROM #testis
WHERE ISDATE(c1)=0

c1
--------
19990229
```

This query returns 19990229 because 1999 wasn't a leap year, making February 29 an invalid date.

DATALENGTH() returns the actual length of the data stored in a column rather than the length of the column itself. Though it can be used with any data type, it's more commonly used with character, binary, and BLOB columns, since they can vary in length. The data length of a fixed data type (such as **int**) never varies, regardless of the value it contains. DATALENGTH() has more uses than you might think, most of them having to do with formatting result sets or data. Here's some sample code from a previous chapter that makes novel use of DATALENGTH():

```
CREATE TABLE #array (k1 int identity, arraycol varchar(8000))
INSERT #array (arraycol) VALUES ('LES PAUL        '+
                                 'BUDDY GUY       '+
                                 'JEFF BECK       '+
                                 'JOE SATRIANI    ')
INSERT #array (arraycol) VALUES ('STEVE MILLER    '+
                                 'EDDIE VAN HALEN'+
                                 'TOM SCHOLZ      ')
INSERT #array (arraycol) VALUES ('STEVE VAI       '+
                                 'ERIC CLAPTON    '+
                                 'SLASH           '+
                                 'JIMI HENDRIX    '+
                                 'JASON BECKER    '+
                                 'MICHAEL HARTMAN')
```

```
-- To set the fourth element
UPDATE #array
SET arraycol =
LEFT(arraycol,(3*15))+'MUDDY WATERS    '+
RIGHT(arraycol,CASE WHEN (DATALENGTH(arraycol)-(4*15))<0 THEN 0 ELSE
DATALENGTH(arraycol)-(4*15) END)
WHERE k1=2

SELECT
   Element1=SUBSTRING(arraycol,(0*15)+1,15),
   Element2=SUBSTRING(arraycol,(1*15)+1,15),
   Element3=SUBSTRING(arraycol,(2*15)+1,15),
   Element4=SUBSTRING(arraycol,(3*15)+1,15),
   Element5=SUBSTRING(arraycol,(4*15)+1,15),
   Element6=SUBSTRING(arraycol,(5*15)+1,15)
FROM #array a
```

(Results abridged)

Element1	Element2	Element3	Element4
LES PAUL	BUDDY GUY	JEFF BECK	JOE SATRIANI
STEVE MILLER	EDDIE VAN HALEN	TOM SCHOLZ	MUDDY WATERS
STEVE VAI	ERIC CLAPTON	SLASH	JIMI HENDRIX

Unusual String Functions

Using **FORMATMESSAGE(),** you can format strings using a printf()-like syntax. It takes a parameter specifying the ID of the message from the master..sysmessages table that you want to use, as well as a list of arguments to insert into the message. FORMATMESSAGE() works similarly to RAISERROR(), except that it doesn't return an error. Instead, it returns the resulting message as a string, which you may then do with as you please. Unfortunately, FORMAT-MESSAGE() is limited to messages that exist in sysmessages—you can't use it to format a plain character string. Here's a technique for working around that:

```
DECLARE @msg varchar(60), @msgid int, @pub_id varchar(10), @inprint int
SELECT @msgid=ISNULL(MAX(error)+1,999999) FROM master..sysmessages WHERE error > 50000
SELECT @pub_id=CAST(pub_id AS varchar), @inprint=COUNT(*) FROM titles GROUP BY pub_id
-- Get the last one
BEGIN TRAN
EXEC sp_addmessage @msgid,1,'Publisher: %s has %d titles in print'
SET @msg=FORMATMESSAGE(@msgid,@pub_id,@inprint)
ROLLBACK TRAN
SELECT @msg
```

```
New message added.

------------------------------------------------------------
Publisher: 1389 has 6 titles in print
```

This approach adds the string to sysmessages within a transaction for the express purpose of manipulating it with FORMATMESSAGE(). Once the string is formatted, it rolls the transaction back so that the message is removed from sysmessages. What you end up with is the ability to format a string without it having to be a permanent member of sysmessages first.

Admittedly, that's a lot of code for a menial task like this. The logical thing to do here would be to generalize the technique by moving the code into a stored procedure. Unfortunately, this isn't easily done because Transact-SQL doesn't support variable stored procedure parameter lists—you can't specify an unlimited number of variably typed parameters, which is what's needed to exploit the capabilities of FORMATMESSAGE().

The system procedure xp_sscanf() provides a similar functionality and can handle a variable number of arguments but, unfortunately, supports only string parameters. It supports a variable number of parameters because it's not a true stored procedure—it's an *extended* procedure, and extended procedures are not written in Transact-SQL. They reside outside the server in a DLL and are usually written in C or C++. For the time being, it would probably be faster to cast nonstrings as strings and either call xp_sscanf() or use simple string concatenation to merge them with the message string.

PARSENAME() is handy for extracting the various parts of an object name. SQL Server object names have four parts:

[server.][database.][owner.]object

You can return any of these four parts using PARSENAME(), like so:

```
DECLARE @objname varchar(30)
SET @objname='KHEN.master.dbo.sp_who'

SELECT ServerName=PARSENAME(@objname,4),
       DatabaseName=PARSENAME(@objname,3),
       OwnerName=PARSENAME(@objname,2),
       ObjectName=PARSENAME(@objname,1)
```

ServerName	DatabaseName	OwnerName	ObjectName
KHEN	master	dbo	sp_who

QUOTENAME() surrounds a string with either double quotation marks (""), single quotation marks (''), or brackets ([]). It can be especially handy when building SQL to execute via EXEC(). Here's a code sample from an earlier chapter that uses QUOTENAME() to create SQL code for execution by EXEC():

```
CREATE TABLE #array (k1 int identity, arraycol varchar(8000))

INSERT #array (arraycol) VALUES ('LES PAUL          '+
                                 'BUDDY GUY         '+
                                 'JEFF BECK         '+
                                 'JOE SATRIANI      ')
INSERT #array (arraycol) VALUES ('STEVE MILLER      '+
                                 'EDDIE VAN HALEN'+
                                 'TOM SCHOLZ        ')
INSERT #array (arraycol) VALUES ('STEVE VAI         '+
                                 'ERIC CLAPTON      '+
                                 'SLASH             '+
                                 'JIMI HENDRIX      '+
                                 'JASON BECKER      '+
                                 'MICHAEL HARTMAN')
```

```
DECLARE @arrayvar varchar(8000), @select_stmnt varchar(8000)
DECLARE @k int, @i int, @l int, @c int
DECLARE c CURSOR FOR SELECT * FROM #array

SET @select_stmnt='SELECT '
SET @c=0

OPEN c
FETCH c INTO @k, @arrayvar

WHILE (@@FETCH_STATUS=0) BEGIN
   SET @i=0
   SET @l=DATALENGTH(@arrayvar)/15
   WHILE (@i<@l) BEGIN
      SELECT @select_stmnt=@select_stmnt+'Guitarist'+CAST(@c as
varchar)+'='+QUOTENAME(RTRIM(SUBSTRING(@arrayvar,(@i*15)+1,15)),'"')+','
      SET @i=@i+1
      SET @c=@c+1
   END
   FETCH c INTO @k, @arrayvar
END
CLOSE c
DEALLOCATE c

SELECT @select_stmnt=LEFT(@select_stmnt,DATALENGTH(@select_stmnt)-1)

EXEC(@select_stmnt)
```

(Results abridged)

```
Guitarist0 Guitarist1 Guitarist2 Guitarist3   Guitarist4
---------- ---------- ---------- ------------ ------------
LES PAUL   BUDDY GUY  JEFF BECK  JOE SATRIANI STEVE MILLER
```

Data Scrubbing

The task of cleaning up data received from sources outside SQL Server is a common one. Whether the data is migrated from a legacy system, generated by hardware, or produced by some other means, it's fairly common to need to scan it for bad values.

The first step in removing bad data is to locate it. To that end, let's consider the problem of finding duplicate values among the rows in a table. It's not enough that we merely return those duplicate values—that would be trivial considering we have GROUP BY and SQL's aggregate functions at our disposal. We need to return the actual rows that contain the duplicate values so that we can deal with them. We might want to delete them, move them to another table, fix them, and so on. Let's assume we begin with the following table of employee IDs and in-case-of-emergency phone numbers. The folks who hired us believe they may have duplicate entries in this list and have determined that the best way to identify them is to locate duplicate ICE numbers. Here's the table:

```
CREATE TABLE #datascrub
(EmpID int identity,
ICENumber1 varchar(14),
ICENumber2 varchar(14))
```

```
INSERT #datascrub (ICENumber1, ICENumber2)
VALUES ('(101)555-1212','(101)555-1213')

INSERT #datascrub (ICENumber1, ICENumber2)
VALUES ('(201)555-1313','(201)555-1314')

INSERT #datascrub (ICENumber1, ICENumber2)
VALUES ('(301)555-1414','(301)5551415')

INSERT #datascrub (ICENumber1, ICENumber2)
VALUES ('(401)555-1515','(401)555-1516')

INSERT #datascrub (ICENumber1, ICENumber2)
VALUES ('(501)555-1616','(501)555-1617')

INSERT #datascrub (ICENumber1, ICENumber2)
VALUES ('(101)555-1211','(101)555-1213')

INSERT #datascrub (ICENumber1, ICENumber2)
VALUES ('(201)555-1313','(201)555-1314')

INSERT #datascrub (ICENumber1, ICENumber2)
VALUES ('(301)555-1414','(301)555-1415')

INSERT #datascrub (ICENumber1, ICENumber2)
VALUES ('(401)555-1515','(401)555-1516')

INSERT #datascrub (ICENumber1, ICENumber2)
VALUES ('(501)555-1616','(501)555-1617')
```

The most obvious way to locate duplicates here is to perform a cross-join of the table with itself, like this:

```
SELECT d.EmpId, d.ICENumber1, d.ICENumber2
FROM #datascrub d CROSS JOIN #datascrub a
WHERE (d.EmpId<>a.EmpId)
   AND (d.ICENumber1=a.ICENumber1)
   AND (d.ICENumber2=a.ICENumber2)
```

```
EmpId        ICENumber1       ICENumber2
-----------  --------------   --------------
2            (201)555-1313    (201)555-1314
4            (401)555-1515    (401)555-1516
7            (201)555-1313    (201)555-1314
9            (401)555-1515    (401)555-1516
```

This approach has a couple of problems—first and foremost is efficiency or, rather, the lack of it. Cross-joins are notoriously inefficient and even impractical for extremely large tables. A better way would be to use a correlated subquery, like this:

```
SELECT d.EmpId, d.ICENumber1, d.ICENumber2
FROM #datascrub d
WHERE EXISTS (SELECT a.ICENumber1, a.ICENumber2 FROM #datascrub a
               WHERE a.ICENumber1=d.ICENumber1
                 AND a.ICENumber2=d.ICENumber2
```

```
GROUP BY a.ICENumber1, a.ICENumber2
HAVING COUNT(*) >=2)
```

This technique uses GROUP BY and COUNT() to identify duplicate values within the subquery and then correlates those values with the outer query to restrict the rows returned. It returns the same result set as the previous query but doesn't require a cross-join. With small tables, the difference this makes won't be noticeable. In fact, the self-join technique may actually be faster with really small tables like this one. However, the larger the table becomes, the more noticeably faster this technique becomes. The optimizer is able to use the EXISTS predicate to return from the inner query as soon as even one row satisfies the conditions imposed.

An even better way of doing this replaces the subquery with a derived table, like so:

```
SELECT d.EmpId, d.ICENumber1, d.ICENumber2
FROM #datascrub d, (SELECT t.ICENumber1, t.ICENumber2 FROM #datascrub t
                GROUP BY t.ICENumber1, t.ICENumber2
                    HAVING COUNT(*) >=2) a
WHERE (d.ICENumber1=a.ICENumber1)
  AND (d.ICENumber2=a.ICENumber2)
```

This technique embeds most of the previous example's subquery in a derived table that it then performs an inner join against. This solution is plain, no-frills Transact-SQL, and it's very efficient, regardless of table size.

I mentioned early on that the first approach to solving this problem had a couple of fundamental flaws. The first of those was inefficiency. We've solved that one. The second one is that neither the initial solution nor any of the code samples presented since finds all duplicate rows. Why? Because the duplicates are disguised a little more cleverly than they might have first appeared. Look closely at the INSERT statements. Notice anything peculiar about any of the ICE numbers? Exactly! Some of them are formatted incorrectly, hiding potential duplicates from our routines. To find all duplicates, we need to standardize the formatting of the columns we're scanning. The best way to do this is simply to remove that formatting—to reduce the data to its bare essence. This is a common situation and, depending on the data, can be critical to a successful scrubbing. Here's a revised query that takes the possibility of bad formatting into account. Check out the difference this makes in the result set.

```
SELECT d.EmpId, d.ICENumber1, d.ICENumber2
FROM #datascrub d, (SELECT ICENumber1=REPLACE(REPLACE(REPLACE(t.ICENumber1,'-',''),
'(',''),')',''),
                        ICENumber2=REPLACE(REPLACE(REPLACE(t.ICENumber2,'-',''),
'(',''),')','')
                FROM #datascrub t
                GROUP BY REPLACE(REPLACE(REPLACE(t.ICENumber1,'-',''),
'(',''),')',''),
                        REPLACE(REPLACE(REPLACE(t.ICENumber2,'-',''),
'(',''),')','')
                HAVING COUNT(*) >=2) a
WHERE (REPLACE(REPLACE(REPLACE(d.ICENumber1,'-',''),'(',''),')','')
       =REPLACE(REPLACE(REPLACE(a.ICENumber1,'-',''),'(',''),')',''))
AND (REPLACE(REPLACE(REPLACE(d.ICENumber2,'-',''),'(',''),')','')
     =REPLACE(REPLACE(REPLACE(a.ICENumber2,'-',''),'(',''),')',''))
```

EmpId	ICENumber1	ICENumber2
2	(201)555-1313	(201)555-1314
7	(201)555-1313	(201)555-1314
3	(301)555-1414	(301)555-1415
8	(301)555-1414	(301)555-1415
4	(401)555-1515	(401)555-1516
9	(401)555-1515	(401)555-1516
5	(501)555-1616	(501)555-1617
10	(501)555-1616	(501)555-1617

Of course, this could be extended to any number of delimiters, including spaces, commas, and so forth. This is one case where stored function support would really be nice. It would allow us to hide all the implementation details of the character stripping in a function that we could then call as needed.

Removing Duplicates

Once the duplicate rows are identified, deleting or moving them to another table is fairly straightforward. You couldn't simply translate the main SELECT into a DELETE statement as that would delete both the duplicate *and* the original. It's easy enough to do but would probably get you fired. Instead, you could use a cursor defined with the same basic SELECT as the code above to cruise through the table. You could save each pair of phone numbers off as you traversed the cursor and then iterate through the duplicates, deleting them as you go.

This would work, but there may be a better way. You may be able to use SQL Server's ability to toss duplicate keys when it builds an index to scrub your data. Here's an example:

```
CREATE TABLE #datascrub
(EmpID int identity,
ICENumber1 varchar(14),
ICENumber2 varchar(14))

CREATE UNIQUE INDEX #datascrub ON #datascrub (ICENumber1, ICENumber2)
WITH IGNORE_DUP_KEY

INSERT #datascrub (ICENumber1, ICENumber2)
VALUES ('(101)555-1212','(101)555-1213')

INSERT #datascrub (ICENumber1, ICENumber2)
VALUES ('(201)555-1313','(201)555-1314')

INSERT #datascrub (ICENumber1, ICENumber2)
VALUES ('(301)555-1414','(301)555-1417')

INSERT #datascrub (ICENumber1, ICENumber2)
VALUES ('(401)555-1515','(401)555-1516')

INSERT #datascrub (ICENumber1, ICENumber2)
VALUES ('(501)555-1616','(501)555-1618')

INSERT #datascrub (ICENumber1, ICENumber2)
VALUES ('(101)555-1211','(101)555-1213')
```

```
INSERT #datascrub (ICENumber1, ICENumber2)
VALUES ('(201)555-1313','(201)555-1314')

INSERT #datascrub (ICENumber1, ICENumber2)
VALUES ('(301)555-1414','(301)555-1415')

INSERT #datascrub (ICENumber1, ICENumber2)
VALUES ('(401)555-1515','(401)555-1516')

INSERT #datascrub (ICENumber1, ICENumber2)
VALUES ('(501)555-1616','(501)555-1617')

SELECT * FROM #datascrub

Server: Msg 3604, Level 16, State 1, Line 0
Duplicate key was ignored.
Server: Msg 3604, Level 16, State 1, Line 34
Duplicate key was ignored.
EmpId       ICENumber1      ICENumber2
----------- --------------- --------------
1           (101)555-1212   (101)555-1213
2           (201)555-1313   (201)555-1314
3           (301)555-1414   (301)555-1417
4           (401)555-1515   (401)555-1516
5           (501)555-1616   (501)555-1618
6           (101)555-1211   (101)555-1213
8           (301)555-1414   (301)555-1415
10          (501)555-1616   (501)555-1617
```

The key here is CREATE INDEX's IGNORE_DUP_KEYS option. Note that you can't build a UNIQUE index over a table with duplicate keys regardless of the IGNORE_DUP_KEYS option—that's why the code above creates the index, then inserts the data. As you can see, attempting to insert a duplicate key value (in this case, we defined the key as the two columns we want to scan for duplicates) generates a warning but otherwise allows the query batch to proceed.

Note that this technique works only with "simple" duplicates—ones that don't involve delimiters and extraneous character removal (i.e., noncharacter types, for the most part). If your needs are as complex as the above technique that made use of nested REPLACE() functions, CREATE INDEX...WITH IGNORE_DUP_KEYS won't get the job done since SQL Server can't detect these more cleverly hidden duplicates.

Iteration Tables

It's common to need to loop through a set of values and perform some sort of computation on them. Normally, this is done in Transact-SQL using the WHILE looping construct, or, if you're a glutton for punishment by your colleagues, an illicit GOTO may do the trick. But there's a better way, if you're willing to give up a tiny amount of disk space for a static iteration table. An iteration table is a simple table containing a sequence of numbers that you use for iterative types of computations rather than looping. It's stored permanently in one of your databases (placing it in **model** will cause it to be copied to **tempdb** with each system restart) and can be filtered like any other table with a WHERE clause. To see how this works, consider the following example.

Let's say that we want to display a table of the squares of all numbers between one and one hundred. If this table already exists:

```
CREATE TABLE iterate (I int identity(-100,1))

DECLARE @loop int
SET @loop=-100

WHILE (@loop<101) BEGIN
   INSERT iterate DEFAULT VALUES
   SET @loop=@loop+1
END

SELECT * FROM iterate

I
-----------
-100
-99
-98
(...)
0
1
(...)
99
100
```

writing the query is simple:

```
SELECT SQUARE=SQUARE(I) FROM iterate
WHERE I BETWEEN 1 AND 100
```

It's fast and far more efficient than having to loop using WHILE every time we need a result set like this. Note the use of the negative seed for **iterate**'s identity column. This allows us to perform computations against negative as well as positive numbers. A nice future SQL Server enhancement would be an automatic table of some sort (along the lines of Oracle's DUAL table) that you specify similarly to an identity column with a seed and an increment during a query. This would alleviate the requirement of a permanent iteration table in the example above.

Summary

This chapter introduced you to an assortment of esoteric and fringe Transact-SQL elements. The functions, commands, and techniques presented here are important but don't seem to fit elsewhere in the book. Like many T-SQL elements, knowing about them may save you real work in your own applications.

Appendix

Suggested Resources

The following is a list of resources that you may find useful in enhancing your knowledge of SQL Server, Transact-SQL, and SQL in general. The list is divided into two groups: Books and Internet Resources.

Books

I owe a great debt to the many wonderful SQL books out there. Here are a few I've found particularly useful in my work:

Bjeletich, Sharon and Greg Mable, et al. 1999. *Microsoft SQL Server 7.0 Unleashed.* Sams Publishing. ISBN: 0-672-31227-1.

Celko, Joe. 1999. *Joe Celko's Data & Databases: Concepts in Practice.* Morgan Kaufmann Publishers. ISBN: 1-55860-432-4.

Celko, Joe. 1997. *Joe Celko's SQL Puzzles & Answers.* Morgan Kaufmann Publishers. ISBN: 1-55860-453-7.

Celko, Joe. 1995. *Joe Celko's SQL for Smarties.* Morgan Kaufmann Publishers. ISBN: 1-55860-323-9.

Date, C. J. 1994. *An Introduction to Database Systems.* Addison-Wesley. ISBN: 0-201-38590-2.

Date, C. J. with Hugh Darwen. 1993. *A Guide to the SQL Standard.* Addison-Wesley. ISBN: 0-201-96426-0.

Groff, James R. and Paul N. Weinberg. 1999. *SQL (The Complete Reference).* Osborne. ISBN: 0-07211845-8.

Kline, Kevin, Lee Gould, and Andrew Zanevsky. 1999. *Transact-SQL Programming.* O'Reilly & Associates. ISBN: 1-56592-401-0.

Melton, Jim and Alan R. Simon. 1993. *Understanding the new SQL: A Complete Guide.* Morgan Kaufmann Publishers. ISBN: 1-55860245-3.

Rozenshtein, David, Anatoly Abramovich, and Eugene Birger. 1995. *Optimizing Transact-SQL: Advanced Programming Techniques.* SQL Forum Press. ISBN: 0-9649812-0-3.

Solomon, David and Ray Rankins, et al. 1996. *Microsoft SQL Server 6.5 Unleashed.* Sams Publishing. ISBN: 0-672-30956-4.

Soukup, Ron. 1997. *Inside Microsoft SQL Server 6.5.* Microsoft Press. ISBN: 1-57231-331-5.

Soukup, Ron and Kalen Delaney. 1999. *Inside Microsoft SQL Server 7.0.* Microsoft Press. ISBN: 0-7356-0517-3.

Internet Resources

The number of SQL Server–related Internet resources has exploded over the last couple of years. The table below lists a few of them:

comp.databases.ms-sqlserver	A general-purpose Microsoft SQL Server newsgroup.
forumsb.compuserve.com/gvforums/default.asp?srv=sqlserver	CompuServe forum dedicated to SQL Server (also accessible via GO MSSQL in CompuServe software).
microsoft.public.sqlserver.programming	A Microsoft-hosted newsgroup dedicated to SQL Server programming issues, especially those related to Transact-SQL.
www.acm.org	The primary public Web site of the Association for Computing Machinery—the world's first educational and scientific computing society.
www.microsoft.com/sql	The section of the primary Microsoft public Web site that's dedicated to SQL Server. You can download a number of useful files from this site, including a demo copy of SQL Server itself.
www.ntfaq.com/sql.html	An FAQ (frequently asked questions) page for SQL Server.
www.sqlwire.com	A site dedicated to tracking SQL Server–related news.
www.swynk.com	A Web site that's independent of Microsoft and provides useful info on several Microsoft products including SQL Server.

Index

Intervals, runs and sequences, 201, 210–212
INTO clause, 6, 98, 270
ISABOUT(), 473
ISAMS and cursors, 251–253
ISDATE(), 518
ISNULL(), 31, 78–79, 206
ISNUMERIC(), 518
Isolation of transactions, 284
items table, 145–147
Iteration advantage of Query Optimizer, 384
Iteration tables, 525–526

J
Jagged (uneven) arrays, 214–215
JOIN, 202, 204, 206, 208, 210, 238
Joins, 13–17
    ANSI/ISO SQL-92 join syntax, 13–16
    FROM clause, 15, 126
    conceptual entities, 13
    condition or criterion, 13
    CROSS JOIN, 17
    EXISTS predicate function and, 136–137
    FULL OUTER JOIN, 17
    inner joins, 13–14, 16
    left joins, 13–16
    legacy join syntax, 13–16
    multilevel joins, 14
    normalization, 13
    NULL, 13–17
    optimizations, 385–386
    order, effect on, 126–128
    OUTER JOINS, 13–17, 126–128, 232
    physical entities, 13
    RIGHT JOIN, 17
    RIGHT OUTER JOIN, 16
    subqueries versus, 142–144
    WHERE clause, 13–16, 127–128
    See also Subqueries (subselect)

K
KEEPIDENTITY keyword, 106
Kenton, H.W.
    on "Don't fix it if it ain't broke," 23
    on engineering's artistic element, 463
    on good engineering, 337
    on intolerance, 511
    on marketing, 251
    on politicians versus engineers, 97

KEY_COLUMN_USAGE system view, 516–517
KEYSET cursors, 253–254, 257–258

L
Leaf nodes, listing, 248
Left joins, 13–16
Legacy join syntax, 13–16
Levenstein, Aaron, on statistics, 173
LIKE mask, 354–355, 357
LIKE predicate function, 48–49, 60, 131–133, 470
LOCAL keyword, 267–268
Local prefix (#), 91–93, 312
Locks, 272
Logging, minimizing, 287
Looping construct, need for, 33

M
Maintenance routines, 432–455
    BULK INSERT, 455
    CREATE INDEX, 437, 525
    CREATE STATISTICS, 433
    DATABASEPROPERTY(), 443
    DBCC DBREINDEX(), 437, 440
    DBCC UPDATEUSAGE(), 435–437
    DROP INDEX, 437
    EXISTS predicate, 445
    INFORMATION_SCHEMA SCHEMATA view, 435
    INFORMATION_SCHEMA view, 435
    INIT_SERVER.SQL, 448–453
    INSERT...EXEC, 453
    model database, 453
    no_output option, 445
    on_success_action, 453
    PRIMARY KEY constraint, 437
    SELECT *, 455
    select into/bulk copy, 65–66, 453
    sp_add_jobserver, 453
    sp_attach_db, 448
    sp_copyfile, 443–445
    sp_dbbackup, 440–443
    sp_dboption, 448
    sp_generate_script, 453
    sp_getSQLregistry, 443, 453
    sp_make_portable, 445–448
    sp_readtextfile, 453–455
    sp_rebuildindexes_all, 437–440
    sp_update_stats_all, 432–435
    sp_updateusage_all, 435–437

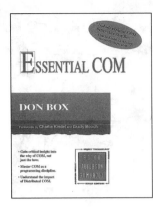

Essential COM

Don Box

Addison-Wesley Object Technology Series

Essential COM helps developers go beyond simplistic applications of COM and become truly effective COM programmers. You will find comprehensive coverage of the core concepts of Distributed COM (interfaces, classes, apartments, and applications), including detailed descriptions of COM theory, the C++ language mapping, COM IDL (Interface Definition Language), the remoting architecture, IUnknown, monikers, threads, marshalers, security, and more. Written by the premier authority on the COM architecture, this book offers a thorough explanation of COM's basic vocabulary, provides a complete Distributed COM application to illustrate programming techniques, and includes the author's test library of COM utility code. By showing you the why of COM, not just the how, Don Box teaches you to apply the model creatively and effectively to everyday programming problems.

0-201-63446-5 • Paperback • 464 pages • ©1998

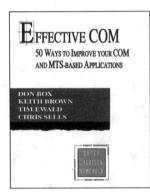

Effective COM

50 Ways to Improve Your COM and MTS-based Applications
Don Box, Keith Brown, Tim Ewald, and Chris Sells
Addison-Wesley Object Technology Series

Written by *Essential COM* author Don Box in conjunction with three other trainers at DevelopMentor, *Effective COM* offers fifty concrete guidelines for COM based on the communal wisdom that has formed over the past five years of COM-based development. This book is targeted at developers who are living and breathing COM, humbled by its complexity and challenged by the breadth of distributed object computing. Although the book is written for developers who work in C++, many of the topics (e.g., interface design, security) are approachable by developers who work in Visual Basic, Java, or Object Pascal. *Effective COM* takes a practical approach to COM, offering guidelines developers can use immediately to become more effective, efficient COM programmers.

0-201-37968-6 • Paperback • 240 pages • ©1999

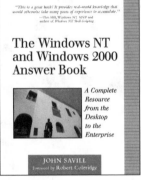

The Windows NT and Windows 2000 Answer Book

A Complete Resource from the Desktop to the Enterprise
John Savill

Rock-solid reliable, independent answers to more than 800 questions that Windows NT and Windows 2000 system administrators and developers most often ask! Here are questions and answers for virtually every key NT topic, including installation and bootup; system, user, and desktop configuration; backup and recovery; managing disks; and much more. You'll find complete chapters on troubleshooting, the Registry, domain management, IP addressing, remote access, printing, batch files and scripting, security, performance, administering Windows 95/98 workstations, and even Internet Information Server and Microsoft Exchange. More than 150,000 professionals rely on John Savill's highly regarded Windows NT FAQ (www.ntfaq.com) every month. Now developers have the site—refined with more detail—packed into this great resource.

0-201-60636-4 • Paperback • 864 pages • ©1999

Developing Applications using Outlook 2000, CDO, Exchange, and Visual Basic

Raffaele Piemonte and Scott Jamison

Written for IT developers who build collaborative and workflow applications, this book is a comprehensive reference to working with Microsoft's powerful collaborative development environment, including Outlook 2000, Exchange Server, Visual Basic, and the Collaboration Data Objects (CDO) Library. It demonstrates ways in which these technologies can be tied together into effective business solutions—from small-scale groupware to large-scale enterprise-wide systems. This book offers an overview of the Microsoft collaborative landscape, and then examines each element of that environment in detail. Numerous examples showcase the applications made possible with these technologies and demonstrate VBScript coding techniques. In addition, this book shows how a number of outside technologies can extend the capabilities of the Outlook/Exchange development environment, including Active Directory services, SQL Server, and ActiveX Data Objects.

0-201-61575-4 • Paperback • 592 pages • ©2000

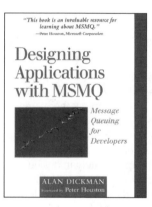

Designing Applications with MSMQ

Message Queuing for Developers
Alan Dickman

Using Web technology effectively to access a vast number of potential customers while keeping customer service levels high is a difficult task. MSMQ (Microsoft Message Queuing) works with MTS (Microsoft Transaction Server) to connect databases and automate responses to external customers (e.g., order processing, customer service issues via email). *Designing Applications with MSMQ* offers a resource for understanding the fundamentals of distributed transactional objects or components. Developing and deploying TP applications has historically been a highly complex task. Microsoft's transaction-processing products, now integrated with Windows NT, make development of mission-critical applications simpler. This book addresses the needs of both Window developers and UNIX TP developers, including software and examples to support the correct design of distributed transactional object systems using MS products, through detailed coverage of online retailing applications.

0-201-32581-0 • Paperback • 400 pages • ©1998

Essential WinInet

Developing Applications Using the Windows Internet API with RAS, ISAPI, ASP, and COM
Aaron Skonnard

This book gives you a complete understanding of *how* the Internet works, *how* to use the most powerful Internet application development tools available today, and *how* to develop complete client/server Internet solutions using WinInet. WinInet, a Win32 API, allows developers to add Internet protocol functionality to Windows applications (HTTP, FTP, or gopher). *Essential WinInet* offers comprehensive coverage and examples, moving behind ISAPI to ASP, COM, and RAS as well. Using WinInet, developers can download web pages, access server applications (CGI, ISAPI, or ASP), upload/download files, and traverse gopher document systems—all within their Windows applications. WinInet can be used to develop sophisticated Internet-centric applications like Web browsers, Internet banking systems (Money98/Quicken), or even an Internet-based real estate management system.

0-201-37936-8 • Paperback • 528 pages • ©1999

ATL Internals

Brent Rector and Chris Sells
Addison-Wesley Object Technology Series

When you are working with COM and C++ and are struggling with understanding how ATL works and how to use it, let ATL experts Brent Rector and Chris Sells show how to use Microsoft's ATL version 3.0. ATL (Active Template Library) is a lighter, faster substitute than MFC for creating COM components. The authors clearly demonstrate how ATL reduces a developer's workload by providing the reader with most of the boilerplate code necessary for developing COM classes and servers. The numerous examples demonstrate how to use ATL for implementing various types of COM objects—simple COM objects, in-proc and out-of-proc COM servers, enumerators, connection point event sources and sinks, windows, controls, and more.

0-201-69589-8 • Paperback • 656 pages • ©1999

The MFC Answer Book

Solutions for Effective Visual C++ Applications
Eugène Kain

Microsoft Foundation Class (MFC) Library is becoming increasingly popular among Windows programmers—more than one million developers use MFC. Although there are many tutorials covering MFC programming, there are few texts that teach you to build sophisticated and professional user interfaces that go beyond Wizard-supplied functionality. *The MFC Answer Book* is specifically designed to help programmers solve their MFC programming problems in the most efficient way possible, both immediately in answer form and through detailed explanations. The techniques covered in this book will save the MFC programmer hours or even days of frustration looking for the right answer to a pressing question. The accompanying CD-ROM contains more than 100 sample programs demonstrating the various solutions discussed in the book, enabling the programmer to immediately reuse those proven techniques in his or her own projects.

0-201-18537-7 • Paperback with CD-ROM • 704 pages • ©1998

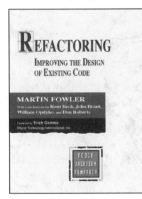

Refactoring

Improving the Design of Existing Code
Martin Fowler with contributions by Kent Beck, John Brant, William Opdyke, and Don Roberts
Addison-Wesley Object Technology Series

In this book, Martin Fowler, well-known author of *Analysis Patterns*, breaks new ground again with the first focused introduction to the process of refactoring. Formerly a tool employed by expert programmers only, refactoring is a method of reworking an existing bad design into a good one. Each refactoring step is simple—seemingly too simple to be worth doing. Refactoring may involve moving a field from one class to another, or pulling some code out of a method to turn it into its own method, or even pushing some code up or down a hierarchy. While these individual steps may seem elementary, the cumulative effect of such small changes can radically improve the existing design and is a proven way to prevent software decay.

0-201-48567-2 • Hardcover • 464 pages • ©1999

Windows™ Sockets Network Programming
Bob Quinn and Dave Shute

Windows Sockets (WinSock), a standard network API for use with Windows, UNIX, and TCP/IP networking environments, is an extraordinary resource for network programmers. This book shows you how to reap WinSock's full benefits to create network-ready applications. In addition to comprehensive coverage of WinSock 1.1 and 2.0 function calls, you will find information on porting existing BSD Sockets source code to Windows, debugging techniques and tools, common traps and pitfalls to avoid, and the many different operating system platforms that currently incorporate WinSock.

0-201-63372-8 • Hardcover with CD-ROM • 656 pages • ©1996

Software Project Management
A Unified Framework
Walker Royce
Addison-Wesley Object Technology Series

This book presents a new management framework uniquely suited to the complexities of modern software development. Walker Royce's pragmatic perspective exposes the shortcomings of many well-accepted management priorities and equips software professionals with state-of-the-art knowledge derived from his twenty years of successful from-the-trenches management experience. In short, the book provides the software industry with field-proven benchmarks for making tactical decisions and strategic choices that will enhance an organization's probability of success.

0-201-30958-0 • Hardcover • 448 pages • ©1998

Win32 Programming
Brent E. Rector and Joseph M. Newcomer

Win32 Programming covers all the material necessary to understand and write 32-bit Windows applications for both Windows 95 and Windows NT 3.5.1. The book details Win32 application programming concepts, approaches, and techniques for the common Application Programming Interface of Windows 95 and Windows NT. It covers basic methods of Windows message handling, advances in mouse and keyboard input handling, and graphical output using the Graphics Device Interface. The CD-ROM is a gold mine of useful programs, with a C template to create your own Windows applications and dozens of other programs.

0-201-63492-9 • Hardcover with CD-ROM • 1568 pages • ©1997

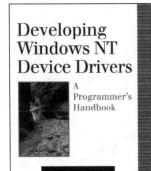

Developing Windows NT Device Drivers

A Programmer's Handbook
Edward N. Dekker and Joseph M. Newcomer

Device drivers are a necessary evil, connecting the operating system with its peripherals. There is not always a need for a custom device driver, but it is difficult to determine when one is necessary until driver fundamentals are clear. This book emphasizes the core techniques of programming device drivers. Without this core knowledge, all of the "advanced" driver techniques (layered drivers, WDM, File System Filters, File System Drivers) are inaccessible. This book covers the components of a Kernel mode device driver for Windows NT. There is also background on the bus interfaces the driver programmer will use, the ISA and the PCI. The authors tackle both existing drivers (the ISA bus and the PCI bus, the primary buses in today's computers).

0-201-69590-1 • Hardcover • 1280 pages • ©1999

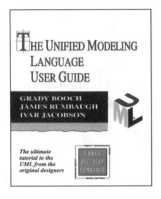

The Unified Modeling Language User Guide

Grady Booch, James Rumbaugh, and Ivar Jacobson
Addison-Wesley Object Technology Series

The Unified Modeling Language User Guide is a two-color introduction to the core eighty percent of the Unified Modeling Language, approaching it in a layered fashion and showing the application of the UML to modeling problems across a wide variety of application domains. This landmark book is suitable for developers unfamiliar with the UML or modeling in general, and will also be useful to experienced developers who wish to learn how to apply the UML to advanced problems.

0-201-57168-4 • Hardcover • 512 pages • ©1999

UML Distilled, Second Edition

A Brief Guide to the Standard Object Modeling Language
Martin Fowler with Kendall Scott
Addison-Wesley Object Technology Series

Thoroughly revised and updated, this best-selling book is a concise overview that introduces you to the Unified Modeling Language, highlighting the key elements of the standard modeling language's notation, semantics, and processes. Included is a brief explanation of UML's history, development, and rationale, as well as discussions on how UML can be integrated into the object-oriented development process. The book also profiles various modeling techniques associated with UML—use cases, CRC cards, design by contract, dynamic classification, interfaces, and abstract classes. The first edition of this classic work was the recipient of *Software Development* magazine's 1997 Productivity Award.

0-201-65783-X • Paperback • 224 pages • ©2000

CD Warranty

Addison-Wesley Professional warrants the enclosed disc to be free of defects in materials and faulty workmanship under normal use for a period of ninety days after purchase. If a defect is discovered in the disc during this warranty period, a replacement disc can be obtained at no charge by sending the defective disc, postage prepaid, with proof of purchase to:

Addison-Wesley Professional
75 Arlington St., Suite 300
Boston, MA 02116

After the 90-day period, a replacement will be sent upon receipt of the defective disc and a check or money order for $10.00, payable to Addison-Wesley Professional.

Addison-Wesley Professional makes no warranty or representation, either expressed or implied, with respect to this software, its quality, performance, merchantability, or fitness for a particular purpose. In no event will Addison-Wesley Professional, its distributors, or dealers be liable for direct, indirect, special, incidental, or consequential damages arising out of the use or inability to use the software. The exclusion of implied warranties is not permitted in some states. Therefore, the above exclusion may not apply to you. This warranty provides you with specific legal rights. There may be other rights that you may have that vary from state to state.

System Requirements

The CD-ROM will run on Windows 95/98 and NT4–Server and Workstation.